AMERICAN FOREIGN POLICY

Past, Present, and Future

ELEVENTH EDITION

GLENN P. HASTEDT

James Madison University

D0249653

ROWMAN & LITTLEFIELD

Lanham • Boulder • New York • London

Executive Editor: Traci Crowell
Associate Editor: Molly White
Senior Marketing Manager: Karin Cholak
Marketing Manager: Deborah Hudson
Interior Designer: Ilze Lemesis
Cover Designer: Jen Huppert Design
Cover Art: Diogo Salles/Getty Images

Credits and acknowledgments borrowed from other sources and reproduced, with permission, in this textbook appear on the appropriate page within the text or in the credits on page 371.

Published by Rowman & Littlefield
A wholly owned subsidiary of The Rowman & Littlefield Publishing Group, Inc.
4501 Forbes Boulevard, Suite 200, Lanham, Maryland 20706
www.rowman.com

Unit A, Whitacre Mews, 26-34 Stannary Street, London SE11 4AB, United Kingdom

Copyright © 2015, 2018 by Rowman & Littlefield
Tenth edition 2015.

British Library Cataloguing in Publication Information Available

Library of Congress Cataloging-in-Publication Data
Names: Hastedt, Glenn P., 1950–
Title: American foreign policy : past, present, and future / Glenn P. Hastedt, James Madison University.
Description: Eleventh edition. | Lanham : Rowman & Littlefield, 2018. | Includes bibliographical references and index.
Identifiers: LCCN 2016044675 (print) | LCCN 2016049417 (ebook) | ISBN 9781442270053 (pbk. : alk. paper) | ISBN 9781442270060 (ebook)
Subjects: LCSH: United States—Foreign relations—Textbooks. | United States—Foreign relations—1945–1989—Textbooks. | United States—Foreign relations—1989– —Textbooks. | United States—Foreign relations administration—Textbooks.
Classification: LCC E183.7 .H27 2018 (print) | LCC E183.7 (ebook) | DDC 327.73—dc23
LC record available at https://lccn.loc.gov/2016044675

♾️™ The paper used in this publication meets the minimum requirements of American National Standard for Information Sciences—Permanence of Paper for Printed Library Materials, ANSI/NISO Z39.48-1992.

Printed in the United States of America

To Thomas Francis

Brief Contents

Contents

4   Learning from the Past   75

5   Society   102

Preface

This eleventh edition of *American Foreign Policy* comes at a time when a growing number of unexpected global challenges confront policy makers and the American public. The death of Osama bin Laden signaled for many the lessening, if not the end, of the terrorist threat to the United States. Instead, the United States finds itself engaged to varying degrees in complex terrorist and civil conflicts in Syria and Africa. Military victories in Iraq and Afghanistan were expected to secure the region from future threats to U.S. security. Instead, these military and state-building efforts are proving to be long-drawn-out affairs from which exiting is difficult. American power, which was believed by many to be without an equal, is being challenged by both a rising power (China) and a supposed failed power (Russia). There is also the emergence of new threats in cyber warfare and the reemergence of past foreign policy challenges in immigration and global health.

Added to this is an unsettled domestic political scene. Foreign policy bipartisanship has been very much in absence of late. Trade, terrorism, immigration, foreign aid, environmental protection, and military policy have all brought forward highly partisan debates that have pitted Democrats against Republicans and created fissures within both parties. On top of this was the 2016 presidential election that at many points divided more than united the American people.

In responding to these foreign policy challenges, American foreign policy today is shaped by three very defining experiences. The first is the Cold War that signaled the end to the notion that the United States might once again embrace an isolationist foreign policy and provided a clearly identified enemy in the Soviet Union on which to center American foreign policy. The second was the Vietnam War, which undercut American optimism that it could play policeman of the world and left in its wake a divided American public. The terrorist attacks of 9/11 were the third defining event. They moved the United States from an ill-defined post–Cold War era in which foreign policy challenges, while numerous, were not major threats to its security into a Global War against Terrorism. Unlike the Cold War, in which deterrence and containment were the key strategic concepts, the War on Terror produced a series of major offensive military undertakings.

Each of these three experiences pull the United States in different directions as it confronts its current foreign policy agenda. The successful conclusion of the Cold War brought with it a sense of optimism about the ability of the United States to accomplish its foreign policy goals along with a sense that true security could be achieved. Vietnam left a sense of powerlessness and suspicion of foreign involvement in its wake. Rather than being a global leader, the legacy of Vietnam suggested that the United States was part of the problem contributing to global unrest and violence. The emerging legacy of the 9/11 attacks combines elements of both. We see the identification of a global enemy and the strong sense of purpose that characterized Cold War foreign policy, yet we also see the sense of powerlessness and frustration that emerged from Vietnam. Most notably, there is no talk of the end of history as there was at the conclusion of the Cold War.

Like its predecessors, this eleventh edition of *American Foreign Policy* does not try to present students with an answer on how best to move American foreign policy forward. Rather, it is designed to help students cultivate the critical thinking skills they need to develop their own answers and participate in current and future debates about the conduct and content of U.S. foreign policy. We do this by raising four key sets of questions over the course of the book: (1) What do we mean by foreign policy and what is the national interest? (2) How did we get here and how do we learn from the past? (3) How is foreign policy made? (4) What next?

The eleventh edition updates information presented in the tenth and adds to that coverage with more extensive discussions of hybrid warfare, cyber wars, and drones in chapter 13. Chapter 2 has been updated to provide an assessment of Obama's foreign policy. The Further Reading sections at the end of each chapter have been updated and include a greater number of journal articles for students to examine on their own.

The chapters in this edition of *American Foreign Policy* contain all of the essential critical thinking materials found in previous editions. The introductory "Dateline" section introduces students to the material being covered by providing them with a short contemporary case study. The "Historical Lessons" section provides a historical context for students to understand current U.S. foreign policy issues and is linked to the "Dateline" section. The "Over the Horizon" section concludes each chapter with a speculative view to the future to spur student thinking about how American foreign policy might evolve in the coming years. Each of these critical thinking sections has been updated and in some cases revised to better capture the current U.S. foreign policy agenda.

In many cases new material appears in these sections to reflect the evolving nature of American foreign policy. New Dateline sections include ISIS (chapter 1), the Libyan intervention (chapter 4), authorization of force resolutions (chapter 6), women in combat (chapter 8), the climate agreement (chapter 10), the Trans-Pacific Trade Agreement (chapter 11), the Iran nuclear agreement (chapter 12), back to Afghanistan (chapter 13), and Obama's opening to Cuba (chapter 14).

New Historical Lessons include the War Powers Act (chapter 6), the integration of the military (chapter 8), the Kyoto Agreement (chapter 10), NAFTA (chapter 11), and into Afghanistan (chapter 13).

New Over the Horizon topics include a millennial foreign policy (chapter 3), an intelligence-industrial complex (chapter 5), a climate coalition of the willing (chapter 10), a Middle East Nuclear Free Zone (chapter 12), the future of COIN (chapter 13), and the new time for a terrorism long telegram (chapter 14).

The eleventh edition is accompanied by a learning package designed to enhance the experience of both instructors and students:

- **Test bank.** I have written a test bank made up of multiple-choice, true/false, and essay questions. The multiple-choice and true/false questions are all referenced by section. The test bank is available in Word to adopters on the text's catalog page at rowman.com. Adopters may also visit the Respondus Test Bank Network to download the test bank for either Respondus 4.0 or Respondus LE.

- **Companion website.** Accompanying the text is an open-access companion website designed to reinforce the main topics. For each chapter, flash cards and self-study quizzes help students master the information they learn in the classroom. Students can access the companion website from their computer or mobile device at textbooks.rowman.com/hastedt11e.

Special thanks to Lydia Andrade, University of the Incarnate Word; Jose de Arimateia da Cruz, Armstrong State University; Simon Peter Gomez, Reinhardt University; Danielle Lupton, Colgate University; Kanishkan Sathasivam, Salem State University; James Seroka, Auburn University; and Clifton W. Sherrill, Troy University. Thanks also to those at Rowman & Littlefield who worked on this project.

Defining American Foreign Policy Problems 1

Dateline: ISIS

Foreign policy problems rarely surface as coherent and neatly bounded challenges that provide policy makers with clear guidance on what conditions produced them or the proper response. Nor do they remain constant over time. Instead they evolve and mutate, sometimes in unexpected ways. Such is the challenge facing the United States in responding to ISIS (the Islamic State of Iraq and Syria), also known as ISIL (the Islamic State of Iraq and the Levant) or as Daesh.

ISIS emerged from the ashes of the Bush administration's successful military operations in Afghanistan and Iraq against al Qaeda. Initially it was viewed as a short-term opponent, one whose challenge could be contained by Iraqi security forces. It was a "low boil" insurgency that might last a decade, a conclusion based on the perception that as terrorists ISIS was interested in promoting violence to bring down the Iraqi government and not to seize and rule over territory.

The primary focus of U.S. foreign policy in Iraq was on the rapid deterioration of the positive relationship between Shiites and Sunnis that had been created by the Anbar Awakening and the U.S. military surge. The United States found itself trapped between Iraqi prime minister Nouri al-Maliki's unwillingness to make concessions and fear that overly aggressive military action by Shiite forces would widen the growing gap and make reconciliation impossible.

ISIS factored into this definition of the Iraq problem largely by virtue of being seen as a group of foreign combatants whose actions threatened to exacerbate matters by stoking the flames of Sunni extremism and as a breeding ground for terrorists who would soon return to their home countries. In his 2012 reelection campaign, President Obama referred to the successor groups to al Qaeda, of which ISIS was one, as being equivalent to a junior varsity team noting, "The analogy we use around here sometimes, and I think is accurate, is if a JV team puts on Lakers' uniforms, that doesn't make them Kobe Bryant."

By 2014 the intelligence community had reached the conclusion that this characterization of ISIS's capabilities and intentions was incorrect. Key to this changed assessment was ISIS's expansion into Syria, where an ongoing and brutal civil war provided it with a safe haven to grow and expand its influence. In its annual global threat report to Congress, the intelligence community reported that that ISIS "will probably attempt to take territory in Iraq and Syria." In June of that year, ISIS declared its intent to create an Islamic caliphate (an Islamic state led by a religious supreme leader who is also its political leader). By the end of 2014, it had captured dams, oil fields, and air bases as well as established a de facto capital in Raqqa, in northeastern Syria. The intelligence community estimated that ISIS had 20,000–31,500 fighters, two-thirds of whom were based in Syria.

As 2014 progressed it became increasingly clear that the Obama administration's policy of abstaining from a direct involvement with ISIS—relying instead on regional allies and Syrian rebels to defeat it—was in need of change. But it was not clear in what direction to move. As Obama noted in August, "We don't have a strategy yet." His administration was torn between the desire "not to get dragged into another ground war in Iraq" and the need to take military action against ISIS's advance on Baghdad and expanding influence in Syria. In June Obama authorized sending up to three hundred military advisors to Iraq. In early August he ordered air strikes against ISIS targets in Iraq for the purpose of protecting American personnel and preventing acts of genocide. In September he announced that the United States would also bomb ISIS targets in Syria. All of this only two years after having backed away from air strikes in Syria in response to the use of chemical weapons by the government of Bashar al-Assad.

Additional changes in U.S. foreign policy followed. In October 2015, following Russia's unexpected military intervention into the conflict, a peace conference was held in Vienna. Unlike in past peace efforts, the United States was willing to obtain an agreement that brought stability to the region even if it meant leaving Assad in power. In 2016 the Obama administration expanded its air strikes against ISIS. In January and February it directed 251 bombs and missiles on ISIS targets in Afghanistan, more than three times the number in those months in 2015. It also struck at ISIS targets in Libya as part of a preemptive strategy to prevent ISIS from expanding even further into North Africa.

By then, however, the ISIS problem had also morphed into something new. Where al Qaeda had risen to prominence by virtue of high-profile terrorist attacks abroad ISIS had focused its violence on targets closer to home. This was no longer the case. In the two-year span from March 2014 to March 2016, ISIS carried out or inspired at least twenty-nine deadly assaults targeting Westerners and killed more than 650 people with the most visible attacks being those in Paris and Brussels.

The war with ISS entered yet another phase in October, 2016 when Kurdish fighters and Iraqi government troops aided by U.S advisors and air power laid siege to Mosul, once Iraq's second largest city. It had become a symbol of ISS' power in the region. This long awaited military offensive brought into focus two new questions. First, did Obama have a plan for governing post ISS northern Iraq after Mosul was liberated or would he repeat Bush's mistake of achieving a military victory without a peace plan? Second, how would ISS respond? The consensus view is that ISS will not go quietly. Rather, it will retreat temporarily into the desert and prepare for a comeback as they did between 2007 and 2013.

No other off-the-shelf solution was available to the Obama administration in responding to ISIS. A series of difficult and interconnected choices had to be made under uncertain conditions and with incomplete information In this chapter, we examine six key issues in constructing a foreign policy: (1) problems must be defined, (2) choices must be made, (3) costs must be assessed, (4) public support must be built, (5) courses of action must be designed, and (6) results must be assessed.

We begin our overview of thinking about foreign policy by examining the legacy that the Obama administration has left to President Trump. We then look more closely at the challenges of constructing a foreign policy and examine these six key issues in more detail. From there we return to look in more detail at selected presidential foreign policy doctrines.

The Obama Foreign Policy Legacy

It is far too early to anticipate the direction that President Trump's foreign policy will take. As the fall of the Soviet Union and the 9/11 terrorist attacks bear witness, unanticipated events can radically alter the nature of foreign policy problems faced and the domestic political context in which decisions are made. What we can do, however, is identify the starting point from which Donald Trump's foreign policy will begin by asking: What is Obama's foreign policy legacy?

Answering this question involves making judgments about its content and consequences. There is no single foreign policy statement that captures the content of Obama's foreign policy. Rather, there appear to have been two "Obama Doctrines." The first is optimistic in its outlook and emerges from a set of speeches that President Obama gave in 2009. As a group they pointed in the direction of an Obama Doctrine that promised to "reset" America's relations with the rest of the world. His foreign policy would be activist in orientation but stress cooperation rather than domination. It would not be consumed 24-7 by a single problem but would adopt a global perspective on the need for American leadership and problem-solving.

Four themes ran through those initial speeches. First, there was a call for a new start in U.S. relations with the world. Second, this new start would be based on a sense of partnership that was open to all who were willing to participate. Speaking in Russia, President Obama said, "There was a time when Roosevelt, Churchill, and Stalin could shape the world in one meeting. Those days are over." Third, he identified a set of common areas of concern. Numbered among them were ridding the world of nuclear weapons; promoting economic prosperity; advancing political, economic, and social rights; and isolating and defeating extremism. Fourth, he noted that success in these areas was a long-term undertaking. In accepting the Nobel Peace Prize, Obama observed that the goal of ending violent conflict would not be achieved in our lifetime.

This Obama Doctrine proved to be short-lived. Optimism about the future gave way to a more somber view of the present as foreign policy challenges in Asia, the Middle East, and Europe mounted. In place of this doctrine rose a second more cautious and pragmatic Obama Doctrine that sought to draw a distinction between a compelling threat to U.S. national security and lesser threats. In his May 2014 graduation speech at West Point, New York, President Obama argued that while America must still play a leader on the world stage, military action cannot be the only or primary component of this leadership in every case.[1] Trying to capture the essence of this second Obama Doctrine, one commentator suggested that it could be found in "a willingness to be the world's police chief but not its policeman."[2]

A wide range of assessments have been put forward concerning the consequences of Obama's foreign policy.[3] At one extreme are critics who see his foreign policy as being that of a softheaded idealist—naïve and "designed to produce American decline." One critic summed up Obama's view of foreign policy saying, "There should be less of it." Found at the other extreme are supporters, one of whom argues Obama's foreign policy "represents the dawn of a new and superior conception of American foreign policy."

In between these extremes are found varying degrees of positive and negative assessments of Obama's foreign policy. Three observations from this center group are particularly relevant to making judgments about its legacy. First, Obama was better at formulating policies than implementing them. As one commentator noted, he got the big issues right but struggled to adapt when they failed. Second, he was determined to avoid mistakes. This frequently translated into a preference for using air strikes over putting troops into combat. One positive of this perspective was to focus on both the short- and long-term effects of using force and to recognize that unintended consequences might result. A negative consequence was that it hampered his ability to calm public fears or create a public consensus behind his policies. Third, Obama's foreign policy was plagued by a large gap between his declaratory and action foreign policy. **Declaratory policy** consists of proclamations that state the intent of the United States to pursue a line of action. **Action policy** is what the United States actually does. It is what we tend to think of when we study U.S. foreign policy. The most notable example of this during the Obama administration came with his bold statement about a "red line" warning to Syria over the use of chemical weapons. Five times he warned the Syrian government about the consequences of doing so, yet no action was taken.

Thinking about Foreign Policy Problems

There is no such thing as a typical foreign policy problem. Presidents discover three truths very quickly. First, most foreign policy problems contain a bundle of distinct policy problems or issues that intersect in complicated ways. This makes deciding how to approach a problem difficult because of uncertainty over just what the problem is or how attacking one aspect of the problem will affect its other dimensions. Here is what then national security advisor Condoleezza Rice told the 9/11 Commission in 2004 about the Bush administration's antiterrorism policy: "You didn't have an approach against al Qaeda because you didn't have an approach against Afghanistan. And you didn't have an approach against Afghanistan because you didn't have an approach against Pakistan. And until we could get that right, we didn't have a policy."[4]

Second, foreign policy problems are seldom ever "solved." George Shultz, President Ronald Reagan's secretary of state, noted that policy making does not involve confronting "one damn thing after another . . . it involves confronting the same damn thing over and over."[5] In part this is due to the difficulty of fashioning policies that accurately capture the complexity of the problem being addressed. But, the necessity of dealing with the same problem over and over again may also be a result of the fact that there is no solution. Such problems are often characterized as "wicked problems." Terrorism is seen by many as a wicked problem. No permanent solution exists. Terrorism can be deterred, targets can be protected, the terrorist threat can be managed, but the potential for terrorism cannot be ended.

Third, it is also important to realize that foreign policy problems differ in terms of their history and origin. Some foreign policy problems are inherited from previous administrations. The key dilemma faced by presidents is whether to endorse the policy line of their predecessor or move in a new direction. President Obama inherited an American on-the-ground military presence in Iraq and Afghanistan from President Bush that he was determined to end. Now, President Trump has inherited a similar military presence in Iraq and Afghanistan, a proxy war in Syria, along with a policy of air strikes against ISIS targets in Libya. A second category of foreign policy problems are the result of a president's own policy. Bill Clinton's foreign policy was widely criticized for its inconsistency and his lack of decisiveness. Zbigniew Brzezinski, President Jimmy Carter's national security advisor, described Clinton's foreign policy as being an "enemy du jour" foreign policy.[6] Important political calculations follow from whether a foreign policy was inherited or of one's own making: Only inherited policy problems can be blamed on one's predecessor. Third, some foreign policy problems are new. One of the most significant events of this type in recent times was the collapse of communism and the breakup of the Soviet Union that confronted the administration of George H. W. Bush in 1989. A similarly momentous new problem faced President George W. Bush in the war against global terrorism following the attacks of September 11, 2001. The last category of foreign policy problems consists of problems rooted in long-term structural features of world politics. The impact of globalization on the U.S. economy is one such problem. Another is the existence of a trade-off between military power and economic growth.[7] It is held by many that Great Powers continually overspend on the military. They succumb to "imperial overreach," setting in motion the long-term decline of their economies which leads to a "fall" from Great Power status.

Choices

Foreign policy is about choices: choices about what goals to pursue, what threats to protect against, what costs to bear, and who should bear those costs. Choices always exist. President George W. Bush, when asked if the president ever had a last card to play in foreign policy before having to walk away and accept defeat, replied, "There is always another card." However, those choices might not always be as great as a president wants. In reflecting on the four military options presented to him on Afghanistan, Obama noted that two were basically alike and two were unclear.[8]

Just as there are always options once a conflict is under way, so too there are always choices about what problems to place on the foreign policy agenda. Two different lines of thinking have been used to make foreign policy choices: one involves asking what it is that Americans want and the other asking what it is that the United States should do. Answers to the first are generally found in public opinion polls. Answers to the second are typically sought in the concept of the national interest.

What Do Americans Want in Foreign Policy?

The public's sense of what is in the U.S. national interest has remained relatively stable over the years. When asked in a 2013 public opinion poll what foreign policy goals they held to be very important, 81 percent said protecting the jobs of American workers.[9] In 2010, 79 percent identified this goal as important and in 1978, 78 percent did so. In 2014 this goal came in second to protecting the United States from terrorist attacks (83 percent). In addition to protecting American jobs and protecting the United States from terrorism, more than 50 percent of the American public identified preventing the spread of weapons of mass destruction (73 percent), reducing dependence on imported energy (61 percent), and combatting international drug trafficking (57 percent) as foreign policy priorities in 2013. At the other end of the public opinion spectrum, we found that in 2013 only 33 percent supported a policy of promoting human rights. This number was consistent with past polls. In 2008, 31 percent voiced support for human rights as a high priority in U.S. foreign policy and in 1978, 39 percent did so.[10]

Beneath this long-term stability we do see changes in how the public rates the importance of issues. A December 2014 Pew Research Center open-ended poll found that only 1 percent of the public identified terrorism as the most important problem facing the United States. In December 2015 that number rose to 18 percent.[11] Overall these two polls showed a sharp increase in the importance Americans attached to foreign policy and international foreign policy issues. Only 9 percent cited them as most important in 2014 while 32 percent did so in 2015.

The National Interest

For those who pose the question of selecting goals in terms of the demands of foreign policy rather than the wishes of the American people the answer is found in defending and pursuing the American **national interest**, the fundamental goals and objectives of a country's foreign policy. The term "national interest" is unmatched in its emotional impact and ability to shape a foreign policy debate. It conveys a sense of urgency, imminent threat, and higher purpose. All other foreign policy objectives pale in comparison to those promoting the national interest. It is advanced with great certainty and talked about as if there could be no doubt as to its meaning.

Students of world politics have struggled with little success to give concrete meaning to the term "national interest."[12] Various formulations are used to separate threats and problems into different categories. Some employ a pyramid in which core national interest problems are found at its apex and are few in number. Beneath it are found larger numbers of long-range societal goals and goals that advance the interests of specific groups within a country. Others using the same logic divide foreign policy problems into three categories: "A"-list threats are those that pose a direct and immediate challenge to U.S. survival. "B"-list threats involve challenges to immediate U.S. interests, but not to U.S. survival. "C"-list threats indirectly affect the U.S. national interest but are not immediate or direct.

The implication of both frameworks is the same. Policy makers need to concentrate resources on addressing the most important foreign policy issues if they do not wish to jeopardize the U.S. national interest. The ever-present danger is that not enough resources will be available to successfully deal with a core or A-list threat should it appear.

Regardless of the approach used, the fundamental problem remains one of deciding what category a foreign policy problem should be placed in. This is a judgment call and has led to two major lines of dissent in discussing the national interest. One argues that since it is not possible to rank the importance of foreign policy goals in some abstract fashion, the national interest should be defined by a country's actions. If a country is willing to allocate significant resources to a problem, then solving that problem is in the national interest. A second dissenting voice calls for reexamining the issues we debate for inclusion in these ranking schemes. They want greater attention paid to **public goods**. These are goods such as a clean environment that are not owned by any one country but belong to everyone in the international community; consequently they tend to be devalued in discussions of the national interest.

Costs

Foreign policy comes with a price tag. This is true whether we are dealing with declaratory policy or action policy. At the most basic level, the price tag of action policy can be readily calculated in monetary terms. According to the Defense Department the United States spent an average of $11 million per day between September and November 2014 fighting ISIS. Spanning from 1965 to 1975, the Vietnam War cost an estimated $111 billion ($686 billion in 2008 dollars). One study placed the total cost of the Iraq and Afghan wars at $4.4 trillion at the end of 2014. Far more difficult to calculate are the intangible costs such as the loss of lives and the impact a foreign policy may have on raising or lowering a country's international prestige or its willingness to engage in future activities of a similar kind. Obama spoke to this in 2014 in announcing that the United States would send military advisors to Iraq. Asserting that this would not lead to a combat presence as occurred in the Iraq War he said, "Recent days have reminded us of the deep scars left by America's war in Iraq. What's clear from the last decade is the need for the United States to ask hard questions before we take action, particularly military action."

Two additional dimensions of the cost problem also need to be taken into account when looking at action policy. The first is **opportunity cost**. Resources devoted to one foreign policy problem cannot be used on another or on domestic problems. Not only are resources not unlimited, but the foreign and domestic policy goals that policy makers may decide to pursue have no natural limit.

The difference between the resources (power) available to pursue goals and the list of goals being pursued is often referred to as the **"Lippmann Gap"** in honor of columnist Walter Lippmann, who in 1947 observed that a recurring problem in American foreign policy was an imbalance between American power and the goals it sought.[13] When this occurred, he found American foreign policy to be mired in domestic conflict and ineffective abroad. Most notably, conflicts were not adequately prepared for and peace agreements were too hastily constructed.

The second additional dimension to the cost problem is that policies have unintended consequences. **"Blowback"** is the term commonly used to capture the essence of this phenomenon.[14] It was first used by the Central Intelligence Agency (CIA) to characterize problems that came about as a result of covert action programs. An example of blowback can be found in the war on terrorism. After defeating Iraq the United States instituted a policy of de-Baathification. Under Order #2 Iraq's military was dissolved. All soldiers were dismissed but allowed to keep their weapons. With no possibility of employment many joined ISIS and came to hold important military leadership positions.

Declaratory policy also has its costs. The perennial danger exists that declaratory and action policies will be out of sync with one another, creating what some refer to as the "say-do" problem.[15] The lack of fit between declaratory and action foreign policy has repeatedly dogged presidents in the area of human rights and democracy promotion which have received a great deal of declaratory policy support but little action policy support. Beyond creating the say-do problem many argue that this discrepancy also undermines American global leadership by denying presidents "the global bully pulpit" from which to build a global consensus for action.[16]

Building Consensus

In order to succeed, a foreign policy must be supported by the American public. American policy makers have long recognized this reality. Dean Acheson, who served as secretary of state from 1949 to 1953, once commented that 80 percent of the job of conducting foreign policy was managing one's domestic ability to make policy.[17] The term long used to convey this sense of support is "**bipartisanship**." It refers to the ability of both Democrats and Republicans to unite behind a course of action. Unity at home is seen as sending a message to adversaries that they cannot "wait out" a president in hopes of getting a better deal with his successor or to try and appeal to Congress to undercut his foreign policy. Recent presidents have found bipartisanship to be in increasingly short supply. Rather than serving to unite the public, high-profile foreign policy issues such as the Iraq War and the attack on the U.S. consulate in Benghazi have become the center of political controversy. Many now question of how normal or natural bipartisanship is. Should the periodic lack of consensus be expected, or is it an indication of a fundamental change in the domestic politics of American foreign policy? Writing prior to the 2008 election, long-serving American diplomat Richard Holbrooke said that the core challenge of the next president "will be nothing less than to re-create a sense of national purpose."[18] That challenge continues.

Because it is such a powerful symbol, the national interest is a key instrument presidents and others have used to build public support for their foreign policies. While it may not dictate a specific course of action, invoking the national interest places opponents on the defensive and provides a point for the public to unite behind the president.[19]

At the same time invoking the national interest in making foreign policy can also trap policy makers. Having justified a course of action as being in the national interest, it is politically difficult to do an about-face and declare that this is no longer the case. Typically, in these cases, we find policy makers insisting that their policy is correct, but altering the definition of the national interest used as a justification. The Iraq War is a case in point. In 2003 President George W. Bush stated that the purpose of the Iraq War was "to disarm Iraq, free its people and defense [*sic*] the world from grave danger [of weapons of mass destruction]." In 2005, he characterized the Iraq War as a step toward quarantining terrorist groups that might otherwise attack the United States. In 2007 he compared America's enemies to communists.[20]

Invoking the national interest as a means of building public support may also trap presidents by blinding them to other foreign policy problems. By the end of Bush's presidency the excessive focus on Iraq began to trouble Secretary of State Condoleezza Rice and others. They sought to get him to tone down his rhetoric fearing that by making Iraq the "be-all, end-all test" of American strength, U.S. standing and interests in other parts of the world were being harmed.[21]

Selecting a Policy Instrument

Policy makers must decide not only what goals to pursue but also how to pursue them. A prime consideration in selecting a policy instrument is the context in which it will operate. Power is not like money. It cannot be used with equal effectiveness anywhere. Economic strategies that worked well in an era when the United States was a hegemonic economic power may prove less useful in a period of economic decline or parity. Similarly, covert action policies successful in one country may fail in another.

Hard Power and Soft Power

At a most general level, policy makers have two forms of power around which to build their foreign policies. The first is **hard power**, which is coercive power and the traditional means by which states protect and advance their national interests. While most often employed against an enemy, hard power can also be used against a reluctant ally. It is designed to force or compel another state to act in a prescribed fashion. As much as possible, hard power tries to limit the range of choices open to another state so that the state will act in accordance with U.S. wishes. Hard power is most often associated with military power, but virtually all instruments of foreign policy can be employed in this fashion.

The second is **soft power**, which is the power to influence and persuade. It is rooted in the power of attraction seeking to convince states to willingly identify with the United States and support the U.S. position. Domination is replaced by cooperation. Examples would include using the military for disaster and humanitarian relief efforts, providing economic and medical assistance to those in need, and strengthening democratic institutions and civil society in states making the transition to democracy. In each of these cases, a reservoir of goodwill is created, which the United States can draw upon in carrying out its foreign policy.

Observers of U.S. foreign policy are divided as to whether hard power or soft power is preferable. Hard power supporters note that soft power is difficult to use. Many of the resources associated with it, such as the appeal of American values and American democracy, are beyond the control of policy makers and not easily mobilized. Soft power supporters note that while hard military power can defeat an enemy, it cannot produce peace. Robert Gates, who served in both the George W. Bush and Obama administrations, cautioned that "we cannot kill our way to victory."[22]

Grand Strategy

No matter how wisely or carefully they are chosen, selecting a set of foreign policy instruments will not automatically result in a successful foreign policy. Decision-makers must also devise an overall course of action that brings these policy instruments together into a unified and coherent whole. **Grand strategy** is the linchpin that unites goals and tactics. It differs from military strategy or diplomatic strategy in its scope. Where they are concerned with the effective use of hard power or soft power, grand strategy is concerned with a government-wide approach that brings together all elements of power. At the same time, constructing an effective grand strategy is also a very political undertaking and a difficult task. In 2005 Secretary of State Rice stated that the U.S. strategy in Iraq was "clear, hold, and build." To others, including General George Casey, who then was the commanding general in Iraq, this was not a strategy. It was little more than a bumper sticker.[23]

Several factors contribute to the problem of constructing a grand strategy. The first is our incomplete knowledge of cause and effect. We do not understand democratization, terrorism, or other challenges well enough to formulate overarching grand strategies to deal with them. A second limitation is found in the organizational and political barriers one encounters in trying to implement grand strategy. The inevitable problem of getting bureaucracies to work together virtually guarantees that grand strategy in action will fall far short of grand strategy on paper. Third, there are perceptual and psychological barriers to how accurately policy makers see the world and understand their own motives. President George W. Bush spoke of the United States having "freedom hegemony" in the Middle East, a condition many critics of U.S. policy in other countries would characterize as imperialism.[24]

Some believe that we should not try and construct a grand strategy.[25] Supporters of this perspective argue it is more appropriate to proceed on a case-by-case method in which pragmatism rather than broad principles rule. They stress that constructing an effective foreign policy is better seen as a test of wills than as constructing a blueprint. Still, most believe that there is little choice but to try and craft grand strategies if for no other reason than it forces policy makers to look beyond what President Truman's secretary of state Dean Acheson referred to as the "thundering present" and think about the big picture and ask big questions.

Historical Lesson

The Monroe Doctrine

In the early 1820s, the United States faced a new challenge for which it needed a foreign policy. Napoleon had been defeated and the conservative states of Europe were successfully putting down a series of revolutions in southern Europe. The possibility now presented itself that France and Spain together might try to reestablish their influence in the Western Hemisphere, where states throughout Central and South America had taken advantage of the conflict in Europe to declare their independence.

In August 1823 the British contacted the U.S. minister to Great Britain and suggested a joint American-British declaration intended to prevent France from interfering into the affairs of these new democracies or gaining territory in the Americas through conquest or cession.

The U.S. minister welcomed the idea, but lacking the authority to accept the British proposal he sent it on to Washington.

President James Monroe was inclined to accept the British offer. He consulted with former presidents James Madison and Thomas Jefferson, both of whom supported it. Secretary of State John Quincy Adams opposed the idea. He felt that the possibility of a European intervention into Latin America was remote. Adams was also confident that if France and Spain tried to do so, Great Britain would be forced to counter it with or without an agreement with the United States. He was also concerned that the language in the proposed statement could also be interpreted to mean the United States had to abandon hopes of acquiring Texas, California, and Cuba. Finally, Adams resisted the idea of playing a secondary role to Great Britain in a matter involving the defense of the Western Hemisphere.

Adams's position carried the day, and the question now became how to proceed with a unilateral American statement. Adams preferred a series of diplomatic notes. Monroe preferred including it in his regular message to Congress. The first draft presented to the cabinet in November 1823 was defiant in tone. Adams objected and succeeded in having the speech toned down substantially.

As presented to Congress on December 2, 1823, the Monroe Doctrine had three parts. The first part was primarily directed at Russia and warned it not to try and establish a colonial presence in North America by moving down southward from Russian Alaska. In the next section, Monroe warned the European monarchies that the United States would view "any attempt on their part to extend their system to any portion of this hemisphere as dangerous to our peace and safety." He continued, "We could not view any interposition for the purpose of oppressing them, or controlling in any other manner their destiny . . . in any other light as the manifestation of an unfriendly disposition toward the United States." Monroe concluded that the policy of the United States continued to be one of not interfering in the internal concerns of any European power.

Monroe's pronouncement were met with widespread approval within the United States, although some questioned his positioning of the United States as protector of newly established democracies and feared that this position would involve the United States in foreign conflicts. European powers reacted with displeasure, terming it arrogant and blustering. Great Britain reacted with a mixture of support and muted anger. It knew that it would be the British navy and not the U.S. navy or army that would guarantee the independence of the former Spanish colonies. For their part, the newly independent states of Latin America responded with caution. They too recognized the importance of the British navy. Moreover, when Colombia, Brazil, and Mexico proposed an alliance with the United States based on Monroe's address, they were turned down.

Some eighty years later in December 1904, President Theodore Roosevelt added what came to be known as the Roosevelt Corollary to the Monroe Doctrine. It stated that it was now necessary for the United States to act as a hemispheric policeman punishing wrongdoing and establishing domestic order when governments were incapable of doing so. Roosevelt was moved to announce his Corollary because European states were becoming angry with Latin American states for their failure to pay debts owed to them and began to use force to obtain payment. Roosevelt at first approved of their plans but then became concerned with the precedent they set.

Applying the Lesson

1. Some argue that the Bush Doctrine is based on the Monroe Doctrine and turns it into a global document. Do you agree or disagree?
2. Is the original Monroe Doctrine or the Roosevelt Corollary most important for U.S. foreign policy today?
3. Which foreign policy problem was more difficult to create a response to, that faced by Condoleezza Rice or that faced by James Monroe?

Presidential Foreign Policy Doctrines

The earliest grand strategy in American diplomatic history was put forward in President George Washington's Farewell Address, when he called for avoiding entanglement in foreign alliances. It provided the conceptual foundation for a policy of isolationism that in various forms was embraced by many of his successors. The Monroe Doctrine, calling for a policy of activism and creating a U.S. sphere of influence in Latin America in return for in European affairs; Manifest Destiny, or a policy of continental expansion; and the Open Door, as a strategy for establishing an American presence in Asia, are other examples of notable early American foreign policy grand strategies.

The grand strategy of U.S. foreign policy has come to be associated with a series of presidential doctrines that set forward the goals, means, and objectives of U.S. foreign policy. In Box 1.1, we highlight five doctrines that have been particularly important for signaling shifts in the agenda of U.S. foreign policy. We discuss them in more detail here and then turn to the challenge of evaluating foreign policy.

Box 1.1

Selected Presidential Foreign Policy Doctrines

The Truman Doctrine

The gravity of the situation which confronts the world today necessitates my appearance before a joint session of the Congress. The foreign policy and national security of this country are involved. One aspect of the present situation, which I wish to present to you at this time for your consideration and decision, concerns Greece and Turkey. . . . The United States has received from the Greek government an urgent appeal for financial and economic assistance. . . . The very existence of the Greek state is today threatened by the terrorist activities of several thousand armed men, led by Communists. . . . The United States must supply that assistance.

. . . There is no other country to which democratic Greece can turn. . . . The future of Turkey as an independent and economically sound state is clearly no less important to freedom-loving peoples of the world . . . [its] integrity is essential to the preservation of order in the Middle East. . . . I am fully aware of the broad implications involved if the United States extends assistance to Greece and Turkey.

. . . One of the primary objectives of the foreign policy of the United States is the creation of conditions in which we and other nations will be able to work out a way of life free from coercion. . . . I believe that it must be the policy of the United States to support free people who are resisting attempted subjugation by armed minorities or outside pressures. I believe that we must assist free people to work out their own destinies in their own way. . . . If we falter in our leadership, we may endanger the peace of the world—and we shall surely endanger the welfare of our own nation.

Source: Address before a joint session of Congress, March 17, 1947

The Nixon Doctrine

A nation cannot remain great if it betrays its allies and lets down its friends. Our defeat and humiliation in South Vietnam without question would promote recklessness in the councils of those great powers who have yet to abandon their goals of world conquest. . . . I laid down in Guam three principles as guidelines for future American foreign policy toward Asia. First, the United States will keep its treaty commitments. Second, we shall provide a shield if a nuclear power threatens the freedom of a nation allied with us or of a nation whose survival we consider essential to our security. Third, in case involving other types of aggression, we shall furnish military and economic assistance when requested in accordance with our treaty commitments. We shall look to the nation directly threatened to assume primary responsibility of providing the manpower for its defense. . . . The defense of freedom is everybody's business, not just America's business.

Source: President Nixon's address to the nation, November 3, 1969

The Carter Doctrine

The 1980s have been born in turmoil, strife, and change. This is a time of challenge to our interest and our values and it's a time that tests our wisdom and our skills.

. . . I am determined that the United States will remain the strongest of all nations, but our power will never be used to initiate a threat to the security of any nation or to the rights of any human being. We seek to be and to remain secure — a nation at peace in a stable world. But to be secure we must face the world as it is. . . . The region which is now threatened by Soviet troops in Afghanistan is of great strategic importance. . . . Let our position be absolutely clear: an attempt by any outside force to gain control of the Persian Gulf region will be regarded as an assault on the vital interests of the United States of America, and such an assault will be repelled by any means necessary, including military force.

Source: State of the Union address, January 23, 1980

The Reagan Doctrine

We must stand by all our democratic allies. And we must not break faith with those who are risking their lives — on every continent from Afghanistan to Nicaragua — to defy Soviet-supported aggression and secure rights which have been ours from birth.

. . . The U.S. must rebuild the credibility of our commitment to resist Soviet encroachment on U.S. interests and those of its allies and friends, and to support effectively those Third World states that are willing to resist Soviet pressures or oppose Soviet initiatives hostile to the United States, or are special targets of Soviet policy.

Source: Reagan Doctrine, U.S. Department of State

The Bush Doctrine

Today, at the start of a new century, we are again engaged in a war unlike any our nation has fought before — and today like Americans in Truman's day, we are laying the foundations for victory. The enemies we face are different in many ways from the enemy we faced in the Cold War. In the Cold War, we deterred Soviet aggression through a policy of mutually assured destruction. . . . The terrorists have no borders to protect, or capital to defend. They cannot be deterred — but they will be defeated.

. . . In this new war we have to set a clear doctrine. . . . America will not wait to be attacked again. We will confront threats before they fully materialize. We will stay on the offense against the terrorists, fighting them abroad so that we do not have to face them at home. . . . The security of our nation depends on the advance of liberty in other nations. . . . So we are pursuing a forward strategy of freedom in the Middle East. I believe the desire for liberty is universal, and by standing with democratic reformers across a troubled region we will extend freedom to millions who have not known it — and lay the foundation of peace for generations to come.

Source: Commencement address at the United States Military Academy at West Point, May 27, 2006

The Truman Doctrine

On March 12, 1947, in a speech to a special joint session of Congress, President Harry S. Truman asked for $400 million for economic assistance to Greece and Turkey to help them resist Soviet-inspired aggression. In making his request, he asserted, "It must be the policy of the United States to support free peoples who are resisting attempted subjugation by armed minorities or outside pressures." Prior to the speech, Secretary of State Dean Acheson met with congressional leaders and outlined the need for action, citing "a highly likely Soviet breakthrough" in Greece and the danger of "infection" elsewhere by this "eager and ruthless opponent." Congressional leaders agreed to support the request provided Truman made his case to the full Congress and the American people.

Greece was involved in a civil war that pitted a pro-British government against leftist rebels led by the communist-controlled opposition National Liberation Front. Turkey was involved in an ongoing dispute with the Soviet Union over control of the Dardanelles Straits that linked Soviet ports along the Black Sea with the Mediterranean Sea. From the Soviet point of view, access to the Mediterranean was crucial to its ability to act as a Great Power, but it was also a security threat. During World War II, Turkey had permitted German naval forces to enter the Black Sea. Stalin now insisted on international control over the straits, a demand that Turkey interpreted as a threat to its national sovereignty.

Truman's speech is widely seen as the equivalent to a U.S. declaration of Cold War against the Soviet Union. It firmly rejected the pre–World War II U.S. foreign policy of isolationism and provided a rationale for U.S. activism in world affairs by declaring that the world was "divided between two antithetical ways of life: one based on freedom, another on coercion" and that "we shall not realize our objectives . . . unless we are willing to help free peoples to maintain their free institutions and their national integrity." The Truman Doctrine, as the contents of this speech came to be known, also identified a universal enemy with its references to aggression by "totalitarian regimes." This phrase was applied almost exclusively to the Soviet Union and its allies.

Although the Truman Doctrine did not specify a set of actions to be taken, its implementation quickly came to center on two concepts: containment and deterrence. Central to both the concepts was a status quo orientation to the events in the world. U.S. foreign policy would not actively seek to roll back the Iron Curtain so much as it would work to stop the further expansion of the Soviet Union and its sphere of influence.

Containment became identified with three sets of policies. The first was encircling the Soviet Union and its allies in a ring of alliances and bilateral security agreements that would contain them. The most significant alliances were the North Atlantic Treaty Organization (NATO), the Central Treaty Organization (CENTO) in the Middle East, and the Southeast Asia Treaty Organization (SEATO). Important bilateral agreements were signed with Japan, the Philippines, and South Korea. Covert military action was a second important instrument of containment. It was directed at key countries that were being threatened by communist takeovers or had just fallen victim to them, such as Iran, Guatemala, Cuba, and Indonesia. Finally, foreign aid was used to help assure the loyalty and support of key governments and to promote economic prosperity as a way to dampen the appeal of communism. Deterrence came to be associated with nuclear weapons and the recognition that they were no longer effective instruments of war. Instead, their primary purpose was to stop conflicts from erupting.

The Nixon Doctrine

The Nixon Doctrine was part of an attempt by Nixon to formulate a policy that would allow the United States to remain the dominant power in the international system after Vietnam, but not require that it send troops abroad to contain the spread of communism. The Nixon Doctrine stated that the United States would help free countries defend themselves, but that these countries must provide for their own military defense, with the United States providing both military and economic assistance. In short, there would be no more Vietnams.

In addition to the Nixon Doctrine, the Nixon administration pursued two other initiatives as part of its strategy to redirect American foreign policy. The most narrowly constructed was Vietnamization, which sought to turn over responsibility for defending South Vietnam to the South Vietnamese. In an effort to buy sufficient time for Vietnamization to work, Nixon ordered the invasion of Cambodia and Laos in order to eliminate communist sanctuaries there. That strategy failed when, in spring 1972, North Vietnamese forces attacked across the 17th Parallel into the South, forcing Nixon to "re-Americanize" the war. The second and more broadly conceived policy initiative was détente. It sought to engage the Soviet Union and China in a dialogue that would transform their relationship with the United States from one of competition and open distrust to one of limited cooperation and muted conflict. The most significant accomplishments of détente were the opening to China and the signing of Strategic Arms Limitation Talks (SALT) arms control agreements with the Soviet Union.

A major consequence of the Nixon Doctrine was a massive increase in the level of arms transfers to regional powers. Providing allies with military aid was necessary because while détente reduced the level of tension between the United States and the Soviet Union, it did not do away with the fact that they were still engaged in competition for global influence. Indonesia, the Philippines, Saudi Arabia, Iran, Pakistan, and South Korea became prime recipients of this aid. A particularly troubling situation developed in the Middle East. The rapid increase in oil prices brought on by the Organization of Petroleum Exporting Countries (OPEC) allowed these states to purchase weapons rather than receive them as foreign aid. This resulted in ever-more sophisticated weapons flowing into the region.

The Carter Doctrine

The Carter Doctrine is the name given to the policy announced by President Jimmy Carter in response to the Soviet Union's December 1979 invasion of Afghanistan. Carter stated that the United States would treat an "attempt by any outside force to gain control of the Persian Gulf region as an assault on the vital interests of the United States and such force will be repelled by any means necessary, including military force."

The Carter Doctrine represented a virtual about-face for Carter's foreign policy toward the Soviet Union. Carter had campaigned on a platform that rejected power politics and promised to replace it with an emphasis on human rights and morality. He quickly moved to negotiate a new Panama Canal Treaty, and in September 1977, two treaties were signed that would transfer sovereignty over the canal to Panama on January 1, 2000. The following year, in September 1978, Carter arranged for a summit conference at the presidential retreat at Camp David between Israeli prime minister Menachem Begin and Egyptian president Anwar Sadat, at which both leaders agreed to a "just, comprehensive and durable settlement for the Middle East conflict."

The inevitable consequence of Carter's foreign policy was to deemphasize the importance of the Soviet Union to U.S. foreign policy and to draw attention to how the Soviet Union treated its citizens. Both moves offended Soviet leaders and U.S.-Soviet relations deteriorated. Only after two-and-a-half years of difficult negotiations was a SALT II agreement reached in 1979. That agreement, already controversial, was never voted on by the Senate. Carter withdrew it from consideration because of the Soviet invasion of Afghanistan.

A 1973 coup d'état deposed the king of Afghanistan. A struggle for power ensued that resulted in the pro-Soviet wing of the Marxist People's Democratic Party taking power. In 1979 they were overthrown by a rival Maoist group. Both groups attempted to undertake radical social reforms that were being resisted by Islamic groups. In December 1979, faced with a chaotic situation in Afghanistan and the possible triumph of opposition Islamic forces, the Soviet Union sent an invasion force of over fifty thousand soldiers into Afghanistan and placed exiled pro-Soviet Communist Party leader Babrack Karmal in power.

The Soviet action caught the Carter administration off guard and called into question the wisdom of Carter's foreign policy agenda. As part of his response, Carter requested an increase in annual defense spending and expanded the American naval and air presence in the Persian Gulf. Though this action was generally applauded, some commentators criticized Carter's response as overreacting and motivated by domestic political concerns. They argued that while the Soviet invasion of Afghanistan was deplorable, it did not represent a calculated

Soviet move to control the Persian Gulf. This debate, however, was soon overshadowed by the Iranian hostage crisis and the Carter administration's inability to secure the release of the Americans taken hostage in the American embassy.

The Reagan Doctrine

Unlike Nixon and Carter, for most of his presidency, Reagan saw the Soviet Union as a state to be challenged and not worked with. Early in his administration, he referred to the Soviet Union as an "evil empire," charging that "the only morality they recognize is what will further their cause; meaning they reserve unto themselves the right to commit any crime, to lie, to cheat."[26] A prerequisite for dealing effectively with such a state was a major buildup of American military strength and a toughened stance toward arms control. To these ends, Reagan called for a $16 billion increase in defense spending over five years, the deployment of the MX missile system, the renewed production of poison gas, the development of the neutron bomb, and the beginning of a long-term research plan—the Strategic Defense Initiative ("Star Wars")—to build a missile defense system. On arms control, his administration went public with a series of accusations of Soviet arms control cheating.

In his 1985 State of the Union speech, Reagan asserted, "We must not break faith with those who are risking their lives—on every continent from Afghanistan to Nicaragua—to defy Soviet aggression and secure rights which have been ours from birth. Support of freedom fighters is self-defense." By speaking in this manner, Reagan signaled an important shift in his foreign policy from that of his predecessors. The United States would now do more than contain the spread of communism; it would also work actively to remove communists and their allies from power. In fact, the Reagan administration was already doing so.

Reagan saw Central America as a major front in the conflict between the United States and Soviet Union. His administration considered El Salvador a textbook case of communist aggression and contended that a large part of the problem in this country was due to Russian and Cuban military support for leftist rebel forces, which was being funneled through Nicaragua. In a move to cut off the supply of weapons, Reagan signed a presidential finding in March 1981 authorizing the CIA to organize and fund moderate opponents of the Sandinista Nicaraguan government. These forces came to be known as the Contras.

The administration's unwavering support for the Contras became one of the most controversial features of its foreign policy. Where Reagan characterized the Contras as the "moral equivalent of the founding fathers," human rights groups complained at length about their brutality. In 1984 Congress cut off funding for the Contras. In an effort to circumvent this ban, the Reagan administration undertook a failed secret initiative that became known as the Iran-Contra Affair. It proposed that American weapons intended for Israel would be sold to Iran, and Israel would receive new weapons. In return, Iran would help secure the release of American hostages in Lebanon. Money from the weapons sales would be used to fund the Contras.

The Reagan administration was also deeply involved in Afghanistan by 1985. The primary Afghan group opposing the Soviet Union's invasion was the Mujahadin. It proved to be a formidable fighting force not only because of its tenacity but also because of the American aid it received. In 1984 the Reagan administration was underwriting the Mujahadin to the tune of $120 million. By 1987 this figure had increased to $630 million. The success achieved by the Reagan administration in tying down the Soviet Union in Afghanistan was not without its long-term costs. This policy resulted in a large amount of U.S. arms flowing into the hands of Afghan groups that combined forces with the Taliban-led government that came into power after the Soviet Union left and were later used against U.S.-supported interests.

Near the end of his administration, Ronald Reagan did a seeming about-face in his foreign policy. He and Soviet leader Mikhail Gorbachev became regular partners at summit conferences, meeting five times during Reagan's last term. It was their second summit at Reykjavik, Iceland, that provoked the most controversy. Given insufficient preparation, the Reagan administration was caught off guard by Gorbachev's proposal that both sides eliminate all offensive strategic nuclear weapons. Reagan accepted the proposal, only to back off later because of his personal attachment to the Star Wars program.

The Bush Doctrine

Although the Bush Doctrine first appeared as a unified statement in the September 2002 *National Security Strategy of the United States of America*, its key themes were already visible by then.[27] Speaking to a joint session of Congress following the 9/11 terrorist attacks, President George W. Bush stated that the United States "would make no distinction between the terrorists who committed these acts and those who harbor them" and that "we will pursue nations that provide aid or safe haven to terrorism. Every nation, in every region, now has a decision to make. Either you are with us or you are with the terrorists." In a June 2002 speech to the graduating class at West Point, Bush stated, "Our security will require all Americans to be forward-looking and resolute, to be ready for preemptive action when necessary to defend our liberty and to defend our lives." He also asserted, "The gravest danger to freedom lies in the crossroads of radicalism and technology." To these observations, the *National Security Strategy* added that "we cannot let our enemies strike first," that the United States will use its power to encourage free and open societies, and that it will never allow its military supremacy to be challenged.

The Bush Doctrine provided the intellectual framework for launching the Global War on Terrorism, the invasion of Afghanistan to remove the Taliban from power, and the invasion of Iraq. Central to the administration's argument for the Iraqi invasion was the latter's possession of weapons of mass destruction, a claim that later proved to be false. Where the Taliban in Afghanistan and Saddam Hussein in Iraq were removed from power with relative ease, capturing Osama bin Laden and establishing democracy in Iraq proved to be a far greater challenge. Bin Laden succeeded in escaping U.S. forces and fled to Pakistan. In

Iraq, rather than being greeted as liberators, U.S. forces soon came to be viewed as occupiers and became the target of terrorist attacks. The conflict also brought forward vivid images of mistreatment of prisoners by American military personnel at Abu Ghraib prison, which served to inflame anti-American sentiment in Iraq and antiwar feelings in the United States. A sense of stability returned to Iraq near the end of the Bush administration as a change in strategy that sought to achieve victory through counterinsurgency principles which emphasized working with Iraqis rather than trying to secure victory through battlefield successes against them led to a reduction in the violence.

Problems began to resurface in Afghanistan, where the Taliban had regrouped and were now once again viewed as a significant national security threat that demanded a U.S. military presence. More generally, a sense had developed that the administration's goal of spreading democracy through the region had been replaced by a preference for stability.

Assessing Results

Judging the consequences of a foreign policy is a complicated task. A major problem is that success and failure are often treated as absolute categories, yet this is seldom the case. Far more typical are situations in which success and failure are both present in varying degrees. A state rarely has only one goal when it undertakes a course of action, and the reality of multiple goals further complicates the calculations of costs and benefits. Estimates of success and failure also depend on one's time frame. Economic sanctions work slowly, but that does not mean that they are any less effective than fast-acting ones. They might even be preferable, because they minimize the risk of miscalculation that occurs during crisis situations.

Political considerations also cloud any evaluation of the effectiveness of a policy instrument. In 2003 Libya announced that it was giving up its pursuit of nuclear weapons. The George W. Bush administration quickly hailed the announcement as evidence that its tough post-9/11 military stance, including the doctrine of preemption, was succeeding. Others countered that the success really should be attributed to years of behind-the-scene diplomacy and economic sanctions.[28]

Beyond questions of success or failure we can also judge past, present, and future U.S. foreign policies in terms of their underlying characteristics. In this section we introduce three such standards: (1) their intellectual coherence, (2) the extent to which they are motivated by domestic politics rather than foreign events, and (3) the consistency with which they are applied to foreign policy problems. To a greater or lesser extent, each of these reference points has been found to be a problem in the five foreign policy doctrines we examined earlier.

Intellectual Coherence

The foreign policy of containment that grew out of the Truman Doctrine was grounded in two very different views of the Soviet Union, both of which could not be correct. One view, championed by George Kennan, saw Soviet expansion largely as defensive and reactionary. It saw Soviet leaders as more concerned with staying in power than with spreading communism. The authors of National Security Council document #68 (NSC-68) rejected this perspective. They saw Soviet hostility to the United States as unrelenting and based on Marxist-Leninist ideological principles. Moreover, its leadership was committed to spreading communism throughout the world. For Kennan, American power could be applied selectively around the world. From the perspective of NSC-68, it had to be applied wherever communists were present or threatened.

Nixon's policy of détente was rooted in National Security Advisor Henry Kissinger's belief that the most stable international system was one in which all major powers viewed the international system as legitimate, something the Soviet Union and China could not do so long as they were the target of American containment efforts.[29] Conservative critics took exception to Nixon's willingness to accept the Soviet Union as a full partner in the family of nations maintaining that little if anything had changed in communist foreign policy other than the Nixon administration's evaluation of it.

Carter's foreign policy was characterized by sympathetic observers as "the hell of good intentions" for its immature and mistaken belief that it could push U.S.-Soviet relations to the sidelines while addressing human rights problems.[30] Jeanne Kirkpatrick, who would go on to serve as ambassador to the United Nations in the Reagan administration, criticized Carter's human rights policy arguing that it did not recognize the difference between right-wing governments and totalitarian governments such as that of the Soviet Union.[31] The former could make a transition to democracy, whereas the latter could not. Accordingly, far greater pressure needed to be put on totalitarian governments than on right-wing dictatorships.

Reagan's view of the Soviet Union was challenged by most on the political left, as was the presumed linkage between the Reagan administration and the fall of communism. One observer asserted that the principal reasons for Reagan's success had little to do with administration policy, but rather resulted from "forces and trends outside the control of the United States and of measures undertaken by others and occasionally even opposed by Mr. Reagan."[32] Interestingly, Reagan's foreign policy near the end of his administration, with its interest in arms control and willingness to push American allies such as Philippine President Ferdinand Marcos on human rights and pro-democracy issues, led some conservatives to characterize it as "Carterism without Carter."

Several aspects of the Bush Doctrine brought forward questions about the strength of its intellectual foundations. Most fundamentally it sparked a debate over the purposes of American power that pitted realist conservatives against neoconservatives.[33] Both groups were in agreement on the importance of military power, but conservative realists called for restraint in its use while neoconservatives advanced an ambitious agenda that included spreading democracy.

The most prominent point of controversy about the implementation of the Bush Doctrine involved the concept of preemption. At issue here was the blurring of a long-standing distinction in international politics between preemption and prevention.[34] Both are based on the principle of striking first in self-defense. In the case of preemption, the feared attack is imminent. In the case of prevention, it is more general and future-oriented. International law recognizes the legitimacy of preemptive strikes, but not necessarily of preventive strikes on an enemy. Critics argued that in casting the Iraq War as a preemptive one, the Bush administration used the imagery of preemption in a situation to justify a preemptive war.

A related criticism questioned the administration's assertion that containment and deterrence could not work against rogue regimes and supporters of international terrorism because of the irrational nature of these regimes.[35] Defenders of containment and deterrence argued that rationality is a matter of degree and not an all-or-nothing quality. Rogue regimes concerned with their survival could be expected to act rationally enough in the face of U.S. deterrence threats.

The Dominance of Domestic Politics

Truman resisted adopting the changes suggested in NSC-68 because of their budgetary implications, especially the need to fight communism everywhere in the world. Only after the outbreak of the Korean War and the changed domestic climate at home did he embrace a more expansive and expensive definition of containment. Nixon's embrace of détente and the shifting of defense responsibilities on to allies were likewise heavily influenced by the unwillingness of the American public to pay for the Vietnam War. Carter announced his doctrine and abandoned détente with the Soviet invasion of Afghanistan and a reversal in American thinking about what it is willing to pay for national security. Reagan and Bush represent interesting cases. Both pursued aggressive foreign policies that required large-scale military spending. Yet, as even sympathetic critics of each pointed out, neither called on the American public to sacrifice. As one observer put it about Reagan's foreign policy, its great appeal was that it demanded so little from the public while promising to deliver so much.[36] When costs were encountered, such as the attacks on the marine barracks in Lebanon in 1983 that killed 241 marines, the policy was quickly terminated by Reagan. Bush, by contrast, held firm in his commitment to victory in Iraq even after the 2006 midterm elections indicated widespread public disapproval for the war. Still, there was no call for greater public sacrifice. Additionally, some assert that the invasion of Iraq was not dictated by the War on Terror but was an opportunistic response to the events of 9/11 that allowed the administration to pursue its goal of removing Saddam Hussein from power.

Inconsistency of Application

Critics have charged that no administration fully succeeded in using its doctrine as an organizing device to guide all of its foreign policy decisions. Inconsistencies are always present. Carter succumbed to offering arms sales to states whose human rights record his administration had criticized. Reagan did little to aid Eastern European states seeking to break away from the Soviet Union, and he entered into negotiations with supporters of terrorism as part of the Iran-Contra Affair. He also entered into arms control talks with the Soviet Union near the end of his presidency. Bush engaged in a preemptive war with one member of the "axis of evil" (Iraq), but found it necessary to enter into negotiations with another that obtained nuclear weapons (North Korea) and struggled to get support from the international community to block the efforts of the third to get nuclear weapons (Iran).

On one level, the existence of a gap between declaratory policy and action policy is unavoidable and on occasion may actually be prudent. George H. W. Bush and Bill Clinton were often criticized for their lack of a guiding foreign policy doctrine in the early years of the post–Cold War international system. Many defended Bush's failure to do so, arguing that, given the uncertainty associated with this new world, the benefits of pragmatism far outweighed the benefits of an overarching vision of American foreign policy that would guide decision-making. Bill Clinton, by contrast, was roundly criticized for his indecision and frequent changes of direction over the use of military force in Somalia, Haiti, and Bosnia.

Over the Horizon: Citizen Power?

We noted earlier in this chapter that selecting a policy instrument is central to the construction of a successful foreign policy. Today, the debate is largely over the relative merits of hard and soft power. Recently, a new form of power is gaining attention. It is referred to as citizen power and highlights the growing ability of the public around the world to create highly fluid and far-reaching interactive platforms such as YouTube, podcasts, wikis, Facebook, and text messaging that have the ability to distribute information to large numbers of people and facilitate political activity.[37]

Writing in November 2010, only months before the advent of pro-democracy demonstrations and rebellions in North Africa and the Middle East, Eric Schmidt and Jared Cohen, both affiliated with Google, suggested that "governments will be caught off guard when large numbers of their citizens, armed with virtually nothing but cell phones, take part in mini-rebellions that challenge their authority."[38] More recently it has been argued that "the forces of technology are ushering in a new age of openness" that will put people in a position to better observe and critique the policies of countries at home and around the world.[39] In this world it is not only individuals who will be empowered but also organizations and political movements. Commercial satellite imagery, for example, can be easily purchased. One think tank has used this imagery to detail China's efforts to reclaim land in the South China Sea. Another research organization has used it to track North Korean nuclear test preparations. A pro-Ukrainian volunteer regiment used drone images to expose large Russian bases in their country.

One foreign policy area where citizen power has received considerable attention is arms control. Under the heading of societal verification or public verification it sees the potential for ordinary citizens to use modern technology to provide information that supplements standard international safeguard and verification practices.[40] Another area where citizen power is potentially important, for better or worse, is terrorism. As ISIS campaigns in Syria have demonstrated, social media and images taken by citizens have become both a source of great propaganda value to terrorists and a valuable source of information about their activities that would otherwise not be available.

Continuing to rely simply on soft and hard powers may result in U.S. foreign policy either playing a reactive role to developments in the international system or being reduced to the role of spectators. Citizen power can also be seen as creating two over-the-horizon dangers for the United States. First, the communication technologies that support citizen power are also available to oppressive governments, terrorists, and drug dealers making citizen power a competitive arena. Second, citizen power can also be used to force the United States into a position of acting where it might otherwise not. Images of civilians killed in drone attacks targeted on terrorists are intended to turn local populations against the United States. An attempt to prod the United States and others into action was the primary goal of photos released containing images of chemical attacks in Syria. Images of beheadings by ISIS were intended to have the opposite effect.

Critical Thinking Questions

1. Identify ten foreign policy problems facing the United States today. Divide them into A-, B-, and C-list problems. On what basis did you make your decisions?
2. What type of foreign policy problems do hard power and soft power work best on?

3. Pick a foreign policy problem. What standards should be used to evaluate U.S. efforts to address it?

Key Terms

action policy, 4
bipartisanship, 9
blowback, 8
declaratory policy, 4
grand strategy, 10
hard power, 10

Lippmann Gap, 8
national interest, 6
opportunity cost, 8
public goods, 7
soft power, 10

Further Reading

Richard Betts, "Is Strategy an Illusion?" *International Security* 25 (2000), 5–50.

A frequently heard recommendation for improving American foreign policy is to develop a more coherent grand strategy. This important essay raises the question of whether it can be done.

Ted Galen Carpenter, "The Case for Moral Realism," *The National Interest* 140 (November 2015), 51–58.

The starting point of this article is that not all interests are created equal. The author divides them into four categories: vital, conditional, peripheral, and barely relevant. The article then discusses the challenge of making moral compromises in foreign policy making.

Daniel Drezner, "Military Primacy Doesn't Pay (Nearly As Much As You Think)," *International Security* 38 (2013), 52–79.

This article argues that there is little evidence to support the position that military primacy results in significant geoeconomic gains. The major foreign policy benefits of military power occur when military primacy is coupled with economic primacy.

Paul Kennedy, ed., *Grand Strategies in War and Peace* (New Haven: Yale University Press, 1991).

The essays in this volume present a historical and comparative perspective on the challenges of developing grand strategy.

Paul D. Miller, "Obama's Afghanistan," *The American Interest* 11 (Summer 2016), 56–64.

A former director for Afghanistan and Pakistan under George W. Bush, the author is critical of Obama's Afghanistan policy arguing that while it had elements of the right approach, it was never provided the time or resources needed to succeed.

Joseph Nye, *Soft Power: The Means to Success in World Politics* (New York: PublicAffairs, 1994).

This volume introduces readers to the concept of soft power and discusses its ability to advance foreign policy and further the national interest.

Bruno Tertrais, "Drawing Red Lines Right," *Washington Quarterly* 37 (Fall 2014), 7–24.

The author notes that red lines have a mixed record of success. This article examines the circumstances under which they will fail and makes recommendations for how to improve the chances of success.

Notes

[1] http://www.whitehouse.gov/the-press-office/2014/05/28/remarks-president-west-point-academy-commencement-ceremony.

[2] David Ignatius, "Obama Speech Offers Clarity on Libya Policy," *Washington Post*, March 29, 2011.

[3] For a sampling, see Fred Kaplan, "Obama's Way," *Foreign Affairs* 95 (2016), 46–63; Gideon Rose, "What Obama Gets Right," *Foreign Affairs* 94 (2015), 2–12; Bret Stephens, "What Obama Gets Wrong," *Foreign Affairs* 94 (2015), 13–17; Jeffrey Goldberg, "The Obama Doctrine," *The Atlantic* (April 2016); and Ganesh Sitaraman, "Progressive Pragmatism," *The American Interest* 9 (May 2014), 68–75.

[4] Steve Strasser, ed., *The 9/11 Investigations* (New York: PublicAffairs, 2004), 233.

[5] Jim Hoagland, "Why Clinton Improvises," *Washington Post*, September 25, 1994, C1.

[6] Zbigniew Brzezinski, *Second Chance: Three Presidents and the Crisis of American Superpower* (New York: Basic Books, 2007), 183.

[7] Paul Kennedy, *The Rise and Fall of the Great Powers* (New York: Random House, 1987).

[8] Bob Woodward, *Obama's Wars* (New York: Simon & Schuster, 2010), pp. 278–79.

⁹ Dina Smeltz, *Foreign Policy in the New Millennium* (Chicago: Chicago Council on Global Affairs, 2012), 14.

¹⁰ Pew Research Center, "Americans' Foreign Policy Priorities for 2014," http://www.pewresearch.org/fact-tank/2013/12/31/americans-foreign-policy-priorities-for-2014.

¹¹ Pew Research Center, "The 2016 Election: American Foreign and Economic Policy Views," http://www.pewglobal.org/2016/01/15/2016-election-american-foreign-and-economic-policy-views-presentation.

¹² For recent efforts, see Ted Galen Carpenter, "Dealing with Bad Allies: The Case for Moral Realism," *The National Interest* 140 (2015), 51–58; Derek Reveron and Nikolas Gvosdev, "(Re) Discovering the National Interest," *Orbis* 59 (2015), 299–316; and Bruce Jentleson, "Strategic Recalibration," *The Washington Quarterly* 37 (2014), 115–36.

¹³ Walter Lippmann, *The Cold War: A Study in U.S. Foreign Policy* (New York: Harper, 1947). Also see Michael Mazarr, "A Strategy of Discriminate Power," *The Washington Quarterly* 37 (2014), 137–50.

¹⁴ Chalmers Johnson, *Blowback* (New York: Owl Books, 2000).

¹⁵ Humphrey Taylor, "The Not-so-Black Art of Public Diplomacy," *World Policy Journal* 24 (2007/8), 51–59.

¹⁶ "The Price of Detachment," *The Economist*, March 23, 2013, 37.

¹⁷ Charles Kupchan and Peter Trubowitz, "Grand Strategy for a Divided America," *Foreign Affairs* 86 (2007), 82.

¹⁸ Richard Holbrooke, "The Next President," *Foreign Affairs* 87 (2008), 2.

¹⁹ John P. Lovell, "The Idiom of National Security," *Journal of Political and Military Sociology* 11 (1983), 35–51.

²⁰ Glenn Kessler and Robin Wright, "A Case for Progress amid Some Omissions," *The Washington Post*, June 29, 2005, A1; Dan Fromkin, "White House Briefing," January 24, 2005, http://www.washingtonpost.com/wp-dyn/politics/administration/briefing; Omar Fekeiki, "The Toll of Communism," *Washington Post*, June 13, 2007, C1.

²¹ Bob Woodward, *The War Within* (New York: Simon & Schuster, 2008), 189.

²² Ann Scott Tyson, "Gates Warns of Militarized Policy," *Washington Post*, July 16, 2008, A6.

²³ Woodward, *The War Within*, 32.

²⁴ Ibid., 425.

²⁵ Richard Betts, "Is Strategy an Illusion?" *International Security* 25 (2000), 5–50.

²⁶ The speech can be found at http://www.nationalcenter.org/ReaganEvilEmpire1983.html

²⁷ *National Security Strategy of the United States,* 2002, http://georgewbush-whitehouse.archives.gov/nsc/nss/2002.

²⁸ George Joffe, "Libya: Who Blinked and Why," *Current History* 103 (May 2004), 221–25.

²⁹ Henry Kissinger, *A World Restored* (New York: Grosset & Dunlap, 1964).

³⁰ Stanley Hoffmann, "Requiem," *Foreign Policy* 42 (1981), 3–26.

³¹ Jeanne Kirkpatrick, "Human Rights and American Foreign Policy: A Symposium," *Commentary* (November 1981), 42–45.

³² Michael Mandelbaum, "The Luck of the President," *Foreign Affairs* 64 (1986), 393–413.

³³ G. John Ikenberry, "The End of the Neo-conservative Moment," *Survival* 46 (2004), 7–22; Francis Fukuyama, *America at the Crossroads* (New Haven: Yale University Press, 2006).

³⁴ On the distinction between preemption and prevention, see Lawrence Freedman, "Prevention, Not Preemption," *Washington Quarterly* 26 (2003), 105–14.

³⁵ Robert F. Trager and Dessislava P. Zagorcheva, "Deterring Terrorism: It Can Be Done," *International Security* 30 (2005/6), 87–123; Jeffrey Record, "The Bush Doctrine and War with Iraq," *Parameters* (Spring 2003), 4–21.

³⁶ Robert Tucker, "Reagan's Foreign Policy," *Foreign Affairs* 68 (1989), 1–27.

³⁷ Eric Schmidt and Jared Cohen, "The Digital Disruption," *Foreign Affairs* 89 (2010), 75–85.

³⁸ Ibid.

³⁹ Sean Larkin, "The Age of Transparency," *Foreign Affairs* 95 (May 2016), 136–46.

⁴⁰ For an early argument for societal verification, see Seymour Melman, *Inspection for Disarmament* (New York: Columbia University Press, 1958). A more recent discussion is found in Nina Gerami, "Attracting a Crowd," *Bulletin of the Atomic Scientists* 69 (May/June 2014), 14–18.

The Global Context **2**

Dateline: The South China Sea

Foreign policy is outward looking and seeks to promote the national interest. This much is agreed upon. Where disagreement exists is over how best to anticipate threats and recognize opportunities found beyond their borders. Do we look at the structure of the international system, changing relations between countries, or specific events? Each of these possible focal points presents itself to the United States as it formulates a foreign policy to respond to Chinese actions in the South China Sea.[1]

Some 648,000 square nautical miles, the South China Sea is one of the world's largest semi-enclosed seas. Five countries (six if Taiwan is counted) with a combined population of about 270 million are found along its borders: China, Vietnam, the Philippines, Brunei, and Malaysia. All claim sovereignty over some or all of it. China argues that these islands have been Chinese territory "since antiquity." At issue is not only control over the waters of the South China Sea and the airspace above it, but control over some four hundred to six hundred rocks, reefs, atolls, and islands. The two largest groupings of land are the Spratly and Paracel Islands. Both have been the focal point of military-political conflicts involving competing claims made by China, Vietnam, and the Philippines. Officially the United States has taken no position on these conflicting territorial claims other than rejecting China's claim to sovereignty over virtually all of it.

Three geostrategic factors come together to frame the South China Sea foreign policy problem facing U.S. foreign policy. First, the South China Sea is a critical passageway for global commercial shipping and naval operations linking the Middle East and Africa to Asia. The amount of oil passing through its waters is six times larger than that going through the Suez Canal. Second, evidence points to the presence of potentially significant natural energy reserves beneath the South China Sea. The Chinese media refers to it as "the second Persian Gulf." Third, the South China Sea is of great strategic importance to China. It is often spoken of in terms comparable to how the United States traditionally has looked at the Caribbean Sea. To a considerable degree it was in recognition of China's growing economic and military power along with the key role that the South China Sea played in China's foreign policy thinking that President Obama called for a "pivot' to Asia when he became president.

Tensions between the United States and China have grown noticeably. In November 2013, after China unilaterally claimed the right to police a contested portion of the airspace over the South China Sea, the United States sent two B-52 bombers into that zone without asking permission. In May 2014 without notice China unilaterally placed a $1 billion deepwater oil drilling rig of the shore of an island claimed by both China and Vietnam. The move was described in the press as a possible "game changer" because logically it would require China to expand its navy in order to protect its investment. Three months later China rejected a U.S. call for a freeze on "provocative acts" in the South China Sea stating that "as a responsible great power, China is ready to maintain restraint but for unreasonable provocative activities, China is bound to make a clear an firm reaction."[2]

Matters escalated considerably in 2015 when China began to build a "Great Wall of Sand" in the South China Sea, defined by China as a "lawful and justified" land reclamation project within its own borders. The project involves the construction of coral reefs and rocks with the Spratly Islands along with harbors, piers, helipads, and possibly an airstrip. State Department officials characterized it as an unprecedented attempt to "militarize outposts on disputed land features." Secretary of Defense Ashton Carter responded by stating, "We're going to meet it. We will remain the principal security power in the Asia-Pacific for decades to come." By early 2016 China had moved forward by placing surface-to-air missiles with a range of 125 miles on a disputed island. In a counter move the United States announced that it was on track to reposition 60 percent of the navy to the Pacific by 2020. The Philippines, Japan, and Australia have all agreed to new military basing rights for the United States.

Tensions continued to rise in fall, 2016. The U.S. Navy sent a destroyer near a contested island claimed on the first of what it described as regular operations to challenge China's "excessive maritime claims." China countered by carrying out one of its regular military exercises in disputed waters. Adding to the complexity of the situation was the emergence of a dispute between the U.S. and the Philippines which found President Rodrigo calling for a withdrawal of U.S. troops from the Philippines in two years and agreeing to reopen talks with China on disputes between them on the South China Sea.

This chapter lays out the foundation for developing a deeper understanding of the foreign policy problem the United States faces in the South China Sea and elsewhere by presenting three broad international political perspectives used to study world politics and then moving to identifying key structural features in world politics. We next turn our attention to the contemporary international system. We examine three important issues (terrorism, globalization, and American hegemony) and compare American and non-American views of the world today.

Historical Lesson

The First Asian Pivot: Commodore Perry's Opening of Japan

President Obama's Asian Pivot was not the first time that the United States had come to recognize the potential importance of Asia to its military and economic security. A first Asian Pivot occurred more than a century ago when Commodore Matthew Perry led four ships into Tokyo Bay on July 8, 1853.

For some two centuries, Japan had managed to severely limit the access foreigners had to its territory. Japanese leaders had expelled missionaries whom they had come to consider as overly zealous and foreign traders whom they saw as taking advantage of their people in 1639. By the mid-1800s this policy was becoming harder to maintain. Already in the 1830s U.S. naval vessels stationed in China had made several voyages to Japan in an effort to establish relations.

By the time Commodore Perry set sail to Japan a combination of factors had come together to make the opening of Japan a high-priority foreign policy issue. The annexation of California now provided the United States with Pacific Ocean ports, raising the possibility of expanding U.S. trade with China. Japan's geographic location and rumors that it held large coal reserves made access to Japanese ports an important part of any move to increase the U.S. economic presence in Asia. American missionaries also lobbied for access to Japan, convinced that Protestant religions would be accepted by the Japanese, who had earlier rejected Catholicism. Stories of Japanese mistreatment of shipwrecked American sailors gave rise to yet additional calls for opening Japan.

Perry presented Japanese leaders with a letter from President Millard Fillmore outlining U.S. objectives. He then left, informing them that he would return the following year for an answer. Return he did and on March 5, 1854, the Treaty of Kanagawa was signed; it was subsequently ratified unanimously by the Senate. It provided the United States with two coaling stations and provided protection for shipwrecked sailors, but it did not give the United States commercial concessions or the guarantee of trading rights. These rights would not come into existence until 1858 when a follow-on treaty gave the United States two additional coaling stations as well as trading rights. It also established the principle of extraterritoriality according to which American citizens arrested in Japan would be tried by U.S. courts. This provision was common to treaties Western powers signed with Asian states at the time. From their perspective they came to be referred to as the unequal treaties.

Within a decade, Japan turned these agreements to their fullest advantage, using them to spur reforms to its feudal political and economic systems. The resulting Meiji Restoration transformed Japan into an industrial and military power, as testified to by its victories in the Sino-Japanese War of 1894 and the Russo-Japanese War of 1904 that gave it control over Taiwan and over much of Manchuria, as well as a dominant position in Korea. Theodore Roosevelt won the Nobel Peace Prize for helping bring about an end to the latter war.

Japan's growing power also set the stage for a series of military and diplomatic interactions with the United States over the next several decades that would steadily deepen America's involvement in Asian regional politics. One of the first points of dispute between the two countries was the U.S. annexation of Hawaii in 1898. The Taft-Katsura Agreement of 1905 was designed to prevent future disputes over areas of influence. In return for recognizing American control over the Philippines, the United States recognized Japan's dominant role in Korea.

In short order this agreement was followed by an American show of military strength and another agreement. In 1907 President Theodore Roosevelt sent the entire American battle fleet of sixteen ships on an around-the-world tour. Japan was one of its most important ports of call. At the time, the United States had the world's second largest navy and Japan the fifth largest. The next year the Root-Takahira Agreement was signed, in which both countries promised to respect the political-military status quo in the Pacific and support the Open Door policy in China as well as respect China's political independence and integrity. This agreement failed to hold, as during World War I Japan sought to extend its dominance over China by issuing the 21 Points and seizing control of Germany's Asian colonial holdings.

Applying the Lesson

1. To what extent are the motivations behind Obama's Asian Pivot and the pivot to Asia symbolized by Commodore Perry's opening of Japan similar?

2. What lessons does Admiral Perry's opening of China and the subsequent pattern of U.S.-Japanese relations hold for the current Asian Pivot?

3. How would realists, neoliberals, and constructivists evaluate U.S foreign policy toward Japan as described here? How would this assessment compare to what they would say about President Obama's Asian Pivot?

Thinking about the World

Disagreement about the causes and consequences of foreign policy decisions are an enduring feature of the commentary on American foreign policy. For example, some argue that Russia's intervention into the Ukraine in 2014 was provoked by Western military and economic expansion toward its borders causing Russian president Vladimir Putin to push back. Others counter that full responsibility lies with Russia. It was a product of Russian domestic politics, most notably Putin's declining popularity.[3] A basic reason for disagreements over such an important issue in foreign policy is that observers hold different theoretical perspectives about the fundamental nature of world politics. Three perspectives are particularly important for understanding the larger debate over what American foreign policy should be and what it can be.

Realism

The first theoretical perspective is **realism**, which was the dominant intellectual perspective used for studying world politics in the twentieth century.[4] For realists, world politics involves a constant struggle for power that is carried out under conditions that border on anarchy. There is little room for embracing universal principles or taking on moral crusades. The acknowledged founding voice of American realism was Hans Morgenthau, who captured the essence of realism in stating that leaders "think and act in terms of interests defined as power." For realists, peace defined as the absence of war is possible only when states follow their own narrowly defined national interests. Where early realists stressed human nature as the central driving force in world politics, later realists focused their attention on the central role played by the structure of the international system. Once in place, international systems become a force that states cannot control but one that controls states.

Neoliberalism

A second theoretical perspective is **neoliberalism**.[5] While conceding that in many respects the international system is anarchic, it rejects the pessimistic conclusion reached by realists that world politics is essentially a conflictual process from which there is no escape. Instead, neoliberalism sees world politics as an arena in which all participants (states and nonstate actors) can advance their own interests peacefully without threatening others. This becomes possible when conditions are created that allow the inherent rationality of individuals to come to the forefront. Among the primary factors that promote peaceful intercourse are democracy, respect for international laws, participation in international organizations, restraints on weapons, and free trade. President Woodrow Wilson, who championed the League of Nations after World War I, is the American statesperson most associated today with neoliberalism although many of his views are closer to traditional liberalism. Long dismissed by realists as idealistic, Wilsonianism began to reassert itself as a powerful voice in American foreign policy after Vietnam.

Constructivism

The third theoretical perspective is **constructivism**.[6] While realism and neoliberalism differ in their interpretations of the essential features of world politics, they both share the conviction that the nature of world politics is fixed and that objective rules for conducting foreign policy can be derived from them. Constructivism takes issue with this. Constructivists assert that international politics is not shaped by fixed underlying forces but by our perceptions of them. Ideas and cultural and historical experience give meaning to what we see. For example, free trade is not inherently a force for peace or a cause of war. How it is evaluated depends on one's personal and societal experiences with free trade.

Our ways of looking at the world are capable of changing over time as we interact with others. An entire generation of Americans has grown up after the end of the Cold War and sees American global dominance as natural. As a result, many in the United States have trouble understanding how revolutionary and unnatural this can appear to others.[7] One year after it was announced, a commentator noted that from China's perspective Obama's Asian Pivot "was pulled right out of the old Cold War playbook. . . . Washington is trying to inflame new tensions by isolating it and emboldening the countries China has territorial disputes with."[8] The administration soon quietly dropped "Asian Pivot" and begin speaking about the U.S. "rebalancing" to Asia.

International System: Structural Constants

In this and the following two sections, we present a survey of those forces in the international system that are most often seen as driving state behavior. We group them into three categories: structural constants, Cold War trends, and the dominant features of the contemporary international system. While realists, neoliberals, and constructivists would disagree on how to rank their relative importance, all would agree that an effective U.S. foreign policy requires thinking critically about them.

Decentralization

The first enduring feature of the international system is its decentralized nature. No central political institutions exist to make laws or see to their enforcement in the international arena nor is there a common political culture to anchor an agreed-on set of norms governing the behavior of states. The combined result is a highly competitive international system in which there is a constant expectation of violence and very little expectation that either international law or appeals to moral principles will greatly influence the resolution of an issue.

Decentralization does not mean that the international system operates in a state of anarchy. For realists, "ordered anarchy" would be a more apt characterization. Enforceable laws and common values may be absent, but rules do exist that lend a measure of predictability and certainty to international transactions. They do so by indicating the limits of permissible behavior and the directions to follow in settling disputes. Rules are less permanent than laws, are more general in nature, and tend to be normative statements rather than commands. They grow out of the basic principles of self-help and decentralization and are rooted in the distribution of power in the international system. As this distribution of power changes, so will the rules.

Neoliberals hold a different interpretation of how the international system is ordered and becomes governed by rules. In their view, rules are negotiated into existence by states. They are voluntarily entered into and obeyed by states trying to advance their national interests. What is significant from the perspective of neoliberals is that, once established, these rules often demonstrate a remarkably long life span that outlasts the specific problem they were designed to address or the identity and power of those who negotiated them into existence.

Self-Help System

The second structural constant in the international system grows out of the first: The international system is a self-help system. States must rely on themselves to accomplish their foreign policy goals. To do otherwise runs the risk of manipulation or betrayal at the hands of another state. It is important to stress that Great Powers as well as smaller powers need to heed the admonition to avoid excessive dependence on others. One of the recurring problems that have confronted American policy makers is that U.S. foreign policy has often become hijacked or captured by allies in less powerful states. Often, these leaders were put into power through U.S. intervention and relied heavily on U.S. support to maintain power. Their very weakness becomes a lever to use against the United States when it seeks to force them into policies they do not like.[9]

The self-help principle challenges policy makers to bring goals and power resources into balance. Pursuing more goals than one has the resources to accomplish or squandering resources on secondary objectives saps the vitality of the state and makes it unable to respond effectively to future challenges. Vietnam is argued by many to be a classic example of the inability to balance goals and resources and its crippling consequences. American policy produced steady increases in the level of the U.S. commitment to the war, but it did not bring the United States any closer to victory. Instead, the reverse occurred: The longer the United States remained in Vietnam and the greater its commitment, the more elusive victory became. Neoliberals reject this emphasis on self-help. From their perspective the ability of states and individuals to recognize the costs and benefits of different strategies will allow them to pursue cooperative, mutually beneficial solutions to problems and avoid the use of force in settling disputes.

A Stratified System

The third structural constant in the international system is its stratified nature. The equality of states embedded in the concept of **sovereignty** is a legal myth. The principle of sovereignty dates back to the Treaty of Westphalia and the beginnings of the modern state system in 1648. It holds that no legal authority exists above the state except that which the state voluntarily accepts. The reality of international politics is quite different, and sovereignty is a matter of degree rather than an absolute condition. States are "born unequal."[10] The resources they draw on for their power are distributed unequally across the globe. As such, the ability of states to accomplish their foreign policy objectives (as well as their very choice of objectives) varies from state to state.

The principle of stratification leaves open the question of how unevenly power is distributed. The three most commonly discussed forms of stratification are **unipolar**, **bipolar**, and **multipolar**. In a unipolar system, one state possesses more power than any other. No other state or alliance of states can match it. In a bipolar system, two relatively equal states exist above all others. Typically, permanent alliance systems form around them. A multipolar system is characterized by the presence of a core group of states that are relatively equal in power. Floating coalitions rather than permanent alliances form as states join and leave coalitions to accomplish goals and protect their interests.

Neoliberals would argue that this picture is overdrawn. Rather than organized around the global or regional distribution of power, the international system should be seen as organized around issue areas, regimes, each of which is organized around its own set of rules and norms. Here again, there is the expectation that enlightened self-interest will produce regimes based on accommodation rather than domination.

International System: Evolutionary Trends

Although the basic structure of the international system has endured over time, the system itself is not unchanging. Four post–World War II trends are especially notable for their ability to influence the conduct of U.S. foreign policy. They are: a diffusion of power, issue proliferation, actor proliferation, and regional diversity.

Diffusion of Power

Power is the ability to achieve objectives. It is typically viewed as something one possesses—a commodity to be acquired, stored, and manipulated. But power must also be viewed as a relational concept. What is ultimately at issue is not how much power a state has, but how much power it has in a specific issue compared to those with whom it is dealing.

The postwar era has seen a steady diffusion of power. It is not so much that the quantity of power possessed by the United States has declined. U.S. dominance in nuclear weapons remains unchallenged. The same holds true for conventional weapons. What has changed is the ability of other states to exploit points of sensitivity and vulnerability. The causes for the diffusion of power are many. Robert Gilpin, after examining the decline of empires throughout history, asserts that we can identify a cycle of hegemonic decline.[11] As the cycle progresses, a combination of the burdens of imperial leadership, increased emphasis on the consumption of goods and services, and the international diffusion of technology conspires to sap the strength of the imperial state and bring about its decline.

The success and failure of foreign policies can also contribute to the diffusion of power. The effect of foreign policy failures is relatively easy to anticipate. In the wake of defeat, follow the search for scapegoats, disillusionment with the task undertaken, and a desire to avoid similar situations. The Vietnam War is held by many to have been responsible for destroying the postwar domestic consensus on the purpose of American power. Economic sanctions directed against Fidel Castro in Cuba in the 1960s failed to bring down his regime and only made him more dependent on Soviet support.

American foreign policy successes have also hastened the decline of U.S. dominance. The respective reconstructions of the Japanese and Western European economies rank as two truly remarkable achievements. In a sense, U.S. foreign policy has been almost too successful here. These economies are now major economic rivals of the U.S. economy and often outperform it. But as the Japanese case also illustrates there is nothing inevitable about the process of power diffusion. In the 1960s observers spoke of the Japanese economic miracle and the threat it presented to U.S. economic power. In the 1990s reference was instead being made to Japan's lost decade and the many economic problems it faced.

A similar scenario may be unfolding with regard to the BRICS (Brazil, Russia, India, China, and South Africa). As the twenty-first century dawned they were seen by many as the center of political and economic influence in a new world order crowding out American dominance. Their first international summit conference in June 2009 ended with a call for establishing a multipolar international system. By 2016 there was little evidence of sustained or meaningful economic, political, or military cooperation between the BRICS that would support the view that they were a "harbinger of a profoundly novel global order."[12]

Issue Proliferation

The second area of evolutionary change in the international arena is issue proliferation. Not long ago, one could speak of a clear-cut foreign affairs issue hierarchy. At the top were a relatively small number of high-politics problems involving questions of national security, territorial integrity, and political independence. At the bottom were the numerically more prevalent low-politics issues of commerce, energy, environment, and so on. Although largely intuitive, the line between high and low politics was well established. The positions occupied by issues in this hierarchy were also relatively fixed. This allowed policy makers to develop a familiarity with the issues before them and the options open to them. Today, this is no longer the case.

The high-politics category has become crowded. Natural resource scarcity moved from a low-politics to high-politics foreign policy problem after the 1973 OPEC oil embargo. In 2014 the Defense Department's Quadrennial Defense Review along with other studies pointed to the growing national security threat posed by global climate change. Issues may also change position for political reasons. Human rights, which was a major concern for the United States when Jimmy Carter was president, returned to a low-politics position when Reagan took office.

The high-low politics distinction was implicitly based on the existence of a prior distinction between foreign and domestic policy. This distinction has become increasingly difficult to maintain. How, for example, do we classify attempts to fight international drug cartels? On one level this is a foreign policy problem. The United States is actively engaged with helping the Mexican government combat the drug cartels operating out of that country. These organizations realize more than $20 billion in profits from sales in the United States alone. Yet this is also a matter of domestic policy as some states decided to legalize the recreational use of marijuana.

The term that is increasingly being used to characterize these and other issues with significant domestic and international dimensions is "**intermestic**" (*inter* from "international" and *mestic* from "domestic").[13] Another prime example of an emerging intermestic policy area is food safety. Traditionally, food safety issues have been treated as a domestic policy matter. This is no longer realistic. Food production has become globalized and with that has come expressions of concern about its quality. Between 2000 and 2006, the value of food imports doubled to $2.2 trillion; yet, traditionally, the Food and Drug Administration inspects less than 1 percent of the imported food products under its jurisdiction. Both Congress and the George W. Bush administration moved to change this situation by toughening inspection standards on imported food.

Actor Proliferation

The third evolutionary feature of the international system is actor proliferation. On the one hand, actor proliferation has taken the form of an expansion in the number of states. Today, there are 190 countries. This compares to 58 states in 1930. The United States has diplomatic relations with all but 3, 4 if Taiwan is counted. This expansion in the number of states has brought with it a corresponding expansion in the number of views that can be found on any given problem. Whereas 84 states attended the first United Nations Conference on the Law of the Sea (UNCLOS I) in 1958, 185 countries attended the Paris Climate Summit conference along with the EU and others bringing the total number of participants to 196 in 2015. The vast number of states and the diversity of views expressed in these global meetings now present great obstacles to achieving an agreement.

Although the growth in the number of new states has slowed, continued growth is taking place in a second area: nonstate actors. States have never been the only actors in world politics. Yet it is only comparatively recently that nonstate actors have appeared in sufficient numbers and possessed control over enough resources to be significant actors in world politics. Three categories of nonstate actors may be identified. They are intergovernmental organizations (IGOs) such as the United Nations, NATO, and the Organization of American States; nongovernmental organizations (NGOs) such as General Motors, the International Red Cross, the Catholic Church, and the Palestine Liberation Organization; and subnational actors such as the Defense Department, New York City, and Texas.

Statistically, the growth in the number of nonstate actors has been explosive. On the eve of World War I, there were only 49 IGOs and 170 NGOs. In 1951 the numbers had grown to 123 IGOs and 832 NGOs. The 2015/2016 edition of the *Yearbook of International Organizations* identified 273 conventional IGOs and 3,189 conventional NGOs. Overall, it lists almost 70,000 international organizations: 7,757 IGOs and 60,272 NGOs.[14]

Actor proliferation has altered the context within which American foreign policy decisions are made in three ways. First, it has changed the language used in thinking about foreign policy problems. The state-centric language of the Cold War now competes with the imagery of interdependence and globalization for the attention of policy makers. Second, nonstate actors often serve as potential instruments of foreign policy. By not being identified as part of a state, their actions may be better received by other actors. The third impact that nonstate actors have on U.S. foreign policy is that they often limit the options open to policy makers. Their ability to resist and frustrate state initiatives can necessitate that states consider courses of action they otherwise would likely reject, including inaction. Two recent examples are the lack of a credible pro-Western rebel group in Syria to support and the inability to take quick action in Nigeria against the Boko Haram Islamic militant group.

Regional Diversity

As a superpower, the United States is concerned not only with the structure and operation of the international system as a whole but also with the operation of its subsystems. Three subsystems are especially important to it. Each presents it with different management problems and thus requires a different solution.[15] While the language used to describe them comes out of the Cold War era, the differences among regions they highlight remain important factors in the way international politics is conducted and which foreign problems are held to be important.

The first subsystem is the Western system, which is made up of the advanced industrial states of the United States, Canada, Western Europe, and Japan. The principal problem in the Western system is managing interdependence. At issue is the distribution of costs and benefits. U.S. leadership and initiative in the realm of national security policy, once so eagerly sought by its allies, is now often resisted. For its part, the United States has begun to question the costs of leadership and seeks to have its allies pick up a larger share of the defense burden. A similar situation holds for economic relations. Many in the United States are no longer willing to underwrite a free trade system or to accept economic discrimination in the name of alliance unity.

The second subsystem is the North-South system. Instead of expectations of sharing and mutual gain, the South views matters from a perspective rooted in the inequalities and exploitation of colonialism. Thus, when NATO and U.S. forces intervened in Libya and removed Muammar Qaddafi from power in the name of Responsibility to Protect, many in the South saw this humanitarian doctrine as nothing but a cover for another instance of Western imperialism. Whereas solutions to the problems of interdependence lie in the fine-tuning of existing international organizations and practices, solutions to the problems of dependence and domination require constructing a new system that the South is willing to accept as legitimate and in which it is treated as an equal.

The third subsystem of concern to the United States is the remnants of the Cold War East-West system. The fundamental management problem here is one of reintegration. The Cold War divided the East and West into two largely self-contained, competing military and economic parts. Détente brought about a limited reintegration of the East and West in the 1970s through arms control and trade agreements. The opportunity for full-scale integration of these states into the international system came with the demise of communism and the collapse of the Soviet Union and has to some extent been realized. Russia became a member of the G8 and both China and Russia joined the World Trade Organization. Still, the task of reintegration is incomplete as evidenced by Russia's military intervention into Ukraine to reclaim the Crimea, China's growing assertiveness in the South China Sea and its aggressive overseas economic policies, and ongoing concerns for the status of human rights in both countries.

Dominant Features Today

In many ways the contemporary international system lacks a defining identity. For some it is the post-9/11 era. Others argue while looking back at 9/11 that not much has changed in world politics.[16] Still others see the current international system as one marked by the resurgence of Great Power politics with the rise of Russia and China. Regardless of how it is defined, it is clear that the structure of the international system has become more complex. It has become a three-dimensional chessboard, with different problems and dynamics on each board. There is a traditional hard-power-driven security chessboard, a soft-power-driven economic chessboard, and a third chessboard dominated by the activities of nonstate actors where power is diffuse and hard to define. Each of these poses its own challenges to the United States. Here, we isolate one challenge on each chessboard.[17]

Terrorism

Terrorism dominates the third chessboard. For many it is the most prominent feature of the contemporary international system. Box 2.1 presents a snapshot of the scope of the terrorism problem as it existed in 2014, a point in time just ahead of the attacks in Paris (November 2015) and Brussels (March 2016) and the series of attacks in Turkey, Bangladesh, and Iraq that occurred within one week of each other in June–July 2016. Used in its most value-free and politically neutral sense, terrorism is violence for the purpose of political intimidation.[18] Terrorism is not a new phenomenon nor is it the exclusive tool of any political ideology or political agenda. It does not specify an organizational form. Governments as well as nonstate actors may engage in terrorism.

Box 2.1

Snapshot of Global Terrorism

Number of times since 2000 a country has been ranked among the top ten countries affected by terrorism:

1. India   14
2. Afghanistan   13
2. Pakistan   13
4. Iraq   12
5. Algeria   9
5. Russia   9

Number of deaths due to terrorism in 2014: 32,685

Increase in deaths due to terrorism in 2014 from 2013: 18,111. Largest one year increase (80%)

Top five countries with regard to deaths due to terrorism:

1. Iraq
2. Nigeria
3. Afghanistan
4. Pakistan
5. Syria

Five largest increases in deaths due to terrorism in 2014 from 2013:

1. Nigeria   +5,662
2. Iraq   +3,532
3. Afghanistan   +1,391
4. Ukraine   +665
5. Syria   +593

Five largest reductions in deaths due to terrorism in 2014 from 2013:

1. Pakistan   −596
2. Algeria   −82
3. Russia   −80
4. Lebanon   −65
5. Philippines   −51

Five most frequent targets of terrorism in 2014 (excluding "other"):

1. Private citizens and property
2. Police
3. Government
4. Business
5. Military

Three most frequently used weapons in terrorist attacks in 2014:

1. Explosives, bombs, dynamite   58%
2. Firearms   28%
3. Other   14%

The five most deadly terrorists groups in 2014 that accounted for 84% of all deaths:

1. Boko Haram   6,644
2. ISIL/ISIS   6,073
3. Taliban   3,477
4. Fulani militants   1,229
5. Al-Shabaab   1,021

Lone wolf attackers account for 70% of all deaths from terrorism in the West since 2006; 80% of deaths caused by lone wolf terrorists in the West were driven by right-wing extremism, nationalism, antigovernment sentiment, and other forms of political extremism and supremacy.

In 2014, 88% of terrorist attacks were successful (the attack was carried out). This is down from 97% that were successful in 2007.

Source: Institute for Economics and Peace, *Global Terrorism Index, 2015.*

Today's brand of terrorism dates from 1979. It is the fourth wave of terrorism that has arisen since the 1880s.[19] The preceding three waves each lasted a generation. If this pattern holds, the current wave of terrorism will not lose its energy until around 2025. The first, anarchist wave of terrorism began in Russia and was set in motion by the political and economic reform efforts of the czars. The second, anticolonial wave of terrorism began in the 1920s and ended in the 1960s. The third, New Left wave of terrorism was set in motion by the Vietnam War. It was made up of Marxist groups such as the Weather Underground and separatist groups that sought self-determination for minority groups felt to be trapped inside larger states, such as the Palestine Liberation Organization.

The defining features of the current wave of terrorism are twofold. The first is its religious base. Islam is at its core. Its initial energy was drawn from three events in 1979: the start of a new Muslim century, the ouster of the shah in Iran, and the Soviet invasion of Afghanistan. The United States is the special target of this religious wave of terrorism. Iranian leaders have long referred to the United States as the "Great Satan," and the common goal shared by Islamic terrorist groups was to drive the United States out of the Middle East. Before 9/11, this wave had produced a steady flow of terrorist attacks on U.S. facilities. Marine barracks were attacked in Lebanon in 1983, the World Trade Center was struck in 1993, American embassies were attacked in Kenya and Tanzania in 1998, and the USS *Cole* was attacked in 2000. The second defining attribute is the specter of mass casualties. Whereas earlier waves of terror focused on assassinating key individuals or the symbolic killing of relatively small numbers of individuals, today we also see terrorist attacks resulting in large numbers of deaths.

As recently as 2015 U.S. officials struggled with the question of whether al Qaeda or ISIS (Islamic State of Iraq and Syria) posed the greatest terrorist threat to the U.S. homeland. The FBI, the Justice Department, and the Department of Homeland Security rated ISIS as the higher threat while the Defense Department, the National Counterterrorism Center, and intelligence agencies tended to place al Qaeda ahead of it. At the heart of this debate were questions surrounding which would be most able to strike U.S. targets and which could cause the greatest damage? As one member of Congress put it before the 2015 Paris attacks, "ISIS is all about the quantity of attacks, Al Qaeda . . . is about the quality of the attack." One day before the Paris attack that debate was settled when Secretary of State John Kerry called ISIS "the gravest threat faced by our generation and the embodiment of evil in our time."

ISIS emerged from the ashes of the defeated al Qaeda in Iraq and blossomed in the dead space created by the Syrian civil war. Some describe it as an insurgency or rebellion rather than a terrorist group. Audrey Cronin characterizes it as a post–al Qaeda jihadist threat which uses terrorism as a tactic but is not really a terrorist organization.[20] From her perspective ISIS operates as a pseudo-state, controlling oil-producing operations in Iraq and Syria along with extortion, taxes, and selling goods such as abandoned U.S. weapons and antiques on the black market.

One of the challenges the United States faces in dealing with ISIS is similar to that it faced in dealing with al Qaeda: ISIS has begun to decentralize its decision-making structure. In the case of al Qaeda decentralization took the form of a series of concentric rings with al Qaeda central at its core surrounded by additional rings composed of al Qaeda affiliates and associates such as Al Qaeda in the Arabian Peninsula (AQAP), which is very active in Yemen; al Qaeda locals; and finally the al Qaeda network made up of homegrown radicals with no direct connection to al Qaeda but who are drawn to its ideology and act in support of it.[21] ISIS has followed a similar logic in delegating decision-making power to mid-level military commanders in Iraq and Syria, seeking out foreign affiliates, and actively recruiting and training disenchanted individuals and criminals to return to their home countries and engage in terrorist attacks.

Of special concern to the United States has been the ability of al Qaeda and ISIS to establish affiliates in North Africa. Noteworthy additions include al Qaeda in the Islamic Maghreb which began operations in 2007, the al Shabab East African terrorist movement which declared its loyalty to al Qaeda in 2012, the establishment of the Islamic State of Libya in Libya in 2014, Boko Haram which declared an Islamic caliphate in Nigeria and pledged it allegiance to ISIS in 2015, and the merger of the Mali terrorist group al Mourabitoun with al Qaeda in 2015. While such mergers make headlines, it is not clear how much they benefit al Qaeda or ISIS.[22] A study of al Qaeda found that the divergent preferences and priorities of al Qaeda central and its affiliates created a host of problems limiting its effectiveness.

This line of inquiry leads to the largely unanswered question of how terrorist groups end.[23] This question became especially pressing in 2016 when ISIS began to lose control of territory in Syria and Iraq as well as experience serious monetary loses due to U.S. air strikes on its oil and banking operations leading some to speculate that its caliphate could soon be brought to an end. With no warning it went on the offense employing with great psychological affect al Qaeda's strategy of global suicide attacks. They were made possible in large part by the presence of large numbers of followers and combatants who had returned home from Syria and Iraq. These attacks were characterized not so much as lone wolf attacks as wolf pack attacks, some of which were centrally planned by ISIS and others inspired by ISIS or entirely the product of decisions made by local groups.

Globalization

Globalization dominates the second chessboard. For those who see it as the primary structural feature of the emerging international system, globalization is a reality and not a choice.[24] The problem facing the United States is not whether to participate in a globalized economy but how to participate. And, as with all underlying structural aspects of the international system, globalization places limits on state behavior—rewarding states with correct foreign and domestic policies and punishing them for adopting inappropriate ones.

A central problem in formulating a foreign policy based on globalization is that it is a vaguely defined term that is often used interchangeably with internationalization, Westernization, and Americanization. Most commentators define "globalization" as an economic process that centers on the speed with which economies interact with one another and the intense and all-encompassing nature of those interactions. Economies do not simply trade with one another; they are transformed by their interactions. For globalization's supporters, this transformation will lead to economic benefits and prosperity.

Globalization, however, is much more than just an economic process. It is a dynamic mix of economic, political, social, and cultural forces that holds the potential for bringing about both positive and negative changes within states and among them. Globalization may unleash the forces of democracy, but it may just as easily unleash a fundamentalist and defensive cultural backlash by those who feel threatened. Similarly, globalization accelerates the diffusion of technology and knowledge among people, which may help solve global health and environmental problems, but it also allows terrorist groups to communicate with one another and travel more efficiently as well as potentially gain access to weapons of mass destruction.

Globalization did not arrive on the scene suddenly or in one fell swoop. It emerged bit by bit over time. Although some commentators trace its foundations back to the eighteenth century, most identify its beginnings with the post–World War II era and the establishment of the Bretton Woods monetary system and its core institutions: the World Bank, the International Monetary Fund, and the General Agreement on Tariffs and Trade (GATT). Together, they laid the foundation for an international economic system that facilitated and encouraged an ever-expanding and accelerating cross-border flow of money, commodities, ideas, and people. This foundation set in motion a chain reaction producing what Thomas Friedman refers to as the "flattening of the world."[25]

Those who embrace globalization as the dominant structural feature of the contemporary international system see it as an irreversible process. Others are not convinced of this. Niall Ferguson raises the possibility that at some point globalization may collapse and we may enter into a post-globalist era.[26] He sees economic and political parallels between the current period of globalization and that which existed prior to the outbreak of World War I and the Great Depression of the 1930s.

Ian Bremmer does not see globalization as ending, but he raises the possibility that it has entered a new phase, one dominated by state capitalism.[27] In it governments rather than private businesses are the driving force behind investment decisions. The goal now is to increase state power, not to maximize profit. Prominent forms of state capitalism include government-owned or -controlled natural resource companies; national champions or firms that receive special tax incentives and other benefits from the state; and sovereign wealth funds that the states control and invest in key firms and industries. State capitalist firms have many short-term competitive advantages over private companies, but Bremmer warns that in the long run their inherent inefficiencies due to the role that politics plays in their operation and investment decisions could harm global economic growth.

American Hegemony

American **hegemony** is the principal issue on the first chessboard, the traditional hard-power security-dominated chessboard. The term "hegemony" implies control, dominance, or preeminence. It was used to describe the United States' position on this chessboard after the end of the Cold War, when for all practical purposes it was the last superpower left standing on the chessboard. Part of the difficulty in making judgments about the present condition of this first chessboard lies in the terms commonly used to describe hegemonic power.

Some observers refer to the United States as an empire. Not surprisingly, this characterization is controversial.[28] In its most neutral sense, an "empire" is a state with "a wide and supreme domain." The political, economic, and military reach of the United States fits that criterion. However, the term "empire" also carries very negative connotations. An empire is viewed as a state that imposes its will on others and rules through force and domination. Military occupation and the arbitrary use of military power typify an empire's foreign policies. These are charges that have frequently been leveled at American foreign policy. Critics of the empire label assert that what is being confused today is a negative reaction to the reach of American foreign policy, which is imperial in the sense that it is global, and the political ambition of the United States to control vast expanses of territory beyond its borders, which does not exist.

A quite different view holds that America's unchallenged dominance allows it to act as the functional equivalent of a world government. It provides services that are needed for the effective functioning of the international system, such as military security, stewardship of the global economy, and emergency humanitarian aid. Were the United States not to carry out these and other crucial tasks, the international system might cease to function effectively, because no other state possesses the resources to do them, and a true world government is not likely to come into existence. One need not go this far to see American hegemony as being beneficial rather than exploitive. As one supporter of this position noted, it is in both America's and the world's interests that American primacy last as long as possible.[29]

In between these two views of American hegemony lies a third perspective. It stresses the limits that global politics places on U.S. hegemony. One variant of this perspective sees the United States has having sat atop a Unipolar Concert for most of the post–Cold War era.[30] The United States did not dominate global politics singlehandedly but did so with the acquiescence of the next two major powers in the international system (China and Russia) who both chose not to try and balance the United States as they benefitted greatly from the international system as it operated under U.S. leadership.

Each of these three perspectives finds itself challenged to answer the question of how long this hegemonic position can continue. For those who adopt the American empire perspective, the historical reality is that good or bad empires come with expiration dates. They do not last forever. And modern empires tend to have much shorter life spans than did ancient and early modern ones. The average Roman Empire lasted 829 years. The British Empire lasted 336 years. Twentieth-century empires on average lasted only 57 years.[31]

For those who adopt the United States as global government perspective the principal challenge facing the United States in playing this role is its ability to simultaneously provide possession and milieu goals. Possession goals are zero sum in nature. If one country rules a territory, others do not. If five countries control the international oil market, others do not. Milieu goals are owned by no country, but they are circumstances and conditions which are necessary for countries to achieve their possession goals. Prominent among milieu goals are peace, a healthy global environment, and freedom of the seas and skies. Both are in the national interest but they are often in conflict. The more the United States uses its position to advance possession goals and the less it advances milieu goals, its ability to serve as a legitimate surrogate global government will be challenged.

The key longevity issue for those who stress the continuing importance of power politics to U.S. dominance is the extent to which credible challengers to U.S. power exist or will surface. Some see the United States as being a remarkably secure country. Foreign policy problems are many, but individually and collectively they do not constitute security threats.[32] Stephen Brooks and William Wohlforth argue that such challenges will not materialize soon.[33] They note that while China's rise in power today is very real, the distance China must travel from being a great power to becoming a superpower is far bigger than successful challengers have faced in the past. Others take a more pessimistic view arguing that power balancing by Russia and China is already under way to the point that the unipolar concert has unraveled bringing with it a series of regional challenges to U.S. influence.[34]

Fu Ying, chair of China's Foreign Affairs Committee of the National People's Congress, takes a relatively optimistic view of the stability of the current global order.[35] He sees a triangular strategic partnership existing among Russia, China, and the United States that is the cornerstone of global stability. In this triangle the greatest distance separates the United States and Russia. Chinese-Russian relations are the most positive and stable. U.S.-China relationships show frequent ups and downs.

The Obama administration's pivot to Asia was not the first time U.S. foreign policy turned its attention to that region of the world. In Box 2.2 we look at the first such Asian pivot, Commodore Perry's opening of Japan.

Box 2.2

Military Power of the Republic of China, 2013

The People's Republic of China (PRC) continues to pursue a long-term, comprehensive military modernization program designed to improve the capacity of its armed forces to fight and win short-duration, high-intensity regional military conflict. Preparing for potential conflict in the Taiwan Strait appears to remain the principal focus and primary driver of China's military investment. However, as China's interests have grown and it has gained greater influence in the international system, its military modernization has also become increasingly focused on investments in military capabilities to conduct a wider range of missions beyond its immediate territorial concerns, including counter-piracy, peacekeeping, humanitarian assistance/disaster relief, and regional military operations. Some of these missions and capabilities can address international security challenges, while others could serve more narrowly defined PRC interests and objectives, including advancing territorial claims and building influence abroad.

To support the Chinese People's Liberation Army's (PLA) expanding set of roles and missions, China's leaders in 2012 sustained investment in advanced short- and medium-range conventional ballistic missiles, land-attack and anti-ship cruise missiles, counter-space weapons, and military cyberspace capabilities that appear designed to enable anti-access/area-denial (A2/AD) missions (what PLA strategists refer to as "counter-intervention operations"). The PLA also continued to improve capabilities in nuclear deterrence and long-range conventional strike; advanced fighter aircraft; limited regional power projection, with the commissioning of China's first aircraft carrier, the Liaoning; integrated air defenses; undersea warfare; improved command and control; and more sophisticated training and exercises across China's air, naval, and land forces.

Source: "Executive Summary," *Military Power of the Republic of China, 2013*, Annual Report to Congress, Office of the Secretary of Defense.

America and the World: Attitudes and Perceptions

As constructivists remind us, the global setting of American foreign policy involves more than just a series of contemporary problems and underlying structural features. It also consists of attitudes and perceptions about the world. As evidenced by responses to global public opinion polls conducted in the United States and other countries in 2014 it is increasingly obvious that Americans and non-Americans do not always see the world the same way.[36] Seventy percent of Americans polled said that the United States takes into account the interests of other countries in making foreign policy decisions. Little consensus on this point existed abroad. At one extreme only 13 percent of Pakistanis said that the United States considers their country's interest a great deal or a fair amount. At the other extreme 85 percent of Filipinos said the United States considers their country's interests.

Global public opinion polls also show differences in how Americans and citizens of other countries view policy problems. A 2014 survey showed that 50 percent of Americans believe that foreign trade destroys jobs compared to 38 percent in Japan. A 2015 survey found that concern about global climate change was highest in Latin American where 74 percent thought it was a very serious problem; 64 percent of respondents in sub-Saharan Africa held this view; and only 45 percent of Americans gave this answer with 25 percent holding climate change not to be a serious problem at all.[37]

Widely different views also exist on the exercise of American power. Of 20 countries surveyed in 2013, most (41 percent) continued to see the United States as the leading economic power. However, this was down from 47 percent in 2008, and a majority of people in 23 of 39 countries surveyed felt that China had already replaced the United States as the dominant economic power or would soon do so. In the area of soft power widely different views emerged when respondents were asked about their feelings toward the spread of American ideas and customs. The median positive response in Latin America was 32 percent and in Africa it was 56 percent. A similarly lukewarm response was given to questions about U.S. ideas on democracy. Here the range of positive attitudes ran from a low of 38 percent in Argentina and Bolivia to a high of 82 percent in Kenya.

An even more politically significant indicator of differences in global outlook is found in the periodic anti-American protests that erupt around the world, which are widely interpreted both as signs of displeasure with specific American foreign policies and as pent-up resentment of Western powers more generally. A notable recent example occurred in 2012 when often violent anti-American protests spread rapidly through some 20 countries in North Africa, the Middle East, Central and South Asia, and Indonesia following the release of a video that was seen as insulting Islam.

In seeking to understand the motivations and logic of such anti-American demonstrations observers have made distinctions among four different types of anti-Americanism.[38] First, there is liberal anti-Americanism. It is commonly found in other advanced industrial societies. At its core is the charge that the United States repeatedly fails to live up to its own ideals in conducting its foreign policy. A second strain of negative feelings toward the United States is social anti-Americanism. Here, the complaint concerns the United States' trying to impose its version of democracy and its definition of rights on others while being insensitive to local societal values and norms. Third, there is sovereign anti-Americanism. This version of anti-Americanism focuses on the threats the United States presents to the sovereignty and to the cultural and political identity of another country. It matters not whether the country is powerful or weak for there to be a nationalistic backlash. Finally, there is radical anti-Americanism. It defines American values as evil and subscribes to the notion that only by destroying them can the world be made safe.

The world is not solidly anti-American. Positive and negative views coexist in most cases and much of the anti-American sentiment is mild and shallow.[39] Majorities in 28 of the 38 foreign countries surveyed expressed an overall favorable opinion of the United States. Pro-American views tend to be most pronounced among those aged 60 and older, a factor many attribute to American foreign policy initiatives during the Cold War. Another group that has solidly pro-American sentiments is made up of young people identified as "aspirational." They are upwardly mobile or would like to be. They do not fit easily into any demographic category, some come from low-income or low-education backgrounds, while in other cases, they are among the younger and wealthier citizens of a country.[40]

Over the Horizon: 2030

Our account of the global context within which the United States conducts its foreign policy highlights three important points when looking over the horizon. First, the international system is multilayered. Second, foreign policy challenges and opportunities can arise from a variety of factors. Third, not everyone will define upcoming foreign policy problems the same way. Perceptions and ideas matter.

What then might the future hold? Periodically the National Intelligence Council (NIC) addresses this question. Its peeks into the future are not meant to be taken as predications or forecasts but as attempts to help policy makers focus on trends and aspects of the international system that have the potential to shape U.S. foreign policy for better or worse.

According to the NIC's *Global Trends 2030* report, the world will be radically transformed by 2030.[41] It foresees an international system where no state will be a hegemonic power. *Global Trends 2030* goes on to identify two megatrends, individual empowerment and the diffusion of state power, that will drive this transformation. What exact path this transformational process will proceed down is not fixed. The report identifies six game changers that will help determine this along with a series of black swans or specific events that could also change the direction of the future. The key game changers are: (1) crises in the global economy, (2) global governance shortfalls, (3) the potential for increased conflict, (4) increased regional instability, (5) the impact of new technologies, and (6) the uncertain role the United States will play in world politics. Numbered among the possible black swans are a democratic China, nuclear war, a global health pandemic, and the collapse of the European Union. *Global Trends 2030* concludes by presenting four alternative futures.

Stalled Engines. Defined as a plausible worst case scenario it sees the United States and Europe as turning inward and no longer exercising global leadership as a new "great game" in Asia erupts. Regional powers step into the power vacuum but will not fully succeed. While globalization is not reversed economic growth will falter and a global economic recession will set in.

Fusion. This is the best case scenario. Here, conflict in south Asia triggers the formation of a coalition composed of United States, China, and Europe that intervenes and imposes a cease-fire. In its aftermath this coalition begins working together to address a series of global challenges. The end results are stronger international institutions and global economic prosperity.

Gini Out of the Bottle. This is a world of extremes as countries are divided into two opposing camps: winners and losers. As a whole the world is reasonably wealthy but states are increasingly insecure. The United States has gained energy independence and is still the dominant power but no longer plays the role of policeman of the world.

Nonstate World. In this world nonstate actors take the lead in confronting global challenges. States do not disappear, but they play a less central role in world affairs and find it difficult to advance their national interests. This patchwork of global governance produces uneven results. Economically, the global system is relatively well off. The major shortcoming is in the area of responding to security threats.

Critical Thinking Questions

1. Which of the three theoretical perspectives we introduced (realism, neoliberalism, and constructivism) is best suited for guiding thinking about U.S. foreign policy today?

2. Which of the possible global futures is most likely? How should the United States prepare for it?

3. Which features of the international system are most influential in determining the success or failure of U.S. foreign policies?

Key Terms

bipolar, 34

constructivism, 32

globalization, 29

hegemony, 29

intermestic, 36

multipolar, 34

neoliberalism, 31

realism, 31

sovereignty, 27

terrorism, 29

unipolar, 34

Further Reading

Stephen Brooks and William Wohlforth, "The Rise and Fall of Great Powers in the Twenty-First Century," *International Security* 40 (Winter 2015), 7–53.

This article examines the rise of China as a challenger to U.S. unipolarity. It concludes that while China's rise in power is real, the United States will likely long remain the only superpower.

Chester Crocker, "The Strategic Dilemma of a World Adrift," *Survival* 57 (February 2015), 7–30.

The author argues that the international system is in a rudderless transition. It is partially re-polarized creating a toxic mix of normative issues and power dynamics. With no one being in charge of global order the key question is of how one gains and uses strategic leverage.

John Lewis Gaddis, *The United States and the End of the Cold War: Implications, Reconsiderations and Provocations* (New York: Oxford University Press, 1992).

Authored by a leading diplomatic historian, this volume looks back to the end of the Cold War for insight both as to why it ended and what that means for the future of American foreign policy.

Ted Hopf, *Reconstructing the Cold War* (New York: Oxford University Press, 2014).

Uses a social constructivist theoretical perspective to examine the Cold War period with an eye toward explaining the many abrupt changes in policy that took place in its early years.

John Ikenberry, ed., *America Unrivaled* (Ithaca, NY: Cornell University Press, 2002).

Using the concepts of unipolarity and hegemony as their starting points, the essays in this book present arguments from a variety of theoretical perspectives on the future shape of the international system and America's place in it.

Anthony Richards, "Conceptualizing Terrorism," *Studies in Conflict and Terrorism* 37 (March 2014), 18–29.

This article presents a solid overview of the concept of terrorism which it defines as a method of political violence. It then examines the implications of this definition for the debate over how to think about terrorism in world politics.

Alexander Wendt, *Social Theory of International Relations* (New York: Cambridge University Press, 1999).

The author is one of the founding scholars of the constructivist school of international relations theorizing. This book introduces readers to this approach and illustrates its utility through an examination of key concepts in the study of international relations and foreign policy.

Notes

[1] Robert Kaplan, "The South China Sea is the Future of Conflict," *Foreign Policy* 188 (2011), 78–85.

[2] Anne Gearon, "U.S.,. China Tussle Over Sea Claims," Washington Post, August 10, 2014. https://www.washingtonpost.com/world/us-china-tussle-over-sea-claims/2014/08/10/2f613504-2085-11e4-8b10-7db129976abb_story.html.

[3] For this debate, see John Mearshimer, "Why the Ukraine Crisis Is the West's Fault," *Foreign Affairs* (2014), 77–89, and the exchange between Mearshimer and Michael McFaul and Stephen Sestanovich in the following issue of *Foreign Affairs* (167–78).

[4] Kenneth Waltz, *Theory of International Politics* (New York: McGraw-Hill, 1979).

[5] Andrew Moravcsik, "Taking Preferences Seriously: A Liberal Theory of International Politics," *International Organization* 51 (1997), 513–53.

[6] Alexander Wendt, *Social Theory of International Politics* (New York: Cambridge University Press, 1999).

[7] David Calleo, "The Tyranny of False Vision: America's Unipolar Fantasy," *Survival* 50 (2008), 61–78.

[8] "Troubled Waters, Murky Commitments: How Asia Sees Obama's Pivot to the Pacific," *Washington Post*, November 20, 2012, http://article.wn.com/view/2012/11/20/troubled_waters_murky_commitments_How_Asia_sees_obama_s_pivo. Also see Andrew Nation and Andrew Scobell, "How China Sees America," *Foreign Affairs* 91 (2012), 32–47.

[9] John Tower et al., *The Tower Commission Report* (New York: Bantam, 1987), 137.

[10] Robert Tucker, *The Inequality of Nations* (New York: Basic Books, 1977).

[11] Robert Gilpin, *War and Change in World Politics* (New York: Cambridge University Press, 1981). For a dissenting view on the decline of U.S. power, see Bruce Russett, "The Mysterious Case of Vanishing Hegemony; or, Is Mark Twain Really Dead?," *International Organization* 39 (1985), 207–32.

[12] Marcos Degaut, *"Do the BRICS Still Matter?"* (Washington, DC: Center for Strategic and International Studies, October 2015).

[13] Bayliss Manning, "The Congress, the Executive and Intermestic Affairs: Three Proposals," *Foreign Affairs* 56 (1977), 306–24.

[14] For discussions of the growth of nonstate actors, see Werner Feld, *International Relations, a Transnational Approach* (Sherman Oaks: Alfred, 1979); Harold K. Jacobson, *Networks of Interdependence* (New York: Knopf, 1979). For statistics, see the *Yearbook of International Organizations*, http://www.uia.be/ybvol1.com.

[15] The three subsystems as well as the management problems they present are taken from Joan Edelman Spero, *The Politics of International Economic Relations*, 3rd ed. (New York: St. Martin's Press, 1985), 13–19.

[16] William Dobson, "The Day Nothing Much Changed," *Foreign Policy* 156 (2006), 22–25.

[17] Joseph Nye, "The Future of American Power," *Foreign Affairs* 89 (2010), 2–12.

[18] For a discussion of the concept of terrorism, see Anthony Richards, "Conceptualizing Terrorism," *Studies in Conflict and Terrorism* 37 (2014), 213–236.

[19] David C. Rapoport, "The Four Waves of Modern Terrorism," and Audrey Kurth Cronin, "The Sources of Contemporary Terrorism," in Audrey Kurth Cronin and James Ludes (eds.), *Attacking Terrorism* (Washington, DC: Georgetown University Press, 2004), 19–45.

[20]   Audrey Cronin, "ISIS Is Not a Terrorist Group," *Foreign Affairs* 94 (2015), 87–98.

[21]   Bruce Hoffman, "From Global War on Terror to Global Counterinsurgency," *Current History* 105 (December 2006), 423–29.

[22]   Daniel Byman, "Buddies or Burdens?" *Security Studies* 23 (2014), 431–70.

[23]   Audrey Kurth Cronin, "How al-Qaida Ends: The Decline and Demise of Terrorist Groups," *International Security* 31 (2006), 7–48.

[24]   Richard Haass and Robert Litan, "Globalization and Its Discontents: Navigating the Dangers of an Entangled World," *Foreign Affairs* 77 (1998), 2–6.

[25]   Thomas Friedman, *The World Is Flat* (New York: Farrar, Straus and Giroux, 2005).

[26]   Niall Ferguson, "Sinking Globalization," *Foreign Affairs* 84 (2005), 64–77.

[27]   Ian Bremmer, *The End of the Free Market* (New York: Penguin, 2010).

[28]   Alexander Motyl, "Empire Falls," *Foreign Affairs* 85 (2006), 190–94.

[29]   Michael Mandelbaum, *The Case for Goliath* (New York: Public Affairs Press, 2005).

[30]   Thomas Wright, "The Rise and Fall of the Unipolar Concert," *The Washington Quarterly* 37 (2015), 7–24.

[31]   Niall Ferguson, "Empires with Expiration Dates," *Foreign Policy* 156 (2006), 46–52.

[32]   John Mearsheimer, "American Unhinged," *National Interest* 129 (January/February 2014), 9–30; Micah Zenko and Michael Cohen, "Clear and Present Safety," *Foreign Affairs* 91 (2012), 79–93.

[33]   Stephen Brooks and William Wohlforth, "The Rise and Fall of the Great Powers in the Twenty First Century," *International Security* 40 (2015/16), 7–53.

[34]   Niall Ferguson, "Complexity and Collapse," *Foreign Affairs* 89 (2010), 18–32.

[35]   Fu Ying, "How China Sees Russia," *Foreign Affairs* 95 (2016), 96–105.

[36]   Pew Global Attitudes Project, http://www.pewglobal.org/2013/07/18/americas-global-image.

[37]   See Pew Research Center Studies: Faith and Skepticism about Trade, Foreign Investment (2014); and Global Concern about Climate Change (2015).

[38]   Peter Katzenstein and Robert Keohane, "Anti-Americanisms," *Policy Review* 139 (2006), 25–37.

[39]   Giacomo Chiozza, *Anti-Americanism and the American World Order* (Baltimore: Johns Hopkins University Press, 2009).

[40]   Anne Applebaum, "In Search of Pro-Americanism," *Foreign Policy* 149 (2005), 32–40.

[41]   *Global Trends 2030: A World Transformed* (Washington, DC: National Intelligence Council, 2012).

The American National Style 3

Dateline: The Mexican Border

In responding to foreign policy challenges the United States is influenced as much by ideas as by events. In the case of border security the idea that technological or engineering solutions exist to political problems has been especially influential. In his presidential campaign Donald Trump embraced such a solution in calling for a wall to be built along the border as a means to reduce illegal immigration and drug smuggling from Mexico into the United States. His proposal brought forward a firestorm of controversy. A closer look reveals that for over a decade the United States has been seeking a technological solution to the border problem.

The U.S.-Mexico border is 1,969 miles long. It is the world's most frequently crossed international border. While many enter and exit the United States legally, it also has the highest number of illegal border crossings, with an estimated five hundred thousand illegal entries taking place every year. It is also a deadly border. From 1998 to 2004, 1,954 migrants died trying to cross it.

In 1994 President Bill Clinton authorized Operation Gatekeeper to "to restore integrity and safety to the nation's busiest border" by stopping illegal immigration. Prior to this point only about some eighty miles of barriers and fencing existed along the U.S.-Mexico border in Texas and California. Operation Gatekeeper was targeted at the San Diego border sector. It involved doubling the Border Patrol's force, building more fences and walls, and implementing high-tech land and air surveillance along the border.

In 2006 President George W. Bush signed the Secure Fence Act, stating, "This bill will help protect the American people. This bill will make our borders more secure." This legislation called for creating a double-reinforced fence along 700 miles of the border. When Barack Obama took office in 2009 more than 580 miles of fence was in place although only a small portion was double-layered. By 2012 the total length of fencing had increased to 649 miles consisting of some 300 miles of vehicle barriers and 353 miles of pedestrian barriers.

In 2014 Rep. Duncan Hunter, chair of the House Armed Services Committee, argued for constructing a reinforced two-layer fifteen-feet parallel steel and wire fence separated by a one-hundred-yard gap along the entire border. His plan also included additional physical barriers to entry, extensive lighting systems, and sensors to detect attempted illegal border crossing.

Constructing the border fence as it currently exists was controversial for many of the same concerns leveled at Trump's Great Wall proposal. The first is cost. Trump proposed that Mexico pay the cost. The fourteen-mile San Diego fence was to cost a total of $14 million. The first eleven miles ended up costing $42 million. The initial costs of pedestrian fencing averaged $3.9 million per mile while that of vehicle fencing ranged from $200,000 to $1.8 million. The projected cost of upkeep of the fencing system in Bush's plan was $66.5 billion over the next twenty years. According to the Department of Homeland Security the fence was breached over four thousand times in FY 2010 with an average repair cost of $1,800 per breach.

Second, there is the question of its effectiveness. As the fence is constructed and passageways into the United States blocked, illegal crossing did not so much end as move on to other points. Where once the Tucson enforcement zone was the most active point of entrance, it is now the Rio Grande Valley. In a six-month span covering late 2013 and early 2014 more than ninety-seven thousand illegal migrants were arrested in the Rio Grande Valley, a 69 percent increase from the previous year. Moreover, just as technology in the form of fencing has been used to stop border crossings, it has been used to overcome it. In a two-week period three smuggling tunnels were found along with over forty tons of marijuana. The tunnels were equipped with lighting, ventilation, and in one case a railcar system.

Defenders of the border fence system cite both the overall reduction in the rate of Mexican emigration to the United States and the steep drop in the number of Mexican migrants apprehended at the border as proof of its success. The net migration of Mexicans to the United States is at a low level not experienced since the 1940s with the number of border arrests at its lowest level in nearly fifty years. Critics of the border fence assert that these figures are better attributed to a decrease in the number of jobs open to Mexican immigrants in the United States, better law enforcement of migration laws, and a decline in the percentage of Mexicans aged fifteen to twenty-nine.

A third point of controversy has been the manner in which the fence was constructed. More than thirty legal waivers were used to bypass existing laws and regulations. Among those acts from which the project received exemptions were the Endangered Species Act, the Clean Water Act, and the National Historic Preservation Act. Michael Chertoff, secretary of the Homeland Security Department, justified the legal waivers arguing that criminal activity will not stop while public debates and legal activity drag on. States and communities along the border registered objections to the concept of a fence because of the negative impact it had on the economic health of their areas.

Fencing is not the only technological solution the United States has embraced in an effort to secure its border with Mexico. It is now also employing the same drone aircraft used to hunt out terrorists in Pakistan, Afghanistan, and Iraq (without their missile packages). In 2011 eight Predator drones flew missions on the U.S. side of the Rio Grande in search of illegal border-crossing activity. Originally plans called for having twenty-four drones in service by 2016 with the ultimate goal of giving the Border Patrol the right to have one airborne anywhere in the continental United States on a three-hour notice. Those plans have been scaled back due to concerns over the effectiveness of the drone program. In 2011 each drone cost $20 million. The Government Accountability Office estimated that an hour of flight time cost $3,600 and that it cost $7,054 for each illegal immigrant or smuggler caught.

Moreover, the Mexican border is not the only border the United States has sought to close off using technology. In 1991–92 some 40,000 Haitians sought to reach the United States by boat. Poverty and political oppression were the primary forces producing this mass exodus. President George H. W. Bush ordered that their boats be intercepted before reaching the United States and returned to Cuba. A decade earlier President Reagan ordered the Coast Guard to stop refugees from reaching the United States by boat. His announcement came after an estimated 125,000 Cubans arrived in Florida on boats of varying sizes and degrees of safety in 1980 in what was known as the Mariel Boatlift. Unexpectedly, Cuban premier Fidel Castro had announced that anyone wishing to leave Cuba for the United States would be permitted to do so. Almost instantly Cuban Americans in Miami organized a boatlift operation. In his 1992 campaign President Bill Clinton promised to change this policy. As inauguration day approached fears grew of another mass exodus from Haiti. Shortly after taking office he revoked his pledge and kept in place the 1981 Reagan order.

Embracing engineering solutions as a means to deal with political problems is only one of the ways in which ideas shape the content and conduct of U.S. foreign policy. In order to get a fuller picture this chapter will examine the concept of an American **national style** to foreign policy with special attention to its sources and consequences. Later in the chapter we will look at the way in which past approaches to foreign policy influence the contemporary U.S. debate over foreign policy giving special attention to Wilsonianism.

The Importance of Ideas

Policy makers come and go, but ideas and ways of thinking endure. George W. Bush's major foreign policy innovation, moving from **containment** and **deterrence** to **preemption**, strikes many as a radical departure from the past, but others see in it the long reach of American history.[1] The same holds true for **neoconservatism**, the set of foreign policy ideas that formed the conceptual foundation for the Bush Doctrine, with its emphasis on preemption, unilateral action, and support for democratization. To many, it is neither "neo" nor "conservative." Its core ideas of moralism, idealism, exceptionalism, militarism, and global ambition have deep intellectual roots in the American foreign policy tradition.[2] More recently, Barack Obama's foreign policy received a great deal of criticism for embracing the idea of "leading from behind." It was rejected by many as ill-conceived, un-American, and bound to fail. Regardless of the merits of these critiques few pointed out the similarities between leading from behind and the post-Vietnam Nixon Doctrine which called for providing weapons to regional allies so that American troops would not have to be used to contain the spread of communism.[3]

The importance of ideas as a force in foreign policy decision-making stems from both their immediate and long-term effects.[4] In the short run, shared ideas help policy makers and citizens cope with the inherent uncertainty involved in selecting from competing policy lines. Consistency with the principles of free trade or isolationism may not produce the "correct" policy, but these criteria do provide a basis for the selection or rejection of policies.

Ideas also become institutionalized as organizations and laws are designed around them. Because organizations and laws are slow to change, they become an anchor for any future reform debate. Once they are in place, political constituencies coalesce around policies rooted in these ideas and lobby for their continued existence. As a result, ideas continue to exert an influence on policy long after they have lost their vitality and after those who espoused them have passed from the scene.

Viewed over the long term, the result of this interplay of policies and ideas is a layered pattern in which policies reflecting different sets of ideas and pulling in different directions are combined, with little overall coherence. This pattern is very much evident in American trade policy. Conventional explanations of American trade policies focus on the political leverage of societal interest groups or the demands of the international system.[5] Others argue that only by looking at ideas can one explain America's movement from a protectionist cycle that began in the early nineteenth century and culminated in the highly protective tariffs of the 1930s to a free-trade cycle that now contains elements of both free trade and fair trade.

The national security policy arena provides an even clearer picture of the influence of shared ideas and ways of acting on American foreign policy. Throughout most of the Cold War period, these ideas and actions were embodied in the concept of containment. The first public statement of containment came in an article in *Foreign Affairs* written by George Kennan. In it, he argued:

> Soviet pressure against the free institutions of the western world is something that can be contained by the adroit and vigilant application of counter-force at a series of constantly shifting geographical and political points, corresponding to the shifts and maneuvers of Soviet policy.[6]

The logic of containment became embodied in a wide range of U.S. foreign policy initiatives including the Truman Doctrine, which pledged U.S. support to all states coming under pressure from international communism; early U.S. foreign aid programs intended to rebuild the economies of Western Europe (the Marshall Plan) and bring economic development to the Third World (the Four Point Program); and the creation of military alliances on the perimeter of the Soviet Union including the North Atlantic Treaty Organization (NATO), the Southeast Asia Treaty Organization (SEATO), and the Central Treaty Organization (CENTO).

Even the Nixon administration's much heralded shift to a policy of **détente** could be comfortably fitted into the larger strategy of containment. Détente was designed to protect U.S. influence as much as possible in an era of lessened power abroad and increasingly isolationist feeling at home. Confrontation and crisis management were now too expensive to be the primary means for stopping Soviet expansion. Détente sought to accomplish this end by creating a framework of limited cooperation within the context of an international order that recognized the legitimacy of both U.S. and Soviet core security goals.[7]

Isolationism versus Internationalism

U.S. foreign policy is frequently discussed in terms of a tension between two opposing general foreign policy orientations: **isolationism** and **internationalism**. From the isolationist perspective, American national interests are best served by "quitting the world" or, at a minimum, maintaining a healthy sense of detachment from events elsewhere. It draws its inspiration from Washington's Farewell Address, in which he urged Americans to "steer clear of permanent alliances with any portion of the foreign world" and asserted that "Europe has a set of primary interests which to us have none or very remote relations."[8] Among the major foreign policy decisions rooted in the principles of isolationism are the Monroe Doctrine, the refusal to join the League of Nations, the neutrality legislation of the 1930s, and, more loosely, the fear of future Vietnams. The internationalist perspective sees protecting and promoting American national interests as requiring an activist foreign policy. Internationalists hold that the United States cannot escape the world. Events abroad inevitably impinge upon U.S. interests, and any policy based on the denial of their relevance is self-defeating. Such widely divergent undertakings as membership in the United Nations and NATO, the Marshall Plan, the Helsinki Human Rights Agreement, and involvement in Korea and Vietnam can be traced to the internationalist perspective on world affairs.

The oscillation between isolationism and internationalism has not been haphazard. An underlying logic appears to guide the movement from one to the other. Five earlier periods of U.S. foreign policy of twenty to thirty years' duration have been identified; each combines an introvert (isolationist) and extrovert (internationalist) phase.[9] According to this line of analysis, the United States has left the last phase of an internationalist phase, with the next isolationist phase having begun in 2014. Evidence that this may be occurring is readily found in public opinion polls that indicate while the American public remains internationalist it has become less supportive of the use of military force abroad and majority now sees both the Afghanistan and Iraq war as mistakes.

Introvert	Extrovert
1. 1776–98	1. 1798–1824
2. 1824–44	2. 1844–71
3. 1871–91	3. 1891–1918
4. 1918–40	4. 1940–67
5. 1967–87	5. 1987–2014
6. 2014–34?	

In each of these periods, U.S. policy makers had to confront a major foreign policy problem. In period one, it was independence; in period two, issues involving manifest destiny were dominant; and in period three, it was the process of becoming an industrial power. The crisis of world democracy dominated period four, and in the fifth period the need to create a stable world order has been the main challenge facing U.S. foreign policy. In each period, the dominant cycle (introversion or extroversion) imposes limits on the types of solutions that can be considered by policy makers and predisposes the public to accept certain courses of action. The cyclical movement between isolationism and internationalism is seen as being spiral in nature. Each movement toward internationalism is deeper than the one before it, and each reversal to isolationism is less complete than the one preceding it.

Disagreement exists over the mechanism that triggers a shift from one phase to the next. A number of possibilities have been suggested. One possibility is that shifts in foreign policy orientations may be tied to the business cycle.[10] Some have found that in periods of economic recovery U.S. foreign policy takes on a belligerent tone. Similarly, the more stable the economy, the more moderate is U.S. foreign policy. In a similar vein, it has been argued that the periodic outward thrust of U.S. foreign policy is a product of domestic frustrations and disappointments.[11] Foreign policy successes are sought as a sign that the American dream is still valid and capable of producing victories.

Whatever is the specific trigger, the movement from isolationism to internationalism and back again is made possible because both general foreign policy orientations are very much a part of the American national style. One does not represent the American approach to world affairs, and the other its denial. They are two different ways in which the patterns of American foreign policy, its fundamental building blocks, come together.[12] Both are united in the conviction that the institutions and ideals brought forward by the American experience need protection. The approaches differ on how best to provide for their continued growth and development. Isolationism seeks to accomplish this end by insulating the American experience from corrupting foreign influences. Internationalism seeks to protect them by creating a more hospitable global environment.

Sources of the American National Style

The sources of the American national style are found in many places.[13] One of the most frequently talked about influences is the conditions under which earlier generations of American policy makers operated and the ideas that guided their thinking and produced a sense of American exceptionalism that continues even today.

Few nations can look back on as favorable a set of conditions in which to grow and develop. The vast size of the United States brought with it an abundance of natural resources on which to build a prosperous economy. Just as important for the development of the American national style is the fact that this economic growth took place without any master plan. Individual self-reliance, flexibility, and improvisation were the cardinal virtues in developing America. Guided by these principles, the United States has become a "how-to-do-it" society, whose energies are largely directed to the problem at hand and whose long-range concerns receive scant attention.[14]

This economic growth also occurred in an era of unparalleled global harmony. With the exception of the Crimean War, from the Congress of Vienna in 1815 until the outbreak of World War I in 1914, the Great Powers of Europe were largely at peace with one another. The defense of America's continental borders never required the creation of a large standing army or navy. Peace and security seemed to come naturally. They were widely accepted as the normal condition of world affairs. The links between American security and developments abroad went unnoticed. Democracy, rather than the strength of the British navy or the European balance of power, was seen as the source of American security.

The faith in the power of democracy reflects the extent to which American political thought is rooted in the eighteenth-century view of human nature. Most important to the development of the ideas that have guided U.S. policy makers is the work of John Locke, who argued that people are rational beings capable of determining their own best interests. The best government was held to be that which governed least. To Locke, the historical record indicated that the exercise of power led inevitably to its abuse and corrupted the natural harmony that exists among individuals. Conflicts between individuals could be settled without the application of concentrated state power. The wastefulness and destructiveness of war disqualified it as a means of conflict resolution. Negotiation, reason, and discussion are sufficient to overcome misperceptions and reconcile conflicting interests.

In contrast to war, trade is seen as a force promoting the peaceful settlement of disputes. The dynamics of the marketplace bind individuals together in mutually profitable exchanges. The power of the marketplace is seen as endangered or frustrated by the power of governments. The greater the power of one over society, the lesser the power of the other. Because commerce creates a vested interest in peace, logic again points to limiting government powers. The American historical experience seemed to offer vivid proof of the correctness of the liberal outlook on human affairs.

Much attention, of late, has also been given to the influence of religion on American foreign policy.[15] Four components of this religious frame to American foreign policy are especially important. First is the idea of America as God's "chosen nation." Second, America has a special mission or calling to transform the world. Third, in carrying out this mission, the United States is engaged in a struggle against evil. Finally, American foreign policy has come to be characterized by an apocalyptic outlook on world affairs. Change will come about not through gradual or subtle changes but through a cataclysmic transformation in which evil is encountered and then decisively and permanently defeated.

One must be careful, however, to recognize that not all religions necessarily view world politics or America's role in the world in the same way. For example, within Protestantism, three different schools of thought speak to the conduct of American foreign policy.[16] They are fundamentalism, evangelicalism, and liberal Christianity. Liberal Christianity provided the worldview for such key members of the founding generation of "Cold Warriors" as Secretaries of State Dean Acheson and John Foster Dulles. It is now in decline and has been replaced by fundamentalism and evangelicalism as the politically dominant forces among Protestantism.

Fundamentalism and evangelicalism each provide a different lens for looking at America's place in the world. Fundamentalists are deeply pessimistic about the possibility of bringing about a new world order and see a deep divide separating believers and nonbelievers. Defensive and self-confident, they hold an apocalyptic view of the future and are not particularly interested in cooperating with those with whom they disagree. Evangelicals also divide the world into believers and nonbelievers, but they are far more optimistic than fundamentalists in their view about the potential for progress and cooperation among different people. Here again, caution must be exercised in making generalizations. Some sixty or seventy different evangelical/fundamentalist groups exist, and they do not all hold identical foreign policy positions. In fact, for many of these groups, foreign policy is quite secondary in importance to domestic social policy.[17]

Taken as a whole this reading of the American past has led to a sense of American exceptionalism that continues today. By one count the phrase "American exceptionalism" appeared 4,172 times in national U.S. publications from 2010 to 2012.[18] Accompanying this sense of exceptionalism is the perceived need (right) to a leadership role in world affairs.[19] During isolationist periods, leadership takes the form of standing apart from international politics and leading by example. In internationalist periods, it is revealed in attempts to transform the international system. In 1998 Secretary of State Madeleine Albright asserted that "if we use force, it is because we are America. We are the indispensable nation. We stand tall. We see farther into the future." Vice President Dick Cheney spoke in equally expansive terms in 2002, stating, "America has friends and allies in this cause, but only we can lead." Exceptionalism was at the center of President Obama's speech to the nation on Libya in March 2011 when he asserted that "for generations the United States of America has played a unique role as anchor of global security and as an advocate for human freedom" as well as in 2014 at West Point when he "asserted America must always lead on the world stage."

Before proceeding a caveat is in order. Ours is not the only way to characterize the American historical experience, value system, or national style.[20] For some, the United States has been antirevolutionary, seeking to prevent social change and stop Third World revolutionary movements that might threaten its dominant position in world affairs. This view is often found in the writings of revisionist historians who find U.S. foreign policy to be imperial in nature and rooted in the expansionist needs of capitalism. Others see U.S. foreign policy as racist, as evidenced by its immigration policy, which systematically discriminated against the Chinese and other non-Western Europeans; its hesitancy to support international human rights conventions; and its attitude toward the suitability of Hawaii, Puerto Rico, and the Philippines for either statehood or independence. Finally, some argue that what we have called internationalism is better defined as interventionism: a tendency to intervene in the affairs of other states to a degree far beyond any reasonable definition of U.S. national interest. In this view, there is no competing theme of isolationism but only opposition to specific cases of intervention on pragmatic or tactical grounds.

Patterns

Three patterns of thought and action provide the building blocks from which the American national style emerges. They are unilateralism, moral pragmatism, and legalism. In this section we examine each in turn.

Unilateralism

The first pattern is **unilateralism**, or a predisposition to act alone in addressing foreign policy problems.[21] Unilateralism does not dictate a specific course of action. Isolationism, neutrality, activism, and interventionism are all consistent with its basic orientation to world affairs. The unilateralist thrust of U.S. foreign policy represents a rejection of the balance-of-power approach associated with the European diplomatic tradition. It reflects the American sense of exceptionalism and is often perceived by others to be an insensitive and egoistic nationalism.

The best-known statement of the unilateralist position is the Monroe Doctrine. With the end of the Napoleonic Wars, concern arose that Spain might attempt to reestablish its control over the newly independent Latin American republics. Great Britain approached the United States about the possibility of a joint declaration to prevent this from happening. The United States rejected the British proposal, only to turn around and make a unilateral declaration to the same end: The United States would not tolerate European intervention in the Western Hemisphere, and in return, it pledged not to interfere in European affairs. In 1904 the Roosevelt Corollary to the Monroe Doctrine was put forward. Spurred into action by the inability of the Dominican Republic to pay its foreign lenders, President Theodore Roosevelt sent in U.S. forces. The Roosevelt Corollary established the United States as the self-proclaimed policeman of the Western Hemisphere. It would play that role many times. The years 1904–34 saw the United States send eight expeditionary forces to Latin America, conduct five military occupations ranging in duration from a few months to nineteen years, and take over customs collections duties twice. The legacy of the Monroe Doctrine continues into the post–World War II era. The Central Intelligence Agency (CIA)-sponsored overthrows of the Arbenz government in Guatemala and the Allende government in Chile, U.S. behavior in the Bay of Pigs and the Cuban missile crisis, the 1965 invasion of the Dominican Republic, the 1983 invasion of Grenada, and the 1989 invasion of Panama testify to the continued influence of unilateralism on U.S. behavior in the Western Hemisphere.

The nature of the American participation in World War I and the subsequent U.S. refusal to join the League of Nations also reflect the unilateralist impulse. Official World War I documents identify the victors as the Allied and Associated Powers. The only Associated Power of note was the United States. For U.S. policy makers, this was more than a mere symbolic separation from its European allies. Woodrow Wilson engaged in personal negotiations with Germany over ending the war without consulting the allies about the terms of a possible truce. The United States was also the only major victorious power not to join the League of Nations. This abstention is often attributed to isolationism, but it can also be seen as a triumph of unilateralism.[22] Membership would have committed the United States to a collective security system that could have obliged it to undertake multilateral military action in the name of stopping international aggression.

The impact of unilateralist thinking also comes through clearly in the neutrality legislation of the 1930s. These acts placed an embargo on the sale of arms to warring states. Because arms sales were seen as the most likely method of U.S. entry into a war, they had to be prohibited regardless of the consequences that the embargo might have on events elsewhere. The post–World War II shift from isolationism to internationalism did not bring about an abandonment of unilateralism; it only placed a multilateral façade over it. Control over NATO's nuclear forces remains firmly in the hands of the United States. The presence of the UN flag in Korea and references to SEATO treaty commitments in Vietnam could scarcely conceal the totally U.S. nature of these two wars. In the United Nations, the United States' veto power protects its vital interests from the intrusion of other powers, and the system of weighted voting used in international financial organizations guarantees the United States a preponderant voice in their deliberations.

The American penchant for unilateralism was never far beneath the surface in its dealings with allies during the later years of the Cold War. Nowhere was this more evident than at the Reykjavik summit meeting with Soviet leader Mikhail Gorbachev. James Schlesinger observed at the time that in proposing to eliminate all ballistic missiles within ten years "the administration suddenly jettisoned 25 years of deterrence doctrine . . . without warning, consultation with Congress or its allies."[23]

The Global War on Terror did not change this unilateralist impulse; if anything, it reinforced it. In his January 2002 State of the Union address President George W. Bush gave notice to the world that he was prepared to act unilaterally against terrorism. "Some governments will be timid in the face of terror. . . . If they do not act, America will." Obama embraced unilateralism, as well as moral pragmatism, which we will address next, in his use of drones to kill terrorist leaders.[24]

Moral Pragmatism

The second pattern in American foreign policy is **moral pragmatism**.[25] The American sense of morality involves two elements. The first is that state behavior can be judged by moral standards. The second is that American morality provides the universal standard for making those judgments. By definition, American actions are taken to be morally correct and justifiable. Flawed policy initiatives are routinely attributed to leadership deficiencies or breakdowns in organizational behavior and not to the values that guided that action. In the aftermath of World War I, the Nye Committee investigated charges that the United States had been led into war by banking interests, and the McCarthy investigations looked into alleged communist penetration of the State Department following the "loss of China."

In judging state behavior by moral standards, the United States typically makes the leap of placing responsibility for foreign policy problems on the evil nature of the opponent rather than on the underlying dynamics of world politics or its own actions. George Kennan, the author of the containment doctrine, put it this way: "There seems to be a curious American tendency to search, at all times, for a single external evil, to which all can be attributed."

In line with Kennan's observation Paul Pillar, a CIA officer who once served as national intelligence officer for the Middle East, has gone so far as to argue that the United States needs a villain in making foreign policy and that in Iran it found one.[26] The end result is that United States becomes preoccupied with Iran to a far greater extent than is warranted by the threat they pose. Pillar argues that by casting an adversary as a villain several harmful by-products follow for U.S. foreign policy, all of which have surfaced in negotiations to limit Iran's quest for nuclear weapons: in the process the United States (1) comes to deny that any reasonable basis for the adversary's action exists; (2) underestimates how much support that government may have among its people; and (3) misjudges the adversary's willingness to compromise.

American pragmatism takes the form of an "engineering approach" to foreign policy problem-solving.[27] U.S. involvement is typically put in terms of "setting things right." It is assumed that a right answer does exist and that it is the

American answer. Moreover, the answer to the problem is seen as being permanent in nature. Foreign policy crises arise when others do not see the problem
in similar terms. To some, this has been especially evident in U.S.-Soviet arms
control talks, where the American approach to strategic thinking treated nuclear
war as a "mathematical exercise."[28] Operating on the basis of a very different historical experience, the Soviets viewed war in quite different terms. It was marked
by much uncertainty for which no engineering solution existed.

The preferred American method for uncovering the solution is to break the
problem into smaller ones—the same way an engineer may take a blueprint and
break a large task down into smaller ones. An organizational or mechanical solution is then devised for each of the subproblems. In the process, it is not unusual
to lose sight of the political context of the larger problem being addressed. When
this happens, the result can be the substitution of means for ends, improvisation,
or reliance on canned formulas to solve the problem.

The neutrality legislation of the 1930s provides an example of moral pragmatism at work. As first put forward, the legislation was easy to implement but paid
little attention to the political realities of the day. Weapons were not to be sold
to either side. Yet, refusing to sell weapons to either participant guaranteed victory to the stronger side and invited its aggression. The neutrality legislation was
repeatedly amended in an effort to close the gap between technique and political
reality. In 1937 the president was given the authority to distinguish between civil
strife and war. In 1939 the neutrality legislation permitted the cash-and-carry
purchase of weapons by belligerents. This allowed the United States to sell weapons to Great Britain but made a mockery of the neutrality principle.

The potential dangers of rooting U.S. foreign policy on a foundation of moral
pragmatism came through quite clearly in the Iran-Contra fiasco. Convinced of
the moral correctness of the goal of freeing American hostages in Lebanon, the
Reagan administration proceeded to sell arms to Iran and then diverted monies
gained through these sales to the U.S.-backed Contras fighting the Sandinista
government in Nicaragua. The reliance on engineering solutions and formulas
to solve problems also reached excess here, as witnessed by National Security
Council (NSC) staffer Lieutenant Colonel Oliver North's equation for achieving
the release of the American hostages, part of which read: 1 707 w/300 TOWs
(Tube-launched Optically tracked Wire-guided missiles) = 1 AMCIT (American
citizen). More recently, this tendency to see the solution to foreign policy problems as lying in designing blueprints and putting them in place is evident in
the American tendency to equate building democracy with holding elections and
writing a constitution.

A frequent complaint leveled at U.S. Cold War foreign policy was its overre-
liance on ritualistic solutions such as treaties, foreign aid, and pledges of support
to right-wing dictators in the name of freedom to stop the spread of communism. One author argued that the anticommunist impulse was used to sanction
almost any course of action, no matter how immoral, if it bought about the
greater goal of stopping communism.[29] In the view of many this attitude has
carried over to the Global War on Terrorism. In his address to the American people following the 9/11 attacks, George W. Bush declared, "Either you are with

the U.S. or you are with the terrorists." He would go on to call for Osama bin Laden's capture "dead or alive." Establishing secret interrogation centers for the questioning of suspected terrorists using techniques commonly considered to fall under the heading of "torture" were justified by the magnitude of the threat. So too was a policy of secret National Security Agency (NSA) surveillance on electronic communications of Americans. The policy was justified on the grounds that Americans were not the target of the collection program and that any information collected on them was accidental and "miniscule." Moreover, it was necessary to stop future terrorist attacks on the United States.

Legalism

The third pattern in U.S. foreign policy is **legalism**. It grows out of the rejection of the balance of power as a means for preserving national security and the liberal view that people are rational beings who abhor war and favor the peaceful settlement of disputes.[30] A central task of U.S. foreign policy, therefore, is to create a global system of institutions and rules that will allow states to settle their disputes without recourse to war. The primary institutional embodiments of the legalist perspective are the League of Nations and the United Nations. Also relevant are the host of post–World War II international economic organizations that the United States joined (i.e., the World Bank and International Monetary Fund). Just as commerce between individuals binds them together, international trade is assumed to bind states together and reduce the likelihood of war.

The rule-making thrust to legalism is found in the repeated use of the **pledge system** as an instrument of foreign policy.[31] In creating a pledge system, the United States puts forward a statement of principle and then asks other states to adhere to it either by signing a treaty or by pledging their support for the principle. Noticeably absent is any meaningful enforcement mechanism. The Open Door Notes exemplify this strategy for world affairs problem-solving. In the Notes, the United States unilaterally proclaimed its opposition to spheres of influence in China and asked other powers to do likewise, but it did not specify any sanctions against a state that reneged on its pledge. The Washington Naval Disarmament Conference of 1922 and the 1928 Kellogg-Briand Pact are also part of the pledge system. The Washington Naval Disarmament Conference sought to prevent war by establishing a fixed power ratio for certain categories of warships. The agreement failed to include inspection or enforcement provisions. Its restraining qualities were soon overtaken by a naval arms race in areas left uncovered by the agreement and by a general heightening of international tensions. The Kellogg-Briand Pact sought to outlaw war as an instrument of foreign policy. Yet, true to its unilateralist impulse, the United States stated that signing the pact would not prevent it from enforcing the Monroe Doctrine or obligate it to participate in sanctions against other states. The SALT I and SALT II (Strategic Arms Limitation Talks) agreements followed the tradition of the pledge system. They specified in broad terms the nuclear inventories that the Soviet Union and the United States were permitted to have, but without creating any enforcement provisions.

Variations of the pledge system have become a prominent feature of U.S. contemporary bilateral and multilateral trade policy. Confronted with an intransigent Japan in 1993, U.S. negotiators settled for a "framework" agreement that specified how future agreements would seek to resolve issues of trade imbalances and barriers to trade without detailing the particulars of the agreement. The New START arms control agreement signed between the United States and Russia in 2010 contained no enforcement procedures. Neither did the 2015 Paris Climate agreement. Countries were expected to set their own reduction standards. International shaming was to serve as the enforcement mechanism.

Legalism has also placed a heavy burden on U.S. foreign policy. In rejecting power politics as an approach for providing for U.S. national security, policy makers have denied themselves the use of the "reasons-of-state" argument as a justification for their actions. Instead, they have sought to clothe their actions in terms of legal principles. Post–World War II examples include fighting the Korean War under the UN flag, seeking the approval of the Organization of American States for a blockade during the Cuban missile crisis, and citing a request by the Organization of Eastern Caribbean States as part of the justification for going into Grenada. This pattern has continued in the post–Cold War era. Obama obtained UN support for his air attacks on Libya, George H. W. Bush moved forward with his military campaign against Iraq after getting UN support, and Bill Clinton did the same for his use of force in Haiti. George W. Bush continued this reliance on legalism even though he acted without UN support. His administration argued that no new UN resolution was necessary, because Saddam Hussein had violated previous UN resolutions and was thus in violation of an international agreement. In Bush's words, Iraq "had answered a decade of UN demands with a decade of defiance."

Consequences of the American National Style

As suggested earlier, these three patterns come together to support both isolationism and internationalism. They also produce four consequences for the overall conduct of U.S. foreign policy. The first consequence is a tendency to "win the war and lose the peace." As Robert Osgood wrote in 1957:

> The United States has demonstrated an impressive ability to defeat the enemy. Yet . . . it has been unable to deter war; it has been unprepared to fight war; it has failed to gain the objectives it fought for; and its settlements have not brought satisfactory peace.[32]

For many his observation rings true today.

This condition stems from the American tendency to see war and peace as polar opposites. War is a social aberration, whereas peace is the normal state of affairs. Strategies and tactics appropriate for one arena have no place in the other. The two categories must be kept separate to prevent the calculations of war from corrupting the principles of peace. In times of peace, reason, discussion, and trade are relied on to accomplish foreign policy objectives. In times of war, power is the appropriate tool. The absence of a conceptual link between war and peace means that war cannot serve as an instrument of statecraft and that war plans will be drawn up in a political vacuum. The objective of war is to defeat the enemy as swiftly as possible. Only when that is accomplished can one return to the concerns of peace.

Historical Lesson

The Bracero Program

World War II led to a significant demand for additional workers in the United States, most notably in agriculture and the railroad industry. This demand was filled by Mexican workers, "braceros," who crossed into the United States as part of a guest worker program negotiated between the two countries. Officially known as the Mexican Contract Labor Program, it existed from 1942 to 1964. The wartime years produced the smallest migrant flow of any of these years, with 49,000–82,000 Mexican workers crossing the border. From 1947 to 1954, the average annual migration was 116,000–141,000 per year. In the last ten years of the Bracero Program, there were on average 333,000 migrant worker contracts.

This was not the first attempt to regulate the entry of Mexican labor across the border. In 1909 President William Howard Taft signed an executive agreement with Mexico permitting thousands of Mexican contract workers to harvest sugar beets in Colorado and Nebraska. When the United States entered World War I, restrictions on the number of contract workers permitted into the United States were eased, and the number of Mexican workers increased to 73,000. The Mexican government viewed this situation with some alarm. The Mexican Constitution of 1917 contained a provision that sought to safeguard the rights of emigrant workers, and it attempted to discourage workers from going to the United States unless they already had contracts that provided such protections. These efforts were largely ineffective. In 1929, with the depression under way in the United States and large numbers of Mexicans returning home due to lack of jobs, the Mexican government sought but failed to obtain a bilateral agreement with the United States that would allow it to jointly manage the flow of workers across the border.

At the outset of the Bracero Program, Mexico possessed significant bargaining strength that allowed it to insert provisions protecting migrant rights, such as insisting that the braceros be paid the prevailing wage in the community they were working in and prohibiting Mexicans from being rejected at "white" restaurants and other facilities in the American South. Mexico blacklisted Texas because of its discrimination policies and would not allow braceros to go there. Gradually, however, Mexico's leverage began to weaken.

One important reason for this was the growing phenomenon of illegal, or wetback, immigration into areas such as Texas, where demand for migrant labor was great. In 1943 Congress passed Public Law 45 that gave legal status to the agreement reached with Mexico in 1942. One of its key provisions was that the United States could unilaterally declare an "open border" if need be. This power was used in May 1943 to grant one-year entrance permits. Texan farmers rushed into Mexico and began recruiting migrants, and the process undermined the orderly bilateral recruitment of workers. Lax border control enforcement in the early 1950s further contributed to the flow of illegal migrant workers.

In the late 1940s and early 1950s, the United States sought to deal with the problem of illegal migrant labor by transforming it into legal labor. This was done by mass deportations and mass legalizations. The scope of the problem was immense. From 1955 to 1959, 18 percent of all seasonal farm laborers were braceros. In New Mexico, braceros made up 70 percent of the seasonal labor force. From 1947 to 1949, the President's Commission on Migratory Labor estimated that 142,000 deportable Mexicans in the United States were legalized as braceros. In 1950 slightly more than 19,800 new bracero contracts were awarded, but an estimated 96,200 illegal Mexicans were working in the United States.

The legacy of the Bracero Program is found in many areas. Seasonal and regional concentrated agricultural jobs, as opposed to establishing permanent residences, became the norm for Mexicans coming to the United States. Part of the Mexican government's response to the end of the Bracero Program was to create jobs along the U.S. border for returning migrants. This became the Border Industrialization or Maquiladora Program.

It has not worked as expected, since these firms have preferred to hire young Mexican women rather than returning braceros.

Within the United States, the end of the Bracero Program has not ended the debate over how to address the problem of illegal Mexican workers in the United States or how to provide sanctioned labor to employers. The Reagan administration proposed a pilot program giving 50,000 Mexicans temporary work permits each year. The George W. Bush administration floated the idea of a massive amnesty program for illegal Mexican migrants in the months prior to the 9/11 attacks. When the administration dropped these plans, Mexico called for establishing a new guest worker program.

Applying the Lesson

1. What elements of the American national style can be found in the idea of a fence to control immigration and the Bracero Program?
2. Rate the importance of foreign policy and domestic policy considerations in these two policies.
3. Should we think about immigration primarily as an economic problem or as a national security problem?

The closing stages of World War II illustrate the problem inherent in the war-peace dichotomy. Should U.S. forces have pushed as far as possible eastward for the political purpose of denying the Red Army control over as much territory as possible, or should they have stopped as soon as the purely military objectives of the offensive were realized and not risked the lives of U.S. soldiers on nonmilitary goals? The latter course of action was selected, and the Cold War East-West boundary in Europe reflected this choice. The George W. Bush administration was not immune from this artificial separation of war and peace. A sharp distinction between war and peace was evident in planning for the Iraq War. The original war plan expected that U.S. troops would be withdrawn within six months of the invasion and planning for the postwar transition to democracy was virtually absent. The presence of a sharp war-peace distinction and impatience were evident in Obama's accelerated efforts to leave Afghanistan as the victor after bin Laden's death and the quick exit of American forces from Libya after Muammar Gaddafi was removed from power.

The second consequence is the existence of a double standard in judging the behavior of states. Convinced of its righteousness and the universality of its values, and predisposed to act unilaterally, the United States has often engaged in actions that it condemns when they are practiced by other states. The United States can be trusted to test and develop nuclear weapons, but other states, especially Third World states, cannot. Soviet interventions in Afghanistan and Czechoslovakia are condemned as imperialism, while U.S. interventions in the Dominican Republic, Grenada, and Panama are held to be morally defensible. The United States urges its allies not to sell weapons to terrorists or those who support them, while it sells weapons to Iran in the hopes of securing the release of U.S. hostages in Lebanon. The reverse condition also holds. Activities considered by most states to be a normal part of world affairs have been highly controversial in the United States. The clandestine collection of information and covert attempts to influence developments in other states are cases in point. Both are long-standing instruments of foreign policy. The notion that different rules might apply to the United States than to other states surfaced after revelations of widespread abuse by American interrogators at Abu Ghraib prison. President Bush dismissed as "absurd" an Amnesty International report charging the administration with having created a gulag at the Guantanamo Bay detention facility.

The third consequence is an ambivalence toward diplomacy. In the abstract, diplomacy is valued as part of the process by which states peacefully resolve their disputes. Along with international law and international organizations, diplomacy occupies a central place in liberal thinking about the proper forums for conducting foreign relations. The product of diplomacy, however, is viewed with great skepticism. If the U.S. position is the morally correct one, how can it compromise (something vital to the success of diplomacy) without rejecting its own sense of mission and the principles it stands for? As John Spanier notes, under these conditions compromise is indistinguishable from appeasement.[33] It does not matter whether the other party to the negotiations is a twentieth-century communist state or an eighteenth- or nineteenth-century European state. In either case, the fruits of diplomacy have been looked on with suspicion.

For the George W. Bush administration, this skepticism over the value of negotiating with the enemy was evident in its dealings with North Korea over its violation of the Agreed Framework that had been negotiated by the Clinton administration. "Talking" with North Korea was seen as tantamount to "caving in" to a government that the administration had labeled as being part of an "axis of evil." This ambivalence to negotiating with the enemy was also evident in negative comments made after the Obama administration announced an exchange of prisoners with the Taliban that freed an American soldier who had been held for five years. Those objecting argued it was morally wrong to negotiate with terrorists and that it would just lead to future abductions and captures by the Taliban.

The fourth consequence is impatience. Optimistic at the start of an undertaking and convinced of the correctness of its position in both a moral and a technical sense, Americans tend to want quick results. They become impatient when positive results are not soon forthcoming. A common reaction is to turn away in frustration. The next time a similar situation presents itself and U.S. action is needed, none may be taken. Calls for "no more Vietnams" reflect this sense of frustration. So, too, did the demand to get U.S. Marines out of Lebanon following the terrorist attacks on the U.S. compound during the Reagan administration.

The desire for quick and visible results is seen by many as creating a bias for the use of the military as an instrument of foreign policy. Neither diplomacy nor economic power offers quick results. Both are slow working and work best when used out of the public eye. A vicious circle thus can be created. The demand for quick results leads to a reliance on military power, but the rigid distinction between war and peace makes it difficult to use that power effectively. Its use may be marked by a double standard or, as Osgood observed, may simply fail to meet its political objectives. If that is the case, then diplomacy may be considered as an option. Yet here again, the results are likely to be slow in coming, and the settlement will be looked on with skepticism. Frustration will set in and dominate U.S. foreign policy until a consensus exists supporting new foreign policy initiatives. Finally, impatience was evident in the expectation that the United States could oversee an election for an interim Iraqi government, the writing of a constitution, its ratification, and the election of a permanent government in twelve months. The problem is, as one columnist noted, that Iraq does not operate on Washington's clock.[34]

Voices from the Past

As we have seen, the four broad historical patterns of thought have come together to support a variety of foreign policies. Their influence continues to be felt in the debate over which past presidential foreign policies should serve as reference points against which to judge current actions. In this section we will examine those past presidential foreign policies most frequently cited as precedents for today's foreign policy.

A Revival of Wilsonianism

Early evaluations of Wilson's foreign policy held it to be naively idealistic and fundamentally flawed. This is no longer the case. While conceding that the Wilsonian vision was ill-suited to the first decades of the twentieth century, many assert that **Wilsonianism** is quite relevant to the conditions of the post–Cold War era. Rather than characterizing Wilson as an idealist, he is seen by many who embrace his foreign policy principles as a vindicated visionary, one who possessed a "higher realism" in his handling of foreign affairs.[35]

After the 9/11 terrorist attack, George W. Bush, who had promised a moderate foreign policy, began to sound very much like Wilson. In his 2002 State of the Union address, Bush stated, "America will lead by defending liberty and justice because they are right and true and unchanging for people everywhere. . . . We have no intention of imposing our culture. But America will always stand firm for the nonnegotiable demands of human dignity."

Proponents of Wilsonianism as the basis for post–Cold War American foreign policy center their attention on his Fourteen Points. Presented in a speech Wilson delivered before Congress in 1918, the Fourteen Points constituted an outline for constructing a new world order. They included proposals for laying the foundation for a new, "open" era of international politics and for creating "a general association of nations" that would provide guarantees of "political independence and territorial integrity to great and small states alike."

Looking beyond the Fourteen Points themselves, the Wilsonian vision of world politics rested on four elements: first, promoting democracy; second, encouraging free trade; third, controlling weapons. Together, these three elements would place restraints on the exercise of power by governments and provide space for the development of individual liberty. The fourth element was the League of Nations. It would provide an alternative to balance-of-power politics as a means of providing for national security.[36]

Those who advocate adopting neo-Wilsonian foreign policy have not gone unchallenged. Some opponents assert that the term lacks clear meaning to the point that virtually all recent presidents could be termed Wilsonians.[37] For example, the Reagan Doctrine could be seen as the ultimate embodiment of the Wilsonian legacy given its commitment to expand democracy. In the same vein, Robert Tucker offers another critique. He argues Wilson's internationalism approach to foreign policy is not as unique as many of its supporters argue and that it shares much in common with that of Jefferson, who is cited by many as an early advocate of isolationism. They both rejected amoral European-style diplomacy and sought to replace it with a new diplomacy that rested on the will of the people. They were united in the belief that American interests could only be safeguarded by a reformed international system.[38]

David Fromkin poses another problem with Wilsonianism as a model for contemporary American foreign policy.[39] He concludes that one of its core assumptions is the importance of a strong presidency. Wilson saw the president's control of foreign policy as "very absolute." He believed that the Senate had no choice but to ratify any treaty submitted to it by the president, regardless of any doubts about its wisdom or the secrecy with which it may have been negotiated. Wilson also advocated the Espionage Act of 1917. Edward Snowden (NSA leaks), Daniel Ellsberg (Pentagon Papers), and Julius and Ethel Rosenberg (stealing atomic secrets for the Soviet Union) are among those charged with violating it.

Other Voices

Woodrow Wilson's is the most frequently cited voice from the past but not the only being rediscovered as the United States searches to define its place in the world today. Isolationists point to the writings of John Adams. According to Adams, American foreign policy should be based on the principle that the United States is "the well-wisher to the freedom and independence of all" but "the champion and vindicator only of her own."[40] Adams was putting forward an argument for nonintervention into the affairs of others and advocating a foreign policy that was to be based on the "power of example." To go further, he warned, would involve the United States in "wars of interest and intrigue, of individual avarice, envy, and ambition." Conservative internationalists point to Theodore Roosevelt's writings.[41] They would replace liberal internationalism's conception of humanitarian intervention as a philanthropic exercise with one rooted in a sense of nationalistic patriotism. Writing before the Spanish-American War, Roosevelt stressed that "the useful member of a community is the man who first and foremost attends to his own rights and duties . . . the useful member of the brotherhood of nations is that nation which is most thoroughly saturated with the national ideal."

In addition to these two, other voices from the past continue to exert an influence on the present.[42] Alexander Hamilton speaks to those who see the primary purpose of American foreign policy as the promotion of American economic strength at home and abroad. After World War II, this required an American foreign policy that worked with other states to promote and protect an open international economic order. Andrew Jackson's writings and actions provide a foundation for those who stress the populist principles of courage, honor, and self-reliance in the conduct of American foreign policy. Suspicious of outsiders and their values, Jacksonians champion a foreign policy of constant vigilance backed by overwhelming might that may be employed with few, if any, constraints.

Some commentators see in the Tea Party movement evidence of a revival of Jacksonianism. A closer look shows that the Tea Party's foreign policy agenda contains strains from both Jacksonianism and other voices from the past.[43] One wing is strongly internationalist and conservative in outlook. Sarah Palin has advanced this perspective favoring a foreign policy that seeks to defeat the enemy rather than withdraw from the world. A competing perspective argues for a selective and more isolationist-oriented involvement in foreign affairs but it is not of one mind on how to proceed. Senator Ron Paul has advanced a libertarian foreign policy agenda that is Jeffersonian in outlook expressing concern for the corrupting effects of global involvement on American democracy.[44] This has been particularly notable in his opposition secret to the NSA domestic surveillance program.

We close this section by once again noting that the American national style does not produce a single type of foreign policy nor are its various elements always present to the same degree. It can accommodate a variety of foreign polices ranging from internationalism to isolationism. For example, Obama's foreign policy broke ranks with some of the characteristics of the American national style we have presented in its willingness to engage in arms control negotiations with Iran but embraced others in its accelerated use of drones to target terrorists and its willingness to continue the NSA's domestic surveillance program.

Over the Horizon: A Millennial Foreign Policy?

The key question looking over the horizon for the U.S. national style is can it change in a way to adapt to future foreign policy challenges or will traditional ways of defining problems and solutions continue? Will engineering solutions continue to dominate thinking about protecting U.S. borders or will other approaches be used? The American national style should not be seen as frozen in place. Change is possible. In the eyes of some observers change might come as a result of the increased presence of women, blacks, and Hispanics in the policy-making process.[45] Their histories read quite differently from those presented in the standardized accounts of the American past, and they may bring to the policy process a very different style of acting and thinking about solutions of foreign policy problems.

Another potential source of change in the American national style is the coming into political power a new generation: the Millennials. Born between 1980 and 1997 they make up almost one-quarter of the adult U.S. population. They reached adulthood after the Cold War ended and have few memoires of the pre-9/11 world with its terrorist attacks and Middle East wars. Moreover, they are also far more likely than older generations to see the United States as having provoked 9/11 through its foreign policy actions.

Research shows that Millennials differ from older Americans in their foreign policy outlooks in three critical ways: (1) they see the world as significantly less threatening and are less worried about national security; (2) they are more supportive of international cooperation; and (3) while compared to older generations they are more hesitant to support using military force, in specific cases they do not reject using force out of hand. They are more supportive of multilateral military efforts than undertaking unilateral action.

Beneath this layer of agreement points of disagreement and division can be found among Millennials suggesting that their impact on policy may be somewhat uncertain. Perhaps most significantly, partisanship is present with Millennial Democrats and Millennial Republicans disagreeing on foreign policy priorities once one moves beyond preventing the spread of nuclear weapons, fighting terrorism, reducing U.S. dependence on foreign oil, and protecting American jobs.[46]

Critical Thinking Questions

1. Could the United States become isolationist again?
2. What is the most important element in the American national style for understanding U.S. foreign policy?
3. How difficult would it be for the U.S. national style in foreign policy to change?

Key Terms

containment, 54
détente, 55
deterrence, 54
internationalism, 55
isolationism, 54
legalism, 59
moral pragmatism, 59

national style, 53
neoconservatism, 54
pledge system, 63
preemption, 54
unilateralism, 59
Wilsonianism, 54

Further Reading

Andrew Bacevich, *The New American Militarism: How Americans Are Seduced by War* (New York: Oxford University Press, 2005).

The author traces the history of militarism in American political thought and argues that after Vietnam, both the American political left and right have embraced militarism as a means of advancing their political agendas.

Judith Goldstein, *Ideas, Interests, and American Trade Policy* (Ithaca, NY: Cornell University Press, 1993).

This book shows how new ideas shape foreign policy decisions long after they have been introduced by becoming embedded in political institutions.

John G. Ikenberry, et al., *The Crisis of American Foreign Policy: Wilsonianism in the 21st Century* (Princeton: Princeton University Press, 2009).

This volume presents a collection of essays on the meaning of Wilsonianism and its impact on contemporary American foreign policy. Special attention is given to the Iraq War and the Bush administration.

Gabriel Kolko, *The Roots of American Foreign Policy* (Boston: Beacon, 1969).

This classic volume presents a "revisionist" interpretation of American foreign policy, one that draws heavily on the influence of special interests and capitalism as its driving force.

Walter Russell Mead, *Special Providence* (New York: Routledge, 2002).

This book presents an interpretive history of the different ways in which Americans have come to view the world and the proper foreign policy response. Four different foreign policy traditions are identified.

Henry Nau, *Conservative Internationalism* (Princeton: Princeton University Press, 2013).

Traditional foreign policy debates often stress the tension between liberal internationalism and nationalism. This book examines another perspective, conservative internationalism, and traces its development from Jefferson to Reagan.

Robert Tomes, "American Exceptionalism in the Twenty-First Century," *Survival* 56 (February 2014), 27–50.

This essay begins with the observation that exceptionalism is not simply a rhetoric device. It is deeply embedded in the American worldview. The author traces its development over time.

David Unger, "A Better Internationalism," *World Policy Journal* 29 (2012), 101–10.

Liberalism internationalism is pictured as having become a code language for U.S. pressure against other governments. It has become reduced to a tool for crisis management. In its place there needs to be a policy of constructive internationalism.

Notes

[1] Michael Desch, "America's Liberal Illiberalism: The Ideological Origins of Overreaction in U.S. Foreign Policy," *International Security* 32 (2007/08), 7–43.

[2] Robert Kagan, "Neocon Nation: Neoconservatism, c. 1776," *World Affairs* 170 (2008), 13–35.

[3] Derek Reveron and Nikolas Gvosdev, "(Re)Discovering the National Interest," *Orbis* 59 (2015), 299–316.

[4] Judith Goldstein, *Ideas, Interests, and American Trade Policy* (Ithaca, NY: Cornell University Press, 1993), 1–18.

[5] Ibid.

[6] George Kennan, "The Sources of Soviet Conduct," *Foreign Affairs* 25 (1947), 576.

[7] For discussions of containment and détente, see John Spanier, *American Foreign Policy since WW II*, 10th ed. (New York: Holt, Rinehart & Winston, 1985), 23–29, 189–200, 304–306, and 316–21; Charles W. Kegley, Jr., and Eugene R. Wittkopf, *American Foreign Policy: Pattern and*

Process, 2nd ed. (New York: St. Martin's, 1982), 48–69; Henry T. Nash, *American Foreign Policy: A Search for Security,* 3rd ed. (Homewood, IL: Dorsey, 1985), 44–48 and 249–50.

8 Howard Bliss and M. Glen Johnson, *Beyond the Water's Edge: American Foreign Policy* (Philadelphia: Lippincott, 1975), 52–53.

9 Frank Klingberg, *Positive Expectations of America's World Role* (Lanham, MD: University Press of America, 1996).

10 Dexter Perkins, *The American Approach to Foreign Policy* (Cambridge, MA: Harvard University Press, 1962), 154.

11 Robert Dallek, *The American Style of Foreign Policy, Cultural Politics and Foreign Affairs* (New York: New American Library, 1983).

12 Max Lerner, cited in Cecil Crabb, Jr., *American Foreign Policy in the Nuclear Age,* 4th ed. (New York: Harper & Row, 1983), 47; Richard Ullman, "The 'Foreign World' and Ourselves: Washington, Wilson and the Democratic Dilemma," *Foreign Policy* 21 (1975/76), 97–125.

13 For a discussion of these points, see Stanley Hoffmann, *Gulliver's Troubles, or the Setting of American Foreign Policy* (New York: McGraw-Hill, 1968); Spanier, *American Foreign Policy since WW II;* Perkins, *The American Approach to Foreign Policy;* Amos Jordan and William J. Taylor, Jr., *American National Security, Policy and Process* (Baltimore: Johns Hopkins University Press, 1981).

14 Kenneth Keniston, quoted in Bliss and Johnson, *Beyond the Water's Edge,* 110.

15 John Judis, "The Author of Liberty," *Dissent* (Fall 2005), 54–61. See also the special issue, "Religion and the Presidents," *Review of Faith and International Affairs* 9:4 (2011).

16 Walter Russell Mead, "God's Country," *Foreign Affairs* 85 (2006), 24–43.

17 Peggy Shriver, "Evangelicals and World Affairs," *World Policy Journal* 23 (2006), 52–58.

18 Cited in Robert Tomes, "American Exceptionalism in the Twenty-First Century," *Survival* 56 (2014), 27.

19 Stanley Hoffmann, "Foreign Policy Transition: Requiem," *Foreign Policy* 42 (1980/81), 3–26.

20 For a discussion of alternative interpretations of U.S. foreign policy and national style, see Kegley and Wittkopf, *American Foreign Policy,* 69–81. See also Bear Braumoeller, "The Myth of American Isolationism," *Foreign Policy Analysis* 6 (2010), 349–72.

21 For a discussion of unilateralism, see Gene Rainey, *Patterns of American Foreign Policy* (Boston, MA: Allyn & Bacon, 1975), 19–43.

22 Robert Tucker, *The Radical Left and American Foreign Policy* (Baltimore: Johns Hopkins University Press, 1971), 34.

23 James Schlesinger, "Reykjavik and Revelations: A Turn of the Tide?" *Foreign Affairs* 65 (1987), 431.

24 Trevor McCrisken, "Obama's Drone War," *Survival* 55 (2013), 97–122.

25 For a discussion of American foreign policy highlighting these themes, see Arthur Schlesinger, Jr., "Foreign Policy and the American Character," *Foreign Affairs* 62 (1983), 1–16.

26 Paul Pillar, "The Role of Villain," *Political Science Quarterly* 128 (2013), 211–31.

27 Hoffmann, *Gulliver's Troubles,* 150.

28 Freeman Dyson, "On Russians and Their Views of Nuclear Strategy," in Charles W. Kegley, Jr., and Eugene R. Wittkopf (eds.), *The Nuclear Reader* (New York: St. Martin's, 1985), 97–99.

29 David Watt, "As a European Saw It," *Foreign Affairs* 62 (1983), 530–31.

30 For a critical discussion of the impact of legalism, see George Kennan, *American Diplomacy, 1900–1950* (New York: Mentor, 1951).

31 Rainey, *Patterns of American Foreign Policy,* 36.

32 Robert E. Osgood, *Limited War: The Challenge to American Strategy* (Chicago: University of Chicago Press, 1957), 29.

33 Spanier, *American Foreign Policy since WW II,* 11.

34 Jackson Diehl, "War against Time," *The Washington Post,* January 8, 2007, A15.

35 Charles W. Kegley, Jr., "The Neoidealist Moment in International Studies: Realist Myths and the New International Realities," *International Studies Quarterly* 37 (1993), 131–46; Arthur S. Link, *The Higher Realism of Woodrow Wilson* (Nashville, TN: Vanderbilt University Press, 1971).

[36] Michael Mandlebaum, "Bad Statesman, Good Prophet: Woodrow Wilson and the Post–Cold War Order." *National Interest* 64 (2001), 31–41.

[37] Robert W. Tucker, "The Triumph of Wilsonianism?" *World Policy Journal* 10 (1993), 83–100.

[38] Ibid.; Tony Smith, "Making the World Safe for Democracy," *Washington Quarterly* 16 (1993), 92–102.

[39] David Fromkin, "What Is Wilsonianism?" *World Policy Journal* 11 (1994), 100–12.

[40] George Kennan, "On American Principles," *Foreign Affairs* 74 (1995), 116–26.

[41] The material and quotation in this section are found in Adam Wolfson, "How to Think about Humanitarian War," *Commentary* 110 (July/August 2000), 44–48.

[42] Walter Russell Mead, *Special Providence* (New York: Routledge, 2002). Mead also identifies two other American traditions—one is associated with Wilson and the other with Jefferson.

[43] Brian Rathbun, "Steeped in International Affairs? The Foreign Policy Views of the Tea Party," *Foreign Policy Analysis* 9 (2013), 21–37.

[44] Walter Russell Mead, "The Tea Party and American Foreign Policy," *Foreign Affairs* 90 (2011), 28–44.

[45] Ernest J. Wilson III, ed., *Diversity and U.S. Foreign Policy: A Reader* (New York: Routledge, 2004).

[46] A. Trevor Thrall and Erik Goepner, *Millennials and U.S. Foreign Policy* (Washington, DC: CATO Institute, 2015).

Learning from the Past 4

Dateline: Libya

When asked to identify the biggest mistake of his presidency President Barack Obama pointed to the lack of planning for the post-Gaddafi era that followed the 2011 bombing of Libya. Few argue with the description of post-intervention Libya as teetering on the edge of civil war and constituting a threat to regional and perhaps global security. But what lessons should be drawn? For some, the greater mistake was intervening in the first place.[1]

Protests against the government of Muammar Gaddafi began in mid-February 2011. Earlier that year April Spring uprisings in Egypt and Tunisia were largely peaceful and resulted in the removal of longtime pro-Western leaders. Libya was different. Gaddafi had long opposed the West and was a supporter of international terrorism. Few expected the protests in Libya to remain peaceful.

The Obama administration's initial response to events in Libya was marked by caution. Given its oil holdings instability in Libya would hurt the global economy; the United States was already viewed with suspicion in many parts of the Moslem world for its removal of Saddam Hussein from power; and the anti-Gaddafi forces were largely unknown to the United States. Many suspected them of having ties to al Qaeda. Further complicating the administration's decision-making process was what one official called the "shadow of uncertainty" as to Gaddafi's intentions and the competence of rebel leaders.

The administration's first concrete action came on February 25 when Obama signed an Executive Order freezing $30 billion in assets in the United States belonging to Gaddafi's family and key Libyan government organizations. This was done only after the last Americans were evacuated from Libya. The American embassy had expressed concern that if the United States took forceful declaratory or action-oriented foreign policy initiatives, American citizens might be taken hostage.

Obama's advisors disagreed over using military force to protect Libyan civilians and remove Gaddafi from power. Secretary of Defense Robert Gates warned against becoming involved in another big land war asking, "Can I finish two wars before you guys go looking for a third one." Director of National Intelligence James Clapper raised the likelihood that the end result of the crisis would be the emergence of two or three ministates. Secretary of State Hillary Clinton joined with National Security Council staffer Samantha Powers and United Nations ambassador Susan Rice in supporting military action as concerns grew that Gaddafi was about to unleash a military attack on civilians and rebels in Benghazi. She called for arming rebel forces and obtained an agreement from Arab states and North Atlantic Treaty Organization (NATO) allies to support a UN resolution calling for imposing a no-fly zone and "using all necessary means" to protect civilians on March 17.

Later that day, Obama approved military action with the caveat that no U.S. troops would be involved and that it would be a limited and finite operation. Operation Odyssey Dawn began on March 19 with air attacks on armored Libyan government units near Benghazi and on Libya's air defense system. The U.S. contributions to the military intervention included a naval force of eleven ships including guided missile destroyers and a nuclear attack submarine, A-10 ground aircraft, F-16 fighters, U-2 reconnaissance planes, drones, and covert CIA agents on the ground. The operation ended on October 31. Gaddafi died at the hands of rebel forces.

Operation Odyssey Dawn was hailed by many in the West as a success, a model of humanitarian intervention. It was not long before pessimism set in. In less than four years Libya had seven prime ministers. Forming a national unity government proved to be impossible. The Libyan government failed to disarm rebel forces some of whom declared their own state in oil-rich eastern Libya. Human rights violations continued moving the Human Rights Watch to define the situation as one "that may amount to crimes against humanity." Especially disturbing to the Obama administration was that Libya had become a jihadist magnet attracting as many as sixty-five hundred fighters to ISIS (Islamic State of Iraq and Syria) training camps. Not only did these recruits pose a threat to stability in Libya and Africa more broadly, they also presented a major obstacle to defeating ISIS in Syria, Iraq, and Afghanistan.

In response to these developments, in November 2015, the U.S. conducted air strikes against an ISIS training center in Libya. In February 2016 the Pentagon presented a plan to attack thirty to forty ISIS targets in hopes of killing key ISIS leaders and providing an opening for Western-backed Libyan forces to defeat ISIS fighters on the ground.

Calls to learn from the past are commonplace. Yet, what should President Trump learn from Libya? History suggests remarkably little learning from the past takes place.[2] In this chapter we look at the challenges faced in learning from the past. We ask how and what policy makers learn: the types of events they learn from, the types of calculations they make, and the lessons they learn. We then turn our attention to Vietnam and Iraq as important sources of lessons for today's policy makers.

How Do Policy Makers Learn from the Past?

Policy makers learn by matching the known with the unknown.[3] This is not a passive act. They do not sit back and simply accept data as a given, but actively interact with data.[4] In deciding how to respond to the humanitarian crisis in Kosovo Bill Clinton and his advisors drew upon **analogies** from at least four different events from the past, each of which suggested a different definition of the problem and response: Vietnam, the Holocaust, Munich, and the outbreak of World War I.[5]

In addition to selecting reference points for evaluating information, policy makers must make judgments about what is a piece of information (**signal**) and what is unimportant (**noise**). Discriminating between the two is no easy task. Having identified a piece of data as a signal does not tell the policy maker what to do; it only sets in motion the process of learning. Information received in the Philippines that Pearl Harbor was under attack did not tell them they were the next target or what steps to take to defend themselves. In the period before Pearl Harbor, fifty-six separate signals ranging in duration from one day to one month pointed toward the Japanese attack, but there was also a good deal of evidence to support all of the wrong interpretations. Surprise occurred not because of a lack of signals, but because there was too much noise.[6]

Policy makers discriminate between the signals and noise by making a series of assumptions about what motivates the behavior of others or what constitutes the underlying dynamics of a problem confronting them. Consider the intercepted Japanese directive to its U.S. embassy and consulates to burn their codes. In retrospect, this is taken as a clear indication that hostilities were imminent. But during the first week of December 1941, the United States ordered all of its consulates in the Far East to burn their codes, and no one took this to be the equivalent of a U.S. declaration of war against Japan.

The assumptions that policy makers bring to bear on foreign policy problems are influenced by their long-term experiences and immediate concerns. Long-term experience provides policy makers with a database against which to evaluate an ongoing pattern of behavior. For Franklin Roosevelt and other U.S. policy makers, personal experiences and their reading of history led to a conclusion that the presence of the U.S. fleet at Pearl Harbor was a deterrent to a Japanese attack. They failed to appreciate that it also made a fine target. For their part, Japanese leaders drew on their 1904 war-opening attack in the Russo-Japanese War as the model for how to deal with a more powerful enemy.

Once they are in place, perceptual systems are not readily changed. They easily become obsolete and inaccurate. The principle involved here is **cognitive consistency**.[7] Individuals try to keep their beliefs and values consistent with one another by ignoring some information, actively seeking out other data, and reinterpreting still other information so that it supports the individuals' perception of reality. As a result instead of being a continuous and rationally structured process, learning is sporadic and constrained. Policy makers do not move steadily from a simplistic understanding of an event to a more complex one as their experience and familiarity with it build. New information and new problems are fitted into already well-established perceptual systems. Learning, thus, rarely produces dramatic changes in priorities or commitments, and changes in behavior tend to be incremental.

A well-documented case of this process at work is John Foster Dulles's perception of the Soviet Union.[8] Dulles was Eisenhower's secretary of state and had a **closed belief system**. He saw the Soviet Union as a hostile state and interpreted any data that might indicate a lessening of hostility in such a way that it reinforced his original perceptions. Cooperative Soviet gestures were not a sign of goodwill but the product of Soviet failures and represented only a lull before the Soviet Union would engage in another round of hostilities.

Events Policy Makers Learn From

The sporadic and constrained nature of the learning process means that not all aspects of the past are equally likely to serve as the source of lessons. Two categories of events are especially important. The first is the dramatic and highly visible event. Policy makers turn to these events out of the conviction that because they are so dramatic and visible, they must contain more important information than do commonplace happenings. The scars they leave in defeat and the praises sung in victory can become deeply entrenched in the collective memory of society. Events of this magnitude are often referred to as **generational events**, because an entire generation draws on them for lessons. War is the ultimate dramatic event. A policy maker need not have been involved in the negotiations at Munich in 1938 to invoke the analogy and point to the dangers of appeasement.

The corollary to paying a great deal of attention to highly dramatic events is to all but ignore the nonevent. The crisis that almost happened but did not is not learned from. Warnings about the weakness of the shah of Iran were heard as early as 1961, when members of the Senate Foreign Relations Committee warned the incoming Kennedy administration that no number of weapons could save the shah. Mass unrest and corruption, they argued, doomed him to defeat. Senator Hubert Humphrey declared: "This crowd they are dead. They just don't know it. . . . It is just a matter of time."[9] The more often the warning is given and no attack occurs, the easier it is for policy makers to dismiss the next warning. The November 27, 1941, warning to Pearl Harbor that a Japanese attack was possible was not the first one received. An alarming dispatch had been received in October, and no attack had followed.

The second type of highly influential event is one that the policy maker experienced firsthand. Especially important are those experiences that took place early in the policy maker's career. The lessons drawn from events experienced firsthand tend to be overgeneralized, to the neglect of lessons that might be drawn from the careful analysis of the experiences of others.[10] U.S. thinking about the post–World War II role of the atomic bomb provides an example of the pull of personally experienced events on policy making.[11] The initial decisions were made by the men who had defeated Germany and Japan. In formulating ideas about the uses to which the bomb might be put, they drew heavily on these experiences. From 1945 to 1950, the Soviet targets identified for destruction by the atomic bomb duplicated those emphasized in the U.S. World War II policy of targeting commercial and industrial centers. To these men, the atomic bomb was not a qualitatively new weapon for which a new strategy had to be developed. It was only the latest and most powerful weapon developed to date. It would be left to politicians to put forward the first strategy tailored to the political and technological realities of the postwar era.

Firsthand experiences that occur early in a policy maker's career are especially important because perceptual systems are resistant to change. Individuals are most open to competing images of reality when they confront a situation for the first time. Once a label or category is selected, it establishes the basis for future comparisons. These early firsthand experiences are not necessarily related to foreign policy problems. They may be ways of thinking about problems that proved successful in the past, positions taken on issues that produced the desired outcome, or strategies used in winning political office.[12] Early firsthand experiences are also of special significance because of the conditions under which policy makers must try to learn from the past. Henry Kissinger spoke to these problems in his memoirs when he stated that "policy makers live off the intellectual capital they have brought with them into office; they have no time to build more capital."[13]

Types of Calculations Made

When an event is recognized as a possible source of lessons, policy makers frequently engage in two types of calculations. First, they pay attention to *what* happened and seldom to *why*. The Iron Curtain descended across Europe; Vietnam fell; and the American embassy in Iran was attacked and hostages were taken. Focusing on what happened rather than on why creates a type of tunnel vision that obscures the differences between the present situation and earlier ones. What can one conclude from the fact that for the 1968 invasion of Czechoslovakia, the 1979 invasion of Afghanistan, and the 1981 non-invasion of Poland, the Soviet Union required three months' preparation time? Perhaps not very much.[14] Policy makers could not assume that the Soviets would need three months to prepare for the next invasion. None of these were extremely urgent cases demanding a more rapid mobilizations or precluded one starting at a higher stage of readiness.

Second, in examining what happened, policy makers tend to dichotomize the outcome into successes and failures. They tend to forget that most policy initiatives are designed to achieve multiple objectives, that success and failure are rarely ever total, and that neither success nor failure is permanent. Problems are not so much solved as redefined and transformed into new challenges and opportunities.

When a policy is defined as a success, policy makers are especially prone to ignore three considerations in applying it as a lesson: (1) its costs, (2) the possibility that another option would have worked better or produced the same result at lesser cost, and (3) the role that accident, luck, and chance play in affecting the outcome of events. When an event is defined as a failure, a different set of biases tends to grip policy makers' thinking. There is (1) the presumption that an alternative course of action would have worked better and that policy makers should have known this and (2) an unwillingness to admit that success may have been unattainable or that surprise is inevitable. The congressional investigation into Pearl Harbor takes up thirty-nine volumes, and the success of the Japanese attack continues to bring forward a never-ending series of books asserting that U.S. policy makers knew of the attack and permitted it to happen.

Lessons Learned

Three lessons are most often learned by policy makers from their studies of history. The first is to expect to see more of the same. The shah of Iran was expected to continue in power in 1979 simply because he had ruled for so long. Iran without the shah seemed inconceivable. The grain shortage of 1973 caught U.S. policy makers by surprise because for them "the grain problem" was always one of too much grain. It did not occur to policy makers that the combination of large-scale Soviet purchases of grain plus global drought would send the price of grain in the United States skyrocketing.

A second lesson learned is to expect continuity in the behavior of others. In part this occurs because policy makers are insensitive to the perceived costs of inaction as viewed by another state. The United States made this mistake at Pearl Harbor. U.S. estimates of Japanese behavior were based on the cost of attacking the United States. Insufficient attention was given to the costs that the Japanese would experience if they did nothing and allowed the status quo to continue into the future. For similar reasons, the hostile acts or words of allies surprise policy makers more than the hostility of an enemy.

Third, policy makers learn to avoid policies that failed and repeat policies that brought success. This would be fine if two conditions did not work against the continued success of a policy. First, successful policies get overused. They are applied to problems and situations for which they were not intended. Second, a successful policy often changes the situation in ways that will frustrate its future use. In the 1960s, military aid to the shah may indeed have been responsible for averting the coup predicted by members of the Senate Foreign Relations Committee; but it also changed the situation so that by the late 1970s, continued military aid became part of the shah's problem instead of the answer.

These three frequently learned lessons cast a long shadow over U.S. foreign policy making in the lead-up to the Iraq War. First, policy makers expected to see more of the same. The dominant view was that nuclear proliferation is a "strategic chain reaction," with Iraq under Saddam Hussein being the most recent addition to this chain.[15] Second, it was assumed that Saddam Hussein was evil and could not be trusted to change his policies or at a minimum be contained as a security threat. Moreover, Saddam Hussein was engaged in an ongoing game of deception and obstruction with UN weapons inspectors. Why would he do this unless he was trying to hide something? When no weapons of mass destruction were found, an unexamined possibility emerged as the best explanation.[16] Other available explanations include that Saddam Hussein was acting out of a fear that if his bluff was exposed, his enemies within Iraq would be emboldened and his hold on power seriously weakened, and that his bluff was directed at intimidating neighboring states such as Iran and Saudi Arabia. Finally, the George W. Bush administration was determined to avoid what it saw as the central mistake made by George H. W. Bush in the Persian Gulf War. The administration would remove Saddam Hussein from power.

Historical Lesson

Bosnia

Bosnia (more formally Bosnia and Herzegovina) emerged as an independent country in April 1992 from the break-up of Yugoslavia. Dating back to when it was a province within the Ottoman Empire, Bosnia had been a multi-political unit. The 1991 census defined its population as being 44 percent Muslim ("Bosniak"), 32.5 percent Serb, 17 percent Croat, and 6 percent Yugoslav. This split made it an inviting target for other states as they gained independence from the collapsing Yugoslavia. A March 1991 agreement reportedly included provisions to split Bosnia between Serbia and Croatia, two other former Yugoslav provinces. The depth of the problem facing Bosnia was evident in a statement by Serb leader Radovan Karadzic that October. "In just a couple of days Sarajevo [Bosnia's capital] will be gone and there will be five hundred thousand dead, in one month

Muslims will be annihilated in Bosnia and Herzegovina."

A series of international efforts sought to prevent Bosnia from becoming a war zone. The European Union called for ethnic power-sharing at all levels of government. The UN imposed an arms embargo on all former Yugoslav territories as violence grew and attacks began. While neutral on the surface, the embargo hurt Bosnia because its military lacked weapons. Serbia had taken control over most of Yugoslavia's military weapons and Croatia was able to obtain smuggled weapons because of its location on the Mediterranean Sea. After gaining independence Bosnia lobbied to have the arms embargo lifted. Great Britain, France, and Russia opposed doing so. Twice Congress voted to send weapons to Bosnia. Each time President Bill Clinton vetoed the bill although his administration did support efforts to smuggle weapons into Bosnia.

The same month that it obtained its independence the forty-four-month-long siege of Sarajevo began. Bosnian Serbs with the support of Serbia began attacking Bosnian Muslim villages within Bosnia, and Croatia moved to expand its control over ethnic Croatian portions of the country. By June an estimated 2.6 million people had become internally displaced people or refugees. In May 1993 the UN set up "safe areas" in an attempt to protect civilians; however the highly restrictive rules of engagement placed on UN forces left civilians exposed to Serb and Croat attacks which were often followed by the establishment of concentration camps and the systematic use of rape and torture. Collectively these acts came to be defined as "ethnic cleansing."

One safe area was Srebrenica. A predominantly Muslim city at various points in time it was under Serbian and Bosnian control. In 1995 UN forces controlled the city but in July they failed to stop Serbian military units and Bosnian Serb paramilitary forces from capturing the city. In genocide that followed some 8,000 Muslim men and boys were killed. In 2016 Karadzic was convicted by the International Criminal Court of genocide for the Srebrenica massacre.

During his campaign Bill Clinton asserted that "ethnic cleansing could not stand." However, as president he had been reluctant to take military action. His support for Bosnia was largely rhetorical. This began to change in the months prior to Srebrenica. David Halberstam notes he came to feel that the future of his presidency was at stake. Still, he had no policy and he wanted to move forward with minimum risk, something that would no longer be possible if the UN forces left as they were scheduled to and required

the assistance of U.S. soldiers in doing so. The need for action was real: "we have a war by CNN . . . our position is unsustainable."[17]

The answer chosen was Operation Deliberate Force, a NATO bombing campaign led by the United States in August and September 1995 in which 400 aircraft dropped over 1,200 bombs on over 300 Serbian targets. Combined with a ground operation conducted by Croatian and Bosnian military forces Serbia found it necessary to halt its military operations and enter peace talks which produced the November 1995 Dayton Accords. With the fighting over, Bill Clinton sent 20,000 U.S. troops to Bosnia as part of a NATO peacekeeping force.

At its conclusion the Bosnian bombing campaign was hailed as a major success. Not only did it bring peace but it reestablished NATO's credibility as a fighting force and resulted in few casualties. A more complex picture would emerge. Three years after the fighting ended Bosnia remained an ethnically divided and tension-filled state. Economic reconstruction was slow, few war criminals had been indicted, and only about 300,000 of 1.8 million Bosnian refugees had returned home. War also continued. It had moved to Kosovo where Serbs again sought ethnic cleansing. NATO again conducted a bombing campaign. Before NATO intervened some 2,500 people had died in Kosovo. After eleven weeks of bombing the Serbs had killed an estimated 10,000 people.

Applying the Lesson

1. Was intervening in Bosnia in the U.S. national interest?
2. Was the Bosnian peacekeeping operation a success?
3. Are there any lessons policy makers might have learned from Bosnia that applied to the Libyan case?

Case Studies

Our attention now shifts to an examination of Vietnam and the Iraq War as case studies of learning from the past. Through the phrases "Vietnam syndrome" and "**Iraq syndrome**" they have become primary reference points for thinking about the war in Afghanistan and the merits of intervention in to Libya, Syria, and elsewhere. Vietnam is used to provide a look at the range of lessons used by policy makers in making decisions about how to fight the war and to illustrate the range of lessons that American elites have drawn from U.S. involvement. Because events in Iraq are so close to us, bringing together the words *learning* and *Iraq* is not easy. Our focus here is on the initial stages of the war and reconstruction efforts because it is where most of the lessons of Iraq are directed. It also means that our discussion of lessons learned and the Iraq War is more speculative in nature.

The Vietnam War

America's involvement in Vietnam spanned six presidents. The cost of the war and its level of destruction were enormous: 55,000 American dead; a maximum American troop presence of 541,000 men; a total cost of $150 billion; untold numbers of Vietnamese dead and wounded; 7 million tons of bombs dropped; and 20 million craters left behind. In spite of these grim statistics, much confusion exists over the Vietnam War. A public opinion poll taken between March 21 and March 25, 1985, revealed that only three of five Americans knew that the United States supported South Vietnam. In a press conference on February 18, 1982, in response to a question about covert operations in Latin America, President Reagan stated:

> If I recall correctly, . . . North and South Vietnam had been, previous to colonization, two separate countries [and] provisions were made that these two countries could, by the vote of their people together, decide whether they wanted to be one country or not. . . . Ho Chi Minh refused to participate in such an election. . . . John F. Kennedy authorized the sending of a division of Marines. And that was the first move toward combat troops in Vietnam.[18]

Table 4.1 presents a chronology of major events in the history of the U.S. presence in Vietnam.

Vietnam Chronology The first president to have to deal with Vietnam was Truman. Initially, his views on Indochina resembled those held during World War II by Roosevelt, who was sympathetic to Ho Chi Minh's efforts to establish independence for the region and unsympathetic to French attempts to reestablish their prewar position of colonial domination. In 1947 Truman resisted French requests for U.S. aid and urged France to end the war against Ho Chi Minh, who, while being one of the founders of the French communist party, had proven himself a valuable ally and nationalist in defeating Japan

Truman's views were soon to undergo a stark and rapid transformation. By 1952 the United States was providing France with $30 million in aid to defeat Ho Chi Minh, and in 1953, when Truman's presidency ended, the United States was paying one-third of the French war cost. Ho Chi Minh was also redefined from a nationalist into a communist threat to U.S. security interests. Nothing had changed in Indochina to warrant this new evaluation of the situation. Dramatic events, however, were taking place elsewhere as Cold War competition took root. France was reluctant to participate in a European Defense System, something the United States saw as vital if Europe was to contain communist expansionist pressures. In a virtual quid pro quo, the United States agreed to underwrite the French war effort in Indochina, and France announced its intent to participate in plans for the defense of Europe.

The Eisenhower administration began by reaffirming Truman's financial commitment to France and then enlarged upon it. By the end of 1953, U.S. aid rose to $500 million and covered approximately one-half of the cost of the

---

TABLE 4.1 **Chronology of U.S. Involvement in Vietnam**

September 1940	France gives Japan right of transit, control over local military facilities, and control over economic resources in return for right to keep nominal sovereignty.
March 1945	Gaullist French forces take over administration of Vietnam from pro-Vichy French troops.
September 1945	Ho Chi Minh declares Vietnam to be independent.
February 1950	United States recognizes French-backed Bao Dai government.
March 1954	French forces defeated at Dien Bien Phu.
April 1954	Geneva Peace Talks begin; end in July.
September 1954	SEATO created.
July 1956	No elections held in Vietnam.
October 1961	Taylor-Rostow mission sent to Vietnam; 15,000 advisers sent in as a result.
November 1963	Diem and Kennedy assassinated.
August 1964	Gulf of Tonkin incident.
February 1965	Pleiku barracks attacked; eight U.S. soldiers dead and sixty injured; Operation Rolling Thunder launched in retaliation.
May 1965	General Westmoreland requests 80,000 troops.
July 1965	President Johnson announces an additional 125,000 troops to be sent to Vietnam.
January 1968	Tet Offensive.
March 1968	Bombing halted; Johnson steps out of presidential race.
April 1970	Cambodia invaded.
March 1972	Major North Vietnamese offensive launched.
April 1972	B-52 bombings of Hanoi and Haiphong.
May 1972	North Vietnamese harbors mined.
December 1972	Peace talks collapse and then resume after heavy bombing.
January 1973	Peace agreement signed.
March 1975	North Vietnamese offensive begins.
April 1975	South Vietnam surrenders.

French war effort. For Eisenhower and Secretary of State John Foster Dulles, expenditures of this magnitude were necessary to prevent a Chinese intervention that they both felt was otherwise likely to occur. Unfortunately for the French, U.S. aid was not enough to secure victory, and Eisenhower was unwilling to go beyond financing a **proxy war**.

The end came for the French at Dien Bien Phu. With its forces under siege there, France informed the United States that unless it intervened, Indochina would fall to the communists. With no aid forthcoming, the process of withdrawal began. France's involvement in Indochina officially came to an end with the signing of the 1954 Geneva Peace Accords. According to this agreement, a "provisional demarcation line" would be established at the 17th Parallel. Vietminh troops loyal to Ho Chi Minh would regroup north of it, and pro-French Vietnamese forces would regroup south of it. Elections were scheduled for 1956 to determine who would rule over the single country of Vietnam. The Geneva Accords provided the French with the necessary face-saving way out of Indochina. Ho Chi Minh's troops controlled three-quarters of Vietnam and were poised to extend their area of control. All parties to the agreement expected Ho Chi Minh to win the 1956 election easily.

The United States did not sign the Geneva Accords but pledged to "refrain from the threat or use of force to disturb" the settlement. However, only six weeks after its signing, the United States helped set up the Southeast Asia Treaty Organization (SEATO) as part of an effort to halt the spread of communism in the wake of the French defeat. A protocol extended coverage to Laos, Cambodia, and "the free people under the jurisdiction of Vietnam." The Vietminh saw the protocol as a violation of the Geneva Accords because it treated the 17th Parallel as a political boundary and not as a civil war truce line. Political developments below the 17th Parallel supported the Vietminh interpretation. In 1955 the United States backed Ngo Dinh Diem, who had declared himself president of the Republic of Vietnam. With U.S. support, he argued that because South Vietnam had not signed the Geneva Accords, it did not have to abide by them and hold elections. The year 1956 came and went with no elections. By the time Eisenhower left office, U.S. military aid had reached one thousand U.S. military advisers stationed in South Vietnam.

The landmark decision on Vietnam during the Kennedy administration came in October 1961 with the Taylor-Rostow Report. Receiving contradictory information and advice on how to proceed, Kennedy sent General Maxwell Taylor and Walt Rostow to Vietnam on a fact-finding mission. They reported that South Vietnam could only be saved by the introduction of eight thousand U.S. combat troops. Kennedy rejected this conclusion, but he did send an additional fifteen thousand military advisers. Kennedy's handling of the Taylor-Rostow Report is significant for two reasons. First, the decision was typical of those he made on Vietnam. He never gave the advocates of escalation all they wanted, but neither did he ever say no. Some increase in the level of the American military commitment was always forthcoming. Second, in acting on the Taylor-Rostow Report, Kennedy helped shift the definition of the Vietnam conflict from a political problem to a military one. Until this point, Vietnam was seen by the Kennedy administration as a **guerrilla war** in which control of the population was key. From now on, control of the battlefield was to become the priority item.

Under President Lyndon Johnson, U.S. involvement in the war steadily escalated. Pressures began building in January 1964, when the Joint Chiefs of Staff (JCS) urged Johnson to put aside U.S. self-imposed restraints so that the war might be won more quickly. The JCS especially urged aerial bombing of North Vietnam. In August 1964 this bombing began in retaliation for an incident in the Gulf of Tonkin. The United States stated that two North Vietnamese Patrol Torpedo (PT) boats fired on the *C. Turner Joy* and the *Maddox* in neutral waters. President Johnson went to Congress for a resolution supporting his use of force against North Vietnam. The Gulf of Tonkin Resolution passed by a unanimous vote in the House and by an 88–2 vote in the Senate. It gave the president the authority to "take all necessary measures to repel any armed attack against the forces of the United States and to prevent further aggression." The incident itself is clouded in controversy. Later studies suggest that the incident was staged or that it never occurred. These views hold that Johnson was merely looking for an excuse to begin bombing.[19] The Gulf of Tonkin Resolution became the functional equivalent of a declaration of war.

From that point forward, the war became increasingly Americanized. *Operation Rolling Thunder*, a sustained and massive bombing campaign, was launched against North Vietnam in retaliation for the February 1965 Vietcong attack on Pleiku. In June the military sought two hundred thousand ground forces and projected a need for six hundred thousand troops. By 1967 U.S. goals were also changing. A Pentagon Papers memorandum put forward the following priorities: 70 percent to avoid a humiliating defeat; 20 percent to keep South Vietnam from China; and 10 percent to permit the people of South Vietnam to enjoy a better, freer way of life.[20]

The Tet Offensive in January 1968 brought a final challenge to the Johnson administration. It was a countrywide assault by communist forces on South Vietnam that penetrated Saigon, all of the provincial capitals, and even the U.S. embassy compound. The U.S. response was massive and expanded bombings of North Vietnam. In the end, the communist forces were defeated. As a final thrust to take control of South Vietnam, the Tet Offensive had been premature, but it did demonstrate the bankruptcy of U.S. policy. Massive bombings and hundreds of thousands of U.S. combat troops had not brought the United States closer to victory. In March 1968 Johnson announced a halt in the bombings against North Vietnam and that he was not a candidate for reelection.

Establishing détente was Richard Nixon's primary concern, and this policy could be threatened by any weakness or vacillation in U.S. policy on Vietnam. American commitments to Vietnam had to be met if the Soviet Union and China were to respect the United States in the post-Vietnam era. The strategy selected for accomplishing this was Vietnamization. Gradually, the United States would reduce its combat presence such that by 1972 the South Vietnamese army would be able to hold its own when supported by U.S. air and naval power and by economic aid.

The inherent weakness of Vietnamization was that it could succeed only if the North Vietnamese did not attack before the South Vietnamese army was ready. Nixon and Kissinger designed a two-pronged approach to lessen this possibility. Cambodia was invaded with the hope of cleaning out North Vietnamese sanctuaries, and the bombing of North Vietnam was increased. Nevertheless, the potential danger became a reality when in the spring of 1972 North Vietnam attacked across the demilitarized zone (DMZ). At this point, Nixon was forced to re-Americanize the war in order to prevent the defeat of South Vietnam. Bombing of North Vietnam now reached unprecedented levels, and North Vietnamese ports were mined.

The Paris Peace Talks were being carried out against the backdrop of this fighting. They had begun in earnest in 1969 but had made little progress. With this escalation of the war, Nixon also offered a new peace plan, which included a promise to withdraw all U.S. forces after an Indochina-wide cease-fire and exchange of prisoners of war. Progress was now forthcoming. Hanoi was finding itself increasingly isolated from the Soviet Union and China, both of which had become more interested in establishing a working relationship with the United States than in defeating it in Vietnam. It was now South Vietnam that began to object to the peace terms and stalled the negotiating process. In early December 1972 the "final talks" broke off without an agreement. On December 18 the United States ordered the all-out bombing of Hanoi and Haiphong to demonstrate U.S. resolve to both North and South Vietnamese leaders. On December 30 talks resumed and the bombing ended. A peace treaty was signed on January 23, 1973.

President Gerald Ford was in office when South Vietnam fell in 1975. What began as a normal military engagement ended in a rout. On March 12, 1975, the North Vietnamese attacked across the DMZ. On March 25, Hue fell. Five days later, Da Nang fell. The United States evacuated on April 29, and on April 30, South Vietnam surrendered unconditionally.

Lessons Used by Policy Makers In examining the lessons used by policy makers in their decision-making on Vietnam, our focus is on the Kennedy and Johnson administrations because it was during this period that the major escalations in the U.S. commitment took place. We can identify two broad types of lessons of the past held by U.S. policy makers. The first are political lessons, and the second are strategic and tactical ones.

The political lessons of the past for elected and appointed policy makers had the same bottom line: Personal survival in the upper circles of decision-making in Washington required creating an image of toughness. The source of this lesson for elected officials was the "loss" of China. The Republicans had successfully leveled this charge against the Democrats. Kennedy applied the same strategy against Nixon in 1960, accusing the Eisenhower administration of losing Cuba. Politically, Kennedy saw Vietnam as his China. Johnson stated many times that he did not intend to be the first U.S. president to lose a war.

The national security managers also drew on the fall of China for lessons. To this they could add lessons from decision-making in the Korean War. In each case, the implications were the same: A reputation for toughness was the most highly prized virtue that one could possess.[21] The bureaucratic casualties in the decision-making process on China were those who, even though they were correct, had become identified with the "soft" side of a policy debate. Those who had been hawkish—though wrong—emerged relatively unscathed from McCarthyism. To a lesser extent, Korea produced a similar pattern. Dean Rusk, who had failed to predict the Chinese entry into Korea but was staunchly anti-communist, did not pay a price for being wrong. In 1961 he became Kennedy's secretary of state.

Standing out among the host of strategic and tactical lessons of the past that were drawn on by policy makers on Vietnam was the Munich analogy and the danger of appeasement. Munich had become a symbol for a generation of policy makers.[22] Its impact was so great that even those with no personal contact with the European peace efforts in the late 1930s could draw on it for insight. Lyndon Johnson, for example, saw the central lesson of the twentieth century as being that the appetite for aggression is never satisfied. It was Dean Rusk who drew most openly and repeatedly on the Munich analogy. Although he recognized that differences existed between the aggressions of Ho Chi Minh and those of Hitler, the basic point remained the same: "Aggression by any other name was still aggression and . . . must be checked."[23]

Very different lessons could be drawn from the French experience in Indochina. It was on the mind of every participant in the debate on the Taylor-Rostow Report.[24] Yet, it had a negligible effect on American thinking, falling far short of being a generational experience on the order of Munich. Only George Ball who worked for France at the Geneva negotiations drew actively on it. To him, the war was unwinnable. Ball warned Kennedy that if he sent the fifteen thousand combat troops to Vietnam as recommended, the commitment would escalate to three hundred thousand men.

Ball became concerned with U.S. policy in Vietnam because he feared that it was diverting attention from Europe. This Europeanist orientation to world politics was not unique within the Kennedy-Johnson administrations. McGeorge Bundy was "totally a man of the Atlantic." He was also very much a product of the 1950s and the Cold War, so when he entered the debate on Vietnam, he was an advocate of the U.S. presence. Kennedy's first ambassador to Vietnam was also a Europeanist who was ignorant of Asia and Asian communism. The predominance of Europeanists illustrates the interaction of political, strategic, and tactical lessons of the past. A president concerned with making sure Vietnam did not become his China had limited options in making appointments because a residue of doubt continued to hang over the credentials of most Asian experts. Even though they lacked knowledge about Asian affairs, a president could feel politically safe with Europeanists in key decision-making positions.

The lack of knowledge about Asia on the part of key policy makers comes through in the strategic and tactical lessons they drew from Asian events. Kennedy's favored set of lessons of the past was Magsaysay's struggle against the Huk guerrillas in the Philippines and the British experience in Malaysia. Both contests were of a far different order from what was being contemplated in

Vietnam. For example, the Malaysian analogy was flawed in at least five respects, according to the U.S. military:

1. Malaysian borders were far more controllable.
2. The racial characteristics of the Chinese insurgents in Malaysia made identification and segregation a relatively simple matter compared with the situation in Vietnam.
3. The scarcity of food in Malaysia compared to the relative plenty in South Vietnam made the denial of food to the guerrillas a far less usable weapon.
4. More important, in Malaysia, the British were in actual command of military operations.
5. Finally, it took the British twelve years to defeat an insurgency that was less strong than the one in South Vietnam.[25]

The professional military also proved unable to draw on Asia for insights into how to fight in Vietnam. General Westmoreland was "a conventional man in an unconventional war." Vietcong challenges brought only a request for more and more men and more bombing. The approach of General Maxwell Taylor, the chairman of the JCS, was not very different. While he spoke of the challenge of brush-fire wars, he was not really talking in terms of fighting a guerrilla war. His solution was additional troops; political reforms were not mentioned. Taylor's analogy was with Korea. Looking at Korea, he drew favorable comparisons with battlefield conditions and terrain. Taylor overlooked the differing nature of the two wars. Korea had been a conventional war begun with a border crossing by uniformed troops who fought in large concentrations.[26] This was not Vietnam in 1964.

The lessons drawn by two other policy makers deserve mention. The first is Walt Rostow, who brought to Vietnam decision-making a firm set of beliefs on how to win the war and of the necessity of winning it. In his eyes, communist intervention had taken place in South Vietnam, breaking the first rule of peaceful coexistence. The boundaries of the two camps were immutable, and any effort to alter them had to be resisted. His solution was air power. Rostow had selected bombing targets during World War II and was convinced that massive bombing would bring North Vietnam to its knees.

The second person worth looking at is Lyndon Johnson, who drew heavily on his experience in Texas politics in formulating his Vietnam strategy. He had opposed the idea of a coup against Diem. That simply was not the way things were done in Texas: "Otto Passman and I, we have our differences, . . . but I don't plan his overthrow."[27] Beyond that, the United States had given its word to Diem, and you don't go back on your word. Johnson also felt that displays of toughness were prerequisites for dealing with the Vietnamese. Here, he drew on analogies to his dealings with Mexicans: "If you don't watch they'll walk right into your yard and take it over . . . but if you say to 'em right at the start, 'Hold on just a minute,' they'll know they are dealing with someone who'll stand up. And after that you can get along just fine."[28]

Lessons Learned Vietnam had a tremendous impact on public opinion and elite attitudes. It destroyed the postwar consensus on the ends and means of

U.S. foreign policy and left in its place three competing belief systems: Cold War internationalism, post–Cold War internationalism, and neo-isolationism. The existence of these three competing outlooks would greatly complicate future U.S. foreign policy making.

In identifying the specific lessons of Vietnam, we rely on a survey conducted by Ole Holsti and James Rosenau.[29] They identify seven groups holding different notions about the sources, consequences, and lessons of Vietnam. These groups covered the entire range of opinion from consistent critics to consistent supporters. Fully 30 percent of the sample falls at the extremes, confirming the depth of the impact Vietnam had on American attitudes. Looking first at the sources of failure, Holsti and Rosenau were able to identify twenty-one reasons why the United States lost in Vietnam. The depth of the disagreement is great. Not only are the sources of failure ranked differently by the various groups, no one explanation appears among all seven groups. Only three explanations appear among six of these groups: the United States' lack of clear-cut goals, the presence of Soviet and Chinese aid, and North Vietnamese dedication.

A more coherent picture emerges when we look at the consequences of Vietnam. Supporters cited international system-related concerns as the most important consequences of Vietnam. Critics cited Vietnam's domestic impact as most significant. Only one consequence was cited by all seven groups, but not with the same relative importance: The United States will limit its conception of its national interest. The picture becomes cloudy again when turning to the lessons of Vietnam. Thirty-four lessons were cited. No one lesson appears among all seven groups. Only two appear among six groups: executive-legislative cooperation is vital; and Russia is expansionist.

The Iraq War

Military planners describe six linked phases of military activity. They are depicted in Figure 4.1. In the Shape Phase (Phase 0), normal and routine military operations take place. In the Deter Phase (Phase I), military action seeks to deter the enemy by demonstrating resolve and capabilities for action. In the Seize Initiative Phase (Phase II), military force is used to execute offensive operations.

In the Dominate Phase (Phase III), military forces focus on breaking the enemy's will for organized resistance by engaging in a full deployment of force. The Stabilize Phase (Phase IV) is required when there is no functioning legitimate government or there is only a minimally functioning one. Here military forces are required to perform limited local governance activities. Finally, in the Enable Civil Authority Phase (Phase V), the objective of the military is to support the civil authorities. Whereas great praise surrounded the initial military operation in Iraq, the lack of connections between the first three phases and Phase IV as well as the conduct of Phase IV became the subject of much criticism.[30]

Iraq War Chronology The prelude to the Iraq War found the United States engaged in diplomatic efforts at the UN Security Council to gain its approval for

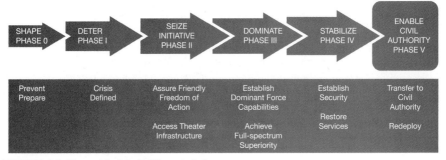

FIGURE 4.1 Phase Model of Military Activity

military action against Iraq. President George W. Bush addressed the UN General Assembly in September 2002, calling on it to move quickly to enforce the resolution demanding Iraq's disarmament while making it clear that the United States was prepared to act on its own. With the prospects for an affirmative vote by the UN Security Council virtually nonexistent, on March 16 President Bush met with British Prime Minister Tony Blair and leaders from Spain and Portugal in the Azores to announce that the "moment of truth" had arrived for Saddam Hussein. The following day Bush issued an ultimatum requiring Saddam to leave Iraq in forty-eight hours, and on March 19 Bush ordered the invasion of Iraq. A **"shock and awe"** military campaign began that was designed to overwhelm and demoralize Iraqi forces, allowing the coalition forces to move swiftly to Baghdad. On April 9 Baghdad came under the control of U.S. forces, and on May 1 President Bush declared an end to major combat operations. At this point, the administration began Phase IV. A chronology of major events in the Iraq War is presented in Table 4.2.

By all accounts, the Bush administration entered Phase IV without a great deal of forethought, expecting it to be completed in about six months. Calls for additional forces were rejected as unnecessary, and postwar planning carried out in the State Department and the CIA received little attention in the Pentagon. On May 12 Paul Bremer arrived in Iraq as head of the new Coalition Provisional Authority (CPA). Bremer's first two orders proved to be highly controversial. CPA Order 1 attempted to "de-Baathify" Iraqi society. All full Baath Party members were immediately dismissed from their government positions and banned from future government employment. CPA Order 2 dissolved the Iraqi army along with Saddam Hussein's bodyguard and special paramilitary. The result of these two decisions was to drive into the opposition many highly trained individuals who were not necessarily supporters of Saddam Hussein and on whom the United States would have otherwise been able to rely on to help stabilize the military and political situation in Iraq.

Establishing political stability, much less creating a democratic government, proved an elusive goal. Political milestones were realized, but the creation of a functioning government supported by the all sectors of the Iraqi

TABLE 4.2	Chronology of Major Events in the Iraq War
January 2002	In his State of the Union address, President Bush identifies Iraq, Iran, and North Korea as an "axis of evil."
September 2002	Bush addresses the UN General Assembly and challenges it to confront "the grave and gathering danger" of Iraq or become irrelevant.
December 2002	Bush approves deployment of U.S. forces to the Persian Gulf.
February 2003	The United States, Spain, and Great Britain introduce a resolution in the Security Council authorizing the use of military force against Iraq. Russia, Germany, and France oppose it.
March 17, 2003	Bush gives Saddam Hussein a forty-eight-hour ultimatum to leave Iraq.
March 19, 2003	Operation Iraqi Freedom begins with a "decapitation" air strike against leadership targets in Baghdad.
March 21, 2003	Major fighting begins.
May 1, 2003	Bush declares an end to major combat operations.
December 2003	Saddam Hussein is captured.
April 2004	Photos are aired showing torture and mistreatment of prisoners by U.S. personnel at Abu Ghraib prison.
June 2004	United States transfers power to a new interim Iraqi government.
September 2004	U.S. casualties reach the 1,000 mark.
December 2004	United States announces its plans to expand its military presence in Iraq to 150,000 troops.
January 2005	Iraq holds its first multiparty election in fifty years.
May 2006	Nouri al-Malaki forms Iraq's first permanent democratically elected government.
December 2006	The Iraq Study Group Report (Baker-Hamilton Report) is released.
January 2007	President Bush announces a surge of U.S. forces into Iraq to stem the violence and create conditions for peace.
March 19, 2008	Fifth anniversary of the start of the Iraq War.
September 2008	The United States transfers responsibility for security in Anbar Province, the heart of the Sunni insurgency, to the Iraqi military and police.
November 2008	The Iraq cabinet approves a status of forces agreement that will govern the U.S. presence in Iraq through 2011.
January 2009	Iraq holds local elections that are free from violence.
August 2010	Last U.S. combat brigade leaves Iraq.
December 2011	President Obama declares the Iraq War to be over.

population was not achieved. On May 28, 2004, Iyad Allawi was selected as prime minister of the interim Iraqi government. One month later, sovereignty was transferred to this government, and Paul Bremer left Iraq. On October 13, 2005, a national referendum was held on Iraq's constitution, and in May

2006 Nouri al-Malaki formed Iraq's first permanent democratically elected government. President Bush praised his government as having "strong leaders that represent all of the Iraqi people" and signaling a "decisive break with the past," but by the end of 2006, U.S. national security advisor Stephen Hadley was questioning the will and capacity of the al-Malaki government to take the necessary military and political steps to bring the sectarian violence in Iraq under control. Al-Malaki's ability to do so was central to the success of Bush's surge plan, announced in January 2007, which sent additional U.S. forces to Iraq.

Bush's decision was controversial because it contradicted the central thrust of the Iraq Study Group's report.[31] It recommended a phased exit of U.S. forces from Iraq as well as talks with Syria and Iran. In June it was announced that the surge was complete, with 28,500 more U.S. forces in the country. This brought the total number of U.S. forces in Iraq to 165,000, the largest to date.

U.S. strategy in Iraq began to move in a new direction in 2007 when General David Petraeus took command of the military operation there. Prior to assuming this post, he oversaw the writing of the Army's new counterinsurgency manual.[32] It was the first new manual on counterinsurgency (COIN) operations produced by the army in twenty years and now became the basis of U.S. operations in Iraq. The manual states that the central issue in insurgencies and counterinsurgencies is political power. The long-term success of COIN requires that people take charge of their own affairs and consent to the government's rule.

The combination of the surge, the change of strategy to COIN, and a Sunni tribal uprising that produced the "Anbar Awakening" had the effect of altering the military landscape in Iraq. From 2004 until mid-2007 Iraq averaged more than fifteen hundred civilian deaths per month with the U.S. military experiencing almost one hundred dead and seven hundred wounded. By the end of 2007, U.S. fatalities fell to an average of twenty-three per month and from June 2008 to June 2011 this number fell by just over one half.[33]

By 2013, two years after Obama declared the Iraq War over, a much different picture was in place. A series of political protests accompanied the insurgency-led violence in Iraq after the withdrawal of U.S. forces. A common focal point was on failings of the Iraqi government to end corruption and provide public services. Significant protests in the name of democracy took in Iraqi Kurdistan. Sunni Arabs protested what they saw to be their marginalization in Iraq's new economic and political order. The net result of this deteriorating situation was that most of the military gains prior to 2011 were gone. Led by al Qaeda-linked insurgents, suicide attacks were once again common, and in 2013 some 7,800 civilians and 1,000 Iraq security troops died in attacks.

By 2014 references to an Iraq insurgency were increasingly replaced by ones identifying the situation in Iraq as a civil war. Both politically and militarily, the tipping point came in 2014 with the announcement by Islamic State of Iraq and the Levant (ISIL/ISIS) of the creation of a worldwide caliphate which claimed religious, optical, and military authority over all Muslims. In June 2014 ISIS took control of Fallujah and some 70 percent of Anbar Province. In response Obama sent additional forces to Iraq. Later that year he announced a renewal of significant U.S. military operations in Iraq. It would be 2016 before Fallujah was retaken by Iraqi forces.

Analogies with Past Conflicts   In this section we examine three lessons from the past American policy makers drew upon in making strategic decisions about the Iraq War (the Cold War and the Vietnam and Korean Wars) and two sets of operations decisions about how to fight the war (COIN and rebuilding Iraq).

The Cold War   The George W. Bush administration cast the Global War against Terrorism as a long war and identified Iraq as the central front in that war, thus inviting comparisons with the Cold War. One factor that stands out in many analyses of how the Cold War was played, especially in the Third World, is the challenge that nationalism presented to U.S. foreign policy as it sought to counter the influence of the Soviet Union and communism.[34] Both the Soviet Union and the United States were most effective when they cast their arguments in terms of local conditions and nationalist sentiment. They were least effective when trying to couch a local conflict in global terms. The United States also encountered difficulties because it tended to ignore the differences among local enemy forces, grouping them all together under the heading of communists or communist sympathizers and to ally with leadership forces that were often seen by local political forces as part of the problem. This same set of problems in dealing with nationalism was a central challenge faced in Iraq.

A rather ominous reading of the past is presented by Andrew Bacevich.[35] He sees the Cold War and the Iraq War as firmly linked. In his view, they are World War III and part of World War IV, respectively. Periodically during the Cold War, the Middle East and the Persian Gulf, in particular, had been a major concern of U.S. policy makers, but this concern was almost always overshadowed by other conflicts. This changed just as the Cold War was ending, with the Soviet invasion of Afghanistan and the Iranian hostage crisis. Bacevich sees President Jimmy Carter as virtually declaring the start of World War IV and Ronald Reagan as fully committing the United States to the region. The first phase of World War IV concluded in 1990. Iran and the Soviet presence in Afghanistan were the main U.S. enemies at this time. A second phase began with Iraq's invasion of Kuwait and ran through the 1990s. World War IV entered its third phase with the terrorist attacks of 9/11.

The Vietnam War   There are no shortage of comparisons between the Vietnam War and the Iraq War.[36] Nor is there any shortage of controversy over such comparisons. When President George W. Bush invoked the Vietnam comparison in 2007, stating that "one unmistakable legacy of Vietnam is that the price of America's withdrawal was paid by millions of innocent citizens," Senator Edward Kennedy (D. Mass.) countered, saying, "The president is drawing the wrong lessons from history."[37] Among the most often-noted differences are those involving the nature of the military conflict. In Vietnam, the United States entered into an ongoing national war of liberation. It was a war in which the enemy operated as a unified political-military force and engaged in conventional military battles as well as conducting insurgency operations. Violence rarely spread into major South Vietnamese cities. The United States also carried the war on the ground and in the air to North Vietnam and neighboring states that it accused of aiding the enemy. More recently, it has been suggested that the need exists to learn the political lessons of the Vietnam War. Four have been suggested by John Kerry, John McCain, and Bob Kerry: (1) do not confuse a war with the warriors; (2) be honest with Congress and the American people; (3) exercise humility in assuming knowledge about foreign cultures; and (4) with sufficient effort and will, seemingly unbridgeable differences can be reconciled.[38]

In Iraq, the conflict began with an American invasion. Conventional war fighting soon ended and the conflict became almost entirely a combination of terrorist and insurgency attacks. Opposition forces did not operate as a unified political-military front but as militias, terrorist bands, and death squads under the leadership of a host of leaders. In the process, cities became the battleground and civilians the frequent targets as the various sides fought for dominance and to settle old and new feuds. The United States did not expand the Iraq War beyond that country's borders, even though it asserted that Iran and Syria were harboring and supporting Iraqi insurgents.

It is with the political side of the Iraq War that commentators see far more parallels with the Vietnam War, although not all agree on what they are. Melvin Laird, who served as secretary of defense under Nixon during Vietnam, observed that one point of similarity is that both wars were launched on the basis of faulty intelligence and "possibly outright deception."[39] By "possible deception," he was referring to the weapons-of-mass-destruction charge leveled against Saddam Hussein and the Gulf of Tonkin incident.

Similarities are also found in the decisions made by presidents early in the war and then as they encountered wars in which victory no longer seemed attainable. For Kennedy and Bush, Vietnam and Iraq became testing grounds for new strategic doctrines.[40] For Kennedy, it was an opportunity to move away from Eisenhower's doctrine of massive retaliation to one of graduated escalation. Massive retaliation with its emphasis on the all-out use of nuclear weapons left presidents few options in dealing with regional threats like Vietnam. For Bush, Iraq provided a test case for preemption as the new American strategic doctrine and a replacement for deterrence, which was judged as too passive and unable to dissuade leaders of rogue states.

Nixon and Bush also used similar language in explaining an American exit strategy to the public. Nixon said, "As South Vietnamese forces become stronger, the rate of American withdrawal can become greater." Bush asserted, "As the Iraqi security forces stand up, coalition forces can stand down."[41] Political differences are also present. The depth of support for the Vietnam War was far wider and deeper than it was for the Iraq War. In the early 1960s few questioned the domino theory and the need for an American presence in Vietnam. No equivalent rationale for action existed at the outset of the Iraq War. This was unlike the war in Afghanistan that preceded it, in which the link to the global spread of terrorism seemed evident to most.

The Korean War In June 2007 the Bush administration publicly raised the possibility of a long-term deployment of U.S. troops in Iraq after the present mission ends. The historical analogy put forward is South Korea, where U.S. forces continued to be based for decades after the Korean conflict formally ended. The

Korean model was presented by both Bush and Secretary of Defense Robert Gates as superior to the Vietnam model, which U.S. forces left "lock, stock, and barrel." The analogy is attractive because of the economic prosperity and political stability that South Korea has experienced since the armistice was signed. Critics quickly pointed out, however, that given the animosity toward American forces in Iraq, the continued presence of U.S. troops would likely be a lightning rod in domestic Iraqi politics and a target of military and terrorist attacks. Beirut in the 1980s, where U.S. Marines established a presence after fighting between Lebanon and Israel, was cited as a better analogy. At first welcomed by all factions, a suicide bomber driving a truck struck the Marine barracks in 1983, killing 241 soldiers.

Fighting COIN Operations The recognized differences between the political and military battlefields of Vietnam and Iraq that we noted earlier have led to a major debate over the military lessons of Vietnam for Iraq when it comes to fighting COIN operations. At one end of the debate are those who argue that the most relevant strategy in Vietnam was the abandoned "strategic hamlet" program, in which the United States sought to pacify specific areas and then gradually expand control outward. In Iraq this has been referred to as the "oil spot" strategy.[42] At the other end of the spectrum are those who argue that the different political situations in Iraq and Vietnam negate the relevance of any Vietnam COIN strategy for Iraq. They argue that, in Iraq, the issue is not the people against a government so much as it is a security problem driven by mutual fear of all people about what will happen if the opposing group(s) seizes control of the government. Winning the hearts and minds of the people does not address this problem; nor does promoting democracy. In fact, democratization may only further polarize the situation by increasing anxieties over what the new government will do.[43]

The search for lessons from the past that the United States can use in fighting insurgents in Iraq also yields a cautionary note. David Kilcullen argues that today's insurgents differ greatly from their predecessors in terms of policy, strategy, operational art, and tactics.[44] For example, given the global and instantaneous nature of communications today, the success of the insurgents may not ride on the legitimacy of the local government but on the ability to mobilize public support around the world for their cause. Kilcullen continues by saying that whereas it was once believed that COIN operations were 25 percent military and 75 percent political, they may be 100 percent political today. He concludes by echoing the observation of Bernard Fall, a noted Vietnam-era COIN specialist: "If it works, it is obsolete."

Rebuilding Iraq The post–World War II American occupations of Germany and Japan were put forward by the George W. Bush administration as the starting points for thinking about rebuilding Iraq. He observed, "America has made and kept this kind of commitment before . . . after defeating enemies, we did not leave behind occupying armies, we left constitutions and parliaments."[45] A closer reading of the American experience in Germany and Japan would have provided reason for caution with regard to both process and outcome. Douglas Porch maintains that for nearly a full decade, many of those involved in these reconstruction programs considered their efforts to be nearly a complete fail-ure.[46] Rather than encounter a welcoming population, they found resentment and resistance. Actions taken to bring about reform were often counterpro-ductive. General Lucius Clay, who was in charge of the American occupation zone in Europe, called de-Nazification his biggest mistake. It was in his mind a "hopelessly ambiguous procedure" that linked together small and big Nazis and engendered the hostility of the population at large because the implemen-tation of this policy often appeared arbitrary and hypocritical. Yet, the United States moved quickly to "de-Baathify" Iraq by dismissing party members from government positions and decommissioning the army.

It can be argued that the reasons for the ultimate success of the occupations of Germany and Japan had little to do with American policy or the presumed natural inclination of people liberated from tyranny for democracy. Rather, it had to do with such factors as enlightened domestic leadership, economic miracles fueled by the Marshall Plan in Europe, and the Korean War in Asia, along with the prior experience of democracy and entrepreneurship in these two states. The key American contribution was creating domestic and regional security, laying the ground rules for democratic reform, and then getting out of the way.

Germany and Japan were not the only efforts at reconstruction (or, more broadly, nation building) that might have been looked to for lessons. Fourteen other cases exist including Cuba (1898–1902, 1906–1909, and 1917–22), the Dominican Republic (1916–24, 1965–66), South Vietnam, Cambodia, and Afghanistan.[47] In only two of these cases, Panama (1989) and Grenada, was democracy in place after ten years. In seven cases, the United States established governments that almost totally depended on it for their survival. In none of these cases did democracy emerge. One lesson drawn from these experiences is that the ideal form of transition involves a quick transfer of power to legitimately elected local leaders, but this presupposes a functioning electoral system and moderate local leaders who have genuine support among the populace.

Over the Horizon: The Challenge of R2P

Learning from the past is not easy. Its successes and failures are often obscured by the pressing foreign policy issues of the day. Deputy Secretary of State Rich-ard Armitage gave voice to this political reality when not long after 9/11 he asserted, "History starts today."[48] Yet the pull of the past is never completely gone. As much as Obama wished to escape the Vietnam syndrome, he could not. When members of his administration brought up Vietnam all Obama could say was "ghosts."[49]

As we look over the horizon, the 2011 Libyan intervention potentially holds two very different lessons for American foreign policy. The first involves the process by which the intervention began. Was it a calculated decision or, as many put it, was it another case of the United States stumbling into war. The second, and the one we will focus on here, is what it tells us about the future of Responsibility to Protect (R2P). Will it continue to serve as a guideline for interventions or will it fall by the wayside? R2P holds that sovereignty is not just the right of a government to rule but it also brings with it responsibility for protecting and advancing the lives of its citizens. When a government is unable to do so, the international community has a responsibility to intervene with force if necessary and as a last resort. R2P also obligates intervening countries to help rebuild the affected country.

Proponents argue that R2P saves lives and is ethically required. It provided the justification for intervening into Libya and has been a primary rationale advanced by those favoring intervention into Syria. Many speculate that it will be a primary motivation behind future U.S. interventions. Opponents argue that R2P either simply postpones an inevitable civil war or serves as a cover for countries to intervene to protect their own narrowly defined national interests. In between these two positions are those who see the value of R2P but question the heavy reliance on military force and who see a near complete neglect of the obligation to help rebuild societies.

In examining the Libyan intervention Alan Kuperman draws three R2P lessons.[50] First, interveners should be sensitive to the possibility of deliberate misinformation and inaccurate reporting in deciding to act. Second, humanitarian intervention contains the risk of unexpected consequences. It may escalate rebellions and spill them across borders. Third, R2P may be prone to mission creep. While it is intended to protect citizens, many fear that intervening governments may also use it to seek regime change. Doing so may encourage the government to continue fighting where a negotiated settlement leaving it with some power might end the violence more quickly.

Critical Thinking Questions

1. What is the most important lesson that can be learned from the U.S. experience in Vietnam?
2. What lessons does Iraq hold for an involvement in Afghanistan?
3. What are the dangers of looking to the past for lessons on how to deal with current foreign policy problems?

Key Terms

analogies, 77
closed belief system, 78
cognitive consistency, 78
generational events, 78
guerrilla war, 86

Iraq syndrome, 83
noise, 77
proxy war, 85
shock and awe, 91
signal, 77

Further Reading

David Fitzgerald, *Learning to Forget* (Stanford: Stanford University Press, 2013).

This author focuses on the evolution of COIN doctrine beginning with Vietnam and continuing through to Iraq and emphasizes the difficulty of learning from the past and how military leaders used history in formulating policy.

Robert Gallucci, *Neither Peace nor Honor: The Politics of American Military Policy in Vietnam* (Baltimore: Johns Hopkins, 1975).

The U.S. experience in Vietnam has produced many excellent volumes. This book is particularly noteworthy for its treatment of bureaucratic politics and the overall decision-making process.

Kristen Harkness and Michael Hunzeker, "Military Maladaptation: Counterinsurgency and the Politics of Failure," *Journal of Strategic Studies* 38 (2015), 777–800.

Examining the U.S. and British experience in COIN this article argues that the primary impediment to incremental bottom-up small-scale learning by the military lies in the political realm.

Robert Jervis, *Perception and Misperception in International Politics* (Princeton, NJ: Princeton University Press, 1976).

This classic volume introduces readers to the many ways in which perceptions and misperceptions manifest themselves in foreign policy decisions.

Yuen Foong Khong, *Analogies at War: Korea, Munich, Diem Bien Phu and the Vietnam Decision of 1965* (Princeton: Princeton University Press, 1992).

This book examines the process of analogical reasoning and shows how policy makers used three key analogies from the past to make a key decision in the Vietnam War.

Ernest May, *"Lessons" of the Past: The Use and Misuse of History in American Foreign Policy* (New York: Oxford University Press, 1978).

This foundational work on analogies and American foreign policy advances three arguments: policy makers are influenced by what they believe history teaches them; they tend to use history badly; and they are capable of using history better.

Ben Roswell, "Solving the Statebuilders' Dilemma," *The Washington Quarterly* 35 (2012), 97–114.

Using Afghanistan as a starting point the author examines the problem of state-building. He identifies the need to replace the double compact between the international community and the host government in carrying out state-building tasks with a triple compact that includes the public.

Notes

[1] Alan Kuperman, "Obama's Libya Debacle," *Foreign Affairs* 94 (2015), 66–77.

[2] Richard K. Betts, *Surprise Attack: Lessons for Defense Planning* (Washington, DC: Brookings, 1982), 8.

[3] Richard Ned Lebow, *Between Peace and War: The Nature of International Crisis Behavior* (Baltimore: Johns Hopkins University Press, 1981), 199.

[4] Roberta Wohlstetter, *Warning and Decision* (Stanford: Stanford University Press, 1962), 70.

[5] Roland Paris, "Kosovo and the Metaphor War," *Political Science Quarterly* 117 (2002), 423–50.

[6] Wohlstetter, *Warning and Decision*, 388.

[7] On cognitive consistency and its application to world politics, see Robert Jervis, *Perception and Misperception in International Politics* (Princeton: Princeton University Press, 1976); John D. Steinbruner, *The Cybernetic Theory of Decision: New Dimensions of Political Analysis* (Princeton: Princeton University Press, 1974); Lebow, *Between Peace and War*.

8 Ole Holsti, "The Belief System and National Images: A Case Study," *Journal of Conflict Resolution* 6 (1972), 244–52.

9 *Washington Post*, December 23, 1984, 11.

10 An example of this is the lack of U.S. learning from Russia's experience in Afghanistan. See Larry Goodson and Thomas Johnson, "Parallels with the Past—How the Soviets Lost in Afghanistan, How the Americans Are Losing," *Orbis* (2011), 577–99.

11 These points are discussed in George Quester, *Nuclear Diplomacy, The First Twenty-Five Years* (New York: Dunellen, 1970); Michael Mandelbaum, *The Nuclear Question: The United States and Nuclear Weapons, 1946–1976* (New York: Cambridge University Press, 1979).

12 Jervis, *Perception and Misperception*, 249–50.

13 Henry Kissinger, *The White House Years* (Boston: Little, Brown, 1979), 54.

14 Betts, *Surprise Attack*, 8.

15 Scott Sagan, "Why Do States Build Nuclear Weapons?," *International Security* 21 (1996–97), 58.

16 Kenneth Pollack, "Spies, Lies, and Weapons," *Atlantic Monthly* 293 (January 2004), 78–92.

17 David Halberstam, *War in a Time of Peace* (New York: Touchstone, 2001), 307, 313, and 317.

18 Results of the public opinion poll are found in the *New York Times*, March 31, 1985, sec. 6, 34. Reagan's comments can be found in the *Weekly Compilation of Presidential Documents* 18 (February 18, 1982), 185.

19 John Stoessinger, *Why Nations Go to War*, 3rd ed. (New York: St. Martin's Press, 1982), 101.

20 *The Pentagon Papers as published by the New York Times* (New York: Quadrangle, 1971), 263.

21 On this point, see Richard Barnett, *The Roots of War* (New York: Penguin, 1973), Chapters 4 and 5.

22 Ernest May makes this point in his treatment of Vietnam in *"Lessons" of the Past: The Use and Misuse of History in American Foreign Policy* (New York: Oxford University Press, 1978).

23 Robert Gallucci, *Neither Peace nor Honor: The Politics of American Military Policy in Vietnam* (Baltimore: Johns Hopkins University Press, 1975), 33.

24 May, *"Lessons" of the Past*, 94.

25 Ibid., 98–99.

26 David Halberstam, *The Best and the Brightest* (Greenwich: Fawcett, 1969), 212.

27 Ibid., 356.

28 Ibid., 643.

29 Ole Holsti and James N. Rosenau, "Vietnam, Consensus, and the Belief Systems of American Leaders," *World Politics* 32 (1979), 1–56.

30 For a first wave of writings on the Iraq War, see Larry Diamond, "What Went Wrong in Iraq," *Foreign Affairs* 83 (2004), 34–56; Bob Woodward, *State of Denial* (New York: Simon & Schuster, 2006); Thomas Ricks, *Fiasco* (New York: Penguin, 2006); Rajiv Chandrasekaran, *Imperial Life in the Emerald City* (New York: Alfred A. Knopf, 2007).

31 *The Iraq Study Group Report* (New York: Vintage, 2006).

32 FM 3–24, *Counterinsurgency*. Available at Army Knowledge Online, www.us.army.mil.

33 The extent to which the surge and COIN versus the Anbar Awakening are responsible for this drop in violence is a point of debate. See Stephen Biddle, Jeffrey Friedman, and Jacob Shapiro, "Testing the Surge," *International Security* 37 (2012), 7–40.

34 Anatol Lieven and John C. Hulsman, "Neo-conservatives, Liberal Hawks, and the War on Terror: Lesson from the Cold War," *World Policy Journal* (Fall 2006), 64–74.

35 Andrew Bacevich, "The Real World War IV," *Wilson Quarterly* (Winter 2005), 36–61.

36 For comparisons of Vietnam and Iraq, see Stephen Biddle, "Seeing Baghdad, Thinking Saigon," *Foreign Affairs* 85 (2006), 2–14; Frederick Kagan, "Iraq Is Not Vietnam," *Policy Review* 134 (2005–2006), 3–14; Andrew Krepinevich Jr., "How to Win in Iraq," *Foreign Affairs* 84 (2004), 87–104.

37 Michael Fletcher, "Bush Compares Iraq to Vietnam," *Washington Post*, August 23, 2007, A1.

38 John Kerry, John McCain, and Bob Kerry, "Lessons and Hopes in Vietnam," *New York Times*, May 24, 2016, A21.

39 Melvin Laird, "Iraq: Learning the Lessons of Vietnam," *Foreign Affairs* 84 (2005), 22–43.

40 Lawrence Freedman, "Iraq, Liberal Wars and Illiberal Containment," *Survival* 48 (2006), 51–65.

[41] Quoted in Biddle, "Seeing Baghdad, Thinking Saigon," 4.

[42] Krepinevich, "How to Win in Iraq."

[43] Biddle, "Seeing Baghdad, Thinking Saigon."

[44] David Kilcullen, "Counter-insurgency *Redux*," *Survival* 48 (2006), 111–30.

[45] Bush's speech can be found at: http://www.cbsnews.com/news/bush-speech-full-text/

[46] Douglas Porch, "Occupational Hazards," *National Interest* (2003), 35–46.

[47] Minxin Pei, "From Victory to Success: Afterwar Policy in Iraq," *Foreign Policy* 137 (July 2003), 1–55.

[48] Bacevich, "The Real World War IV," 60.

[49] Bob Woodward, *Obama's War* (New York: Simon & Schuster, 2010), 97.

[50] Alan Kuperman, "A Model Humanitarian Intervention?" *International Security* 38 (2013), 105–36.

5 Society

Dateline: NSA Electronic Surveillance

Observers are divided over the role the public should play in the making of foreign policy. James Billington argues for an active and involved public: "International affairs cannot be a spectator sport. . . . Many must be involved; many more persuaded."[1] Walter Lippmann presents the opposite position, "The people have imposed a veto upon the judgment of the informed and responsible officials. . . . They have compelled the governments . . . to be too late with too little, or too long with too much."[2] This disagreement is very much in evidence in the controversy surrounding Edward Snowden's June 2013 leak of documents reporting the existence of a secret National Security Agency (NSA) domestic surveillance program.

Snowden was an NSA contractor. The documents he leaked revealed the NSA had obtained a ruling from the Foreign Intelligence Surveillance Court (FISC) directing Verizon Business Network Services to provide it "on a daily basis" with all call logs "between the United States and abroad" or "wholly within the United States, including local telephone calls." The directive did not include the content of the communications but only metadata: the beginning and end points of a communication and its length. The Obama administration initially declined comment but confirmed it the following day. Subsequent leaks revealed that the NSA had also been secretly monitoring the communications of key U.S. allies.

Supporters of these programs quickly moved to defend them. President Obama proclaimed that "nobody is listening to your telephone calls." NSA officials asserted that it might "incidentally acquire" information about Americans and foreign residents but it could not intentionally target any U.S. citizen. The program was defended as legitimate because it was authorized by law and known to Congress. It was also asserted that the NSA program had helped thwart dozens of potential attacks. NSA defenders also attacked Snowden. Speaker of the House John Boehner called him a "traitor."

Critics challenged all of these assertions. They claimed no evidence had been produced to show that the NSA programs played a major role in stopping terrorism. They noted that from 1979 to 2012 the FISC had approved 33,942 of 33,949 electronic warrant requests and that Congress had been lax in carrying out its oversight responsibilities. Most importantly, they argued that the NSA program was in violation of Second Amendment rights barring unreasonable searches and seizures.

Supporters did not waver, but as revelations continued to mount Obama felt compelled to act and in January 2014 announced modifications in the program. After failing to pass reform legislation in 2014, Congress did so in September 2015. A classic compromise, it fully satisfied neither opponents of the program nor its supporters. The bill requires that the government now obtain targeted warrants to collect phone metadata from telecommunications companies. It also authorized the NSA to temporarily resume its collection program before adopting a new system.

In this chapter, we will examine the major avenues available to the public in exercising its voice on foreign policy matters: elections, public opinion, interest group activity, and political protest. We will then turn to the role of the media in formulating public perceptions. Before turning our attention to how policy makers view the public voice in making foreign policy we will also take a brief look at how states increasingly are becoming involved in foreign policy.

Public Awareness of Foreign Policy Issues

Before examining the avenues of influence open to those seeking to influence U.S. foreign policy, three stage-setting observations are necessary. First, it needs to be recognized that not everyone is equally interested in or aware of foreign policy issues. A commonly used framework divides the American public into four groups based on their level of awareness. First, a large group is unaware of all but the most significant international events. Members of this group have at best vague and weak opinions. Second, there exists another large group which is aware of many major international events but is not deeply informed about these. The remainder of the American public, generally seen as comprising 25 percent, are generally knowledgeable about foreign issues and hold relatively firm convictions. They are referred to as "opinion holders." Within this group, there is a smaller set of activists, 1–2 percent, who serve as opinion mobilizers for the other segments of the public.

Second, it matters where the public gets its information from. Opinion polling in the months following the invasion of Iraq found that many Americans were wrong about key facts such as the existence of evidence linking Iraq and al Qaeda (45–52 percent of Americans said it existed) and the finding of weapons of mass destruction (about 25 percent believed this). Fox was the news source of choice for those who had the most misperceptions, while NPR listeners held the fewest misperceptions. Another study found that those who are not very attentive to foreign affairs get most of their news on international events from talk shows that emphasize soft news stories and tended to hold isolationist attitudes.[3]

Third, as we shall see in more detail later, even though the public may not know the facts about a foreign policy issue they tend to feel confident about what ought to be done. This holds true for both the substance of policy and how it is made. With regard to the substance of American foreign policy a classic example comes from a 1988 poll in which less than 50 percent of Americans could locate South Africa on a map. Nonetheless, 87 percent disapproved of its policy of apartheid. A 2014 poll asked Americans to rank on a scale of 1–10 how much influence various groups had on American foreign policy with 10 being the highest. Respondents ranked the public as having the second to lowest amount of influence (4.8). When asked how much influence these groups should have, public opinion was ranked the highest (7.9). The president came in second (7.5).[4]

Public Opinion

Public opinion provides a first avenue for the public to express its views on foreign policy. Every president since Richard Nixon has employed pollsters to learn just that.[5] Yet, the public is not convinced anyone is listening. The same 2014 poll we cited earlier found that from the American public's point of view the gap between the views of the American public and the decisions taken by policy makers was considerable: 42 percent said it was very large and 45 percent said it was somewhat large.

Interpreting a public opinion poll is not always easy. The public's response can easily be swayed by the wording of a question. For example, before the Persian Gulf War, when asked if the United States should take all action necessary, including military force, to make sure Iraq withdrew from Kuwait, 65 percent said yes. Only 28 percent said yes when asked if it should initiate a war to force Iraq out of Kuwait. Questions on trade policy show a similar sensitivity to wording with responses varying depending upon whether exports or imports are asked about and whether the question asks about the impact of trade on wages or economic growth.[6]

Trends and Content

Because of this sensitivity to wording looking at the responses to questions over time is a better way of uncovering what Americans think about foreign policy issues than looking at one-time polls. Approached this way, public opinion polls have captured several clearly identifiable changes in the structure of American public opinion about foreign affairs issues.

The pivotal event for the first change was World War II. Public opinion polls before World War II suggested a strongly isolationist outlook. In 1939, 70 percent of opinion holders said that American entry into World War I was a mistake, and 94 percent of the people polled felt that the United States should "do everything possible to stay out of foreign wars" rather than try to prevent one. The outbreak of fighting in Europe had little impact on U.S. attitudes.[7] This changed dramatically following the attack on Pearl Harbor. Internationalist sentiment now came to dominate public perceptions about the proper U.S. role in the world. Between 1949 and 1969, 60–80 percent of the American public consistently favored active U.S. participation in world affairs.[8]

Before the Vietnam War, virtually all internationalists were in fundamental agreement on several key points. Among their core beliefs were that the United States had both the responsibility and the capability to create a just and stable world order, peace and security are indivisible, the Soviet Union was the primary threat to world order, and containment was the most effective way of meeting the Soviet challenge.[9] Foreign policy based on these beliefs could expect to receive the support of the American people. When disagreements arose, they tended to be about the process of making foreign policy rather than about its substance.

Vietnam changed public attitudes.[10] It produced a steady and precipitous erosion of internationalist sentiment, with internationalism only reemerging as the majority perspective in 1980. In 1964, 65 percent of the public was defined as internationalist. This fell to 41 percent in 1974. That year also saw a dramatic increase in the number of isolationist responses, from 9 percent in 1972 to 21 percent. No single pivotal event is associated with this rebirth of internationalism. Instead, the American public gradually came to see the international system as threatening and out of control and developed a renewed willingness to use U.S. power and influence to protect U.S. national interests. Among the events that contributed to this shift were the 1979 Iranian coup, the 1979 Soviet invasion of Afghanistan, and the 1980 U.S. Olympic boycott.

Internationalism is under siege today. The Pew Research Center characterized the public mood in the months preceding the 2016 election as one of isolationism with a very, very big stick.[11] Polls then showed that a majority of the American public (57 percent) favored letting other countries deal with their own problems and concentrating on problems in the United States; only 46 percent held this view in 2010. In 2008, 60 percent of Americans felt the next president should concentrate on foreign policy over domestic policy. In 2016 only 17 percent held this position. Yet, alongside of these attitudes we find that 55 percent of the American public favors policies that would allow the United States to maintain its status as the only superpower. Only about one-third see it as acceptable for another country to rival the United States as a world superpower.

From 2013 to 2016 there has been a 12-point increase in the number of Americans favoring increased defense spending. The public is divided on how to best protect the United States. By far and away they see Islamic militants as the major national security threat (80 percent). But, while 47 percent favor using overwhelming amounts of force against terrorism to defeat it, 47 percent also feel that using too much force will lead to an increase in terrorism.

A significant factor feeding into this change in outlook is a loss in confidence in America's world involvement. Almost one-half polled in 2016 felt the United States was less powerful than it was a decade ago. A poll taken in late 1998 found the American public to be self-confident, with 50 percent feeling that the United States played a more important and more powerful role in the world than it had ten years earlier.[12] As recently as 2008, 63 percent of those questioned favored the United States taking an "active role" in world affairs.[13]

The downward trend of American support for the Afghanistan War captures the public's current outlook. Immediately after the 9/11 attacks, 94 percent of Americans favored military action in Afghanistan. By 2007 only 56 percent said the war was worth fighting. A December 2013 poll found that 66 percent of Americans felt the war in Afghanistan was not worth fighting, with 50 percent "strongly" believing it was not worth the cost. A majority believes that the United States is less powerful today than it was ten years ago.

Public Opinion and the Use of Force

A particularly important question for policy makers is the willingness of the public to support the use of military force. Here too, attention must be paid to wording and context. A 2012 poll regarding U.S. policy toward Syria showed that almost 75 percent of Americans opposed military action but 62 percent supported creating no-fly zones. Polling done that year also revealed that 70 percent of Americans favored using drones to fight terrorism.[14]

The conventional wisdom inherited from the Vietnam War era is that the public is unwilling to support the use of force if it results in casualties. Known as the **"Vietnam syndrome,"** the policy implication of this reading of the public led policy makers to either avoid the use of force altogether or use it only in highly controlled settings such that military force could be applied quickly and in an overwhelming fashion to ensure a short conflict with few American casualties.

The accumulated evidence on the use of force from the 1960s through the 1990s now points in a different direction and raises questions about the policy implications of the Vietnam syndrome. The public is not totally gun-shy. It will support the use of military force even when casualties occur, depending on (1) the policy purpose behind its use, (2) the success or failure of the undertaking, and (3) the degree of leadership consensus.

Of particular interest for the question of purpose is a study undertaken by Bruce Jentleson,[15] who argues that the American public is most likely to approve military force when the purpose is to restrain the foreign policy actions of a hostile state and least likely to do so when the purpose is to bring about internal political change.

Public support for U.S. military involvement in the Middle East fits this pattern. During the Persian Gulf War it was highest for Operation Desert Shield and

Operation Desert Storm, which were designed primarily to curb Iraqi foreign policy adventurism by defending Saudi Arabia and liberating Kuwait. Public support dropped sharply when the question put was one of overthrowing Saddam Hussein. This overall pattern held true in the Obama administration. When asked about the Libyan military operation, 65 percent said they supported military action to protect civilians from Gaddafi but only 48 percent supported the use of military force to remove him from power. Polling on Syria also supports this argument.[16] An online poll running from December 2015 to April 2016 showed only 35 percent of Americans favored removing Assad from power. As many as 66 percent favored using force against Assad if he had been found to use chemical weapons against Syrian opponents and after the 2015 Paris bombings 60 percent supported military action including ground troops to fight ISIS (Islamic State of Iraq and Syria).[17]

Studies also suggest that the public is sensitive to the domestic costs of foreign policy activism. The more serious the domestic problems relative to the external challenge, the more powerful will be the public's isolationist impulse. Thus, the weaker the economy, the less support a president is likely to find for an activist foreign policy. This logic helps explain support for the Iraq War, which was fought without a tax hike and cost less than 1 percent of the gross domestic product (GDP). In comparison, the Vietnam War cost 9 percent of the GDP, and at one point, the Korean War cost 14 percent of the GDP.[18]

The impact of race and gender also has been an important area of inquiry in the study of public opinion and the use of force. When the Iraq War started, only 29 percent of blacks polled supported it. Hispanics were also far less likely than whites to support it. Over 60 percent of all Hispanics disapproved of the Iraq War.[19] A similar pattern held in 2014 when a poll questioned Americans on their support for air strikes against Sunni insurgents in Iraq. Now, 58 percent of whites voiced their support for air strikes while only 50 percent of blacks and 43 percent of Hispanics did so.[20]

Research on gender also shows differences (Table 5.1).[21] The 2014 poll cited earlier showed that 64 percent of men supported air strikes against the Sunni insurgents while only 44 percent of women did. On average, regardless of the purpose, women are less supportive of the use of military force. They are also more sensitive to humanitarian concerns and the loss of life. Having said this, women by and large are not pacifists. The differences between men and women on the use of force tend to occur at the margins and are a response to specific circumstances.

Beyond race and gender, party identification also affects public opinion on the use of military force. Afghanistan and Syria reveal similar divisions along party lines. In 2013, 67 percent of Democrats believed the war was not worth fighting while only 54 percent of Republicans took this position. Only three years earlier when Bush was president a mere 27 percent of Republicans held the Afghan War not to be worthwhile. On Syria, 80 percent of Democrats supported Obama's decision to delay air strikes against Syria while only 56 percent of Republicans did.

TABLE 5.1	Gender-Based Differences on Use of Military Force	
Policy Issues	Female (% in favor)	Male (% in favor)
Conflict		
War against Terror	70.5	80.0
Persian Gulf War	49.8	66.8
Somalia	52.6	61.4
Kosovo/Serbia	47.0	54.4
Type of Military Action		
Air/missile strikes/bombing	54.1	66.6
Send troops abroad	48.1	60.0
Policy Objectives		
Foreign policy restrain	54.9	68.1
Humanitarian intervention	63.4	68.1
Internal political change	43.8	53.2
Peacekeeping	43.4	49.6
Mention of Casualties		
War on Terror/no casualties mentioned	73.8	82.4
War on Terror/casualties mentioned	58.0	71.5
Haiti/no casualties mentioned	31.3	42.5
Haiti/casualties mentioned	26.0	37.7

Source: Adapted from Richard Eichenberg, "Gender Differences in Public Attitudes toward the Use of Force by the United States, 1990–2003," *International Security* 28 (2003), 110–41, tables 2–5.

Impact

The question of how much influence public opinion has on American foreign policy can be answered in two ways: We can look (1) to the type of impact it has and (2) to the conditions necessary for it to be heard. Public opinion can have three types of impact on American foreign policy. It can serve as a constraint on innovation, a source of innovation, and a resource to be drawn on by policy makers in implementing policy. Public opinion acts as a constraint by defining the limits of what is politically feasible. To the extent the public is subject to having unstable moods about foreign policy issues as was frequently believed in the early Cold War period and some see today in the war against terrorism, public opinion may act as a powerful constraint on U.S. foreign policy. A case can also be made that the existence of too firm an outlook or too rigid a division of opinion is just as much a constraint. The deeply entrenched isolationist outlook of the American public during the 1930s made it extremely difficult for President Franklin Roosevelt to prepare the United States for World War II. A firm but divided opinion is cited by one major study as being responsible for the prolonged U.S. presence in Vietnam.[22] Faced by a "damned if they do and damned if they don't" dilemma, successive administrations are seen as having followed a strategy of perseverance until a public consensus developed for either a strategy of victory or withdrawal.[23]

Observers generally agree that public opinion rarely serves as a stimulus to policy innovation. One commentator argues that "no major foreign policy decision in the U.S. has been made in response to a spontaneous public demand."[24] Although this may be the case, public opinion today does appear to be capable of placing new items on the political agenda. What it tends to lack is the ability to overcome forces that push policy makers in the opposite direction. Such appears to be the case with regard to humanitarian interventions. In examining U.S. humanitarian interventions into Haiti, Bosnia, Somalia, and Kosovo one study found that public support for humanitarian intervention did increase congressional support but that political partisanship and ideology were strong enough to block congressional action.[25] Other examples where public opinion moved policy makers to action but did not result in a wholesale change in policy include the nuclear freeze movement in the early 1980s and the public outcry over NSA violations of civil liberties revealed by Snowden's leaks.

With regard to the second point, work by public opinion pollsters suggests that we might think about the influence of public opinion on foreign policy in terms of "**tipping points**."[26] Policies that have reached the tipping point at which public opinion begins to exert an influence share three characteristics: (1) A majority of the public is in support of or opposed to a particular policy, (2) they feel intensely about it, and (3) they believe that the government is responsible for addressing the problem. Public opinion on most foreign policy issues does not meet these requirements. Recent current issues that are at the tipping point or have crossed over it are the Iraq War, ISIS terrorism, illegal immigration, and outsourcing jobs.

Elections

Almost invariably, the winning candidate in an election cites the results as a mandate for their policy program. Do elections really serve as a mechanism for translating the public voice into policy? The evidence suggests that claims of popular mandates are often overstated and based on a flawed reading of election returns.

A look back at the Lyndon Johnson-Barry Goldwater election of 1964 shows just how deceptive electoral outcomes can be. In 1964 Johnson won a landslide victory over Goldwater, who had campaigned on a platform of winning the war against communism in Vietnam "by any means necessary." The results were commonly interpreted as a mandate for continued restraint in the war effort. However, national surveys revealed that 63 percent of those who favored withdrawal and 52 percent of those who favored a stronger stand, such as invading North Vietnam, supported Johnson.[27]

For elections to confer a mandate on the winner, three demands are made of the voters: (1) they must be knowledgeable, (2) they must cast their ballots on the basis of issue preferences, and (3) they must be able to distinguish between parties and candidates.

Voting and Foreign Policy

Evidence on the first point is not encouraging. The lack of widespread public understanding about foreign affairs issues never ceases to amaze commentators. Consider the following:

1964: 38 percent knew that Russia was not a member of NATO.

1966: Over 80 percent failed to properly identify the Vietcong.

1979: 23 percent knew the countries involved in the Strategic Arms Limitation Talks.

1993: 43 percent could not identify which continent Somalia was on.

2003: 68 percent believed that Iraq played an important role in the terrorist attacks of 9/11.[28]

Do candidates win because of their policy preferences, or in spite of them? Historically, foreign policy has not been a good issue on which to conduct a campaign.[29] Party identification, candidate image, incumbency, or some other nonissue factors generally play important roles in deciding how the public votes. The "bump" a president gets from a foreign policy success may also be short lived and is not easily transferred to other issues on the agenda. After Saddam Hussein was captured, George W. Bush's ratings went up eight points. Three months later that bump was gone. Obama's approval rating immediately jumped nine points after Osama bin Laden was killed. It too soon returned to its prior level and the jump had virtually no impact on his low approval rating on economic issues.

Charles Whalen, a former six-term congressman, sees the sporadic interest and low information level of constituents regarding foreign policy matters as a point of vulnerability to incumbents.[30] Challengers attempt to create an image of having policy differences with the incumbent and to cast the incumbent in a negative light. They find a powerful weapon in foreign affairs voting records. These issues are often complex, and when taken out of context, they can put the incumbent on the defensive. In 2000 the Cuban American National Foundation (CANF), a powerful anti-Castro lobbying force, targeted members of Congress who supported lifting U.S. economic sanctions against Cuba. Advertisements asserted that by voting to lift these sanctions, voters would be strengthening Castro, allowing him to continue to engage in forced child labor and child prostitution, sponsor international terrorism, and imprison political prisoners.

This dynamic also holds true at the presidential level where foreign policy setbacks provide a strategic opening for the opposition party to put the president on the political defensive. The congressional hearings on the Obama administration's response to the attacks on the U.S. diplomatic outpost in Benghazi, Libya, are a case in point, but it is not a unique case. Over the course of over a century the party out of power has sought to exploit setbacks in U.S.-China relations as evidence of incompetent or weak presidential leadership.[31] In the 1870s Democrats called for a policy of curbing Chinese immigration into the United States; in the 1950s Republicans blamed Truman for losing China; and in the 1990s Democrats attacked George H. W. Bush for his response to China's handling of the Tiananmen Square protests.

The third prerequisite for elections to serve as a mandate is that voters must be able to distinguish between party and candidate positions. In U.S. elections this is rarely the case. When choice is present in a presidential campaign it generally takes place in primaries where candidates seek to separate themselves from their competitors by advancing boldly stated **positional issues** that lack detail but carve out valuable political turf.[32] During the general election presidential candidates of both parties tend to stress **valence issues** which find most people on the same side of the issue out of the need to form and hold together broad electoral coalitions.

In line with this reasoning we saw that early in the 2015–16 primary season Donald Trump called for building a wall along the U.S.-Mexico border and making Mexico pay for it and advocating torture as a weapon to defeat terrorists; he also called upon South Korean and Japan to develop nuclear capabilities. As the Republican convention neared and with his nomination appearing certain Trump's tone changed. He now promised that "America is going to be strong again; America is going to be great again; it's going to be a friend again . . . we are going to finally have a coherent foreign policy, based on American interests and the shared interest of our allies . . . . we want to bring peace to the world."

Impact

What then is the impact of elections on U.S. foreign policy? For many observers, the greatest foreign policy impact of elections is not found in a single election but in the cycle of elections that defines a president's term in office.[33] The first year in office is characterized generally by policy experimentation, false starts, and overly zealous goals due to inexperience and the continued influence of overly simplistic foreign policy campaign rhetoric. During the second year in office, pragmatism becomes more evident. This is because of both the increased knowledge and skill of the administration and the realization that a foreign policy mishap may lead to the loss of House and Senate seats in the midterm elections. In the third year, foreign policy issues are evaluated largely in terms of their potential impact on the presidential reelection campaign. Potential successes are pursued vigorously even if the price tag is high, while the administration will try to disengage itself from potential losses. The final year brings stalemate to the foreign policy process. "Foreign governments have long understood the difficulty of doing business with the U.S. in election years."[34] Foreign policy initiatives come to a halt as all sides await the outcome of the election. One negative consequence of this stalemate is that can provide adversaries with a window of opportunity to advance their interests. Commentators suggested that is exactly what Russia was doing in its assault on rebel opponents of Syrian President Bashar al-Assad in Allepo.[35]

The most propitious time for foreign policy undertakings is held to be the first year and a half of a second term. Here, one finds an experienced president who has a foreign policy agenda and is operating under the halo effect of a reelection victory. By late in the second year of a president's second term, electoral considerations begin to overwhelm foreign policy again, as jockeying begins in both parties for their respective presidential nominations. At some point, the president comes to be regarded both at home and abroad as a "lame duck," which limits his or her ability to conduct foreign policy.

The influence of the election cycle is evident in the George W. Bush administration's efforts to deal with Iraq in his second term.[36] Fear of an explosive news story before the 2006 midterm elections delayed a serious strategic review of Iraq policy, even though it was acknowledged within the White House that the current strategy was not working. We can also see the influence of the electoral cycle in Obama's administration. His first year in office was marked by frequent calls for resetting American foreign policy. His second year saw him adopt a pragmatic surge in troops to Afghanistan, and following the midterm elections he moved to clear his foreign policy agenda by gaining high-stakes victories on the New START Treaty and ending the ban on gays in the military. In his third year, Obama announced the beginning of troop withdrawal from Afghanistan and moved on getting much-delayed trade legislation through Congress. In March 2012 Obama confided in Russian President Dmitry Medvedev that no agreement could come before the presidential election. After the election he would have "space." Obama's second term has not fully followed the script outlined by the election cycle argument. Partisan divisions between Republicans and Democrats and divisions within the Republican Party stalled efforts to pass immigration reform legislation in his second term, but near the end of his presidency he did succeed in getting fast track authority and a nuclear arms agreement with Iran through Congress.

Historical Lesson

The Pentagon Papers

The Pentagon Papers was a forty-seven-volume history of the U.S. involvement in Vietnam from World War II through 1967. Officially known as *United States-Vietnam Relations, 1945–1967*, it was secretly commissioned by Secretary of Defense Robert McNamara in June 1967 and completed in 1969 just prior to Richard Nixon's inauguration. The Pentagon Papers contained 3,000 pages of commentary and analysis and 4,000 pages of documents, which included highly classified reports, memos, cables, and analyses. Only fifteen copies were printed.

The first installment of the "Pentagon Papers" appeared on the front page of the *New York Times* on June 13, 1971. Three days later, the Nixon administration obtained a federal court injunction to stop further installments from appearing in the paper. This did not bring an end to the Pentagon Papers, as the *Washington Post* and fifteen other papers began printing it. On June 30 the Supreme Court ruled 6–3 against the Nixon administration, opening the way for newspapers to print the entire Pentagon Papers. The day before, Senator Mike Gravel (D. Alaska) had entered over 4,000 pages of the Pentagon Papers into the official record of the Subcommittee on Public Buildings and Grounds to ensure they would be made public. In making its ruling the Supreme Court found that the Nixon administration had not made a case for prior restraint of free speech to block the continued publication of the Pentagon Papers. The nine justices of the Supreme Court wrote nine different opinions in reaching this overall conclusion.

The Pentagon Papers created an immediate sensation. It revealed information that had not been covered in the press, such as U.S. bombings of Cambodia and Laos as well as military raids into North Vietnam that were designed to provoke a North Vietnamese response. Some argued that it represented a dangerous breach of national security secrecy, while others considered it a historical document that might cause embarrassment but was not a security threat. What was not in doubt was that the information it contained about military actions in Vietnam differed dramatically from that which was depicted in government policy statements. Most pointedly, it showed that presidents had lied about their intentions not to fight a wider war (Johnson) or that they actually had already done so (Nixon).

The source of the leaked Pentagon Papers was Daniel Ellsberg, a RAND think tank analyst. A military analyst during the Vietnam War, he had worked on the report for several months and was able to obtain a copy and photocopy it. After failing to interest Nixon's

national security advisor Henry Kissinger or Senators George McGovern and William Fulbright in the report, Ellsberg approached the *New York Times* in February 1971. He gave them forty-three volumes of the study. The four remaining volumes contained what he felt was particularly sensitive information and he kept them back.

Ellsberg went into hiding after the *New York Times* began publishing the Pentagon Papers. He surrendered to police two days before the Supreme Court decision. He went on trial in 1973 for violating the 1917 Espionage Act and other statutes. The case was dismissed after it became known to the court that Ellsberg's psychiatrist's office had been targeted as part of the Watergate break-ins.

Applying the Lesson

1. Where is the dividing line between the public's right to know and the need for secrecy?

2. What motivations might McNamara have had in ordering the Vietnam study?

3. To what extent are the Pentagon Papers and the National Security Agency leaks similar and different?

Interest Groups

The third avenue open to the public for expressing its outlook on foreign policy issues is interest group activity. A wide variety of groups actively try to influence U.S. foreign policy. Consider U.S. policy toward China.[37] A representative list of interest groups active in this policy area includes such diverse groups as the AFL-CIO, Amnesty International, the Christian Coalition of America, the Committee of 100 for Tibet, and the U.S.-China Business Council.

Groups wishing to influence U.S. foreign policy make their views known to policy makers either directly or through interest brokers. Not surprisingly, former policy makers are among the most prominent interest brokers because of their access to policy makers and policy-making institutions. Among the key recent foreign policy officials who established lobbying or strategic consulting firms after leaving office are Condoleezza Rice (secretary of state and national security advisor under George W. Bush), Stephen Hadley (his onetime national security advisor), and Robert Gates (secretary of defense). Together they formed RiceHadleyGates LLC. Among the recent congressional leaders who entered the consulting field are former Senate majority leader Trent Lott and former House majority leader Richard Gephardt.

Types of Interest Groups

We can divide the most active foreign policy interest groups into four broad categories: business groups, ethnic groups, foreign interests, and ideological public interest groups.

Business Groups   The long-standing cliché at the heart of business lobbying is that "what is good for General Motors is good for the United States." It is a view endorsed both by those who feel threatened by foreign competition and seek protection, such as the auto, steel, and textile industries and farmers, and by those who depend on open access to foreign markets, such as Wal-Mart. Nowhere is business foreign policy lobbying more controversial than when it is carried out by defense industries. Their activities bring forth images of what President Dwight Eisenhower referred to in his farewell address as the **military-industrial complex**.[38]

At the core of this negative image is the assertion that there exists within U.S. policy-making circles a dominating political force consisting of professional soldiers, industrialists, and government officials. Acting in unison, they determine policy on defense-related matters.[39] The resulting policies are based on an ideology of international conflict that requires high levels of military spending, a large defense establishment, and a belligerent, interventionist foreign policy. In the 1960s, the concept of a military-industrial complex became a major theme in writings of those who opposed the U.S. involvement in Vietnam. Concerns about its influence waned in the 1970s with the shift in emphasis from confrontation and containment to détente but have returned with the large increases in defense spending that have accompanied the Global War on Terrorism and the wars in Afghanistan and Iraq.

One key dimension to the operation of the military-industrial complex is its complex network of linkages to Congress as illustrated by the extensive lobbying efforts of defense contractors. In 2011 Lockheed Martin, General Dynamics, and Raytheon spent a combined total of $33.4 billion on lobbying. Representative Ike Skelton, who chaired the Armed Services Committee in 2010, received some $150,000 in campaign contributions from General Dynamics, Boeing, Northrop Grumman, and other firms. The centerpiece of Lockheed-Martin's lobbying efforts is saving the F-35 fighter. Production of the F-35 is spread to some nine hundred suppliers in forty-five states. Its price tag of $160 million per plane makes it the most expensive plane ever built but one which in 2016 after nine years of development was still not ready for combat.

A second key dimension is the ties between the military-industrial complex and the government bureaucracy. A 2012 study found that 70 percent of the retired three- and four-star generals took jobs with defense contractors or as consultants. In October 2012 alone, the Defense Department issued contracts valued at some $37.4 billion. Weapons manufacturers are not the only firms making large profits. During the Iraq War, Halliburton was awarded many non-bid contracts and saw its net profit for the second quarter of 2003 reach $26 million as compared to a second-quarter 2002 loss of $498 million.

Ethnic Groups   The most successful ethnic lobbies have relied on three ingredients to give them political clout: (1) the threat of switching allegiances at election time, either from one party to another or from one candidate to another in the same party; (2) a strong and effective lobbying apparatus; and (3) the ability to build a case around traditional American symbols and ideals.[40]

The Jewish American lobby possesses the most formidable combination of these elements. The centerpiece of the Jewish lobbying effort for Israel is the highly organized, efficient, and well-financed American Israel Public Affairs Committee (Aipac), which serves as an umbrella organization for pro-Israeli groups. It "promptly and unfailingly provides all members [of Congress] with data and documentation, supplemented, as circumstances dictate, with telephone calls and personal visits on those issues touching upon Israeli national interests."[41]

High levels of funding for pro-Israeli candidates are a key component of the lobbying strategy followed by pro-Israeli political action committees (PACs). A study by the Federal Election Commission found that from 1998 to 2006 Jewish PACs made over $13 million in contributions to congressional candidates. The next highest ethnic PAC was Cuban Americans ($1 million). Another core component of its lobbying strategy is to take U.S. officials to Israel for visits. In August 2010, eighty-one members of Congress traveled to Israel at its expense for briefings.

Money alone does not explain the strength of Jewish American lobbying efforts. It has also been successful because the message it sends resonates well with Americans: a country founded by settlers who were displaced from their homelands with a common sense of destiny and mission as a chosen people who are threatened by enemies.[42]

One of the challenges Aipac faces in looking to the future is that the demographics of its support base are changing. Where its primary supporters were once liberal Democrats, they are now found among conservative Republicans and especially evangelical Christians. African Americans were once staunch supporters of Israel but now increasingly align with Palestinian causes. Aipac's core base has also become old. A 2008 poll showed that while more than one-half of Jewish Americans older than sixty-five years felt that the Israel-Palestine relations were a major issue in the U.S. election, more than 66 percent of young non-Orthodox Jewish students did not feel this way. This changed support base has contributed to the emergence of challenger groups to Aipac.[43] The most significant of these is J Street, which was formed in 2008 and defines itself as "the political home for pro-Israel, pro-peace Americans" and advocates a two-state solution to the Israeli-Palestinian conflict.

Aipac suffered what the press described as a stinging defeat in 2015 when it was unable to mobilize sufficient votes in Congress to block Obama's nuclear deal with Iran. Citizens for a Nuclear Free Iran, an Aipac affiliate, worked with a $20 million advertising budget to stop the agreement and ran ads in forty states. Aipac also organized a fly-in campaign in which hundreds of its supporters flew into Washington to urge their senators to vote against the agreement. For its part, J Street unleashed a $5 million advertising campaign in support of the agreement.

A closer look reveals that this is not the first time presidents have succeeded in acting in opposition to Aipac's position. In 2013 Aipac failed to get Congress to impose economic sanctions on Iran. This legislation was strongly opposed by Obama. Here again J Street lobbied against them. Decades earlier, in 1981, Ronald Reagan agreed to sell AWACS (Airborne Warning and Control Systems aircraft) to Saudi Arabia over its objections in what was then the largest arms sale in U.S. history.[44]

No Arab American lobbying force equal to Aipac has yet emerged.[45] In 1972 a central organization, the National Association of Arab Americans (NAAA), was founded, and in the mid-1980s it had field coordinators in every congressional district and a membership of some one hundred thousand Arab American families. Also active in encouraging the participation of Arab Americans in the political process is the Arab American Institute, which was founded in 1985. From 1998 to 2006 Arab American PACs spent some $500,000 on congressional campaigns.

A major obstacle to creating an effective Arab lobbying force is the ethnic diversity of Arab Americans. Until 1948 most Arabs coming to the United States were Christians from Syria and Lebanon. Since 1978 most have been Muslims. The result is that no single political agenda exists for Arab Americans. A consensus exists only on the broad issues of pursuing a comprehensive peace plan in the Middle East and establishing better U.S. relations with the Arab world.

By the mid-1980s, African Americans had made great strides toward meeting two of the three prerequisites listed here. First, as the Reverend Jesse Jackson's 1984 bid for the presidency made clear, blacks make up an important constituency within the Democratic Party. Second, an organizational base, TransAfrica, now exists. The major focus of black lobbying in the mid-1980s was reorienting U.S. policy toward South Africa. With this issue behind it, African Americans have had a more difficult time mobilizing on foreign policy issues.[46] Combating genocide and dealing with the HIV/AIDS epidemic have emerged as top priorities. On genocide in Rwanda, the African American community evidenced an overall lack of interest. This has been explained by the absence of a clear-cut black-white dimension to the problem.

Ethnic diversity is a problem for Hispanic American lobbying on foreign policy.[47] Mexican immigration which has been motivated largely by economic considerations is concentrated in the Southwest and is largely Democratic. In 1980, Jimmy Carter got 72 percent of this vote. Cuban immigration is concentrated on the East Coast. It has been motivated largely by foreign policy concerns and is politically conservative and Republican. Ronald Reagan got 59 percent of Florida's Hispanic vote. To this, one must also add Puerto Ricans, who are concentrated largely in the Midwest and Northeast and who generally vote Democratic.

Two additional fissures within the Hispanic community make the establishment of an effective lobbying force difficult. One pits American-born Hispanics against immigrants.[48] The only real area of overlapping concerns is immigration policy. When questioned regarding their policy priorities, American-born Hispanics give greatest weight to domestic issues such as education, crime, economic growth, and the environment. The second fissure is generational. This came through clearly in the differing reactions to George W. Bush's June 2004 imposition of tight restrictions on travel to Cuba and on the practice of sending money to relatives still there. The ban was supported by the 250,000 remaining "historic exiles" who fled Cuba right after Castro seized power but was opposed by those who fled more recently. This generational divide surfaced again when President Obama announced that the United States and Cuba would move toward establishing normal diplomatic relations. Many longtime Cuban exiles in Florida denounced Obama as a traitor and liar while many younger Cuban Americans expressed the view that the time was right for a change in U.S.-Cuba relations.

The most famous Hispanic lobby is the CANF (Cuban-American National Foundation).[49] Vehemently opposed to Fidel Castro and intent on ending communist rule in Cuba, CANF opposed any change in American policy toward Cuba. Its Free Cuba PAC made some $250,000 in campaign contributions to congressional candidates from 1998 to 2006. This figure was far surpassed by the U.S. Cuba Democracy PAC established in 2003. It gave $760,000 to congressional candidates during this period. Among the major pieces of legislation CANF supported was the 1992 Cuban Democracy Act. Passed by Congress in an election year and endorsed by both presidential candidates in an effort to gain the support of the Cuban American community, it prohibited foreign affiliates of U.S. firms from doing business in Cuba. The legislation was derided by its critics as an "economic declaration of war" against Castro and a violation of international free trade agreements.

CANF did a dramatic about-face in April 2009. Just days before President Obama announced that he was lifting long-standing restrictions on family and remittances to Cuba, CANF issued a white paper for calling for a new direction in U.S.-Cuba relations built upon people-to-people exchanges, promoting Cuban civil society, and targeted bilateral and multilateral diplomacy. It continued to follow this new line in 2015 when in speaking to the possible ending of the U.S. embargo against Cuba it urged all presidential candidates "to prioritize human rights and democracy in Cuba above political expediency."

The end of the Cold War ushered in a new era of ethnic interest group lobbying. The 1996 senatorial race in South Dakota saw a battle in which the Democratic candidate raised over $150,000 from Pakistani American groups, while the Republican candidate (who authored legislation cutting U.S. foreign aid to Pakistan) raised approximately the same amount from Indian American sources. The influence of these groups is now also found in the halls of Congress. In 2006 Indian American lobbying pressured Congress to approve the U.S.-India nuclear agreement at a time when its passage was in doubt.[50]

Foreign Lobbyists Not surprisingly both foreign governments and foreign firms engage in lobbying but so too do politically active ethnic groups and opposition groups. A recent example of nonstate foreign lobbying involved supporters of an Iranian opposition group, Mujahadin-e-Khalq (MEK), three thousand of whose members are living in exile. The State Department listed MEK as a terrorist organization, although it formally renounced terrorism in 2001. Among those speaking out on its behalf were former CIA directors Porter Goss and James Woolsey, former FBI director Louis Freeh, and former Joint Chiefs of Staff chairman Hugh Shelton. A point of controversy behind their lobbying efforts was the legal requirement that advocates of foreign organizations register as lobbyists and provide details of their fees and activities. MEK supporters argue they are not lobbyists but legitimately acting as individuals to promote good foreign policy decisions. Secretary of State Hillary Clinton removed MEK from the terrorist list in 2012.

While the most common concerns of foreign governments are foreign aid legislation and arms sales, foreign governments pursue a wide range of interests when lobbying including persuading American firms to invest in their country, promoting security ties with the United States, and improving its image in Washington.[51] More often than not foreign lobbying is done quietly and out of sight, but on occasion it has been highly visible and controversial. A case in point is Israel's lobbying efforts to get Congress to block the Obama administration's nuclear deal with Iran. Prime Minister Benjamin Netanyahu addressed a joint session of Congress, Israel's ambassador to the United States spoke to some sixty members of Congress, and Netanyahu spoke to a delegation of U.S. legislators visiting Israel at a trip paid for by the American Israel Education Foundation, an affiliate of Aipac. In each of these cases Israeli officials sought to downplay the challenge this presented to Obama's policy by arguing they were merely providing information and were not lobbying.

The primary concern of foreign firms engaged in lobbying is their ability to conduct business in the United States. Indian high-tech firms, for example, have joined in with American firms to lobby against provisions in any immigration bill that would limit the ability of highly skilled foreign workers to come to the United States. Of particular concern at state and local levels are taxation, zoning, and labor laws. Once, Sony threatened not to build new plants in California and Florida unless those states changed certain tax codes. They did.

Congress and the White House are not the only targets of foreign lobbying. Kurds have targeted much of their efforts on the bureaucracy. One of their goals was to obtain $18.4 billion from U.S. construction funds dedicated to the Kurdish region of Iraq. The State Department opposed their efforts. Kurdish lobbying effort then successfully switched its focus to the Commerce Department, which identified Kurdistan as the "gateway" for U.S. firms going to Iraq.

Ideological Public-Interest Groups   A wide variety of groups fall into this category. At one extreme are highly institutionalized and well-funded organizations that one does not normally think of as interest groups. These are **"think tanks"** that have as part of their mission the propagation and advancement of ideas on how to address public policy problems. The Brookings Institution was for a long time the most prominent foreign policy think tank advancing a liberal-democratic foreign policy agenda. Over the years it has become more moderate and centrist in its orientation. Two of the most visible think tanks now occupy positions at the conservative end of the political spectrum: the Cato Institute, a libertarian organization that has advanced a restrictive if not isolationist foreign policy agenda; and the Heritage Foundation which in the view of many of its past supporters is moving away from its traditional orientation of serving as a source of conservative ideas about a foreign policy based on a strong military defense, limited involvement in humanitarian undertakings, and free market principles in international trade to a more activist and combative lobbying orientation. Also playing prominent roles as producers of ideas are the American Enterprise Institute, New America, and the Center for Strategic and International Studies (CSIS).

Think tanks make their mark in Washington in many ways. Their members serve as a source of expertise for administrations and congressional committees to draw on as either outside experts or employees. Less visibly but perhaps most significantly, they serve as a focal point for bringing like-minded individuals together to address common concerns. For example, think tanks were prominent members of the "blue team," a loose alliance of members of Congress, staffers, conservative journalists, and lobbyists for Taiwan who worked to present China as a threat to the United States. More recently the Heritage Foundation, AEI, and the Foreign Policy Institute joined forces in a "defend defense" initiative to protect the Pentagon's budget from major cutbacks.

Recently think tanks have come under close scrutiny for receiving large sums of money from foreign governments without acknowledging it.[52] Since 2011 at least sixty-four foreign governments and their officials have contributed money to twenty-eight major U.S. research organizations. CSIS has disclosed a list of thirteen foreign government donors including Germany and China. The Atlantic Council has acknowledged accepting funds from twenty-five countries since 2008. Neither think tank identified the amount of money involved. Norway signed an agreement with the Center for Global Development for $5 million to promote its request for doubling the amount of foreign aid it receives from the United States. These revelations prompted members of Congress to propose legislation requiring think tanks to disclose their sources of funding and to request the Justice Department begin an investigation to see if federal laws had been broken.

Also included in this category are more traditional societal groups, the most prominent of which today may be the "religious right."[53] Pat Robertson's Christian Broadcasting Network gave $3–$7 billion to U.S.-backed anticommunist forces in Central America. In 2003 Robertson defended Liberian leader Charles Taylor against charges that he was a war criminal. He later called for the assassination of Venezuelan president Hugo Chavez.

Evangelical groups became especially active in shaping U.S. foreign policy to Africa during the administration of George W. Bush.[54] The U.S. policy on AIDS was heavily influenced by its beliefs and lobbying by the Focus on the Family group. Bush also created a new Center for Faith-Based and Community Initiatives within the U.S. Agency for International Development. Sudan emerged as a high-priority country in evangelical African lobbying efforts due to the limitations it placed on religious freedom and the continued presence of slavery. Christian Solidarity International has been particularly active on questions of slavery.

The religious right does not hold a monopoly on interest group activity by religious organizations. The prelude to the Iraq War found groups active on both sides. Whereas fundamentalist groups tended to support the war, the Catholic Church, the Religious Society of Friends (Quakers), the United Church of Christ, the World Council of Churches, the Muslim Peace Fellowship, and the Shalom Center all spoke out against it.

Impact

Establishing the influence of an interest group on a specific policy is difficult. More is required than just revealing the presence of group activity. A concrete link must be established between the group's actions and the actions taken by those who were influenced. Efforts to establish the validity of assertions about the influence of the military-industrial complex on U.S. foreign policy have produced mixed results. One observer suggests that the competing judgments can be reconciled if we make a distinction between major political decisions, which set into motion high rates of defense spending, and legislative and administrative decisions, which translate them into concrete programs. The influence of the military-industrial complex is greatest in the industrial area and far less in the military complex, where it faces strong competition from ideological, economic, and other nonmilitary influences.

Additionally, it needs to be recognized that lobbying success is not an all-or-nothing condition. Consider recent lobbying efforts to bring about comprehensive immigration reform. This legislation was supported by George W. Bush and Obama, yet Congress was reluctant to act largely due to splits within the Republican Party and concerns about potential voter backlash. This outcome would suggest failure, yet a case can also be made that without the coordinated activity of lobbying groups immigration reform would be much further away from becoming a reality than it is today.

Political Protest

The public voice on foreign policy matters is expressed not only through officially sanctioned avenues. It can also be heard in a variety of forms that challenge policy makers to take notice of positions that are often at variance with official policies. Such protests range in form from the acts of single individuals, such as Cindy Sheehan challenging President George W. Bush's position on the Iraq War by camping outside his ranch in Crawford, Texas, to antiwar marches such as that in Washington, DC, in 2010 on the seventh anniversary of the Iraq War.

Modern technology has added a new dimension to protest movements, the "virtual protest march." In October 2003, when tens of thousands of protesters marched in Washington calling for an end to the occupation of Iraq, other protesters flooded congressional offices with e-mails stating their opposition to the war. A similar tactic was used to pressure Congress into investigating the prewar intelligence claims made by the George W. Bush administration. More than four hundred thousand people from every state contacted members of Congress.

Political protests are valued for their ability to alter the political landscape by bypassing existing power centers and introducing new or marginalized voices into the political debate. In the case of the antiglobalization protests, it ensured that environmental, labor, and democracy issues could not be totally ignored. In the case of pro-immigration forces, it brought many Hispanics into the political process for the first time. Protestors on Darfur hoped to bring greater attention to this issue among an American public that is largely unfamiliar with Africa.

The ability for political protests to have this impact may be especially important today in large part because an "apathetic internationalism" is reshaping American politics, encouraging policy makers to ignore foreign policy problems and empowering "squeaky wheels," those who make the loudest noise about foreign policy problems. More often than not, this condition favors those organized interests that can mobilize their supporters most effectively to pressure policy makers. But when thousands of protesters repeatedly take to the streets, a new element is added to the equation.[55]

There is nothing automatic about the success of protest movements. Major foreign policies are not easily reversed, and it is often difficult to sustain the political momentum needed to change policies. Such was the situation facing antiglobalization protestors at a 1999 meeting of the World Trade Organization in Seattle and climate change protestors in 2014 who marched in New York City. Protest movements can also give birth to counterprotests that can be cited by policy makers as justifying their policies. Such was the case in September 2005, when pro–Iraq War individuals marched in Washington, DC.

The Media and American Foreign Policy

To this point we have looked at how the public conveys its views to policy makers. We have not yet examined how the public obtains its information about the world. In looking at this issue, we first examine the sources of information that the public relies upon and then how those sources can shape their thinking.

Newspapers and Television

For generations of Americans newspapers were the primary if not the only means of keeping up with news. One of the most cited early examples of the influence of the media on U.S. foreign policy is the Spanish-American War. At the turn of the twentieth century, the Hearst and Pulitzer newspaper chains engaged in sensationalistic "**yellow journalism**" to increase circulation. Their sensationalist coverage of the sinking of the USS *Maine* in Havana Harbor is routinely cited as contributing to the onset of the war by stirring up American public opinion. More recent scholarship cites the greater importance of more fundamental foreign policy issues dividing the United States and Spain but the imagery of the press being able to lead the United States to war remains strong.

The advent of competing sources of news has cut sharply into the ability of the press to shape public opinion. By 1993 slightly more Americans reported watching network news regularly than they did reading the newspaper (60 percent to 58 percent), but by 2008 more people were going online three or more times per week (37 percent) or listening to radio news (34 percent) than reading the newspaper (34 percent). Television suffered an even more dramatic decline, with only 29 percent of those responding to the 2008 poll saying they watched network news regularly.[56]

Increased competition and rising operating costs have translated into significant declines in the overseas news collection activities of television and newspapers.[57] In 2003 newspapers and chains reported having 307 full-time foreign correspondents. In 2016 the *Washington Post*, listed 16 foreign bureaus, less than one-half of which had both a bureau chief and a foreign correspondent. Not surprisingly, one result of these types of cutbacks is that the percentage of front-page foreign news stories in U.S. newspapers has steadily declined. In 2007 it was at 14 percent, down from 27 percent in 1987 and 1977.

To note that the number of those watching network newscasts has decreased significantly does not do full justice to the transformative impacts that television as a medium has had on the reporting of foreign policy news. Network evening news broadcasts were only fifteen minutes long in 1962 and relied heavily on video of international events that were at least a day old. Consider how differently the October 1962 Cuban missile crisis might have played out had it occurred in the 1990s.[58] Robert McNamara, President Kennedy's secretary of defense, observed, "I don't think that I turned on a television set during the whole two weeks of that crisis."[59] During the Cuban missile crisis, the Kennedy administration knew about the missiles in Cuba six days before the information was broadcast to the American people. Using military force was the first option embraced by the Kennedy administration, but it was abandoned as the week progressed in favor of a blockade. McNamara, for one, is uncertain that the same decisions would have been reached in an altered decision-making environment.

The arrival of 24-7 news coverage that began with the debut of CNN in 1980 has changed the political time open to presidents to develop foreign policy responses. News reports and images of terrorist attacks, starving people, and military conflict now require immediate comments. The inability to produce a response or to provide one that is soon undermined by unfolding events leads to charges of policy incoherence and policy failure as well as providing administration critics with an opportunity to put forward demands that the United States must do "something."

Today, the bottom line is that presidents must develop a television policy to accompany their foreign policy. They have not always succeeded. In the Persian Gulf War, the George H. W. Bush administration was able to frame the policy issue on its own terms and to control the media's coverage of it.[60] Uncertain about how to proceed in Haiti, Bosnia, and Somalia, his administration and that of Bill Clinton were unable to present a coherent story with which the media could frame its pictures.[61]

In response to charges that they are not fairly portraying American foreign policy in their reporting many in the traditional media make two points. First, very often, administrations have developed television policies but not foreign policies. If what the media shows does not correspond to the declaratory statements of American foreign policy, it is not the media's fault. Second, the clearest way to limit the influence of the media is to enunciate a clear policy.

Drawing on his experience as a historian and CNN commentator, Michael Beschloss offers a set of lessons to presidents as they make foreign policy in the television age. A sampling is found in Table 5.2.

The New Media and American Foreign Policy

Not only have the Internet and other methods of electronic communication become a major source of foreign policy news and information but in some cases they have become the dominant or preferred source of information. For example, by 2003, 77 percent of Americans who used the Internet did so to get or share information on the Iraq War. One in five Internet users stated that it helped shape their thinking about the war.[62] We can identify at least three ways in which the new media helps shape public views on foreign policy.

TABLE 5.2   Media Lessons for Modern-Day Presidents

1. Television offers presidents a superior weapon for framing issues and selling policy in crisis.
2. Television also amplifies public opposition.
3. Television can encourage presidents to favor crisis management over long-term planning.
4. Television can drastically reduce the time, secrecy, and calm available to a president for deliberating with advisers on an urgent foreign policy problem.
5. Presidents cannot presume that they can maintain a monopoly on information for long.
6. Television allows presidents to communicate with adversary leaders and populations.
7. Television can seriously affect relations with allies.
8. Unexpected events shown on television can have an inordinate influence on the public's perception of a foreign crisis.
9. When appearing on television during a crisis, a president and his high officials must be absolutely honest with the public.
10. Censorship can risk a damaging backlash.
11. Television can help create an unexpected agenda, especially during the run-up or endgame of a war.
12. Presidents who fail to craft an implicit or explicit television strategy while dealing with a foreign crisis do so at their own peril.

Source: Hearings, Committee on Foreign Affairs, House of Representatives, 103rd Congress, April 26, 1994 (Washington, DC: U.S. Government Printing Office, 1994), 52–53.

First, it serves as a source of raw information. One way it does this is through leaking secret documents. Nowhere was this more in evidence than in July 2010 when WikiLeaks released over ninety-one thousand secret documents about Afghanistan and other foreign policy matters on its website. Prior to this it had released more than seventy-six thousand documents under the heading "Afghan War Diary." A second way is by serving as virtually the sole source of information on areas that reporters for safety and other reasons cannot get to. This has occurred in the Syria civil war where videos from independent news sources and social media sites have been used by such traditional media outlets as ABC News, Reuters, and the *New York Times.*

Second, beyond providing information, the Internet and social media are sources of images of foreign policy. Despite the army's best efforts to contain their use, by mid-2007 more than seven thousand video clips of combat footage from Iraq were available on YouTube. A cell phone camera videotaped the execution of Saddam Hussein for the world to see. In 2012 a YouTube feature on Joseph Kony, who is wanted by the International Criminal Court for crimes against humanity, went viral, attracting more than fifty million views and raising hundreds of thousands of dollars

Third, the Internet allows individuals to connect in a personal and direct manner with U.S. foreign policy. Foreign policy blogs abound. The White House arranged for President Obama's June 2009 speech in Cairo to be sent out in text-message format in four languages, translated into thirteen languages, and broadcast on Facebook. In 2010, the day on which the United States condemned North Korea for an artillery attack on a South Korean island, the *Washington Post* ran a poll asking readers to "weigh in" on how the United States should proceed.

Shaping the Public's View

While it has become commonplace to speak of the media as driving foreign policy decisions, that is, the **"CNN effect**," a more complex relationship exists between the media and policy makers that drives coverage of foreign events. Evidence suggests that the media does not so much discover foreign policy problems as it takes cues about what to report from the political debate in Washington. This is referred to as "indexing." If there is no debate in Washington, then there is no debate in the media, and coverage of a topic may all but disappear. In the case of the Iraq War, the drop in coverage, from an average of 15 percent of the news content in July 2006 to 3 percent in February 2007, coincided with a drop-off from 35 percent to 23 percent in the number of Americans who could correctly estimate the number of U.S. fatalities in the war.

In reporting on foreign policy problems, journalists look first to the White House for cues on how to define a problem. This is important because first impressions are often difficult to challenge. With this frame of reference established, journalists then go to other lesser news sources such as members of Congress, ex-government officials, and outside experts for commentary and input. This is referred to as the opinion cascade, and according to some, including former

White House press secretary Scott McClellan, it makes the media a "complicit enabler" of the Bush administration's case for going to war with Iraq.

The Iran nuclear agreement provides another example of how the White House attempts to orchestrate press coverage of foreign policy. Deputy National Security Advisor Ben Rhodes observed: "All of these newspapers used to have foreign correspondents. Now they don't. They call us to explain to them what's happening in Moscow and Cairo . . . They literally know nothing." His office also set up a team of staffers to provide talking points for foreign policy experts who the media was known to consult. "The [the experts] were saying things that validated what we had given them to say." The end result according to Rhodes was an echo chamber.[63]

Two very different consequences follow from the manner in which the media frames its foreign policy stories. The first is the **rally-around-the-flag effect**, in which the public moves to support the president in times of conflict and crisis. Initially, the American public was sharply divided on using military force against Iraq in 1991. Support for war hovered around the 50 percent mark until President George H. W. Bush's January 16, 1991, speech announcing the beginning of the bombing campaign. Support then shot up to 72 percent.

There is nothing in presidential speeches that automatically produces a significant boost in support for the administration's foreign policy. The changing face of the American media with the growth of cable outlets makes it increasingly difficult for presidents to move large numbers of the public to support their policies because with the growth of options viewers in search of news increasingly go to those channels whose views they support. Thus, conservative Republicans tend to watch Fox News and liberal Democrats tend to watch CNN or MSNBC. Indicative of this new reality is the fact that on Obama's announcement that he was willing to use force against Syria, the American public remained opposed to military action by a 48 percent to 29 percent margin.

The second consequence is a **"spiral of silence."** Here, when individuals hold opinions that they do not hear reaffirmed in the voices of others they exercise self-censorship as a way of protecting themselves from criticism. The opposite reaction takes place among those who receive positive reinforcement for their views. They become even more vocal and confident in their beliefs, leading the dissenters to exercise even more self-censorship. Many see it at work in public opinion on the Persian Gulf War. Networks all but ignored antiwar stories in the lead-up to the war. Of 2,855 minutes of network news coverage of the war in this period only 29 minutes showed popular opposition to the ongoing American military buildup.

It also should be noted that questions exist about the media's objectivity and independence. With regard to the traditional media concern exists over its dependence on military sources for information. The main issue here is the growing phenomenon of embedded reporters who file reports based on their travels with the military on combat missions. As one critic observed, "We can't understand what we don't see; we can't explain a conflict if we hear only from one side."[64] With regard to the new media concerns have been raised that an illusion of objectivity exists surrounding the images transmitted through Facebook, YouTube, and twitter accounts. This has been especially true for the Syrian civil war, a conflict described as the most socially mediated conflict in history. One recent study found that Syrian social media images were carefully managed by "gatekeepers." Violent images were designed to delegitimize the Assad regime to the outside world, encourage further extremism and polarization in the conflict, and demobilize others from intervening militarily for fear of becoming the next victims. It is notable in this regard that early social media transmissions from Syria were in English and that only as the civil war progressed did Arabic emerge as the dominant language.[65]

States and Foreign Policy: The New Battleground

Before turning to the question of how policy makers respond to the public voice in making foreign policy decisions one further observation needs to be made as to how the public makes its views known. Because the foreign policy agenda has increasingly become one in which both domestic and foreign policy concerns are present simultaneously (intermestic policies) it is not surprising to find that with increasing frequency the public voice on foreign policy is being directed away from Washington and to state capitals.

The most prominent policy area at the state level relating to foreign policy is immigration. In 2016 the Supreme Court on a tie vote supported legal challenges to Obama's immigration policy ending that program. This was not the first challenge to come from states. Angered by ongoing border violence and reacting to citizen demands that illegal immigration be curbed, Arizona earlier passed a state law that among other provisions allows police to arrest suspected illegal immigrants without a warrant. Other states such as Alabama have enacted or are considering similar legislation. The Justice Department has challenged the constitutionality of these laws and Arizona, in turn, sued the federal government for its failure to provide border security with Mexico. Eleven countries, including Mexico, asked the courts for permission to file friend-of-the-court briefs in the Arizona case because they had an interest in ensuring they have "reliable relations" with the United States. A 2012 Supreme Court decision struck down portions of it but left others standing. In 2014 a judge in Oregon ruled that an immigrant's rights were violated when she was held in jail as a result of a request from the deferral immigration emergency agency. After the verdict sheriffs in nine Oregon counties said they would no longer honor such federal requests. Michigan governor Rick Snyder and Sen. Rand Paul put forward still another proposal for dealing with immigration: states would be allowed to create regional visa programs permitting immigrants to obtain short-term work visas that would serve as the starting point for eventual permanent residency in the United States.[66]

Policy Makers' Response

The prevailing view among policy makers holds that foreign policy is too important to be rooted in public perceptions of world affairs. Public attitudes are something to be formed and shaped rather than followed. Consider comments made by two past secretaries of defense. Leon Panetta (under Obama) told a press conference, "We cannot fight wars by polls." Dick Cheney (under George H. W. Bush) said, "I do not look upon the press as an asset. Frankly, I look on it as a problem to be managed."[67]

The tendency of policy makers to discount the positive contribution of the public voice to foreign policy making also shows up when they look to uncover the public voice. A State Department official observed, "If a given viewpoint different from our own does not have congressional expression, forget it."[68] A congressional staffer could not remember the last time he was asked to do a foreign policy poll. The inevitable result of this perspective is to greatly narrow the range of public attitudes that are taken into account in making policy. Additionally, policy makers often appear not to understand how the public thinks about foreign policy issues. In a 2004 poll 76 percent of the public said the United States should participate in the International Criminal Court. When asked before the poll results were released, only 32 percent of government officials and 15 percent of congressional staffers anticipated that a majority of the public would hold this view.[69]

Policy makers may not be totally off base in their lack of attention to public opinion. One study suggests that presidents can safely ignore what the public thinks depending on the type of foreign policy problem they are dealing with. For a noncrisis what matters to the public is that the president takes action. Judgments of success and failure do not enter into its thinking because of the long time needed for such issues to be resolved. Crises are different. In crises what matters to the public is not the decision of whether or not to use force or intervene. What matters is if it failed or succeeded.[70]

Over the Horizon: An Intelligence-Industrial Complex?

Earlier in this chapter we noted that in his farewell address President Eisenhower warned about the need to guard against the influence of the military-industrial complex. The revelations by Snowden regarding the existence of a secret NSA domestic electronic data gathering program has many warning against a new threat to the public's ability to effectively express its voice on foreign policy matters: an intelligence-industrial complex. As with the military-industrial complex critics see the intelligence-industrial complex as a largely unaccountable political force whose roots are found in the perception of significant national security threats to the United States. Where the military-industrial complex gains its influence through the production of military power the intelligence-industrial complex gets its influence through the collection and production of information. As former NSA director Lt. Gen. Keith Alexander put it the challenge they face is "you need a haystack to find a needle"

In the early postwar era Western Union, RCA Global, and ITT provided intelligence agencies access to telegraph communications. Later the intelligence community turned to AT&T which had discovered a method for tapping into underwater fiber cables. More recently Microsoft provided the NSA with the capability to circumvent its own encryption program. For the NSA and other intelligence agencies building a haystack requires the cooperation of commercial communication firms.[71]

Critics see it as having come into existence through a combination of jaw-boning, stealth, legal protections, and monetary rewards. Legal protection came in the form of the granting telecoms immunity from prosecution from any lawsuits brought against them for their having cooperated with government requests to turn over information. Jawboning took many forms. Appeals to patriotism played a central role. So too did indirect pressure when those appeals failed. As one Verizon executive noted, "At the end of the day, if the Justice Department shows up at your door, you have to comply." To cement its working relationship with communication firms the Security Affairs Support Association (now the Intelligence and National Security Alliance) was created in 1979.

Contracting and consulting firms are another part of the intelligence-industrial complex. Originally seen as a surge capability NSA's use of them has become a permanent fixture: 70 percent of the intelligence budget ($56 billion out of $80 billion) now goes to private contractors. Booz Allen Hamilton (BAH) for whom Snowden worked is one such contractor. Obama's director of national intelligence (DNI) James Clapper was a former BAH executive. Mike McConnell, who served as President Bill Clinton's NSA director, left to work for BAH and then returned to government service as George W. Bush's DNI and has since returned to BAH. Of its twenty-five thousand employees, 75 percent hold security clearances and 50 percent hold top secret clearances. For these firms the contracts have been significant. A computer systems contract awarded to BAH by the Department of Homeland Security for $2 million escalated $124 million.

Evidence that the intelligence-industrial complex may not be monolithic and that it contains potentially significant internal divisions is found in the response of prominent former national security officials who supported Apple in its rejection of the FBI's request that it unlock the mobile phone used by the attacker in the San Bernardino shootings. They include heads of the CIA, NSA, and Homeland Security. All now work for technology consulting firms, some of which they founded.

The issue of whether or not the intelligence-industrial complex represents a threat to American civil liberties as critics argue finds Americans divided. A March 2016 CBS poll found that 50 percent supported the FBI's insistence that Apple unlock the mobile phone linked to the 2015 San Bernardino terrorist attack and 43 percent supported Apple's refusal to comply.

Critical Thinking Questions

1. Which of the means of exercising the public voice discussed in this chapter (public opinion, elections, lobbying, and political protest) is most effective?

2. Is the media best seen as a threat to the president's ability to conduct foreign policy or an important tool he can use?

3. Should policy makers listen to the public or use their professional judgment in making foreign policy decisions?

Key Terms

CNN effect, 124

military-industrial complex, 127

positional issues, 111

rally-around-the-flag effect, 125

spiral of silence, 125

think tanks, 118

tipping point, 109

valence issues, 111

Vietnam syndrome, 106

yellow journalism, 121

Further Reading

Gabriel Almond, *The American People and Foreign Policy* (New York: Praeger, 1960).

This is an early attempt to address the question of how the public thinks about foreign policy. It provides a solid foundation for raising the issue of the public's proper role in foreign policy making.

Robert Entman, *Projections of Power: Framing News, Public Opinion and U.S. Foreign Policy* (Chicago, IL: University of Chicago Press, 2004).

This book brings together the nature of public opinion, the manner in which the news media covers foreign policy, and the influence of the White House into a model of how foreign policy problems come to be defined and framed.

Peter Gries, *The Politics of American Foreign Policy* (Stanford: Stanford University Press, 2014).

This author argues that ideology shapes American foreign policy. He finds Americans to be less united on a multilateral foreign policy strategy than is commonly held to be the case and rejects the argument that an Israeli lobby determines U.S. Middle East policy.

Erika King, *Obama, the Media and Framing the U.S. Exit from Iraq and Afghanistan* (Burlington, VT: Ashgate, 2014).

This volume looks at the narratives presented by both the Bush and Obama administrations in exiting these two wars alongside of how the mass media framed these stories. It finds an interpretive disconnect between the political and media accounts.

William Lynn III, "End of the Military-Industrial Complex," *Foreign Affairs* 89 (September 2014), 97–108.

This article identifies four periods of the military-industrial complex. It raises the issue of the ability of the Pentagon to adapt to globalization and argues that the Pentagon should go abroad to partner with foreign firms

Helen Milner and Dustin Tingley, *Sailing the Water's Edge* (Princeton: Princeton University Press, 2016).

This book examines how domestic politics influences foreign policy since World War II. It finds that presidents have more control over some policy instruments than others. One result is the militarization of foreign policy.

Peter Trubowitz, *Defining the National Interest: Conflict and Change in American Foreign Policy* (Chicago, IL: University of Chicago Press, 1998).

The author argues that regional economic diversity and America's uneven integration into the global economy are the central factors shaping the debate over the national interest.

Notes

[1] James Billington, "Realism and Vision in Foreign Policy," *Foreign Affairs* 65 (1987), 630.

[2] Walter Lippmann, quoted in Amos Jordan and William J. Taylor Jr., *American National Security Policy and Process* (Baltimore: Johns Hopkins University Press, 1981), 43.

[3] Matthew Baum, "Circling the Wagons: Soft News and Isolationism in American Public Opinion," *International Studies Quarterly* 48 (2004), 313–38.

[4] Craig Katura and Dina Smeltz, "Who Matters for US Foreign Policymaking?" Chicago Council on Global Affairs, June 19, 2015.

[5] Kathryn Tempas, "Words vs. Deeds," *The Brookings Review* (Summer 2003), 33–35.

[6] On trade, see Max Ehrenfreund, "What Americans Really Think About Free Trade," *Washington Post*, https://www.washingtonpost.com/news/wonk/wp/2016/03/25/what-americans-really-think-about-free-trade/.

[7] Robert Erikson, Norman Luttbeg, and Kent Tedin, *American Public Opinion* (New York: Wiley, 1980), 44.

[8] Barry Hughes, *The Domestic Context of American Foreign Policy* (San Francisco: Freeman, 1978), 31.

[9] Ole R. Holsti and James N. Rosenau, *American Leadership in World Affairs: Vietnam and the Breakdown of Consensus* (Winchester: Allen & Unwin, 1984), 218–20.

[10] Lloyd Free and William Watts, "Internationalism Comes of Age . . . Again," *Public Opinion* 3 (1980), 46–50.

[11] "American Isolationism, With a Very, Very Big Stick," *Foreign Policy*, May 17, 2016, http://foreignpolicy.com/2016/05/17/american-isolationism-with-a-very-very-big-stick-trump-clinton-election/.

[12] John Reilly, "Americans and the World: A Survey at Century's End," *Foreign Policy* 114 (1999), 97–113.

[13] David Skidmore, "The Unilateral Temptation in American Foreign Policy," in Steven Hook and James Scott (eds.), *U.S. Foreign Policy Today: American Renewal?* (Washington, DC: CQ Press, 2012), 37.

[14] See Scott Clement, "Poll: Americans Also See Chemical Weapon 'Red Line' in Syria," *Washington Post*, December 20, 2012; Scott Clement, "Majority of Americans Say Afghan War Has Not Been Worth Fighting, Post-ABC News Poll Finds," *Washington Post*, December 12, 2013; Pew Research Center for the People and the Press, "Public Backs Diplomatic Approach in Syria, but Distrusts Syria and Russia," September 16, 2013.

[15] Bruce W. Jentleson, "The Pretty Prudent Public: Post-Vietnam American Opinion on the Use of Military Force," *International Studies Quarterly* 36 (1990), 49–74.

[16] Steven Kull, "Framing of Syria Issue Key to Public Support," CNN.com Blogs, http://globalpublicsquare.blogs.cnn.com/2013/09/06/framing-of-syria-issue-keyto-public-support.

[17] See https://www.isidewith.com/poll/1591613755 and http://thehill.com/policy/defense/260940-large-majorities-of-americans-favor-ground-troops-against-isis-new-poll-says.

[18] Miroslav Nincic, "Domestic Costs, the U.S. Public, and the Isolationist Calculus," *International Studies Quarterly* 41 (1997), 593–610; Robert Hormats, *The Price of Liberty: Paying for America's Wars* (New York: Times Books, 2007).

[19] Marisa Abrajano and R. Michael Alvarez, "Hispanic Public Opinion and Partisanship in America," *Political Science Quarterly* 126 (2011), 255–85.

[20] Washington Post-ABC Poll, August 13–17, reported in the *Washington Post*, https://www.washingtonpost.com/page/2010-2019/WashingtonPost/2014/09/09/National-Politics/Polling/release_361.xml?tid=a_inl.

[21] Richard Eichenberg, "Gender Differences in Public Attitudes toward the Use of Force by the United States, 1990–2003," *International Security* 28 (2003), 110–41.

[22] Leslie Gelb and Richard K. Betts, *The Irony of Vietnam: The System Worked* (Washington, DC: Brookings, 1979).

[23] Richard Sobel, *The Impact of Public Opinion on U.S. Foreign Policy since Vietnam* (New York: Oxford University Press, 2001).

[24] Richard J. Barnett, *The Roots of War* (New York: Penguin, 1977), 243.

25 Timothy Hilderbrant, Courtney Hiderbrant, Peter Holm, and Jon Pevehouse, "The Domestic Politics of Humanitarian Intervention," *Foreign Policy Analysis* 9 (2013), 243–66.

26 Daniel Yankelovich, "The Tipping Points," *Foreign Affairs* 85 (2006), 115–25; "Poll Positions," *Foreign Affairs* 84 (2005), 2–16.

27 Gerald M. Pomper, *Elections in America: Control and Influence in Democratic Politics* (New York: Dodd, Mead, 1968), 251.

28 The figures through 1979 are discussed in ibid., 19; and Hughes, *Domestic Context of American Foreign Policy*, 91. The 1993 data are from *Time* (October 4, 1993). The 2003 data are from Steven Kull, Clay Ramsey, and Evan Lewis, "Misperception, the Media, and the Iraq War. Political Science Quarterly 118 (2003), 569–598.

29 Michael Abramowitz, "Terrorism Fades as Issue in 2008 Campaign," *Washington Post*, September 11, 2008, A6.

30 Charles Whalen, *The House and Foreign Policy* (Chapel Hill: University of North Carolina Press, 1982).

31 Peter Turbowitz and Jungkun Seo, "The China Card," *Political Science Quarterly* 127 (2012), 189–211.

32 William Schneider, "Conservatism, Not Interventionism: Trends in Foreign Policy Opinion, 1974–1982," in Kenneth Oye, Robert Lieber, and Doanld Rothchild (eds.), *Eagle Defiant: United States Foreign Policy in the 1980s* (Boston: Little, Brown, 1983).

33 William B. Quandt, "The Electoral Cycle and the Conduct of American Foreign Policy," *Political Science Quarterly* 101 (1986), 825–37.

34 Laurence Radway, "The Curse of Free Elections," *Foreign Policy* 40 (1980), 61–73.

35 Michael Gordon and Neil MacFarquhar, "Election In U.S. Offers Kremlin Opening in Syria," *New York Times*, October 4, 2016, A1.

36 Bob Woodward, *The War Within* (New York: Simon & Schuster, 2008), 320–21.

37 Kerry Dumbright, "Interest Groups," in Ramon Hawley Myers, Michel Oksenberg, and David L. Shambaugh (eds.), *Making China Policy* (Lanham: Rowman & Littlefield, 2001), 149–72.

38 C. W. Mills, *The Power Elite* (New York: Oxford University Press, 1956).

39 See Steven Rosen, ed., *Testing the Theory of the Military Industrial Complex* (Lexington: Heath, 1973).

40 Martin Weil, "Can the Blacks Do for Africa What the Jews Did for Israel?," *Foreign Policy* 15 (1974), 109–29.

41 Charles McMathias Jr., "Ethnic Groups and Foreign Affairs," *Foreign Affairs* 59 (1981), 975–99.

42 Walter Russell Mead, "The New Israel and the Old: Why Gentile Americans Back the Jewish State," *Foreign Affairs* 87 (2008), 28–46.

43 Michael Abramowitz, "Jewish Liberals to Launch a Counterpoint to AIPAC," *Washington Post*, April 15, 2008, A13.

44 Mark Lander, "Potent Pro-Israeli Group Finds Its Momentum Blunted," *New York Times*, February 3, 2014, 4.

45 David J. Sadd and G. Neal Lendenmann, "Arab American Grievances," *Foreign Policy* 60 (1985), 17–29.

46 Fran Scott and Abdulah Osman, "Identity, African-Americans and U.S. Foreign Policy," in Thomas Ambrosio (ed.), *Ethnic Identity Groups and U.S. Foreign Policy* (Westport: Praeger, 2002), 71–92.

47 Bill Richardson, "Hispanic American Concerns," *Foreign Policy* 60 (1985), 30–39.

48 Michael Jones-Correa, "Latinos and Latin America," in Ambrosio (ed.), *Ethnic Identity Groups and U.S. Foreign Policy,* 115–30.

49 See Shawn Miller, "Trade Winds Stir Miami Storm," *Insight*, June 7, 1993; Carla Anne Robins, "Dateline Washington: Cuban-American Clout," *Foreign Policy* 88 (1992), 165–82.

50 James Kirk, "Indian-Americans and the U.S.-India Nuclear Agreement: Consolidation of an Ethnic Lobby," *Foreign Policy Analysis* 4 (2008), 275–300. See also Swaminathan Aiyar, "India and the United States: How Individuals and Corporations Have Driven Indo-U.S. Relations," CATO Institute, *Policy Analysis* 713 (December 11, 2012).

[51] "Shadow Diplomacy," http://100r.org/2013/07/shadow-diplomacy-african-nations-bypass-embassies-tap-lobbyists.

[52] Eric Lipton, Brooke Williams, and Nicholas Confessore, "Foreign Powers buy Influence at Think Tanks," *The New York Times*, September 7, 2014, p. A1.

[53] William Martin, "The Christian Right and American Foreign Policy," *Foreign Policy* 114 (1999), 66–80.

[54] Asteris Huliaras, "The Evangelical Roots of U.S. Africa Policy," *Survival* 50 (2008–2009), 161–82.

[55] James Lindsay, "The Apathy: How an Uninterested Public Is Reshaping Foreign Policy," *Foreign Affairs* 79 (2000), 2–8.

[56] John Hamilton, *Journalism's Roving Eye: A History of American Foreign Reporting* (Baton Rouge: Louisiana State University Press, 2009), 459.

[57] Priya Kumar, "Foreign Correspondents," *American Journalism Review* (December/January 2011), http://ajrarchive.org/article.asp?id 4997.

[58] See prepared statement by Michael R. Beschloss, "Impact of Television on U.S. Foreign Policy," hearing before the Committee on Foreign Affairs, House of Representatives, 103rd Congress, second session, April 26, 1994.

[59] See, "News Release," John F. Kennedy Library, January 24, 2012, https://www.jfklibrary.org/About-Us/News-and-Press/Press-Releases/JFK-Library-Releases-Remaining-Presidential-Recordings.aspx

[60] Trevor Thrall, "The Gulf in Reporting the Gulf War," *Breakthroughs* 2 (1992), 9–13.

[61] Jacqueline Sharkey, "When Pictures Drive Foreign Policy," *American Journalism Review* 15 (December 1993), 14–19.

[62] Lee Raine, Susannah Fox, and Deborah Fallows, *The Internet and the Iraq War, the Internet and American Life Project* (Washington, DC: The Pew Foundation, 2004).

[63] Paul Farhi, "Obama Official Says He Pushed a 'Narrative' to Media to Sell the Iran Nuclear Deal," *The Washington Post*, May 6, 2016, https://www.washingtonpost.com/lifestyle/style/obama-official-says-he-pushed-a-narrative-to-media-to-sell-the-iran-nuclear-deal/2016/05/06/5b90d984-13a1-11e6-8967-7ac733c56f12_story.html.

[64] David Ignatius, "The Dangers of Embedded Journalism, in War and Politics," *Washington Post*, May 2, 2010, B1.

[65] Marc Lynch, Deen Freelon, and Sean Aday, *Syria's Socially Mediated Civil War* (Washington DC: U.S. Institute of Peace, Peaceworks No. 91, 2014).

[66] Brandon Fuller and Sean Rust, "State-Based Visas," CATO Institute, *Policy Analysis*, 748 (April 23, 2014).

[67] Cheney, as quoted in Herbert Abrams, "Weapons of Miller's Descriptions," *Bulletin of the Atomic Scientists* 60 (July/August 2004), 63; for Panetta's quote, see http://www.cnn.com/2012/03/27/politics/panetta-afghanistan/.

[68] Bernard Cohen, *The Public's Impact on Foreign Policy* (Boston: Little, Brown, 1973), 117.

[69] David Skidmore, *The Unilateralist Temptation in American Foreign Policy* (New York: Routledge, 2011), 36–38.

[70] Thomas Knecht, *Paying Attention to Foreign Affairs* (University Park, PA: Penn State University Press, 2010).

[71] Michael Hirsh, "How America's Top Tech Companies Created the Surveillance State," *National Journal*, July 25 2013.

Congress

Dateline: 2015 Authorization of Military Force Resolution

No shortage of views exists regarding the role that Congress plays in making foreign policy. In the press it is frequently characterized as an obstacle course that presidential foreign policy initiatives must navigate. One dissenting view holds that in reality Congress is not much of an obstacle course for presidents to run.[1] A second dissent argues that even if it is a hard obstacle course, congressional participation in foreign policy making is not an evil to be avoided because it raises the public's awareness about issues, provides additional information to policy makers, and, in the long run, may improve the quality of U.S. foreign policy.[2] President Obama's 2015 request to Congress for an Authorization of Military Force (AUMF) resolution provides a starting point for looking at this debate.

In February 2015, some six months after his administration began its air war against the Islamic State of Iraq and Syria (ISIS), Obama formally requested a declaration of congressional support. In presenting Congress with a draft AUMF to vote upon Obama made it clear that in his view he already possessed the constitutional authority to conduct military operations against ISIS. Obama was seeking an AUMF in order to add further legitimacy to the actions he would take as commander in chief.

The administration's AUMF set a three-year limit on military engagements against ISIS and prohibited the use of "enduring offensive ground forces" but did not exclude the possibility of limited ground action or the use of Special Operations forces. The AUMF also did not place geographic limits on where military operations might be conducted and affirmed that they could be used against ISIS as well as "associated forces."

Obama's 2015 AUMF resolution would rescind the last war-fighting authority granted by Congress to a president. In 2002 President George W. Bush obtained an AUMF that was used to fight the Iraq War. Obama's proposed AUMF left untouched, however, the 2001 AUMF resolution passed after 9/11 which gave Bush the authority to "use all necessary and appropriate force against anyone who committed or aided the attacks of September 11, 2001 or harbored such an organization or person in order to prevent a future attack." As passed it is of unlimited geographic scope and duration and has been used by Bush and Obama to justify their use of military force throughout the Middle East.

The 2015 wording of the administration's AUMF was designed to appeal to those in Congress (mostly Democrats) who feared it would justify another open-ended war in the Middle East and those who sought a more robust war effort (mostly Republicans). It satisfied neither. The proposed AUMF never reached the House or Senate floor for a debate and vote.

A Republican senator who opposed Obama's handling of foreign policy because it was not robust enough nonetheless supported the AUMF because it would show allies and enemies that the United States was united. Another Republican senator said he would vote yes but had concerns, "You go to war with the president you've got." A Democratic representative worried that the AUMF was not a "constraining document" and needed revision. A Democratic senator feared its passage would "reward a decade of mismanagement in the Middle East.

Constitutional questions also surfaced. Senator Bob Corker, who chaired the Senate Foreign Relations Committee, wondered why Congress would bring the AUMF up for a vote when there was not an obvious need to do so adding that it would only make us appear to be divided over ISIS. Senators Tim Kaine and Jeff Flake countered saying by that not voting Congress had abdicated its responsibility to influence the war on ISIS. Representative James McGovern accused Congress of "moral cowardice" for refusing to debate the AUMF.

The question of an AUMF Resolution for military action against ISIS was rejoined by Obama in his 2016 State of the Union address when he stated, "If this Congress is serious about winning this war, and wants to send a message to our troops and the world, you should finally authorize the use of military force against ISIL. Take a vote. But the American people should know that with or without congressional action, ISIL will learn the same lessons as terrorists before them." A few days later Senate Majority Leader Mitch McConnell said the Senate would only pass an AUMF against ISIS if Obama agreed that it would not contain any limits on where or for how long U.S. troops, including ground forces, could fight. In April McConnell introduced a revised AUMF to that effect.

In this chapter we look at the constitutional basis of Congress's power to participate in foreign policy and the methods at its disposal to exercise its voice. First, we will look at the constitutional powers on which its participation is based. Next, we will examine how Congress's operating structure and procedure impact on its participation in foreign policy making. We conclude by looking at how its relationship with the president in making foreign policy has changed over time.

Constitutional Powers

The division of power found in the Constitution provides the foundation on which congressional participation in foreign policy rests. It comprises four powers: (1) the power of advice and consent in making treaties, (2) the power to confirm presidential appointments, (3) a set of war powers, and (4) the power to regulate commerce.

Treaty-Making Power

The Constitution states that the president, by and with the advice and consent of the Senate, has the power to make treaties. The president's role in the treaty-making process generally has not been a source of serious controversy. The president nominates the negotiators, issues instructions to them, submits the treaty to the Senate for its advice and consent, and, if consent is given, decides whether to **ratify** the treaty and make it a law. Far more controversial have been the nature of senatorial advice and consent, the topics to be covered by treaties, and the role of the House of Representatives in the treaty-making process.

Senatorial Advice and Consent President Obama received the Senate's approval for the New START Treaty in December 2010 by a vote of 71–26 after a hard-fought political battle. The treaty had received the endorsement of all living presidents, secretaries of state, and commanders of U.S. nuclear forces. It was sent to the Senate prior to the 2010 midterm elections, but the administration lacked the necessary support to bring it to a vote. Those elections saw the Republicans win control of the Senate and called for postponing a vote until the new Congress was sworn in. To secure support for the treaty and block crippling amendments, the administration agreed to spend an additional $84 billion over ten years to modernize the U.S. nuclear weapons program.

The Senate has given its consent to over fifteen hundred treaties and rejected only twenty-two. Fifteen of those rejections occurred from 1789 to 1920.

Among the recent treaties rejected by the Senate was an International Disability Treaty that was signed by President George W. Bush and supported by Obama. It was defeated by a 61–38 vote in December 2012, five short of the 66 votes needed. Supporters of the treaty argued it is modeled on the American Disability Act. Conservative opponents argued it undermined U.S. sovereignty and the ability of American citizens to hold policy makers accountable for their actions by allowing international authorities to dictate the treatment of Americans with disabilities as well as threaten home-schooling programs and encourage abortions.[3] A list of rejected treaties is presented in Table 6.1.

These figures do not tell the full story. Omitted in this counting are treaties negotiated by presidents but never voted on by the Senate or those the Senate consented to only after prolonged delays. In 1988 the Senate gave its consent to a Convention on the Prevention and Punishment of Genocide that was first submitted to the Senate by President Harry Truman in 1949.

In 2015 thirty-eight treaties had been submitted to the Senate for its advice and consent and not yet voted on. The most recently negotiated treaty was signed in 2014 to create a nuclear free zone in central Asia. The oldest was a 1949 International Labor Organization Convention that supported labor's right to organize. President Jimmy Carter's withdrawal of the SALT II treaty from consideration after the Soviet invasion of Afghanistan is only one example of major Senate "nonrejections." Truman negotiated a

---

TABLE 6.1 **Rejected Treaties**

Bilateral	Multilateral
Suspension of Slave Trade/Columbia, 1825	Treaty of Versailles, 1920
Property Rights/Switzerland, 1836	World Court, 1935
Annexation/Texas, 1844	Law of Sea Convention, 1960
Commercial Reciprocity/Germany, 1844	Montreal Aviation Protocol, 1983
Transit and Commercial Rights/Mexico, 1860	Comprehensive Test Ban, 1999
Cuban Claims Commission/Spain, 1860	Convention on the Rights of Persons with Disabilities, 2012
Arbitration of Claims/United Kingdom, 1869	
Commercial Reciprocity/Hawaii, 1870	
Annexation/Dominican Republic, 1870	
Interoceanic Canal/Nicaragua, 1885	
Fishing Rights/United Kingdom, 1888	
Extradition/United Kingdom, 1889	
Arbitration/United Kingdom, 1897	
Commercial Rights/Turkey, 1927	
St. Lawrence Seaway/Canada, 1934	

Source: http://www.senate.gov/artandhistory/history/common/briefing/Treaties.htm#4.

treaty establishing an International Trade Organization that was to be part of the Bretton Woods system. Because of certain Senate opposition, Truman never submitted the treaty for advice and consent, and the interim General Agreement on Tariffs and Trade (GATT) became the formal international vehicle for lowering tariffs. A 2013 arms trade treaty negotiated by the Obama administration that would have established international norms regulating the sale of weapons including small handguns was "dead on arrival" when even before the U.S. officially signed the treaty over fifty senators made their opposition known citing a desire not to "subject the U.S. to the influence of internationally defined norms."

An overall tally, such as the one in Table 6.1, also makes no mention of the senatorial attempts to change the treaties. Between 1947 and 2000, the Senate attached reservations to 162 of the 796 treaties that came before it.[4] In the heated debate over the Panama Canal Treaties, 145 amendments, 76 reservations, 18 understandings, and 3 declarations were proposed. The Senate's attachment of amendments and reservations to treaties is far from random.[5] The subject matter of the treaty matters. "High politics" treaties—those dealing with national security issues and questions of U.S. sovereignty—are far more likely to be saddled with reservations. Economic treaties are also likely to attract reservations. Beginning with the Vietnam War, ideology has been an important factor shaping Senate treaty votes. Today, conservative senators tend to vote for arms control agreements only when the president is a member of their party. Liberal senators, in contrast, tend to support arms control agreements regardless of the party that occupies the White House.

The motivations behind introducing treaty amendments are many. They include the desire to protect domestic economic interests, to reassert senatorial powers by insisting on increased reporting and certification provisions as a condition for giving advice and consent to a treaty, or to make a policy statement—such as the 1997 Chemical Warfare Convention, which directed the secretary of defense to increase U.S. military ability to operate in areas contaminated by chemical and biological weapons. Not all senatorial changes to treaties are alike.[6] Some senatorial changes are designed to improve a treaty; others are meant to kill it by introducing unacceptable provisions. This was the motivation behind some of the amendments to immigration reform legislation. Among the more than three hundred amendments considered were killer amendments (poison pills) that would have required a 90 percent apprehension rate of illegal border crossings before the undocumented immigrants could begin the process of gaining citizenship.

Finally, we should note that the president and Senate may continue to clash over the provisions of a treaty long after senatorial advice and consent has been given. The issue here is over who has the power to interpret treaty language and thus potentially change the meaning of the treaty. A significant presidential-congressional clash over the language of the Antiballistic Missile (ABM) Treaty spanned three presidencies. The centerpiece of the dispute was whether a president could reinterpret the language of a treaty without congressional approval. President Reagan did so, and on the basis of this new interpretation, his administration asserted that it could legally test elements of his Strategic Defense Initiative shield. The controversy continued when the Clinton administration approached Russia about modifying the language of the treaty to permit the deployment of mobile defensive systems against intermediate missiles. The administration said its proposal was intended only to clear up ambiguities in the treaty. Senate leaders responded that the administration should not try to put any change into effect without the approval of the Senate. The Clinton administration ultimately conceded this point and recognized the Senate's right to review the revised treaty language. President George W. Bush formally withdrew the United States from the ABM Treaty in June 2002. Thirty-one members of Congress unsuccessfully brought legal action against the administration, asserting that the president lacked the constitutional power to do so.

The Role of the House   The Constitution gives the House no formal role in the treaty-making process, and traditionally it played the part of a spectator. This is changing as the House has seized upon its budgetary powers as the vehicle for making its will known to both the Senate and the president. Treaties are not always self-executing. They typically require enabling legislation and the expenditure of funds before their provisions take effect. The Constitution gives the House control over the budget and in the process the ability to undo what the Senate and the president have agreed on.

A case in point is the Panama Canal Treaties. According to one observer, the House came quite close to destroying these treaties by inserting into the implementing legislation language that disagreed with and contradicted parts of one of the treaties just approved by the Senate by identical 68–32 votes.[7]

The Carter administration's implementing legislation was assigned to four House committees. Primary jurisdiction was held by the Merchant Marine and Fisheries Committee, whose chair, Representative John Murphy, opposed the treaty. He proposed his own version of the implementing legislation, which gave Congress a continuing say in supervising the Panama Canal for many years to come. Eventually, the Carter administration found it necessary to abandon its own bill in favor of the Murphy bill. This angered Panamanian leaders, who cited almost 30 articles of the House bill that violated provisions of the negotiated treaty. Final congressional approval was given to the implementing legislation only four days before the treaty was scheduled to take effect.

Appointment Powers

As originally envisioned, the power to approve or reject presidential appointments was closely related to the power to give advice and consent to treaties. By exercising a voice in who negotiated the treaty, the Senate would be able to influence its content. In practice, this linkage was never fully put into place, and it has long since unraveled. The Senate has failed to actively or systematically exercise its confirmation powers. Frequently, it has not hesitated to approve ambassadors appointed solely for political purposes and without any other apparent qualifications for the post. Such appointments are heavily criticized by Foreign Service professionals due to their lack of expertise but defended by others who argue that political appointees bring more political clout with them to the position of ambassador than do careerists and therefore can be of value to the president. Typically 30 percent of ambassadorial positions are now going to political appointees or non-careerists. In the Reagan administration this number reached as high as 38 percent. Under Clinton and Carter it fell to 27 percent. Obama was near the high end with 35 percent. His political ambassadorial appointments gave $13.6 million to democratic campaigns. Under George W. Bush many ambassadorships went to "Pioneers," individuals who had raised a minimum of $100,000 for his presidential race.

Normally when the Senate raises its voice in opposition to an appointment, the concern has been directed more toward making a policy statement than questioning the qualifications of the nominee. In 2014 over fifty ambassadorial nominees were awaiting approval by the Senate, and forty-nine of them were careerists. In one case Roberta Jacobson was unanimously confirmed as ambassador to Mexico in 2016 after her nomination was put on hold by Senator Marc Rubio for eleven months. Jacobson had been assistant secretary of state for the Western Hemisphere and played an important role in normalizing relations with Cuba, a policy that Rubio opposed. In return for dropping his hold the Obama administration agreed to a number of his demands including annual reports on forty topics such as religious freedom, Hong Kong autonomy, and anti-Semitism.

War Powers

The war powers of the Constitution are split into three basic parts. Congress is given the power to declare war and the power to raise and maintain an army and a navy, while the president is designated as commander in chief of the armed forces. In the abstract these powers fit together very nicely, but in practice the exact meaning of these powers is unclear. Alexander Hamilton saw them as a symbolic grant of power, with the actual power to decide military strategy and tactics being held by professional soldiers. Many presidents have taken this grant of power quite literally. Franklin Roosevelt participated actively in formulating military strategy and tactics during World War II, and Lyndon Johnson took part in selecting bombing targets during Vietnam.

An additional problem is defining when a state of war exists. Is it any instance where U.S. troops are placed into combat, or must a war be declared into existence? In its Prize Cases decision of 1862, the Supreme Court ruled that the existence of a war was found in the prevailing conditions and not in a formal congressional declaration. U.S. practice has borne this out. Congress has declared only 5 of the over 125 "wars" that the United States has fought: the War of 1812, the Spanish-American War, the Mexican War, World War I, and World War II.

The most visible means available to Congress in trying to limit the president's use of force is the 1973 **War Powers Resolution**, which was passed over President Nixon's veto. It requires the president to do the following:

1. "In every possible instance," consult with Congress before committing U.S. troops in "hostilities or into situations where imminent involvement in hostilities" is likely.
2. Inform Congress within forty-eight hours after the introduction of troops if there has been no declaration of war.
3. Remove U.S. troops within sixty days (or ninety days in special circumstances) if Congress does not either declare war or adopt a concurrent resolution approving the action.

Congress also can terminate U.S. military involvement before the sixty-day limit by passing a concurrent resolution. Such a resolution does not require the president's signature and therefore cannot be vetoed.

As of April 2014 presidents submitted 160 reports to Congress.[8] In doing so, they have not recognized the constitutionality of the War Powers Resolution. In reporting the Mayaguez rescue operation in 1975, President Gerald Ford stated that he was "taking note" of the War Powers Resolution but asserted that he acted on the basis of his commander-in-chief powers. President Obama used language frequently employed by past presidents in 2011 when he did not seek congressional approval in establishing the no-fly zone in Libya. In his notification to Congress he stated that "this is a limited . . . operation which does fall in the president's authority" and that he was informing Congress "consistent" with the War Powers Resolution. He used identical language in sending his Six Month Consolidated War Powers Resolution report to Congress in 2015.[9]

In preparing for the Iraq War, the George W. Bush administration put forward two arguments for why the War Powers Resolution did not apply.[10] First, it argued that the 1991 resolution passed before the Persian Gulf War provided continuing military authority to the president. Second, it maintained that the use of force was authorized by the 1998 Iraq Liberation Act, which called on the president to provide for the overthrow of Saddam Hussein. In fact, the act specifically stated that none of its provisions "shall be construed to authorize or otherwise speak to the use of United States Armed Forces . . . in carrying out this Act." In place of a War Powers Resolution vote, the George W. Bush administration obtained an AUMF for the Iraq War authorizing the administration to enforce the UN resolution on Iraq's weapons of mass destruction and to protect the United States from Saddam Hussein. This AUMF is presented in Box 6.1.

One object of presidential hostility to the War Powers Resolution is the provision granting Congress the right to terminate hostilities after they have begun through the use of a **legislative veto**. It allows Congress to approve or disapprove executive branch actions after the fact, in a form short of legislation. In addition to the War Powers Resolution, Congress has inserted legislative vetoes into a wide range of foreign policy legislation, including arms sales and the export of nuclear fuel and facilities.[11] Presidents have maintained that only congressional action that has been approved by the president or is passed by Congress over a presidential veto is legally binding. On January 23, 1983, in a landmark case, the Supreme Court agreed with the presidential interpretation in making its ruling in *U.S. v. Chadha*. The closest it came to being used was with the transfer of nuclear material to India in 1980 and the sale of an AWACS and F-15 enhancement package to Saudi Arabia in 1981.

Another sore point with presidents is the sixty-day time limit imposed by the War Powers Resolution. Presidents have challenged the time limit on constitutional grounds and ignored it in practice. In 1999, for example, U.S. military operations in Kosovo passed the sixtieth day. Bill Clinton did not seek a thirty-day extension. Thirty-two members of Congress and others brought the case to court to try and block continued military action. The court ruled that they did not have legal standing and dismissed it. A more recent controversy over the sixty-day limit came during the Obama administration when it argued that no report back to Congress was necessary since the operations being conducted in Libya did not qualify as "engaging in hostilities." Ten congressmen filed a lawsuit to end the military mission. Obama responded with a letter of explanation documenting that his administration had engaged in forty-six separate briefings with Congress on Libya.

Commerce Powers

The Constitution gives Congress the power to regulate commerce with foreign nations. In theory, this power belongs exclusively to Congress. In practice, power sharing between the two branches has been necessary. Congress may have the power to regulate foreign commerce, but only the president has the power to negotiate treaties.

Power sharing in the area of commerce has produced cooperation as well as conflict. The first innovative power-sharing arrangement is found in the 1934 Trade Agreements Act, by which Congress delegated to the president the authority to "implement into domestic law the results of trade agreements as they relate to tariffs." This authority greatly enhanced the president's power position in multilateral trade negotiations by removing the threat of congressional obstructionism in the formal approval and implementation of the negotiated agreement. Congress periodically renewed this grant of authority for a succession of presidents, changing only the time frame involved and the value of the reduction permitted and inserting legislative veto provisions.

The Trade Reform Act of 1974 introduced the second major innovative power-sharing arrangement when it created a "fast-track" reporting procedure. Under it, Congress was required to vote "yes" or "no" within ninety days on trade legislation that came before it and was prohibited from adding any amendments. Presidents have found it difficult to obtain this negotiating authority, now renamed "**trade promotional authority**." Legislators repeatedly have raised concerns over the lack of consultation between presidents and Congress. They also fear that presidents will enter into trade-offs in such areas as environmental protection, food safety, intellectual property rights, and labor standards in the name of furthering free trade. Proponents of fast-track authority argue that without it countries are unwilling to enter into agreements with the United States since Congress may reject or amend the agreements. They also argue that fast-track authority is valuable because it protects Congress from domestic trade protectionist pressures.

Bill Clinton was forced to allow his fast-track authority to lapse as part of the political price for getting the Senate to ratify the treaty establishing the World Trade Organization. In December 2001 the House of Representatives passed a bill restoring fast-track authority to George W. Bush by a vote of 215–214. Bush's fast-track authority expired on July 1, 2007. Obama succeeded in obtaining fast-track authority in 2015, but it did not come easily. It was seen by observers as necessary if the Trans Pacific Partnership and the Europe-focused Transatlantic Trade and Investment Partnership then being negotiated were to be approved by the Senate. The legislation gave fast-track authority to the president for three years, and it could be extended for an additional three years. Obama succeeded by forming a political coalition with the leadership of the congressional Republican Party. Lined up against them were Liberal Democrats and Tea Party Republicans.

Even before it was introduced Senate Democrats threatened a filibuster unless fast-track authority was combined with a separate bill that would require the president to take countermeasures against countries that manipulated their currencies to gain a trade advantage. The country most fitting this description is China. When they successfully blocked consideration of the bill giving him fast-track authority Obama quickly worked with Republican leaders and the few Senate Democrats who supported it to devise a new strategy. Under it the Senate would take a series of trade votes beginning with one on a trade enforcement bill that included provisions to punish currency manipulating countries (it passed 78–20). It would then vote on an African trade preference bill (it passed 97–1). Finally, it would vote on a separate fast-track bill that contained worked protection provisions (it passed 62–37). Efforts by opponents to include the currency provision in the bill failed by a 48–51 vote.

Supporters of the fast-track legislation agreed that the House and Senate had to pass the same bill, otherwise the conflicting bills would be sent to a conference committee and then resubmitted to the House and Senate for another round of votes, a situation they wanted to avoid. The House was expected to be an even tighter vote. Only 17 of 188 Democrats announced their support for fast-track authority. When the Senate bill came up for a vote in the House, Democrats voted against the worker protection provisions of the fast track authority bill as a way to defeat the bill even though they favored those provisions. The fast-track authority bill without the worker protection provisions then passed 219–211, but since it was different from the Senate bill the two would have to be reconciled in a conference committee. Once again fast-track supporters found it necessary to construct a complex package of votes to secure victory. Rather than send the two bills to the conference committee votes would be taken on what technically would be new bills. The House would first vote in favor of a stand-alone fast track authority bill which would be sent to the Senate where it would be approved. The Senate would then attach the worker protection legislation it had originally included in its bill to the African preferential trade bill and send it to the House where it would be approved. The strategy worked.

Congressional Structure and Foreign Policy

The four constitutionally based powers are brought to bear on foreign policy problems through Congress's internal structure and its standard operating procedures. In this section, we highlight four important by-products of these features: the reliance on blunt foreign policy tools, the absence of a single voice that can speak for Congress, the presence of policy entrepreneurs, and the significant power possessed by staff aides.

Historical Lesson

War Powers Act

The 1973 War Powers Resolution is the starting point for most contemporary discussions about the proper relationship between Congress and the president. It was a highly controversial piece of legislation when passed and continues to be so today. The bill was passed over President Nixon's veto. No president has yet recognized the constitutionality of the War Powers Resolution. Members of Congress and scholars have called for its repeal. Others have proposed amendments.

Crises in both foreign policy and domestic policy provided a highly charged backdrop for a multiyear political tug-of-war between Nixon, the House, and the Senate over the question of placing limits on the president's ability to deploy troops into combat upon his own authority and without prior consultation with Congress. The principal foreign policy crisis was the Vietnam War. Congress provided President Lyndon Johnson with the authority to take "all necessary measures" to repel any armed attack against the forces of the United States and to prevent further

aggression in the 1964 Gulf of Tonkin Resolution. The facts of this incident in which U.S. naval vessels were attacked by North Vietnamese forces remain contested even today. Johnson maintained that he did not need this congressional endorsement to carry out the U.S. war effort.

Nixon took the same position in continuing and expanding the war to include the 1970 invasion of Cambodia. On the domestic scene increased opposition to the Vietnam War and controversies surrounding the 1972 presidential election campaign created an electrifying political atmosphere that spurred congressional efforts to control presidential war powers. One incident was the 1972 Watergate break-in at the Democratic Party Headquarters and subsequent efforts to cover it up. A second was the October 1973 Saturday Night massacre in which Nixon's attorney general and his deputy both refused to fire Archibald Cox, who was the special prosecutor appointed to investigate the Watergate affair. Both of them along with Cox resigned in protest.

The Senate acted first. In 1969 it passed a resolution that proclaimed U.S. forces could not be committed to combat "only from affirmative action taken by the executive and legislative branches . . . by means of a treaty, statue, or concurrent resolution." In 1970 the House approved legislation that required presidents to report to Congress after they had placed troops into combat on the circumstances that led to this action and the scope of the military action being undertaken. A House Foreign Affairs subcommittee considered seventeen war powers bills and resolutions in putting forward the bill. No prior approval from Congress was required by the bill. The House passed the legation by a 2889–39 vote. Congress adjourned without the Senate taking any action.

In 1971 the House again passed this legislation. The Senate Foreign Relations Committee took up the proposed House bill. Its approach to limiting presidential war-making power was quite different. The legislation it sent forward specified conditions under which a president could commit troops to combat without congressional approval and set a time limit for how long such a deployment could last without gaining such approval. The competing House and Senate bills eventually went to a conference committee. Only one meeting took place and Congress adjourned without an agreement having been reached.

In 1972 both the House and Senate acted quickly to reintroduce their respective War Powers legislation. Significant points of disagreement remained over limiting the president's right to send troops into combat without prior consent and the timeline by which the president must report to Congress to gain its consent. The House had a 120-day reporting deadline while the Senate's deadline was 30 days. In July the competing versions of the bill again went to a conference committee. On October 4 it emerged and was approved by both the House (238–123) and the Senate (75–20). As promised, President Nixon vetoed the bill on October 24. There was no doubt that the Senate would vote to override Nixon's veto. The House vote was less certain. Presented as a vote that pitted congressional power against presidential power, the House voted to override Nixon's veto by 4 votes; 18 House members who voted against the bill nevertheless voted to override Nixon's veto while 15 who supported the bill supported Nixon's veto.

From the outset, the War Powers Resolution has been controversial. Senator Jacob Javits saw in it the basis for a new foreign policy compact between the president and Congress. Senator Thomas Eagleton, originally a supporter of the legislation with Javits, voted against it because he claimed that it gave the president powers he never had—the power to commit U.S. troops abroad without prior congressional approval.

Applying the Lesson

1. What does the War Powers Resolution case tell us about Congress's ability to influence the use of military force by the president?
2. Which is preferable: the War Powers Resolution or an Authorization of Military Force Resolution?
3. What is the proper role of Congress in making decisions about the use of military force?

Blunt Foreign Policy Tools

Foremost among the tools on which Congress relies to influence policy are its general legislative, budgetary, and oversight powers. Although these are formidable powers, Congress often finds itself frustrated in its efforts to fine-tune the U.S. foreign policy or give it a new sense of direction, because of their bluntness and essentially negative character.

General Legislative Powers Four basic forms of congressional action exist. Included are the simple resolution, which is a statement made by one house; the concurrent resolution, a statement passed by both houses; and the joint resolution, a statement made by both houses that is signed by the president. None of these carries the force of law; they are simply statements of opinion by Congress. Last, there is the legislative bill, which is passed by both houses and is signed by the president (or passed over the president's veto) and becomes law. Such was the case near the end of the Obama administration when just prior to the 2016 presidential election the Senate voted 97-to-1 and the House voted 348-to-77 to override Obama's veto of a bill that would allow families of those killed in the 9/11 attack to sue Saudi Arabia if it were found to have aided Al Qaeda. Obama had opposed it for setting a possibly dangerous precedent that other countries might use against U.S. in response to military or intelligence activities.

An early post–World War II study of Congress found that while presidential policy proposals were primarily presented as bills, congressionally initiated actions tended to be expressed as simple resolutions.[12] The situation today is much the same, although the volume of legislation that passes through Congress has grown exponentially. The 1960 edition of *Legislation on Foreign Relations* ran only 519 pages. The 2008 edition contained over 5,000 pages.

The challenges facing legislation originating in Congress is illustrated by the fate of comprehensive immigration reform. The foundational law governing U.S. immigration and citizenship policy is the 1952 McCarren-Walter Act. It was vetoed by President Truman for being un-American and discriminatory and then passed over his veto. The last comprehensive immigration reform legislation passed by Congress occurred in 1986 under the Reagan presidency.

Both George W. Bush and Barack Obama identified comprehensive immigration reform as high-priority items and failed. Under Bush the 2007 Comprehensive Immigration Reform Act was introduced in the Senate but never voted on. Earlier in Bush's presidency two other major pieces of immigration reform legislation were introduced. They ranged in length from some five hundred to eight hundred pages. One bill was introduced in the House. It was successfully passed out of three committees and passed by the full House in December 2005. A second bill was introduced in the Senate where bipartisan supporters of the bill were unable to invoke closure on the Senate debate on the bill. When it finally passed it was different from the House bill. When House and Senate leaders were unsuccessful in forming a conference committee to reconcile the differences between the two bills immigration legislation expired with the end of the congressional session.

After Obama's reelection a bipartisan group of eight senators sought to secure passage of a comprehensive immigration reform bill. In January 2014 Speaker of the House John Boehner indicated he was prepared to support such a bill only to reverse course the next month as Republican opposition to the bill held firm. With congressional action stalled, Obama then announced he would begin using his executive powers to bring about immigration reform. That plan came to a halt later in 2014 when a dramatic surge took place in the number of illegal border crossings which made immigration reform politically "toxic" for both parties.

"**Barnacles**" is the term often used to describe the amendments that Congress attaches to foreign policy legislation sought by the president.[13] One type of barnacle is to earmark or designate funds contained within a piece of legislation for a specific country. Foreign aid earmarks for Israel are among the most prominent and recurring examples of funds being designated for specific purposes. For example, the December 2010 budget resolution directed that $205 million be given to Israel to help construct a missile defense system. A different type of barnacle can be found in the House 2014 budget bill. It forbade the Obama administration from spending funds to transfer detainees at Guantanamo Bay to the United States and from U.S. military involvement in Syria unless it was approved by Congress.

Budgetary Powers Congress's budget powers are equally blunt and difficult to use. The omnibus spending bill passed by the House in January 2014 comprised funds found in twelve different spending bills. This situation reflects the fact that while the final decision on the overall budget ceiling is made by Congress as a whole, the budget is put together in multiple locations. Authorization decisions are made separately by the committees with legislative jurisdiction over the policy area. Appropriations decisions are made by the House and Senate Appropriations Committees and their subcommittees.

Three problems stand out for foreign and defense policy as a result of this process. The first is coherence. The 2014 omnibus defense spending bill marked the first time in four years that the House and Senate have agreed on budget resolution and were not funding defense and foreign policy spending through the use of continuing resolutions that leave such spending at the previous year's level. The year 2015 saw a return to past practices. In June the Senate passed a $600 billion defense policy bill that among other things would ban the use of torture and authorize the sale of lethal offensive weapons to the Ukraine. It then voted down a bill authorizing the government to spend money to pay for it.

The second problem is inconsistency in application. Foreign aid allocated by the State Department comes under far more scrutiny than that distributed by the Pentagon. In Afghanistan, for example, the State Department must verify among other things that the programs are sustainable and transparent, and that the Afghan government is taking steps to reduce corruption, empower women, and protect human rights before releasing its funds. The Pentagon faces no such constraints.

Third, it permits end runs. The primary vehicle is the Overseas Contingency Operations (OCO) account. It was created to fund temporary war-related costs in frontline states, most notably Afghanistan, Pakistan, and Iraq. But it has become used to fund war-related operations in places such as Yemen, the Horn of Africa, and the Philippines, where they might encounter serious objections if they surfaced in other spending bills. The OCO account is also not subject to the automatic budget cuts adopted by Congress in 2011. It was in large part because Congress included $39 billion more than he requested in the OCO account in the 2015 National Defense Authorization Act that Obama vetoed this bill. In 2016 Obama again threatened vetoes of both the House and Senate versions of the bill. Both bills provided for higher levels of defense spending than Obama wanted. The Senate version also contained a number of provisions which the administration said were unwarranted attempts to micromanage defense policy such as restricting his ability to transfer prisoners from the Guantanamo Bay military prison, setting conditions on establishing military relations with Cuba, and limiting the size of the National Security Council staff.

Box 6.1

Excerpt: House Resolution Authorizing the Use of Force Against Iraq, October 2, 2002

Section 1

This joint resolution may be cited as the "Authorization for the Use of Military Force Against Iraq."

Section 2: Support for United States Diplomatic Efforts

The Congress of the United States supports the efforts by the president to:

a. strictly enforce through the United Nations Security Council all relevant Security Council resolutions applicable to Iraq and encourages him in those efforts; and

b. obtain prompt and decisive action by the Security Council to ensure that Iraq abandons its strategy of delay, evasion and noncompliance and promptly and strictly complies with all relevant Security Council resolutions.

Section 3: Authorization for Use of United States Armed Forces

a. Authorization. The president is authorized to use the Armed Forces of the United States as he determines to be necessary and appropriate in order to

1. defend the national security of the United States against the continuing threat posed by Iraq; and

2. enforce all relevant United Nations Security Council Resolutions regarding Iraq.

b. Presidential determination. In connection with the exercise of the authority granted in subsection (a) to use force the president shall, prior to such exercise or as soon thereafter as may be feasible, but no later than 48 hours after exercising such authority, make available to the Speaker of the House of Representatives and the president pro tempore of the Senate his determination that

1. reliance by the United States on further diplomatic or other peaceful means alone either (A) will not adequately protect the national security of the United States against the continuing threat posed by Iraq or (B) is not likely to lead to enforcement of all relevant United Nations Security Council resolutions regarding Iraq, and

2. acting pursuant to this resolution is consistent with the United States and other countries continuing to take the necessary actions against international terrorists and terrorist organizations, including those nations, organizations or persons who planned, authorized, committed or aided the terrorists attacks that occurred on Sept. 11, 2001.

c. WAR powers resolution requirements.

1. Specific statutory authorization. Consistent with section 8(a)(1) of the War Powers Resolution, the Congress declares that this section is intended to constitute specific statutory authorization within the meaning of section 5(b) of the War Powers Resolution.

2. Applicability of other requirements. Nothing in this resolution supersedes any requirement of the War Powers Resolution.

Section 4: Reports to Congress

a. The president shall, at least once every 60 days, submit to the Congress a report on matters relevant to this joint resolution, including actions taken pursuant to the exercise of authority granted in section 2 and the status of planning for efforts that are expected to be required after such actions are completed, including those actions described in section 7 of Public Law 105338 (the Iraq Liberation Act of 1998).

b. To the extent that the submission of any report described in subsection (a) coincides with the submission of any other report on matters relevant to this joint resolution otherwise required to be submitted to Congress pursuant to the reporting requirements of Public Law 93-148 (the War Powers Resolution), all such reports may be submitted as a single consolidated report to the Congress.

c. To the extent that the information required by section 3 of Public Law 102-1 is included in the report required by this section, such report shall be considered as meeting the requirements of section 3 of Public Law 102-1.

An additional problem with using the budget as an instrument to shape the direction of U.S. foreign policy is that programs cost money but "policies" may not. What policies are able to do is raise expectations, place U.S. prestige on the line, or commit the United States to a course of action in the eyes of other states. Congress tends to find that it has little choice but to support— fund— the policy initiative, at least on a cosmetic basis. Senator John Kerry spoke to this point in expressing his opposition to the congressional resolution supporting the Persian Gulf War. He noted: "I hear it from one person after another—I do not want the President to look bad. . . . The President got us in this position. I am uncomfortable—but I cannot go against him."[14]

A final limitation of Congress's ability to use its budgetary powers to influence foreign policy lies with the implementation of congressional budgetary decisions. In 1971 Congress appropriated $700 million for a new manned bomber. The funds went unspent by the Nixon administration because it opposed the project. The reconstruction of Iraq provides another example of the limited ability of Congress's budgetary powers to influence the implementation of American foreign policy. In 2003 the Bush administration called for a quick infusion of money into Iraq to speed its recovery and transformation in the aftermath of the war. Yet in June 2004, just days before power was transferred to a new Iraqi government, none of the $500 million for health care, $400 million for roads and bridges, or $4.2 billion for water and sanitation improvements had been spent.

An ironic twist of the budgetary process is that Congress often makes foreign policy bureaucracies spend money in ways that they feel are wasteful. In 2010, 173 members of Congress, Republicans and Democrats, signed a letter to Secretary of Defense Leon Panetta in support of continuing production of the Abrams tank for which the House had included funds in the budget and which the army does not want to buy. Its preference is to pause production and stop buying tanks until 2017, when production of a newly designed tank would begin.

Oversight This refers to the actions of Congress regarding the bureaucratic implementation of policies. **Oversight** is no easy matter. Three major types of **reporting requirements** are traditionally used by Congress. One standard tool is to require government agencies to provide it with reports on their activities and events abroad. The 2015 annual State Department report on human trafficking placed twenty-three countries in Tier 3 which is defined as those countries whose policies do not meet minimum standards and who are not making an effort to improve. Included among them were Iran, Russia, Libya, Kuwait, and Venezuela. Its 2014 Religious Freedom Report cited Nigeria, Pakistan, Sri Lanka, Vietnam, China, Syria, Iran, India, and Burma for failures to respect religious freedom or take action to protect individuals from persecution by nonstate actors. Typically countries identified as not meeting U.S. performance standards in a policy area must be recertified in order to qualify for foreign aid and trade preferences. For example, a 1986 law requires that the State Department annually certify that recipients of U.S. foreign aid are "fully cooperating" in eradication efforts and the worldwide fight against drugs. Most of these reporting requirement penalties contain presidential escape clauses that allow the president to get around them.

A second type is the notification that a particular type of foreign policy action has been taken or will be taken. Most of these reports do not concern politically charged issues and involve changes in the distribution of foreign aid funds, arms sales, and arms control initiatives. One sensitive area involves covert action. As we note later in this chapter, the CIA is required to report covert actions to Congress. The military is not required to do so with its special operations and these have become increasingly common. It is partly for this reason that in 2014 Congress acted to prevent the Obama administration from shifting control of the drone antiterrorist campaign from the CIA to the Pentagon after it approved legislative language that required U.S. intelligence agencies to make this information public. The third type of reporting requirement is a onetime report. For example, in the 1986 Anti-Apartheid Act, Congress identified ten issues on which it wanted the president to furnish information.

An important variation on the idea of reporting requirements is found in congressional oversight of intelligence. Initially, there was little if any meaningful congressional control over the CIA. When asked if the committee he chaired had approved funding for a 36,000-man "secret" army in Laos, Senator Allen Ellender, chairperson of the Senate Appropriations CIA subcommittee, replied, "I did not know anything about it . . . I never asked. . . . It never dawned on me to ask about it. I did see it published in the newspaper some time ago."[15]

Beginning in 1974, Congress's attitude toward the intelligence community began to change.[16] One factor prompting the new outlook was a series of revelations about CIA wrongdoing and excess. The two most publicized ones implicated the CIA in a destabilization campaign directed at bringing down the socialist government of Salvador Allende in Chile and included allegations that the CIA had violated its charter by undertaking surveillance of U.S. citizens inside the United States. In their aftermath, Congress passed the Hughes-Ryan Amendment to the 1974 Foreign Assistance Act. It required that, except under exceptional circumstances, the CIA inform members of six congressional committees "in a timely fashion of the nature and scope of any CIA operation conducted for purposes other than obtaining information."

According to the terms of the Hughes-Ryan Amendment, the president was also required to make a "finding" that each covert operation is important to national security. **Presidential findings** have included such information as the time and duration of the activity, the risks involved, funding restrictions, their relationship to prior National Security Council (NSC) decisions, policy considerations, and the origin of the proposal.[17] This has not always meant that Congress has been well informed by the presidential finding. The presidential finding for the Iran arms transfers carried out by the NSC was signed after the operation began, and Director of Central Intelligence William Casey was instructed not to inform Congress. This is presented in Box 6.2. The 1975 presidential finding supporting U.S. activities in Angola was so vague that only Africa was identified as the location of the operation. The stated purpose was to provide "material, support, and advice to moderate nationalist movements for their use in creating a stable climate in order to allow genuine self-determination."[18]

There is nothing automatic about information being furnished to Congress by the intelligence community or other agencies. One controversial case involves a Senate Intelligence Committee study of interrogation at Guantanamo Bay. In 2012 the committee sent the report to the CIA and other agencies for comment and verification. In June 2013 new CIA director John Brennan delivered a 122-page rebuttal to the report's conclusion that the interrogations had produced little valuable intelligence. Committee member Senator Mark Udall then revealed in December that the committee had learned that the CIA's own internal supported many of the findings of the committee's report. Brennan, in response to questioning by Udall, denied that such a review existed (calling it a summary) or that he had read it.

> ### Box 6.2
>
> ## Presidential Finding on CIA Involvement in Arms Shipments to Iran
>
> I hereby find that the following operation in a foreign country (including all support necessary to such operation) is important to the national security of the United States, and due to its extreme sensitivity and security risks, I determine it is essential to limit prior notice, and direct the Director of Central Intelligence to refrain from reporting this Finding to the Congress as provided in Section 501 of the National Security Act of 1947, as amended, until I otherwise direct.
>
> Scope
> Iran
>
> ### Description
>
> Assist selected friendly foreign liaison services, third countries, which have established relationships with Iranian elements, groups, and individuals] sympathetic to U.S. Government interests and which do not conduct or support terrorist actions directed against U.S. persons, property, or interests for the purpose of: (1) establishing a more moderate government in Iran, and (2) obtaining from them significant intelligence not otherwise obtainable, to determine the current Iranian Government's intentions with respect to its neighbors and with respect to terrorist acts, [and (3) furthering the release of the American hostages held in Beirut and preventing additional terrorist acts by these groups.][19] Provide funds, intelligence, counterintelligence, training, guidance and communications, and other necessary assistance to these elements, groups, individuals, liaison services and third countries in support of these activities. The USG will act to facilitate efforts by third parties and third countries to establish contact with moderate elements within and outside the Government of Iran by providing these elements with arms, equipment, and related material in order to enhance the credibility of these elements in their effort to achieve a more pro-U.S. government in Iran by demonstrating their ability to obtain requisite resources to defend their country against Iraq and intervention by the Soviet Union. This support will be discontinued if the U.S. Government learns that these elements have abandoned their goals of moderating their government and appropriated the material for purposes other than that [sic] provided by this finding.
>
> Source: President's Special Review Board, *The Tower Commission Report* (New York: Bantam, 1987), 217–18.

The Absence of a Single Voice

Traditionally, the work of Congress was done in committees. It was here that the political deals were made and the technical details of legislation were worked out. Congress as a whole was expected to quietly and expeditiously give its consent to committee decisions, and more often than not, it did. Beginning in the early 1970s, the focus of decision-making shifted from the full committee to the subcommittee. The result has been an even greater decentralization of Congress, which is visible in a number of ways.

First, there is the increased attention that the executive branch must give to the foreign policy views of all members of Congress because foreign-policy-relevant legislation now springs from a greater variety of sources. In 2000 legislation allowing the sale of food to Cuba was part of an agricultural spending bill. A prohibition on spending funds for planning related to the Kyoto Protocol was inserted as an amendment to an appropriations bill for the Environmental Protection Agency. As one State Department official put it, "It used to be that all one had to do was contact the chairman and a few ranking members of a committee, now all 435 members plus 100 senators have to be contacted."[20] Second, there is the growing tendency for prospective pieces of legislation to be referred to more than one committee. Multiple referrals are necessary because of the lack of fit between the jurisdictions of congressional committees and policy areas. This is true for new and old policy areas. At least three Senate committees and seven subcommittees claim jurisdiction over cybersecurity. A dozen Senate committees are involved in foreign economic policy, and nearly fifty subcommittees are involved in foreign policy regarding the Third World.[21] Finally, there is the potential for comments made by individual members of Congress to foreign policy problems. In 2011 a House Foreign Affairs subcommittee was on an investigative trip to Iraq. While there, Representative Dana Rohrabacher told the prime minister that his committee was investigating the killing of Iraqi dissidents by government forces. He told the press this probably was a crime against humanity. The government immediately demanded that the entire delegation leave Iraq. The following year the Obama administration asked him to cancel a planned visit to Afghanistan for fear his sharp criticism of President Hamid Karzai would undermine relations with his government and undercut U.S. efforts to start peace talks with the Taliban.

Policy Entrepreneurship

A change in attitude has accompanied the trend toward increasing decentralization. Policy individualism has replaced party loyalty as the motivation behind much congressional action. As a result, the long-standing congressional norms of deference and apprenticeship have been replaced by expectations of power sharing and policy input. "Entrepreneurship" is the label frequently attached to this new outlook. A **policy entrepreneur** is someone who is looking for opportunities to make political capital out of policy gaps.[22] Many saw policy entrepreneurship in the establishment of a select committee to investigate the Benghazi attacks six months before the midterm elections amid repeated allegations that the Obama administration gave a "stand down" order to a potential rescue mission to Benghazi. Prior investigations into the incident, including one by Congress, found no evidence to support the charge. This conclusion was reinforced by comments made by Republican House Majority Leader Kevin McCarthy in 2105 after the committee turned its attention to Hillary Clinton's use of her personal e-mail server as secretary of state, a position she held at the time of the Benghazi attack while secretary of state. In TV interviews he stated that the hearings had achieved its desired results as Hillary Clinton's positive image in polling about democratic presidential candidates had declined.

The entrepreneur is different from the traditional foreign policy "**gadfly**," who raises issues to influence the terms of the policy debate and is concerned with long-term policy gains.[23] Gadflies are found across the political spectrum. Among the most outspoken gadflies today are John McCain and Ron Paul. McCain was a strong backer of more open and forceful support for Libyan rebels who opposed Muammar Gaddafi and made a highly visible surprise visit to Benghazi to help their cause. He would later travel to Syria, where he called for U.S. military intervention to support the rebels. For his part, Paul has been a leading congressional critic of the NSA electronic surveillance program. In 2015 he sought to prevent reauthorization of the Patriot Act by speaking for almost eleven hours.

Staff Aides

A shortage of information has always been a problem for Congress when it comes to making foreign policy. Few members can hope to acquire the background and expertise to understand the full range of topics that may come before them. The emergence of numerous and well-informed staff aides has given the problem a new focus.[24] The problem is no longer just one of acquiring needed information from the executive branch or party leaders. It is also now one of using information in a controlled and coherent fashion. In 1947 there were roughly five hundred committee and two thousand personal staffers. By the 1990s the House was employing some eleven thousand staffers and the Senate another six thousand. The major House and Senate foreign policy committees (Armed Services and Foreign Affairs/Foreign Relations) each have over fifty staffers.

Concerns have been expressed about whether (1) the staffers are serving Congress or just leading willing members from issue to issue and (2) an activist staff might be overloading Congress with new issues, thereby robbing it of the time needed for debate and deliberation. As evidence of these dangers many site the frequency with which staffers travel abroad on information trips at the expense of foreign governments. From 2006 to 2011 staffers reported taking 803 trips to foreign countries. China was the primary destination: More than 200 trips were taken there at the expense of the Chinese government or a foundation that received funding from U.S. businesses such as Wal-Mart. In 2013 ten members of Congress and thirty-two staffers went on an all-expense-paid trip to a conference at a resort on the Caspian Sea that was paid for by the state-owned oil company of Azerbaijan. Air fare was estimated to cost $112,899 with gifts received ranging from $2,500 to $10,000. In 2012 this oil company was one of several that sought to be exempted from U.S. economic sanctions imposed on Iran for a Caspian Sea natural gas pipeline project they were engaged in.

Congress as a whole has also increased its information-gathering and information-processing capabilities by establishing or increasing the size of the Congressional Research Service (established in 1914), the Government Accountability Office (which dates back to 1921 under a different name), and the Congressional Budget Office (1974). Representatives and senators can also draw on the products of private nonprofit research institutes and think tanks such as the Brookings Institution, the Cato Institute, and the Heritage Foundation.[25]

Until the 1970s, think tanks were relatively few in number. Today, they are prominent fixtures on the Washington, DC, political landscape.

Influence of Party and Region

It is clear that the difficulty Congress has speaking with one voice on foreign policy greatly complicates its efforts at efficiency. We can bring this difficulty into even greater focus by examining the influence of party and region on foreign policy decisions. The overwhelming majority of votes occur along party lines, and this tendency has become more pronounced since the 1980s. Strong as it may be, party affiliation cannot withstand all of the competing pressures that representatives and senators face when they vote.

Republicans largely deserted George W. Bush on two major issues in 2007. The first was immigration reform, where a coalition of Republicans and Democrats united to allow a filibuster to continue and block consideration of reform legislation supported by the president. The second issue was the Iraq War, where a series of Republican senators led by Richard Lugar and Pete Domenici called for a policy change. In 2015 Republicans split over the future of the Export-Import Bank. Tea Party Republicans favored terminating it characterizing it as wasteful spending and an example of crony capitalism. The pro-business wing of the party saw it as vital to the success of American firms trying to compete in the global marketplace. Democrats are not immune from internal divisions. As we noted earlier, Democrats largely deserted Obama in his quest for fast-track authority.

Splits within the Republican and Democratic parties are a recurring problem. In the late 1990s senior Republican leaders embraced an internationalist outlook rooted in Cold War foreign policy triumphs, while more junior Republicans tended to have a different worldview.[26] They opposed supporting loan guarantees to Mexico and expensive new weapons systems, favored privatization of foreign aid, and showed little interest in bipartisan resolutions supporting the president in Bosnia or elsewhere.

The arrival of Tea Party members into Congress after the fall 2010 election has accentuated this split. A revolt against Republican leadership by its members defeated legislation that would have extended the provisions of the Patriot Act for one year. This necessitated introducing the bill a second time to get it passed. Tea Party members also tend to be "budget hawks" who are less willing to spare the defense budget from cuts than is the party leadership as a whole. This divide was quite visible as Congress grappled with how to respond to Obama's call for a vote on military action in Syria. Traditional conservative hawks led by McCain supported it, while noninterventionist Republicans led by Paul opposed it.

The Democratic Party is beset with its own internal struggles on foreign policy that have split conservatives and liberals. This came through quite clearly in the conflict over revelations that the National Security Agency had engaged in a covert electronic communications collection program that gathered data on Americans. Democratic Senator Dianne Feinstein, chair of the Senate Intelligence Committee, strongly supported the NSA. Democratic committee members Mark Udall and Ron Wyden were vocal opponents of the program, arguing that it violated the Fourth Amendment.

One area where partisanship appears to trump all other factors in influencing congressional involvement in foreign policy involves controlling presidential war powers.[27] The single best predictor of whether or not Congress will remain quiet or vocally oppose presidential calls for war is its partisan composition. When the opposition party is in control, Congress raises its voice. Congressional opposition inspired by party politics may not prevent a president from acting, but it is capable of raising the political costs of military action and leading presidents to alter their plans or abandon them entirely. It was, thus, not surprising that Obama ran into difficulties with Congress over his refusal to cite the War Powers Resolution in 2011 when the United States helped establish a no-fly zone in Libya or in his efforts to get Congress to obtain AUMF resolutions for air strikes in Syria and against ISIS.

Geographic interests are also significant factors in influencing congressional votes. Today, as in the past, U.S. involvement in the global economy has an uneven impact on different areas of the country and produces regional conflict over how to define the American national interest.[28] Thus, U.S. foreign policy can be seen as driven by a coalition of the South and the West, regions that benefit from a foreign policy designed to promote free trade and assure international stability. Opposed to it is the Northeast, which, though it once benefited from such policies, now sees itself as economically disadvantaged by them and favors protectionism and cuts in defense spending. Geography and economics also come together to influence foreign policy votes in other ways. Those representing districts negatively affected by foreign imports from oppressive regimes raise human rights issues more so than do those whose districts rely more heavily on foreign markets.[29]

Members of Congress are also especially protective of how their constituents fare in receiving government funds. Senator Henry "Scoop" Jackson, who sat on the Armed Services Committee, was known as the "Senator from Boeing" for his ability to steer aircraft contracts to the Boeing Company, which was headquartered in Washington. This concern for "pork" extends beyond the committee system. At one time, the contract for the B-1 bomber had 400 subcontracts in over 400 of the 435 districts of the House.

Outsourcing Foreign Policy

With increasing frequency Congress has turned to another mechanism for overcoming the many forces that impede efficiency in making policy and exercising oversight: the special commission. These may be composed of outside experts, retired government officials, or handpicked members of Congress. Commissions deal with the inefficiency problem in a number of ways. First, the appointment of a commission represents a positive symbolic response to a perceived foreign policy problem. Second, it allows Congress to proceed in a non-accusatory fashion, thereby dampening the flames of partisanship. Commissions take political pressure off policy makers by providing them with political cover for making difficult decisions. Third, commissions provide an opportunity for educating the public and for information gathering that extends beyond the closed network of congressional staffers, committee and subcommittee chairs, and executive branch officials.

Commissions have been created to deal with several different types of problems. One type is formed to investigate and make recommendations on a particular policy issue or problem. The National Commission on Terrorist Attacks upon the United States (the 9/11 Commission) was this type of committee. A second type of committee is set up to investigate and report back on an ongoing problem. The Commission on Wartime Contracting is such a commission. Of particular concern to this commission have been questions of waste, fraud, and financial abuse stemming from the increased use of private contractors in combat theaters. The third type of committee is created to provide Congress with a policy option(s) to deal with a problem. The Defense Base Realignment and Closure (BRAC) Commission was created for this purpose. Closing military bases is a politically unpopular decision given the economic impact it would have on local communities but a necessary budget move when combined with the military realities of downsizing the armed forces. Rather than have Congress identify which bases to cut, the BRAC Commission was established. Five BRAC rounds have taken place, in 1988, 1991, 1993, 1995, and 2005. More than 350 military installations have been closed by this process.

Establishing a commission is no guarantee that the problem will be solved, or even that its recommendations will be listened to or even welcomed. Virginia Senator John Warner, in objecting to the BRAC Commission's recommendation to shut down major facilities in Virginia, referred to its decision-making process as "rigged." In 2012 the Pentagon requested two new BRAC rounds. Not only did Congress not vote to establish these new rounds, but the House Armed Services Committee added a provision to the budget forbidding the Pentagon from spending any funds "to propose, plan or execute" the base closing process. Many of the recommendations of the 9/11 Commission were ignored. The December 2005 "report card" issued by members of the 9/11 Commission gave the administration five Fs and 12 Ds for its follow-through in implementing its recommendations. It received only one A, and that was for its antiterrorism finance efforts.[30]

Not all are pleased with this increasingly frequent use of commissions. Senator Trent Lott addressed the Senate on September 23, 2002, on the subject of special commissions, specifically the creation of the 9/11 Commission. He observed that, in his opinion, congressional commissions were "an abdication of responsibility." Why, he wondered, "do we have an Armed Services Committee, an Intelligence Committee, a Government Affairs Committee, or a Foreign Affairs Committee?"[31]

Congress and the President: The Changing Relationship

The relationship between Congress and the president is not static. Viewed over time, congressional-presidential relations have shown a great deal of variation. One way to capture the changing relationship is by looking at the degree to which Congress has been assertive and active in its dealings with the president on foreign policy matters.[32] Combining these two dimensions produces four patterns. A *competitive* Congress is both active and assertive in foreign policy and thus quite willing to challenge a president's lead. A *disengaged* Congress is neither active nor assertive and tends to readily follow a president's foreign policy preferences. A *supportive* Congress is one that is active but not aggressive. It cooperates with the president on a broad range of foreign policy initiatives without challenging him. Finally, a *strategic* Congress is not particularly active but is willing and capable of challenging a president on specific issues that conflict with its foreign policy agenda.

From the end of World War II until about 1958, a *supportive Congress* existed. Relations between the two branches were largely harmonious. Bipartisanship was the order of the day. The president was the acknowledged architect of American foreign policy, and Congress's role was to reaffirm his policy initiatives and provide him with the means to act. Often its participation took on a plebiscitary character, with the passage of area resolutions such as those on the Middle East, Taiwan, and Latin America. Periods of dissent did occur, such as after the "loss of China" and during the McCarthy hearings, but overall, the Cold War consensus held.

The next decade, 1958–68, saw the emergence of a *strategic Congress*. The Cold War principles around which the earlier bipartisan consensus was built had begun to fray. Congress was not in open revolt against the president; proclamations of support were still present, most notably for the Gulf of Tonkin Resolution, and failures such as the Bay of Pigs did not evoke partisan attacks. But pockets of resistance had now formed, and Congress did move to challenge the president selectively. Two key points of confrontation were the Vietnam War and the existence of a missile gap.

From 1968 into the mid-1980s, Congress was both active and assertive. This *competitive Congress* not only sought to limit the president's ability to conduct foreign policy by passing such measures as the War Powers Resolution and the Case-Zablocki Act, but it also resisted many of the president's most important foreign policy initiatives. The Jackson-Vanik Amendment undermined Nixon's détente policy, Carter was challenged on the Panama Canal Treaties, and Ford was rebuffed on an arms sales agreement to Turkey.

The period from the mid-1980s until September 11, 2001, marked a return to a *strategic Congress*. Once again, Congress selectively engaged the president on foreign policy issues. In some cases, such as the annual vote on most favored nation status for China, the interactions became almost ritualistic. On other occasions, such as the Comprehensive Nuclear Test Ban Treaty, ratification of NAFTA, and granting of fast-track trade authority, the conflicts were highly partisan and spirited.

The terrorist attacks of 9/11 led to the emergence of a *disengaged Congress*, one that was willing to cede the authority to make crucial foreign policy decisions to the president. Nowhere is this more evident than in George W. Bush's ability to obtain an AUMF resolution from Congress against Iraq by votes of 77–23 in the Senate and 296–133 in the House. Congress was not totally compliant, but it did not directly challenge the president. Objections to the Bush administration's proposed language authorizing the president "to use all means that he determined to be appropriate" were addressed in behind-the-scenes meetings and led to mutually acceptable language being found. This disengaged Congress did not last long. It soon showed signs of moving back toward a *strategic Congress*, which by 2005 was firmly in place as Bush and Congress began to spar regularly over the conduct of the Iraq War.

By the end of Obama's presidency a *competitive Congress* had reemerged. With increasing intensity Congress and Obama found themselves at odds over virtually every administration foreign policy initiative with Congress often acting in a preemptive manner as highlighted by three examples from 2015.

In March, Israeli prime minister Benjamin Netanyahu addressed a joint session of Congress at the invitation of House Speaker John Boehner. Obama was not consulted on the invitation, and in his speech Netanyahu spoke out strongly against a nuclear arms agreement with Iran. Also in March forty-seven Republican senators sent an open letter to Iranian leaders telling them that any agreement they reached with Obama on nuclear weapons without congressional approval could be reversed by the next president. In December, hours after Obama promised world leaders at the Paris climate conference that the United States would be in the leading in responding to global climate change the House passed a resolution already approved by the Senate to prevent the Environmental Protection Agency from taking action to enforce tighter standards.

Indicative of both the difficulty that the Congress and the president have in working together when Congress adopts a competitive orientation and evidence that it can be done is the innovative way in which Congressional participation in approving the Iranian nuclear accord was handled. Obama initially had claimed he had the authority to enter into a nuclear agreement with Iran without congressional approval. This proved to be a politically untenable and after threatening to veto legislation giving Congress a voice Obama agreed to a compromise. According to the terms of the compromise Iran Nuclear Review Act the administration had to submit its agreement with Iran to Congress as soon as it was completed along with classified material. Congress then had sixty days within which to review it at which point Congress either voted its approval or disapproval of lifting congressionally imposed sanctions. If Congress voted to disapprove of the agreement, Obama had twelve days to decide whether or not to veto it, and if he used his veto power Congress got ten days to attempt to override the veto. Finally, if the agreement went into effect the president had to submit periodic reports to Congress on Iran's ballistic missile program and its support for terrorism. Not long after Obama and congressional leaders agreed upon this compromise a revolt within the Republican Party threatened to undermine it. Killer amendments were unsuccessfully proposed including ones that Iran recognize Israel and that the Iran nuclear agreement be defined as a treaty which would require a two-thirds affirmative vote by Congress.

Structured this way, the agreement allowed Congress to exercise its voice, which all assumed would be to reject the agreement but at the same time gave Obama the upper political hand since his veto of a disapproval resolution would be difficult to overcome. In fact, Obama obtained a veto proof majority in the Senate before it voted 58–42 against the agreement guaranteeing it would go into effect.

Over the Horizon: A New War Powers Act?

The fundamental problem facing Congress in exercising its foreign policy voice in the future will continue to be the challenge of managing the contradictory pressures for efficiency and participation. Nowhere does this challenge appear more difficult to resolve than in the exercise of congressional and presidential war powers. The focal point of the debate over how to proceed is, as it has been from its coming into law in 1973, the War Powers Act. Obama's repeated interest in obtaining AUMF resolutions is seen as potentially complicating future debates over the reach of the War Powers Resolution and likely raising the political cost to a president who does not go to Congress or acts against its wishes in using force.

In 2014 Senators Tim Kane and John McCain put forward the War Powers Consultation Act which they characterized as bipartisan legislation to strengthen the ineffective the consultative process that currently exists between Congress and the president on whether and when to engage in military action. It was based upon a 2008 bipartisan National War Powers Commission report.[32] Among its key provisions was that the president must consult with Congress before deploying U.S. troops into significant armed conflict; the creation of a permanent Joint Congressional Consultation Committee; and a congressional yes/no vote on significant armed conflicts within thirty days.

For some this did not go far enough. In November 2014 Senator Rand Paul called for Congress to vote on a declaration to proclaim war against ISIS. His declaration would have limited military action to one year and placed significant restrictions on the use of ground forces.

A very different challenge to the president's power to engage in war with ISIS came in May 2016 when Army Captain Nathan Michael Smith, who supports the war effort, brought a lawsuit against President Obama arguing that he lacked proper authorization from Congress to wage a war against ISIS. Along with prior AUMF the Obama administration could argue that as with the Vietnam War and other military conflicts Congress has implicitly authorized the war by providing money for fighting it. The consequences of such a suit are hard to predict. In late November, after the 2016, election a federal judge rejected the suit asserting that it was not a matter for the courts to decide but one that Congress and the president must determine.

Critical Thinking Questions

1. Is there a need for a new War Powers Act?
2. Is party identification or geography (what state or district they represent) a more important influence on how members of Congress vote on foreign policy issues?
3. What changes would you make to Congress's internal structure and operating procedures to make its voice more effective in foreign policy?

Key Terms

barnacles, 146

gadfly, 153

legislative veto, 140

oversight, 145

policy entrepreneur, 143

presidential finding, 150

ratify, 135

reporting requirement, 149

trade promotional authority, 141

War Powers Resolution, 141

Further Reading

Michael Allen, *Blinking Red* (Washington, DC: Potomac Books, 2013).

This book chronicles the often tense and combative congressional politics which went into the creation of the Office of the Director of National Intelligence following the 9/11 attacks.

Colton Campbell, Nicol Rae, and John Stack, Jr., (eds.), *Congress and the Politics of Foreign Policy* (Upper Saddle River, NJ: Prentice Hall, 2003).

Collectively, the essays in this volume examine the changing pattern of congressional-presidential interactions over foreign policy. Increasing congressional assertiveness is a key dimension to this relationship.

Linda Fowler, *Watchdogs on the Hill* (Princeton: Princeton University Press, 2015).

This book examines the decline of congressional oversight of U.S. foreign policy. Using case studies she attributes this decline to several factors. The author argues for the importance of oversight in generating information for the public and proposes reforms to improve oversight.

Louis Henkin, *Foreign Affairs and the Constitution* (Mineola, NY: Foundation Press, 1972).

This classic account looks at American foreign policy making from a constitutional perspective that emphasizes the distribution of powers in the Constitution and the legislative legacy that follows from it.

William Howell and Jon Pevehouse, *While Dangers Gather: Congressional Checks on Presidential War Powers* (Princeton, NJ: Princeton University Press, 2007).

Relying on both quantitative and case study analyses, the authors argue that a full understanding of the conditions under which Congress challenges the president's war powers must examine both formal legislative action and informal actions on the part of Congress.

John Kyl, Douglas Feith, and John Fonte, "War of Law," *Foreign Affairs* 92 (July 2013), 115–25.

This article defends congressional record of rejecting treaties and international agreements on the ground that international law subverts U.S. sovereignty and lessens accountability of the government to voters.

Jordan Tama, "Independent Commissions as Settings for Civil-Military Deliberation," *Armed Forces and Society* 42 (April 2016), 407–26.

This article examines the activities and impact of three independent advisory commissions established by Congress to examine issues related to women in the military.

Notes

[1] Norman Ornstein and Thomas Mann, "When Congress Checks Out," *Foreign Affairs* 85 (2006), 67–82.

[2] Douglas Bennett Jr., "Congress in Foreign Policy: Who Needs It?" *Foreign Affairs* 57 (1978), 40–50.

3 For a statement of this position, see Jon Kyl, Douglas Feithr, and John Fonte, "The War of Law: How New International Law Undermines Democratic Sovereignty," *Foreign Affairs* 92 (2013), 115–25.

4 David Auerswald and Forrest Maltzman, "Policymaking through Advice and Consent: Treaty Consideration by the United States Senate," *Journal of Politics* 65 (2003), 1102.

5 Ibid., 1097–110; C. James DeLaet and James M. Scott, "Treaty-Making and Partisan Politics: Arms Control and the U.S. Senate, 1960–2001," *Foreign Policy Analysis* 2 (2006), 177–200.

6 See David Auerswald, "Senate Reservations to Security Treaties," *Foreign Policy Analysis* 2 (2006), 83–100.

7 William L. Furlong, "Negotiations and Ratification of the Panama Canal Treaty," in John Spanier and Joseph Nogee (eds.), *Congress, the Presidency, and American Foreign Policy* (Elmsford: Pergamon, 1981), 77–107.

8 Matthew Weed, The War Powers Resolution (Washington, DC, Congressional Research Service, April 3, 2015), https://www.fas.org/sgp/crs/natsec/R42699.pdf.

9 The report can be found at https://www.whitehouse.gov/the-press-office/2015/06/11/letter-president-six-month-consolidated-war-powers-resolution-report.

10 On the Iraq War, see Louis Fisher, "Deciding on War against Iraq," *Political Science Quarterly* 118 (2003), 389–410; Fisher, "Presidential Wars," in Eugene Wittkopf and James McCormick (eds.), *The Domestic Sources of American Foreign Policy*, 4th ed. (Lanham: Rowman & Littlefield, 2004), 155–70.

11 Congressional Research Service, *Foreign Policy Effects of the Supreme Court's Legislative Veto Decision* (Washington, DC: Congressional Research Service, February 23, 1984).

12 James A. Robinson, *Congress and Foreign Policy Making: A Study in Legislative Influence and Initiative* (Homewood: Dorsey, 1962), 110.

13 I. M. Destler, "Dateline Washington: Congress as Boss," *Foreign Policy* 42 (1981), 161–80.

14 *The Congressional Record*, January 11, 1991, S250–S251.

15 Quoted in Victor Marchetti and John Marks, *The CIA and the Cult of Intelligence* (New York: Dell, 1980), 324.

16 For an account of why little has really changed, see Amy Zegart, "The Domestic Politics of Irrational Intelligence Oversight," *Political Science Quarterly* 126 (2011), 1–25.

17 William Corson, *Armies of Ignorance: The Rise of the American Intelligence Empire* (New York: Dial, 1977), 472.

18 John Stockwell, *In Search of Enemies* (New York: Norton, 1978), 47.

19 Point (3) did not appear in the first draft.

20 Roger H. Davidson, "Subcommittee Government: New Channels for Policy Making," in Thomas E. Mann and Norman J. Ornstein (eds.), *The New Congress* (Washington, DC: American Enterprise Institute, 1981), 130.

21 Thomas L. Brewer, *American Foreign Policy: A Contemporary Introduction*, 2nd ed. (Englewood Cliffs, NJ: Prentice Hall, 1986), 119.

22 David Price, *Who Makes the Laws?* (Cambridge, MA: Schenkman, 1972), 330.

23 Joshua Muravchik, *The Senate and National Security: A New Mood*, Washington Paper #80 (Beverly Hills: Sage, 1980), 57–60.

24 For a discussion of congressional staffs, see Michael J. Malbin, "Delegation, Deliberation, and the New Role of Congressional Staff," in Mann and Ornstein (eds.), *The New Congress*, 134–77; Muravchik, *The Senate and National Security*.

25 James A. Smith, *The Idea Brokers: Think Tanks and the Rise of the New Policy Elite* (New York: Free Press, 1991); David Newsom, *The Public and Foreign Policy* (Bloomington: Indiana University Press, 1996).

26 James Kitfield, "The Folk Who Live on the Hill," *National Interest* 58 (1999/2000), 48–55.

27 William Howell and Jon Pevehouse, "When Congress Stops Wars," *Foreign Affairs* 96 (2007), 95–107.

28 Peter Trubowitz, *Defining the National Interest* (Chicago: University of Chicago Press, 1998).

[29] Ellen Cutrone and Benjamin Fordham, "Commerce and Imagination," *International Studies Quarterly* 54 (2010), 633–56.

[30] Dan Eggen, "U.S. Is Given Failing Grades by 9/11 Panel," *Washington Post*, December 6, 2006, A1.

[31] Trent Lott, "Special Commissions," *Congressional Record*, September 23, 2002, S9050–S9053.

[32] James Scott and Ralph Carter, "Acting on the Hill," *Congress and the Presidency* 29 (2002), 151–69; Ralph Carter and James Scott, "Striking a Balance: Congress and U.S. Foreign Policy," in Steven Hook and James Scott (eds.), *American Foreign Policy Today: American Renewal?* (Washington, DC: CQ Press, 2012), 36–53.

[33] Miller Center of Public Affairs, University of Virginia, *National War Powers Commission Report* (2008).

Presidency 7

Dateline: Obama's First 100 Days

Presidential performance in foreign policy, as well as in domestic policy, can be judged by any of a number of different standards. One that continues to be embraced is what did they accomplish in their first 100 days? It builds on a sense of high expectations (and sometimes fear) that the newly elected president will move quickly to implement campaign promises. Here, we look at Barack Obama's first 100 days (January 20–April 29, 2009) as a point of reference for evaluating President Trump's first 100 days of making foreign policy.

On January 22 Obama issued an executive order that the Guantanamo Bay prison be closed within one year, something Congress prevented him from doing, and declared that the United States would not engage in torture or other coercive interrogation techniques including waterboarding. The following day Obama also announced he was reversing the Mexico City policy under which the United States did not fund international organizations that performed or provided information on abortions. Later that week Obama would be interviewed on Arab television news and state "Americans are not your enemy."

On February 27 Obama announces that all U.S. combat forces will leave Iraq by August 2010 but that some ten thousand support troops would remain behind carrying out training and support missions. One month later, on March 27, Obama announced a comprehensive review of U.S. military strategy in Afghanistan and Pakistan along with a decision to send some four thousand military trainers to Afghanistan. On April 9 he asked Congress for an additional $83.4 billion for military and diplomatic operations in Iraq and Afghanistan.

President Obama did not make his first visit to a foreign country until February 19, 2009, when traveled to Canada. His first extended trip abroad did not occur until late March to early April. On March 31 he began an eight day-six country tour of Europe and the Middle East. His first stop was Great Britain where the G-20 economic summit was being held. Prior to the start of that conference he met with Russian president Dmitry Medvedev. They announced the start of negotiations on a new strategic arms control treaty. From there Obama went to Strasbourg where a NATO summit took place. At that meeting Obama obtained a pledge from NATO to send an additional five thousand military trainers and police to Afghanistan. Next Obama went to Prague where he gave a speech on the need for ridding the world of nuclear weapons. Before returning to the United States he also went to Turkey where he addressed its parliament assuring them that "the United States is not, and will never be, at war with Islam," and made a surprise visit to U.S. troops in Iraq where he also met with Iraqi leaders.

Obama returned to the United States and on April 13 announced that Cuban Americans would now be permitted to transfer unlimited sums of money to relatives in Cuba and make trips to visit them. His executive order also permitted American first to provide high technology and information services in Cuba. Three days later Obama made his first trip to Mexico where he met with Mexican president Felipe Calderon to discuss the problem of drug violence along the U.S.-Mexico border. On April 18 Obama attended the Summit of the Americas meeting in Trinidad and Tobago where he called for a new beginning in U.S. relations with Cuba. At the summit he shook hands with Venezuelan president Hugo Chavez who once referred to George W. Bush as a devil.

The historical record suggests that focusing too heavily on a president's first 100 days is not necessarily a good indicator of what foreign policy is to come in the 1,361 days that follow. Yet the standard will continue to be used and comparisons made. In this chapter, we look at the president and foreign policy from various perspectives to give us a better foundation from which to make evaluations. We first look at the president's constitutional powers. Then we turn our attention to the president as a person and then to the presidency as an institution.

Weak President or Strong President

For those who see the president as a weak leader, they often appear to be little more than a clerk because they lack the power to command others to act and must instead rely on the ability to persuade.[1] Far from running the government, the president struggles simply to comprehend what is going on.[2] Information does not come to presidents automatically, nor can they count on speed and secrecy in making and carrying out decisions. In 2003 George W. Bush had a conversation with Secretary of Defense Donald Rumsfeld and Jerry Brenner, who headed the Coalition Provisional Authority in Iraq. Bush asked who was in charge of finding weapons of mass destruction in Iraq. Rumsfeld said Brenner was; Brenner said Rumsfeld was.[3]

This view is challenged by those who see the president as at least potentially a strong and powerful leader, capable of unilateral action.[4] By acting first and alone they argue the president places political competitors in the position of having to undo what they have just done. Unilateral presidential action is not a matter of presidents usurping congressional powers as much as it is being able to take advantage of ambiguities in the constitutional distribution of powers, the existence of vaguely worded and ambiguous legislative language, and the inherent difficulties that Congress, the courts, and other political competitors face in acting in a unified fashion. The **unilateral president** has many tools at his disposal, ranging from issuing executive orders and national security directives to setting up new organizations and redefining their responsibilities.

The President and the Foreign Affairs Constitution

In the previous chapter, we introduced the constitutional distribution of powers within which the president operates in making foreign policy. The Constitution binds both the president and Congress, but over time the president has developed a number of strategies for circumventing these restrictions. In this section, we examine four of the most important strategies that are at the president's disposal: using executive agreements, issuing signing statements, using unofficial ambassadors, and engaging in undeclared wars. This does not mean that presidents will always get their way or that it will not be challenged. When Congress did not act on immigration reform Obama issued an executive order that provided deportation relief to illegal immigrants in the United States. A federal court judge ruled it unconstitutional and the administration was forced to appeal the case to the Supreme Court. On a tie vote the Supreme Court held that Obama's immigration reform policy was illegal.

Executive Agreements

The U.S. Constitution specifies that the Senate shall give its advice and consent to treaties, but it does not define what a treaty is or what international agreements are to be made in this form. From the outset, presidents have claimed the constitutional authority to engage in international agreements by means other than treaties. This alternative is known as an **executive agreement**, and over time it became the favored presidential method for entering into understandings with other states. Unlike a treaty, an executive agreement does not require the consent of the Senate before coming into force. The U.S. Supreme Court has ruled that it carries the same legal force as a treaty. The principal limit on its use is political, not legal: the fear that an angry Congress would retaliate by blocking other presidential foreign policy initiatives.

The number of executive agreements compared to treaties has increased steadily over time. Between 1789 and 1839, the United States entered into 60 treaties and 27 executive agreements. A century later, between 1889 and 1939, those numbers had grown to 524 treaties and 917 executive agreements. Bill Clinton signed 365 executive agreements and George W. Bush entered into 291. Because Obama preferred to act through executive orders and memorandums, he did not make as much use of executive agreements as did his predecessors. Midway through his last year in office Obama had entered into 183 executive agreements. Many of them, however, were for high-profile foreign policy issues, such as a 2012 strategic partnership agreement with Afghanistan that established the outlines for U.S.-Afghanistan relations after U.S. combat forces left in 2014, the 2015 climate agreement, and the nuclear agreement with Iran.

The Senate has attempted to curb the president's use of executive agreements on a number of occasions. Two efforts have been particularly noteworthy. The first was the **Bricker Amendment**. It would have required that executive agreements receive the same two-thirds vote of approval from the Senate that treaties must get. In 1954 the Bricker Amendment failed by one vote to get the two-thirds majority needed in the Senate to set into motion the amendment ratification process at the state level.

The second was the 1972 Case-Zablocki Act, which required that Congress be informed of all executive agreements. The goal was to give Congress the opportunity to take action to block these agreements if it saw fit.[5] It was seen as necessary because executive agreements have not always been made public. Particularly revealing in this regard is the history of secret presidential agreements with Saudi Arabia.[6] In 1947 President Harry Truman entered into an agreement with King Ibn Saud in which the United States promised to take "energetic measures" to ward off aggression. President John Kennedy also entered into a secret agreement with Saudi Arabia authorizing the use of force to protect it under certain circumstances. The Case-Zablocki Act has not ended the practice of secret executive agreements. In part, the problem is definitional. In 1975 Representative Les Aspin estimated that four hundred to six hundred agreements had not yet been reported to Congress because the White House claimed that they were understandings, oral promises, or statements of political intent but not executive agreements.[7] Included among these were a 1973 secret message that President Nixon had sent to North Vietnam promising reconstruction aid in return for a peace agreement, Henry Kissinger's 1975 understanding with Israel and Egypt that U.S. personnel would be stationed in the Sinai as part of the disengagement process, and the 1975 Helsinki Accords.

Signing Statements

Presidents may also act unilaterally to thwart Congress by issuing **signing statements**. Some signing statements amount to little more than claiming credit for a piece of legislation or thanking key supporters. Other times, they are statements of constitiutional rights and prerogatives. Such was the case in 2005 upon the passage of the anti-torture legislation. Two weeks after its public signing, Bush quietly attached a statement dealing with the rights of detainees. It stated he would interpret the legislation "in a manner consistent with the constitutional authority of the President to supervise the unitary executive branch and as Commander in Chief and . . . in achieving the shared objective of the Congress and the President in . . . protecting the American people from further terrorist attacks."[8] The effect of this statement was to claim presidential authority to conduct the War on Terror as the executive saw fit. Of forty foreign policy bills he signed, Bush issued fourteen constitutional signing statements, and he also issued seventeen such statements in signing thirty-five pieces of national security legislation.[9]

In spite of his criticism of Bush's use of signing statements as a senator, Obama did not abandon the practice. In June 2009 he signed a spending bill that placed conditions on money given to the World Bank and International Monetary Fund. In his signing statement, Obama stated he would not allow this legislation to interfere with his authority as president to conduct foreign policy and negotiate with other countries. In signing the 2012 National Defense Authorization Act, Obama embraced Bush's language cited earlier, stating he would interpret its language "consistent with my constitutional authority as Commander in Chief."

Executive Orders, Spending, and Administrative Powers

Presidents also have a number of more subtle options to pursue their foreign policy agendas.[10] One is to issue executive orders. Obama had done so in a variety of foreign policy areas. In 2016 he signed an executive order ending a twenty-year-old economic sanctions program against Iran for its pursuit of nuclear weapons. The order revoked four previous executive orders and modified a fifth. Eight executive orders imposing sanctions on Iran remained in place. Another particularly controversial executive order, one which prompted a political response from Congress, was that which closed the Guantanamo Bay military prison. It remained open because of congressional legislation that made it extremely difficult if not impossible to transfer the remaining prisoners to other facilities.

In his second term Obama issued controversial executive orders involving cyber security. One centered on protecting critical elements of the U.S. information and economic infrastructure from cyber-attacks. The House and Senate had considered cybersecurity legislation in 2012, but no legislation was passed due to a Republican filibuster in the Senate. Obama's executive order provided for expanded information sharing and collaboration between the government and private sector and developing a voluntary framework for cybersecurity standards and best practices. In 2015 he signed an executive order allowing the administration to impose sanctions on groups or individuals who engage in cyber-attacks or commercial espionage in cyberspace.

Presidents may also use their spending and administrative powers to advance foreign policy initiatives blocked by Congress. In 1999 the Senate rejected the

Comprehensive Nuclear Test Ban Treaty. Yet Bill Clinton helped fund a global network of monitoring stations that were vital to detecting illegal tests. The United States has not yet signed the 1997 treaty banning land mines, yet it has avoided producing, transferring, or deploying new land mines. It is also the world's leading funder of de-mining projects and helps fund follow-up meetings on the treaty's progress. The United States has not signed the treaty establishing an International Criminal Court (ICC), yet Bush supported a UN resolution referring Darfur to the ICC and Obama sent U.S. forces to Africa to help capture ICC fugitive Joseph Kony and turned over a Congolese warlord to the ICC after he surrendered to a U.S. embassy.

Informal Ambassadors

The Constitution gives the Senate the power to approve or reject presidential appointments. By having a voice in who is appointed to negotiate treaties and run departments, it was thought that the Senate would be able to influence policy. In practice, this linkage between people and policy has never fully materialized. Appointees see themselves as agents of the president. It is his agenda they seek to advance and not that favored by members of Congress.

Presidents have also turned the confirmation powers into something less than what was originally intended by using personal representatives as negotiators. President Franklin Roosevelt relied heavily on Harry Hopkins in making international agreements, leaving Secretary of State Cordell Hull to administer "diplomatic trivia." President Jimmy Carter had Hamilton Jordan conduct secret negotiations during the Iranian hostage crisis, and in the Reagan administration, National Security Council (NSC) staffers and private citizens were relied on to carry out the Iran-Contra initiative. A similar problem confronts the Senate if it wishes to influence the type of advice the president gets. Presidents are free to listen to whom they please. Under Woodrow Wilson, Colonel House, a friend and confidant, was more influential than Secretaries of State William Jennings Bryan and William Lansing. Today, it is widely recognized that the national security advisor often has more influence on presidential thinking than does the secretary of state. Yet the former's appointment is not subject to Senate approval.

Obama turned to informal ambassadors for dealing with a number of high-profile foreign policy problems, most notably reopening relations with Cuba, negotiating a nuclear agreement with Iran, and greenhouse gas emissions with China. All were carried out largely in secret. The Cuban negotiations, for example, were conducted by two White House officials and begun without the knowledge of Secretary of State John Kerry.

Undeclared Wars

By one count, the United States has used force over three hundred times.[11] Only five times has it declared war. The passage of the 1973 War Powers Resolution did little to redress this imbalance. Rather than willingly abide by it, presidents have submitted reports to Congress declaring that they were doing so voluntarily and characterized their decision to use force as lying beyond the jurisdiction of the War Powers Resolution. Carter did not engage in advance consultations with Congress in carrying out the hostage rescue effort. He claimed that it was a humanitarian action. Reagan used the same logic in bypassing Congress on the invasion of Grenada. He would later argue that because U.S. Marines were invited in by the Lebanese government, they were not being sent into a combat situation, and the War Powers Resolution did not apply. This assertion lost much of its support when 241 U.S. soldiers were killed in a terrorist attack. Even though George H. W. Bush did obtain congressional resolution supporting the 1991 Persian Gulf War, he continued to stress that "I don't think I need it . . . I feel that I have the authority to fully implement the United Nations resolution." In a twist, President Grover Cleveland went so far as to tell Congress that even if it declared war against Spain over Cuba, he would not honor that vote and begin a war.

Historical Lesson

John F. Kennedy's First 100 Days

The mystique surrounding a president's first 100 days in office began with the election of Franklin Roosevelt in 1932 at the height of the depression. In his first 100 days Congress passed fifteen major pieces of legislation as part of the New Deal economic recovery program. FDR also began his famous series of radio fireside chats. Presidential performance in their first 100 days since then has been spotty, especially in the area of foreign policy. Dwight Eisenhower concentrated on ending the Korean War. In his presidential camping he had pledged to bring it to an end and actually went to Korea weeks after being elected. Richard Nixon went on a five country tour of Europe, announced the end of the draft, and that the United States would deploy an anti-ballistic missile defense system in his first 100 days. Jimmy Carter announced he was pardoning Vietnam draft evaders. Bill Clinton announced a controversial plan to allow gays in the military.

George W. Bush announced the United States was withdrawing from the Kyoto Climate accord.

John Kennedy's first 100 days in office were among the most active insofar as foreign policy was concerned. The results were both good and bad. Kennedy was inaugurated on January 21, 1961. Three days later he announced that via an executive order he was establishing the Peace Corps as a pilot program. Congress would be asked to establish it on a permanent basis. George McGovern was named its director.

On February 22, Kennedy sent a letter to Nikita Khrushchev, head of the Soviet communist party, in which he extended an invitation to hold personal talks on foreign policy matters of interest to both countries. Khrushchev had earlier sent Kenney a congratulatory letter after the election. The meeting was held in Vienna in June, after the 100-day period. Berlin and Laos were the major points of discussion. Kennedy's advisors urged him not to hold such a meeting. They feared he would misread Khrushchev's personality and intentions. Initially the summit was seen as a diplomatic success but that assessment soon changed. Kennedy did not fare well in the private discussions, and Khrushchev appears to have come away from the summit with the view the Kennedy was an inexperienced leader whom he could outmaneuver.

In March Kennedy announced an ambitious ten-year plan for economic growth and development in the Western Hemisphere. A central feature of the plan was to be an economic partnership between the United States and Latin American countries. This became the Alliance for Progress which officially came into existence in August 1961. The short-term impact of the Alliance for Progress was significant as the amount of U.S. foreign aid to the region virtually tripled. Long-term assessments were not as positive as much of the money flowing into the region benefited U.S. corporations who returned profits to the United States more than it did local economies.

The most significant foreign policy decision made by Kennedy in his first 100 days came on April 1961 when he approved the Bay of Pigs operation. It called for covertly training Cuban exiles into a paramilitary force to overthrow Castro. They would covertly be sent back to Cuba where they would help spawn a popular uprising against Castro. The plan was developed by the CIA during the Eisenhower administration's final year in office. During the 1960 presidential campaign both Kennedy and Richard Nixon called for taking a hard line stance against Castro with Kennedy asserting that Eisenhower had not done enough to end his rule. Kennedy was elected president on November 8, 1960. On November 18 he was briefed on the invasion plan. On January 3, 1961, the Eisenhower administration broke diplomatic relations with Cuba. Kennedy was briefed again on January 28, 1961. At these briefings he called for changes in the invasion plan, one of which was to move the landing to the Bay of Pigs in order to further hide its link to the United States. At an April 12 press conference when asked what the United States would do to help support anti-Castro Cubans Kennedy said that the United States had no intention of intervening in Cuban affairs.

The Bay of Pigs invasion took place on April 17. Little went right. Overwhelmed by Cuban military forces the U.S.-backed Cubans quickly surrendered. When confronted with news of the invasion's imminent collapse Kennedy rejected calls for openly providing additional U.S. assistance. The failure was not a surprise to many. Both the chairman of the Joint Chiefs of Staff and secretary of defense had voiced their doubts about the CIA plan as did former secretary of state Dean Acheson and current members of Kennedy's State Department.

Applying the Lessons

1. What standard should be used in assessing presidential performance in the first 110 days?

2. How deeply should presidents be involved in the decision-making process?

3. What is more important in the first 100 days of a presidency: continuity with the past or changing the direction of foreign policy?

Obama's thinking on presidential war powers evolved during his presidency. As a presidential candidate in 2008 Obama stated "the president does not have the power under the Constitution to unilaterally authorize a military attack in a situation that does not involved stopping an actual or imminent threat to the nation." By 2011 his position was consistent with that of past presidents. Obama sought congressional approval neither for military action against Gaddafi nor for the continuance of military operations there after the mandated sixty-day reporting period established by the War Powers Resolution. Approval, he held, was not necessary because it was a humanitarian operation. Later, he asserted the sixty-day reporting requirement did not apply because U.S. military activities in Libya fell short of "hostilities."[12] As we noted in the previous chapter Obama moved somewhat in the opposite direction in his handling of the U.S. involvement in the Syrian civil war twice going to the Senate for authorization of military force resolutions. He presented it as constitutionally unnecessary but desirable as a means of producing increased support for U.S. military action. Critics saw them as attempts to spread the blame to Congress should military action fail.

When Does the President Matter?

In a study of twentieth-century U.S. foreign policy, John Stoessinger was struck by how few individuals made crucial decisions shaping its direction.[13] He found that "movers" (exceptional individuals who, for better or worse, not only find turning points in history but help create them) have been far outnumbered by "players" (individuals caught up in the flow of events, who respond in a standard and predictable fashion). One explanation for this imbalance is that there may exist relatively few situations in which the personal characteristics of the president or other policy makers are important for explaining policy.

A useful distinction can be made between action indispensability and actor indispensability.[14] **Action indispensability** refers to situations in which a specific action is critical to the success or failure of a policy. The identity of the actor is not necessarily a critical factor in explaining the action. It is possible that any individual (player) in that situation would have acted in a similar manner. **Actor indispensability** refers to those situations in which the personal characteristics of the involved are critical to explaining the action taken. In Stoessinger's terms, the individual involved is a mover. This is someone who increases the odds of success or failure by bringing his or her unique qualities to bear on a problem.

A crucial element of action indispensability is the degree to which the situation permits restructuring. Some situations are so intractable or unstable that it is unreasonable to expect the actions of an individual policy maker to have much of an impact. In concrete terms, we can suggest that the identity of the president will have the greatest impact on policy under four conditions. The first is when the issue is new on the agenda. Jimmy Carter's involvement in human rights policy and Ronald Reagan's championing of the Strategic Defense Initiative are cases in point. The second is when the issue is addressed early in the administration. Carter's decision to not simply wrap up the SALT II package left him by

Gerald Ford but to negotiate his own treaty illustrates this point. Bill Clinton's handling of Somalia is another example. Third are those ongoing issues in which the president is deeply involved. Vietnam was such an issue for Lyndon Johnson and Richard Nixon. Finally, we can expect presidential personality to matter when the issue is in a state of precarious equilibrium and events are primed to move in any number of directions.

All four of these conditions are met by the events of 9/11. The issue was new on the agenda. Although the administration of Bill Clinton had given terrorism more attention than did the incoming George W. Bush administration, no firm plan of action was in place. The attack occurred early in the Bush administration. And certainly from the viewpoint of key individuals in the administration, the terrorist attacks presented the United States with a unique opportunity to remake the political map of the Persian Gulf.

Students of the presidency have focused most heavily on two aspects of the president as individual in attempting to understand U.S. foreign policy. The first is presidential personality. The second is the president's managerial or leadership style. We will look at each in turn.

Presidential Personality

Textbooks and newspaper accounts of U.S. foreign policy are dominated by references to policies that bear a president's name, such as the Monroe Doctrine, the Truman Doctrine, or the Bush Doctrine. Personalizing the presidency this way suggests that the identity of the president matters greatly and that if a different person had been president, U.S. foreign policy would have been different. Yet is this really the case?[15] A persuasive case can be made that situational factors, role variables, and the common socioeconomic backgrounds of policy makers place severe constraints on the impact of personality on policy. In this section, we first look at a leading effort to capture presidential personality and then examine under what conditions we should expect presidential personality to make a difference.

The most famous effort to classify presidential personality and explore its implications for policy is that of James David Barber, who defines "personality" in terms of three elements.[16] The first element is *worldview*, which Barber defines as an individual's politically relevant beliefs. The second element is *style*, which refers to an individual's habitual ways of responding to political opportunities and challenges through "rhetoric, personal relations, and homework." Both are heavily influenced by the third and most important component of personality: *character*, which develops in childhood. Character is the way individuals orient themselves toward life and involves two dimensions. The first is the amount of energy they put into the presidency. Presidents are classified as either passive or active. The second dimension is whether the president derives personal satisfaction from the job. A president who does is classified as positive, and one who gets no personal satisfaction from being president is classified as negative. Together these two dimensions produce four presidential personalities. Each type of **presidential personality** has different implications for U.S. foreign policy.

Active-positive presidents, such as Truman, Kennedy, Carter, Clinton, George H. W. Bush, and Obama, put a great deal of energy into being president and derive great satisfaction from doing so. They are achievement oriented, value productivity, and enjoy meeting new challenges. *Active-negative* presidents, such as Johnson and Nixon, are compulsive individuals who are driven to acquire power as a means of compensating for low self-esteem. Active-negatives adopt a domineering posture toward those around them and have difficulty managing their aggressive feelings. *Passive-positives* are directed individuals who seek affection as a reward for being agreeable. Passive-positive presidents such as Reagan do not make full use of the powers of the presidency but feel satisfied with the job as they define it. *Passive-negatives* such as Eisenhower get little satisfaction from the job and use few of the powers available to them. They are in politics only because others have encouraged them to be, and they feel a responsibility to meet these expectations. Their actions are plagued by low self-esteem and feelings of uselessness. They do not enjoy the game of politics. Rather than bargain and compromise, they seek to avoid confrontation by emphasizing vague principles and procedural arrangements.

Carter's handling of the Panama Canal Treaties illustrates the ability of active-positives to engage productively in coalition-building efforts and to accept the compromises necessary to get a policy measure passed. Carter's presidency also illustrates the problem with active-positive presidents: They may overextend themselves by pursuing too many goals at once, and they may be insensitive to the fact that the irrationalities of politics can frustrate even the best-laid plans. Carter was roundly criticized for being too flexible in the search for results and for trying to do too many things at the outset of his administration: negotiate a SALT II treaty, negotiate a Panama Canal treaty, and reorder U.S. foreign policy priorities by emphasizing human rights and economic problems over the Soviet threat.

Barack Obama fits comfortably into the active-positive category.[17] He is portrayed as a listener, someone who conveys a sense that he is open to the views of others. At the same time, he is seen as being ambitious, self-confident, and predisposed to advancing his own positions on issues at his own pace. In describing his approach to foreign policy making Obama once said, "I want a president who has the sense that you can't fix everything" but "if we don't set the agenda, it doesn't happen."[18] With this perspective comes an ability to avoid being locked into large numbers of losing positions or those where victory comes with a high political price tag. The primary danger facing Obama, as it does all active-positives, is the possibility that his pragmatism will be seen as "flip-flopping" and being too detached from events to energize the public to support his policies. Signs of this scenario played themselves out in his changing policies to military action in Libya, which he first opposed and then endorsed on short notice, and his policy toward military strikes against Syria for its use of chemical weapons and against ISIS.

The great danger of active-negatives is that they will adhere rigidly to a disastrous foreign policy. Woodrow Wilson did so during the League of Nations controversy; Johnson, with Vietnam; and Nixon, with his actions in the Watergate scandal and the impeachment proceedings. Passive presidents are especially prone to two problems. The first is policy drift. Problems may go unaddressed and opportunities for action may be missed. This situation results from both a general disinterest in using the powers of the presidency and a reluctance to engage in the nitty-gritty political work necessary to forge a consensus and move ahead. The second potential danger is the absence of accountability. Without the energetic involvement of the president in making policy, the inevitable question arises of "Who is in charge?"

Placing a president in one of Barber's categories involves a great deal of subjective judgment. Consider the case of Eisenhower, who was defined as a passive-negative president by Barber. Recent evidence suggests that this may not be the case.[19] Eisenhower may have deliberately cultivated the image of not being involved in policy making in order to deflect political pressures. His "hidden-hand leadership" employed a behind-the-scenes activism combined with a low profile in public.

An even more significant complicating factor is that Barber's personality traits may not be as permanent or enduring as the term implies. Change may occur over time because multiple traits are present. George W. Bush is a case in point.[20] Bush can be seen as passive in his delegation of authority to others, his preference for focusing on a few select themes, and his engaging in binary black-and-white thinking that allowed him to make decisions without getting into the deeper questions involved in an issue. At the same time, we can see a very active side to Bush. Bob Woodward, who chronicled the Bush administration's decisions to go to war in Afghanistan and Iraq, said Bush's decision-making style "bordered on the hurried. He wanted actions, solutions. Once on course, he directed his energy at forging on, rarely looking back, scoffing at—even ridiculing—doubt and anything less than 100 percent commitment."[21]

Presidential Managerial Style

Presidents do not lead by personality alone. Just as important to the outcome of their presidency is the managerial style they embrace to get others to follow. And, while we might expect presidential personality to have its greatest influence under a limited set of conditions, a president's managerial and leadership style could be expected to have a more uniform effect on U.S. foreign policy. Getting others to follow is not easy. In accepting the resignation of Alexander Haig as secretary of state, Ronald Reagan wrote in his diary that "actually the only [foreign policy] disagreement was over whether I made policy or the Sec. of State did."[22]

Presidential managerial styles can be described in any number of ways. Zbigniew Brzezinski gave the following thumbnail sketches of how the first three post–Cold War presidents managed foreign policy.[23] George H. W. Bush had a "top-down" managerial style that placed him firmly in command of decisions. This did not mean that he was always happy with the way the system worked. Commenting on discussions about dealing with Soviet pressure on Lithuania, Bush later said, "I was dissatisfied with this discussion since it did not point to action and I wanted to take action."[24] Bill Clinton had a "kaffeeklatsch" (informal get-together over coffee) approach to decision-making. His meetings lacked an agenda, rarely began or ended on schedule, frequently were marked by the spontaneous participation of individuals who had little reason to be there, and often ended without any clear sense that a decision had been reached. George W. Bush is described as having "strong gut instincts" along with a "propensity for catastrophic decisiveness" and a temperament prone to "dogmatic formulations."

Viewed from a more analytical perspective, we find that four basic managerial options have been employed by presidents to bring order and coherence to their foreign policy.[25] None is by definition superior to another. All have contributed to foreign policy successes and failures. The first is a **competitive system**, in which a great deal of emphasis is placed on the free and open expression of ideas. Jurisdictions and grants of authority overlap as individuals and departments compete for the president's attention in putting forward ideas and programs. Franklin Roosevelt is the only president who successfully employed such a model. Johnson is seen as having tried and failed. A second leadership style involves setting up a **formalistic system**, in which the president establishes orderly routines and procedures for organizing the administration's policy deliberations. The system is hierarchically structured, with the president deeply involved as the final arbitrator in defining strategy and policy choices. Truman, Eisenhower, Nixon, Ford, and Reagan set up formalistic systems. The third management style centers on the creation of a **collegial system**, in which the president tries to bring together a group of advisors to operate as a problem-solving team. Kennedy, Carter, George H. W. Bush, and Clinton set up this type of system.

The fourth management style, employing a **chief executive officer (CEO) system**, was introduced by George W. Bush. In spirit, it harkens back to a Nixon-style attempt to govern by stressing loyalty, tightly controlling the flow of information, and surrounding himself with an "iron triangle" of aides to the exclusion of others in the White House. There were noticeable differences. Whereas the Nixon NSC system stressed hierarchy and centralized control, Bush put into place a flattened power structure in which the president set the overall direction of policy but delegated responsibility for carrying through on policy to key individuals.

In some respects Obama returned to the operating style of the Nixon White House. He was routinely characterized as running the most centralized White House decision-making system since Nixon. Leon Panetta, who served under Obama as CIA director and defense secretary, complained about "the increasing centralization of power at the White House" and its "penchant for control." And like Nixon, Obama closely held on to final decision-making power. Obama surprised his advisors with his "red line" speech about chemical weapons in Syria. Secretary of Defense Leon Panetta admits that "I did not know it was coming." Just as surprising was his decision to forego military action. With the decision to act militarily having been made, Obama and Chief of Staff Denis McDonough took a walk. When they returned Obama announced he had changed his mind.[26]

Where Obama's managerial style differs from that of Nixon is in its emphasis on a highly structured decision-making process in which competing and dissenting views are aired and which moves to a decision in a deliberate fashion.[27] While consensus is sought, Obama has left little doubt that he is the manager of the decision-making process, assigning papers to be written, guiding debates, and ultimately making the decision.

The downside to Obama's blend of competitive and formalistic decision-making styles is that it often results in a lengthy and slow-moving decision-making process that can create an image of indecisiveness. One official described the decision-making process as "groundhog day." Deciding to approve sending a weapons shipment to Egypt after the coup that removed Mohammed Morsi from power in 2013 took eighteen months (the key issue was officially defining the take over as a coup since under the Leahy Act the United States could not send weapons to the new government) and produced a decision to approve the sale that Obama noted "will likely piss everybody off."[28]

The National Security Council

Leadership requires more than getting individuals to work together toward a common set of goals. It also has an organizational foundation. Bureaucracies are needed to provide advice, develop policy alternatives, and implement policies. Experience has taught presidents that bureaucracies are not easily moved. As a result, presidents have been forced to look elsewhere for organizations that will allow them to lead. The central foreign policy structure that presidents have grown to rely on is the NSC system, which is composed of three parts: an advisory body of cabinet rank officials, a national security advisor, and a professional staff.

According to the 1947 National Security Act, the purpose of the NSC was to advise the president "with respect to the integration of domestic, foreign, and military policies relating to national security."[29] Its history can be broken down into four phases, each of which has altered the manner in which foreign policy problems come to the president.

The first phase of the NSC's history ran from 1947 to 1960. During this period, the NSC gradually became overly institutionalized. Truman was the first president to have the NSC, and he was cautious in using it. He particularly wanted to avoid setting any precedents that would give the NSC the power to supervise executive branch agencies or establish a norm of group responsibility for foreign policy decisions. For Truman, foreign policy was the responsibility of the president alone. The NSC was to be an advisory body and nothing more. To emphasize this point, Truman did not attend early meetings of the NSC. The outbreak of the Korean War changed Truman's approach to the NSC. He started to use it more systematically and began attending its regularly scheduled meetings. All national security issues were now to be brought to his attention through the NSC system, the NSC staff was reorganized, and the emphasis on outside consultants was replaced by a senior staff served by staff assistants.

The institutionalization and involvement of the NSC in policy making continued under Eisenhower, who created a Planning Board to develop policy recommendations for the president and an Operations Coordinating Board to oversee the implementation of national security decisions. Eisenhower also established the post of assistant for national security affairs (commonly known as the president's national security advisor) to coordinate the national security decision-making process more forcefully. This NSC system never really functioned as envisioned. Instead of producing high-quality policy recommendations, decisions were made on the basis of the lowest common denominator on which all could agree. As a result, rather than increasing presidential options, it limited them. Policy implementation continued to be governed by departmental objectives and definitions of the problem rather than by presidential goals and perspectives.[30]

The second phase of the NSC's history, in which it became overly personalized, began with the Kennedy administration and lasted until 1980. Under Kennedy, the NSC system Eisenhower created declined in importance. Kennedy adopted an activist approach to national security management that was grounded in informal operating procedures. The emphasis was on multiple lines of communication, direct presidential contacts with second- and third-level officials, and securing outside expert advice. Ad hoc interagency task forces replaced the formal NSC system as the primary decision-making unit. Within the NSC system, emphasis switched from the council itself to the NSC staff.

In Kennedy's revamped management system, the national security advisor played a key role. This person was responsible for ensuring that the staff operated from a presidential perspective. McGeorge Bundy held this post under Kennedy and in the first part of the Johnson administration. He was replaced by Walt Rostow in 1966. The change in advisors brought with it a change in operating style. Bundy saw his role as a facilitator or honest broker whose job was to encourage the airing of ideas and policy alternatives. Rostow was more of an ideologue, concerned with policy advocacy over process management.

Like Kennedy, Lyndon Johnson took an activist stance and favored small, informal policy-making settings over the formal NSC system. Major decisions about Vietnam were made at the Tuesday lunch group that brought together Johnson and his key foreign policy advisors. The Tuesday lunch group was a "procedural abomination," lacking a formal agenda and clearly stated conclusions, wearing on participants, and confusing to those at the working levels.[31] The NSC coordinating system was overwhelmed by the pressures of Vietnam and was often bypassed by the tendency of the White House to make key policy decisions.

Nixon began his presidency with a pledge to put the NSC system back at the center of the foreign policy decision-making process.[32] This was achieved by first selecting Henry Kissinger as his national security advisor and William Rogers as his secretary of state. The combination of a strong, opinionated, and activist national security advisor and a secretary of state with little foreign policy experience guaranteed that foreign policy would be made in the White House. Second, Nixon created an elaborate NSC committee and staff system with Kissinger at its center. With this structure, Kissinger was able to direct the flow of paper in the direction he wanted, bringing the NSC system into play on certain issues and cutting it out of others. By the end of the Nixon administration, the NSC was largely on the outside looking in. It met only three times in 1973, compared with thirty-seven times in 1969. Such important decisions as the invasion of Cambodia, Kissinger's trip to China, the Paris peace negotiations, bombing in Vietnam, and putting U.S. troops on worldwide alert during the Yom Kippur War in the Middle East were made outside the NSC system.

Carter dismantled the elaborate Nixon-Ford-Kissinger committee system in favor of two committees. The Policy Review Committee was charged with handling long-term projects. A Special Coordinating Committee was created to deal with short-term problems, crisis situations, and covert action. Collegiality also returned, as evident in the prominent policy-making roles played by the Friday foreign policy breakfasts (attended by Carter and his key foreign policy advisors), but it came at a price. The Friday foreign policy breakfasts became substitutes for full NSC meetings, and decisions arrived at during the breakfasts were not always fully integrated into the NSC system, nor did they necessarily result in clearly articulated positions.[33]

During the Reagan administration, the NSC entered a third phase. Pledging to depersonalize the system, Reagan pushed too far in the opposite direction, causing it to go into decline. The national security advisor became a "nonperson" with little foreign policy influence or stature. With no force able to coordinate foreign policy, an unprecedented degree of bureaucratic infighting and fragmentation came to characterize (and paralyze) Reagan's foreign policy. The NSC staff moved in two different directions. On the one hand, it became preoccupied with bureaucratic trivia. (There were twenty-five committees, fifty-five midlevel committees, and some one hundred task forces and working groups.) On the other hand, it became involved in the actual conduct of foreign policy in the Iran-Contra initiative. Only with the arrival of Colin Powell as national security advisor and the passing from the Cabinet of such powerful and highly opinionated figures as Secretary of Defense Caspar Weinberger and Director of Central Intelligence William Casey did a coherent foreign policy agenda appear.[34]

In the George H. W. Bush and Clinton administrations, decision-making in the NSC transformed again, becoming more collegial in nature. Both presidents selected low-key national security advisors who were expected to stay out of the public limelight. The move to collegiality was applauded by most as a necessary step to overcome many of the past excesses of the NSC system. In each case, however, the final result was less than had been hoped for. The primary problem encountered in George H. W. Bush's administration was too much homogeneity in outlook. All of the participants, including the president, were confident that they understood the world, and they were slow to adapt to the end of the Cold War. Bill Clinton failed to make his collegial system work because he was unable to provide a constant vision to guide his team or to construct an effective division of labor among its members.

George W. Bush and Obama continued to try and construct a collegial system. Central to George W. Bush's advisory system was the "War Cabinet," consisting of some twelve key Bush advisors on the war against terrorism. Instead of operating in a collegial fashion, however, this system became highly competitive and split over how to conduct foreign policy. The meetings became highly formalized with no real discussions taking place. Instead, key officials holding strong views on policy issues, such as Secretary of Defense Donald Rumsfeld and Vice President Dick Cheney, routinely employed back channels to communicate with Bush privately about policy matters.[35] One CIA official commenting on the decision to invade Iraq recalled that "there was no meeting; no policy options papers, no showdown in the Situation Room where the wisdom of going to war was debated or the decision to do so made."[36]

In setting up his NSC system President Obama set up an advisory system that emphasized his role as the key foreign policy decision-maker. Most significantly, he did not select a national security advisor whose thinking he would depend on or adopt. Rather, as many commentators have noted, Obama served as his own Kissinger. The predictable result was that Obama's national security advisor's influence on policy was often marginalized as was the case with James Jones, the national security advisor whom Obama routinely bypassed while seeking advice from others, such as Chief of Staff Rahm Emanuel. In surveying this state of affairs, Director of National Intelligence Dennis Blair was moved to note that at any one time there was not one national security advisor in the Obama administration but at least three and as many as five.[37]

Obama's NSC system came to be viewed with suspicion by many in the bureaucracy. At the center of their concerns were its large size and the inexperienced foreign policy backgrounds of many who served as staffers. In both cases we can see long-term trends at work. The NSC system had been growing consistently. Under Carter it had twenty-five staffers; under George W. Bush it had reached two hundred. Under Obama it doubled in size to four hundred staffers, who increasingly were perceived as lacking in professional expertise. One can trace the beginnings of this tension to the Kennedy administration where the staff came to be viewed less as a body of professionals who would stay on from administration to administration and more as a group that identified closely with the current administration and was loyal to it. Defenders of the growth in size of the NSC system and its partisan outlook see it as reflective of the changed nature of foreign policy making. Increasingly, they note, domestic political considerations play an important role in foreign policy making requiring that the White House take a more active and central role in coordinating foreign policy.

Other White House Voices

The NSC system is not the only body close to the president that exercises influence over the making of U.S. foreign policy. Four other voices that have grown in prominence are that of the vice president, the U.S. trade representative (USTR), the president's chief of staff (COS), and the first lady.

The Vice President

Political folklore assigns the vice president little more than a ceremonial position in the policy-making process, barring the death of the president. There is often great truth in these images. Harry Truman spoke with Franklin Roosevelt only eight times and knew nothing of the development of the atomic bomb or discussions that Roosevelt had with Winston Churchill and Joseph Stalin on the shape of the post–World War II international system. Of late, however, much has changed. More and more vice presidents are playing selective but important foreign policy roles.[38] Dan Quayle, George H. W. Bush's vice president, became the administration's most active voice on Latin American affairs, and his decidedly pro-Israel position was important in maintaining the Persian Gulf War alliance against Iraq. Al Gore, Bill Clinton's vice president, established himself as a key administration expert on Russia and some of the important newly emerging states, such as Kazakhstan and Ukraine.

The foreign policy roles played by Quayle and Gore were, however, pale in comparison to that of Dick Cheney, George W. Bush's vice president. Cheney laid a solid structural foundation from which to exert his influence on foreign policy matters. He assembled a national security staff larger than that of any previous vice president. Cheney also brought a clear-cut perspective on foreign policy matters and considerable foreign policy experience to the vice presidency. He had served as secretary of defense under George H. W. Bush and had established himself as the most aggressive member of that administration's inner circle in dealing with the collapse of communism and the end of the Cold War, arguing that "we ought to lead and shape events."[39]

After the 9/11 attacks Cheney became a powerful voice for taking the war to Iraq, often engaging in spirited exchanges with Secretary of State Colin Powell, who opposed such a move. Both before and after the invasion of Iraq, Cheney vehemently asserted in public that Iraq possessed weapons of mass destruction and that a link existed between Iraq and al Qaeda. His behind-the-scenes efforts to root out intelligence supporting this position and his preoccupation with discrediting opponents of the war are among the most controversial aspects of the Bush administration's handling of prewar intelligence. Bush and Cheney were not always in agreement in foreign policy matters, however, and by the end of his presidency the distance separating their views had grown as Bush became more pragmatic in his foreign policy outlook.[40]

Joe Biden continued in the role of activist vice president as part of the Obama administration, although more in the mode of Al Gore than Dick Cheney. In 2013 Biden traveled to China, where he played the administration's "bad cop," publicly criticizing Chinese leaders for their attempts to silence criticism by American media in China by blocking their websites and not renewing visas of correspondents. Within the White House Biden was an active participant in deliberations over sending more troops to Afghanistan, arguing against a surge and a vigorous counterinsurgency policy in favor of a more aggressive counterterrorism policy (counterterrorism plus) targeted at killing or capturing al Qaeda leaders and training Afghan police and army forces.

The U.S. Trade Representative

Up until the early 1960s, the State Department had primary responsibility for conducting international economic negotiations. That changed with the passage of the 1962 Trade Expansion Act, which created the Office of the Special Trade Representative to head an interagency trade organization located in the White House. The move, which was led by Congress, was seen as necessary because the State Department was not viewed as a strong enough advocate of American economic interests.

The USTR is charged with the responsibility of overseeing U.S. activity in multilateral trade negotiations and of negotiating trade issues with other states and within the UN system of organizations. Thus, it was Robert Zoellick, rather than Colin Powell, who accompanied George W. Bush to Quebec to meet with Latin American leaders in hopes of laying the foundation for the Free Trade Area of the Americas. It was Zoellick who announced that the United States and the European Union had reached an agreement resolving a long-standing dispute over trade in bananas. It was Zoellick who accompanied Bush to the G8 economic summit in Genoa, and it was Zoellick who supervised U.S. negotiations at the Doha Round of World Trade Organization talks. When President Obama went to Italy in July 2009 to attend the meeting of the G8 nations, it was USTR Ron Kirk who accompanied him.

The USTR came in for unwelcomed scrutiny when WikiLeaks published information relating to intellectual property rights agreements that it was negotiating as part of the TransPacific Partnership trade agreement. While the USTR has long been recognized as a strong advocate for promoting global trade the WikiLeaks documents pictured the USTR as holding a clear bias in support of stronger copyright protection and intellectual property rights positions held by major U.S. firms many of which now employ former USTR officials and negotiators. Also coming in for criticism was USTR's lack of transparency. Here the issue was its reliance on a series of sixteen industry trade advisory groups to provide it with advice. These groups received access to confidential negotiating positions and issues that public interest groups do not have.

The White House Chief of Staff

By convention, a division of labor has evolved in White House decision-making circles between the COS and the national security advisor. Each acts as a principal source of advice for the president—the COS for domestic policy and the national security advisor for foreign policy. In addition, the COS acts as a **gatekeeper**, regulating those who have access to the president. This latter power is seen as making the COS more of a political (and powerful) figure than the national security advisor.[41] This division of labor is disappearing, and more and more the COS has come to have an important voice in foreign policy matters too.

The influence of domestic considerations as filtered through the COS's office reaches not only to what decisions are made but also to how foreign policy decisions are communicated. Brent Scowcroft, George H. W. Bush's national security advisor, noted that he had expected the NSC to write the first draft of the president's national security speeches because the language was so very important, but that this was not the case. Instead, the White House speech writers took the lead, with the result that foreign policy speeches often sounded like campaign speeches laced with dramatic rhetoric.

Several reasons stand out for why the COS is now a potentially important foreign policy voice. Foremost among them is the blurring of the boundary between foreign and domestic policy. Today many traditional foreign policy problems have characteristics of both and can be characterized as intermestic issues. One consequence of this is to make the COS's domestic political expertise relevant for how many foreign policy issues are decided. As Hamilton Jordan recalls, he sought to play the role of an early warning system to alert officials to potential domestic political problems embedded in foreign policy decisions. A second consequence of the intermestic nature of foreign policy problems is that presidents have increasingly turned to advisory groups to help manage and coordinate policy decisions in these areas. The COS's role as power broker and gatekeeper has become crucial for ensuring that the president stays on top of the policy process. Leon Panetta, Bill Clinton's second COS, insisted that all decision papers, including those from the NSC, go to the president only after his review. If he felt that not enough options were being given to Clinton, the paper was returned.

Examples of the prominent foreign policy role played by the COS in the George W. Bush and Obama administrations are easy to find. Andrew Card, who was Bush's first COS, was widely associated with an early Bush immigration initiative designed to garner Hispanic votes for the Republican Party. After 9/11, he was one of those placed in charge of the Homeland Security Council. As the Bush administration moved toward war with Iraq, Card established the White House Iraq Group to make sure that the various parts of the White House were working in harmony on Iraq. In spring 2006 Card was replaced by Josh Bolten, who is credited with arranging for meetings between Bush and critics of the Iraq War as part of a strategy of puncturing the protective information bubble that had come to engulf the president.

Obama chose Rahm Emanuel to be his COS. Emanuel and other political advisors soon came to be seen by Obama's national security advisor James Jones as short on foreign policy knowledge and as major obstacles to developing and deciding on a coherent foreign policy.[42] Collectively Jones referred to them as water bugs, the Politburo, and the Mafia.[43] True to the domestic politics orientation held by chiefs of staff, Emanuel repeatedly raised questions about the cost of the surge and gaining congressional approval for it during deliberations over sending additional troops to Afghanistan. On detainee policy, Emanuel often opposed Attorney General Eric Holder's positions, urging Obama to be more sensitive to the domestic political aspects of decisions related to closing Guantanamo Bay, releasing sensitive photos, and bringing suspected terrorists to trial in civilian courts.[44] Secretary of Defense Gates was highly critical of Thomas Donilon, who replaced Jones as COS, complaining that decisions about military intervention into Libya were made without significant military input. At one point Gates told the Pentagon not to give the White House staff too much military information because they did not understand it. At another point he told Donilon and Vice President Biden, "The last time I checked neither of you are in the chain of command."

The First Lady

In the George W. Bush administration, Laura Bush filled the traditional and largely ceremonial foreign policy role bestowed upon first ladies. She was seen much more than heard but did have a focal point for her foreign policy activities, in this case freedom in Burma. It is important to recognize that this role, while the most common, is not the only role that first ladies have played in U.S. foreign policy making.

First ladies have long been involved informally in making U.S. foreign policy. Abigail Adams lobbied President John Adams on a treaty with the Netherlands in 1799. Edith Wilson served as Woodrow Wilson's communication link with both foreign governments and others in the U.S. government while he was incapacitated by a stroke. While generally neutral on policy matters, she tried but failed to get Wilson to accept Senator Henry Cabot Lodge's reservations on the League of Nations. Eleanor Roosevelt engaged in a wide series of debates with President Franklin Roosevelt during his presidency.

Two recent first ladies who adopted a much more visible and active role in foreign policy were Rosalynn Carter and Hillary Clinton. The signature foreign policy undertaking of Rosalynn Carter's stay in the White House was a June 1977 trip to Latin America. With Jimmy Carter heavily involved in completing the Panama Canal Treaties, the Middle East peace process, and arms control talks with the Soviet Union, the decision was made to send her to Latin America as a sign of the U.S. interest in the region and its commitment to human rights. In preparation for the trip, Rosalynn Carter met with scholars and representatives from the State Department, Treasury Department, National Security Department, and Organization of American States.

Hillary Clinton's signature foreign policy initiative involved advocacy for women's rights and her attendance at the Fourth United Nations Conference on Women, held in Beijing in September 1995. In addressing that body, she strongly criticized China's treatment of women. Hillary Clinton's preparation for this trip included discussions with representatives from the State Department, the NSC, the office of the U.S. ambassador to the UN, and nongovernmental organizations.

Michelle Obama, however, took a step back from active engagement in foreign policy. Her primary area of international involvement was "youth engagement," which was the focus of her first solo official trip abroad, to Mexico in 2010, as well as a principal theme of her 2011 official trip to South Africa and Botswana. This second trip became the object of political controversy as some Obama supporters used it to express disappointment over the continued lack of attention being given to Africa in U.S. foreign policy. Her 2014 trip to China was organized around the promotion of "people-to-people exchanges" but also found her speaking out on Internet freedom and minority rights.

Over the Horizon: Improving Presidential Transitions

At the outset of this chapter we noted that for many, the first 100 days of Donald Trump's presidency will be widely seen as sending important signals as to what type of president he will be. For others, just as important—and perhaps even more important—are the seventy-two days between his election as president on November 8, 2016, and his inauguration on January 20, 2017, when the transition from one president to another takes place.

Prior to 2008 very little formal transition planning took place. Transitions were largely ad hoc affairs consisting of occasional national security briefings after the election. 9/11 changed that. As one senior George W. Bush administration official who was involved in both the 2000 and 2008 transitions noted, "Thank goodness it was September 11 and not February 11 because we would have been completely incapable of dealing with them." The Bush administration was committed to creating a more efficient transfer of power. Still, another official noted that in 2008 "we were kind of making it up as we went along." The 9/11 Commission Report added credence to this observation noting that it was not until six months into his presidency that George W. Bush had a full set of senior officials in place. Another study found that historically, on an average, fifty days passed between the confirmation of a department head and the confirmation of the second-ranking person in that department.

The desire to better prepare a presidential candidate to become president led to the creation of the nonpartisan Partnership for Public Service. In studying the 2008 transition it found both McCain and Obama began transition planning in spring 2008 with McCain's campaign being less aggressive believing that he would face fewer problems succeeding a Republican president. Fears of appearing overly presumptuous or overly confident about victory were major psychological and political impediments to transition planning. Its report recommended future presidential candidates appoint transition directors within two weeks of gaining the nomination and that by January 1 the president-elect should give Congress the names of its nominees for the top fifty State Department, Defense Department, national security, and economic positions. The Senate should vote on them on or shortly after inauguration day.

In March 2016 Congress passed legislation which Obama signed into law that established a set of deadlines that both presidential candidates and the administration had to meet. That very month transition coordinators from some forty different agencies met to discuss transition planning. The legislation had established a May deadline, six months before the election, for a president to create a transition coordinating council at the White House and in federal agencies.

Critical Thinking Questions

1. Where does presidential responsibility begin and end in foreign policy making?
2. Is there a "best" type of presidential personality for foreign affairs?

3. What is more important in determining presidential success in foreign policy, the way the NSC is organized or presidential management style?

Key Terms

action indispensability, 171
actor indispensability, 171
Bricker Amendment, 166
CEO system, 175
collegial system, 175
competitive system, 175

executive agreement, 165
formalistic system, 175
gatekeeper, 181
presidential personality, 172
signing statements, 165
unilateral president, 165

Further Reading

Michael Armacost, *Ballots, Bullets and Bargains: American Foreign Policy and Presidential Elections* (Stanford: Stanford University Press, 2015).

This book examines the way in which the electoral process influences how candidates define their foreign policy positions. Particular attention is paid to how sitting presidents select foreign policy problems to fix and the pressures on newly elected presidents to act boldly.

James David Barber, *The Presidential Character: Predicting Performance in the White House* (Englewood Cliffs, NJ: Prentice Hall, 1985).

This study popularized the concept of presidential character and presents a still widely used framework for studying presidential personality and its impact on foreign policy.

Matthew Eshbaugh and Christopher Linebarger, "Presidential and Media Leadership of Public Opinion on Iraq," *Foreign Policy Analysis* 10 (2014), 351–69.

Examining presidential speeches, news coverage, and levels of public support for the Iraq War the authors find that while the tone of media coverage drove support for the president, the tone of presidential rhetoric influenced the public's assessment of George W. Bush's handling of it.

David Kaye, "Stealth Multilateralism," *Foreign Affairs* 92 (September 2013), 113–24.

This article highlights the extent to which presidents have managed to circumvent congressional rejection of foreign policy initiatives which they hold to threaten U.S. sovereignty. It concludes by noting the limitations of these work-around tactics.

Richard Neustadt, *Presidential Power* (New York: Free Press, 1960).

This classic account of presidential power emphasized the weaknesses of the president in pursuing his foreign policy agenda.

Paul Rutledge and Heather Larson-Price, "The President as Agenda Setter-in-Chief," *Policy Studies Journal* 42 (2014), 443–64.

This article examines the influence of the presidency on setting the congressional policy agenda in six areas from 1956 to 2005. It finds compelling evidence of presidential leadership and a reactive congress. This is especially true for international affairs issues.

Elizabeth Saunders, *Leaders at War* (Ithaca, NY: Cornell University Press, 2011).

This is a study on how presidents shape decisions on military intervention. A typology is developed and applied to cases that stress how threats are defined and the nature of the intervention strategy selected.

Notes

[1] Richard Neustadt, *Presidential Power* (New York: Free Press, 1960).

[2] Hugh Heclo, "Introduction: The Presidential Illusion," in Hugh Heclo and Lester M. Salamon (eds.), *The Illusion of Presidential Government* (Boulder: Westview, 1981), 1.

[3] Bob Woodward, *State of Denial* (New York: Simon & Schuster, 2006), 212.

[4] Terry Moe and William G. Howell, "Unilateral Action and Presidential Power: A Theory," *Presidential Studies Quarterly* 29 (1999), 850–72.

[5] James A. Nathan and Richard K. Oliver, *Foreign Policy Making and the American Political System* (Boston: Little, Brown, 1983), 115.

[6] Walter Pincus, "Secret Presidential Pledges over Years Erected U.S. Shield for Saudis," *Washington Post*, February 9, 1992, A20.

[7] Charles W. Kegley Jr. and Eugene R. Wittkopf, *American Foreign Policy: Pattern and Process*, 2nd ed. (New York: St. Martin's Press, 1982), 418.

[8] George W. Bush, "Statement on Signing the Department of Defense, Energy Supplemental Appropriations to Address Hurricanes in the Gulf of Mexico and Pandemic Influenza Act, 2006," *Weekly Compilation of Presidential Documents* (December 30, 2005), 1918–19.

[9] Christopher Kelley and Bryan Marshall, "The Bush Presidencies and the Unitary Executive Theory: The Implications of Presidential Signing Statements," *White House Studies* 7 (2007), 144–62.

[10] David Kaye, "Stealth Multilateralism," *Foreign Affairs* 92 (2013), 113–24.

[11] Ryan Hendrickson, *The Clinton Wars: The Constitution, Congress, and War Powers* (Nashville: Vanderbilt University Press, 2002), 1.

[12] Charlie Savage, "2 Top Lawyers Lost to Obama in Libya War Policy Debate," *New York Times*, June 17, 2011, 1.

[13] John Stoessinger, *Crusaders and Pragmatists: Movers of Modern American Foreign Policy* (New York: W. W. Norton, 1979).

[14] Fred I. Greenstein, *Personality and Politics* (Chicago: Markham, 1969).

[15] Robert Jervis, "Do Leaders Matter and How Would We Know," *Security Studies* 22 (2013), 153–79.

[16] James David Barber, *The Presidential Character: Predicting Performance in the White House*, 3rd ed. (Englewood Cliffs, NJ: Prentice Hall, 1985). Also see Alexander George, "Assessing Presidential Character," *World Politics* 26 (1974), 234–82. For other formulations of presidential personality, see Lloyd S. Etheridge, "Personality Effects on American Foreign Policy, 1898–1968: A Test of Interpersonal Generalization Theory," *American Political Science Review* 72 (1978), 434–51; Stoessinger, *Crusaders and Pragmatists*.

[17] See, for example, Stanley Renshon, "Psychological Reflections on Barack Obama and John McCain: Assessing the Contours of a New Presidential Administration," *Political Science Quarterly* 123 (2008), 391–433. For a more recent and different interpretation of Obama's foreign policy by Renshon, see his "Understanding the Obama Doctrine," *White House Studies* 12 (2012), 187–202.

[18] Jeffrey Goldberg, "The Obama Doctrine," *The Atlantic*, April 1, 2016, 23.

[19] Fred I. Greenstein, *The Hidden Hand Presidency: Eisenhower as Leader* (New York: Basic Books, 1982).

[20] See Ilan Peleg, *The Legacy of George Bush's Foreign Policy* (Boulder: Westview, 2009), 75–98. Peleg classifies Bush as an active-negative.

[21] Bob Woodward, *Bush at War* (New York: Simon & Schuster, 2002), 256.

[22] Ronald Reagan, *The Reagan Diaries*, edited by Douglas Brinkley (New York: HarperCollins, 2007); also Howard Katz, "Ronald Reagan, in His Own Words," *Washington Post*, May 2, 2007, A1.

[23] Zbigniew Brzezinski, *Second Chance: Three Presidents and the Crisis of American Superpower* (New York: Basic Books, 2007), 11, 86–87, 137.

[24] George Bush and Brent Scowcroft, *A World Transformed* (New York: Vintage, 1998), 225, 381.

[25] Donald M. Snow and Eugene Brown, *Puzzle Palaces and Foggy Bottom: U.S. Foreign and Defense Policy-Making in the 1990s* (New York: St. Martin's Press, 1994), 44–70.

[26] Goldberg, "The Obama Doctrine," 23.

[27] Stephen Wayne, "Presidential Character and Judgment: Obama's Afghanistan and Health Care Decisions," *Presidential Studies Quarterly* 41 (2011), 291–306.

[28] Karen DeYoung, "How the Obama White House Runs Foreign Policy," *The Washington Post*, August 4, 2015.

[29] Zbigniew Brzezinski, "The NSC's Midlife Crisis," *Foreign Policy* 69 (1987/88), 80–99.

[30] For a reinterpretation of the Eisenhower NSC experience, see Fred Greenstein and Richard Immerman, "Effective National Security Advising: Recovering the Eisenhower Legacy," *Political Science Quarterly* 115 (2000), 335–45.

[31] William Bundy, "The National Security Process: Plus Change . . .," *International Security* 7 (1982/83), 94–109.

[32] On the Nixon NSC system, see John Leacacos, "Kissinger's Apparat," *Foreign Policy* 5 (1971), 2–27.

[33] Robert E. Hunter, *Presidential Control of Foreign Policy: Management or Mishap*, Washington Paper #91 (New York: Praeger, 1982), 35–36.

[34] Terry Diehl, "Reagan's Mixed Legacy," *Foreign Policy* 75 (1989), 34–55.

[35] Colin Campbell, "Unrestrained Ideological Entrepreneurship in the Bush II Advisory System," in Colin Campbell and Bert Rockman (eds.), *The George W. Bush Presidency* (Washington, DC: Congressional Quarterly Press, 2004), 73–104.

[36] Paul Pillar, "Intelligence, Policy and the War in Iraq," *Foreign Affairs* 85 (2006), 18–32.

[37] Bob Woodward, *Obama's Wars* (New York: Simon & Schuster), 289.

[38] Paul Kengor, "Cheney and Vice Presidential Power," in Gary Gregg II and Mark Rozell (eds.), *Considering the Bush Presidency* (New York: Oxford University Press, 2004), 160–76; "The Vice President, Secretary of State, and Foreign Policy," *Political Science Quarterly* 115 (2000), 175–99.

[39] James Oliver, "Pragmatic Fathers and Ideological Suns: Foreign Policy in the Administrations of George H. W. Bush and George W. Bush," *White House Studies* 7 (2007), 203.

[40] Peter Baker, *Days of Fire* (New York: Doubleday, 2013).

[41] David Cohen, Chris Dolan, and Jerel Rosati, "A Place at the Table," *Congress and the Presidency* 29 (2002), 119–49.

[42] Woodward, *Obama's Wars*, 137.

[43] Ibid., 138.

[44] Bush and Scowcroft, *A World Transformed*, 49.

8 Bureaucracy

Dateline: Women in Combat

Viewed solely in terms of lines on an organizational chart the foreign affair bureaucracy provides presidents with a powerful set of tools to use in promoting their foreign policy agenda. Looked at more closely, these organizations cannot be used as freely as would be liked. They have their own histories, operating styles, and concerns that require attention. We begin this chapter by looking at the interplay of these forces in the decision to allow women into combat.

On December 3, 2015, Secretary of Defense Ashton Carter announced that the Defense Department would open all combat jobs to women. "There will be no exceptions . . . they'll be allowed to drive tanks, fire mortars, and lead infantry soldiers into combat. They'll be able to serve as Army Rangers and Green Berets, Navy SEALS, Marine Corps infantry, Air Force parajumpers and everything else that was previously open only to men." The decision was announced three months prior to the deadline President Barack Obama had given the military earlier in his presidency. When announced the Navy and Air Force had already opened most of their combat positions to women, and the Army was moving in that direction. The Marine Corps which was 93 percent male had asked for an exemption in September for its infantry and armor positions. With this announcement their request was denied. An estimated 220,000 military jobs were now available to women.

While the history of women serving in combat positions in the military goes back to the American Revolution it was not until 1901 with the passage of the Army Reorganization Act that women could formally join the military and then it was through the Army Nurse Corps. A shortage of manpower to meet the combat needs of the armed forces during World War II provided the impetus for expanding the role of women in the military. By the end of World War II almost 400,000 women had served in the military, and 543 women died in the line of duty during that war. The 1948 Women's Armed Forces Integration Act gave women a permanent place in the U.S. military, but it also limited the number of women to 2 percent of the enlisted force and 10 percent of the officer corps.

The formation of an All-Volunteer military following the end of the draft in 1973 created another era of manpower shortages for the military and helped foster a further expansion in the positions women held. The Navy and Air Force opened pilot training to women, and in 1975 Congress passed legislation that permitted women to attend the military academies. In 1977 the Army opened many previously closed military positions to women but continued to exclude them from combat roles.

By the late 1970s it had become clear to many in Congress and the military that the term "combat mission" no longer provided clear guidance for what positions women could hold. Consequently, in 1988, the military adopted a "risk rule" which barred women from noncombat units if the risks to which they would be exposed were equal to or greater than the risks in the combat units they supported. In 1994 Secretary of Defense Less Aspin officially rescinded the risk rule putting in its place a Direct Combat Exclusion Rule which limited the exclusion of women to units below the brigade level whose primary mission was to engage in direct combat on the ground. Aspin's actions followed lobbying efforts by civil rights and women's advocacy groups to end the risk rule and a study by a Presidential Committee on the Assignment of Women in the Armed Forces that called for determining military assignments on the basis of qualifications and not gender.

The War on Terrorism along with military conflicts in Afghanistan and Iraq again overtook efforts to define combat situations from which women were to be excluded. They were wars without clear front lines and wars in which it was difficult to identify which units had direct combat as their primary mission. Increasingly women soldiers searched homes and people for weapons, engaged in door-to-door neighborhood patrols, and were embedded in special operations forces. By the end of 2015 at least 161 women had died and 1,016 had been injured in these conflicts. In the wake of these events there followed a series of military commissions and Pentagon reviews that called for the end to combat exclusion policies.

In March 2016 Ashton Carter authorized the military to begin integrating female combat soldiers "right away." His decision was announced after the thirty-day period within which Congress had to act to stop his December decision from going forward. Carter recognized the challenges in implementing this policy. He expected some units to remain largely male and that opposition could be expected from Defense Department officials and military personnel who believe that opening combat positions to women would reduce the effectiveness of the military. Marine Corps General John Kelly, who headed the U.S. southern Command, put his opposition in these terms: the sole reason for change in the military should be if it makes the units more lethal.

In this chapter, we will examine the organization structure and the internal value systems of three organizations that dominate the foreign affairs bureaucracy: the State Department, the Defense Department, and the Central Intelligence Agency (CIA). We then take a brief look at key bureaucracies that have traditionally been classified as domestic but that now also have a foreign policy role. Finally, we examine how policy makers respond to the challenges of dealing with the foreign affairs bureaucracy.

The State Department

The State Department, then called the Department of Foreign Affairs, was created in 1789. It was the first department created under the new Constitution. According to historical tradition and government documents, the president looks first to the State Department in making foreign policy.

Structure and Growth

The State Department serves as a transmission belt for information between the United States and foreign governments and as a source of expertise and skills for senior policy makers to draw on. These are daunting tasks. Dean Rusk, secretary of state under Presidents John Kennedy and Lyndon Johnson, estimated that he saw only six of every one thousand cables sent to the State Department each day, and that the president saw only one or two.[1] By the end of the twentieth century, the State Department was electronically processing over fourteen thousand official records and ninety thousand data messages each day along with over twenty million e-mail messages per year.

The full magnitude of this explosion of electronic messaging came into focus when the congressional investigation into the terrorist attack on the U.S. consulate in Benghazi began to inquire into Hillary Clinton's use of a personal computer to engage in official business. A Freedom of Information Act request yielded over thirty thousand e-mails from her private server. Some two thousand contained redacted information considered confidential. Of these three-quarters dealt with "foreign government information," which is a catch-all category of information obtained through meetings and conversations with foreign officials. Typical of what was found involved a case where the assistant secretary of state for Near Eastern affairs sent an e-mail to over twenty-four people telling them that Saudi Arabia was sending troops into Bahrain to put down antigovernment protests. It produced ten responses in one day. Besides Hillary Clinton others in the e-mail conversation were the former ambassador to Kuwait and the director of the CIA.

Annually, the State Department represents the United States in over fifty major international organizations and at over eight hundred international conferences. In 2016 the United States had some three hundred embassies, consulates, and diplomatic missions. U.S. relations with India involve twenty-two different agencies. The U.S. embassy in Islamabad, Pakistan, includes four hundred and fifty diplomats. Present in a typical embassy are representatives from the U.S. Agency for International Development, the Defense Department, CIA, Agriculture, Commerce, Treasury, the Centers for Disease Control and Prevention, and Export-Import Bank. The concept of a **country team** was developed to bring coherence to the welter of agencies and programs that are now represented at an embassy.

As chief of mission, the ambassador heads the country team. In practice, ambassadors have found it quite difficult to exercise enough authority to transform a set of independent and often competing policies into a coordinated and coherent program. For example, in 2005, the Pentagon requested to be allowed to put special operations forces into a country without the explicit approval of the ambassador. Also complicating the problem is the background of the ambassador. Frequently, the ambassador is not a career diplomat. A study of ambassadorial appointments from 1960 to 2014 found that in twenty-nine countries and diplomatic missions such as the United Nations, 81–100 percent of ambassadors were political appointees. At the other extreme, in sixty-five countries 0–10 percent of the ambassadors were political appointees.

The State Department's basic structure remained largely unchanged for the duration of the Cold War. Beneath the secretary of state were two deputy secretaries of state and six undersecretaries with responsibility for such matters as political, economic, international security, and management affairs. The remainder of the State Department was organized around geographical areas and functional tasks. While the number and identity of the regional areas remained steady, the functional bureaus showed considerable change over time, as certain units such as the education and culture bureau disappeared and others such as the refugee bureau and a bureau responsible for human rights and humanitarian affairs were created.

In part, this organizational stability was realized by setting up semiautonomous organizations to deal with three of the more pressing problem areas of Cold War diplomacy: foreign aid, arms control, and dispersal of information. The United States Agency for International Development (USAID) was established in 1961 and was responsible for administering the U.S. foreign economic aid program. The Arms Control and Disarmament Agency (ACDA) was also established in 1961 and was responsible for such activities as conducting studies on arms control and disarmament policies, providing advice to key officials including the president on these matters, and managing U.S. participation arms control and disarmament negotiations and agreements. The United States Information

Agency (USIA) was established in 1953 and was charged with promoting a better understanding of the United States in other countries. The Voice of America is one of its best-known undertakings.

Today, the State Department is undergoing two profound organizational changes. One change involves the State Department's "shrinking presence" overseas. In June 2008 there were 6,636 **Foreign Service Officers** (FSOs) and 4,919 support staff in the State Department. This was just 10 percent more than twenty-five years earlier. In an attempt to rectify this problem a hiring initiative, Diplomacy 3.0, was begun with the goal of increasing the size of the Foreign Service by 25 percent by 2013. This goal was not met, and the target date for achieving it has been put back to 2023.

The second change is organizational. USIA and ACDA have been brought into the State Department ending their status as semiautonomous agencies. Secretary of State Condoleezza Rice combined arms proliferation and arms control bureaus into a Bureau of International Security and Nonproliferation, and a director of foreign assistance was placed over all foreign aid programs, whether they are administered by the State Department or by the USAID. Secretary of State Hillary Clinton instituted additional changes based on the State Department's first Quadrennial Diplomacy and Development Review (QDDR) issued in 2010. They included creating an undersecretary for civilian security, democracy, and human rights within the State Department and making USAID the lead agency for presidential initiatives on food security and global health.

The State Department's Value System

Capturing the essence of the State Department's value system is best done by looking at how secretaries of state have defined their role and how the FSO corps approach their job.

The Secretary of State The job of secretary of state is not an easy one. All too frequently it seems that post–World War II secretaries of state have left under a cloud of criticism. Among the charges leveled are lack of leadership (Dean Rusk), aloofness and arrogance (Dean Acheson), and overly zealous attempts to dominate foreign policy making (Henry Kissinger). Secretaries of state have also found themselves excluded from key decisions. Cyrus Vance resigned from the Carter administration partly in protest over his exclusion from decision-making on the Iranian hostage rescue effort.

In order to participate effectively in foreign policy making, secretaries of state, as do their counterparts at Defense and the CIA, need a power base from which to work. In practice, this has required that they must either become advocates of the State Department perspective or serve as the loyal ally of the president.[2] Neither guarantees success, and each power base has its dangers and limitations. Adopting the first perspective makes one suspect in the White House, while the second makes one suspect within the State Department and runs the risk of letting it drift for lack of effective oversight. The greatest danger comes with the failure to establish any power base, a situation said to have been experienced by Madeleine Albright, who served as secretary of state in the Clinton administration.

President George W. Bush's two secretaries of state adopted both of these role orientations. Colin Powell's primary role orientation was as a spokesperson for the State Department perspective. Condoleezza Rice built her power base around the close personal ties she had developed with Bush during the campaign and as national security advisor. As a strong political figure in her own right, Hillary Clinton, President Barack Obama's secretary of state in his first term, arrived at the State Department with a unique power base. Within State she proved herself to be a competent manager who lobbied on its behalf and restored much of the luster it had lost in previous years. At the policy level, she became the "bad cop" or "realist hawk" to Obama's "good cop" although she struggled to integrate herself into Obama's inner decision-making circle noting that she saw the president at least once a week while Kissinger saw Nixon every day.[3]

More generally, Hillary Clinton is seen as having done much to advance American soft power and promote people-to-people diplomacy while leaving crisis diplomacy to presidentially appointed special envoys. Walter Russell Mead judges her overall record as secretary of state to be mixed with Libya and Egypt seen as failures and her outreach to Burma that pulled it out of China's sphere of influence as an important success.[4] John Kerry, who was secretary of state in Obama's second term, came to the position with a strong personal connection to Obama from having worked with him on foreign policy issues as a special envoy in his first term. As was the case with Hillary Clinton, Kerry was not able to establish himself as a force in Obama's tightly controlled foreign policy decision-making process. What he did succeed in doing was creating an effective division of labor in foreign policy becoming the highly visible voice of an activist U.S. foreign policy in negotiations with Russia and in the Middle East. As one administration official summed up Kerry's deep commitment to negotiating difficult foreign policy problems: that's Kerry's thing, but we will back him if he appears to be succeeding.[5]

Foreign Service Officers

At the heart of the State Department system is its FSO corps. The Foreign Service was created in 1924 by the Rogers Act. Foreign service officers were intended to be generalists, "trained to perform almost any task at any post in the world."[6] The principal organizational device for producing such individuals is to rotate them frequently among functional tasks and geographic areas. The civil service, which existed apart from the FSO corps, was relied on to perform the State Department's "lesser" technical and administrative tasks. Increasingly FSOs feel themselves under siege by increasing politicization within the State Department where senior positions are routinely filled with short-term political appointees, a process referred to as **political creep**, and the blurring of the line between civil service and Foreign Service personnel.

From 1975 to 2013 the number of FSOs in senior positions, those at or above the rank of assistant secretary, declined from 60 percent to between 25 and 30 percent. Additionally in 2015 there were more than forty-five diplomatic assignments headed by individuals with titles such as special envoy and ambassador-at-large.

These individuals and their staffs are appointed outside of the standard process for hiring people in the State Department and often operate with little interaction with or regard for Foreign Service careerists. The end result of this "spoils system" according to a report by the American Academy of Diplomacy is a significant decline in professional input into the decision-making process.[7]

The distinction between FSOs and civil servants in the Foreign Service has long been the subject of controversy. In 1954 a reorganization proposal developed by Harry Wriston led to the merger of these two personnel systems. "Wristonization" was not a complete success. The hope had been this merger would "Americanize" the Foreign Service by bringing in individuals with pasts different from the eastern, Ivy League, and upper-class backgrounds associated with it. This broadening of outlook was seen as necessary because many viewed FSOs with suspicion for having becoming aloof and separate from American society. They were a prime target of the McCarthy investigations into un-American activities. In 1953 alone, some 70–80 percent of the highest-ranking FSOs were dismissed, resigned, or were reassigned to politically safe positions.[8] Today the concern is with the increased blurring of the line separating the Foreign Service and civil service which from the FSO perspective has resulted in a downgrading of professional experience in foreign policy decisions. For example, at issue is the decision to refer to FSOs as foreign service generalists or simply generalists in internal documents.

These concerns do not diminish the significance of two frequently identified ongoing problems with the FSO system. First, the representativeness of the FSO corps continues to be a major problem. In 1976 a class action discrimination lawsuit was brought against the State Department. That year only 9 percent of FSOs were women. In late 1993, 56 percent of the FSO corps was white male, 24 percent white female, 7 percent minority male, and 4 percent minority female. Additional problems surround the nature of key overseas appointments. Under George W. Bush, there were only three Hispanic FSOs serving as ambassadors and all were in Latin America. Only one of thirty-two diplomats heading embassies or U.S. missions in Europe in 2009 was black. No blacks held either of these positions in South and Central Asia or the Near East, but eleven of thirty-seven missions in Africa were headed by blacks.[9]

The second continuing problem is the FSO corps value system. It consists of a clearly identifiable world outlook and set of guidelines for survival within the State Department bureaucracy.[10] Most argue that this value system is not conducive to the formulation and administration of U.S. foreign policy and is one reason for the State Department's declining influence on foreign affairs. Central to this value system is the dual conviction that the only career experience relevant to the work of the State Department is that gained in the foreign service, and that the core of this work lies in the areas of political reporting, negotiating, and representing U.S. interests abroad. The FSO is empirical, intuitive, and cautious.[11] Risk taking in the preparation of analysis or processing of information is avoided. As one observer put it, the "desk officer 'inherits' a policy toward country X, he regards it as his function to keep that policy intact."[12]

Changes are coming to the FSO system and the culture of the State Department. One change is in how FSOs are selected. A new selection process has been put in place for selecting applicants for the Foreign Service. It changes the focus from competing in a lengthy national exam to emphasizing team-building abilities and résumés. A second change is found in the 2015 QDDR. Among its recommendations is the call for building a culture of collecting, using, and sharing data that would promote data driven policy making. Commentators note that this represents a significant change from the traditional FSO and State Department approach of working in highly decentralized units and emphasizing personal knowledge and contacts in making foreign policy.[13]

Impact on Foreign Policy

The State Department, once the centerpiece of the foreign affairs bureaucracy, has seen its power and influence steadily erode. It has gone from being the leading force behind such policies as the Marshall Plan, NATO, and containment to largely playing the role of the critic who finds fault with the proposals of others. It has become defensive and protective in interdepartmental dealings, unable to centralize and coordinate the activities of the foreign affairs bureaucracy.

Two complaints frequently are voiced about the State Department's performance. First, its recommendations are too predictable. Regardless of the problem, the State Department can be counted on to advocate minimizing risks, avoiding quick action, and adopting a long-term perspective on the problem. Second, its recommendations are insensitive to the presidential perspective on foreign policy matters. It fails to frame proposals in ways that will produce political support or at least minimize the political costs to the president. The combined result is that State Department recommendations are easily dismissed. In the eyes of many, it has become more of a spokesperson for foreign viewpoints within the U.S. government than an advocate of U.S. national interests. This situation is not condemned by all. To some, it is the role the State Department should play and that it should stop trying to perform functions for which it is no longer suited.[14]

The State Department's inability to exercise leadership in foreign policy has repeatedly produced calls for reform. The most recent effort is its first QDDR. Modeled on the **Quadrennial Defense Review** (QDR), this review was mandated by Hillary Clinton. Its central theme was the need to lead through civilian power. This is seen as deemphasizing the role of the military in societal reconstruction and development efforts and giving chiefs of mission greater power, expanding the skill set of FSOs, and turning to the expertise of other federal agencies before turning to private contractors.

The Defense Department

For most of its history, the military security of the United States was provided by forces under the command of the War Department and the Department of the Navy. No political or military authority other than the president existed above these two departments to coordinate and direct their affairs. During World War II, the ineffectiveness of this system became apparent and led U.S. policy makers to take a series of ad hoc steps to bring greater coherence to the U.S. war effort. In 1947 the National Security Act formalized many of these arrangements by establishing a Department of the Air Force and giving legal standing to the Joint Chiefs of Staff (JCS). It also created a National Military Establishment and the position of secretary of defense. Further changes were made in 1949, when the National Military Establishment was redesignated as the Department of Defense.

Structure and Growth

A number of different organizational reform issues have arisen since the Defense Department was created. In the early 1980s the pressing issue was improving the operational efficiency of the armed forces. The failed 1979 hostage rescue effort, the 1983 terrorist attack on the marines in Beirut, and problems encountered in the 1983 invasion of Grenada were cited by military reformers as proof that reforms were needed, beginning at the very top.[15] Congress shared these concerns. Over the objections of the executive branch and many in the military, in 1986 it passed two pieces of legislation designed to remedy the perceived shortcomings. The Goldwater-Nichols Act strengthened the position of the JCS relative to that of the individual services. It also gave added weight to those parts of the Pentagon that had an interservice perspective. The second piece of legislation, the Cohen-Nunn Act, established a unified command for special operations and created an assistant secretary of defense for special operations and low-intensity conflict.

More recently, four challenges have dominated the military reform agenda. The first three involve personnel issues. One is the need to find a response to the personnel crunch facing the military. The Army has experienced this problem most acutely. In 1990, at the end of the Cold War, the Army had 732,403 active-duty soldiers. This number was down to some 486,000 in 2002 before rebounding to 598,000 in May 2009. A 2014 Pentagon study projected a 420,000-person army in 2019.

One part of the solution has been to **outsource** many tasks to private contractors. These tasks range from cleaning military facilities to supervising supply lines, operating combat systems, and training troops. More than sixty private firms with twenty thousand employees were in Iraq at one point. In 2016 the Air Force planned to outsource the day-to-day management of its satellite communications system. While typically turned to as a means of saving money and dealing with personnel shortfalls, outsourcing can also be turned to for political purposes such as when the use of U.S. forces would arouse negative public opinion or run against congressional limits on the size of U.S. military operations such as was the case in Colombia during its civil war.

Another part of the solution to the personnel shortage problem has been to rely more heavily on National Guard and reserve forces. By 2005 almost 400,000 of the nearly 870,000 members of the reserves have been activated since 9/11. This represents the greatest proportional use of the National Guard and reserves since World War II. Still another move has been to step up its recruitment efforts, but this in turn has brought with it new problems.[16] One issue is that recruitment standards have been lowered. In 2007 only 79 percent of those enlisted had completed high school. This compares to 90 percent in 2001.

Historical Lesson

Integrating the Military

On July 26, 1948, President Harry Truman signed Executive Order 9981:

WHEREAS it is essential that there be maintained in the armed services of the United States the highest standards of democracy, with equality of treatment and opportunity for all those who serve in our country's defense:

NOW THEREFORE, by virtue of the authority vested in me as President of the United States, by the Constitution and the statutes of the United States, and as Commander in Chief of the armed services, it is hereby ordered as follows:

1. It is hereby declared to be the policy of the President that there shall be equality of treatment and opportunity for all persons in the armed services without regard to race, color, religion or national origin. This policy shall be put into effect as rapidly as possible, having due regard to the time required to effectuate any necessary changes without impairing efficiency or morale. . . .

Executive Order 9981 went on to create a President's Committee on Equality of Treatment and Opportunity in the Armed Services one of whose tasks was to examine how rules, procedures, and practices might be altered or improved upon to carry out this policy.

The history of black American participation in the military shows a continued pattern of white reluctance to allow it along with the military necessity that it occur. From the very outset free and slave blacks fought in the American Revolution on both sides. New England states offered freedom to slaves who fought as a means of meeting their quota of troops in the Continental Army. Some southern states did likewise but to a lesser degree. It is estimated that one-fifth of the Northern Army was black. After the war many of those promised freedom remained in slavery. For its part the British also offered freedom to blacks who joined with them. In the Civil War, manpower shortages led Congress to pass legislation to allow blacks to fight but required them to fight in racially segregated military units; 180,000 blacks fought for the North. After the war four black regiments were established, and they fought in the Indian wars and the Spanish-American War. This policy of segregated military units was in effect when World War II began. Also now in effect was a quota system which limited the number of blacks in the military to their percentage of the total American population. Once again pressures of wartime led to de facto changes in policy. With an insufficient number of Allied forces available to counter the German offensive at the Battle of the Bulge black soldiers were allowed to volunteer to fight alongside white soldiers rather than serve in support roles although they were placed in separate platoons.

After the end of World War II political pressures mounted for ending segregation. A 1945 Army report called ending discrimination a desirable goal but concluded it was impractical. In 1947 the Army permitted states to determine the level of integration of their National Guard above the company level. New Jersey ended military segregation at that point. The end result was a situation in which some states had partially integrated reserve units and the active military was segregated. In 1947 A. Philip Randolph helped establish the Committee Against Jim Crow in Military

Service and Training as part of a broader civil rights movement effort to end discrimination in the military. The focal point of their concern was Truman's plan for universal military service which while it did not endorse discrimination was perceived by Committee founders to endorse segregation. It was against this backdrop that Truman issued his executive order. It came shortly after he was nominated to run for president, an election many expected him to lose especially since southern democrats unhappy with the party's endorsement of civil rights decided to run their own candidate for president under the banner of the Dixiecrats.

Truman's executive order encountered resistance and was not uniformly accepted. In 1949 the secretary of the army was forced into retirement for refusing to desegregate the army. That same year 32 percent of white army personnel opposed integration in any form. During the Korean War a shortage of white enlisted men and increasing black enrollment created yet another crisis. 98 percent of blacks still served in segregated units and black soldiers were trained at a segregated military base. In 1951 while General MacArthur was still the commanding officer in Korea, evidence surfaced that far more black soldiers were being court martialed than were white soldiers. Thurgood Marshall was sent by the National Association for the Advancement of Colored People (NAACP) to investigate. He defined the military situation there as one of "rigid segregation." As a result of his investigations charges against most black soldiers were dropped. It would be under the Eisenhower administration in September 1954 that the last all back military unit was abolished. Many consider the endpoint of segregation in the military to be July 26, 1963, when Secretary of Defense Robert McNamara ordered an end to discrimination against blacks outside of military bases.

Applying the Lessons

1. How similar were the integration histories for women and blacks?
2. To what extent should the military be representative of all groups in society?
3. How does one measure the extent to which real change takes place in the military, the foreign service, intelligence agencies, or other national security bureaucracies?

The second personnel issue involves the treatment of individuals in the military, most notably gays and women. A "don't ask, don't tell" policy was put in place in 1994 that allowed gays to serve in the military, but it did not stop gays from being discharged. In December 2010, after months of political maneuvering by opponents in Congress along with a Pentagon study that supported it, President Obama signed legislation repealing the "don't ask, don't tell" policy. The policy formally came into effect in September 2011.

The role of women continues to be a major issue for the military. At the outset of the chapter we noted that in January 2013 the military formally lifted the ban on women in combat, but this is not the only issue involving the treatment of women in the military. Another controversy surrounds the problem of harassment. In 2015 the Pentagon reported 6,131 cases of sexual assault, a number that is more than double that in 2007. While this increased level of reporting of sexual harassment has brought greater awareness of the problem, obstacles remain. One report found that the military failed to take action against 30 percent of those accused of sexual assaults in 2010. There have also been repeated cases where senior officers charged with these offenses have been shielded by the system. Senator Kirsten Gillibrand introduced legislation that would remove sexual assault cases from the jurisdiction of military commanders. The Pentagon strongly opposed this measure, and it was defeated by a vote of 55–45 with 60 votes having been needed to break the filibuster that had been blocking its consideration.

The fourth issue is the size of the Defense Department's budget. Obama's proposed FY 2017 defense budget was $524 billion. This figure is considerably lower than the $671 billion actually spent by the Pentagon in FY 2010, and under terms of the 2011 Budget Control Act the Pentagon's budget must be reduced by some $487 billion over the next ten years. Additional funding was requested for Iraq and Syria ($59 billion) and to fight ISIS ($7.5 billion, up from $50 billion in FY 2015 with $200 million of that funding targeted on North and West Africa) bringing the total 2017 military budget to $583 billion. In breaking down the Pentagon's operating budget approximately two-thirds of the money is scheduled to finance the Pentagon's day-to-day operating costs including pay and benefits. The remaining one-third is directed to address future defense needs such as modernizing equipment and facilities. Compensation costs for active duty service members have risen 57 percent over the past decade with some estimates projecting that by FY 2021 military personnel related costs could consume 46 percent of the Defense Department budget.

The Defense Department's Value System

Understanding the Defense Department's internal value system requires that we look at how secretaries of defense have defined their job as well as how the professional military approaches its job.

Secretary of Defense Secretaries of defense generally have adopted one of two roles.[17] The first is that of the generalist. The generalist recognizes and defers to military expertise. He is concerned with coordinating and integrating the judgments he receives from the military professionals. He sees himself as being the Defense Department's representative in the policy process. In contrast, the functionalist is concerned with consolidating management and policy control in the office of the secretary of defense. The functionalist rejects the notion that there exists a unique area of military expertise, and he sees himself as first among equals in defense policy decision-making. Above all, the functionalist seeks to manage the system efficiently in accordance with presidential policy objectives.

James Forrestal, the first secretary of defense, adopted the generalist perspective. As secretary of the Navy, he had opposed creating a unified military establishment, and his tenure as secretary of defense was marked by repeated efforts by the services to protect their standing as independent organizations.

Robert McNamara, who served as secretary of defense during the Vietnam War, was a functionalist who sought to move decision-making power out of the hands of the military services and into the civilians in the Office of the Secretary of Defense. To do so, he brought Planning, Programming, and Budgetary System (PPBS) analysis to the Defense Department. Instead of organizing the budget by department (Army, Navy, Air Force), the PPBS examined spending by its principal missions such as conventional defense of Europe or nuclear deterrence.[18]

Donald Rumsfeld, George W. Bush's first secretary of defense, established himself from the very outset of the administration as a functionalist who intended to alter the fundamental direction of American military policy and organization. Military professionals saw his presence as a "hostile takeover."[19] Victory against the Taliban in Afghanistan and the early military success in Iraq appeared to vindicate his positions. Subsequent problems with the occupation and reconstruction of Iraq led to open questioning of his ideas and management style. Rumsfeld was replaced by Robert Gates, who stayed on in the Obama administration and moved to restore the working relationship between the civilians and the professional military officers in the Pentagon. Gates was not a generalist, however. He quickly established himself as a functionalist, moving aggressively to restructure defense-spending priorities away from advanced technology, high-cost, long lead time weapons systems as well as traditional military priorities such as aircraft carriers and the U.S. missile defense system to simpler systems that could be put into combat quickly. Ashton Carter, Obama's last secretary of defense, was also a functionalist who was committed to reducing the size of the military budget but also had had good working relations with military professionals having previously served as the Pentagon's chief of technology and weapons-buying programs. He replaced Chuck Hagel, an independent-minded Republican who had been highly critical of defense spending while in the Senate but failed to establish an effective working relationship with either the White House or the Pentagon.

Professional Military To understand the system of values inside the Defense Department, we need to examine the outlook of the professional military toward policy making at three different levels. At the highest level we have the general pattern of **civil-military relations**. Two different general sets of perspectives have long shaped thinking about this relationship.[20] The traditional view of civil-military relations sees the professional soldier as being above partisan politics. Professional soldiers are expected to restrict themselves to speaking out only on those subjects that fall within their sphere of expertise and stay out of politics. In the fusionist perspective, the professional soldier must acquire and use political skills if he or she is to exercise an effective voice on military matters.

In practice, neither is without its problems. The line separating military decisions from political ones is anything but clear making it difficult if not impossible for the professional to stand above politics. The challenges to a president created by an embrace of the fusionist perspective were fully evident in the dilemma facing the Obama administration on how to proceed in Afghanistan. General Stanley McChrystal's public evaluation of the situation there as dire and his call for a significant increase in the U.S. presence put him at odds with many civilians in the administration and helped create a politically charged domestic political climate within which Obama had to make his decision.

If we look down one level further, we see differences in outlook among the military services. They each have different "personalities."[21] The Navy, it is said, worships at the altar of tradition, the Air Force at the altar of technology, and the Army at that of country and duty. They also have different views of their own identities. The Navy sees itself above all as an institution whose stature and independence must be protected. The Air Force sees itself as the embodiment of the idea that air power is the key guarantor of national security in the modern age. The Army views itself as artisans of warfare. One of the challenges facing the U.S. Army today is how to conceptualize modern warfare. Two competing perspectives exist. The success of the Persian Gulf War in 1991 gave impetus to the idea of a **Revolution in Military Affairs** in which technological advances are central to success on the battlefield. At the opposite extreme is the development of counterinsurgency warfare thinking (COIN) which emphasizes the solider and their interaction with the local population.

At the most basic level concern focuses on the outlooks of individual soldiers. Most troubling here is the behavior of the officer corps. All of the services have been affected. At one point five active duty and former generals were reprimanded or investigated in a two-week period. Charges against them and other senior officers ranged from alcoholism to sexual assaults and misuse of government funds. In another case the Air Force suspended thirty-four officers responsible for launching nuclear weapons for cheating on exams that measure their knowledge of how to operate nuclear warheads.

Impact on Foreign Policy

The professional military's impact on foreign policy is a subject that is often discussed with great emotion. While some believe that military professionals are more aggressive than their civilian counterparts, evidence suggest otherwise.[22] Where the military professional and the civilian policy maker part company is over how and when to use force, not over whether to use it. The military prefers to use force quickly, massively, and decisively, and it is skeptical of making bluffs that involve the threatened use of force. Diplomats, on the other hand, prefer to avoid using force as long as possible, because they see its use as an indication of a failure in policy, but they are positively predisposed to making military threats.

The military's real policy influence comes through its ability to set the context of a decision through the presentation of information, capabilities, and tactics. Bob Woodward, author of *The Commanders*, similarly reflects on how variable the influence of the military is on decisions regarding the use of force.[23] The Pentagon, he notes, "is not always the center of military decision making." It was in the months before the George H. W. Bush administration's invasion of Panama, when the attention of the White House was on other matters. In the case of the Persian Gulf War, the White House paid attention to little else. "When the President and his advisors are engaged, they run the show."

One of the major ways in which the military can exercise this type of foundational and behind-the-scenes influence is through its planning process. Every four years, the Defense Department undertakes a QDR. The 2014 QDR identified three strategic pillars to guide military planning: defense of the U.S. homeland, building security globally, and projecting power and winning decisively. Critics argue that while the QDR identifies missions it fails to prioritize them thus limiting the military's ability to influence policy. Gates once noted that planning meetings with the Pentagon "seemed to be about some distant threshold war." The military seemed to be gearing up to fight wars of the future while ignoring wars of the present.[24]

CIA and the Intelligence Community

The intelligence community comprises sixteen agencies plus the Office of the Director of National Intelligence (ODNI). The director of national intelligence (DNI) is the head of the intelligence community. Until this position was created in 2004, the director of central intelligence (DCI) served as both head of the CIA and the intelligence community. Members of the intelligence community are charged with working independently and collaboratively to gather the information necessary to conduct foreign relations and national security activities. The requested National Intelligence Program budget for FY 2017 was $53.5 billion. The FY 2013 budget was officially listed at $40 billion after sequestration reductions. The largest share according to documents leaked to the press went to the CIA ($14.7 billion), the National Security Agency (NSA; $10.8 billion), and the National Reconnaissance Office ($10.3 billion). Funding for the CIA increased by 56 percent from 2004 and that for the NSA was up 33 percent.

Structure and Growth

Two points need to be stressed before turning our attention to three of the most prominent members of the intelligence community: the CIA, the NSA, and the ODNI. First, the intelligence community is not a static entity. Its composition, as well as the relative importance of its members, has changed over time as new technologies have been developed, the international setting has changed, and bureaucratic wars have been won and lost. The status of charter member is best conferred on the CIA; the State Department's intelligence unit, the Bureau of Intelligence and Research (INR); and the intelligence units of the armed forces. All of these were given institutional representation on the National Security Council at the time of its creation in 1947. Three institutions that have a long-standing but lesser presence in the intelligence community are the Federal Bureau of Investigation (FBI), the Treasury Department, and the Atomic Energy Commission (AEC), which is now found in the Energy Department. The newest addition to the intelligence community is the Department of Homeland Security.

Second, the concept of a community implies similarity and likeness. It suggests the existence of a group of actors who share common goals and possess a common outlook on events. In these terms, the U.S. intelligence community is a community only in the loosest sense. More accurately, it is a federation of units existing with varying degrees of institutional autonomy in their contribution to the intelligence function that both work together and challenge each other.

This point can be illustrated through several examples. The CIA and the Defense Intelligence Agency (DIA) have often been in conflict over matters of intelligence analysis. DIA was created in 1961 for the purpose of unifying the overall intelligence efforts of the Defense Department. During the Vietnam War, the CIA and DIA were often at odds over estimates of North Vietnamese and Viet Cong troop strength with CIA estimates being far more pessimistic than those of the DIA. During the Iraq War, the challenge to the CIA came from a newly created Office of Special Plans (OSP) within DIA whose mission it was to provide an independent review of raw intelligence and dispute the mainstream interpretations given to it by the intelligence community. More recently the CIA and DNI engaged in a bureaucratic conflict over who would select the covert action station chief. This traditionally had been a CIA responsibility but the DNI now claimed it. The final White House decision largely supported the CIA.

We begin our selective examination of members of the intelligence community looking at the CIA. For most Americans, the CIA is the public face of the intelligence community. And, since until the DNI came into existence, its director was also the head of the intelligence community, and it long enjoyed the status of first among equals within the intelligence community.

The organizational predecessor of the CIA was the Office of Strategic Services (OSS). It was created by a 1942 military order and tasked with collecting and analyzing strategic information and conducting special operations. At the end of World War II Truman disbanded the OSS and assigned its intelligence duties to units within State, and the Army and Navy. The 1947 National Security Act reestablished the CIA as a stand-alone intelligence unit.[25]

The CIA began a major reorganization in 2015. According to CIA director John Brennan the goal is to break down organizational "stove pipes" that artificially separate CIA personnel into different operating units making communication between them difficult. Central to the new organizational structure are ten mission centers that will bring together analysts and covert action operators on a day-to-day basis. The mission centers are modeled on the CIA's Counterterrorism Center and will focus on such issues as terrorism, weapons proliferation, global issues, and the Middle East. Up until now analysts were housed in the Directorate of Intelligence and operators were in the Directorate of Operations. These units were two of the four major operational arms of the CIA. The Directorate of Intelligence has been the primary producer of government intelligence documents, which range in frequency from daily briefs to weekly, quarterly, and yearly summaries, to occasional special reports. The best known of these reports are the National Intelligence Estimates (NIEs). The Directorate of Operations, more recently identified as the National Clandestine Service, has had three basic missions: the secret collection of information, counterintelligence, and covert action. They will continue to exist but will now focus on recruiting and training personnel who will be assigned to the centers. The two other directorates (the Directorate of Science and Technology and the Directorate of Personnel) will also continue to operate.

These four directorates will be joined by a new directorate: the Directorate of Digital Innovation. It is tasked with such responsibilities as cyber espionage, protecting the CIA's internal e-mail system, and monitoring global social media and other open source information sources. No timetable has been set for completing the reorganization.

The second prominent member of the intelligence community we will examine is the NSA. The NSA was the first major addition to the intelligence community. It came into existence in 1952 and operates as a semiautonomous agency of the Defense Department.[26] The NSA became the unwanted center of public attention in 2013 when the media began reporting on the existence of a secret domestic surveillance program under which it had been collecting information from various communication platforms including e-mail, chat services, videos, and file transfers. NSA argued that the program was approved by Congress and the courts. It maintained that the contents of these communications were not collected but only metadata, the beginning and endpoints of communication and its length, were being targeted. Any information gathered on Americans was termed "incidentally acquired" and "miniscule" in amount. Critics argued that the NSA was violating the Fourth Amendment which prohibits unreasonable searches and seizure, and that oversight by Congress and the courts was largely absent.

It too has recently undergone a major internal organizational change. In 2016 the NSA announced that the Signals Intelligence Directorate which was responsible for its offense mission of spying on foreign targets and the Information Assurance Directorate which was responsible for the NSA's defensive mission of defending classified networks from hostile attacks were to be merged into a single Directorate of Operations.

An earlier organizational change occurred in 2010 when the NSA's director also became the commander of the U.S. Cyber Command. Its initial focus was to be on developing policy and legal frameworks for the defense of the military's computer systems along with protecting private sector computers which provide a potential entry way into government computer systems from attack. In 2013 following a Defense Department study that concluded the military was unprepared for a full-scale cyber-attack the Pentagon began a major expansion of its cybersecurity force capabilities. Three different missions now have been identified for the expanded Cyber Command: (1) national mission forces to protect computer systems and other infrastructure s from foreign attack, (2) combat mission forces to plan and execute offensive operations, and (3) cyber protection forces to strengthen the Defense Department's computer networks. The combat mission force is expected to grow to fifteen units by the end of 2015. Additional teams would be created to support military commands.

The third organization we will examine is the newest agency involved in intelligence—the ODNI, which came into existence as part of the post-9/11 reforms of the intelligence community. Its head, the DNI, is identified as the principal intelligence advisor to the president and is charged with overseeing and directing the implementation of the National Intelligence Program. The two principal organization subunits within the ODNI focus on collection and analysis.

Two broad areas of concern have been raised about the operation of the ODNI. The first is its size. As originally envisioned, the ODNI was to be a lean management organization sitting atop the intelligence community. It quickly grew into an organization with a staff of over fifteen hundred people. In 2010 the President's Intelligence Advisory Board concluded that the ODNI had become "bureaucratic and resource heavy" to the point where it impeded its ability to coordinate the intelligence community. A second concern is with the powers of the office, in particular his budgetary powers and ability to shape intelligence programs. Only the CIA exists as a separate organizational entity within the intelligence community. All others are parts of larger departments, most often the Defense Department. Consequently, the other members of the intelligence community look with only one eye to what the DNI demands while keeping the other eye firmly fixed on departmental positions and priorities. Shortly after its creation, the FBI moved 96 percent of its intelligence budget into units that were not under the jurisdiction of the DNI. More recently, the DNI reached an agreement in principle with the Defense Department that the civilian portion of the Pentagon's intelligence budget will come under his control. The Pentagon's covert action/spy budget will remain under its jurisdiction.

The Intelligence Community's Value System

Periodically throughout its history the CIA has found itself an institution under siege both because of covert action and intelligence failures. Senator Daniel Patrick Moynihan was so outraged over the CIA's failure to anticipate the fall of communism in the Soviet Union that he called for its abolition.[27] One area that has received a great deal of attention is the manner in which both its top leadership and professionals approached their job. The Senate Intelligence Committee's report placed a major portion of the blame for the intelligence failures on Iraq and before 9/11 on "a broken corporate culture and poor management." It is to the informal organizational side of the CIA we now turn.

Director of Central Intelligence Because the DCI was simultaneously head of the intelligence community and the CIA, he had many role orientations available to choose from. Few sought and none achieved real managerial control over the intelligence community. The most recent to try was Stansfield Turner, President Carter's DCI, who ran into stiff and successful resistance from Secretary of Defense Harold Brown.

When defining their role as head of the CIA, three outlooks have been dominant: managerial, covert action, and estimating. Only John McCone (1961–65) gave primacy to the intelligence-estimating role, and he was largely an outsider to the intelligence process before his appointment. Allen Dulles (1953–65) and Richard Helms (1966–73) both stressed the covert-action side of the agency's mission. Since the replacement of Helms by James Schlesinger, DCIs have tended to adopt a managerial orientation. Although their particular operating styles have varied, a common theme to these managerial efforts was to increase White House control over the CIA.

According to critics of this role orientation one frequent result of this outlook is that the heads of the CIA have politicized the intelligence process. By this it is meant that they have used their managerial control over intelligence products to ensure that its findings are consistent with the policy preferences of the administration and do not reflect the judgment of intelligence professionals. **Politicizing intelligence** was a charge directed at William Casey, Robert Gates, and most recently George Tenet, who resigned in June 2004 after having become a central figure in the debate over whether the CIA as an organization or he personally had overstated the case for war with Iraq.

Director of National Intelligence The DNI is torn by the same types of role conflicts that have afflicted DCIs: the need to establish a power base and the need to define an orientation to intelligence. In a little more than five years, there were four DNIs. John Negroponte, the first DNI, moved quickly to solidify his position as the president's primary intelligence advisor by personally presenting the president's daily intelligence briefing. Later DNIs, however, struggled to establish both an effective working relationship with President Obama and with the intelligence community. One, Dennis Blair, resigned having failed to establish an effective power base with either.

Intelligence Professionals In order to understand how the intelligence professional thinks about intelligence, we first need to note how the consumers of intelligence think about it, because it is their demands and inquiries to which the intelligence professional responds.[28] First is the conviction that analysts should furnish information and nothing more. Exploring alternatives or coming to conclusions is the responsibility of the consumer. The underlying logic is one of "connecting-the-dots." Facts are seen as self-interpreting, and if all the facts are known, then any question can be answered. Second, it is assumed that experience rather than the application of analytical techniques to a problem provides the most insight into the meaning of raw data. Third is an emphasis on current events. The perceived need is for up-to-the-minute information to solve an ongoing problem. A final shared attitude toward intelligence is the tendency to treat it as a free good. Intelligence is seen as something "on tap" and always on call.

The views on intelligence within the intelligence community are far from uniform. Differences exist both between and within organizations.[29] For example, some suggest that within the cyber command four different outlooks can be identified all of which should be present: cyber priests (who think in terms of deterrence), cyber prophets (adaptation), cyber designers (resilience), and cyber detectives (resistance).[30]

With this qualification in mind, it is possible to identify four tendencies in the approach to intelligence adopted by members of the intelligence community.[31] One tendency is to be current events oriented and to be a "butcher," cutting up the latest information and presenting the choicest pieces to the consumer. A second tendency is for analysts to adopt a "jigsaw theory" of intelligence. The analyst here acts like a "baker"; everything and anything is sought after, classified, and stored, on the assumption that at some point in time, it may be the missing ingredient to solving a riddle. Similar to the butcher's role, the baker's role orientation is consistent with the policy maker's notion of intelligence as a free good and the assumption that the ambiguity of data can be overcome by collecting more data.

A third tendency is for the production of "intelligence to please" or "backstopping." Often, when consumers of intelligence stress current data, they combine it with known policy preferences. The analyst is then placed in a very difficult position. Efforts at providing anything but supportive evidence will be ignored. The final role orientation is that of the "intelligence maker," who acts as an organizational broker, forging a consensus on the issue at hand. Because a consensus is needed for action, this role orientation is valuable, but a danger exists in that the consensus does not have to be based on an accurate reading of events. Facts bargained into existence provide an equally suitable basis for a consensus.

Impact on Foreign Policy

Intelligence is not easily integrated into the policy process.[32] The relationship between intelligence and policy makers is marked by a series of tensions that often serve to make the impact of intelligence on policy less than what it could be under optimum circumstances. As Paul Pillar who once served as deputy director of the CIA's counterterrorism center observed about the Iraq War: "Had Bush read the intelligence community's report, he would have seen his administration's case for the invasion stood on its head."[33]

The first tension is between the logic of intelligence and the logic of policy making.[34] The logic of intelligence is to reduce policy options by clarifying issues, assumptions, and consequences. The logic of policy making is to keep options open for as long as possible. One way to do this is to keep secrets from intelligence agencies. The second tension is between the type of information the president wants to receive and the type of information that the intelligence community is predisposed to collect and disseminate. Policy makers are most eager to get information that will help them convince Congress or the public about the merits of a policy. They are most frustrated with information that is politically impossible to use and generally skeptical about the incremental value of added information for policy-making purposes.[35] Third, intelligence produced by the intelligence community is not the only source of information available to policy makers. Interest groups, lobbyists, the media, and personal acquaintances all compete with it, and presidents are free to choose which intelligence they wish to listen to. No one can make a policy maker accept or act on a piece of intelligence.

The Domestic Bureaucracies

The most recent additions to the foreign affairs bureaucracy are organizations that traditionally have been classified as domestic in their concerns and areas of operation. Their foreign policy involvement parallels a process that happened after World War II when the Defense Department, rather than the State

Department, was instrumental in shaping global arms development programs and international security arrangements.[36]

Integrating these newcomers into the foreign affairs bureaucracy has not been an easy task. At the core of the problem is finding an agreed-on balance between foreign policy and domestic concerns. In the early post–World War II period, the foreign policy goal of containing communism dominated over private economic goals, but, more recently, domestic goals have become dominant and are often pursued at the cost of broad foreign policy objectives.

Treasury, Commerce, and Agriculture

Of all the domestic bureaucracies, the Treasury Department plays the most prominent role in foreign policy so much so that by the mid-1970s, the State Department had become more of a participant than a leader in the field of international economic policy. The two departments approach international economic policy from quite different perspectives. Like the other domestic bureaucracies, the Treasury Department takes an **"America first" perspective** and places the needs of its clients at the center of its concerns. One author describes it as having an "undifferentiating adversary attitude" toward world affairs.[37] This is in contrast to the State Department's tendency to adopt a long-range perspective on international economic problems and one sensitive to the position of other states. A type of standoff currently exists between the State Department and Treasury Department for influence in the policy process although Treasury has been ascending in importance due to rise in the use of economic sanctions, the recent global economic downturn, and the central role played by China in holding U.S. debt and maintaining an undervalued currency. It is not unusual to find top treasury officials in negotiations with Chinese leaders. It now takes a strong secretary of state to neutralize the influence of the Treasury Department and its domestic allies.[38] Treasury gained additional importance as a foreign policy actor when along with trade restrictions economic sanctions began to include financial constraints directed at individuals. As a step in tightening sanctions against North Korea in 2016 the Treasury designated it as a "primary money launderer," a designation which makes it more difficult for North Korea to obtain funds from international financial institutions.

The Commerce Department has also emerged as a major foreign affairs bureaucracy, but its influence is not on the same level of the Treasury Department. It still functions as somewhat of a junior partner and is more involved in operating issues than in policy ones. Until 1969 the Commerce Department's primary foreign policy involvement stemmed from its responsibility for overseeing U.S. export control policy. These controls were aimed largely at restricting the direct or indirect sale of strategic goods to communist states. Since 1980, the Commerce Department has become the primary implementer of nonagricultural trade policy and the chief administrator of U.S. export and import programs. The Commerce Department is not without its own challengers for influence on trade policy. The Office of the U.S. Trade Representative has also benefited at the expense of the State Department, and it enjoys a great deal of congressional support for its activities.

The Agriculture Department also remains a junior partner in the foreign affairs bureaucracy. It is active in administering U.S. food export programs. Its best-known foreign policy role is as the administrator of P.L. 480, the Food for Peace program, which provides for the free export of government-owned agricultural commodities for humanitarian and developmental purposes. In 2003 the Agriculture Department became embroiled in controversy for providing export help to American tobacco companies. The Foreign Agriculture Service provided market information to firms about where the demand for American cigarettes was high and where control laws were weak.

Numerous others play occasional roles as well. The Drug Enforcement Agency (DEA) has eighty-six foreign offices in sixty-seven countries where they carry out bilateral investigations; sponsor and conduct counter-narcotics training; participate in intelligence gathering activities; and provide assistance in developing drug control laws and regulations. The DEA gained notoriety recently when its agents accompanied Honduran counter-narcotics police in two firefights with cocaine smugglers. One of these incidents left four people dead leading to demands that it leave the country. The Food and Drug Administration has become more active in foreign policy issues though its inspection program of drug and food imports into the United States. Some one hundred and fifty countries export FDA-regulated products to the United States. As of 2008 the FDA operated foreign offices in China, India, as well as countries in Europe and Latin America.

Homeland Security

The Department of Homeland Security is an uneasy fit in the foreign affairs bureaucracy. It has elements of both a foreign policy organization and a domestic one given the wide range of activities that fall under its jurisdiction. The Department of Homeland Security was established on November 25, 2002, as a response to the terrorist attacks of 9/11. Its creation combined twenty-two different agencies from eight different departments with a projected budget of $37.45 million and 170,000 employees into one. It absorbed all of the Federal Emergency Management Agency (FEMA), the Coast Guard, the Secret Service, the Immigration and Naturalization Service, and the Customs Service, along with the new Transportation Security Administration. The FBI and CIA were not directly affected by the creation of the Department of Homeland Security, but the new department was given an "intelligence and threat analysis" unit that would serve as a customer of FBI and CIA intelligence for assessing threats, taking preventive action, and issuing public warnings.

Where the Defense Department has been described as a bureaucratic battleship that can only change directions very slowly, Homeland Security has been likened to a speedboat that keeps turning and shifting gears but goes nowhere. In virtually all aspects of its work, Homeland Security has encountered problems, beginning with its ineffective color-coded terrorist warning system that was put into place after 9/11 and continuing on to its tracking of the activities of peaceful war protestors. Among those groups it placed under surveillance were

Amnesty International, CASA, and People for the Ethical Treatment of Animals. Most recently, Homeland Security found itself at the center of the political controversy over immigration reform. As a consequence for three months in 2015 Congress refused to appropriate money for its operation with the result that the Department of Homeland Security faced the possibility of having to shut down. Congress finally passed funding providing them with six months of continued funding.

Policy Makers' Response

According to Henry Kissinger, "The purpose of bureaucracy is to devise a standard operating procedure that can cope effectively with most problems."[39] Doing so frees high-level policy makers to concentrate on the unexpected and the exceptional and to pursue policy innovations. While true in theory, this view is misplaced. In practice two problems arise. First, policy makers expect far more from bureaucracy than help in dealing with the normal—probably too much. Consider President Gerald Ford's statement about the U.S. involvement in Vietnam: "We could have avoided the whole darn Vietnam War if somebody in the Department of Defense or State had said, 'Look here. Do we want to inherit the French mess?'"[40] As we saw in chapter 4, the reality of the U.S. involvement in Vietnam is far more complex. Second, policy makers often feel trapped by the bureaucracy. Obama put it this way: "There's a playbook in Washington that presidents are supposed to follow. It's a playbook that comes out of the foreign policy establishment. . . . But the play book can also be a trap that can lead to bad decisions."[41]

Policy makers have adopted three different strategies for dealing with bureaucracies that are perceived to be failing them.[42] The first is to replace senior leaders. The second is to reorganize bureaucracies. Rare is the bureaucracy that is simply eliminated. Instead, the solution is to combine the offender with another or rearrange its internal structure. In the extreme, this solution takes the form of creating a new bureaucracy to address an ongoing problem. Finally, policy makers may simply choose to ignore the bureaucracy, either by becoming their own experts or by establishing an informal in-house body of experts to produce policy guidance.

It also needs to be noted that bureaucrats have their own view of the problem of integrating the bureaucracy with policy makers. When asked by President Kennedy what was wrong with the State Department, career diplomat Charles Bohlen replied, "You are."[43] Indications that this sentiment still exists came through in June 2016 when fifty-one State Department employees signed a letter to President Obama that was leaked to the press. In it they asserted his policy toward Syria would not end the civil war and called for the ouster of Syrian president Assad. Secretary of State Kerry met with eight FSOs days later to assure them that the issues they raised had been considered. At virtually the same time it was reported that generals in charge of the Iraq War were becoming frustrated and wanted Obama to deploy more troops.

Over the Horizon: Rethinking the All-Volunteer Army

Change does not come easily to bureaucracies. One of the great challenges in constructing foreign policy bureaucracies is to ensure that not only do they contribute to addressing current problems but that they will be able to help policy makers deal with future problems, many of which cannot be completely foreseen. For the military, this is the challenge of building the **military after next**: the military to address tomorrow's national security threats.[44] Debates over how to do this cover many topics. Ones that we will discuss in later chapters include the use of drones, cyber warfare, and the value of counterinsurgency warfare.

Karl Eikenberry, who served as ambassador to Afghanistan from 2009 to 2011 and as head of the U.S.-led Coalition of Forces in Afghanistan from 2005 to 2007, argues that the beginning point for thinking about the military after next is to rethink the all-volunteer army. Military conscription in the United States ended in 1973 for a variety of reasons: demographics, cost, moral arguments about imposing military service, and opposition to Vietnam were among the leading arguments made for ending the draft.

Without formally calling for a return to the draft, Eikenberry argues that for two reasons the advantages of an all-volunteer army over one based on conscription are less certain today than some forty years ago when the all-volunteer army came into existence. First is the question of political ownership of the military: To whom is the military responsible? Ending the draft weakened the connection between military policy and the average citizen. More and more the military has come to rely on young men and women from economically depressed rural areas. There has also been a decline in the number of African American recruits. These trends have given rise to concerns about the representativeness of the military in American society.

Second is the decrease in congressional and media oversight that holds military professionals accountable for their actions. Few members of Congress rigorously challenge military spending patterns or management practices. The Defense Department has gone twenty years without a financial audit and is the last federal department yet to conduct one. The new deadline is 2017. The media focuses on soldiers (embedded reporting) and procurement scandals but seldom on the big picture. One result of the removal of these domestic constraints is that policy makers now have a freer hand to engage in military interventions. As Eikenberry puts it, "The U.S. military has . . . become Thor's hammer that makes increasing numbers of foreign policy appear to be nails."[45]

Another chapter in the debate over the merits of the all-volunteer army versus the draft has recently begun. Opening combat to women soldiers has brought forward calls for requiring women to register for the draft as men do. The heads of all the military services have come out in support of doing so while also asserting they are not interested in reinstating the draft. In June 2016 the Senate passed legislation requiring women to register for the draft. The bill was then sent to the House where Republican opposition existed. The call for registering women for the draft has brought renewed attention on questions concerning the ability of the all-volunteer army to meet future national security needs. Andrew Krepinevich is doubtful, "The risk is that our desire to ask only those who are willing to fight to do so is pricing us out of some kinds of warfare."[46]

Critical Thinking Questions

1. What is more important to the quality of bureaucratic performance—its formal structure or the value system of its members?
2. Is there a place for the domestic bureaucracies we identified in making American foreign policy or should their tasks be taken over by more traditional foreign policy agencies?
3. Can the State Department lead in the making of U.S. foreign policy? Should it lead? If not, who should lead?

Key Terms

"America first" perspective, 208
civil-military relations, 200
country team, 191
foreign service officers, 193
military after next, 211

outsource, 196
political creep, 193
politicizing intelligence, 206
Quadrennial Defense Review, 195
Revolution in Military Affairs, 201

Further Reading

Gordon Adams and Shoon Murray, eds., *Mission Creep* (Washington, DC: Georgetown University Press, 2014).
This book argues that a militarization of U.S. foreign policy has taken place as a result of the Defense Department's involvement in the implementation and formation of foreign policy programs in nontraditional areas such as foreign aid, public diplomacy, economic development, and covert action.
American Diplomacy at Risk (Washington, DC: American Academy of Diplomacy, April 2015).
This study of American diplomacy is critical of the politicization of American diplomacy which it argues has contributed greatly to the disappearance of foreign service professionals. It concludes with recommendations to improve the State Department's organization and management.
Roger George and James Bruce, *Analyzing Intelligence*, 2nd ed. (Washington, DC: Georgetown University Press, 2014).
The authors provide an excellent overview of the analytic challenges facing the intelligence community and the dynamics of intelligence analyst—policy maker relations.
John Harr, *The Professional Diplomat* (Princeton, NJ: Princeton University Press, 1969).
This book provides an early but still valuable and frequently cited study of the attitudes and values of professional diplomats.
Benjamin Jensen, *Forging the Sword* (Stanford: Stanford University Press, 2016)

This book traces the process of doctrinal reform within the U.S. Army. It finds that central to bringing about change in military organizations are "incubators" and advocacy networks. Together they can bring about changes in elite thinking that otherwise would not occur.

Thomas Mackubin, "Military Officers: Political without Partisanship," *Strategic Studies Quarterly* 9 (Fall 2015), 88–101.

According to tradition, military officers are to remain apolitical in carrying out their duties. This essay examines this tradition and several ways in which military officers exercise influence in public debates over military policy.

Amy Zegart, *Flawed by Design* (Stanford: Stanford University Press, 1999).

This book examines the creation of the Central Intelligence Agency. It argues that the politics surrounding this process produced an organization designed as much to protect existing bureaucratic interests as it was to solve the intelligence problem.

Notes

[1] On the volume of State Department message traffic, see Werner Feld, *American Foreign Policy: Aspirations and Reality* (New York: John Wiley, 1984), 61; Gene Rainey, *Patterns of American Foreign Policy* (Boston: Allyn & Bacon, 1975), 175.

[2] J. Anthony Holmes, "Where Are the Civilians: How to Rebuild the U.S. Foreign Service," *Foreign Affairs* 88 (2009), 148–60.

[3] Christopher Jones and Kevin Marsh, "Conducting Diplomacy," in Steve Hook and James Scott (eds.), *U.S. Foreign Policy Today: American Renewal?* (Washington, DC: CQ Press, 2012), 162–80; and Peter Baker, "Emails Show Hillary Clinton Trying to Find Her Place," *New York Times*, July 2, 2015, A1.

[4] Walter Russell Mead, "Was Hillary Clinton a Good Secretary of State?" *Washington Post*, May 30, 2014, https://www.washingtonpost.com/opinions/was-hillary-clinton-a-good-secretary-of-state/2014/05/30/16daf9c0-e5d4-11e3-a86b-362fd5443d19_story.html.

[5] Peter Baker, "John Kerry Rushes in Where Obama Will Not Tread," *New York Times*, September 30, 2015, A1.

[6] Donald Warwick, *A Theory of Public Bureaucracy: Politics, Personality and Organization in the State Department* (Cambridge: Harvard University Press, 1975), 29–30.

[7] *American Diplomacy at Risk* (Washington, DC: American Academy of Diplomacy, April 2015).

[8] Henry T. Nash, *American Foreign Policy: A Search for Security*, 3rd ed. (Homewood: Dorsey, 1985), 141.

[9] Paul Richter and Tom Hamburger, "Few Blacks Serve in Top U.S. Diplomatic Posts," *Los Angeles Times*, March 16, 2010.

[10] In addition to other studies cited in this chapter, see Andrew Scott, "The Department of State: Formal Organization and Informal Culture," *International Studies Quarterly* 13 (1969), 1–18; Andrew Scott, "Environmental Change and Organizational Adaptation: The Problem of the State Department," *International Studies Quarterly* 14 (1970), 85–94.

[11] John Harr, *The Professional Diplomat* (Princeton: Princeton University Press, 1969), 197–98.

[12] I. M. Destler, *Presidents, Bureaucrats, and Foreign Policy: The Politics of Organizational Reform* (Princeton: Princeton University Press, 1972), 158.

[13] QDDR II.

[14] Robert Pringle, "Creeping Irrelevance at Foggy Bottom," *Foreign Policy* 29 (1977/78), 128–39; Warwick, *A Theory of Public Bureaucracy*, 72.

[15] For a discussion on the pros and cons of reorganizing the JCS system, see William J. Lynn and Barry R. Posen, "The Case for JCS Reform," *International Security* 10 (1985/86), 69–97; MacKubin Thomas Owen, "The Hollow Promise of JCS Reform," *International Security* 10 (1985/86), 98–111; Edward Luttwak, *The Pentagon and the Art of War* (New York: Touchstone, 1985).

[16] Ann Scott Tyson, "Youths in Rural U.S. Are Drawn to Military," *Washington Post,* November 4, 2005, A1; Josh White, "Steady Drop in Black Army Recruits," *Washington Post,* March 9, 2005, A1.

[17] James Roherty, "The Office of the Secretary of Defense," in John E. Endicott and Roy W. Stafford (eds.), *American Defense Policy,* 4th ed. (Baltimore: Johns Hopkins University Press, 1977), 286–96.

[18] Amos A. Jordan and William J. Taylor Jr., *American National Security: Policy and Process* (Baltimore: Johns Hopkins University Press, 1981), 185.

[19] Bob Woodward, *State of Denial: Bush at War, Part III* (New York: Simon & Schuster, 2006), 39.

[20] John H. Garrison, "The Political Dimension of Military Professionalism," in Endicott and Stafford (eds.), *American Defense Policy,* 578–87.

[21] Carl Builder, *The Masks of War* (Baltimore: Johns Hopkins University Press, 1989).

[22] Richard K. Betts, *Soldiers, Statesmen, and Cold War Crises* (Cambridge, MA: Harvard University Press, 1977), 4–5.

[23] Bob Woodward, *The Commanders* (New York: Simon & Schuster, 1991), 33.

[24] Bob Woodward, *Obama's War* (New York: Simon & Schuster, 2010), 20–21.

[25] Mark Lowenthal, *U.S. Intelligence,* Washington Paper #105 (New York: Praeger, 1984), 89–92; Stafford Thomas, *The U.S. Intelligence Community* (Latham: University of America Press, 1983), 45–63.

[26] James Bamford, *The Puzzle Palace: Inside the National Security Agency* (Baltimore: Penguin, 1982).

[27] See, for example, Herbert Meyer, "Reinventing the CIA," *Global Affairs* 7 (1992), 1–13; Marvin Ott, "Shaking up the CIA," *Foreign Policy* 93 (1993), 132–51.

[28] Roger Hilsman, *Strategic Intelligence and National Defense* (Glencoe: Free Press, 1956), 37–56.

[29] For a discussion of these points, see Patrick J. McGarvey, *The CIA: The Myth and the Madness* (Baltimore: Penguin, 1973), 148–59; Victor Marchetti and John D. Marks, *The CIA and the Cult of Intelligence* (New York: Dell, 1974), 235–77.

[30] Chris Demchak, "Conflicting Policy Presumptions about Cybersecurity," *Atlantic Council Issue Briefs,* http://www.acus.org/files/publication_pdfs/403/_Demchakbrief.pdf.

[31] Hilsman, *Strategic Intelligence and National Defense,* 199–222; Thomas L. Hughes, *The Fate of Facts in a World of Men,* Headline Series #233 (New York: Foreign Policy Association, 1976), 36–60.

[32] Sherman Kent, *Strategic Intelligence for American World Policy* (Princeton: Princeton University Press, 1966); Willmoore Kendall, "The Functions of Intelligence," *World Politics* 2 (1949), 542–52.

[33] Paul Pillar, "Think Again: Intelligence," *Foreign Policy* 191 (January/February 2012), 52.

[34] Hughes, *Fate of Facts in a World of Men,* 47.

[35] Thomas Hughes, "The Power to Speak and the Power to Listen: Reflections on Bureaucratic Politics and a Recommendation on Information Flows," in Thomas M. Franck and Edward Weisband (eds.), *Secrecy and Foreign Policy* (New York: Oxford University Press, 1974), 18.

[36] Raymond Hopkins, "The International Role of 'Domestic Bureaucracies,'" *International Organization* 30 (1976), 411.

[37] Stephen D. Cohen, *The Making of United States International Economic Policy: Principles, Problems, and Proposals for Reform,* 2nd ed. (New York: Praeger, 1981), 40.

[38] Ibid., 41.

[39] Henry Kissinger, "Conditions of World Order," *Daedalus* 95 (1966), 503–29.

[40] "No Point in Being Bitter," *Washington Post,* December 31, 2006, B1.

[41] Jeffrey Goldberg, "The Obama Doctrine," *The Atlantic,* April 1, 2016, Atlantic

[42] Morton Abramowitz and Leslie Gelb, "In Defense of Striped Pants," *National Interest* 79 (2005), 73–77.

[43] Quoted in Destler, *Presidents, Bureaucrats, and Foreign Policy,* 155.

[44] Paul Bracken, "The Military after Next," *Washington Quarterly* 16 (1993), 157–74.

[45] Karl Eikenberry, "Reassessing the All-Volunteer Force," *Washington Quarterly* 36 (2013), 7–24; see also William Hauser and Jerome Slater, "The Call-Up: Conscription Again," *World Affairs* 172 (2010), 75–82.

[46] Quoted in "Who Will Fight the Next war," *The Economist,* October 24, 2015.

Policy-Making Models 9

Dateline: Drone Policy

In chapter 1 we noted that not all foreign policy problems are alike. To fully understand U.S. foreign policy we must move beyond this observation and understand the decision-making process by which a policy comes into existence. Here we provide a brief overview of key decisions the Obama administration had to make in setting its drone policy, a policy area within which great controversy exists. For some drones are the weapon of choice in the war against terrorism. To others drones are highly questionable instruments of war that have come to be used with effective oversight.

A first decision is how often should drones be used? No agreed upon figure exists on how many drone strikes have been carried out. A gap exists between the administration's declaratory policy and its action policy. In 2013 Obama promised to release drone strike and casualty figures in the interest of making the drone program more transparent. By June 2016 his administration had not yet done so. One commentator using figures from multiple sources concluded that Bush authorized some 50 drone strikes that killed 296 terrorists and 195 civilians in Yemen, Pakistan, and Somalia, and that by 2016 Obama authorized 506 strikes that killed 3,040 terrorists and 391 civilians. In 2016 the administration began to use drone strikes against terrorists in Libya and Somalia.

A second decision is how to approve drone strikes. Under Obama an elaborate and highly structured system existed on paper. A "disposition matrix" serves as a database for targeted killings. The National Counterterrorism Center develops a target list. A third element is a "legal architecture" for choosing targets. The need for this set of criteria grew out of the controversy surrounding the drone killing of Anwar al-Awlaki in 2011. Al-Awlaki was an Islamic cleric who also was an American citizen. He helped put together the failed terrorist strike on an airliner on Christmas Day in Detroit in 2009. At issue was whether killing rather than capturing him was violation of his constitutional right to due process. Information leaked by a whistleblower to the press suggests a less rigorous decision-making process. While Obama gave his permission for each target chosen in Yemen and Somalia (the Central Intelligence Agency (CIA) selects its own targets in Pakistan) he did not know when and where the attack would take place or the specific risk to civilians. His approval was simply for a sixty-day window for the strike(s) to take place.

A third decision is who should carry out the drone strikes? Initially drone strikes primarily were carried out by the CIA. Obama indicated he wanted primary responsibility turned over to the military so that the CIA could concentrate on its intelligence gathering and analysis missions. Critics held this change in operational responsibility was to escape the requirement that Congress be informed in advance of CIA covert action activities (the drone strike). No such advance reporting requirement exists for military action taken by the Pentagon. Some observers suggest that no real decrease in CIA drone strikes actually took place. The administration also came under pressure from members of Congress including the Republican chair and Democratic vice chair of the Senate Intelligence Committee to allow the CIA to carry out more drone strikes on the grounds that they produced fewer civilian casualties than did military drone attacks.

A fourth decision is are there alternatives to drones? Making a judgment about alternatives involves establishing evaluative standards. No agreed upon standard exists. During the Bush administration when drones were less frequently used the alternative employed was to rely on local forces. The end results were often that the target escaped and/or that the military action resulted in human rights abuses, torture, and extrajudicial killings. However, it is argued that drone strikes create blowback against the United States among the local population because of the number of civilian deaths. Weighing and constructing alternatives also involves asking ethical (are drone strikes different from assassinations) and legal questions. On this later point Obama asserted drone strikes did not represent a violation of the War Powers Resolution because they did not involve the presence of U.S. ground troops or U.S. casualties or create a serious threat that this would happen. He further argued they were permitted under the Authorization of Military Force Resolution passed by Congress after the 9/11 attacks.

It is one thing to recount key aspects of an important foreign policy decision, but how do we decide what were the important influences shaping the key decisions. One way to answer these questions is to employ a foreign policy decision-making model. In this chapter, we survey five of the most frequently used **models** of U.S. foreign policy making, highlighting both their strengths and weaknesses.[1] We illustrate how these models can be used to understand U.S. foreign policy making by looking at the Cuban missile crisis from three different vantage points.

Foreign Policy Decisions and Models

One former foreign policy maker has observed that "the business of Washington is making decisions."[2] But what is a foreign policy decision? What is it we are trying to understand? Answering these questions is complicated by a number of factors. First, the notion of a decision is itself somewhat misleading. It suggests the existence of a specific point in time at which a conscious judgment is made on what to do about a problem. Reality is often far less organized. Decisions are seldom final or decisive; they tend to lack concrete beginning and endpoints; and they often amount to only temporary breathing spells or truces before the issue is raised again. Decisions are also often made with far less attention to their full meaning and consequences than is commonly recognized. "A government does not decide to inaugurate the nuclear age, but only to try and build the bomb before its enemy does."[3]

A second factor complicating efforts to understand how policy is made is the relationship of the policy process to policy outcomes. Our intuitive sense is that if the policy process can be made to work properly, then the policy outcome should also work. Accordingly, bad policy can be attributed to bad decision-making. Unfortunately, the link between the two is imperfect. Good decision-making does not ensure good policy. A provocative account of the U.S. experience in Vietnam argued that the fundamental irony of Vietnam is that while U.S. policy has been roundly criticized, the policy-making system worked.[4] It achieved its basic purpose of preventing a communist victory until domestic political opinion coalesced around a strategy of either victory or withdrawal. The political system produced policies that were responsive to the wishes of the majority and near the political center while at the same time allowing virtually all views to be aired. The bureaucracy selected and implemented measures designed to accomplish these ends, and these policies were undertaken without illusions about their ultimate chances of success.

In an effort to make sense out of the complicated business of making decisions, models have been developed to help explain, describe, predict, and evaluate how U.S. foreign policy is made. Models are analytical tools that are designed to serve as simplified representations of reality. As simplifications, they leave out much of the detail and texture of what goes on in the policy-making process. Models can be distinguished from one another in terms of how they seek to capture and depict reality.

Before turning our attention to the models, two caveats need to be raised. First, we are not arguing that policy makers consciously choose one of these models and act accordingly. We are arguing only that these models can help us understand what is happening during the policy-making process. Second, these models should not be judged in terms of being right or wrong. A more useful standard is how helpful the model is for explaining, describing, or evaluating the workings of the foreign policy process for the policy being studied.

The Rational Actor Model

The most frequently employed policy-making model is the **rational actor** model. At its core is an action-reaction process. Foreign policy is viewed as a calculated response to the actions of another actor. This action then produces a calculated response that in turn causes the state to reevaluate and readjust its own foreign policy. In carrying out these calculations, the state is seen as being unitary and rational. By unitary, it is meant that the state can be viewed as calculating and responding to external events as if it were a single entity. There is no need for the analyst to delve into the intricacies of governmental organization, domestic politics, or personalities in trying to understand why a policy was selected. The state can be treated as a **black box**, responding with one voice to the challenges and opportunities confronting it. We implicitly employ this model when we speak of Israeli goals, Argentine national interests, or Soviet adventurism.

The basic elements of a rational decision process are that (1) goals are clearly stated and ranked in order of preference, (2) all options are considered, (3) the consequences of each option are assessed, and (4) a value-maximizing choice is made. Broadly speaking, there are two ways of carrying out a rational actor analysis of policy making. The first is inductive. It is frequently employed in diplomatic histories. The analyst tries to understand the foreign policy decision by placing himself or herself in the position of the government taking the action. The objective is to appreciate the situation as the government sees it and to understand the logic of the situation. The second approach is deductive. It is best exemplified by game theory and is frequently employed by military strategists and deterrence theorists. Here it is assumed that "a certain kind of conduct is inherent in a particular situation or relationship."[5] Rather than relying on actual events to support its analysis, the deductive approach relies on logical and mathematical formulations of how states should (rationally) behave under given conditions.

The rational actor model is attractive because it places relatively few informational demands on the observer. It is also frequently criticized for essentially the same reason. Foreign policy is not just made in response to external events; it is heavily influenced by domestic political calculations, personalities, and organizational factors. In addition, the rational actor model assumes that "important events have important causes." By doing so, it downgrades the importance of chance, accidents, and coincidence in foreign affairs. Critics also contend that the model's information-processing demands exceed human capabilities. Goals are seldom stated clearly or rank ordered. The full range of policy options and their consequences is rarely evaluated. And in making decisions, the need for value trade-offs is denied more than it is faced.

In place of the assumption of rationality, critics often advance two other models. One is based on the concept of incremental decision-making in which goals are only loosely stated, a limited range of options is examined, and the policy selected is one that "satisfies" (from satisfactory to sufficient) rather than optimizes.[6] Another decision-making model asserts that individuals tend to value what they have more than what they do not have; they prefer the status quo more often than one would predict; and they tend to be risk-averse with respect to gains and risk-accepting when it comes to losses. Known as **prospect theory**, it implies that leaders will take more risks to defend their state's international position than to enhance it, and that after a loss, leaders will have a tendency to take excessive risks to recover their positions.[7]

A final challenge to the rational actor model centers on its methodology. Carried out either inductively or deductively, the rational actor model relies heavily on intuition and personal judgment in interpreting actions or placing weights on policy payoffs. Graham Allison has captured this criticism in his rationality theorem.[8] He states that there is no pattern of activity for which an imaginative analyst cannot find objectives that are maximized by a given course of action.

The Bureaucratic Politics Model

Bureaucratic politics is the "process by which people inside government bargain with one another on complex public policy questions."[9] As this definition suggests, the **bureaucratic politics** model approaches policy making in a completely different way from the rational actor model. Policy making is seen as a political process dominated by conflict resolution and not problem solving. Politics dominates the decision-making process because no individual is in a position to decide matters alone. Power is shared, and the individuals who share power disagree on what should be done because they are located at different places within the government and see different faces of the problem.

Using military force to punish terrorists looks different to a secretary of state, who must balance the diplomatic pluses and minuses of such a move, than it does to the military chiefs of staff, whose forces would be used, or to a presidential aide, who is most sensitive to the domestic implications of the success or failure of such a mission. Not everyone in the government is a participant in a particular policy-making "game." Fixed organizational routines define the issue, produce the information on which policy decisions are made, link institutions and individuals together, and place limits on the types of policy options that can be implemented.

Furthermore, the players in the game are not equal in their ability to influence the outcome of the bargaining process. Deadlines, the rules of the game, and **action channels** confer power to some and deny it to others. Rules determine what kind of behavior is permitted and by whom. Can unilateral statements be made? Can information be leaked? Action channels link policy makers together and determine who is in the best position to make a unilateral statement or to be included in a committee that approves action. Deadlines force issues by accelerating the tempo of the decision-making process and creating pressure for an agreement. They come in many forms, such as a meeting with a foreign head of state, a presidential speech, or congressionally established reporting deadlines for the State Department.

Rarely do policy problems enter or leave the policy process in a clearly definable manner. More frequently, they flow through it in a fragmented state and become entangled in other ongoing policy issues. The result is that policy is not formulated with respect to any underlying conception of the U.S. national interest. Instead, its content is heavily influenced by the way in which the problem first surfaces and how it interacts with the other issues on the policy agenda.

A recent example comes from the Obama administration. Director of National Intelligence (DNI) Dennis Blair claimed the right to determine which intelligence officer in an embassy would be designated as the senior intelligence representative. This position has been held for fifty years by the CIA station chief. Leon Panetta, director of the CIA, resisted the move, just as his predecessor resisted efforts by previous DNIs to accomplish this change in authority and power in U.S. embassies. The dispute worked its way up to the White House, where after several months National Security Advisor James Jones supported the CIA's position.

In putting all of the foregoing together, advocates of the bureaucratic politics model argue that policy is not, and cannot be, a product of deliberate choice. Instead, policy is either a result of a political bargaining process or the product of organizational **standard operating procedures**.[10] In either case, the new policy arrived at is not likely to differ greatly from the existing policy. This is because bargaining is a time-consuming and expensive process. The policy makers also are often quite deeply committed to their positions. The need for agreement pushes policy makers toward accepting a minimal decision, one that will allow all sides to claim a partial victory. The inflexible and blunt nature of organizational routines and procedures reinforces the tendency for policy to change only at the margins. Administrative feasibility is a constant check on the ability of policy makers to tailor policy options to meet specific problems. In sum, from the bureaucratic politics perspective, the best predictor of future policy is not the policy that maximizes U.S. national interests but that which is only incrementally different from current policy.

The bureaucratic politics model makes important contributions to understanding U.S. foreign policy by highlighting the political and organizational nature of policy making. However, it has also been the subject of extensive criticisms. First, by emphasizing compromise, bargaining, and standard operating procedures, the bureaucratic model makes it very difficult to assign responsibility for the decisions being made.[11] Second, it misrepresents the workings of the bargaining process by overstating the extent to which policy simply emerges from the policy process.[12] Third, the bureaucratic politics model is chastised for artificially separating the executive branch bargaining process from the broader social and political context. In this view, Congress and domestic political forces cannot be treated as interlopers in the policy process. Attention must also be given to the values of policy makers and not just the policy-making games they play. Finally, the model is criticized for being too complex, a virtual "analytic kitchen sink" into which almost anything can be thrown that might be related to how an issue is resolved.[13] The result is a story that may make for interesting reading but that violates one of the most fundamental rules of explanation: All things being equal, simple explanations are better than complex ones.

The Small-Group Decision-Making Model

A third policy-making model focuses on the dynamics of small-group decision-making. Advocates of this perspective hold that many critical foreign policy decisions are made neither by an individual policy maker nor by large bureaucratic forces. From a policy maker's perspective, small-group decision-making offers a number of advantages over its bureaucratic counterpart. Among its perceived advantages are the following:

> The absence of significant conflict, because there will be few viewpoints to reconcile
>
> A free and open interchange of opinion among members, because there will be no organizational interests to protect
>
> Swift and decisive action
>
> Possible innovation and experimentation
>
> The possibility of maintaining secrecy[14]

Three different types of small groups can be identified.[15] First is the informal small group that meets regularly but lacks a formal institutional base. The Tuesday lunch group in the administration of Lyndon Johnson and the Friday breakfast and Thursday lunch groups of the administration of Jimmy Carter are prominent recent examples. Second is the ad hoc group that is created to deal with a specific problem and then ceases to function once its task is completed. In the first week of the 1950 Korean crisis, six small-group meetings were held. During the Cuban missile crisis, the key decisions were made by the Executive Committee (ExCom), an ad hoc group of about fifteen individuals brought together by President John Kennedy specifically to deal with this problem. The third type of small group is permanent in nature, possesses an institutional base, and is created to perform a series of specified functions. The subcommittees of the National Security Council (NSC) fall into this category. During the Carter administration, a Special Coordinating Committee (SCC) was set up to deal with crisis situations. During the Iranian hostage crisis, Robert Hunter, an NSC official in the Carter administration, reported:

> Throughout the hostage crisis, the SCC met at 9:00 A. M.—at first daily and later less frequently—with an agenda coordinated with the government by the NSC staff in the early hours of the morning. Discussion was brisk, options were presented crisply, and recommendations were rapidly and concisely formulated for presidential decision. . . . The results of the days' labors were reported back; new wrinkles in the crisis were assessed; and the SCC was ready to act again the next morning.[16]

Following the terrorist attacks of September 11, 2001, the George W. Bush administration established a "war cabinet" consisting of some dozen people including Vice President Dick Cheney, Secretary of State Colin Powell, Secretary of Defense Donald Rumsfeld, and National Security Adviser Condoleezza Rice. In spite of its advantages, small-group decision-making often results in policy decisions that are anything but rational or effective. Pearl Harbor, the Bay of Pigs invasion, and key decisions in Korea and Vietnam have all been analyzed from a small-group decision-making perspective.[17]

Policy failures from the perspective of this model are the result of strong in-group pressures on members to concur in the group's decision. This pressure produces a "deterioration of mental efficiency, reality testing, and moral judgment" that increases the likelihood of the group's making a potentially defective decision.[18] Irving Janis coined the term **"groupthink"** to capture this phenomenon. He also identified eight symptoms that indicate its presence. He divided them into three categories: overestimation of the group's power and morality, closed-mindedness, and pressures toward conformity. Janis argued that the more symptoms are present, the more likely it is that concurrence-seeking behavior will result and that defective decisions will be made. Table 9.1 presents a series of observations in the Tower Commission Report about the decision-making on the Iran-Contra Affair against the symptoms mentioned by Janis. Although the match is not perfect (e.g., illusion of unanimity is better seen as an illusion of presidential support), the parallels are striking.

Groupthink is a phenomenon that occurs regardless of the personality traits of group members. It is not an inevitable product of a tight-knit decision group, nor is it necessarily the cause of a policy fiasco. Poor implementation, changed circumstances, or accidental factors also produce policy failures. Groupthink exists as a tendency that is made more or less likely by three sets of antecedent conditions: the coherence of the decision-making group, structural faults of the organization, and the nature of the decision context. At its core is the assumption that concurrence-seeking behavior is an attempt on the part of group members to cope with stress by developing a mutual support base.[19]

Because groupthink is a tendency and not a condition, in theory, it can be avoided. Recognizing that each proposed solution has its own drawbacks, Janis puts forward several measures that he feels would improve the quality of small-group decision-making.[20] They include modifying leadership strategies so that impartial and wide-ranging discussions of alternatives will take place, establishing multiple groups for the same task (multiple advocacy), establishing a devil's advocate, and having a "second chance" meeting at which decisions can be reconsidered one final time.

Three general lines of criticism have been directed at the groupthink approach to small-group decision-making. First, the proposed solutions probably will not work. Consider the idea of multiple advocacy, which attempts to ensure that all views, "however unpopular," will receive serious attention.[21] Two dangers exist here. In each case, they are brought on by overloading the intellectual capabilities of policy makers and by highlighting the ambiguity of the evidence before them. One outcome is that policy makers will simply choose whatever policy option is in accord with their preexisting biases. If a wide range of options are all made to appear respectable and doubts exist about the effectiveness of each, why not "let Reagan be Reagan" and select the one that best fits his image of the world? The other, equally undesirable, outcome is paralysis. Confronted with too many policy options, all of which appear to have problems, policy makers may end up doing nothing.

Second, criticism is directed at the criteria used to establish a good decision.[22] The standard used (vigilant appraisal) virtually duplicates the logic of the

TABLE 9.1 Groupthink and the Iran-Contra Affair

Element of Groupthink	Findings of the Tower Commission Report
Illusion of invulnerability	The president "was all for letting the Israelis do anything they wanted at the very first briefing" (McFarlane, p. 131).
Unquestioned belief in group's morality	The president distinguished between selling [weapons] to someone believed able to exert influence with respect to the hostages and dealing directly with the kidnappers (p. 39). The administration continued to pressure U.S. allies not to sell arms to Iran and not to make concessions to terrorists (p. 65).
Collective efforts to discount warnings	"There is a high degree of risk in pursuing the course we have started, we are now so far down the road that stopping . . . could have even more serious repercussions. We all view the next step as confidence building" (North, p. 167).
Stereotyping the enemy	Release of the hostages would require influence with the Hezbollah, which could involve the most radical elements of the Iranian regime. The kind of strategy sought by the United States, however, involved what were regarded as more moderate elements (p. 64).
Self-censorship	Evidence suggests that he [Casey] received information about the possible divergence of funds to the Contras almost a month before the story broke. He, too, did not move promptly to raise the matter with the president (p. 81). Secretary Shultz and Secretary Weinberger, in particular, distanced themselves from the march of events (p. 82).
Illusion of unanimity	"I felt in the meeting that there were views opposed, some (presidential support) in favor, and the President didn't really take a position, but he seemed to, he was in favor of this project somehow or other" (Shultz, p. 183). "As the meeting broke up, I had the idea the President had not entirely given up on encouraging the Israelis" (Casey, p. 198).
Direct pressure against	"Casey's view is that Cap [Weinberger] will continue to create roadblocks until he is told by you that the President wants this move NOW" (North to Poindexter, p. 232).
Emergence of mindguards	"I don't want a meeting with RR, Shultz, and Weinberger" (Poindexter, p. 45). North directed that dissemination be limited to Secretary Weinberger, DCI Casey, McFarlane, and himself. North said McFarlane had directed that no copy be sent to the secretary of state and that he, McFarlane, would keep Secretary Shultz advised orally on the NSC project (p. 149).

Source: President's Special Review Panel, *The Tower Commission Report* (New York: Bantam, 1987). Citations from Robert McFarlane, national security advisor, 1983–85; Col. Oliver North, national security council staffer; George Shultz, secretary of state; William Casey, director of central intelligence; Adm. John Poindexter, national security advisor, 1985–86; Caspar Weinberger, secretary of defense.

rational actor model. The point remains: If the rational actor model is an unrealistic benchmark against which to judge decision-making, isn't the same true for vigilant appraisal? A third criticism is more theoretical in nature. The groupthink approach is grounded in a conflict model of individual decision-making. According to this model, individuals often confront decision-making situations in which they feel "simultaneous opposing tendencies to accept and reject a given course of action."[23] Vigilant appraisal is realized when individuals address this stress successfully and groupthink occurs when they do not. The "cybernetic" approach to policy making suggests an alternative starting point to understanding individual decision-making. According to this perspective, individuals do not even attempt to resolve the value conflict and tensions involved in making such a decision.[24]

Based on this line of argument, John Steinbruner suggests that, in place of the calculating policy maker, we focus our attention on three types of thinkers, each of whom avoids the need for making value trade-offs.[25] The uncommitted thinker has difficulty making up his or her mind on an issue and is very susceptible to the arguments and positions of others; the theoretical thinker approaches an issue from an ideological perspective; and the grooved thinker deals with a problem by placing it into a limited number of preexisting categories.

Even with these problems, recent decision-making studies continue to point to the importance of groupthink.[26] The approach has also been extended from just explaining a defective decision to explaining shifts in a stream of policy decisions such as the War on Terrorism and the invasion of Iraq.[27]

Elite Theory and Pluralism

During the 1960s and early 1970s, elite theory and pluralism served as the focal point for an intense debate that raged among political scientists over how best to understand the process by which public policy is made. Although no longer the center of attention, they remain important approaches for understanding how U.S. foreign policy is made.

Elite theory represents a quite different perspective on foreign policy making than do the three approaches that we have examined so far. It is concerned with the identities of those individuals who make foreign policy and the underlying dynamics of national power, social myth, and class interests. It stresses the ties that bind policy makers together rather than the forces that divide them.

From the elite theory perspective, foreign policy is formulated as a response to demands generated by the economic and political system. Not all demands receive equal attention, and those that receive the most attention serve the interests of only a small sector of society. These special interests are transformed into national interests through the pattern of office holding and the structure of influence that exists within the United States. Those who hold office are seen as being a stable and relatively cohesive group who share common goals, interests, and values.

Disagreements exist only at the margins and surface most frequently as disputes over how to implement policy and not over the ends of that policy. Those outside the elite group are held to be relatively powerless, reacting to the policy initiatives of the elite rather than prompting them. Furthermore, public reactions are often "orchestrated" by the elite rather than being expressions of independent thinking on policy matters. This explains why certain policy proposals routinely fail to attract serious attention: Ideas that do not build on the relatively narrow range of value assumptions shared by the elite and rooted in the underlying dynamics of the socioeconomic structure are rejected as unworkable, fundamentally flawed, or fatally naïve. Elite theory also suggests that the basic directions of U.S. foreign policy will change slowly, if at all.

Within this broad consensus, elite theorists disagree on a number of points. First, disagreement exists over the constraints on elite behavior. Some see few, if any, constraints on the type of policies that elites can pursue. Others see a more open policy process that is subject to periodic "short-circuiting" by the public. Disagreement also exists over how conspiratorial the elite is. Some elite theorists pay great attention to the social backgrounds and linkages among members of the elite class, whereas others deemphasize these features in favor of an attention to the broader and more enduring forces of a capitalistic economic system that drives U.S. foreign policy to be expansionist, aggressive, and exploitive.[28]

Several recent administrations have been the subject of conspiratorial-style elite analysis. In the case of the Carter administration, the object of attention was the presence of large numbers of members of the Trilateral Commission in policy-making positions. The Trilateral Commission was formed in 1973 to foster cooperation between the United States, Western Europe, and Japan. In the Reagan administration, the focus was on links between his appointees and the Committee on the Present Danger, a group established in the 1970s to warn against the continuing threat posed by the Soviet Union. In the George W. Bush administration, the focus was the influence neoconservatives had on foreign policy decisions. Unlike the other two groups, the neoconservatives do not have an institutional embodiment. Rather, "neoconservative" refers to a broad philosophical outlook on America's role in world politics.

Pluralism is regarded as the orthodox interpretation of how the U.S. policy-making system works. Just as with elite theory, no single comprehensive statement of the argument exists. Still, six common themes can be identified:

1. Power in society is fragmented and diffused.
2. Many groups in society have power to participate in policy making.
3. No one group is powerful enough to dictate policy.
4. An equilibrium among groups is the natural state of affairs.
5. Policy is the product of bargaining between groups and reflects the interests of the dominant group(s).
6. The government acts as an umpire, supervising the competition and sometimes compelling a settlement.

Pluralists acknowledge that power resources are not evenly distributed throughout society. However, they hold that merely possessing the attributes of power (wealth, status, etc.) is not equal to actually possessing power itself.[29] This is because the economic and political sectors of society are held to be separate. In addition, power resources may be substituted for one another. Large numbers may offset wealth; leadership may offset large numbers; and commitment may overcome poor leadership. **Pluralism** would point to the grassroots movement in the United States to force South Africa to end apartheid as evidence of the validity of their case. What began as a movement on college campuses to force companies to disinvest from South Africa gradually succeeded in sensitizing policy makers and the American public to the problem, with the result that, in 1985, U.S. policy toward South Africa began to show signs of change.

A number of flaws have been suggested in the pluralists' argument.[30] Pluralists assume that competition between groups produces policy makers who compete over the content of policy. What happens when policy makers do not compete over policy but instead are so fragmented that they rule over separate and self-contained policy areas? Theodore Lowi suggests that these conditions better describe the operation of the U.S. government than does the pluralist model, and that when this happens, the government is not an umpire but a holding company. Pluralism then exists without competition as interest groups capture different pieces of the government and shape its policies to suit their needs. New groups or the poorly organized are effectively shut out of the decision-making process. Just as important, interest-group liberalism reduces the capacity of the government to plan, because it is unable to speak with one voice or examine problems from a national perspective.

Historical Lesson

The New Look

Dwight Eisenhower was elected president in 1952. Two years earlier the United States had been caught off guard by North Korea's invasion of South Korea. While the Cold War was already under way, the focus of U.S. military and diplomatic efforts was on containing the spread of communism in Europe. The United States had security commitments in place to defend selected countries in Asia, such as Japan, the Philippines, and Australia, but not South Korea. In fact, key statesmen made speeches indicating it was not covered by a U.S. security pledge. In response to North Korea's attack, President Harry Truman sent military forces to help defend South Korea as part of a United Nations effort, dramatically increased U.S. defense spending, and strengthened U.S. security commitments to allies around the world.

Eisenhower did not doubt the seriousness of the communist threat to U.S. national security. Where he parted company with Truman was with the twin assumptions that (1) a specific period of maximum danger existed and (2) that the high levels of defense spending begun by Truman could be sustained over the long run. The foreign policy problem facing the United States as Eisenhower saw it was that the United States had entered what promised to be a prolonged period of "no peace, no war." High levels of defense spending could not be continued indefinitely into the future without undermining the strength of the U.S. economy. Moreover, Eisenhower feared that continued high levels of defense spending would drive the United States "into some form of dictatorial government." The solution Eisenhower would come to embrace as the means for maintaining a strong defense capable of protecting the United States in a period of no peace/no war was to replace a reliance on manpower with an emphasis on technology.

Upon becoming president, Eisenhower quickly began to redirect U.S. national security thinking. In May 1953 he organized the Solarium exercise in which three separate task forces were established to examine alternative directions that American foreign policy might take. One reevaluated containment in light of the desire to cut back defense spending. The second examined issues involving nuclear deterrence. The third considered the possibility of a foreign policy based on rolling back the Iron Curtain.

This was followed by a series of National Security Council (NSC) meetings that in October produced NSC 162/2, the document that replaced NSC 68, on which Truman had based his new defense policy with its high level of military spending. The NSC meetings revealed a sharp difference of opinion between the Joint Chiefs of Staff and others who supported a defense policy that was largely consistent with that of Truman and those who agreed with Eisenhower. In the end NSC 162/2 was a compromise between these two positions.

The compromise did not last long. In November Eisenhower met with the secretaries of defense, treasury, and state. They agree to a sharp reduction in the size of the armed forces. Yet when the budget for fiscal year 1955 was drawn up and presented to Eisenhower in December, it showed the Pentagon asking for an increase in the defense budget and the number of men in uniform. Eisenhower was reported to be furious and directed his secretary of defense to get the military to cut 400,000 troops from its request in order to get the maximum savings possible. This was not the first time Eisenhower had crossed paths with his military advisors. In the deliberations over NSC 162/2 he refused to include a formal dissent by the Joint Chiefs of Staff in the final document, observing that "the Joint Chiefs of Staff were, after all, his military advisors; he made the decisions."

As these deliberations were going on, key administration foreign policy officials such as Secretary of State John Foster Dulles and Chair of the Joint Chiefs of Staff Admiral Arthur Radford were making a series of public speeches advancing Eisenhower's new defense policy. The press began to refer to it as the New Look. Its core elements were: (1) the U.S. military needed to adopt a long-haul strategic planning outlook; (2) American forces were to be substantially reduced; (3) the United States needed to be prepared to use nuclear weapons to deter or counter communist aggression; and (4) the United States needed to rely more on collective security in the future. While the third point highlighted the role of technology in Eisenhower's thinking and is often seen as the centerpiece of the New Look, the fourth point is also important. Eisenhower was confident the United States could reduce the size of its armed forces not only because of technology but because he was counting on allies to commit troops in cases where nuclear weaponry was not sufficient to deter communist aggression.

It was not long after references to the New Look began to emerge with regularity that France was forced out of South Vietnam by Ho Chi Minh and the communists. This event set in motion yet another period of debate over the future of U.S. military strategy, with the dominant sense being that greater flexibility was needed in U.S. security thinking than was provided by such a heavy reliance on nuclear technology. Some referred to this change in approach as the New New Look. Under President John F. Kennedy it came to be known as flexible response.

Applying the Lesson

1. To what extent are Eisenhower's reliance on nuclear technology and Obama's reliance on drone technology different from and similar to one another?

2. To what extent can technology solve political problems?

3. Does the phrase "no peace/no war" apply equally to the situation the United States faces today? What elements of the New Look remain relevant for U.S. security policy?

Integrating Models

It stands to reason that, given the complexity of the situations faced and the variety of factors that might go into selecting a course of action, no single foreign policy model standing alone will be able to help us fully understand a foreign policy decision or outcome. This will often require integrating several different models. Typically, there are four ways in which this integration can be attempted. The first is to shift from model to model as the focus of the analysis changes. For example, from the rational actor perspective, the decision to send U.S. troops to Korea in 1950 is a single decision. From the bureaucratic or small-group perspective, a series of separate decisions might be identified. A distinction can also be made between the sociopolitical aspects of policy making and the intellectual task of choosing a response.[31] The pluralist and bureaucratic politics models help us understand why policy makers act as they do once they are "in place," but they tell us little about how they got there or the values they bring to bear in addressing a problem. To answer these questions, we might want to turn to insights from elite theory or the rational actor model.

A second way to integrate policy-making models is to recognize that some models are more appropriate for analyzing some problems, or issue areas, than they are for others. The general argument is that the more open the policy process and the longer the issue is on the policy agenda (as is typically the case for structural and strategic issues), the more useful will be the bureaucratic and pluralist models. The more closed the process and the quicker the response, the more useful will be the rational actor, elite theory, or small-group model.

A third way to integrate these models is to shift from one to another as the policy problem develops over time. Thus, the elite or rational actor model might be especially helpful for understanding how the United States got involved in Vietnam; the small-group or bureaucratic politics model might be most helpful for understanding key decisions during the course of the war. The **poliheuristic decision-making** model suggests another way to combine them. It argues that individuals only engage in a rational calculation of the costs and benefits of a limited number of alternatives in a second stage of decision-making, after most alternatives already have been eliminated for other reasons.[32]

Similarly, individuals are likely to approach implementing a policy differently from selecting a policy.

A final way of integrating these models is based on the values that guide one's analysis. We have already suggested that although the rational actor model may be deficient as a description of the policy-making process, it is still valuable if the purpose is to evaluate the policy process. One must be careful in using models in this way, for embedded in each are assumptions about how policy should be made that are not always readily apparent. For example, implicit in the rational actor model is a belief in the desirability of a strong president and the ability to act quickly. The model does not place great value on widespread participation in decision-making or on a system of checks and balances.

The Cuban Missile Crisis

In this section, we examine one of the most important events in U.S. foreign policy, the Cuban missile crisis. For many, it was the defining foreign policy crisis of the Cold War. We first present an overview of how the crisis unfolded and then employ three models—rational actor, bureaucratic politics, and groupthink—to show how models can help us understand foreign policy.

The Crisis: An Overview

The Cuban missile crisis, which took place over thirteen days (October 16–28, 1962), is widely regarded as a major turning point in the Cold War.[33] Never before and never after did the United States and the Soviet Union appear to be on the brink of nuclear war. At the time of the crisis, President John Kennedy estimated that the odds of averting such an outcome were from one in three and even.[34]

Soviet weapons shipments to Cuba had been taking place since the summer of 1960. A slowdown in these shipments occurred in early 1962, but the pace quickened again in late July. By September 1 the inventory of Soviet equipment in Cuba included surface-to-air missiles (SAMs), cruise missiles, patrol boats, and large quantities of transportation, electrical, and construction equipment, as well as over five thousand technicians and other military personnel.[35] The first strategic missiles arrived secretly in Cuba on September 8. They were medium-range ballistic missiles (MRBMs) with a range of eleven hundred nautical miles. Forty-two of these missiles reached Cuba before the crisis was resolved. Equipment also began arriving for the construction of intermediate-range ballistic missiles (IRBMs) and IRBM sites, although no IRBMs actually reached Cuba. Finally, Soviet shipments in September included IL-28 jet bombers and MIG-21 jet fighters, plus additional SAMs, cruise missiles, and patrol boats.

Intelligence on the exact dimensions of the Soviet buildup in Cuba came from a number of different sources: refugee reports, CIA agents operating in Cuba, analyses of Soviet shipping patterns, and U-2 spy plane overflights. Not all of the information from these sources was equally reliable, nor did it all come together at the same time and place for analysis. For example, refugees were reporting the presence of Soviet missiles in Cuba before Cuba began receiving weapons of any kind from the Soviet Union, and great care had to be taken in processing reports from agents operating inside Cuba. The United States Intelligence Board met on September 19 and approved an intelligence estimate that indicated the Soviet Union would not introduce offensive missiles into Cuba.

This conclusion was not uniformly shared in the administration. In late August director of central intelligence (DCI) John McCone told President Kennedy, Secretary of Defense Robert McNamara, and Secretary of State Dean Rusk that he believed that the Soviet Union was preparing to place offensive missiles in Cuba. In late September others began to agree with McCone, and on October 4 the Committee on Overhead Reconnaissance (COMOR) approved a U-2 overflight over western Cuba. No U-2 overflights had been authorized over this area since September 5 because of recent mishaps with U-2 overflights in Asia. Fearful that all U-2 flights might be canceled if another incident were to occur, COMOR had decided not to send any U-2s over western Cuba, where SAM sites were known to be under construction. A jurisdictional dispute between the Defense Department and the CIA over who would fly such a mission led to an unsuccessful flight on October 9, and it was not until October 14 that a successful U-2 flight took place. Its photographs firmly established the presence of Soviet offensive missiles in Cuba. On October 22 President Kennedy went on national television to announce the discovery.

Kennedy called together a special ad hoc advisory group known as the ExCom of the NSC to deal with the crisis. ExCom's first meeting took place on October 16, and it began to identify the options open to the United States. Six major options surfaced: (1) no action, (2) diplomatic pressures either at the United Nations or at the Soviet Union, (3) a secret approach to Castro with the option of "split or fall," (4) invasion, (5) a surgical air strike, and (6) a naval blockade.[36] The first option seized on was the surgical air strike.[37] The blockade was not lobbied for strongly until the end of the day, and Kennedy's initial response to this option was one of skepticism, because he was not sure how a blockade would get Soviet missiles out of Cuba.

By the end of the first day, Kennedy identified three options. Participant accounts suggest that attention focused primarily on two of these, the surgical air strike and the blockade. (The third option appears to have been invasion.) In his October 22 statement, Kennedy also announced that, on October 24, a naval quarantine would be imposed on Cuba, and he threatened future action if the missiles were not removed. The blockade was chosen both for what it did and for what it did not do. It was a visible, forceful, military response, but it did not put the Soviet Union into a position where it had no choice but to fight. In fact, it placed responsibility for the next move back on Soviet Chairman Nikita Khrushchev. A number of additional measures were taken publicly to impress on the Soviets the depth of U.S. resolve and to make credible Kennedy's threat of additional action: Squadrons of U.S. tactical fighters were moved to points from which they could attack Cuba; an invasion force of two hundred thousand troops was readied in Florida; some fourteen thousand air force reserves were called up; and U.S. forces around the world were put on alert.[38]

The air strike remained a live option. An air strike had tentatively been scheduled for October 20 but was postponed in favor of the blockade. On October 27, one day before Khrushchev offered to remove the missiles, Kennedy approved plans for an October 29 air strike on Soviet missile silos, air bases, and Cuban and Soviet antiaircraft installations. At that same meeting, ExCom also concluded that an invasion would follow. McNamara held that an "invasion had become almost inevitable," and he felt that at least one missile would be successfully launched at the United States.[39]

The blockade did bring an end to Soviet military shipments to Cuba, but it did not bring a stop to the construction of Soviet missiles and missile sites in Cuba. SAMs became operational during the crisis and shot down a U-2 on October 23. President Kennedy's original orders were that if this happened, the United States would destroy the site that had launched the missile. However, when the incident occurred, Kennedy delayed retaliating in an effort to allow quiet diplomacy some additional time to bring about the withdrawal of the Soviet missiles.

Recent accounts of the Cuban missile crisis suggest that Kennedy would not have ordered an air strike had Khrushchev not responded favorably to U.S. demands, and that the president was prepared to pursue additional negotiations—perhaps through the United Nations—to resolve the crisis.[40] These accounts also argue that U.S. policy makers felt a sense of urgency in their deliberations, not out of a fear that Soviet missiles might soon become operational, but because the longer the missiles remained in Cuba, the more legitimate they would come to be seen by the other states.

On October 28 Khrushchev agreed publicly to remove Soviet missiles in Cuba in return for a U.S. pledge of nonintervention into Cuba. This allowed both sides to achieve their publicly stated goals. The United States got the missiles out of Cuba, and the Soviet Union could claim that it had succeeded in protecting Cuba from U.S. aggression (the justification it gave for having placed the missiles in Cuba when confronted by Kennedy). Recently released documents reveal the existence of a secret agreement between Kennedy and Khrushchev with terms different from those that officially ended the crisis. In order to entice Khrushchev into removing the missiles from Cuba, Kennedy promised to remove U.S. missiles from Turkey. The secret offer was made by Robert Kennedy to Soviet ambassador Anatoly Dobrynin on October 27. Dobrynin was also told that a commitment was needed from the Soviets the next day if the crisis was to end on these terms. For reasons of domestic politics and international prestige, Kennedy had refused to publicly accept this trade-off, which had been repeatedly called for by the Soviets and suggested to him by some members of ExCom. Implementation of the U.S. part of the agreement was made conditional on the Soviets' keeping the agreement secret.

October 28 marks the conventional ending point for the Cuban missile crisis, but it, in fact, continued for several more weeks as both sides struggled with the question of how to implement the agreement. Particularly troublesome issues involved defining what was meant by "offensive" weapons—the United States insisted that the IL-28s must be removed—and establishing a date for ending the blockade—the Soviets wanted the blockade ended and a no-invasion pledge issued before they took out the bombers. Within the U.S. government, there occurred a repeat of the earlier debate on how to proceed: take unilateral military action to resolve the issue, tighten the blockade, or concede the point and go on to other matters. Diplomacy again came to the rescue when, on November 20, Kennedy announced that the Soviet Union had agreed to remove the IL-28s and that the blockade was being ended.

Three Views of the Cuban Missile Crisis

The account of the Cuban missile crisis we have presented is largely consistent with a rational actor interpretation of U.S. foreign policy making. It emphasizes the thorough canvassing of alternatives once a problem has been identified and the selection of a value-maximizing choice. For U.S. policy makers, the goal directing the search for policy options was clear: Get the Soviet missiles out of Cuba without the appearance of having appeased the Soviets and without starting a war. A hard-line stance was in part dictated by domestic political considerations. Cuba had become an important and recurring emotional issue in American electoral politics since Fidel Castro had come to power there in 1959, and Kennedy was vulnerable on Cuba. The Bay of Pigs fiasco had made Cuba Kennedy's political Achilles' heel, raising questions about his judgment and leadership. The Republican Senate and congressional campaign committees had already identified Cuba as the major issue in the upcoming 1962 election. Inaction (a possibility suggested at one point by McNamara) and quiet diplomacy, therefore, were not policy options capable of achieving both the removal of the missiles and a demonstration of political resolve. The air strike was rejected because the air force could not give Kennedy a 100 percent guarantee that the missiles would be knocked out. Similar problems confronted the choice of an invasion. Coupled with highly visible signals of further military action, the blockade was selected as the option that offered the greatest likelihood of getting the missiles out and demonstrating U.S. resolve without running a high risk of setting off a war between the United States and Soviet Union.

As the rational actor model suggests, the blockade itself was structured to fit the needs of U.S. policy makers. It was not implemented until U.S. officials were sure that Soviet leaders had been able to communicate with Soviet ship captains, and the blockade was placed closer to Cuba than was militarily prudent in order to give the Soviet leadership the maximum amount of time to formulate a peaceful response. The first ship stopped was also carefully selected to minimize the possibility of a hostile Soviet response. Two ships that clearly did not carry missiles were allowed to pass through the blockade. The first ship that was stopped also did not carry missiles. It was a U.S.-built World War II Liberty ship, registered in Lebanon, owned by a Panamanian firm, and under lease to the Soviet Union.

A similar analysis of policy options and consequences late in the crisis would identify Kennedy's secret offer to remove U.S. missiles from Turkey as the logical follow-up move. The blockade did buy time and show U.S. resolve, but, in and of itself, it could not remove the missiles. Domestic political considerations again limited Kennedy's options, as did the continued inability of the military to guarantee that an air strike or invasion would not result in one or more Soviet missiles reaching the United States. Kennedy's publicly announced deadline ensured that the military option, with all of its drawbacks, would be used unless Khrushchev could be convinced to take the missiles out of Cuba. The key was to find a face-saving way out for the Soviets that was also true to Kennedy's stated objectives. The combined secret agreement and public pledge of Soviet missiles being removed from Cuba in return for a nonintervention pledge by the United States accomplished this.

The bureaucratic perspective on decision-making during the Cuban missile crisis points to quite a different picture of what transpired. Rather than emphasizing the logic of policy making, it stresses the politics and organizational context of policy making. Politics is evident first in the discovery of missiles in Cuba. Consider the following: As early as August DCI McCone voiced concern about Soviet offensive missiles being placed in Cuba, but he was overruled by McNamara and Rusk; no U-2 flights were directed over the area most likely to have Soviet missiles from September 5 until October 14; the October 14 flight had been authorized on October 4, but a jurisdictional dispute between the Defense Department and the CIA over who would fly the aircraft and which aircraft would be used delayed it. (The solution agreed to was that an air force officer in uniform would fly a CIA plane.) Moreover, evidence now points to the fact that the United States underestimated by one-half the number of troops (forty-two thousand) the Soviet Union had sent to Cuba. Had this figure been known or had the United States discovered the missiles earlier, the nature of policy options considered, the reading of Soviet goals, and U.S. objectives might have been quite different.

The "logic" of the blockade also suffers when the air strike option is examined in closer detail. First, the air force did not specifically design an option to meet ExCom's goal of removing the Soviet missiles. Instead, it merely dusted off an existing contingency plan that also called for air strikes against arms depots, airports, and artillery batteries opposite the U.S. naval base at Guantanamo Bay. Second, air force calculations of its ability to destroy the Soviet missiles were based on an incorrect labeling of the missiles as mobile field-type missiles, although they were actually movable missiles that required six days to be switched from one location to another. Because the air force believed that the Soviet missiles might be moved between the time the last reconnaissance mission was flown and the time of the air strike, it was only able to offer Kennedy a 90 percent guarantee that it could knock out all of the missiles. The limits of rational choice are also revealed in the implementation of the blockade. The navy, like the air force, did not tailor its plans to meet ExCom's needs. After-the-fact reconstructions of the timing of ship stoppings show that, contrary to Kennedy's orders, the navy did not move the blockade closer to Cuba but placed it where it had originally proposed.

The bureaucratic politics model also raises a number of troubling questions about the logic of the agreement that ended the crisis. One point centers on the nature of Soviet goals. No one in ExCom gave serious consideration to the possibility that the Soviet Union was genuinely concerned with deterring a U.S. invasion of Cuba. Evidence now suggests that, along with balance-of-power considerations, this was one of Khrushchev's goals. Moreover, it appears that it was not the threat of nuclear retaliation but the possibility that the United States might use the crisis as a pretext for invading Cuba that led to the decision to remove the missiles. The formal ending of the crisis on the Soviet side also raises troubling questions. Early accounts suggested that Khrushchev was not in full control of the Politburo, and for this reason, contradictory messages were being received in Washington concerning the terms for ending the crisis. Evidence now suggests that this may not have been the case; rather, faulty intelligence may have been responsible. The first and more conciliatory note was sent when Soviet intelligence was indicating an imminent U.S. attack on Cuba. The second and more stringent communiqué was sent once it became clear that there would not be an invasion.

Early accounts of Cuban missile crisis decision-making from the small-group perspective praised ExCom for not falling victim to groupthink. Janis credits ExCom with not stereotyping the Soviets but actively trying to understand what led them to try to place missiles in Cuba secretly.[41] Janis cites Robert Kennedy's concern about a Pearl Harbor in reverse as evidence of a sensitivity to the moral dilemmas involved in the air strike option. He also notes that members of ExCom frequently changed their minds and eventually came to the conclusion that there were no good policy options at their disposal. President Kennedy is credited with having learned from the Bay of Pigs and practicing a leadership style that maximized the possibility that ExCom would produce quality decisions. To encourage free debate, he did not attend all of its meetings, and he split ExCom into smaller groups to debate the issues and reexamine the conclusions reached by other participants.

More recent accounts of ExCom's deliberations suggest that its escape from groupthink was far less complete than was originally believed.[42] At least three decision-making defects surfaced that are fully consistent with the groupthink syndrome. First, ExCom operated with a very narrow mandate: It was to consider the pros and cons of a variety of coercive measures. Kennedy had declared off-limits any consideration of either acquiescence to the Soviet move or diplomacy. ExCom was true to that mandate; 90 percent of its time was spent studying alternative uses of troops, bombers, and warships. Thus, ExCom did not engage in a full search for policy options or operate as an open decision-making forum.

Second, those who sought to expand the list of options under consideration and break out of the group consensus were ostracized. U.S. ambassador to the United Nations Adlai Stevenson initially opposed the use of force and wrote Kennedy a note cautioning him on the dangers of this option. Kennedy was annoyed by the note and blocked efforts by McNamara and Stevenson to include diplomacy on the options list. Stevenson also suggested a trade of Soviet missiles for U.S. missiles in Turkey or for the Guantanamo Bay Naval Base. For these suggestions, he came under sharp personal attack by Kennedy and was frozen out of the core decision-making group.

Third, Theodore Sorensen, special counsel and advisor to President Kennedy, and Attorney General Robert Kennedy acted as surrogate leaders for Kennedy, reporting back to the president on the discussion and pushing group members to reach a consensus. Here, too, the impact was to limit the number of policy alternatives and to stifle discussion. Stevenson observed that "we knew little brother [Robert Kennedy] was watching and keeping a little list where everyone stood." On Friday night, October 25, President Kennedy informed ExCom that he had chosen the blockade. The very next day, the consensus within ExCom for the blockade began to unravel. At that point, Kennedy told his brother to "pull the group together quickly." Sorensen would tell the group that they were "not serving the president well," and Robert Kennedy would tell them that the president could not possibly order an air strike.

Models: A Critique

As we have seen, decision-making models involve dissecting a complex set of political activities. Inevitably, the result is that certain features of the decision-making process receive greater attention and are accorded greater importance than are others. For these reasons, policy makers often are uncomfortable with decision-making models. The models are seen as oversimplifying policy decisions by putting forward a mechanistic and highly segmented interpretation of a process that is better seen as a seamless web of activity involving efforts at consensus-building, problem-definition, and problem-solving. Generalizations about decision-making are dangerous, they contend, because of the uniqueness of each situation, in terms of both the problem at hand and the domestic political context in which decisions are made.

For these reasons, many prefer conveying the intricacies of decision-making through memoirs or historical narratives of the kind written by David Halberstam on Vietnam and Bosnia and by Bob Woodward on Iraq.[43] Constructed as stories, memoirs and historical narratives place individuals at the center of the decision-making process, rather than abstract concepts and forces such as value-maximizing choices, bureaucratic routines, mind guards, and elites. Placing individuals at the center of the decision-making process is necessary, because in their view, it is personal experience, professional skills, and hard work that allow them to succeed.

Proponents of models acknowledge that the potential for distortion is present when models are used, but argue that memoir-type accounts also may distort our understanding of events by overemphasizing the role of individuals or their freedom to act. They suggest that the task facing students of foreign policy making is to blend these models together to produce a picture containing the maximum amount of insight and a minimal amount of distortion on the nature of the policy-making process, without overwhelming them with data demands.[44]

Over the Horizon: Cyber Policy

While the beginning point of the cyber-warfare age is difficult to pinpoint there can be no doubt it has begun. In 2001 Russian hackers penetrated Pentagon computers. In 2010 the United States went on the offensive when along with Israel it launched the Stuxnet virus attack on Iran's nuclear weapon program. By the end of his administration Obama had identified Russia, China, Iran, and

North Korea as having engaged in cyber-attacks on the United States. Cyber-threats have emerged as the newest security problem facing the United States bringing with them images of cyber Pearl Harbors and cyber 9/11s. Yet according to Michael Hayden, former director of the CIA and the NSA, "rarely has something been so important and so talked about with less clarity and understanding" as cybersecurity.

Just as Obama inherited a drone policy that consisted more of tactics than strategy from Bush, so also Donald Trump is inheriting a cyber-policy that consists more of declaratory statements and tactical applications than it does a coherent cybersecurity strategy. This is not altogether surprising since many compare the beginning of the cyber age to the beginning of the nuclear age. Both presented policy makers with a new, powerful weapon for which there were no strategic precedents. Others are not so sure. They see cyber-warfare largely as a continuation of the past; it is best seen as the most sophisticated version of sabotage, espionage, and subversion to date.[45]

In seeking to understand how Obama, Donald Trump, and future presidents construct their cyber-warfare policy commentators will employ many of the policy-making models we have discussed in this chapter. While we cannot pinpoint which they will rely on most heavily, we can identify some of the key cyber-warfare issues that will be examined. First, how are cyber risks to the United States defined: by the target and/or the degree of damage that can be inflicted? Second, can cyber-power be used defensively or must one use it as a first strike or preventive weapons? Third, can cyber-power be used alone or must it be used in conjunction with traditional military or economic weapons? Fourth, can one use cyber-power to deter? Deterrence (and retaliation for an attack when deterrence fails) requires knowing who the adversary is; yet by its very nature it is difficult to tell who is behind a cyber-attack.[46]

Critical Thinking Questions

1. What are the strengths and limitations of using models to understand U.S. foreign policy making?
2. How might the pluralist and elitist models explain the Cuban missile crisis?
3. Which model might be most helpful in trying to understand the foreign policy of China, Iran, or Russia?

Key Terms

action channels, 219
black box, 218
bureaucratic politics, 219
elite theory, 223
groupthink, 222
models, 217

pluralism, 223
poliheuristic decision-making, 228
prospect theory, 219
rational actor, 218
standard operating procedures, 220

Further Reading

Graham T. Allison, *Essence of Decision: Explaining the Cuban Missile Crisis* (Boston, MA: Little, Brown, 1971).
This landmark study of the policy-making process and its impact on policy presents readers with three alternative explanations for the Cuban missile crisis.
John Donovan, *The Cold Warriors: A Policy Making Elite* (Lexington, MA: D.C. Heath, 1974).
This volume examines the backgrounds, careers, thinking, and interactions of key figures in a series of case studies on American foreign policy making during the early Cold War period.
Leslie Gelb and Richard Betts, *The Irony of Vietnam: The System Worked* (Washington, DC: Brookings, 1979).
This provocative study argues that rather than contributing to the failure in Vietnam, as many argue, the American political process worked as intended and can be said to have succeeded.
David Houghton, *The Decision Point* (New York: Oxford University Press, 2013).
This book examines six post–World War II cases in U.S. foreign policy decision-making through bureaucratic, group decision-making and psychological decision-making models.
Irving L. Janis, *Groupthink: Psychological Studies of Policy Decisions and Fiascos*, 2nd ed. (Boston, MA: Houghton Mifflin, 1982).
This classic study examines the dynamics of small-group decision-making and the ways in which they lead to flawed foreign policy decisions.
Alex Mintz and Carly Wayne, "The Polythink Syndrome and Elite Group Decision-Making," *Advances in Political Psychology* 37 (2016), 3–21.
Where groupthink emphasizes conformity in group decision-making, polythink emphasizes the impact of a plurality of opinions and perspectives. This article examines the dynamics and consequences of polythink and makes recommendations to improve group decision-making.
Paul Pillar, "Intelligence, Policy and War in Iraq," *Foreign Affairs* 84 (2006), 15–27.
A retired intelligence professional, the author provides a cogent account of how intelligence and politics interacted in the lead-up to and conduct of the Iraq War.

Notes

[1] A short summary of additional models can be found in Thomas L. Brewer, *American Foreign Policy: A Contemporary Introduction*, 2nd ed. (Englewood Cliffs, NJ: Prentice Hall, 1986), 26–54.
[2] Roger Hilsman, "Policy Making Is Politics," in Charles W. Kegley Jr. and Eugene R. Wittkopf (eds.), *Perspectives on American Foreign Policy: Selected Readings* (New York: St. Martin's Press, 1983), 250.
[3] Ibid., 251.
[4] Leslie H. Gelb and Richard K. Betts, *The Irony of Vietnam: The System Worked* (Washington, DC: Brookings, 1979).
[5] Patrick Morgan, *Theories and Approaches to International Politics: What Are We to Think*, 3rd ed. (New Brunswick: Transaction, 1981), 110.
[6] Herbert A. Simon, *Administrative Behavior: A Study of Decision Making Processes in Administrative Organization*, 3rd ed. (New York: Free Press, 1976).
[7] Jack Levy, "Prospect Theory, Rational Choice and International Relations," *International Studies Quarterly* 41 (1997), 87–112.
[8] Graham T. Allison, *Essence of Decision: Explaining the Cuban Missile Crisis* (Boston: Little, Brown, 1971), 35.

[9] I. M. Destler, *Presidents, Bureaucrats, and Foreign Policy: The Politics of Organizational Reform* (Princeton: Princeton University Press, 1974), 52.

[10] As originally presented by Allison in his *Essence of Decision*, two separate models were used to explain foreign policy making through organizational routines and governmental politics. Subsequently, Allison combined them into one model, as is done here. See Graham T. Allison and Morton H. Halperin, "Bureaucratic Politics: A Paradigm and Some Policy Implications," *World Politics* 24 (1982), 40–79.

[11] Robert L. Gallucci, *Neither Peace nor Honor: The Politics of American Military Policy in Vietnam* (Baltimore: Johns Hopkins University Press, 1975), 153.

[12] Robert J. Art, "Bureaucratic Politics and American Foreign Policy: A Critique," in Robert J. Art and Robert Jervis (eds.), *International Politics: Anarchy, Force, Political Economy, and Decision Making*, 2nd ed. (Boston: Little, Brown, 1985), 471; Stephen D. Krasner, "Are Bureaucrats Important? (Or Allison Wonderland)," *Foreign Policy* 7 (1972), 159–79; Jerel Rosati, "Developing a Systematic Decision Making Framework: Bureaucratic Politics in Perspective," *World Politics* 33 (1981), 234–51.

[13] Jonathan Bendor and Thomas H. Hammand, "Rethinking Allison's Models," *American Political Science Review* 86 (1992), 301–22.

[14] Robert L. Wendzel, *International Politics: Policymakers and Policymaking* (New York: John Wiley, 1981), 439.

[15] Ibid., 438.

[16] Robert E. Hunter, *Presidential Control of Foreign Policy: Management or Mishap?*, Washington Paper #191 (New York: Praeger, 1982), 35–46.

[17] Irving L. Janis, *Groupthink: Psychological Studies of Policy Decisions and Fiascos*, 2nd ed. (Boston: Houghton Mifflin, 1982).

[18] Ibid., 9.

[19] Ibid., 256.

[20] Ibid., 172, 262–71.

[21] Richard K. Betts, "Analysis, War, and Decision: Why Intelligence Failures Are Inevitable," *World Politics* 31 (1978), 61–89.

[22] Carol Barner-Barry and Robert Rosenwein, *Psychological Perspectives on Politics* (Englewood Cliffs, NJ: Prentice Hall, 1985), 247.

[23] Irving L. Janis and Leon Mann, *Decision Making: A Psychological Analysis of Conflict, Choice, and Commitment* (New York: Free Press, 1977).

[24] John D. Steinbruner, *The Cybernetic Theory of Decision: New Dimensions of Political Analysis* (Princeton: Princeton University Press, 1974), 66–67.

[25] Ibid., 125–36.

[26] Mark Schafer and Scott Crichlow, "The Process-Outcome Connection in Foreign Policy Decision Making," *International Studies Quarterly* 46 (2002), 45–68; Alexander George and Erick Stern, "Harnessing Conflicts in Foreign Policy Making," *Presidential Studies Quarterly* 32 (2002), 484–508.

[27] Dina Badie, "Groupthink, Iraq and the War on Terror," *Foreign Policy Analysis* 6 (2010), 277–96.

[28] Compare Gabriel Kolko, *The Roots of American Foreign Policy* (Boston: Beacon, 1969) with C. Wright Mills, *The Power Elite* (New York: Oxford University Press, 1956).

[29] Robert A. Dahl, "A Critique of the Ruling Elite Model," in G. William Domhoff and Hoyt B. Ballard (eds.), *C. Wright Mills and the Power Elite* (Boston: Beacon, 1968), 31.

[30] Theodore J. Lowi, *The End of Liberalism: Ideology, Policy, and the Crisis of Public Authority* (New York: W. W. Norton, 1969).

[31] Glenn H. Snyder and Paul Diesing, *Conflict among Nations: Bargaining, Decision-Making, and System Structure in International Crises* (Princeton: Princeton University Press, 1977), 355.

[32] Alex Mintz, "How Do Leaders Make Decisions? A Poliheuristic Perspective," *Journal of Conflict Resolution* 48 (2004), 3–13.

[33] For a discussion of Cuban missile crisis decision-making, see Graham T. Allison, *The Essence of Decision: Explaining the Cuban Missile Crisis* (Boston: Little, Brown, 1971); Theodore Sorensen, *Kennedy* (New York: Harper & Row, 1965); Richard Ned Lebow, *Between Peace and War: The Nature of International Crisis* (Baltimore: Johns Hopkins University Press, 1981).

34 James A. Nathan and James K. Oliver, *United States Foreign Policy and World Order*, 3rd ed. (Boston: Little, Brown, 1985), 275.

35 Allison, *The Essence of Decision*, 103.

36 Ibid., 58–61.

37 Walter Pincus, "Standing at the Brink of Nuclear War," *Washington Post*, July 25, 1985, A10.

38 Allison, *The Essence of Decision*, 64.

39 "The Decision Would Take Out Only the Known Missiles," *Washington Post*, July 25, 1985, A1.

40 The most important of these is Raymond Garthoff, *Reflections on the Cuban Missile Crisis*, rev. ed. (Washington, DC: Brookings, 1989). The revised edition contains insights into the crisis that came out of a joint U.S.-Soviet conference on the Cuban missile crisis held in 1987.

41 Irving Janis, *Groupthink*, 2nd ed. (Boston: Houghton Mifflin, 1982), 132–58.

42 Lebow, *Between Peace and War*, especially chapter 8.

43 David Halberstam, *The Best and the Brightest* (Greenwich: Fawcett, 1969); *War in a Time of Peace* (New York: Touchstone, 2001); Bob Woodward, *The Commanders* (New York: Touchstone, 1991); *Bush at War* (New York: Simon & Schuster, 2002); *Plan of Attack* (New York: Simon & Schuster, 2004); *State of Denial* (New York: Simon & Schuster, 2006).

44 One model that does try is the decision-making model presented by Richard Snyder, H. W. Bruck, and Burton Sapin in "Decision Making as an Approach to the Study of International Politics," in Richard Snyder, H. W. Bruck, and Burton Sapin (eds.), *Foreign Policy Decision Making* (New York: Free Press, 1963).

45 Thomas Rid, "Cyber War Will Not Take Place," *The Journal of Strategic Studies* 35 (2012), 5–32; and Richard Clarke and Robert Knake, *Cyber War* (New York: Ecco, 2010).

46 On the question of deterrence, see William Lynn, III, "Defending a New Domain," *Foreign Affairs* 89 (2010), 97–108; Mike McConnell, "To Win the Cyber-War Look to the Cold War," *The Washington Post*, February 28, 2010, B1; and Matthew Croston, "World Gone Cyber MAD," *Strategic Studies Quarterly* 5 (2011), 100–16.

10 Diplomacy

Paris, France

Dateline: Paris Climate Agreement

As an instrument of foreign policy, diplomacy is closely identified with **bargaining** and **negotiation**. It is the traditional tool of statecraft. Here we examine the successful effort to negotiate a climate agreement at a conference attended by 195 states and the European Union in Paris from November 30 to December 12, 2015.

Officially known as the 21st United Nations Climate Change Conference (COP) it was the twenty-first annual meeting of the conference which came into existence following the inaugural Rio de Janeiro COP in 1992. The agreement marked the culmination of six years of negotiations to produce a treaty and came into existence after thirty-six consecutive hours of negotiations as the Paris conference was about to adjourn. The agreement needed a unanimous vote and required all sides to compromise on their demands yet also broke new ground in dealing with the problem of climate change.

The Paris agreement sets a goal of reducing the global temperature increase to 1.5°C above preindustrial levels. This target is to be met by having countries submit nationally developed contribution plans. These targets are not legally binding and no enforcement mechanism was put in place. Instead, these national plans represent political and environmental commitments by states who sign the treaty. This marks a change from previous climate treaty attempts which sought to set legally binding commitments and produced opposition from many states including the United States which signed the 1997 Kyoto agreement which was never ratified by the Senate and from which President George W. Bush withdrew U.S. participation.

At Paris, in an attempt to encourage states to meet their national plans, the United States insisted, over the opposition of developing states, that there was a need for an "enhanced transparency framework for action and support." It requires that all states except the least developed and small island states submit on a regular basis reports using agreed-upon measures to judge the progress of their efforts. The first public reports are due in 2023. From the U.S. perspective this was a key ingredient in establishing a "name and shame" agreement verification system in which peer pressure and publicity would serve as the primary enforcement mechanism. Moreover, every state is tasked with resubmitting its national plan targets every five years thus requiring a report in 2020. This is a tighter time frame than some developing countries and high polluters favored. India, for example, sought a ten-year reporting period. These provisions are also significant in that they require all countries to undertake climate mitigation and adaption measures.

A recurring area of controversy in climate negotiations has been the issue of responsibility for the global climate damage. On this point President Obama stated at the opening of the conference that "the United States not only recognizes our role in creating this problem, we embrace our responsibility to do something about it." The Paris agreement states that developed countries should take the lead mobilizing climate finance but does not establish a specific dollar amount they are obligated to provide. The goal of $100 billion per year from rich countries is found in the preamble to the agreement, but it is not legally binding. Many developing countries state that this figure is too low to address the problems they face.

The debate over responsibility has moved on to include who should bear the financial burden of actions needed to address "loss and damage" problems associated with the adverse effects of climate change. At the insistence of smaller island countries the phrase "loss and damage" was included in a climate treaty for the first time. However, at the insistence of developed countries the Paris agreement did not go so far as to establish liability for these problems.

Three factors generally are sighted as contributing to the ability to reach an agreement in Paris. First, there was growing scientific evidence of the damage that has already been done to the environment and concerns regarding the window of opportunity within which to take mitigating and adaptive action. The targets set in Paris were presented as a first and necessary step in that direction but not as accomplishing those goals. Second, months prior to the Paris meeting the

United States and China, the world's first and second leading carbon polluters, agreed upon policies to cut carbon emissions. These bilateral talks were carried out in secret and took nine months to complete. Third, Obama was committed to achieving an agreement. He personally attended the conference and lobbied the heads of key developing countries such as India and Brazil. Periodically during the meeting the State Department made announcements regarding plans to increase the U.S. commitment to aid countries dealing with the effects of climate change. One plan would increase funding from $430 million by 2020 to $860 million. A weakness in the U.S. commitment to an agreement recognized by all was the continuing conflict between Obama and Republicans in Congress over a climate agreement. The additional funding was dependent on congressional approval and prior to the beginning of the conference more than one hundred members of Congress sent a letter to foreign leaders indicating that Obama did not have the support of Congress.

After the European Union ratified the agreement in October, the needed number of countries and polluters had signed the agreement for it to go into effect. This officially took place on November 4, 2016.

As illustrated by the Paris Climate Agreement diplomacy is generally identified with government-to-government bargaining. A far more complex reality exits today. As captured by the concept of public diplomacy, diplomacy today also reaches out directly to the people of a state in hopes of laying a foundation that is favorable to U.S. foreign policy initiatives. It can also involve the use of military power. Here we will introduce the full range of diplomatic options that have been used by the United States.

Process versus Product

For many, diplomacy remains the classic policy instrument and the one best suited to producing lasting and workable solutions to foreign policy problems. Others point out that the use of diplomacy is not without its dangers. Negotiations also hold the potential for exacerbating hostilities, strengthening an aggressor, preparing the way for an attack, and eroding the moral and legal foundations of peace.[1] They do so because, in addition to solving problems, negotiations can also be used to stall for time, obtain information, and make propaganda plays.

The tension described here points to the difference between viewing diplomacy as a process and diplomacy as a product or outcome. According to some observers, this long-standing tension is growing because while interest in diplomacy-as-process is on the rise, the preconditions needed for diplomacy-as-product are on the decline.[2] Three of the most important factors standing in the way of the success of diplomatic efforts today are (1) the absence of shared principles on which to base international agreements, (2) the increased presence of non-negotiable goals, and (3) the growing role of public opinion in foreign policy making. The first two make compromise difficult and greatly reduce the common ground on which solutions can be built. The third complicates the ability of governments to implement agreements.

Bilateral Diplomacy

While countries may prefer to act unilaterally because of the high degree of free-dom it affords them, it is rarely a viable option. For most, including the United States, foreign policy involves partnering or at least interacting with others. The most common form of diplomacy is bilateral diplomacy, in which two states in-teract directly with one another. These relations occur at varying levels, from heads of government and ambassadors down to junior foreign service officers. They also can cover a wide array of subjects, ranging from sensitive security and economic issues to the routine issuing of visas. Bilateral relations are assuming a new prominence today because without the Cold War to frame negotiations, diplomacy has become heavily influenced by country- and situation-specific considerations.

Countries enter into three different types of bilateral relationships, each of which has its own unique set of characteristics: allies, friends, and adversaries. Dealings with allies are marked by high levels of commitment to the negotiation process, a recognition that a wide area of common interests exists, and a willing-ness to address the specific issues involved in a dispute. Leaks of the existence of covert National Security Agency (NSA) communications intercepts programs on foreign leaders brought home the reality that being considered an ally does not preclude being the target of intelligence-gathering efforts. Among those allies whose communications were captured by the NSA were the European Union, Germany, Mexico, Spain, France, and Brazil. The reputed goal was to obtain information regarding their policy positions on global issues. The diplomatic fallout from the leaks escalated into a high-profile conflict between the United States and its allies. In response, a senior NSA official said that identifying the intentions of foreign leaders is a "fundamental given" for intelligence services.[3]

Relations with adversaries are also marked by a high degree of commitment and attention but lack any sense of shared interests. Instead, there is an under-lying sense of conflict and distrust. As a result, much of the bilateral dialogue centers on finding formula-based solutions for problems. Finally, there are bilat-eral relations among friends. These are relations between states that are on good terms but lack extensive dealings with one another. As a result, it is often difficult to strike a deal, as each side advances its own particular interest in the absence of widely perceived common interests.

A fourth category of (non)relations can also be said to exist. During the George W. Bush administration, the most prominent countries with which the United States lacked formal diplomatic relations were the three members of the axis of evil: Iran, North Korea, and Iraq. Consistent with Obama's pledge to reach out to all states the United States began reestablishing relations with sev-eral states, the most prominent of which was Cuba. Others included Myanmar (Burma) on the grounds that the government had made efforts in promoting democracy and respecting human rights and Somalia, where it cited the govern-ment's success in fighting against opposition militant forces.

In some cases, the nature of the bilateral relationship is easy to determine. The United States and Great Britain are long-standing allies. In other cases, determining how to approach another country is not easy. China is a potential military adversary, but it is also a friend and potential ally in managing the international economic system. The Soviet Union and the United States were adversaries during the Cold War, but they found it necessary to cooperate in nuclear arms control initiatives. President Obama made a "reset" in relations with Russia a key feature in his first-term foreign policy. Yet by the second term the United States and Russia were at best uneasy friends in trying to address problems of Syrian chemical weapons and Iranian nuclear arms, and much closer to being adversaries following Russia's involvement in the breakup of Ukraine.

The shifting and muddled nature of bilateral relations is a major problem for the U.S. foreign policy in the Middle East. No one doubts that the United States and Israel are allies yet the two countries are deeply divided over merits of the nuclear agreement with Iran. Saudi Arabia has long been a staunch U.S. ally helping keep the price of oil low and funding U.S. covert operations in the Middle East and Africa. The United States has relied heavily on it to fund antigovernment rebel forces in Syria and covert operations. Yet, as disagreements with the United States mount over its involvement in Yemen's civil war and its policies toward Iraq and Iran it increasingly appears to be more of a friend than an ally. Saudi Arabia increased its military spending so that in 2016 it rather than Russia ranked third in military spending. It also opened up a new arms factory and proposed building a military base on the Horn of Africa. Additional stress in the U.S.-Saudi Arabia relationship stemmed from legislation that would allow Americans to take legal action against states that had given support to the 9/11 terrorists, something which has become the subject of widespread speculation. Saudi Arabia responded to this possibility by threatening to sell off billions of dollars of U.S. assets it controls in retaliation.

One of the perennial problems faced by the United States in carrying out bilateral diplomacy is how to treat opposition leaders and movements as governments of friends, allies, and adversaries are likely to take offense. Angered at the antigovernment protests against his government which he blamed on the United States, Vladimir Putin arranged for passage of a new law that requires all nongovernmental organizations who receive foreign funding to register as "foreign agents." During his rule the United States took great pains not to alienate the shah of Iran and stayed clear of working with or infiltrating groups opposed to his rule.

The decision on how to deal with opposition leaders has become more pronounced in today's international system, where the international politics of democratization and low-level conflicts rooted in local conditions have become much more prominent. The Obama administration had to deal with this question in Egypt (a friend), Libya (an adversary), and Syria (which has been both) in 2011, when pro-democracy Arab Spring protests swept through the region. Similarly, after bin Laden's death, it had to make a decision about more direct negotiations with the Taliban that would permit U.S. forces to leave. Talks were entered into but broke off in 2013 without any agreement.

The changing nature of global politics with its movement away from bloc politics to a greater emphasis on bilateral relations has also brought renewed attention to what has historically been one of the most sensitive topics in bilateral relations: the willingness of countries to allow the United States to station its troops on their territory.[4] The potential scope of the problem is immense. In 1938 the United States had 14 military bases outside of its continental borders. In 2010 there existed 662 military facilities in thirty-eight countries excluding operations in Afghanistan and Iraq.[5]

Basing rights became a high-priority issue during Obama's presidency for two reasons. First, they played an essential role in drone attacks against terrorists. Outside of Afghanistan and Pakistan prominent bases that have been used for this purpose are located in Niger, Djibouti, Seychelles, Yemen, Qatar, Ethiopia, and Saudi Arabia. In 2015 it established a drone base in Cameroon to target the Boko Haram in neighboring Nigeria. Second, they became a signature statement of the depth of his Asia Pivot. His administration entered into basing agreements with Australia that would allow U.S. soldiers to use Australian military bases for training and amphibious exercises; Japan and the United States reached an agreement on moving the Okinawa military base that would keep it operational and permit ten thousand U.S. soldiers to remain in Japan; and the Philippines agreed to allow the United States to increase its military presence there by giving it access to military bases.

Incentives versus Sanctions

One of the most difficult decisions that must be made in bilateral relations involves the choice between employing sanctions and offering incentives. In 2015 the United States decided against lifting a ban on providing Mexico with anti-drug funding because of deficiencies in its human rights policy. In 2016 it lifted relaxed economic sanctions directed at Myanmar as incentive for the government to improve its human rights record while weeks later listing Myanmar as being one of the leading human trafficking countries.

Sanctions are penalties and generally directed at adversaries. The most frequently employed sanctions are economic in nature, and we will discuss them more closely in the next chapter. Diplomatic sanctions also exist. They include threatening to withhold or actually withholding recognition of a government, recalling an ambassador either temporarily (for "consultations") or more permanently, and closing an embassy. Goals behind such actions range from voicing displeasure with a specific policy to attempting to isolate a country.

The historical record shows that sanctions have been used against allies and friends. Chile was warned by Secretary of State Colin Powell that a proposed meeting of United Nations Security Council members opposed to the Iraq War would be seen as an "unfriendly act" and would jeopardize prospects for signing a U.S.-Chile free trade agreement. In fact, many argue that sanctions are most effective against friends, since when relations are minimal or already strained, there may be little additional damage that sanctions can do; so there is little reason for states to comply.

Diplomatic sanctions strike many as more symbolic than economic sanctions and, thus, less costly to employ. Cutting off trade with a country can readily be seen as hurting one's own firms. Observers, however, note that diplomatic sanctions do have costs associated with their use.[6] First, there is a loss of intelligence. Embassies report on events, and without diplomats, a country is potentially blinding itself. When the United States closed its embassy in Kabul, Afghanistan, it lost the ability to engage in human intelligence collection and was forced to rely heavily upon Pakistan's intelligence service for information about the Taliban government. Second, diplomatic sanctions may also lead to misperceptions because of the inability to communicate directly. China's warnings to the United States that it would intervene in the 1950 Korean War went through India because there was no U.S. embassy in China. The warning was not believed. Third, a country loses the ability to promote a positive image. Doing so, under the heading of public diplomacy, is seen as a particularly crucial aspect of U.S. diplomacy today.

Engaging other states through offering incentives is relatively understudied compared to sanctions.[7] Incentives can include the removal of sanctions or the offering of additional trade and foreign aid. Table 10.1 provides an overview of how U.S. foreign aid provided by the State Department and USAID is distributed by objective and program areas. Diplomatic recognition, joint military training exercises, and building people-to-people contacts are also examples of incentives that can be offered. If engagement is chosen, the key decision that policy makers must make is whether the strategy is conditional on the other state undertaking specific actions or if it is unconditional.[8] Offering incentives to a friend or ally is easy. Such a policy is much more controversial when the target state is a foe. Yet it is precisely with these states that the strategy of engagement may offer its greatest benefits, because it provides an avenue for dialogue that did not previously exist. The Clinton administration's policies toward North Korea and Vietnam, for example, were based on engagement rather than sanctions.

The greatest challenge faced by architects of engagement strategies is to avoid the charge that they are appeasing dangerous states rather than providing for U.S. security. The George W. Bush administration faced these very charges from Republicans as it switched strategies in dealing with North Korea, moving from one of confrontation to one that offered incentives or rewards to close down its nuclear facility. Obama encountered similar resistance for removing or suspending economic sanctions against Iran as an inducement to enter into nuclear arms control talks. This problem arises because, when approached as a domestic politics problem, it is far easier to demonize the other state than to engage in negotiations with it. It helps focus public attention on specific aspects of the problem; moral clarity is retained; and attention is deflected from the inconsistencies and indecisions of policies and placed instead on the actions of the other.[9] The downside to a strategy that relies on sanctions and demonizing an opponent is that it limits options for both the current administration and its successors. No case better illustrates this point than American foreign policy toward Cuba, which for over fifty years emphasized nonrecognition and non-negotiation.

Bilateralism versus Multilateralism

In addition to engaging in bilateral diplomacy, or instead of doing so, countries may engage in multilateral negotiations in which many countries participate. A high-profile example came in fall 2009, when the Obama administration

| TABLE 10.1 | Department of State and USAID Foreign Assistance |

Aid Objectives and Program Areas, FY 2015	Planned Allocations (millions of current U.S. dollars)
Peace and Security	*9,070.00*
Counterterrorism	1,260.00
Combating weapons of mass destruction	288.95
Stabilization/security sector reform	6,560.00
Counternarcotics	555.33
Transnational crime	91.24
Conflict mitigation	311.60
Promoting Economic Growth	*3,795.65*
Macroeconomic growth	284.80
Trade and investment	170.25
Financial sector	104.72
Infrastructure	550.85
Agriculture	1,180.00
Private sector competitiveness	522.32
Economic opportunity	271.30
Environment	711.41
Investing in People	*9,870.00*
Health	8,700.00
Education	783.88
Social services/protection of vulnerable	386.12
Governing Justly and Democratically	*2,430.80*
Rule of law and human rights	644.28
Good governance	1,050.00
Political competition	233.43
Civil society	501.72
Humanitarian Assistance	*4,680.00*
Protection, assistance, and solutions	4,500.00
Disaster readiness	149.78
Migration management	30.50

Source: Curt Tarnoff and Marian Lawson, *Foreign Aid: An Introduction to U.S. Programs*. Congressional Research Service, January 29, 2016, 5.

turned to multilateralism in its efforts to curb Iran's pursuit of nuclear weapons. Faced with threats of economic sanctions and coming under increasing pressure to change its policies, it was announced in October 2009 that Iran would meet with representatives from the United States, Germany, France, Great Britain, Russia, and China. This was the first meeting between these states in over a year.

Multilateralism is not without its own problems as a diplomatic problem-solving strategy.[10] One set of obstacles is domestic. Public opinion tends to support acting through the United Nations and other multilateral bodies, but only up to a point, because unilateralism runs deep in the American national style. The division of treaty-making powers between the president and Congress has led to the frequent attachment of reservations, understandings, and declarations to treaties limiting U.S. participation and obligations. As a consequence, U.S. treaty behavior produces confusion and anger abroad, a condition that can easily undermine efforts to promote U.S. security through diplomatic means.[11]

A second set of obstacles is international. How does one enter into a multilateral partnership? The choice at its most fundamental level is between **alliance** members such as those in the North Atlantic Treaty Organization (NATO) or those in economic organizations such as the World Trade Organization (WTO) and creating ad hoc **coalitions** of states that share a common interest with regard to a specific problem, be it genocide, Iraq, or the environment. Permanent allies and organizations can be slow to respond because of conflicts among members or internal decision-making procedures. There is also the ever-present danger of being rejected on a call for support by allies. Creating ad hoc "coalitions of the willing" gets around these problems, but they provide no firm foundation on which to build long-term solutions. They also require the United States to reinvent the solution each time a new problem arises.

Shuttle Diplomacy

In many respects, the choice between bilateral and multilateral diplomacy is a false one. Bilateral diplomacy can be an important component of any multilateral diplomatic undertaking. This is notably the case in **shuttle diplomacy**. Here, the political distance between two states is so great that they are unable to engage in face-to-face negotiations and a trusted third party travels between them in an effort to end the diplomatic stalemate.

Shuttle diplomacy is most famously associated with Henry Kissinger, who served as national security advisor and later secretary of state under President Richard Nixon. His shuttle diplomacy occurred following the 1973 Yom Kippur War. A coordinated surprise attack by Egyptian and Syrian forces seriously weakened Israeli forces and raised the possibility of an Israeli defeat. Eventually, Israeli forces launched a successful counterattack. A UN-arranged truce failed and fighting continued until October 25, when efforts by the U.S. and Soviet Union ended the fighting. A UN peace conference got under way in December and ended in failure in early January 1974. On January 14, 1974, Kissinger flew to Egypt to discuss terms of a possible peace agreement. For the next week Kissinger would repeatedly fly between Egypt and Israel in an effort to narrow the differences between the two states. On January 18 a peace agreement that placed UN peacekeeping forces in the Sinai as a buffer between the two states was announced. Kissinger then turned his attention to the Syrian-Israeli standoff. Beginning in mid-March and running through most of April he met separately and regularly with Syrian and Israeli embassy officials in Washington. Feeling that the foundations of an agreement had been identified, Kissinger left on May 1 for another round of shuttle diplomacy that ultimately produced a peace agreement on May 31. Kissinger undertook one last round of Middle East diplomacy in 1975. This too brought about a peace agreement between Israel and Egypt, but the effort is not considered to have been as successful as the earlier ones, largely due to the amount of U.S. foreign aid that was promised to both sides and because hopes for a broader regional peace agreement were not realized.

Most recently Obama's secretary of state John Kerry engaged in shuttle diplomacy. Again the underlying issue was peace in the Middle East. And, as with Kissinger, his efforts to produce a functioning peace agreement failed. Over the course of five months in 2013 Kerry made six trips to the Middle East and engaged in what were termed "marathon sessions" with leaders on both sides for the purpose of restarting negotiations. Those negotiations resumed in July 2013. By December Kerry had made an additional three trips to the Middle East in an effort to spur both sides to an agreement but with little success. Increasingly Kerry was becoming less of a mediator and more of an active participant in shaping the agreement. As a self-imposed deadline for an agreement approached and with negotiations stalled Kerry returned to the Middle East in late March 2014. He would then schedule a second trip later that week, only to cancel it, saying, "It's reality check time." Kerry pledged to continue to work for a peace agreement but indicated it might be time for the United States to redirect its diplomatic efforts to problems where it might have more success.[12]

Summit Diplomacy

The most visible of all the forms of diplomacy is summit diplomacy, in which heads of state meet personally with one another. **Summit conferences** perform a number of valuable services.[13] Foremost among them is establishing a personal relationship between leaders that sensitizes each to the domestic constraints operating in the other's political system. A second valuable service performed by a summit is that it energizes the bureaucracy and sets a deadline for decision-making. The benefit here is not so much the summit itself but the preparations for the summit.

Aligned against these virtues of summit diplomacy are a number of potentially negative consequences.[14] First, the personal contacts established through face-to-face negotiations may result in an inaccurate reading of the adversary's character and the unclear constraints under which the adversary operates. This appears to have happened at the 1961 Kennedy-Khrushchev summit in Vienna. Khrushchev reportedly came away from it with the impression that Kennedy could be intimidated, and many link the Soviet attempt to place missiles in Cuba to this meeting.

Energizing the bureaucracy does not necessarily guarantee the emergence of a coherent policy. It may only intensify the ongoing bureaucratic struggle so that only a lowest-common-denominator position is taken to the summit. Summit deadlines may also politicize or impede decision-making. This point is most forcefully raised with reference to annual economic summitry, but as the many accounts of U.S.-Soviet arms control talks reveal, it is equally applicable to other forms of international diplomacy.[15] Other commentators suggest that periodic meetings are a questionable device for addressing a continuously evolving problem. Agreements reached in April become obsolete in November, but the next summit is still months away. In addition, summit deadlines offer the recalcitrant state a golden opportunity to exploit the other's eagerness for the summit. One observer suggests that this may have happened with the Carter-Brezhnev summit. Carter's desire for a summit is seen as being partly responsible for his supporting a Soviet initiative to reconvene the Geneva talks on the Middle East. The result, had this actually happened, would have been to give the Soviet Union a voice in the Middle East peace process that was denied to it as long as U.S. peace initiatives dominated the agenda.[16]

Summit conferences have also been criticized for unfairly raising public expectations. A common criticism of high-level diplomacy is that it is part of a cycle characterized by "a burst of publicity about new initiatives or special envoys, followed by policy drift and an unwillingness to push either side," until "eventually the effort goes dormant, sometimes for months, until yet another approach is crafted."[17] The Strategic Arms Limitation Talks (SALT) agreements were negotiated as part of the process of détente, and when détente began to unravel, arms control efforts were one of the main casualties. To deal with many of these shortcomings, President Richard Nixon advocated regular summit conferences as a way of keeping the pressure on the Soviet Union, curbing its behavior, and taking the pressure off getting a major agreement at any one summit.[18]

East-West Superpower Summits

East-West summit conferences were a frequent, if irregularly spaced, feature of the Cold War.[19] The early summits, from 1955 to 1967, dealt with European security issues. Later they became an important mechanism for institutionalizing détente. All told, they produced more than twenty-four agreements, including SALT I and SALT II. Reagan and Gorbachev conducted a series of post-détente summit conferences, the most famous of which was the Reykjavik summit in 1986. There, Reagan proposed abolishing all ballistic missiles, and Gorbachev countered with a proposal to eliminate all strategic arms. Nothing came of these initiatives because they would have prohibited Reagan from engaging in Strategic Defensive Initiative testing beyond the laboratory, something he was determined to do. With the disintegration of the Soviet Union and the end of the Cold War, East-West summits declined in overall strategic importance and became more typical of traditional bilateral relations. Increasingly, they focused on economic assistance and ways to enlist Russian help in the War on Terrorism.

Economic Summits

Beginning in 1975, the heads of state of the six major Western economies (the United States, Great Britain, France, Germany, Japan, and Italy) have been meeting at an annual summit. Originally known as the Group of 6 (G6), today it is the Group of 7 (it was the G8 until Russia was expelled after the Ukraine crisis). These meetings began as a means for informal discussion among the leaders of the major economic powers as they dealt with the effects of the post–Arab-Israeli War oil crisis, global inflation, and the removal of the dollar from the gold standard.

In mid-2007 a financial crisis began to work its way through the international economic system. As the need for a global response rather than separate national responses to the financial crisis became evident, the search for a proper forum for conducting negotiations began. The G8 was seen as having too narrow a membership to construct a global solution and attention shifted to the Group of 20 (G20). It was created as a response to the 1997–98 Asian financial crisis and includes developed and developing economies. Saudi Arabia, Brazil, India, China, Mexico, and South Africa are all members of the G20. The G20 held its first formal summit in 2008 in Washington to address the financial crisis. At the Pittsburgh G8 summit in September 2009, it was agreed that the G20 would replace the G8 as the main forum for international economic discussions.

One common trait shared by all of these forms of economic summitry is that over time military national security questions have become a prominent agenda item.[19] As early as 1996 the G8 agenda was broadened to include terrorism and international crime at the urging of President Bill Clinton. More recently, in a 2012 meeting of G8 foreign ministers hosted by Secretary of State Hillary Clinton, major topics of discussion included possible North Korean missile tests, Iran's nuclear program, and the crisis in Syria. President Obama sought to build global support for a military strike against Syria for its use of chemical weapons at the 2013 G20 summit.

Conference Diplomacy

Conference diplomacy starts from the logic that some problems in international politics affect the interests of too many states to be solved unilaterally, bilaterally, or at summit conferences. What is needed is to bring all of the concerned states together at a regional or global level. One region whose international politics are taking on increasing significance is the Arctic. At the broadest level activities there are regulated by the 1982 UN Convention on the Law of the Sea. Two problems exist with it as a governing document. First, the United States did not sign the treaty. Second, states whose territory borders on the Arctic are seeking to limit the intrusion of other states into the region's decision-making. A preferred site for promoting cooperation and coordination is the Arctic Council. Indigenous communities participate in discussions covering such topics as climate change, oil and gas, and Arctic shipping. One of the major point of controversy facing it are claims by Russia, Canada, and others that certain Arctic waterways are inland passages and thus governed by national laws. The United States assumed the rotating chair of the Arctic Council for the first time in 2015 for a two-year term.

GATT and WTO

The United States has relied heavily on international conferences to accomplish its foreign policy objectives in the area of trade. Historically, the most important of these was the General Agreement on Tariffs and Trade (GATT) talks. The last GATT conference ran from 1986 to 1994. It was known as the Uruguay Round and culminated with the signing of an agreement that established the WTO to supervise international trade law and formally bring the GATT process to an end.

From its first meeting in Geneva in 1947, GATT had been seen as a transitional body that would deal with international trade matters only until an International Trade Organization (ITO) was set up. Because of political opposition in the United States to the broad powers that were to be given to the ITO, President Harry Truman never submitted the treaty to Congress for approval. Similar concerns about the loss of U.S. sovereignty were expressed when the WTO was proposed. Only a last-minute compromise reserving the right of the United States to leave the WTO should it consistently rule against the United States cleared the way for the treaty's approval by the Senate.

Two important early GATT trade negotiation rounds were the Kennedy Round (1964–67) and the Tokyo Round (1973–77). The Kennedy Round reduced barriers to international free trade and marked the high point of international trade cooperation. By the late 1970s, tariffs averaged less than 10 percent. This compared to 25 percent in 1945 and 60 percent in 1934. The Tokyo Round was not as successful. While it made some progress on reducing nontariff barriers to trade through such practices (i.e., government subsidies, dumping, and product standards), little headway was made on liberalizing agricultural trade. Questions of trade in services were not addressed.

Four conflict areas dominated the agenda at the Uruguay Round. They continue to be the principal areas in which meaningful agreements have eluded WTO negotiators. The first is trade in agriculture. At the heart of the problem is the need for more markets for agricultural goods, the widespread presence of subsidies and quotas that protect farmers from foreign competition, and the unwillingness of governments to antagonize the politically powerful agricultural interests in their states. A second area of disagreement involves strengthening international protection for intellectual property. American firms charge that Third World states routinely disregard copyrights and patents in the production of such items as books, compact discs, and computer software. A third area of controversy centers on the demands of the United States and Europe for international labor standards with regard to child labor, convict labor, minimum wages, and unions. Fourth, the United States and Europe have pressed over Third World objections for the establishment of a body to examine the environmental impact of global trade agreements.

The 2001 WTO Doha meeting took place two months after the 9/11 attacks and was viewed by many in the United States and abroad as an opportunity to promote global cohesion. The talks were set to produce an agreement in 2005 before the expiration of President George W. Bush's fast-track trade authority but this did not happen. It was not until December 2013 at Bali, twelve years after it began, that the Doha Round trade talks produced an agreement. The

2013 Bali meeting was generally seen as the last chance for success. Negotiators abandoned any hope of producing a comprehensive trade agreement and instead settled on an agreement on "trade facilitation" by cutting red tape and corruption in customs procedures for bringing goods into a country. Confidence in the WTO's ability to organize and regulate international trade was weakened further in 2014 when negotiators were unable to overcome China's and South Korea's objections to an Information Technology Agreement that would have lowered tariffs on high technology goods.

Historical Lesson

The Kyoto Protocol and Copenhagen Accord

The Paris Climate agreement marks the third time since the initial United Nations Framework Convention on Climate Change was signed in Rio de Janeiro in 1992. Under the terms of that agreement signatory states were required to develop programs to reduce the emission of greenhouse gases. No targets or requirements were included in the treaty. President George H. W. Bush signed the agreement and the Senate ratified it following a promise by him that targets and timetables from future agreements would be sent to the Senate for ratification.

The 1992 agreement mandated annual meetings to continue work on the problem of global warming. The first follow-on agreement came in 1997 with the signing of the Kyoto Protocol which was formally an amendment to the Rio Treaty. It legally required that by 2012 all developed states that signed and ratified the agreement were to reduce their greenhouse emissions by 5 percent from their 1990 levels. Six greenhouse gases were identified as requiring action. Three strategies were identified including removal of greenhouse gases from the atmosphere by such measures as planting trees, investing in clean technologies, and trading emissions. Under this last strategy states that had reduced greenhouse emissions to a point lower than the required target could sell emissions credits to countries that were not meeting them. Countries that failed to meet their targets would be assessed a 30 percent penalty in future reduction rounds. Developing countries, of which China claimed, and continues to claim, it was a part, were exempt from any requirement to reduce greenhouse emissions.

For the Kyoto Protocol to come into force fifty-five countries responsible for at least 55 percent of the total carbon dioxide emissions in 1900 had to ratify the agreement. The fifty-fifth country signed in 2002. The second requirement was not met until 2004 when Russia ratified it. The United States signed the Kyoto Protocol with President Bill Clinton calling it "environmentally strong and economically sound." While it was being negotiated Congress passed a resolution stating that the United States should not sign any climate agreement that did not include targets and timetables for all countries or any agreement that seriously hurt the American economy. President George W. Bush withdrew the United States from the agreement in 2002 without it having been sent to the Senate for ratification calling it "fatally flawed."

The second attempt at negotiating a climate treaty came in Copenhagen in December 2009 when the fifteenth annual meeting following the signing of the Rio Treaty took place. The basic outline of the agenda and the agreement to be negotiated was set two years earlier at the 2007 meeting in Bali. The two weeks of negotiations to flesh out the "Bali roadmap" that took place in Copenhagen were described as raucous, disorganized, and frantic. Documents leaked by Edward Snowden in 2014 revealed that the United States had spied upon other delegations and was in possession of details of their negotiating positions. One account characterized the negotiations as a textbook case of how not to do a deal.

No agreement was in hand as the conference was about to adjourn on December 18. Press reports suggested that only a weak political statement might be announced. At that point foreign leaders had only recently arrived for a ceremonial signing of the final document. President Obama was one of them. What followed in the remaining thirteen hours was intense round-the-clock negotiations between the United States, China, India, Brazil, and South Africa. Obama was particularly active rejecting calls from some states that the United States should simply sign the Kyoto Protocol making an agreement in Copenhagen unnecessary. He also is reported to have entered without an invitation a meeting of Chinese leaders with other heads of state. In the end, an agreement was reached.

Advocates of the agreement called it a historic step forward. Others, however, complained that they had not yet seen the agreement and had been excluded from these last-minute negotiations. This proved to be its downfall. Under United Nations procedures unanimous consent was needed for an agreement to become official. This rule held at Kyoto and Paris. At Copenhagen, angered at their exclusion and objecting to some of its terms, some countries, notably Bolivia, Venezuela, Sudan, and Tuvalu, objected. As a result on December 19, when the meeting conference ended, instead of being adopted the agreement, officially known as the Copenhagen Accord, was merely "taken note of." It was not a legally binding document.

The initial response in the United States was mixed. Obama called it a "meaningful and unprecedented" agreement. Among the breakthroughs contained in the accord were recognition of the need to keep temperatures from rising below 2°C, pledges of aid to developing countries, and a recognition that all countries must reduce emissions. An aide to Senator Richard Lugar called it a "home run." Senator McCain called it a "nothing burger." The longer-term political reaction in the United States and elsewhere was to pull back from seeking a new global climate agreement. The next climate meeting was held in Cancun in December 2010. The Center for Climate and Energy Solutions noted that the Cancun meetings basically stayed close to the script of the Copenhagen Accords leaving all options open and setting no clear path forward to a binding climate agreement.

Applying the Lesson

1. Should all states have an equal say in negotiating a climate treaty? Should there be a unanimity rule?

2. How would you rank Paris, Copenhagen, and Kyoto in terms of their significance?

3. What criteria should be used to measure the success and failure of international conferences?

Environmental Conferences

As we can readily see in the three environmental conferences discussed elsewhere in this chapter (the Paris Climate agreement discussed in the Dateline section and the Kyoto Protocol and Copenhagen Accord discussed in the Historical Box) conference diplomacy is a central vehicle for international environmental policy making. Just as with international economic conference diplomacy, the complexity of these issues coupled with the imperatives of American domestic politics has made it difficult for the United States to exert leadership and has often placed it at odds with the rest of the world. Here we want to introduce and review two of the earliest efforts at environmental conference diplomacy.

The first conference is the 1987 Montreal Protocol on Substances that Deplete the Ozone Layer.[20] The convergence of many factors, not the least of which was the Chernobyl nuclear reactor accident, brought about a policy shift in the Reagan administration position on environmental protect that made the agreement possible. The Montreal Protocol was hailed both for the cuts it was able to make in the production and consumption of ozone-depleting materials and for its procedural approach to the problem. Rather than seek a definitive and comprehensive statement about levels of reduction, funding, and the obligations of signatory states, as had commonly been done in the past, negotiators at Montreal established a framework for addressing the problem and committed themselves to periodic review conferences at which target figures and timetables could be adjusted.

The second conference is the 1992 UN Conference on Environment and Development held in Rio de Janeiro, Brazil. Better known as the Earth Summit, it resulted in the signing of seven major pacts and initiatives. It also found the United States on the defensive again, as the only major state not to sign a biodiversity treaty. The George H. W. Bush administration objected to its provisions calling for all states to protect endangered animal and plant species on the grounds that it did not provide patent protection to U.S. biotechnology firms. The treaty was later signed by Bill Clinton. The United States was also virtually alone in its objections to a treaty on protection against global warming, agreeing to support it only after references to binding targets and timetables were dropped in favor of a more general pledge to reduce the emissions of gases that cause global warming.

Human Rights Conferences

The subject matter of international human rights conferences varies greatly. Topics range from commonly defined rights such as those associated with the 1948 Universal Declaration of Human Rights to concerns of more specific groups of individuals, such as women and children, the disabled, or refugees and displaced persons. The United States generally has been an active participant in these conferences, but at times, it has also opted not to participate or dissented from the agreement. In 2015 the United States played an active role in the September 2015 Global Leaders' Meeting on Gender Equality and Women's Empowerment held in Beijing which commemorated the 4th World Conference on

Women also held in Beijing in 1995. This 1995 conference is seen as notable for having put forward a breakthrough blueprint for advancing women's rights and remembered for Hillary Clinton's statement that "women's rights are human rights." At the 2105 summit the U.S. delegation was led by Samantha Power, the U.S. ambassador to the United Nations, who used the conference as a forum to pressure China and other countries to stop jailing female activists.

The United States has tended not to participate in human rights conferences when the proposed treaty or agenda does not involve advancing and protecting traditionally defined political and civil liberties. One prominent decision to abstain took place in October 1996, when the United States was absent from the Ottawa Conference on land mines, which resulted in a treaty now signed by over 150 countries. India, China, and Russia have also not signed the treaty banning the production and development of antipersonnel mines. One reason given by the United States for not signing the treaty is the continued need for such mines along the demilitarized zone along the North-South Korea border.

The United States has also refused to participate in international conferences on racism because of concerns over language in proposed treaties. A recurring example is a UN conference to end racism and discrimination. In April 2009, President Obama announced he was not going to send a delegation to the Durban Review Conference, which would meet to evaluate progress toward the goals of eliminating racism, racial discrimination, xenophobia, and related forms of intolerance. The principal reason given was the conference's equating of racism with Zionism. The George W. Bush administration balked at participating in the 2001 conference because of this language and the inclusion of a proposal calling for reparations for slavery.

UN Diplomacy

Viewed from one perspective the U.S. diplomatic relationship with the United Nations has shown great variation over time. In its early years, the United Nations existed as a virtual extension of the State Department. Support from the General Assembly could be taken as a given. This began to change in the 1960s as colonial areas gained independence and sought to use the United Nations as a tool for advancing their own agendas. The United States now often found itself on the defensive. It used its veto power in the Security Council for the first time in 1970.

At the same time we can see great consistency in how the United States has approached the United Nations. At any one time, U.S. policy toward the United Nations represents an amalgam of four different roles.[21] First, the United States sees itself as an international reformer. Viewed from this perspective, the United Nations is an important instrument deserving U.S. support, because it holds the potential to transform world politics. Second, the United States sees itself as a custodian. It sometimes usurps or resists the powers of the United Nations because its agenda conflicts with the greater purposes of the United Nations as identified and defined by the United States. The third role is that of spokesperson for the American public. A problem here is that policy makers do not necessarily have a clear sense of what the public thinks. Finally, the United States finds itself in the same role as other states. It seeks to use the UN system to advance and protect American national interests by such actions as applying international sanctions against Iraq, vetoing resolutions condemning Israel, and opposing an international criminal court. Mixed motives are often present behind U.S. actions and the balance among these four role orientations is not fixed. Changes in U.S. policy toward the United Nations thus can be attributed to changes in the intensity of these outlooks and the manner in which they interact.

The Obama administration's UN diplomacy followed this pattern. It continued to seek and obtain UN support for economic sanctions against Iran, which is in line with a national interest approach. It got UN support for establishing a no-fly zone over Libya before taking military action, a decision that put the United Nations in the position of a global reformer. Also, it acted as a custodian, voting against a UN fact-finding report that criticized Israel for killing six passengers on board a Turkish aid flotilla, arguing that the UN Human Rights Council's report was unbalanced and that it had acted too hastily in creating an investigatory panel.

Public Diplomacy and Digital Diplomacy

Public diplomacy consists of the statements and actions of leaders that are intended to influence public opinion in other countries. But public diplomacy is more than just words. It is a set of institutions, programs, and practices designed to accomplish three strategic objectives:

1. Inform the world accurately, clearly, and swiftly about U.S. policy
2. Represent the values and beliefs of the American people
3. Explain how democracy produces prosperity, stability, and opportunity

Public diplomacy is alien to classic diplomacy, which emphasizes secrecy and confidential bargaining among government officials, and, therefore, has been largely neglected and often disparaged as propaganda. This fate befell four Cold War efforts at public diplomacy. Voice of America (VOA) began broadcasting during World War II. Eventually, it came under the control of the U.S. Information Agency (USIA). During the Cold War, USIA radio broadcasts reached into the Soviet Union and Eastern Europe through Radio Liberty and Radio Free Europe. Both were heavily funded covertly by the Central Intelligence Agency. In 1983 the Reagan administration set up Radio Marti to broadcast into Cuba. These efforts at public diplomacy highlight the inherent tension between being an alternate source of information for citizens in these countries and serving as an instrument of U.S. foreign policy. The VOA is the best example of an information source and Radio Marti is the most prominent example of it serving as a foreign policy tool.

President Bill Clinton is widely recognized as one of the most skilled practitioners of public diplomacy. He brought an American-style political campaign atmosphere to his trips abroad that sought to win foreign publics over to his cause. This stands in sharp contrast to President Reagan's forays into public diplomacy, which tended to have a hit-and-run quality to them. Reagan's references to the Soviet Union as the "evil empire" played well at home but scared the public abroad. A similar problem faced George W. Bush, whose black-and-white image of the world and use of phrases associated with the American frontier were off-putting to foreign audiences. Obama's efforts at public diplomacy had a mixed record. On the positive side his foreign policy rhetoric contributed greatly to his winning the 2009 Nobel Peace Prize and reversing negative feelings toward the United States that arose during the Bush administration. On the negative side it later led to feelings of disappointment when Obama's rhetoric was not matched by similarly bold action.

Public diplomacy has received renewed attention today largely because of the revolution in communication technologies and the increased roles that public opinion, nonstate actors, and legislatures play in modern diplomacy. Its importance has also grown because of the increased role that ideas are seen as playing in world politics, as evidenced by the debate over the merits of "soft power." Most pointedly, the War on Terrorism breathed new life into America's public diplomacy through the increased interest in using social media technologies. Some refer to this development as the beginnings of **digital diplomacy** and others as Public Diplomacy II. In 2003 an Office of eDiplomacy was established. By 2012 it was operating an estimated six hundred social media platforms, including blogs (DipNote), Twitter accounts (@StateDept), and Facebook pages (eJournal USA). A Rapid Response Unit was created to monitor social media responses to ongoing situations that impact U.S. national interests.

Neither public diplomacy nor soft power are arenas free from competition.[22] Russia and China have both undertaken major initiatives to improve their global standing and image. Success in these efforts is by no means guaranteed. A recent study of Chinese soft power noted that for all of the funds spent to manage its media image and to promote a positive view of its actions through financing worldwide development projects, China's efforts have produced meager results. Of particular concern to the United States today is the success that ISIS has experienced in using social media to present itself in a positive light to potentially sympathetic Muslims and to intimidate opponents. Assessments by the State Department and others concluded that ISIS was winning the social media war in 2015.[23]

The newfound emphasis on public and digital diplomacy is not without its critics. Three broad sets of criticisms are made. At the strategic level, those who see soft power as being difficult to use or limited in its persuasive abilities perceive public diplomacy as only helping at the margins and not capable of addressing the underlying images of distrust or dislike that may exist abroad.[24] At the tactical level, many are critical of continued attempts to use public diplomacy channels for partisan political purposes, such as presenting President George W. Bush's policies in overly favorable terms or keeping critical stories about the president off the air.[25] Third, digital diplomacy may lead to political problems at home and abroad. This came through quite clearly in a dispute over a Cairo embassy tweet in the context of an incident where protestors stormed the embassy over a film defaming the prophet Muhammad. Occurring in the midst of the 2012 presidential election, the tweet, which was not cleared by Washington, was interpreted by Republicans as an apology to the angry protestors when in fact it was issued before the incident in an attempt by the embassy to reduce tensions.

The Political Use of Force

By its very existence, American military power serves as an instrument of diplomacy. Without ever having to be used or even referred to, it heightens U.S. prestige and gives importance to U.S. proposals and expressions of concern. The knowledge that both conventional and nuclear military power exist in the shadows of international crises influences both the manner in which U.S. policy makers approach problems and the positions adopted by other states.

Coercive Diplomacy

The use of conventional military force for political purposes by the United States is not new. Researchers identified 218 incidents between 1946 and 1975 in which the United States did so.[26] To qualify as a political use of force, the military action had to involve a physical change in the disposition of U.S. forces and had to be done consciously to achieve a political objective without going to war or trying to physically impose the U.S. position on the target state. On average, the political use of force lasted ninety days. Actions taken ranged from a port visit by a single warship to the deployment of major land, sea, and air units in conjunction with a strategic alert and reserve mobilizations. In any one year, as many as 20 incidents and as few as 3 took place.

The end of the Cold War did not end America's interest in using military power for political ends. In fact, a number of factors made the political use of force very attractive. Using a slightly different definition of the political use of force than was used earlier, a recent study examined instances of post–Cold War **coercive diplomacy**. It found that of sixteen cases where military power was used to persuade rather than defeat the opponent, success was realized only five times. It clearly failed in eight cases. The limited success rate is not surprising. Studies of attempts at coercive diplomacy during the Cold War documented an even lower success rate.

Three factors seem to have contributed to what success coercive diplomacy enjoyed, although none guarantees success. First, offering positive inducements to the other state to adjust its policy was important. Second, the timing of the inducement was important. Inducement was most effective when it was offered after the demonstrative use of force or after threatening force. Inducements had little positive effect if they were offered in advance of such shows of resolve. Third, it was important to be able to demonstrate clearly to the opponent what would happen to their military forces should war occur and that their military strategy would fail. Interestingly, the type of demand made by the United States had little relation to success or failure.

The increased prominence of international crises caused by domestic security threats as opposed to cross-border conflicts has created two added problems for the conduct of coercive diplomacy today. First there is the challenge of legitimiz-ing the use of force for political purposes. In the case of Libya in 2011 this was done through a UN resolution invoking the Responsibility to Protect doctrine. In the case of Syria's use of chemical weapons the United States was threaten-ing military action without significant international support. Second, there is the problem of determining where to draw the line for setting in motion military activity. In Libya, that line was never crossed. Rather, there existed the expecta-tion that it was about to be crossed. In Syria, the line established by Obama was crossed and no military action was taken, raising the question of whether another line could be credibly established.

As the Obama administration came to an end there were four major conflicts or potential conflicts in which force was being used for political purposes. The first was the South China Sea, where the United States and China have been engaged in a prolonged series of military provocations and countermoves over the future political, military, and economic status of the region. The second is the Syrian civil war, where military force is being used in an attempt to compel the government and rebel forces to negotiate a solution. The third is in Eastern Europe, where following the Russian interventions into the Crimea and the Ukraine NATO forces have carried out a series of maneuvers and basing deci-sions designed to send a signal of its resolve to Russia and pro-Western political forces in Eastern Europe. The fourth involves Iran. In 2015 the United States sent an aircraft carrier and a guided missile cruiser to the waters off the coast of Iran where they joined ten other U.S. naval vessels in an effort to warn Iran about its deepening involvement with rebels forces in Yemen.

Nuclear Diplomacy

In contemplating using military power for political purposes, American policy makers have not limited themselves to thinking in terms of conventional weap-ons. On at least two occasions, they have threatened to use nuclear weapons in an effort to compel others into action.[27] Evidence suggests that Dwight Eisen-hower made a **compellence** threat in 1953 as part of his plan to bring an end to the Korean War. Richard Nixon also made such a threat in 1969 in an attempt to end the Vietnam War. Unlike the Eisenhower case, when the threat of using nuclear weapons was presented as part of a deliberate U.S. strategy, Nixon cast his in quite different terms, telling his chief of staff H. R. Haldeman:

> I call it the Madman Theory, Bob. I want the North Vietnamese to believe I've reached the point that I might do anything to stop the war. We'll just slip the word to them that "for God's sake, you know Nixon is obsessed about Commu-nism. We can't restrain him when he is angry and he has his hand on the nuclear button." Ho Chi Minh himself will be in Paris in two days begging for peace.[28]

On October 10, 1969, U.S. nuclear forces were put on alert "to respond to possible confrontation by the Soviet Union." The actions taken were designed to be picked up by Soviet intelligence but still not be visible to the American press or public. It was Nixon's hope that this would be part of a lead-up to a massive conventional offensive in Vietnam and would stampede the Soviets into working toward a diplomatic solution to the war. In fact, Nixon had already decided against such a military operation because of the domestic opposition it would unleash in the United States and military doubts about its effectiveness. Soviet leaders do not appear to have responded to this political use of nuclear power in any meaningful way. It does appear that Soviet intelligence recognized the change in nuclear readiness.

Two significant points emerge from a detailed look at the history of this episode. First, the military did not automatically and uniformly implement Nixon's alert order. The Strategic Air Command balked, as did Secretary of Defense Melvin Laird, suggesting that Nixon was in far less control of the U.S. nuclear forces than he believed or most commentators thought. Second, to the Nixon administration, it was obvious this was nuclear signaling over Vietnam. However, at that very moment, the Soviet Union and China were involved in an intense border dispute. Chinese leaders had been evacuated from Beijing, and its nuclear forces were on alert. From both the Chinese and Soviet perspectives, the U.S. nuclear alert could have just as easily been seen in light of this conflict.

The difficulties involved with using nuclear power for political purposes is also seen in Vladimir Putin's March 2015 statement that in the 2104 Crimea crisis he was ready to put Russian nuclear forces on alert. The immediate question this revelation (if true) raised concerned its purpose. Was it designed to strengthen Putin's domestic political position, or was it intended to influence U.S. and NATO decision-making in future crises? If this second interpretation was the intent, it also raises the possibility of a preemptive move by the United States and NATO rather than a conciliatory one.

Arms Transfers

Arms transfers have established themselves as a favorite instrument of policy makers.[29] The Arms Export Control Act of 1976 requires that all arms transfers valued at $25 million or more or those involving the transfer of significant combat equipment be reported to Congress. Soon thereafter one study found that over one hundred were being reported yearly. States sell and buy weapons for a number of different reasons, and the relationship between them has been compared to a reciprocal bargaining process in which each tries to use the other to accomplish goals that are often incompatible.[30]

For arms sellers, three strategic rationales are most often advanced. First, arms transfers can provide influence and leverage abroad by serving as a symbolic statement of support for a regime and providing access to elites. Second, they can be used to protect specific security interests abroad and further regional stability. Third, they can be used as barter in acquiring access to overseas bases.

None of these rationales is without problems. Leverage tends to be a transitory phenomenon in world politics, and an arms transfer relationship can promote friction and set off regional arms races just as much as it can cement ties. Currently, Saudi Arabia is using F-15 fighters in Yemen, the United Arab Emirates is using F-16s to bomb Yemen and Syria, and Qatar is purchasing

Apache helicopters, Patriot missiles systems, and F-15s. On top of this Congress passed legislation in 2008 that required U.S. arms sales to provide Israel with a "qualitative military edge" in the region. This mandate assumed a continuing Arab-Israeli conflict, but today Israel is a de facto ally with several Arab states against Iran. Arms sales can also produce a situation of reverse leverage, in which the recipient state, rather than the seller, exercises the most influence. The United States sold sophisticated weapons to the shah of Iran in the hope that he would use them to contain the spread of communism in the Persian Gulf, while the shah saw those weapons as a way of realizing his dream of making Iran into a regional superpower.

The war against terrorism presents additional problems for arms sales especially in cases where state governments are weak or nonexistent. Libya is a case in point. In 2016 the United States and over twenty countries and international organizations agreed to arms and train Libyan forces and resistance forces against ISIS. The problem as the U.S. military pointed out was that it is unclear which groups are fighting with the government to defeat ISIS and which are really fighting to defeat the government.

There have been five major turning points in the development of U.S. arms transfer policy. The first came in the early 1960s, when the Kennedy administration made a distinction between **arms sales** and arms transferred abroad as foreign aid. Kennedy turned to arms sales in an effort to counter the growing U.S. balance-of-payments problem, which had been brought about in part by the high cost of stationing U.S. troops in Europe. The second turning point came during the Nixon administration. Arms transfers became an important instrument of foreign policy and a cornerstone of the Nixon Doctrine, which stressed the need for Third World allies of the United States to assume the primary responsibility for their own defense. To that end, the United States was prepared to channel aid and assistance, but it would not readily intervene into conflict itself. Sales also replaced aid as the primary vehicle for transferring arms and the quality of the weapons transferred increased dramatically. No longer were arms transfers dominated by obsolete weapons in the U.S. inventory. Now they regularly involved the most sophisticated weapons the United States possessed. Measured in constant dollars, U.S. arms transfers increased 150 percent between 1968 and 1977. Just as important, the Middle East now became the primary area of U.S. arms transfers.

The third turning point in the evolution of U.S. arms transfer policy came with the Carter administration. It represented a turning point for what the administration sought to do rather than for what it accomplished. Carter sought to make arms transfers an "exceptional tool of foreign policy rather than a standard one."[31] The Carter policy had an immediate impact. In the first fifteen months after it was announced, 614 requests from 92 states for over $1 billion worth of arms were turned down.

Gradually, the Carter administration found it difficult to work within its own guidelines. The first major exception to its own rules was approving the sale of the Airborne Warning and Control System (AWACS) for $1.8 billion to Saudi Arabia. The Carter administration also agreed to a large arms package for South Korea in compensation for the reduction of U.S. ground troops to be stationed there. It soon would completely abandon all signs of restraint by approving weapons sales to Israel and Egypt as part of the Camp David Accords and to Saudi Arabia after the shah fell and the Soviet Union invaded Afghanistan.

The fourth turning point in U.S. arms transfer policy came with the arrival of the Reagan administration. It moved quickly to use arms transfers as a tool in its global struggle against communism. In its first three months, it offered approximately $15 billion in weapons and other forms of military assistance to other states, and this pattern would continue and by the end of the Clinton administration the United States was the world's leading arms supplier.

The current period in arms sales policy began after the 9/11 terrorist attacks. One of the most notable features of this period is the embrace of arms transfers to developing countries that were once on restricted lists. Armenia, Azerbaijan, India, and Pakistan, all of which are key allies in the War against Terrorism, now receive U.S. arms. In the case of India, 2002 marked the end of an almost forty-year period in which no export licenses were granted. Before 9/11, the last time Pakistan received funds from the United States to acquire American-made weapons, services, or technology was in 1990, when sales totaled $185 million. In 2002 this number had jumped to $690 million.

Another key feature in this period is the continued growth in arms sales.[32] The total value of arms transfers in 2015 was $10.484 billion. Overall, U.S. arms exports from 2011 to 2015 went to ninety-six countries, 41 percent of which were in the Middle East, and were 27 percent higher than in the 2006–10 time frame. From 2011 to 2015 the United States accounted for 33 percent of the world's arms sales. The top three purchasers of U.S. arms in this period were Saudi Arabia (9.7 percent), the United Arab Emirates (9.1 percent), and Turkey (6.6 percent). Aircraft accounted for 59 percent of all purchases. Table 10.2 presents a breakdown of U.S. arms deliveries to Near Eastern countries from 2007 to 2010 and from 2011 to 2014.

Today, we may be entering a new era of arms transfers. In early 2015 the Obama administration announced that it would allow sales of armed drones to allies. Up until now armed drones have only been sold to Great Britain while unarmed drones, ones used for intelligence gathering, have been sold to NATO allies. The criteria for determining which countries could purchase drones has not been released but the administration said there would be a "strong presumption of denial" in making those decisions.

Over the Horizon: A Climate Coalition of the Willing

According to one unnamed State Department official the War against Terrorism has expanded the role of the military and intelligence agencies to the point where "in a lot of ways, diplomacy is this historical anachronism."[33] Our discussion in this chapter provides evidence that this is not yet the case but it also has identified how difficult and complex diplomacy is today and that many of challenges diplomacy faces have long histories.

TABLE 10.2	U.S. Arms Deliveries to Near East (millions of current U.S. dollars)		
2007–10		**2011–14**	
Saudi Arabia	5,300	Saudi Arabia	9,000
Israel	4,400	Egypt	4,200
Egypt	4,000	UAE	4,000
Iraq	2,000	Israel	3,600
Lebanon	1,400	Iraq	3,100
Kuwait	1,300	Morocco	1,500
Jordan	900	Kuwait	1,400
UAE	800	Jordan	1,200
Bahrain	500	Oman	700
Morocco	200	Bahrain	300
Oman	200	Lebanon	200
		Qatar	100

Source: Catherine Theohary, *Conventional Arms Transfers to Developing Nations, 2007–2014*, Congressional Research Service, December 21, 2015.

No easy solution to these challenges exists.[34] Unilateral, bilateral, and multilateral approaches to diplomatic action all have drawbacks. Looking over the horizon, we may see a middle course of diplomacy emerge under the heading of coalitions of the willing. Protecting the global environment is one policy arena where we have already seen calls for forming coalitions of the willing due to frustration with both the pace of global environmental negotiations and their content. Under this form of diplomacy the United States will partner with interested countries to the exclusion of others.[35] A key area in which climate coalitions of the willing may be able to expand climate protection beyond its current level is in the area of enforcement. The argument made is that given the strong norm requiring universal consensus in international conference decision-making any form of meaningful enforcement may be impossible. It becomes politically more feasible when a smaller group of like-minded countries can agree on credible enforcement obligations and establish sufficient incentives to pursue them.[36]

A variation on this idea is found in the call for creating an informal League of Democracies. It has been endorsed by John McCain in his presidential campaign, advisors to President Barack Obama, and Bill Clinton's secretary of state Madeleine Albright.[37] At its core is the belief that democracies are capable of acting in uniting around a core set of ideas and projecting power on world problems in a just and effective fashion. Designating this group as a League (or a Concert) is meant to convey that it is more unified and permanent than an ad hoc coalition of the willing but less bureaucratic and top heavy than an international organization. Those opposed to its creation note that a League of Democracies is not without its own problems.[38] There the questions of what countries are democracies and how much shared interests do they have. The most vocal critics argue that a League of Democracies may just be a twenty-first-century term for Western imperialism since the majority of its members would likely be rich European states and the target of their policies would be developing countries.

Critical Thinking Questions

1. Are there conditions under which the United States should not enter into diplomatic negotiations with another country or group of countries?
2. Is it wise for the United States to use weapons as an instrument of diplomacy?
3. Confronted with an international crisis, which would you turn to first: bilateral, multilateral, or public diplomacy? Which is most needed to solve the problem in the long run?

Key Terms

alliance, 247

arms sales, 262

arms transfers, 261

bargaining, 240

coalitions, 247

coercive diplomacy, 259

compellence, 260

conference diplomacy, 255

digital diplomacy, 258

negotiation, 240

public diplomacy, 242

shuttle diplomacy, 247

summit conference, 249

Further Reading

Robert Falkner, "A Minilateral Solution for Global Climate Change," *Perspectives on Politics* 14 (March 2016), 87–101.

Gridlock has become common at global climate conferences. The author examines the potential ability of minilateral conferences to produce agreements. He argues that while climate clubs are unlikely to overcome all barriers to reaching an agreement, they offer a more conducive setting for reaching agreements.

Fred Ikle, *How Nations Negotiate* (New York: Harper & Row, 1964).

This is a classic account of the dynamics of international diplomacy and continues to serve as a valuable organizing device for studying the negotiation process.

Paul Meyer, "Seizing the Diplomatic Initiative to Control Cyber Conflict," *Washington Quarterly* 18 (Summer 2015), 47–61.

The article notes that cyberspace is a unique domain that raises special concerns for states. The short history of efforts to negotiate norms for cyberspace is reviewed. The author favors pursuing a global solution rather than a bilateral or regional one.

David Milibrand and Ravi Gurumurthy, "Improving Humanitarian Aid," *Foreign Affairs* 94 (July 2015), 118–29.

The authors argue that a need exists to reconceptualize the provision of foreign aid. They recommend starting with the concept of fragility. They argue that many of the lessons from stable contexts are not transferable and call for a greater emphasis on evidence-based outcomes.

James Peterson, *American Foreign Policy* (New York: Bloomsbury, 2014).
Provides a study of American alliance politics from 1914 to 2014 using a variety of theoretical perspectives. Breaks the time frame into four distinct periods of global warfare.
Jonathan Spalter, "Open Source Diplomacy," *Democracy Journal* 23 (2012), 59–70.
In the wake of the WikiLeaks publication of large number of secret State Department documents the author calls for moving away from secret diplomacy to a more open and transparent diplomacy.
Geoffrey Wiseman, *Isolate or Engage* (Stanford: Stanford University Press, 2015).
This book examines the manner in which U.S. foreign policy interacts with adversarial states through a series of case studies. Of particular importance in shaping this relationship is the role of public diplomacy.

Notes

1 Fred Ikle, *How Nations Negotiate* (New York: Harper & Row, 1964), ix.
2 Jakub Grygiel, "The Diplomacy Fallacy," *American Interest* 3 (2008), 26–35.
3 Michael Schmidt, "NSA Head Says European Data Collected by Allies," *New York Times*, October 30, 2013, http://www.nytimes.com/2013/10/30/us/politics/u-s-intelligence-officials-defend-surveillance-operations-on-capitol-hill.html (accessed November 10, 2103).
4 Catherine Lutz, ed., *The Bases of Empire* (New York: New York University Press, 2009).
5 Department of Defense, *Base Structure Report Fiscal 2010*, http://www.acq.osd.mil/ie/download/bsr/bsr2010baseline.pdf.
6 Tara Miller, "Diplomacy Derailed: The Consequences of Diplomatic Sanctions," *Washington Quarterly* 33 (2010), 61–79.
7 Richard N. Haass and Meghan L. O'Sullivan, eds., *Honey and Vinegar: Incentives, Sanctions, and Foreign Policy* (Washington, DC: Brookings, 2000).
8 Deepak Malhotra, "Without Conditions: The Case for Negotiating with the Enemy," *Foreign Affairs* 88 (2009), 84–90.
9 Stephen Wayne, "Bad Guys and Bad Judgments," in Stanley Renshon and Debroach Welch Larson (eds.), *Good Judgment in Foreign Policy* (Lanham: Rowman & Littlefield, 2003), 103–26.
10 Jonathan Terperman, "Some Hard Truths about Multilateralism," *World Policy Journal* 21 (2004), 27–36.
11 Antonia Chayes, "How American Treaty Behavior Threatens National Security," *International Security* 33 (2008), 45–81.
12 For an early evaluation of Kerry's efforts, see Aaron Miller, "In His Mideast Peace Efforts, John Kerry's Problem Is John Kerry," *Washington Post*, May 25, 2014, B3.
13 For references to the positive contributions of summitry, see Robert Putnam, "Summit Sense," *Foreign Policy* 55 (1984), 73–91.
14 For a discussion of the negative contributions of summitry, see J. Robert Schaetzel and H. B. Malmgren, "Talking Heads," *Foreign Policy* 39 (1980), 130–42.
15 Ibid., 138, for the case of economic summits; see the discussion in Strobe Talbot, *Deadly Gambits* (New York: Vintage, 1984), for examples from arms control talks.
16 Adam B. Ulam, *Dangerous Relations: The Soviet Union in World Politics, 1970–1982* (New York: Oxford University Press, 1983), 186.
17 Quoted in Glenn Kessler, "Road Map Setbacks Highlight U.S. Pattern," *Washington Post*, October 6, 2003, 1.
18 Richard Nixon, "Superpower Summitry," *Foreign Affairs* 64 (1985), 1–11.
19 George de Menil, "The Process of Economic Summitry," in George de Menil and Anthony M. Solomon (eds.), *Economic Summitry* (New York: Council on Foreign Relations, 1983), 55–63.
20 Richard Elliot Benedick, *Ozone Diplomacy: New Directions in Safeguarding the Planet* (Cambridge, MA: Harvard University Press, 1991).
21 This discussion is based on W. Michael Reisman, "The United States and International Institutions," *Survival* 41 (Winter 1999–2000), 62–80, although the definition of roles is slightly different.

22 On China, see David Shambaugh, "China's Soft-Power Push," *Foreign Affairs* 94 (2015), 99–107; on ISIS, see James Farwell, "The Media Strategy of ISIS," *Survival* 56 (2014/15), 49–55.

23 See Mark Mazzetti and Michael Gordon, "U.S. Sees Failure in Fighting ISIS on Social Media," *New York Times*, June 13, 2015, A1; and Scott Shane and Be Hubbard, "ISIS Displaying a Deft Command of Varied Media," *New York Times*, August 31, 2014, A1.

24 Giacomo Chicozza, *Anti-Americanism and the American World* (Baltimore: Johns Hopkins University Press, 2009).

25 Sanford Unger, "Pitch Imperfect," *Foreign Affairs* 84 (2005), 7–13.

26 Barry M. Blechman and Stephen S. Kaplan, *Force without War: U.S. Armed Forces as a Political Instrument* (Washington, DC: Brookings, 1978).

27 Scott Sagan and Jeremi Suri, "The Madman Nuclear Alert," *International Security* 27 (2003), 150–83; William Burr and Jeffrey Kimball, "Nixon's Nuclear Ploy," *Bulletin of the Atomic Scientists* 59 (2003), 28–37, 72–73.

28 Sagan and Suri, "The Madman Nuclear Alert," 156.

29 For background data on arms transfers, their history, the policies of specific states, and a discussion of their rationale, see Stephanie G. Neuman and Robert E. Harkavy, eds., *Arms Transfers in the Modern World* (New York: Praeger, 1980); Andrew J. Pierre, *The Global Politics of Arms Sales* (Princeton: Princeton University Press, 1982); Michael T. Klare, *American Arms Supermarket* (Austin: University of Texas Press, 1984).

30 Edward Kolodiej, "Arms Transfers and International Politics: The Interdependence of Independence," in Neuman and Harkavy (eds.), *Arms Transfers in the Modern World*, 3.

31 Klare, *American Arms Supermarket*, 43–44.

32 Richard Grimmett and Paul Kerr, *Conventional Arms Transfers to Developing Nations, 2004–2011*, Congressional Research Service Report, August 24, 2012.

33 Quoted in Karen DeYoung and Karin Brulliard, "U.S. Breach with Pakistan Shows Imbalance between Diplomatic, Security Goals," *Washington Post*, December 4, 2011.

34 For suggestions of how the United States might proceed, see the symposium "America's Alliances," *American Interest* 6 (Summer 2011), 37–69.

35 Thomas Hale, "A Climate Coalition of the Willing," *Washington Quarterly* 34 (2011), 89–101.

36 Stine Aakre, "The Political Feasibility of Potent Enforcement in a Post-Kyoto Climate Agreement," *International Environmental Agreements* 16 (2016), 145–59.

37 Ivo Daalder and James Lindsey, "Democracies of the World, Unite," *American Interest* 2 (2007), 5–15; G. John Ikenberry and Anne-Marie Slaughter, *Princeton Report on National Security, Forging a World under Liberty and Law* (Princeton: The Princeton Project on National Security, 2006).

38 Thomas Carothers, *Is a League of Democracies a Good Idea?* Carnegie Endowment for International Peace Policy Brief, May 2008.

11 Economic Instruments

Dateline: Trans-Pacific Partnership

Economic statecraft has been described as a "lost art" of U.S. foreign policy.[1] Its advocates consider its disappearance as a foreign policy tool to be harmful to U.S. foreign policy because they see Russia, China, and others embracing it. Here we look at a recent major free trade agreement signed by the United States.

On February 4, 2016, the United States and eleven other states, all of which border on the Pacific Ocean, signed a free trade agreement known as the Trans-Pacific Partnership (TPP). The TPP created the world's largest free trade agreement surpassing the North American Free Trade Agreement (NAFTA). Recent estimates placed the amount of trade between TPP members at $1.5 trillion and trade in services at $242 billion. The TPP is defined as a "living agreement" which other countries can join. South Korea expressed interest in 2014 and the Philippines and China have also shown some interest.

The initial impulse for an Asia-Pacific free trade agreement came from Singapore, New Zealand, and Chile in 2003. In 2006 Brunei joined with them to produce a Trans-Pacific Strategic Economic Partnership. Two years later, in March 2008, President George W. Bush announced the United States would join with these states to negotiate free trade issues relating to investment and financial services. Before the year ended Australia, Peru, and Vietnam joined those negotiations. Late in his first year in office President Obama announced that his administration would continue with these free trade talks. A framework for negotiating an agreement was announced in November 2011 during a meeting of the Asia-Pacific Economic Cooperation summit in Hawaii. In 2012 Canada and Mexico became full partners to the discussions and after a period of intense domestic debate and controversy Japan joined in 2013.

The treaty has thirty chapters on subjects as diverse as the environment, small and medium-sized business, rules of origin, textiles and apparel, intellectual property, and state-owned enterprises. Not surprisingly, TPP negotiations proceeded at an uneven pace. Agreements in some areas were reached with relatively little controversy while talks in others stalemated and threatened to block agreement on a treaty. Five issues were particularly difficult to get agreement on because they raised serious domestic political and economic consequences for some states.[2] One issue was the length of patents for drugs held by pharmaceutical companies. In the final TPP the United States agreed to a shorter patent protection period than currently exists as was advocated by Australia. Under the TPP pharmaceutical companies can keep their formulas secret for five to seven years instead of twelve years. Another set of issues involved protecting the environment, wildlife, and worker rights. Vietnam, Singapore, and Malaysia were particularly opposed to this portion of the agreement. In some cases state-owned enterprises operated with few worker rights. Most of the countries present had never signed a trade agreement that contained economic **sanctions** for failure to protect the environment. A third area of conflict involved tariff protections by the United States, Canada, and Japan for dairy, beef, and poultry producers. All three countries would reduce tariff protections on these products. Fourth, all members of the TPP agreed to open up their automotive industries to foreign completion with Japan being the primary target market here. Finally, the United States obtained agreement on an Investor-State Dispute Mechanism that would allow foreign companies to sue host governments, something pharmaceuticals wanted as they sought to enter protected health care markets in Australia. In return the United States agreed to restrictions on trade of tobacco products.

In the United States the TPP has been the subject of steadily increasing controversy as it moved closer to completion. The Obama administration hailed it as a model twenty-first-century trade agreement that would ensure the competitiveness of U.S. companies and products. Critics argued that its economic benefits were being oversold and that at best they would be distributed unevenly with low income workers and industries benefitting the least. A frequent point of reference made by opponents to TPP was NAFTA. So widespread was opposition to TPP that in the 2016 presidential election campaign both Hillary Clinton and Donald Trump came out against its approval by Congress.

This chapter presents an overview of the major options available in trade and monetary policy that U.S. policy makers can choose from. We look at both the logic behind these policies and examples of their use. We conclude with a more focused look at economic sanctions and foreign aid.

Economic Statecraft

Defined as a deliberate manipulation of economic policy to promote the goals of the state, **economic statecraft** is an age-old instrument of foreign policy, but one that fell into disuse during the Nixon administration. Past examples include the Louisiana Purchase, economic intimidation directed at Great Britain to end its support of the South during the civil war, dollar diplomacy in the late 1800s, Lend-Lease during World War II, and the Marshall Plan for rebuilding Europe.

Critics often see the exercise of American economic power as a part of a foreign policy of **imperialism**. Supporters see its use as part of the legitimate pursuit of American national interest. No matter the purpose for which it is used or the context in which it is used, American economic power exerts its influence by its ability to attract other countries to the U.S. economic system and then trap them in it. For that reason, many refer to it as America's "sticky power."[3]

If the web that the sticky economic power of the United States weaves entraps other countries, it can also entrap the United States. This is true for both commercial and aid-related transactions. China, for example, has jumped to the forefront in recent years as a trading partner and holder of U.S. debt, thus complicating efforts to deal with it in strictly adversarial terms. Pakistan and Afghanistan highlight the problems of providing aid in hopes of both achieving the immediate foreign policy goal of fighting terrorism and the long-range one of increasing U.S. promotion of human rights and democracy. In Pakistan programs financed by the U.S. Agency for International Development have been severely criticized for their minimal impact and because too much money is seen as going to American contractors. In Afghanistan citizens tend to credit the Taliban with the benefits that come from U.S. aid programs. Military aid can result in a different set of problems. Recent evidence suggests that it does not generate additional cooperative behavior on the part of the recipient and may only increase U.S. dependence on the government receiving aid.[4]

A major complicating factor in the use of economic statecraft is uncertainty over judging its successes and failures.[5] All too frequently its supporters argue that economic statecraft is dismissed as ineffective. Advocates of economic statecraft as an instrument of foreign policy make four arguments in its defense.[6] First, day-to-day economic exchanges under the heading of **free trade** are generally defined to be outside the scope of economic power. Second, economic power is often said to fail when they do not produce a change in policy in the target state. Underappreciated is the added cost that economic sanctions place on the target state, even if it does not change its policies. Third, economic power has often been judged a failure because it is examined out of context. Policy makers often turn to it when no other instruments are available or to accomplish the almost impossible, such as removing Fidel Castro from power. Fourth, economic statecraft suffers because writers on world politics underestimate how important symbolic actions are to policy makers and domestic pressure groups.

Nowhere is the challenge of judging success and failure more politically charged than it is with **economic sanctions**. Sanctions against Russia for its annexation of Crimea and role in the Ukrainian crisis are a case in point. In 1954 the Soviet Union transferred control over the Crimea to Ukraine. The action was described as largely symbolic because Ukraine was then part of the Soviet Union. This transfer took on a great deal of significance in 1991 with the fall of the Soviet Union. As an independent country on its borders, the foreign policy of Ukraine was of great importance to Russian leaders, and they were determined to control political events there. Matters came to a head in February 2014 when public protests forced Ukraine's pro-Russian president out of office. Russian ground forces and pro-Russian Ukrainian militia soon seized control of the Crimea. On March 21 the Crimea became part of Russia.

With no credible military options at his disposal, President Obama turned to economic instruments of foreign policy in responding to Russia's annexation. First, Russia lost its membership in the G8, and Obama announced economic sanctions targeting the financial holdings of Putin's key political and economic allies along with Russian banks. In late April additional business leaders and companies linked to Putin's supporters were targeted with financial and travel sanctions. In July sanctions were placed on Russia's largest financial, energy, and defense industries restricting their access to foreign capital. Later in 2014 U.S. companies were prohibited from doing business in the Crimea including imports, exports, and financial transactions.

In responding in this fashion Obama had several goals. One was to help strengthen Ukraine. A second was to inflict economic pain on Putin and his allies and not the Russian people so as to minimize any political backlash against the United States. A third goal was to maintain the support of European allies who, because they were far more dependent than the United States on Russian energy suppliers and markets, were hesitant to invite retaliation by Russia, such as the 44 percent price hike on natural gas it imposed on Ukraine.

Judgments as to the effectiveness of these sanctions are mixed. Defenders argue it has imposed four types of significant costs on Russia: financial, societal, a disruption of consumer markets, and increased tension with allies.[7] Opposed are those who argue whatever successes were realized were not due to the sanctions but to the general downturn in the global economy and price of oil. This view also holds that the sanctions brought unintended consequences and have been counterproductive.[8]

Strategic Outlooks

There is no single strategic outlook that forms the basis for economic statecraft. In this section we examine free trade and strategic trade. We also briefly look at monetary strategies.

Free Trade

Free trade is both an instrument of foreign policy and a strategic orientation to organizing economic power.[9] There is nothing inevitable or natural about free trade. International free trade systems exist because they serve the interests of the dominant power. This was true of Great Britain in the nineteenth century and of the United States in the post–World War II era. From about 1944 to 1962, access to U.S. markets was used as an inducement to get other states to adopt policies favored by the United States. Among those Cold War goals were strengthening military alliances, promoting the economic recovery of Western Europe, ensuring access to strategic raw materials, and stimulating economic growth and political stability in the Third World. American policy makers were also sensitive to the limits of free trade. On a selective basis, they permitted or encouraged discrimination against U.S. goods if it would further these broader U.S. foreign policy goals. At the strategic level, the United States used free trade to create an international system that allowed the U.S. economy to prosper and placed it at the center of international economic trade and monetary transactions.

Bilateral Free Trade

Bilateral free trade agreements govern the terms of trade between two countries. For much of the post–World War II era, bilateral trade agreements were viewed as a second-best method for strengthening the U.S. economy and promoting U.S. interests abroad. Regional and global multilateral agreements were preferred since they promised to open more markets to American goods more quickly than could bilateral trade agreements. This began to change in the post-9/11 era as dissatisfaction grew with regional and global trade agreements.

Virtually all of the bilateral agreements President George W. Bush negotiated ran into domestic political problems. One problem Bush faced was that in 2007 he lost his **fast-track** presidential authority to sign trade agreements and limit Congress to a yes/no vote on the agreement. For different reasons many of these bilateral trade agreements were opposed by domestic interest groups that felt the interests of their constituents would be harmed. With fast-track authority expired, they were now in a position to demand modification of these agreements. Key bilateral free trade agreements approved by Congress were with Singapore, Chile, and Australia. When Bush left office, agreements with South Korea, Colombia, Panama, and Vietnam had not yet been approved.

During the presidential campaign, Barack Obama voiced concern about these treaties, and his administration was largely silent on trade issues in its first year in office. This changed in 2010 when Obama announced a major initiative to double U.S. exports as a way of spurring job growth in the United States. Bilateral export agreements were central to the success of this initiative. Difficult negotiations were entered into with South Korea (over trade in autos and beef imports), Colombia (treatment of union officials), and Panama (taxation policy). Congress approved the agreements in successive separate votes in 2011, with the agreements taking force in 2012.

U.S. domestic politics can also complicate existing bilateral trade agreements. In 2011 the AFL-CIO labor union called upon policy makers to suspend the U.S. free trade agreement with Bahrain, a key ally of the United States in the Persian Gulf. Pro-democracy protests there were met with government resistance that targeted union leaders. The Obama administration limited itself to publicly condemning the violence and mass arrests and called on Bahrain to act with restraint and enter into a dialogue with the protestors.

Regional Trade

In our Dateline and Historical Box sections we examined the TPP and NAFTA, the two most significant regional trade agreements that the United States has negotiated. Here we will look at some of the implications of those two treaties and introduce a major regional trade agreement under negotiation.

For NAFTA the most serious questions surround its future. Most view its economic impact has having been moderate and as being greatly overshadowed by the negative symbolism of a failed treaty that has become its political legacy and has haunted efforts to sell the TPP to the American public. The most pressing question for the future is has NAFTA lost its relevance? Even without the passage of the TPP treaty, the United States, Mexico, and Canada have signed a series of bilateral trade agreements with other countries that basically provide them with the same preferential access to the U.S. market. Similarly, these bilateral agreements as well as the TPP may require that the United States, Canada, and Mexico adhere to a set of stricter regulations and standards than are contained in NAFTA.

Determining what place NAFTA might hold in the future is unclear. Some advocate a more narrow focus such as on improving border cooperation and infrastructure. The concern here is with improving the efficiency of the North American trade in intermediate goods and supply chains that became seriously disrupted with the 9/11 attacks and subsequent efforts at improving border security. Others take a more expansive view of NAFTA's future and call for setting up a North American Customs Union or moving toward developing a common approach on immigration and promoting regional regulatory standardization.

With no past to examine the principal questions being asked of TPP concern its strategic fit in U.S. foreign policy. Many see it as a central ingredient to the U.S. strategy of "rebalancing" to Asia. Not only does it add an economic component to the military rebalancing already taking place but it is argued that the U.S. economy had much to gain by helping develop Asia-Pacific's trading rules rather than leaving that to China. Speculation also centers on TPP's possible impact on World Trade Organization (WTO) negotiations. On the one hand the TPP could be a positive influence. Its expanded set of trade rules could become a model for future WTO negotiations. On the other hand the TPP could help make the WTO irrelevant as more and more countries chose to join it or other regional trade systems. An even larger question is the consequences of either congressional rejection of the TPP or its disavowal by future presidents for U.S. global economic leadership. We noted earlier that Obama campaigned against NAFTA in 2008 and promised to pursue amendments. Once in office, he determined the time was not right for making changes to NAFTA and embraced the TPP.

The regional trade agreement currently being negotiated is the Transatlantic Trade and Investment Partnership (TTIP). If an agreement is reached it would become the world's largest free trade agreement. The concept of a transatlantic free trade area had been raised off and on since the 1990s. Speaking in 2012 Secretary of State Hillary Clinton publicly embraced the idea of a U.S.-Europe free trade area, something she referred to as an "economic NATO." President Obama advocated such a plan in his 2013 State of the Union address. Talks for creating a TTIP began shortly thereafter in July 2013 with November 2014 set as the target date for an agreement.

Although the talks began in an atmosphere of optimism few doubted that it would be a difficult task, primarily because tariffs in U.S.-European trade were already low, which meant negotiators would have to address such domestically sensitive issues as regulations on trading genetically modified crops, safety standards, and financial services. Additional roadblocks to a TTIP agreement come from France, which seeks protection for its film and television industries in the name of protecting cultural diversity, and from civil society groups throughout Europe, which depict TTIP as "an assault on European and U.S. societies" by multinational corporations and are critical of what they describe as the undemocratic closed-door negotiations by which the agreement is being formulated.

Global Free Trade

At the global level, free trade became a major U.S. foreign policy priority for the post–World War II international system. It played a central role in establishing the **Bretton Woods system**. One of its core institutions was the General Agreement on Tariffs and Trade (GATT), which through a series of negotiating rounds succeeded in lowering national tariffs and other barriers to free trade. The Uruguay Round held from 1986 to 1994 was the last series of GATT talks. Out of it came an agreement to set up the World Trade Organization (WTO).

WTO talks encountered opposition from the very outset. A 1999 meeting in Seattle to launch a new Millennium Round of trade talks ended in failure. Not only were the countries attending the meeting divided but it drew large numbers of antiglobalization protestors from across the political spectrum. U.S. interest in a new round of WTO talks only returned after the 9/11 attacks because the Bush administration saw advancing global economic growth as a key part of its strategy to defeat terrorism.

The first round of WTO talks, launched in Doha, Qatar, in November 2001, stalled after a 2003 meeting in Cancun that left rich and poor countries in deep disagreement over free trade in agricultural products. In December 2013 what many saw as a last-ditch effort to save the Doha Round was held in Bali, Indonesia. An agreement was reached when negotiators gave up on achieving a comprehensive agreement in favor of one in which countries simply agreed to cut the red tape and corruption existing in the customs procedures by which goods enter countries.

Representative of the difficulty that the WTO talks have experienced in moving global free trade forward is a 2014 agreement reached in negotiations between India and the United States. WTO rules place strict limits on the amount of food that a country can stockpile because it distorts the global market. India argues it is necessary to feed its population at prices they can afford. The Bali agreement gave developing countries a temporary exception to the stockpiling rule until 2017. The India-U.S. "peace clause" agreement indefinitely extends that exemption.

This agreement was hailed both as a success since it allowed the Bali agreement to move forward and as a failure because it undermined one of the WTO's few major successes: the creation of a dispute settlement procedure. Under GATT a dispute settlement panel was set up only if requested, and its report was adopted only if there was a consensus in favor of it. Under the WTO a standing dispute settlement panel exists, and its report is adopted unless there is a consensus against it. This change transformed the WTO dispute settlement process into a compulsory and automatic instrument for resolving trade disputes.

The United States has both won and lost rulings before the WTO dispute resolution system. Its very existence has produced fears about the potential loss of sovereignty and the nondemocratic nature of the decision-making procedures. In 2015 the WTO ruled in favor of Mexico and Canada and against the United States in a case over meat labeling. U.S. retailers had been identifying where the animal had been born, raised, and slaughtered. Mexico and Canada argued this was a discriminatory trade practice. The year before the WTO sided with the United States in a case against India. Here, the United States charged that India had established rules that placed unfair restrictions on imported U.S. meat and eggs in the name of preventing the spread of avian flu. The United States argued no evidence existed to support this claim.

In the Obama administration, the United States and China frequently accused the other of rule violations on such issues as autos, solar panels, tires, steel, and chicken feet. In 2012 China filed a complaint with the WTO against the United States concerning twenty-four different products. That same year the United States filed a trade complaint charging that China was placing unfair limits on the export of rare-earth minerals that are a crucial element in making iPhones, electric cars, and smart bombs. China replied that it would "vigorously defend its right to control" the export of these minerals. In 2014 the WTO ruled against China, which said it would appeal the ruling. The following year it ruled against China and in favor of the United States which argued China had imposed unfair taxes on imported aircraft thus harming American workers.

Strategic Trade

Competing with free trade as the foundation for American international economic policy is strategic trade.[10] Its advocates argue that current U.S. trade policy cannot be sustained politically or economically because the global market is failing U.S. firms. They maintain that the comparative advantages enjoyed by states in international trade is not due to a country's resource base or historical factors but to imperfections in markets that have been deliberately created by government policy. Only by actively intervening in the international marketplace to create comparative advantages for selected industries can the United States hope to remain a world leader.

The driving force behind strategic trade was the inability of American policy makers (and American industry) to put a dent in the U.S.-Japan trade imbalance. In 1988 concern with the trade imbalance gave rise to the Omnibus Trade and Competitiveness Act. Section 301, commonly referred to as "Super 301," provides for retaliatory sanctions against states that engage in unfair trading practices against the United States. It requires that presidents identify "priority countries" and set a timetable for resolving the dispute, after which time the sanctions will take effect. The 2016 annual report issued by the Office of the U.S. Trade Representative placed eleven countries on its priority watch list, including China, Russia, Venezuela, and India, and twenty-three countries on its watch list. Interest in strategic trade policy increased following the economic crisis of 2008. Elements of it can be found in the stimulus package sponsored by the Obama administration. A prime example is "buy American clauses" such as those requiring the use of U.S.-made iron and steel in certain infrastructure projects.

Strategic trade policy requires two things of the U.S. government. First, it must identify high-growth industries whose health is crucial to the overall global competitiveness of the American economy. Second, it must ensure that these firms are not shut out of foreign markets. Neither task is easy. Identifying industries for special treatment is a politically charged decision that has huge consequences for states and localities. Just as members of Congress fight to prevent military base closures in their districts, they fight to ensure that their districts will get a fair share of research and development money. A related problem is how to address the problems faced by industries such as steel that are no longer competitive internationally but that retain enormous political clout. The problem of ensuring access to foreign markets is complicated by regional trade agreements that limit access by nonmember firms. An overly aggressive strategic trade policy runs the risk of spawning a trade war in which U.S. goods are singled out for retaliation.

For these reasons, critics of strategic trade policy note that it often crosses the line into protectionism. European leaders leveled this charge against the United States in 2010 over the manner in which a $40 billion contract for new aerial refueling tankers was conducted by the Pentagon. Originally, a consortium between European firms and U.S.-based Northrop Grumman won the contract. However, after a strong lobbying campaign from Boeing and pressure from Congress, the Pentagon reopened the bidding and changed the project's specifications, leading Northrop Grumman to pull out and Boeing to get the contract.

Monetary Strategies

The bulk of the discussion in this chapter focuses on trade and aid as the central economic instruments of U.S. foreign policy. It needs to be noted that financial transactions can also be used to further foreign policy goals. This may occur at the strategic level, such as when the United States allowed the value of the dollar to float or provided debt relief funding after the 2008 global financial crisis, and at the tactical level, such as in blocking an individual, corporation, or government's ability to access its funds held in the United States or in other countries.

In addition to GATT, the United States helped create two important international financial institutions as part of the Bretton Woods system. They are the International Monetary Fund (IMF) and the International Bank for Reconstruction and Development (IBRD or, more commonly, the World Bank). The IMF was to regulate international currencies to ensure that they did not suddenly and violently change in value. The World Bank was to provide additional funds that were believed necessary for European economic recovery. Virtually from the outset, the financial aspects of the Bretton Woods system did not function as anticipated. American dollars became the international currency of choice, and American foreign economic and military aid provided the necessary funds for economic recovery.

By 1960, the situation began to change, and the outflow of dollars reached the point where U.S. officials began to worry about the trade deficit. The Bretton Woods system ended in 1971 when President Nixon announced that the U.S. dollar would no longer be convertible to gold. Since then, international monetary management has taken the form of periodic exercises in crisis management rather than systemic reform. The most recent exercise of crisis management came in 2008 with the largest financial and economic crash in over seventy-five years. Under the prodding of France and Great Britain, the G8 met in a special session in Washington in November 2008 to discuss steps that might be taken to deal with the current crisis and avoid similar crises in the future. Subsequent meetings produced an agreement that the G20 rather than the G8 (which was made up only of the major economic powers) would become the primary international forum for making global economic policy.

This economic crisis also set in motion concerns within the United States about two aspects of China's international monetary policy for U.S. economic and national security. The first was China's manipulation of the renminbi, its official currency. At one time its value was pegged, or fixed, against the U.S. dollar, but as China embarked on a development strategy in which exports played a central role, it devalued the renminbi, which made its goods cheaper to buy than those made elsewhere. U.S. officials see the undervalued renminbi as costing American workers jobs and slowing the American economic recovery. In 2015 continued concerns with perceived Chinese currency manipulation along with that of Japan, Malaysia, and other Asian states led to an effort by Congress to attach currency manipulation provisions to Obama's request for fast-track authority.

The second aspect of concern regarding China's international monetary policy is its massive holding of U.S. debt. In 2011 China held $1.16 trillion of U.S. debt, making it the United States' largest debt holder. Many fear that this large debt holding will give China foreign policy leverage over the United States. WikiLeak cables show that Chinese officials believe it might. In October 2008 they discussed limiting further debt purchases due to the U.S. decision to sell arms to Taiwan. This, in turn, led to speculation that China might engage in a massive sell-off of its U.S. debt to drive down the value of the dollar in retaliation for a U.S. foreign policy decision it opposed. Referred to as the "nuclear option," it reportedly was included as a Chinese strategy in a 2009 Pentagon war game.

A recent study suggests that debt power is a potent tool for China to use against the United States when the purpose is to resist pressure from the United States to carry out actions it opposes, but is of limited use as a means to compel the United States to act in ways China would like.[11] In the first instance, China has been able to deflect U.S. pressure on its human rights policy and limit administration (as opposed to congressional) calls for retaliatory action to get China to allow the renminbi to float and increase its value. In the area of compellence, China failed to get the United States to provide special protection for the value of China's dollar-denominated assets or guarantees of access to U.S. markets. China did succeed in getting the Obama administration to drop F-16 fighters from the arms sale to Taiwan but did not succeed in ending the U.S. military commitment to Taiwan. In March 2016 the United States announced an $8 million Taiwanese F-16 modernization program.

Economic Sanctions

Economic sanctions have become a popular way of exercising American economic power. In 2016 the Department of the Treasury was implementing twenty-eight different sanctions programs. Some were directed at specific countries such as Cuba, Iran, and Syria. Others were problem oriented, such as those in place against terrorism, diamond trading, narcotics trafficking, and proliferation.[12]

What constitutes an economic sanction is highly contested. We adopt a middle-of-the road definition. Economic sanctions are "the deliberate withdrawal of normal trade or financial relations for foreign policy purposes."[13] It is important to recognize that sanctions are "not forever." They are intended to bring about change in targeted countries, and when that is accomplished, they are to be removed. Determining when that is the case is no easy matter and not without controversy, any more than is the decision to implement sanctions. Economic sanctions against Cambodia ran for seventeen years (1975–92) while those against Japan in 1985 ran for twenty-four days. Evidence suggests a major factor in determining how long sanctions will stay in place is whether they were imposed by Congress or the president. Presidential sanctions are twice as likely to be lifted after one year. After five years, about 70 percent of congressional sanctions remain in place as compared to some 30 percent of presidential sanctions.[14]

The effectiveness of sanctions can be undermined by a variety of factors. One problem is the pursuit of incompatible goals. For example, in 2004, George W. Bush imposed broad sanctions against Syria for its support of terrorism. Among other measures, it barred all exports to Syria except for food and medicine. Yet Bush delayed implementing the measure and indicated he would continue to permit the sale of telecommunication equipment and aircraft spare parts. The telecommunication exemption was justified on the grounds of the need to promote the free flow of information. Critics argued that Bush did this in order to protect the economic interests of the telecommunication industry.

A second problem is that often economic sanctions are imposed because policy makers find themselves needing to demonstrate resolve when they are unwilling or unable to use military force. In these cases critics argue that sanctions amount to nothing more than "chicken soup diplomacy." They give the appearance of taking action and make one feel good without having to pay a cost.[15] One of those was the Iran-Libya Sanctions Extension Act of 2001. It kept in effect sanctions approved by Congress in 1996 that were about to expire even though no firms had been sanctioned under their terms.

A third problem is the response by other countries. Often described as "black knights," these states provide economic support to the sanctioned country for political reasons that lessen its effectiveness. During the Cold War the Soviet Union was a black knight for Cuba in the face of U.S. sanctions. In the post–Cold War period Venezuela has been Cuba's black knight, while Russia has played that role for Syria and Iran. What holds true for getting around sanctions against governments also holds true for sanctions against rebel groups. In Syria, Sudan sold Chinese-made weapons to Qatar, which arranged for their delivery to Syrian rebels through Turkey. Recent studies suggest help from black knights is of limited valued unless it is accompanied by sanction-busting actions of corporations interested in profit.[16] Cuba, for example, has benefited from investments by Canadian and European firms. Syria was able to obtain funds from Hezbollah that were raised by four Lebanese citizens operating out of West Africa.

Inventory of Options

Should American policy makers decide to employ U.S. economic power against another state they have several options at their disposal.

A **tariff** is a tax on foreign-made goods entering one's country. Typically, tariffs are applied to protect domestic industry against foreign competition or to raise revenue, but they can also be manipulated to serve foreign policy goals. Twice in the post–World War II era, the United States made notable efforts to manipulate its tariff structure to accomplish foreign policy goals. First, the United States used its tariff system as a lever in dealing with communist states. The United States excluded communist states from equal access to the U.S. market. During détente, the United States sought to use access to the U.S. market and most favored nation status as an inducement to the Soviets to cooperate in noneconomic areas such as the Strategic Arms Limitation Talks (SALT) negotiations. The second attempt to use tariffs as an instrument of foreign policy occurred in 1971, when President Nixon placed a 10 percent "surcharge" on all imports not already under a quota. The primary objective behind this move was to force major changes in the trading practices of other states. It failed to do so, and created foreign hostility toward the United States.

The primary danger inherent in the excessive use of tariffs is retaliation. The most serious instance of retaliation took place in the early 1930s, after the United States passed the Smoot-Hawley Tariff. The highest tariff in U.S. history, it taxed imports at an average rate of 41.5 percent of their value. Retaliation by foreign governments led to a sudden and dramatic drop in U.S. exports, which only worsened the ongoing depression, something the Smoot-Hawley Tariff had been intended to help solve. The Trade Agreements Act of 1934 broke the spiral of raising tariffs by authorizing the president to lower existing tariffs by as much as 50 percent to those countries making reciprocal concessions.

Manipulating **nontariff barriers** (NTBs) to trade is a modern variation on this theme. Taking forms ranging from labeling requirements, health and safety standards, and license controls to taxation policy, they have become powerful tools in the hands of policy makers who want to protect local firms from foreign competition or remedy a balance-of-payments problem. U.S. use of NTBs dates at least from the 1930s, when the Buy American Act required the government to purchase goods and services from U.S. suppliers if their prices were not unreasonably higher than those of foreign competitors.

An **embargo** is a refusal to sell a commodity to another state, and it is the third economic instrument of foreign policy. Embargoes (and the more subtle concept of export controls) have long played an important role in U.S. Cold War foreign policy. Building on the Trading with the Enemy Act of 1917, the United States embargoed financial and commercial transactions with North Korea, the People's Republic of China, Cuba, and North Vietnam. Trade with communist states was also controlled by the Export Control Act of 1949. During the Korean War, the list of restricted items reached one thousand in number. Many of these controls are still in place. In 2016 Obama lifted an arms embargo against Vietnam that had been in place since 1975 saying it had made progress on human rights and that the decision was not related to the conflict with China over the South China Sea.

A **boycott** is a refusal to buy a product(s) from another state, and it represents the fourth economic instrument available to policy makers. One celebrated case involved U.S. participation in UN-sponsored sanctions against Rhodesia (Zimbabwe).[17] Off and on, these sanctions lasted for over a decade. They were first imposed by President Lyndon Johnson in a 1968 executive order. Their purpose was to force the white minority Rhodesian government into accepting the principle of majority rule. The U.S. commitment to the boycott was never firm. Congress amended the boycott in 1971 to allow the export of raw chromium and other critical materials to Rhodesia. Upon coming into office, Carter fought a holding action against moves by the Senate to lift the boycott until the British were able to mediate the changeover to majority rule.

The fifth policy tool is the **quota**, which is a quantitative restriction on goods coming from another state. Because of GATT, quotas have not played a large role in foreign economic policy making for most of the post–World War II era. This changed as concerns grew over the international competitiveness of U.S.-made products. Canada has often been the target of U.S. quotas. In 1994 Bill Clinton threatened to limit the amount of Canadian grain entering the United States. In 2004, in an attempt to end a trade dispute, it offered to replace tariffs with a quota system for permitting Canadian lumber to enter the country.

To this list of trade sanctions can be added monetary sanctions designed to deny targeted countries, terrorist groups, and individuals' access to funds. When these monetary sanctions are directed against government officials they are often characterized as **smart sanctions** because they are intended to protect vulnerable social groups from economic harm.

The Obama administrations aggressively employed smart sanctions. We have already noted that Obama targeted Russian advisors and supporters of Putin with sanctions after Russia seized the Crimea from Ukraine. In 2013 Obama identified thirty-seven Iranian firms for sanctions, charging that they were acting as front companies under the control of Iranian leaders. In 2015 the United States announced sanctions against twenty-five individual groups associated with ISIS designed to make it more difficult for them to engage in financial transactions and travel. Initial evaluations of smart sanctions are not encouraging.[18] They do not appear to be significantly more successful than conventional ones. The fundamental problem is the same—a lack of political will to enforce them.

Sanctions in Action

We conclude our discussion of economic sanctions by examining very different types of situations in which the United States has used sanctions: against Iran for its pursuit of nuclear weapons; ending communist rule in Cuba; antiterrorist sanctions against Libya; and cyber sanctions.

Iran Sanctions The United States has a long history of imposing economic sanctions against Iran. Carter ordered a freeze on all Iranian assets under the jurisdiction of the United States after the American embassy was seized and hostages were taken in 1979. Reagan imposed sanctions against Iran for its ties to the bombing of the marine barracks in Beirut in 1984. Bill Clinton instituted a boycott against Iran in response to evidence that it was seeking to acquire nuclear technology. He issued an executive order banning U.S. oil companies and their subsidiaries from trading with Iran. In 1996 Congress passed the Iran-Libya Sanctions Act (now the Iran Sanctions Act), which permitted the United States to place penalties against foreign firms dealing with Iran. Originally set to terminate in 2001, the Iran Sanctions Act has had its life extended several times, with the current expiration date set for 2016. After 9/11, George W. Bush issued an executive order freezing the assets of individuals, organizations, and financial institutions supporting terrorism. Many of those now on the list are Iranian, including corporations, banks, and the Revolutionary Guard.

Obama continued with sanctions against Iran but coupled them with a willingness to engage in talks. With little progress being made in July 2010, he signed the Comprehensive Iran Sanctions, Accountability, and Divestment Act. It amended the Iran Sanctions Act by expanding it to include trade in refined petroleum products and expanded the range of sanctions the president could apply. Under pressure from Congress in 2011 Obama accepted new sanctions against Iran, preventing foreign banks from opening an account in the United States or limiting the funds in an existing account if that bank processed payments through Iran's central bank. The net result of this action was to reduce the ability of Iran to sell oil abroad. In most cases where Congress passes sanction legislation, presidents are permitted to waive sanctions under specified circumstances. In this case Obama could do so if the sanctions led to a rise in the price of oil or if there was a significant reduction in Iranian oil imports to the parent country of the bank being targeted. By mid-2012, twenty countries, including China and all of Iran's major purchasers, had received exemptions.

In 2013 the Obama administration further tightened its sanctions against Iran by enforcing a provision of the Iran Threat Reduction Act that requires that any funds owed to Iran as a result of exempted oil purchases be placed in a local bank and not transferred back to Iran. The election of Hassan Rouhani as president that year led Obama to remove sanctions affecting humanitarian aid by expediting requests for items related to disaster relief, human rights projects, wildlife conservation, and providing health services. When the first round of nuclear talks produced promising results, Obama agreed to lift sanctions freezing Iran's overseas assets in limited amounts and in stages as an encouragement to Iran to continue negotiations. At virtually the same time, in an effort to prevent Congress from imposing additional sanctions, the administration expanded the list of companies and individuals it was placing on the sanctions list for trading in oil or helping Iran's nuclear industry.

Removing Castro from Power   When Castro came to power in 1959, Cuba was heavily dependent on the United States: 67 percent of its exports went to the United States; 70 percent of its imports came from the United States; and under the terms of legislation passed in 1934, the United States purchased the bulk of Cuban sugar at prices substantially above world market rates. Relations between the United States and Castro quickly worsened. In February 1960 Castro concluded a barter deal with the Soviet Union in which Cuban sugar was exchanged for Soviet crude oil. After U.S.-owned oil refineries refused to process the Soviet oil, Castro took them over. The United States responded by terminating all remaining foreign aid programs and canceling all purchases of Cuban sugar for the remainder of the year. Castro retaliated with additional nationalizations of U.S. property. Next, the United States imposed an embargo on all exports to Castro except for food and medicine. Cuba then entered into more economic agreements with the Soviet Union, and, in turn, the United States broke diplomatic relations.

Since then economic sanctions have been tightened periodically, often as a result of electoral considerations. In 1992 Congress passed the Cuban Democracy Act which placed heavy penalties on U.S. firms that engaged in trade with Cuba through foreign subsidiaries. In 1996 the Helms-Burton Act threatened sanctions against countries that provided Cuba with foreign aid and allowed U.S. nationals to sue foreign firms that now controlled properties seized during the Cuban revolution. Opposition from American allies to this last provision has been intense, and presidents have routinely waived it. George W. Bush further tightened the embargo by reducing the amount of time Cuban Americans would be able to visit home and the amount of money they could send home.

Punishing Libya for Supporting Terrorism   Muammar Gaddafi came to power in Libya through a coup in 1969. His nationalization of oil fields produced only a moderate response from the United States, but relations became increasingly tense as his regime became identified with terrorist attacks and hostility toward Israel. The Reagan administration entered office determined to use its Libyan policy as a means of making a statement about America's renewed willingness to flex its power. In 1981 Reagan placed an embargo on crude oil imports from Libya and restricted the export of sophisticated gas and oil equipment to the North African state. In 1985 the importation of refined Libyan oil products was barred. The following year, after a new wave of terrorist violence, Reagan imposed a comprehensive trade embargo that banned all imports and exports. Libyan financial assets in American banks were also frozen. Later in 1986 U.S. oil companies were forced to leave Libya, but were allowed to sign "standstill" agreements permitting the Libyan National Oil Company to run their affiliates until they returned.

The sanctions continued to tighten even after Reagan left office. In 1993 Libya was implicated in the explosion of Pan Am flight 103 over Lockerbie, Scotland, and French UTA flight 772 over Niger. The UN Security Council responded with a new set of global sanctions, which included an oil and gas embargo and the freezing of Libyan funds in foreign banks. In 1996 the U.S. enacted the Iran-Libya Sanctions Act, which put stiff penalties on companies investing more than $40 million in Libya's oil industry. In 1999, after Libya turned over two suspects in the Lockerbie bombing to the World Court, the United Nations suspended its sanctions. They were lifted entirely in 2003, after Gaddafi renounced his support for terrorism.

Cyber Sanctions Cyber threats are among the newest foreign policy target to which sanctions have been applied. A first and ongoing challenge in setting cyber sanctions is to correlate it with the nature of the cyber-attack. Not only do cyber targets vary as some are directed at government agencies while others are targeted on businesses and individuals but the purpose of the attack will vary. The range of cyber-threats facing states may be organized into a conflict ladder that rank orders different types of cyber-threats from high to low. At the top of the ladder is a full range first-strike cyber-attack. Moving downward one would find among other rungs on the ladder retaliatory, symbolic, and crisis management cyber-attacks. At the bottom are criminal, hactivist, and mischief cyber-attacks. A second challenge is determining whether to make public the fact that a cyber-attack has occurred or to remain silent in hopes of acquiring more information about the attackers.

A first round of cyber sanctions put into place by the United States were directed at multinational corporations and countries. Following a 2014 cyber-attack on Sony Pictures, the Obama administration imposed sanctions on ten individuals. Treasury Secretary Jacob Lew stated the action was "driven by our commitment to hold North Korea accountable for it destructive and destabilizing conduct." A second round of cyber sanctions was established by President Obama's April 2015 executive order which authorized sanctions against individuals who engage in "significant malicious cyber-enabled activities that are reasonably likely to result in, or have materially contributed to, a significant threat to the national security, foreign policy, or economic health or financial stability of the United States." Included here are efforts to compromise critical infrastructure, disrupt computer activity, and steal trade secrets personnel identifiers of other sensitive information for corporate or personal gain. The new sanction authority would allow freezing target's assets when they pass through U.S. financial companies and prohibit U.S. firms from doing business with sanctioned individuals.

There have been no shortage of cyber-attacks against the United States. In 2014 Iranian hackers used social media accounts to attack State Department computers. In 2015 Chinese hackers entered the Office of Personal Management's computers giving them the ability to acquire data personal information including fingerprints and socials security numbers on 21.5 million past and present federal employees and contractors. The Obama administration defined it as a classic case of espionage. Chinese officials described it as a crime and not an act of war. The year before Russian hackers were identified as responsible for successful cyber-attacks against ten major financial firms that provided them with information on more than 83 million individuals and businesses. Also in 2014 Russian hackers targeted oil and gas companies along with investment firms.

Foreign Aid

A perennial debate exists over the purpose of U.S. foreign aid. Are its primary goals found in the areas of humanitarian assistance, development, and democratization, or is the purpose of foreign aid to advance core American national security interests? The existence of multiple goals means that foreign aid policy often runs the risk of working at cross-purposes, as in cases where foreign aid given to support governments fighting terrorism or promoting regional stability may negate efforts to promote democracy. This was the case in 2012 when Obama announced that the United States was expanding counterterrorism aid to Cambodia in spite of concerns over its human rights record.

Several underlying conditions need to be kept in mind in thinking about foreign aid as an instrument of foreign policy. First, the size of the U.S. foreign aid program has varied greatly. Calculated in 2015 dollar values, the high point for foreign aid came in 1949 ($65.9 billion) and the low point came in 1997 ($19.5 billion). In 2015 it was estimated at $48.6 billion. Compared to other areas of government spending the foreign aid budget is small, amounting to some 1.3 percent of the total federal budget. Second, U.S. foreign aid is not distributed evenly around the world. It is concentrated on a few states. Table 11.1 provides a comparative listing of the top ten U.S. foreign aid recipients in 1995, 2005, and 2015.

Third, U.S. foreign aid is often given with restrictions, although these restrictions may be overridden by national security concerns. In October 2009 Obama approved a $7.5 billion, five-year aid program to Pakistan, which officials there quickly characterized as "insulting and unacceptable." Among the conditions attached by the United States were the establishment of monitoring mechanisms to see how the money was spent and the establishment of procedures for promoting military officers. In 2012 Obama announced that the U.S. would resume military aid to the new government in Egypt and waive restrictions that made

TABLE 11.1	Top Ten Recipients of U.S. Foreign Assistance from All Sources (millions current U.S. dollars)				
FY 1995		**FY 2005**		**FY 2015**	
Israel	3.010	Iraq	7.767	Afghanistan	5.452
Egypt	2.318	Israel	2.713	Israel	3.100
Russia	543	Egypt	1.791	Iraq	1.829
Turkey	528	Afghanistan	1.730	Egypt	1.456
Ukraine	261	Russia	1.577	Jordan	1.088
Greece	251	Sudan	1.025	Pakistan	805
Palau	245	Colombia	736	Kenya	739
India	166	Pakistan	712	Nigeria	692
Haiti	157	Jordan	647	Ethiopia	650
Rwanda	139	Ethiopia	629	Tanzania	647

Source: State, Foreign Operations, and Related Programs: FY2016 Budget and Appropriations, Congressional Research Service, November 5, 2015, 13.

such aid conditional on progress toward democracy. Fourth, a very high percentage of U.S. foreign aid funds are spent on U.S. products. The Congressional Research Service estimates that 90 percent of food aid is spent on U.S. goods and services. In 2004 United States and British firms had obtained 85 percent of the monies in Iraqi reconstruction contracts, compared to 2 percent for Iraqi firms.

Types of Foreign Aid

There is no standard method for categorizing the different types of U.S. foreign aid programs. One approach used by the researchers of the Congressional Research Service identifies six basic categories, and we will follow that scheme here. Before examining the breakdown of official U.S. foreign aid, however, it is important to note three major developments in the organization and disbursement of foreign aid.

First, remittances, or private foreign aid from individuals living abroad, are now among the most important sources of funds for Third World states. In its 2016 report the World Bank placed U.S. remittances at $56.3 billion. The top three destinations were China ($415.25 billion), India ($10.96 billion, and Mexico ($24.3 billion),. Second, it is becoming increasingly common to speak of a distinction between traditional and nontraditional official foreign aid. Traditional foreign aid is distributed by the State Department and affiliated agencies such as the U.S. Agency for International Development (USAID) and falls under the "150 international affair budget." Nontraditional foreign aid flows from other agencies, such as the Environmental Protection Agency, the National Institutes of Health, the Department of Energy, and most importantly, the Department of Defense.

The third trend to take note of is the increased importance of public-private collaboration and philanthropic foreign aid. The bottom line is that USAID, the primary source of foreign aid in the U.S. government, is now a minority share-holder in foreign aid.[19] One example of public-private collaboration is USAID's Global Development Alliance, which includes such corporations as Coca-Cola and Wal-Mart. The overall goal is to share expertise and information and carry out projects in an efficient manner. Perhaps the best-known foundation engaging in foreign-policy-type activities is the Bill and Melinda Gates Foundation. With an endowment of over $38 billion, it engages in providing financial services for the poor, agricultural development, disaster relief, and health care in developing societies.

The first category of official U.S. foreign aid is *economic aid* given for the purpose of advancing U.S. political and security objectives. This is the biggest category of foreign aid. Monies given in this category have supported such diverse programs as the Camp David Accords, the building of democracy, anti-narcotics efforts, antiterrorism plans, and countering weapons proliferation.

The second largest category of foreign aid is *military assistance*. These monies go to help allies maintain and train their armed forces, as well as to buy U.S. military equipment. Included here are economic support funds. These are loans to countries that are not eligible for development assistance but are considered to be strategically important. Finally, the military assistance grant program provides funds to purchase U.S. military equipment and support military training. Of growing concern here is the inability to account for who has the weapons that were provided. In 2014 the Pentagon found that 156,000 pieces of military equipment valued at almost $500 million could not be found in Afghanistan. Some of this equipment was likely broken and discarded and other pieces were probably stolen and sold to hostile forces.

The third category is *bilateral development assistance*. These aid programs are generally administered by USAID and have a long-term development focus on strengthening the economy, environment, health care delivery systems, and political institutions of recipient states. Funding for the Peace Corps and debt relief falls into this category. One of the major complaints about development assistance aid is that rather than being transitional in nature it has become permanent. In the process it has created dependent societies, stifling development rather than promoting it.[20]

A particularly challenging problem confronting economic aid in the 1980s and 1990s was debt relief. The sums were staggering. In 1988 Mexico's debt stood at $107.4 billion. At first, the Reagan administration approached the problem as one that was solvable through a combination of government austerity measures and prudent lending policies by banks and international organizations. This response proved inadequate, and the Reagan administration sought to increase the level of funding available through the Baker Plan. With the problem continuing, George H. W. Bush devised the Brady Plan, which combined a program of limited and voluntary debt forgiveness with international guarantees of the remaining loan amounts. It too failed to fully solve the debt problem.

The fourth category of foreign aid is *humanitarian economic assistance*. This aid tends to be short term and emergency focused. Refugee assistance, emergency food aid, and disaster relief account for the bulk of this spending.

Bipartisan congressional support for this type of aid has generally been high, although the amount of money involved has fluctuated greatly from year to year, largely because of the unpredictability of the natural disasters that set such aid in motion. In fiscal year 2010 approximately $5 billion was spent on humanitarian programs. This figure was double that from 2006 but still represented only 13 percent of the overall foreign aid budget. Providing humanitarian aid is often complicated by other policy goals. In 2011 the Obama administration had to relax restrictions on giving aid to terrorist groups or their supporters in order to get relief to victims of famine in Somalia.

The fifth category is *multilateral development assistance*. It is the smallest segment of the foreign aid budget and consists of funds contributed to such international development organizations as UNICEF, the United Nations Development Programme, the World Bank, and the African Development Bank. U.S. aid to multilateral organizations is affected by a number of concerns, such as the international planning policies of organizations, the implementation of the Iraq Oil-for-Food program, and the pace and nature of reform efforts at the United Nations.

The final category of foreign aid is *nonemergency food aid*. The Food for Peace program, also known as PL 480, is the primary instrument for distributing this aid. It makes surplus U.S. agricultural goods available to Third World states in local currency and at concessionary prices. Critics of the Food for Peace program have noted that tension has always existed between the humanitarian and political purposes of this aid and that the political purposes tend to triumph. Often, those countries receiving PL 480 funds are not the neediest by objective measures but are valuable U.S. allies. Egypt, for example, has always ranked among the leading recipients of PL 480 funds.

Recently calls have been voiced for moving away from a focus on providing food goods for those in need abroad toward a system of providing those in need with cash that could be spent locally to obtain food at less cost and more quickly than it currently can under the terms of PL 480. A pilot program based on this model was set up during the George W. Bush administration, and in 2014 Obama proposed that 25 percent of Food for Peace's emergency and development aid budget be dedicated to this new program.

Cold War Foreign Aid

The relative importance of military and economic aid varied considerably during the Cold War. The Truman administration's foreign aid program was dominated by economic development initiatives such as the Marshall Plan and the Point Four Program. Ninety-six percent of Truman's foreign aid budgets consisted of development funds. With the outbreak of the Korean War policy makers increasingly viewed foreign aid as an instrument for furthering American national security. More than 60 percent of foreign aid was now given for military purposes. The geographic focus of American foreign aid also changed. Where once Europe received 86 percent of U.S. foreign aid, it received only 6 percent between 1958 and 1961. The share of American aid to the Third World increased to 68 percent during this period.

During the presidency of John Kennedy, the proportion of economic aid to military aid changed again, so that by the mid-1970s, economic aid accounted for 75 percent of all U.S. foreign aid. Within the economic aid category, however, greater emphasis was given to loans (which had to be repaid) than to grants (which did not). With the deepening American involvement in Vietnam, the balance swung back in favor of military aid. By the mid-1970s, it constituted 70 percent of U.S. foreign aid. After the American withdrawal from Vietnam, economic aid reasserted itself, growing to 80 percent of the total. It again faded under the Reagan administration. From 1980 to 1985, economic aid rose from about $7.5 billion to almost $10 billion, while military aid virtually tripled, from $2 billion to almost $6 billion.

Post–Cold War Foreign Aid

During the first decade of the post–Cold War era, three issues dominated the foreign aid agenda. They continue to be controversial, but to some extent all have been overtaken by new foreign aid concerns. The first centered on foreign aid to Russia. The United States targeted two areas for assistance. One was funding economic development. No one denied the need for Russia's economy to grow, but many argued that widespread corruption and government inefficiency made growth impossible. The second was helping Russia denuclearize by providing it with funds to destroy chemical and nuclear weapons, establish safeguards against proliferation, and assess the environmental damage done by nuclear waste. The 1991 Nunn-Lugar Threat Reduction Program was designed with this second goal in mind. Formally terminated in 2013, the Nunn-Lugar remains operational in a modified form that includes a worldwide focus on chemical and biological weapons. As of March 2013 it had helped deactivate 7,616 strategic warheads (82 percent of its goal) and destroy 914 intercontinental ballistic missiles (88 percent of its goal).

Historical Lesson

NAFTA

The North American Free Trade Agreement (NAFTA) between Mexico, Canada, and the United States came into effect in 1994. NAFTA talks began in 1991. On October 7, 1992, a 2,000-page agreement was signed. Congress gave its approval in November 1993 by votes of 234–200 in the House and 61–38 in the Senate. President Bill Clinton signed the agreement into law on December 8, 1993. At the core of the NAFTA agreement were provisions to eliminate most tariffs on goods traded between the three countries. Some were to be eliminated immediately, others were to be phased out over fifteen years. Particularly affected by the NAFTA agreement were agriculture, automobiles, and textiles. Other portions of NAFTA established intellectual property rights protections, labor and environmental safeguards, and a dispute resolution system. George H. W. Bush, whose administration negotiated NAFTA, promised to negotiate labor and environmental protections in order to secure getting fast-track authority from Congress. These safeguards were included in the agreement, but many considered them to be insufficient.

The negotiating path that led to its signing began with President Ronald Reagan's advocacy of a North American Common Market during his 1980 presidential campaign. Armed with fast-track authority that Congress gave him in 1984, the United States and Canada entered into trade negotiations that led to the 1989 Canada-U.S. Free Trade Agreement. The agreement was widely regarded as the most extensive bilateral trade agreement ever negotiated and contained several groundbreaking elements that would appear in later free trade agreements.

By this time Mexico had also become interested in a continent-wide free trade agreement. In the 1960s, Mexico pegged its development hopes on an import-substitution strategy that would protect domestic industries from foreign competition. It was now clear that this strategy had failed. From an economic perspective the most attractive alternative was integration into the U.S. market. Politically, however, this was an unattractive option due to fears that doing so would lead to Mexican dependence on the American economy. Instead Mexico proposed a North American free trade zone.

George H. W. Bush embraced the concept in his 1988 campaign, but once in office his administration was divided over the wisdom of entering into talks with Mexico. The National Security Council, the Commerce Department, and the State Department supported the idea. The Department of Agriculture and the Office of the U.S. Trade Representative were less enthusiastic.

Bush looked on the NAFTA agreement as a vehicle for generating Republican votes in Texas and California in the upcoming 1992 presidential election. Instead, NAFTA became a controversial campaign issue. Leading the early charge against it was onetime supporter Ross Perot, who said NAFTA was the product of a conspiracy among Washington insiders, foreign lobbyists, and huge corporations that would cost the United States some five million jobs. He warned, "You're going to hear a giant sucking sound of jobs being pulled out of this country."[21] Bill Clinton straddled the fence on NAFTA during the presidential campaign. When he finally announced his support for NAFTA, it was conditioned on adding supplemental agreements to cover "serious" omissions dealing with the potential for sudden inflow of large amounts of foreign goods into the U.S. market, the environment, and labor.

Bill Clinton did not immediately push for congressional approval of the NAFTA agreement. Many of those who supported his candidacy for president opposed NAFTA as did a large number of Democrats in Congress. When it did act, it first negotiated a series of executive agreements with Mexico that were not officially part of the treaty and side deals with members of Congress. In one he promised that textile quotas would be phased out over fifteen years instead of ten. In another he pledged to protect peanut, wheat, tomato, and citrus growers by restricting imports to prevent lowering prices. Other side deals had nothing to do with NAFTA such as Bill Clinton's promise to a New York congressman to support a Small Business Administration pilot urban project in his district.

NAFTA continued to be at the center of political controversy after it came into effect in 1994 largely out of concern for its real or perceived impact on American workers, crime, illegal immigration, and drug trafficking. During the 2008 presidential campaign John McCain supported the agreement but the other major candidates attacked it. Barack Obama blamed it for the loss of American jobs. Both he and Hillary Clinton promised to amend the treaty or withdraw from it. Ron Paul called for abolishing NAFTA.

Applying the Lessons

1. Is Fast Trade Authority (trade promotion authority) a good idea? Is it necessary?

2. Are regional trade agreements in the U.S. national interest?

3. Should trade agreements come with expiration dates?

A second area of controversy surrounded funding for combating human immunodeficiency virus/acquired immunodeficiency syndrome (HIV/AIDS). The American response to the AIDS crisis has been caught in a political cross-fire of congressional opposition to foreign aid in general and more general political opposition to any form of aid for family planning programs. In 1984, in what is known as the "Mexico City policy," President Reagan prohibited USAID from providing funds to foreign governments or international and nonprofit organizations that engaged in family planning programs. This ban was suspended by Bill Clinton; put back into place by George W. Bush; and suspended again by Obama.

The third area of controversy involved efforts to stop international drug trafficking. The most ambitious undertaking was Plan Colombia, a $7.5 billion aid package intended to advance the peace process in Colombia, strengthen its national economy, stop the production of drugs, promote justice and human rights, and foster democracy and social development. Critics were fearful that Plan Colombia was all too reminiscent of the 1980–81 period when the United States became embroiled in El Salvador's civil war by its overly close identification with the military.

Both defenders and critics of Plan Colombia acknowledge that drug production has not so much been curtained as it has moved elsewhere, most notably to Mexico. The George W. Bush administration sought to address the problem of Mexican drug trafficking through a $1 billion, two-year foreign aid package in 2007, officially known as the Merida Initiative. Success has been limited by the failure to deliver on the promised aid (less than 2 percent of the promised aerial surveillance aircraft and other equipment were in place in 2009) and by the inability of the Mexican government to control the widespread drug cartel violence.

Post–9/11 Foreign Aid

Since 9/11, foreign aid has come to be viewed in a more positive light by those who long criticized it, under the assumption that it can make a major contribution to the war against terrorism. Almost immediately after 9/11, the George

W. Bush administration sought authority from Congress to waive all existing restrictions on U.S. military assistance and weapons exports for five years to any country he determined was helping in the War on Terrorism. A similar pattern existed in the area of trade. In 2002, for example, the administration proposed dropping trade restrictions on eight Central Asian countries that emerged out of the Soviet Union after its fall. All had questionable records in the areas of human rights and democratization. In addition to being used as a carrot, trade restrictions were also used as a stick. In 2003 the administration announced that it would only allow companies from countries that supported the war against Iraq to bid on prime reconstruction contracts. Also that year, the Bush administration announced that it was suspending military aid to some thirty-five countries because they failed to meet a congressionally imposed deadline exempting Americans from prosecution in the new International Criminal Court. Congress exempted twenty-seven states, including NATO members, Israel, and Egypt, from the loss of aid.

Many traditional supporters of foreign aid are doubtful that these policies will succeed. Instead they place their hopes in the signature development assistance program of the George W. Bush administration, the Millennium Challenge Account (MCA).[22] Targeted toward low-income countries, it was announced in 2002 and began operation in fiscal year 2004 under the jurisdiction of a new independent agency, the Millennium Challenge Corporation (MCC). One of the defining features of the MCC is its narrow focus. Money would be given only to countries that met a demanding set of criteria, and its only purpose would be to support economic growth and reduce poverty. An additional unique feature is that the MCC compact or agreement would be implemented by the recipient country government.

The eighteen different indicators used to judge a country's eligibility are presented in Table 11.2. They fall into three categories: (1) good government, (2) economic freedom, and (3) investing in people. At the end of 2015 twenty-seven compacts had been entered into along with another twenty-six smaller threshold programs. Over time concerns were raised about several aspects of these compacts. First, they all tended to emphasize agricultural and transportation infrastructure projects. More variety had been expected. Second, the funding levels were an issue. In some cases, they were not as high as anticipated, and in other cases, they were seen as far too large to be managed effectively. Third, corruption was a recurring issue. To address such issues in 2016 the MCC put forward a new strategic document, "NEXT: A Strategy for MCC's Future," that reaffirmed its principles and established a set of priority goals.

Of broader concern than the conduct of its country programs was the impact of the MCC foreign aid program on the coherence of U.S. foreign aid initiatives. MCA money was not intended to replace U.S. funding for multilateral foreign aid initiatives or the core development activities of USAID. It is the relationship between USAID and MCC that has received the most attention. Colin Powell described the relationship as one of the MCA "pulling" countries forward and USAID "pushing" them in that direction.[23]

TABLE 11.2	Millennium Challenge Corporation Performance Indicators, FY 2016

Indicator	As Measured By
Ruling Justly	
Civil liberties	Freedom House
Political rights	Freedom House
Freedom of information	Freedom House
Government effectiveness	World Bank, World Governance Indicators
Rule of law	World Bank, World Governance Indicators
Control of corruption	World Governance Indicators
Encouraging Economic Freedoms	
Cost of starting a business	World Bank Group
Inflation	IMF, World Economic Outlook and Country Reports
Fiscal policy	IMF, World Economic Outlook, and Country Reports
Regulatory quality	World Bank Group, world Governance Indicators
Trade policy	Heritage Foundation
Access to credit	International Finance Corporation
Land rights and access	International Fund for Agricultural Development & International Finance Corporation
Gender in the economy	International Finance Corporation
Investing in People	
Public expenditures on health	World Health Organization, UNICEF
Immunization	World Health Organization, UNICEF
Total public expenditures on primary education	UNESCO and national governments education
Girls' primary completion rate or girl's secondary completion	UNESCO
Natural resource management	Center for International Earth Science Information Network, and Center for Environmental Law and Policy

Source: Curt Tarnoff, *Millennium Challenge Corporation*, Congressional Research Service, April 5, 2016.

Over the Horizon: Feed the Future

The focus of policy making tends to be on the immediate problem. This perspective is consistent with the time frame elected officials and bureaucrats think in. Policy makers focus on the next election and bureaucrats deal with an annual budget cycle. Lost in this is a focus on the long term.

Looking just a little over the horizon, we find one program that attempts to break out of this pattern—the Feed the Future (FtF) initiative launched by the State Department in 2010.[24] It is a government-wide response to the problems of hunger, poverty, and malnutrition that brings together units from ten differ-ent agencies and departments. It follows from a U.S. commitment made at the 2009 G8 Summit and has the principal goals of improving agricultural growth, both in livestock and crops, along with the nutritional status of producers and consumers. Central to the FtF initiative is an emphasis on research that will lead to environmentally sustainable productivity gains and a resilient food supply. In 2016 FtF concentrated its efforts on sixteen priority countries with an eye toward address shortcomings in gender/gender development, the environment/human ecology, and climate change. Its core strategy was to use locally adapted technologies to increase agricultural output along with improving local, national, and international markets for the these goods. USAID requested $978 million for FY 2017 for the FtF initiative.

Critical Thinking Questions

1. Which type of free trade agree-ment—bilateral, regional, or global—is of most value to the United States today?

2. Should economic sanctions be used against friends or just foes?

3. What should be the primary ob-jective of U.S. foreign aid—to help the United States or to help the recipient?

Key Terms

boycott, 280

Bretton Woods system, 274

economic sanctions, 269

economic statecraft, 270

embargo, 280

fast track, 272

free trade, 268

imperialism, 270

nontariff barriers, 280

quota, 279

sanctions, 269

smart sanctions, 281

tariff, 269

Further Reading

David Baldwin, *Economic Statecraft* (Princeton, NJ: Princeton University Press, 1985).
This is the classic overview of economic statecraft as an instrument of foreign policy. The author clarifies the concept of economic statecraft and provides examples of its poten-tial and use.
Robert Blackwell and Jennifer Harris, *War by Other Means: Geoeconomics and Statecraft* (Cambridge, MA: Harvard University Press, 2016).
The authors assert that once a mainstay issue in conducting foreign policy, economics has become a neglected and misunderstood foreign policy tool. They call for a new vision of U.S. statecraft to reintegrate economics into U.S. foreign policy.
I. M. Destler, *The Making of Foreign Economic Policy* (Washington, DC: Brookings, 1980).

This book provides a conceptual overview along with several case studies of food trade policy in the 1970s. It examines the nature of the problem, how Congress dealt with it, and how the bureaucracy was organized to deal with it.

Bryan Early, *Busted Sanctions* (Stanford: Stanford University Press, 2015).

This book examines the role of third-party spoilers, "Black Knights," in undermining economic sanctions. The author examines over sixty years of U.S. sanctions. He finds that often U.S. allies are a major impediment to the success of sanctions.

Douglas Irwin, "The Truth about Trade," *Foreign Affairs* 95 (July 2016), 84–95.

The author notes that free trade is often blamed for America's economic problems. He argues that on the whole, trade still benefits the United States. This article examines the validity of complaints leveled against it and examines future options.

Walter Russell Mead, "America's Sticky Power," *Foreign Policy* 141 (2004), 46–53.

This article argues that for too long the United States has overlooked the full potential of its economic power, which has the ability to entrap other countries in positive relationships with it, thereby making global relations more stable and manageable.

Nicoli Nattrass, "U.S. Foreign Aid and the African AIDS Epidemic," *Yale Journal of International Affairs* 8 (2013), 52–61.

This article presents an overview of the content and evolution of U.S. AIDS funding and programs in Africa. The author discusses the merits of critiques of the program and puts forward suggestions for improving it.

Notes

[1] Robert Blackwell and Jennifer Harris, "The Lost Art of Economic Statecraft," *Foreign Affairs* 95:2 (March 2016), 99–110.

[2] http://useconomy.about.com/od/Trade-Agreements/fl/What-Is-the-Trans-Pacific-Partnership.htm.

[3] Walter Russell Mead, "America's Sticky Power," *Foreign Policy* 141 (2004), 46–53.

[4] Patricia Sullivan et al., "U.S. Military Aid and Recipient State Cooperation," *Foreign Policy Analysis* 7 (2011), 275–94.

[5] For a discussion of evaluating economic statecraft that focuses on foreign aid, see Mariann Lawson, *Does Foreign Aid Work?* (Washington, DC: Congressional Research Service, February 13, 2103).

[6] David Baldwin, *Economic Statecraft* (Princeton: Princeton University Press, 1985), makes this point throughout. The statement is found on page 115.

[7] Valdislav Inozemtsev, "Yes, Sanctions Work," *Foreign Affairs* (March 2015), 33–38.

[8] Emma Ashford, "Not-So-Smart Sanctions," *Foreign Affairs* ** (January 2016), 114–23.

[9] Baldwin, *Economic Statecraft*, 44–47, 207–209.

[10] Theodore Moran, "Empirical Studies of Strategic Trade Policy," *International Organization* 50 (1996), 175–205.

[11] Daniel Drezner, "Bad Debts," *International Security* 34 (2009), 7–45.

[12] U.S. Department of the Treasury, *Sanctions Programs*, http://www.treasury.gov/resource-center/sanctions/programs.

[13] Meghan O'Sullivan, *Shrewd Sanctions* (Washington, DC: Brookings Institution Press, 2003), 12.

[14] Emre Hatipoglu, "A Story of Institutional Misfit," *Foreign Policy Analysis* 10 (2014), 431–45.

[15] Meghan O'Sullivan, "Iran and the Great Sanctions Debate," *Washington Quarterly* 33 (2010), 7–21.

[16] Bryan Early, "Unmasking the Black Knights," *Foreign Policy Analysis* 7 (2011), 381–402.

[17] Stephen R. Weissman and Johnnie Carson, "Economic Sanctions against Rhodesia," in John Spanier and Joseph Nogee (eds.), *Congress, the Presidency, and American Foreign Policy* (New York: Pergamon, 1981), 132–60.

[18] Arne Tostensen and Beate Bull, "Are Smart Sanctions Feasible?," *World Politics* 54 (2002), 373–403.

[19] See Carol Adelman, "Global Philanthropy and Beyond," *Georgetown Journal of International Affairs* 13 (2012), 15–24; James Stavridis and Evelyn Farkas, "The 21st Century Force Multiplier," *Washington Quarterly* 35 (2012), 7–20.

[20] *Development and the National Interest* (Washington, DC: Agency for International Development, 1988).

[21] "THE 1992 CAMPAIGN; Transcript of 2d TV Debate Between Bush, Clinton and Perot". The New York Times. New York Times Company. 16 October 1992.

[22] Gene Sperling and Tom Hart, "A Better Way to Fight Global Poverty," *Foreign Affairs* 82 (2003), 9–14; Lael Brainard, "Compassionate Conservatism Confronts Global Poverty," *Washington Quarterly* 26 (2003), 149–69.

[23] Colin Powell, "No Country Left Behind," *Foreign Policy* 146 (January/February 2005), 30–35.

[24] *Feed the Future: Global Food Security Research Strategy*, May 2011, http://www.feedthefuture.gov/documents/FTF_research_strategy.pdf.

12 Military Instruments: Big Wars

Dateline: Iranian Nuclear Agreement

On July 14, 2015, after eighteen months of negotiations and sixteen consecutive days of talks the United States and Iran reached an agreement on limiting Iran's nuclear program to block what the United States characterized as a cover path to nuclear weapons. The agreement is controversial. President Obama stated that it would extend Iran's nuclear breakout time to a year in first decade, up from two to three months at present. In years thirteen, fourteen, and fifteen, however, it will shrink to almost zero. Israeli prime minister Benjamin Netanyahu called it a mistake of historic proportions. Republican members of Congress asserted it would set in motion a nuclear arms race.

From the perspective of the United States and its official negotiating partners, Great Britain, France, Russia, China, plus Germany, collectively known as the P5+1, the goal was to prevent a covert pathway to nuclear weapons by blocking off several different nuclear components. First, Iran's uranium stockpile has been frozen for at least a decade. Second, the number of centrifuges which enrich uranium will be reduced from some nineteen thousand to six thousand, and the level of enrichment allowed will be reduced to below weapons grade for fifteen years. Third, Iran's stockpile of low-enriched uranium will be reduced significantly. Fourth, with international assistance Iran must remove the ore of its heavy water reactor which is capable of producing plutonium. As a side agreement it was decided that existing bans on missile and conventional weapon sales to Iran would continue for eight and five years respectively.

From Iran's perceptive the goal was to remove U.S. and international economic sanctions. The agreement contains a timetable for removing them through a four-step process defined as adoption day, implementation day, transition day, and termination day, which is ten years into the agreement. The agreement also contains provisions for unannounced on-site inspections to all phases of a nuclear development program. Should Iran not comply the United Nations can begin "snap-back" of sanctions.

Iran's path to nuclear weapons began in in the 1970s when with American support the shah of Iran announced plans to build twenty-three nuclear reactors. The seizure of the American embassy in 1979 which resulted in Iran holding fifty-two Americans hostage for fourteen months led to a break in U.S.-Iran relations. An eight-year war with Iraq (1980-88) left both sides seriously weakened. During that war Iran obtained blueprints from Pakistan allowing it to produce enriched uranium. In 2002 it became known that construction was under way to build facilities for this purpose. At this point George W. Bush charged Iran with seeking to become a nuclear power. Iran denied this asserting its pursuit of nuclear power was for peaceful purposes. For the next six years Iran, the UN, and International Atomic Energy Agency (IAEA) officials entered into a series of talks in which agreements were reached but not kept. At the same time the UN and the United States began imposing sanctions. In 2007 a National Intelligence Estimate concluded that "with high confidence" Iran had halted its nuclear program in 2003 and "with moderate confidence" that the program had not resumed.

Upon entering office the Obama administration sought to reach out to Iran's new leader, Ayatollah Ali Khamenei, to no vail. Obama announced that unlike Bush he was willing to enter into talks with Iran before it agreed to UN demands to suspend its nuclear program. He also sent private letters to Khamenei that were met with the announcement that Iran would build more nuclear reactors. Beginning in 2011 mid-level U.S. and Iranian officials secretly began exploratory discussions on the future of nuclear talks. Not all were successful. A March 2012 meeting in which Secretary of State Hillary Clinton participated was characterized as having gone poorly. In March 2013 the secret talks took on a more successful tone as a senior U.S. delegation traveled to Oman to talk with Iranian officials about the possibility of starting bilateral talks. Formal nuclear talks with Iran were taking place as these secret talks were occurring, but as in the past they were making little progress. The secret talks got a major boost in June when Hassan Rouhani was elected president replacing the hard-line Mahmoud Ahmadinejad. Four secret talks soon took place. In October at the formal P5+1 negotiations Iran produce new proposals that were described as containing practical measures to strengthen cooperation and resolve outstanding issues. Neither Israel nor the other P5 countries were told of the secret talks until September 2013. On November 24, 2013, an interim Joint Plan of Action agreement was reached that identified concrete steps to be taken by all parties over the next six months when a full agreement was to be in place.

Implementation of the Joint Plan began in January 2014. In February a new round of talks designed to produce a comprehensive agreement began. Six rounds of talks were undertaken but no agreement was reached by the July deadline. Discussions were then extended until November. Four more rounds of talks failed to produce an agreement and a second extension until July 2015 was agreed to. In April all parties announced agreement on a general framework for a nuclear agreement. The initial July deadline for formalizing that agreement passed without an agreement having been reached. The final 109-page agreement was announced days later after yet another extension of the talks.

In this and the next chapter, we examine the various ways strategists have thought about preventing, fighting, and dealing with the consequences of war. Here we look at the large-scale use of nuclear weapons and conventional weapons for the purposes of preemption, deterrence, and war fighting. We begin here for two reasons. First, possessing military power of this type is a defining feature of a major power status in world politics and presents citizens around the world with the greatest risks. Second, many see parallels between the development, language, and evolution of nuclear strategy and the newest form of warfare, cyber warfare (which we discuss in the following chapter).

Cold War Nuclear Thinking

The United States' nuclear strategy during the Cold War was not static; it changed several times. It was also not always internally consistent. There often was a distinction between what policy makers said their strategy was and what it actually called for. The former is known as declaratory policy, and the latter as action policy. To fully appreciate this difference, we begin by looking at the development of U.S. and Soviet nuclear arsenals and then examine the strategies built upon them.

The U.S. Strategic Arsenal

The first atomic bomb was detonated at 5:30 a.m., on July 16, 1945, in the New Mexican desert. On August 6 Hiroshima was destroyed by an atomic bomb. On August 9 Nagasaki was similarly destroyed by a plutonium bomb. These two attacks effectively depleted the U.S. (and therefore the global) inventory of atomic weapons. The U.S. nuclear arsenal grew slowly. Only two weapons were stockpiled at the end of 1945, nine in July 1946, thirteen in July 1947, and fifty in July 1948.[1] None of these weapons was preassembled; it took thirty-nine people over two days to put them together. The year 1949 marked the end of the U.S. nuclear monopoly, as the Soviet Union detonated its first atomic bomb. Part of the U.S. response to the Soviet Union's acquisition of the nuclear bomb was to develop a more powerful weapon, the hydrogen bomb. The United States successfully tested an H-bomb in November 1952, and the Soviet Union duplicated the feat in August 1953.[2] It is estimated that by 1957, the United States probably had three thousand nuclear bombs, and the Soviet Union had a few hundred.[3]

Reinforcing this U.S. numerical advantage in bombs was a marked superiority in delivery systems. The Soviet bomber fleet was small and could reach the United States only on a one-way mission. The United States did not face a similar handicap because it could use bases in Western Europe to attack the Soviet Union. This advantage disappeared in 1957 when the Soviet Union successfully tested an intercontinental ballistic missile (ICBM) and launched Sputnik into orbit. With these two actions, the Soviet Union demonstrated the theoretical capability to deliver a nuclear attack on U.S. cities and its overseas military bases.

Fearing the development of a "missile gap" in which the Soviet Union would have a significant advantage over it in nuclear weapons, the United States stepped up production of its own ballistic missile force, constructed new early-warning radar systems, and placed the Strategic Air Command (SAC) on a heightened alert status so that almost half of its planes could take off on fifteen minutes' notice. As it turned out, no missile gap developed because the Soviet Union did not engage in a crash buildup of its nuclear forces. The result was an overwhelming U.S. nuclear superiority.

The U.S. nuclear arsenal reached its peak size in 1966 with an estimated 32,000 nuclear warheads. At that time, the Soviet Union possessed about 7,000 nuclear warheads. The long-predicted Soviet buildup got under way in the mid-1960s such that, in 1978, it held a slight numerical advantage over the United States in nuclear warheads: 25,393–24,826. The term "parity" was now used to characterize the U.S.-Soviet nuclear relationship, because although the two nuclear inventories did not match each other for weapon system, they each had compensatory advantages.

U.S. Cold War Nuclear Strategy

For the first eight years of the nuclear age, virtually no such thing as nuclear strategy existed per se at either the declaratory or action level. The uniqueness of nuclear weapons was not yet appreciated. They were simply treated as the largest explosive devices yet created, and it was expected that the next war would be fought along the lines of World War II. Long-range bombers would deliver these weapons against Soviet cities, industries, and military support facilities. When the small stockpile of atomic bombs was exhausted, plans called for using conventional bombs and a general mobilization of U.S. forces.[4] The first war plan to identify atomic bomb target lists was *Broiler* in the fall of 1947. It called for 34 bombs to be dropped on 24 cities. A 1956 war plan listed 1,200 cities in Russia and China for attack; 175 ground zero targets were identified in Moscow and

145 were identified in Leningrad. Additionally 1,100 airfields in Russia, China, and Eastern Europe were designated as targets.[5]

There was a certain degree of unreality to early war plans. Most fundamentally, Bernard Brodie questioned whether nuclear weapons could be used in the same way as other weapons, or if **deterrence** rather than war fighting was their sole credible use.[6] Moreover, if deterrence was to be the principal purpose to which nuclear weapons were put, then some thought was necessary about how to accomplish this purpose. Deterrence could not simply be assumed to exist.

The first formal statement of nuclear strategy was put forward by the Eisenhower administration as part of its New Look defense posture. The nuclear component of this strategy was **massive retaliation**. Massive retaliation was intended to deter a wide spectrum of Soviet attacks, guaranteeing not only the security of the United States but also that of its European and Third World allies by threatening the Soviet Union with massive destruction in retaliation for aggressive behavior. No details were given; all that was promised was "retaliation instantly, by means and places of our own choosing." The lack of specificity was intentional. The Eisenhower administration felt that the Truman administration's pledge of help for any country threatened by communism had given the initiative to the Soviet Union. Massive retaliation was designed to give it back to the United States.

Two recurrent lines of criticism were leveled against massive retaliation. The first concerned its credibility. Critics asserted that deterrence required more than just the capability to inflict damage. The threat also had to be credible. To threaten the Soviet Union with massive destruction for an attack on the United States was one thing; to make the same threat for attacks on Third World states was quite another. Soviet leaders would find the former credible, but not the latter, and therefore, they would not be deterred. The United States would then be left with the distasteful choice of having to implement its threat or do nothing. The second line of criticism was that massive retaliation was ill suited to the changing nuclear relationship between the United States and the Soviet Union. Massive retaliation assumed the existence of an invulnerable retaliatory force, and this was no longer the case because of the growth in the Soviet nuclear arsenal. The growing vulnerability of nuclear forces to attack transformed deterrence from a certainty into an idea based on a "delicate balance of terror."[7]

Massive retaliation was U.S. declaratory policy. Action policy was reflected in U.S. war plans. Evidence suggests that U.S. war plans were not being tailored to meet the two primary contingencies spoken of by policy makers: retaliation and preemption (striking first in self-defense). Instead, U.S. war plans had become capability plans. They were constructed in such a way as to employ all of the nuclear weapons in the U.S. inventory and provide a rationale for acquiring additional weapons.[8] The gap between what the war plans would produce and what policy makers wanted was often quite glaring. For example, in 1955, an SAC officer stated that its plan would leave the Soviet Union "a smoking, radiating ruin at the end of two hours."[9]

The first coordinated effort to establish a nuclear action policy came in 1960 when President Dwight Eisenhower approved the establishment of a National

Strategy Target List (NSTL) and a Single Integrated Operational Plan (SIOP) for using nuclear weapons. Planners selected twenty-six hundred separate installations for attack out of an overall list of forty-one hundred targets.[10] Plans called for launching all thirty-five hundred nuclear warheads if sufficient warning time existed. According to one calculation, the SIOP assigned three hundred to five hundred kilotons of weapons to accomplish the level of destruction caused by a single bomb on Hiroshima.

The Kennedy administration shared its predecessors' conviction that deterrence was the proper role for nuclear weapons. It differed in how to structure deterrence, and it gave attention to a problem that had never been fully addressed in the 1950s: how to fight a nuclear war. Kennedy replaced massive retaliation with the concept of **flexible response**, under which the United States would have a range of conventional and nuclear options to choose from in deterring and responding to Soviet aggression. To make this happen, the Kennedy administration officially incorporated three new features into U.S. nuclear thinking. First, more attention was given to the use of tactical nuclear weapons in the hope that, because of their less destructive nature, they might be more manageable. Second, a new targeting policy was adopted that emphasized attacks on military forces and avoidance of population centers. Third, the Kennedy administration looked into two measures that might limit the damage done to the United States in case of a nuclear war: civil defense and damage limitation.[11]

The value of these changes in nuclear strategy was called into question by the 1962 Cuban missile crisis.[12] Attention now shifted back to formulating a nuclear posture built less on war fighting and more on the ability to inflict widespread devastation on the enemy. To be credible, Robert McNamara initially estimated that U.S. forces must have an **assured destruction** capability to destroy 25–30 percent of the Soviet population and 66 percent of its industrial capacity.

Movement from massive retaliation to flexible response and then to assured destruction implied a parallel set of changes in U.S. targeting policy. Changes in the SIOP did occur, but not necessarily on the scale implied by the change in declaratory policy.[13] The SIOP remained a capabilities plan rather than an objectives plan.[14]

The most significant targeting change to take place was in U.S. declaratory policy, when the Nixon administration introduced the principle of **sufficiency**, which required strategic equality between the United States and the Soviet Union rather than the possession of a minimum level of retaliatory threat.[15]

This was seen as providing crisis stability, so that neither side had an incentive to go first with its nuclear weapons in a crisis. This was followed by the introduction of a new Nuclear Weapons Employment Policy (NUWEP) that emphasized the destruction of Soviet economic recovery assets as the primary objective of U.S. nuclear forces. It stipulated that, under all circumstances, the United States must be able to destroy 70 percent of the Soviet industrial capacity needed for postwar economic recovery. The major notable and controversial addition was made by the Reagan administration, which added the requirement that the United States be able to "prevail" and "force the Soviet Union to seek the earliest termination of hostilities on terms favorable to the U.S."

Historical Lesson

The Baruch Plan

As World War II came to a close, a divided Truman administration looked out to the post–World War II era. Many decisions would have to be made, not the least of which was determining what to do with the nuclear bomb. On one side of the debate was Secretary of War Henry Stimson, who argued that the United States could not for long keep a nuclear monopoly. It would only be a matter of time before the Soviet Union and other countries acquired the scientific knowledge and technological capacity to build nuclear weapons. The answer he favored was placing nuclear power under international control. Aligned against Stimson was a group led by Secretary of State James Byrnes. Distrustful of Soviet motives and fearful of its power, Byrnes argued against any sharing of nuclear secrets. From this perspective, a monopoly over nuclear weapons would be crucial to maintaining the postwar balance of power. Truman was divided on the matter but ultimately supported Stimson's perspective.

The first international discussions about the future of nuclear power took place in Washington in September 1945 between representatives from the United States, Great Britain, and Canada, all of whom had worked on various aspects of the Manhattan Project that developed the bomb. This was followed by a foreign ministers meeting in Moscow in December, where the United States, Great Britain, and Soviet Union agreed in principle to create a United Nations (UN) commission to work for the peaceful use of nuclear power and advise on the destruction of existing nuclear weapons (which only the United States possessed). To help formulate a U.S. position, Stimson appointed Undersecretary of State Dean Acheson to chair a committee in January 1946 that would draft a U.S. nuclear energy policy. Acheson formed a technical advisory group to support his committee's deliberations. It was chaired by David Lilienthal, who also chaired the Tennessee Valley Authority.

The Acheson-Lilienthal Committee issued its report in March 1946. Its fundamental conclusion supported Stimson's position. International inspections of atomic energy facilities were unlikely to stop their spread and the diversion of atomic energy for military purposes. Accordingly, the best solution was to place atomic energy under the control of a new international agency, the Atomic Development Authority, and make it available in small quantities to all countries for peaceful use. In return for the United States taking this step, all other countries would agree not to develop nuclear weapons. The committee's approach was consistent with the prevailing view of the early post–World War II era that the primary obstacles to developing a bomb were not to be found in technological and scientific problems but in the access to the raw materials needed to build the bomb.

After receiving the report, Truman arranged for it to be given to Bernard Baruch, whom he had appointed to be the U.S. representative to the UN Atomic Energy Commission. Baruch proceeded to make important changes in the Acheson-Lilienthal Plan, the most significant of which dealt with changing the enforcement procedures that could be wielded by the new Atomic Development Authority. Baruch eliminated the possibility that decisions by Atomic Development Authority might be vetoed by participating countries. Only then did he believe that the phrase "immediate and direct enforcement" would carry any weight. Additionally, Baruch inserted language that Truman accepted. Baruch's change in wording and the Baruch Plan was presented to the UN Atomic Energy Commission on June 14, 1946. Truman's about-face appears to be tied to steadily deteriorating relations with the Soviet Union that made conflict appear far more likely than cooperation.

Baruch opened his presentation by telling the assembled delegates that they faced a choice between the "quick and the dead." His plan called for giving the Atomic Energy Authority the power to inspect nuclear facilities, made it illegal to possess an atomic bomb, and allowed for the seizure of facilities. The United States would end its nuclear monopoly in stages and destroy its

nuclear weapons only when the Baruch Plan was fully implemented. The Soviet Union quickly rejected the Baruch Plan, objecting to its loss of a veto and calling for the United States to end its nuclear monopoly as a precondition for participating in the plan. In December the Baruch Plan was approved by 10–0 vote, with the Soviet Union and Poland abstaining. Since a unanimous vote of all twelve members of the UN Atomic Energy Commission was needed, the plan was defeated. The Soviet Union detonated its first nuclear device on September 23, 1949.

Applying the Lesson

1. Could the Baruch Plan have slowed down or stopped nuclear proliferation?

2. Some argue that Truman knew the plan would be rejected and was not serious. What do you think?

3. What would a new Baruch Plan have to look like to stop A. Q. Khan?

Post–Cold War Nuclear Thinking

The end of the Cold War did not bring with it an end to nuclear weapons. Questions continue to exist over the proper size of the U.S. nuclear arsenal and strategies for its use.

The U.S. Strategic Nuclear Arsenal

As 2016 began it was estimated that the U.S. nuclear stockpile contained 4,670 nuclear warheads that could be delivered by more than 800 ballistic missiles and aircraft. This is 350 warheads less than were in the 2009 U.S. nuclear stockpile. Of these nuclear warheads, 1,930 are deployed. The remaining 58 percent are in storage and could be reactivated. An additional 2,340 have been retired.[16]

Even though the U.S. (and Russian) nuclear arsenals are reduced in size since the end of the Cold War, the debate over their proper size continues. Former deputy secretary of defense and director of the Central Intelligence Agency John Deutch has called for deploying less than one thousand warheads.[17] Others with extensive government service have called for a nuclear arsenal of five hundred operationally deployed warheads plus five hundred more in reserve.[18] More recently concerns have been expressed that the cuts proposed by Obama (perhaps as many as five hundred warheads) are too severe and that a larger nuclear arsenal is needed if U.S. policy makers are to have a sufficient range of options when dealing with nuclear adversaries.

Embedded in the debate over numbers are two others. One deals with the readiness and reliability of U.S. nuclear warheads, especially those designed in the 1950s and early 1960s. To address this concern in 2005, Congress began funding the Reliable Replacement Warhead program. In 2014 Pentagon studies documents serious deficiencies in the nuclear weapons infrastructure such as aging blast doors in nuclear silos and an aging submarine fleet that will require several billions of dollars to fix. In addition to safety concerns, supporters of the program cite the potential for reducing the size of the U.S. nuclear arsenal by replacing existing warheads with smaller numbers of more reliable ones. The second debate centers on the size and purpose of the warheads. At issue here is the concept of "bunker busters," officially known as Robust Nuclear Earth Penetrators. If they are developed, they would be the first new nuclear weapons designed to implement a policy of preemption rather than deterrence against rogue states.

U.S. Nuclear Strategy: Content

U.S. nuclear thinking continues to bear the imprint of Cold War thinking, with strategic revisions largely being made at the margins. The first presidential statement of U.S. post–Cold War policy came with Bill Clinton's 1997 Presidential Decision Directive 60 (PDD-60). According to it, the U.S. military should no longer prepare to win a protracted nuclear war, but instead to deter the use of nuclear weapons against the United States and its allies. PDD-60 continued to call for the existence of a wide range of nuclear strike options against Russian nuclear forces and against its civilian and military leadership. It also contained a requirement to plan for nuclear strikes against states that have "prospective access" to nuclear weapons or that may become hostile to the United States.

George W. Bush's administration reaffirmed that nuclear weapons play a fundamental role in U.S. force projection capabilities. His major change was to add flexibility to U.S. nuclear strategy by constructing a wider range of scenarios in which nuclear weapons might be employed. In February 2008 it was revealed that Operations Plan (OPLAN) 8010 contained nuclear strike options against combat forces and options to use support equipment against six potential enemies: Russia, China, North Korea, Iran, Iraq, and Syria.

President Obama's nuclear force posture and strategy continue to operate at the margins of Cold War nuclear policy.[19] In June 2013 he announced his intention to pursue additional cuts in the size of the U.S. nuclear arsenal through talks with Russia. He also announced a new NUWEP. It reaffirmed that the "fundamental role" of nuclear weapons is to deter a nuclear attack on the United States and the central role of counterforce targeting in that policy. In doing so it endorsed a targeting policy that is inherently preemptive, yet it also directed the Pentagon to review and potentially reduce the role of "launch on warning" in

U.S. plans. In 2016 the Pentagon was still working on updating the nuclear war plan in keeping with Obama's NUWEP.

A Source of Stability or Instability?

Beyond concerns about the size of the U.S. nuclear arsenal and the content of U.S. nuclear strategy many now question whether nuclear weapons are a stabilizing force in world politics, as they were held to be during the Cold War, or whether they are now a source of instability.[20] Two different dynamics are at work here. On the one hand nuclear weapons are of little value due to the dominant military position of the United States in world politics. No other power represents a significant military threat to the U.S. homeland. On the other hand nuclear weapons do provide a strategic rationale for militarily weak states (and terrorist groups) opposed to the United States. They are sought after both to deter the United States from taking action against them and as offensive weapons to use against it. As the 9/11 attacks demonstrated, this is no idle threat, even though it pales in significance with traditional Cold War security threats.

Bridging the Nuclear-Conventional Divide

This new global context in which U.S. nuclear forces operate has drawn renewed attention to the question of where does one draw the line between using conventional and nuclear weapons. The long-standing fear exists that without a clearly defined "**firewall**" separating the two a conventional war might escalate into a nuclear one.

Careful thinking about the interaction of nuclear and conventional weapons is especially important in two of the most controversial areas of contemporary U.S. military strategy: deterrence and preemption. Deterrence, the use of force to prevent something unwanted from happening, is controversial because some now argue that U.S. enemies cannot be deterred. Preemption, striking first in self-defense when the threat is imminent, is controversial because of its offensive character and the possibility of it being carried out on the basis of incorrect information.

The Korean peninsula provides policy makers with a national security challenge where maintaining the nuclear-conventional firewall may be especially challenging. North Korea exploded its first nuclear device in 2006. In 2015 and 2016 North Korea defied warnings of sanctions by the United States and expressions of displeasure by China by testing a nuclear device it claimed to be a hydrogen bomb and testing rockets that most observers see as a cover for an intercontinental ballistic missile program. Yet, it also experienced a series of failures along with an occasional success in testing missiles capable of striking Japan, South Korea, and U.S. troops in the Pacific. The United States and South Korea responded to North Korea's stepped up nuclear activities by holding a military exercise in 2016 that included preemptive surgical air strikes on its nuclear power plants as well as large-scale ground operations.

Deterrence

The United States is concerned with deterring attacks both on its own home-land and on its allies. The former is known as direct deterrence and the latter as extended deterrence. Up until the terrorist attacks of 9/11, it was taken for granted that direct deterrence was more easily achieved than was extended deter-rence. Now both are suspect.

Two different strategies have been used to implement a deterrence strategy. The first is to set up "trip wires." This typically took the form of American troops stationed abroad, most notably in Germany and South Korea, who would be in the way of any enemy attack. During the Cold War, the presence of American troops abroad was seen as a sign of strength and resolve. Today, the situation is different. They have become targets of opportunity for terrorists and insur-gents. A second strategy is to leave the door open to a nuclear response should deterrence fail. By threatening to take a crisis to the brink of nuclear war, it was assumed that the enemy would abandon its unwanted line of action. Reportedly President Eisenhower threatened the use of nuclear weapons against China if it did not help bring about an end to the Korean War.

We can begin to understand the problems faced in constructing a successful deterrence strategy if we look at how deterrence has failed in the past.[21] Two primary failure patterns exist. In one, deterrence fails through a fait accompli. Hostile policy makers detect no U.S. commitment and feel that they can control their risks in challenging the United States. The 1950 North Korean attack on South Korea is an example of this type of deterrence failure. The attack was not irrational because no clear U.S. commitment existed and the risks appeared to be controllable. Public statements by leading U.S. diplomats and military figures had placed South Korea outside of the U.S. "defense perimeter" and referred to it as a "liability" in the event of war in the Far East. Reinserting U.S. forces into Korea was not expected to be an easy task, so the most likely response to an attack would be diplomatic protest or a minimal military action.

Deterrence can also fail as a result of a limited probe, where the chal-lenging action is easily reversed or expanded depending on the nature of the U.S. response. In these cases, the U.S. commitment is unclear, and the risks still seem to be controllable. The Berlin Wall crisis of 1961 illustrates how deter-rence can fail through a limited probe. The Soviet Union and East Germany moved at midnight on May 12 to close the Berlin border crossing by construct-ing a barbed-wire wall on East Berlin territory. Only when the minimal nature of the U.S. response was clear (the Western powers did not make a protest for four days) did they move to construct a more substantial and permanent wall with only a few well-guarded openings. Problems such as these led the George W. Bush administration to move away from deterrence to **preemption**, which we discuss in this chapter.

Deterrence is not without its defenders. As one observer put it, if deterrence worked against Joseph Stalin, who we knew was determined to get nuclear weap-ons, why did we think it could not work against Saddam Hussein?[22] Deterrence, these analysts argue, has two dimensions. It contains both a threat, "Cross this line and we will attack," and a promise, "If you do not cross this line, we will not harm you." Viewed from this perspective recent U.S. deterrence failures such as against Saddam Hussein Iraq and Bashar al-Assad in Syria result from implementing only the first part of the deterrence equation. Instead of a promise not to do harm the United States has treated the adversary as a villain who could not be trusted and had to be replaced.

It faces a similar problem in East Europe where NATO is moving from a policy of reassurance to one of deterrence. The United States has drawn a line by announcing that NATO is setting up six new commands in East Europe to create a five-thousand-person strong rapid reaction force, the largest military maneuver since the Cold War (Operation Trident Juncture) in October 2015, and followed this up in June 2016 with Operation Anakonda, a ten-day training exercise with more than thirty thousand troops from twenty-four countries (including two non-NATO members) that involves both the deployment of air defense and cyber operations. NATO also established a missile defense base in Romania. It was also announced that beginning in 2017 NATO will deploy four thousand troops to Poland and Baltic States. The key question becomes what is the political message it is sending to Vladimir Putin. Removing him from power is not a realistic option, but will it accept Russian domination over the Ukraine and other borderland areas if he does not undertake aggressive actions? Obama appeared willing to do so but some in Congress called for a stronger military response.

Preemption

Preemption is striking first in self-defense when the threat is imminent. When the threat is not imminent but still held to be real, striking first in self-defense is referred to as a preventive strike. Technically speaking, the George W. Bush administration had ignored this long-standing distinction in putting forward its policy of preemption and combining both scenarios under one heading. Bush advocated preemption as an alternative to deterrence in a speech at West Point in June 2002, and it has become the core concept of what is popularly known as the Bush Doctrine. Preemption is not a new strategy by any means. Ronald Reagan justified the invasion of Grenada in 1983 as a preemptive move. Lyndon Johnson acted in a similar manner, sending troops to the Dominican Republic in 1965. In the more distant past, one could classify Woodrow Wilson's decision to send troops to Mexico in 1914 as consistent with the logic of preemption.

The Iraq War represented the Bush administration's attempt to implement a policy of preemption. Particular attention has been directed at the "shock and awe" strategy used in its opening stage. The expectation was that by rapidly overcoming the enemy's ability and will to fight, the United States would immobilize the enemy and reconstruction would be less expensive. The subsequent occupation problems in Iraq led to debate over the wisdom of using a small military force in this manner. Defenders of the strategy maintain that Operation Iraqi Freedom was not a good test case for "shock and awe." They argue that operational difficulties and the less-than-perfect knowledge of the Iraqi enemy reduced it to a mere slogan instead of a strategy. They cite a conflict with China as a potential case in which it might be better applied.[23]

If the logic of striking first in self-defense is accepted, questions remain to be addressed.[24] For one, should nuclear weapons be used? The official U.S. position is that it will not use or threaten to use nuclear weapons against non-nuclear states who belong to the Nonproliferation Treaty (NPT). In other cases it would "consider the use of nuclear weapons only in extreme circumstances."

Using Conventional Military Force

Conventional military power can be used for many purposes.[25] In this section, we examine the large-scale use of conventional military power for fighting wars. In the next chapter, we return to its use in the context of peacekeeping operations and as a stability force.

During the Cold War, the U.S. military fought two big wars: Korea and Vietnam. Three times since the fall of the Berlin Wall in 1989, the United States has sent large numbers of armed forces abroad to engage the enemy in conflict. The first occurred in 1991, when the United States led a United Nations–sanctioned war against Iraq after its invasion of Kuwait. A massive bombing campaign was initiated on January 17. The offensive military actions that followed met ineffective Iraqi resistance and after one hundred hours of fighting, President George H. W. Bush declared a cease-fire. The 2003 Iraq War got off to a similarly effective start. A massive shock and awe bombing campaign was followed by twenty-one days of combat that began on March 20 and encountered little resistance. Baghdad fell on April 9. There followed, however, a long and protracted unconventional war in which U.S. forces did not fare as well. In October 2011 Obama announced that the last U.S. troops would leave Iraq by the end of the year, bringing the war to a close.

The third major involvement of U.S. forces has been in Afghanistan and can be divided into two phases. The first phase came immediately after 9/11 and had the goal of removing the Taliban from power and capturing or killing Osama bin Laden. It relied heavily on air power and Special Forces that operated in alliance with local resistance leaders. The second phase began in 2008, when U.S. forces began entering Afghanistan in large numbers. The Taliban insurgency had regrouped, forming an alliance with al Qaeda and threatening the control of the U.S.-backed Afghan government. In the judgment of the chair of the Joint Chiefs of Staff, the situation in Afghanistan had become "precarious and urgent." By 2010, the number of U.S. troops in Afghanistan had reached ninety-four thousand. All U.S. combat forces were scheduled to leave Afghanistan at the end of 2014.

War fighting has always been the ultimate measure of a state's military power. For much of the post–World War II period, American military policy was cast in terms of a 2-war capability, meaning that the United States needed the ability to fight two wars at the same time. This has not always been the case. Under Nixon, the standard was 1.5 wars, and under Reagan, it was 3.5 wars. After 9/11 the United States began moving away from this baseline. The 2015 National Military Strategy states that the "if deterrence fails… our military will be capable of defeating a regional adversary in a large-scale, multi-phased campaign while deny the objectives of—or imposing unacceptable costs on—another aggressor in a different region."[26] This has been characterized as a "one plus strategy."

Anticipating where the U.S. forces might engage in war-fighting missions has proven to be a challenge for U.S. planners. After the Persian Gulf War, an early 1990s Defense Department study identified seven potential conflicts, which involved the United States. All of them placed the United States in a reactive mode. Numbered among them were the following scenarios: (1) Russia invades Lithuania. NATO defeats Russia in eighty-nine days of combat; (2) North Korea attacks South Korea. United States and South Korea win after ninety-one days of combat: (3) coup in Panama. United States wins in eight days; and (4) reemergence of a hostile superpower. No outcome is given.[27]

In 2009 a Washington, DC, think tank, the Center for Strategic and Budgetary Assessments, suggested that defense planners consider three potential scenarios that might require the use of large-scale conventional forces: (1) an irregular war between the Nigerian government and an insurgent movement in the oil-rich southern part of the country, (2) a Chinese attempt to incorporate Taiwan through military and economic coercion, and (3) a nuclear-armed Iran that becomes increasingly hostile to the United States and neighboring governments. The three scenarios were said to represent the three major challenges the U.S. military must be prepared to face: state failure and irregular warfare (the Nigeria scenario), confronting a near competitor (the China scenario), and the threat posed by weapons of mass destruction (the Iran scenario).

Of primary concern to war planners today are the possibilities of major military conflict with China and Russia. The possibility of an interstate war with a major power is defined by the National Military Strategy as "low but growing."[28] Concern for possible conflict with China growing out of the dispute over the South China Sea led to the development of the Air-Sea Battle concept in 2010. At the low end of the conflict continuum the Air-Sea Battle strategy was intended to provide policy makers with the ability to maintain the ability to move military forces outside of a specific theater of conflict, conduct a show of force, or engage in limited military strikes. At the higher end of the conflict continuum the Air-Sea Battle strategy was designed to provide an ability to defeat aggression and maintain escalation advantages in the face of advanced weapons systems. One version of the Air-Sea Battle strategy called for U.S. bombers and submarines to incapacitate Chin's long-range intelligence and capabilities and precision missile systems followed by larger air and naval assaults on Chinese targets. In 2015 the Air-Sea Battle strategic framework was replaced by the Joint Concept for Access and Maneuver in the Global Commons. The change is intended to direct attention to two missing elements in the Air-Sea Battle concept: there was no role in it for the Army and no detailed attention was given to the question of what U.S. strategy was after it got access to denied territory.

Both the Air-Sea Battle and the Joint Concept for Access and Maneuver in the Global Commons direct attention to problems of anti-access/area denial (A2/AD). These are ones that have long been a focus of military planners dealing with small war contingencies and are now seen as ones that also confront future large-scale uses of U.S. military force. Anti-access challenges refer to efforts by the adversary to prevent the United States from entering a theater of operation and to prevent it from pre-positioning forces near that area or moving forces to it. Tactics used for this purpose range from denial of basing rights and overflight rights, expulsion from existing bases, terrorism, cyber-attacks, opening alternative fronts which require U.S. military engagement, and the use of weapons of mass destruction and ballistic missiles. Area Denial challenges refer to possible steps taken by an adversary to resist and limit the freedom of action open to the U.S. military once it has entered an area thus making it more difficult and expensive both politically and militarily. Area denial tactics include the use of ballistic missiles, mines, electronic warfare, and social media. They can be employed by individuals, loosely organized groups, terrorist organization, governments, and external countries.

Regardless of the military context, two fundamental political conditions frame the large-scale use of conventional force. The first of these is the domestic political conditions under which conventional military power should be used. This debate has largely been over two different perspectives. One believes that U.S. forces should only be engaged under strictly defined circumstances that included the presence of clearly defined goals, widespread public support, and the clear intention of winning. The second view holds that the United States must be prepared to act even though victory is not assured or that the public strongly supports it. The second framing political consideration is the extent to which the United States can or should act alone. As we noted in our discussion of the American national style, a preference for unilateralism runs deep in American political and strategic thought. Yet this is not always possible. When multilateral action is necessary, problems of speed, efficiency in military operations, and the often time-consuming need for consensus-driven political consultation often arise.

The most notable American alliance is the North Atlantic Treaty Organization (NATO). It was long a Cold War bulwark against communist expansion into Western Europe. With the end of the Cold War NATO became an alliance in search of a mission. Its political and military performance in the Balkans crisis left many wondering if it could adapt to a peacekeeping role. NATO was further beset with internal disagreements about the political goals to be achieved by military action and rules of engagement in Afghanistan. In 2011 the United States turned to NATO as the military instrument for establishing a no-fly zone in Libya and once again found it to be an alliance that was unable to speak with one voice. Just before leaving office, Secretary of Defense Robert Gates warned that unless NATO addressed its lack of political will and low levels of defense spending, the alliance faced a "dim if not dismal future" and "irrelevance."

The Russian annexation of the Crimea in 2014 and its support for pro-Russian militants in eastern Ukraine refocused attention on the original question of NATO's role in Europe. As we noted earlier part of this refocusing has resulted in an increased presence of NATO ground forces and ballistic missiles along the Russian border with East Europe. But problems still remain with using NATO as a military counterweight to Russian influence in Europe, most notably with creating and maintaining a united political and military front. One issue is that the Russian challenge is not simply a land-based one. Russia is modernizing its navy and has altered its naval doctrine to include developing a Russian presence in strategic areas such as the Mediterranean Sea and the blue water Atlantic. In introducing this changed doctrine Russian authorities made explicit reference to NATO saying, "We emphasize the Atlantic because NATO has been developing actively of late and coming closer to our borders."[29] A second factor complicating NATO's recapturing its role as a check on Russian military and political power in Europe is that for some NATO members the greatest threat they face is not from Russia but from instability in North Africa and the Middle East and the influx of large numbers of refugees. Dealing with this issue along with the question of how to prioritize it divides NATO members.

A further unknown in NATO's ability to act as a military counterweight to Russia or respond to terrorist-related issues was the United Kingdom's decision to leave the European Union (Brexit). While NATO and the European Union are separate organizations there is concern that for the next several years British attention and resources will so heavily be directed at the process of exiting it will have little interest or capacity to play a major supporting role for U.S. global defense initiatives.

Reducing the Danger of War: Arms Control and Disarmament

In the earliest years of the Cold War, two general strategies, **arms control** and **disarmament**, were pursued to lessen the likelihood of nuclear war. Disarmament has as its ultimate goal the systematic elimination of weapons, whereas arms control seeks to place restraints on the use of weapons. For the most part, disarmament tended to be pursued through formal treaties and at the level of declaratory policy. Arms control did not always take the form of formal agreements or treaties. Instead, it took the form of more flexible and informal "traffic rules" agreements, such as an agreement to give advance notification of a test or military exercise to reduce the possibility that these actions might be incorrectly interpreted and spiral into a military conflict. The rationale for pursuing such traffic rule agreements was that a treaty in and of itself did not produce arms control. These multiple paths to arms control continue today, as does the tendency for disarmament to remain at the declaratory level. More recently, a third strategy, defense, has also been pursued. We examine each of these now as ways of controlling or preventing big wars. Before doing so we need to note that an often underappreciated dimension to the problem of controlling nuclear weapons involves accidents. In 1979 a training video of a Soviet attack was accidently played and set off warnings of a nuclear attack. Even more serious were a series of Soviet missile, bomber, and submarine accidents from 1983 to 1987 that grew out of a fear of a NATO first strike.[30]

The Cold War Record

From 1946 to 1957, disarmament proposals dominated the international negotiating agenda but little of significance was achieved as proposals were put forward more with an eye to their propaganda and image-creating potential than to their substantive merits. Primary attention was given to the production of nuclear weapons and the formation of nuclear strategy. The first nuclear disarmament proposal to command global attention was the Baruch Plan. Presented by the United States at the United Nations in 1946, it sought to place all aspects of nuclear energy production and use under international control. The Soviet Union rejected it.

Proposals for lessening the danger of nuclear war were not forthcoming again until the Eisenhower administration. Its first proposal was the 1953 Atoms for Peace plan. This was followed in 1957 by the Open Skies proposal. Atoms for Peace was a disarmament plan only in an indirect sense. It sought to get states to cooperate on the peaceful development and use of atomic power. Eisenhower's proposal led to the creation of the International Atomic Energy Agency, but it did not produce movement in the direction of disarmament. The proposed Open Skies Treaty focused on reducing the fear of surprise attack by exchanging blueprints of military installations and allowing each side to carry out aerial surveillance of each other's territory. It too failed to serve as a first step toward disarmament. Rather than accepting the plan as a way of sidestepping the question of on-site inspection, the Soviet Union interpreted it as a device for legitimizing U.S. spying.

The first major breakthrough in arms control came in 1963 following the Cuban missile crisis with the signing of the Limited Test Ban Treaty. It outlawed nuclear explosions (testing) in the atmosphere, under water, and in outer space. A second milestone was reached in 1968 with the signing of the NPT. Up until then the primary **proliferation** concern shared by the United States and the Soviet Union was in stopping the spread of nuclear weapons in Europe, especially to West Germany. With the NPT, attention shifted to the Third World. The NPT represented an agreement between nuclear and nonnuclear states. Those states that had nuclear weapons promised not to provide them to nonnuclear states and to negotiate in good faith among themselves to reduce their nuclear stockpiles. They also pledged to help nonnuclear states develop nuclear energy for peaceful purposes. In return, the nonnuclear states agreed not to try to obtain nuclear weapons.

In addition to spurring interest in multilateral arms control treaties, the Cuban missile crisis also nudged the United States and Soviet Union toward bilateral arms control efforts. The first major product was the hotline (actually a telegraph link) that linked the White House and the Kremlin. During the crisis, it had taken almost twelve hours for a key communication from Soviet leader Nikita Khrushchev to reach President John Kennedy and be decoded. The hotline was first used in 1967 during the Arab-Israeli War, when the Americans and Soviets informed each other of the movement of their navies.

The negotiation of a formal arms control treaty between the United States and Soviet Union had to wait until their nuclear inventories had grown to the point where each side felt that a balance of power existed. The breakthrough agreements came with the 1972 Anti-Ballistic Missile (ABM) Treaty and the Strategic Arms Limitation Talks (SALT) I agreement. The ABM Treaty was of unlimited duration and was modified by a 1975 agreement. Its key provisions limited each side to one ABM deployment area and prohibited the development, testing, or deployment of ABM components. Among the key provisions of SALT I was limits on the number of fixed launchers for ICBMs and numerical limits for submarine-launched ballistic missiles.

The SALT I agreement on offensive forces was set to expire in 1977 and the expectation was that it would lead to SALT II. A first step in this direction was the November 1974 signing of the Vladivostok Accords, which set ceilings on the total numbers of strategic launchers that each side could possess and the number of vehicles that could carry multiple independently targeted warheads. Building on the Vladivostok Accords, the SALT II agreement was to have been completed in the summer of 1973. This deadline was not met in part because Jimmy Carter was elected president, and against Soviet wishes, he sought to achieve deeper cuts. As it finally emerged, SALT II was a complicated, multilayered document to which the U.S. Senate has never given its consent and that has now technically expired.

In his campaign for the presidency, Ronald Reagan attacked the SALT II treaty as fatally flawed because it placed the Soviet Union in a position of military advantage. Accordingly, the first priority of his administration was not arms control but arms modernization and expansion. Reagan's first concrete arms control proposal was directed at the problem of intermediate-range nuclear weapons in Europe. These weapons had become NATO's main defense against the conventional military advantage held by Warsaw Pact troops. By the late 1970s, their military value was seriously challenged by the Soviet Union's introduction of the mobile SS-20 missiles. In November 1981 Reagan presented his solution to this problem. His "zero option" called on the Soviet Union to eliminate its existing intermediate-range ballistic missiles (IRBMs) targeted at Europe in return for a U.S. pledge not to deploy a new generation of missiles there. The idea of a zero option was quickly rejected by the Soviet Union. The resulting deadlock was not broken until September 1987 with the signing of the Intermediate Nuclear Forces (INF) Treaty.

In the same speech in which he unveiled his zero option, Reagan indicated that his administration was preparing proposals for a new round of strategic arms talks, to be known as the Strategic Arms Reduction Talks (START). Little visible movement was forthcoming, and public concern began to mount over the administration's commitment to arms control and its loose language about nuclear war. The nuclear freeze movement became a focal point for efforts to push the administration back to the arms control negotiating table.[31] To blunt this criticism and regain the political initiative on arms control the Reagan administration presented a series of proposals that the Soviet Union rejected as "old poison in new bottles." Still, negotiations continued, and a basic START framework was agreed upon by the time Reagan left office. The agreement was signed by President George H. W. Bush and Mikhail Gorbachev in July 1991.

The Post–Cold War Record

The dynamics of arms control changed with the end of the Cold War. Rather than engaging in many rounds of protracted treaty negotiations, the United States and the Soviet Union entered into a series of unilateral cuts. For example, in September 1991, Bush ordered that (1) all tactical nuclear weapons, except those dropped from planes, be removed from the U.S. arsenal; (2) all nuclear cruise missiles and bombs be taken off naval ships, attack submarines, and land-based naval aircrafts; (3) all strategic bombers be taken off high alert status; and (4) development and deployment of mobile ICBMs be halted. Gorbachev responded by calling for the elimination of all land-based tactical nuclear weapons and the removal of all nuclear arms from ships, submarines, and land-based naval aircrafts.

The failed August 1991 coup against Gorbachev raised concerns in the United States that, should the Soviet Union disintegrate, the government and military's ability to exert command and control over the immense Soviet nuclear arsenal would also disappear, with potentially catastrophic proliferation consequences. To try and minimize the dangers inherent in thousands of "loose nukes," in November 1991, Congress passed the Cooperative Threat Reduction Program, better known as the Nunn-Lugar Program, to help the Soviet leadership secure and dismantle its nuclear stockpile. With the passage of time, the focus has extended to all weapons of mass destruction and the United States now works with Ukraine, Georgia, Kazakhstan, and other countries that were once members of the Soviet Union.

The United States and Russia returned to formal arms control agreements in January 1993 with the signing of START II. It never came into force, although it was ratified in 1996. Domestic and foreign policy issues in both countries led to the treaty languishing in limbo. Russia delayed final approval as a sign of its disapproval of U.S. military action in the Balkans. In the United States attention shifted to the politically charged question of whether it should withdraw from the ABM Treaty so that a national missile defense system could be created. This issue was settled when in December 2001 President George W. Bush gave the required six-month notice that the United States was withdrawing from the ABM Treaty.

Russian President Vladimir Putin called the decision to withdraw from the ABM agreement a "mistake," but it did not stop him from signing a new arms control agreement with the United States in May 2002: the Strategic Offensive Reductions Treaty (SORT), which broke new ground in treaty language. It starts from the premise that Russia is a friend of the United States and not an enemy. The agreement was negotiated in six months and contains only ten sentences. It lacks the appendices, caveats, statements of understanding, and covenants found in earlier arms control agreements. In essence, the treaty permitted each side to do as it pleased so long as its nuclear arsenal was reduced to twenty-two hundred deployed warheads by December 31, 2012. As one U.S. senator observed, "There are no mileposts for performance. There is nothing really to verify except good faith." SORT expired on December 21, 2012.

With START I set to expire in December 2009, President Obama and Russian President Dmitry Medvedev announced at a July 2009 summit meeting that they had agreed upon the outlines of a new arms control agreement: New START. Obama encountered problems in securing support for the treaty both from Russia and from Congress. Putin identified Obama's plans for a missile defense shield as a major impediment to reaching an agreement. Many

Republicans in Congress argued that its inspection provisions were inadequate. Obama succeeded in gaining Senate approval of New START in December 2010 by committing to a ten-year, $85 billion nuclear weapons modernization program. According to the terms of the treaty, both sides can deploy no more than 1,550 strategic warheads and 700 launchers seven years after the treaty is ratified. On-site inspection agreements established in START I also would resume. New START was activated in February 2011 and will remain in force until 2021, with an option to extend its life to 2026.

U.S.-Russian nuclear relations took an antagonistic turn in 2014 when the United States accused Russia of violating the 1987 INF Treaty by testing a prohibited ground launched cruise missile. Russia had begun testing this missile in 2008. Russia responded by asserting that the U.S. decision to place the Aegis missile system that can fire cruise missiles in Romania was in violation of the INF treaty. In 2015 the Obama administration determined that it was not in the interest of the United States to withdraw from the INF treaty because of this violation.[32]

The post–Cold War era has also seen the reemergence of nuclear proliferation as a central national security problem for the United States. In spite of the NPT, nuclear proliferation has been a political and strategic reality. India and Pakistan acquired nuclear weapons in 1974 and 1998, respectively, and Israel is recognized to have possessed them since 1979. South Africa, Iraq, and Libya are known to have had or been in pursuit of nuclear weapons at one time. Attention today is focused on the nuclear ambitions of two states identified by Bush as part of the "axis of evil": Iran and North Korea. As we noted in the "Dateline" opening to this chapter, after lengthy negotiations an agreement was reached with Iran to curb its ability to obtain nuclear weapons.

Negotiations with North Korea have yet to reach the point of seriousness that marked the last two years of negotiating the Iran agreement.[33] Periodic breakthroughs have been negotiated, but they stopped far short of **denuclearizing** North Korea. For example, in 2005, North Korea agreed to abandon its nuclear program and permit on-site inspections in return for food and energy aid. One month later a dispute with the United States over suspected North Korean money laundering led to a breakdown in the talks and in 2006 North Korea conducted its first underground nuclear test. A new agreement was reached in 2007 in which North Korea agreed to freeze its nuclear program in return for energy aid. Within a year this agreement fell apart over its refusal to allow on-site inspections and North Korea restarted its nuclear program. In 2015 North Korea offered to impose a temporary moratorium on its nuclear tests if the United States cancelled the upcoming joint exercise with South Korea. The United States rejected the proposal saying it was inappropriate to link testing nuclear weapons to routine joint maneuvers.

Defense

According to one observer, "The great missing innovation in the nuclear age is the development of means to defend against nuclear attack."[34] Without this ability it is impossible to protect one's population and territory without the cooperation of the enemy. Strategists have established that such tacit cooperation between enemies is possible and often takes place during war.[35] Still, many are troubled that the defense of the United States in the nuclear age is possible only with the cooperation of an adversary. Reagan gave voice to these concerns in a March 1983 speech:

> What if free people could live secure in the knowledge that their security did not rest upon the threat of instant U.S. retaliation to deter a Soviet attack; that we could intercept and destroy their strategic missiles before they reached our soil or that of our allies? Is it not worth every investment necessary to free the world from the threat of nuclear war?[36]

The terrorist attacks of 9/11 added a new dimension to the defense problem. Nuclear weapons did not have to be delivered by long-range missiles or aircraft. They could be assembled in the target or cross-national borders in a variety of ways. Nor would there be a clearly defined set of targets to retaliate against.

The Strategic Defense Initiative

Reagan's solution to this dilemma was the Strategic Defense Initiative (SDI). He defined it as a long-term research and development program designed to identify viable policy options for creating a nuclear defense system. The decision as to which system, if any, to pursue was scheduled to be made in the 1990s. However, in early 1987, the Reagan administration began examining the possibility of an early deployment of SDI. As envisioned by most observers, Reagan's SDI system involved a series of defensive systems layered together in such a way as to create a leak-proof umbrella or protective shield. Each layer in this system was to perform the same tasks: It would search out and detect targets, track them, discriminate between real targets and dummy targets, and intercept and destroy the real targets

Although the goal was never formally abandoned, the scope and funding of a "Star Wars" system were progressively cut back. The George H. W. Bush administration continued to seek funding for it under the guise of "brilliant pebbles." Under it, missiles sent into space would be sent into layered orbits and would possess the ability to detect the launch of enemy missiles. SDI's short-lived existence formally came to an end during the Clinton administration. It was replaced by interest in developing follow-on missiles to the Patriot system used against Scud missiles in the Persian Gulf War. Instead of constructing a nuclear shield over the United States, the new goal would be to prevent attacks by short-range ground-launched missiles.

National Missile Defense Systems

The death of SDI did not mark the end of efforts to establish a national ballistic missile defense system. Surprise missile tests by Iran and North Korea in 1998 provided additional political backing for creating such a system. In 2002 George W. Bush withdrew the United States from the antiballistic missile treaty and put forward a national missile defense system plan calling for ground-based long-range missile interceptors supported by a network of ground-based radars and space-based infrared sensors. Missile defense systems entered a new next phase when his administration signed agreements with Poland and the Czech Republic for the construction of antimissile facilities in those countries to protect Europe from Iranian missiles. Russia responded angrily, claiming that because of the sophistication of the missiles involved this move threatened its security. It responded by suspending its obligations under the Conventional Forces in Europe Treaty and testing a new intercontinental missile.

Obama expressed skepticism about the merits of this missile defense shield during the 2008 presidential campaign, and one of his first foreign policy initiatives was to terminate it. He called for creating a more flexible and extensive system that would be built in four phases through 2020. The first phase was set to become operational in 2011 and involved the use of slower interceptor missiles. Russia responded favorably to Obama's decision and subsequently entered into the New START treaty. In 2013 Obama canceled the fourth and final phase of the planned European missile defense system and in its place he added additional interceptors to the national missile defense system that had been created in California and Alaska. The decision was justified on the grounds of ongoing technical issues and cost. It was also interpreted as an inducement to Russia to engage in more arms control talks.

The most recent developments in constructing a missile defense system have focused on Russia and North Korea. Spring 2013 brought the announcement that the Defense Department was going to spend an additional $1 billion on ballistic missile interceptors along the Pacific Coast, bringing the number of interceptors located there to forty-four by 2017. It was then announced that the United States was moving to place an advanced missile defense system in Guam two years ahead of schedule, as a "precautionary move" to protect U.S. naval and air forces in the Pacific from a North Korean attack. Additionally, the U.S. has begun discussions with Japan and South Korea about constructing a missile defense system. Citing increased Russian aggression Obama reversed his earlier opposition to U.S. supported ballistic missile defense systems in Eastern Europe, and in 2015 the United States established such a system in Romania that is operated by NATO.

The potential benefits of ballistic missile systems are a subject of intense debate. Three issues dominate the discussion. The first is the wisdom of constructing a sufficiently robust system that could potentially negate a Russian or Chinese nuclear capability. Many fear that such a system would force these two states to undertake large-scale expansions of their nuclear programs in order to deter the United States from acting unilaterally against them. Declassified documents reveal that this is how the United States responded in 1968 to the development of a Soviet ABM system. The second debate is about the military value of a more limited system that would be directed at protecting the United States from rogue states with smaller nuclear arsenals. Some see it as a prudent investment in an age of terrorism, whereas others see it as largely symbolic and a response to domestic political pressures. The third issue is its effectiveness.

Missile interceptors currently deployed on the West Coast only have a 50 percent success rate in hitting dummy targets.

Over the Horizon: A Middle East Nuclear-Free Zone?

The signing of an agreement between Iran and the United States in 2015 designed to reduce the short-term threat of an Iranian nuclear breakout is a potentially significant step toward reducing the danger of calculated or accidental nuclear war in the Middle East. But from the perspective of many observers much still remains to be done to bring long-term stability to the region. One course of action that has been advocated but never realized is the creation of a Middle East Nuclear Weans Free Zone (NWFZ) or even more ambitiously, a Weapons of Mass Destruction (WMD) Free Zone that would include a ban on nuclear, chemical, and biological weapons.[37]

Calls for establishing a Middle East NWFZ first appeared at the United Nations in 1974 when Iran, then ruled by the shah, and Egypt put forward a resolution calling for creating one that was approved by the General Assembly. Israel, which still officially denies possessing a nuclear capability but is said to have had one since 1966, presented a counter proposal in 1980. The question remained dormant until 1991 when a UN study outlined confidence-building steps that could be taken to create a Middle East NWFZ. The Security Council passed Resolution 687 endorsing the goal of establishing such a NWFZ. In 1992 regional arms control discussions began under the sponsorship of the Arms Control and Regional Security Group that was formed following the Persian Gulf War, but it soon ended when Egypt and Israel could not agree on the agenda.

In 1995 the NPT Review Conference adopted a resolution calling upon states in the Middle East to begin taking practical steps to bring an NWFZ into existence. It did so again in 2010. In 2012 a conference on establishing an NWFZ was to take place but it was postponed because of disagreements over the agenda. In 2015 the NPT Review Conference yet again took up the idea of an NWFZ. This time, the United States, Great Britain, and Canada objected to the proposed document's language which included a reference to establishing a WMD free zone and it was not adopted.

The historical legacy is not a positive one on which to build a Middle East NWFZ but neither was this the case for Cold War nuclear arms control agreements or the Iranian nuclear accord. Past efforts suggest three major issues to be addressed if an NWFZ is to be created. First, how does one define the Middle East? Early discussions placed the borders at Libya and Iran moving west to east and Syria and Yemen moving north to south. Recent commentaries have called for including Turkey and Pakistan. Second, does an NWFZ come prior to or after true peace is achieved? In one view an NWFZ is part of the pathway to peace. In the other it is a product of peace. Third, how will any agreement be verified? This is one that every arms control agreement has had to address. On-site inspections are the traditional answer but cyber technology may present new alternatives.

Based on previous efforts at arms control observers have suggested a number of steps that might be taken to address these and other issues. They include (1) initially focusing on negotiations at the technical level where political considerations can be best held, (2) creating a coalition of the willing rather than trying to achieve regional unanimity, (3) making use of outside officials to promote negotiations among small groups, (4) pursuing incremental steps forward rather than a comprehensive deal, and (5) obtaining pledges of support from outside powers to uphold the agreement.

Critical Thinking Questions

1. Are nuclear weapons a usable military tool? Under what conditions should their use be considered in place of conventional weapons?

2. Should we be optimistic or pessimistic about the future of arms control efforts?

3. Can arms control efforts become counterproductive?

Key Terms

arms control, 311

assured destruction, 301

denuclearizing, 315

deterrence, 298

disarmament, 311

firewall, 305

flexible response, 301

massive retaliation, 300

preemption, 298

proliferation, 303

sufficiency, 301

Further Reading

Alexei Arbatov, "Saving Nuclear Arms Control," *Bulletin of the Atomic Scientists* 72 (2016), 165–70.
While the number of nuclear arms has decreased greatly from the Cold War period, the probability of their use is higher now than in the past. The main impediment to arms control is that neither side is making it a high priority due to domestic and international impediments.
Richard Betts, eds., *Conflict after the Cold War*, 2nd ed. (New York: Pearson, 2005).
The author has compiled a wide-ranging series of essays, which examine the question of war and conflict from a variety of theoretical perspectives as well as from the vantage point of specific issues such as economics, military doctrine, and democratization.
James Doyle, "Why Eliminate Nuclear Weapons?" *Survival* 55 (2013), 7–34.
The author presents a twofold argument for eliminating nuclear weapons: (1) strategic nuclear deterrence was a "least bad" choice by policy makers and not a desired policy and (2) the conditions of world politics have changed so that a drastically different approach to nuclear weapons is needed.
Alexander George and Richard Smoke, *Deterrence in American Foreign Policy: Theory and Practice* (New York: Columbia University Press, 1974).

This classic study examines the development of deterrence theory and presents eleven different case studies. It includes important essays on the reasons why deterrence fails and the role of theory in policy making.

Gregory Koblentz, *Strategic Stability in the Second Nuclear Age* (New York: Council on Foreign Relations, November 2014).

The first nuclear age was characterized by a superpower arms race and ideological completion. The second nuclear age is defined by the existence of multiple nuclear powers and overlapping levels of cooperation and conflict. This report identifies three major challenges to nuclear stability in this new era.

Matthew Kroenig, "Facing Reality: Getting NATO Ready for a New Cold War," *Survival* 57 (February 2015), 49–70.

This article chronicles NATO's post–Cold War experiences leading up to the challenge presented by Russia in the Ukraine and the Crimea. The author examines these challenge and calls for a new NATO strategy to replace collective security and crisis management.

Michael Mandelbaum, *The Nuclear Question: The United States and Nuclear Weapons, 1946–1976* (Cambridge, MA: Cambridge University Press, 1979).

This book presents an important introduction to arms control and nuclear strategy. It provides an overview of developments in these areas from the beginning of the nuclear age through the 1963 Limited Test Ban Treaty.

Notes

[1] David Alan Rosenberg, "The Origins of Overkill: Nuclear Weapons and American Strategy, 1945–1960," *International Security* 7 (1983), 124.

[2] There is an inherent upper limit to how much power can be generated by fission, but there is no upper limit for fusion.

[3] Harvard Nuclear Study Group, *Living with Nuclear Weapons* (New York: Bantam, 1983), 79.

[4] There are a number of excellent volumes dealing with the development of U.S. nuclear strategy. The major ones relied on in constructing this history are Rosenberg, "The Origins of Overkill," 3–71; Jerome H. Kahan, *Security in the Nuclear Age: Developing U.S. Arms Policy* (Washington, DC: Brookings, 1975); Michael Mandelbaum, *The Nuclear Question: The United States and Nuclear Weapons, 1946–1976* (Cambridge, MA: Cambridge University Press, 1979); Richard Smoke, *National Security and the Nuclear Dilemma: An Introduction to the American Experience* (Reading: Addison-Wesley, 1984).

[5] Thomas Gibbons-Neff, "Declassified: How the Pentagon Planned to Nuke the Soviet Union and China during the Cold War," *The Washington Post*, December 28, 2015.

[6] Bernard Brodie (ed), *The Absolute Weapon* (New York: Harcourt Brace, 1946).

[7] Albert Wohlstetter, "The Delicate Balance of Terror," *Foreign Affairs* 37 (1959), 211–56.

[8] Rosenberg, "The Origins of Overkill"; Peter Pringle and William Arkin, *S.I.O.P.: The Secret U.S. Plan for Nuclear War* (New York: W. W. Norton, 1983).

[9] David Rosenberg, "A Smoking Radiating Ruin at the End of Two Hours: Documents of American Plans for Nuclear War with the Soviet Union, 1954–1955," *International Security* 6 (1982/83), 3–38.

[10] Rosenberg, "The Origins of Overkill," 116–17.

[11] On the ABM decisions, see Morton Halperin, *Bureaucratic Politics and Foreign Policy* (Washington, DC: Brookings, 1974).

[12] Mandelbaum, *The Nuclear Question*, 134.

[13] Rosenberg, "The Origins of Overkill," 178.

[14] Desmond Ball, "U.S. Strategic Forces," *International Security* 7 (1982/83), 34.

[15] Warner R. Schilling, "U.S. Strategic Nuclear Concepts in the 1970s: The Search for Sufficiently Equivalent Countervailing Parity," *International Security* 6 (1981), 59.

16 Hans Kristensen and Robert Norris, "United States Nuclear Forces, 2016," *Bulletin of the Atomic Scientists* 72 (2016), 63–73.

17 John Deutch, "A Nuclear Posture for Today," *Foreign Affairs* 84 (2005), 49–60.

18 Sidney Drell and James Goodby, *What Are Nuclear Weapons For?* (Washington, DC: Arms Control Association, April 2005).

19 Hans Kristensen, "Falling Short of Prague," *Arms Control Today* (September 2013).

20 Kier A. Lieber and Daryl G. Press, "The End of MAD," *International Security* 30 (2006), 7–44.

21 Alexander George and Richard Smoke, *Deterrence in American Foreign Policy: Theory and Practice* (New York: Columbia University Press, 1974).

22 Morton Halperin, "Deter and Contain," *American Prospect* 13 (November 4, 2002), 22–25.

23 Harlan Ullman, "Slogan or Strategy," *National Interest* 84 (2006), 43–49.

24 For a variety of critiques, see the various articles in the symposium "Is Preemption Necessary?," *Washington Quarterly* 26 (2003), 75–145.

25 See Richard Betts, *American Force* (New York: Columbia University Press, 2012), for a discussion of the challenges of using military force today.

26 *The National Military Strategy of the United States of America, 2015*, 6.

27 *Washington Post*, February 20, 1992, A1.

28 *The National Military Strategy of the United States of America, 2015*, 4.

29 See "New Russian Naval Doctrine Enshrines confrontation with NATO," *Moscow Times*, July 27, 2015, http://www.themoscowtimes.com/business/article/new-russian-naval-doctrine-enshrines-confrontation-with-nato/526277.html.

30 Sean Maloney, "Remembering Soviet Nuclear Risks," *Survival* 57 (September 2015), 77–104.

31 For a statement of the nuclear freeze position, see Randall Forsberg, "Call a Halt to the Arms Race: Proposal for a Mutual U.S.-Soviet Nuclear Weapons Freeze," in Burns H. Weston (ed.), *Toward Nuclear Disarmament and Global Security: A Search for Alternatives* (Boulder: Westview, 1984), 384–89.

32 For a critique of the Obama record, see Steven Pifer, "Obama's Faltering Nuclear Legacy: the 3 R's," *Washington Quarterly* 38 (Summer 2015), 101–18.

33 Michael Wallerstein, "The Price of Inattention: A Survivable North Korean Threat?" *Washington Quarterly* 38 (Fall 2015), 21–35.

34 Michael Mandelbaum, *The Nuclear Future* (Ithaca, NY: Cornell University Press, 1983), 43.

35 Thomas C. Schelling, *The Strategy of Conflict* (New York: Oxford University Press, 1960).

36 Reagan's speech is reprinted in Edward Haley, David M. Kethly, and Jack Merritt, eds., *Nuclear Strategy, Arms Control, and the Future* (Boulder, CO: Westview, 1985), 311–12.

37 For views on a NWFT, see Claudia Baumgart and Harold Muller, "A Nuclear Weapons-Free Zone in the Middle East: A Pie in the Sky?" *Washington Quarterly* 28 (2004), 45–58; the Global Forum on this topic in the *Bulletin of the Atomic Scientists* 70 (May 2014), 1–9; and Baria Ahmar, "A Nuclear Free Zone in the Middle East: Realistic or Idealistic?" *Palestine-Israel Journal* 19 (2013), http://www.pij.org/details.php?id=1513.

13 Military Instruments: Small Wars

Dateline: Back to Afghanistan

No clear dividing line or formula exists for distinguishing between big wars and small wars. The number of casualties, length of combat, and the impact on domestic society make up the most frequently cited dividing lines. In spite of the label, small wars have the ability of presenting major challenges to powerful states. Here, we look at one country where small wars have become commonplace: Afghanistan.

Strategically located at the intersection of the Middle East, South Asia, and Central Asia, Afghanistan has long been the object of attention by foreign governments seeking to conquer and control it. These efforts have rarely been successful. Alexander the Great remarked that Afghanistan was easy to march into but difficult to march out of. The United States is the latest country to experience this truth.

On May 27, 2014, President Barack Obama announced that combat missions would end in Afghanistan at the end of the year. Effective January 2015 full responsibility for combat operations and the security of the country would be assumed by the Afghan army. By the end of his presidency virtually all U.S. troops except those guarding the U.S. embassy were to have left Afghanistan. In October 2015 President Obama announced a change in plans. The U.S. military mission in Afghanistan would be extended beyond 2016. Now, fifty-five hundred U.S. troops would remain in Afghanistan at the end of 2016 or early 2017. Obama noted their mission would not change and that the decision had been made in consultation with U.S. military leaders and Afghanistan's president Ashraf Ghani.

As noted earlier, no mention was made of the Taliban as the principal adversary or even a lesser adversary in Obama's May 2014 announcement. The reality on the ground suggested something different. By spring 2015, before Obama's announcement of a revised timeline, the United States had for all practical purposes returned as a fighting force due to the Afghan army's continued troubles and the resurgence of the Taliban. In February five hundred U.S. soldiers were rushed to Helmand province, Afghanistan's largest province located in the south and a prime opium producing area. They came to aid Afghanistan's army which was struggling to defeat advancing Taliban forces. In April thousands of Afghan reinforcements were sent to Kunduz province in norther Afghanistan to turn back a Taliban offensive. Kunduz fell to the Taliban briefly in the fall. By the end of 2015, 102 Afghan generals had been replaced by the Ministry of Defense. During the first three months of 2015 the casualty rate among Afghan military and police rose 54 percent. U.S. and NATO aircraft conducted 128 airstrikes against low-level Taliban forces in the same period.

Air strikes against the Taliban forces are permitted for purposes of force protection. Observers and military officials on the ground noted that this directive was being interpreted loosely. One official noted that "they are putting guys [American advisors] on the ground in places to justify the airstrikes . . . it's not force protection when they are going on the offensive."[1] In February an ex-Taliban leader was killed by a drone strike that was defined as force protection and not counterterrorism by officials even though no American forces had been stationed for years at the place where he was killed. To explain these discrepancies U.S. officials distinguished combat missions from combat situations, and stated that while U.S. forces were allowed to accompany Afghan units into combat they were not to intentionally lead them. When questioned on the drone strike the response was "do you know what was in his mind?"

In February 2016 further steps were taken to aid the Afghan military in its fight against the Taliban. It was announced that some seven hundred to eight hundred additional troops would be sent to Helmand. They would not take part in the fighting. Their missions was to train and protect Afghan forces. They also did not signify an increase in the level of the U.S. military presence as they were replacing units that had been stationed elsewhere in Afghanistan. On May 23, 2016, Obama announced that a U.S. drone strike in Pakistan had killed the Taliban's official leader Mullah Mansour. He described it as "an important milestone" noting that the Taliban were continuing to "plot and unleash attacks on American and coalition forces" and that Mansour was an obstacle to peace talks with the Taliban. Obama also insisted the drone strike did not signal a change in the military mission to Afghanistan. One month later Obama authorized U.S. forces greater leeway in assisting Afghan forces in fighting the Taliban. They now can accompany regular local Afghan forces into battle and not just elite Afghan troops. One consequence of this decision will be to expand the use of air power against the Taliban since more U.S. forces can call in protection.

In July 2016 Obama announced yet another change in plans. Now, rather than reducing the size of U.S. forces in Afghanistan to fifty-five hundred by the end of his presidency, the United States would keep eighty-four hundred troops in Afghanistan. He also noted that U.S. commanders had received new powers to combat the Taliban and other militant groups saying, "The security situation remains precarious" and "the Taliban remains a threat."

Small wars are seen by many as the dominant form of conflict in the future. In this chapter, we examine the range of forms that small wars might take (conventional military force, hybrid wars, covert action, counterinsurgency operations, counterterrorism, and cyber warfare) as well as the role of arms control in such conflicts.

Separating Big Wars from Small Wars

Big wars and small wars tend to have their own language. Large wars have combatants and are fought according to generally accepted (in the West) rules of law. Small wars have insurgents and often appear to be wars without rules. We also use different language to discuss why big and small wars happen. In the case of large wars, we speak of **windows of opportunity**, where leaders calculate they can win; **windows of fear**, where leaders do not believe they can win but see the consequences of inaction as so dire that they feel forced to try to go to war; and accidents, where neither side wanted war but find themselves fighting one. This language also underlies our efforts to stop big wars. Deterrence is intended to convince an opponent that no window of opportunity exists. Arms control seeks to close windows of fear and reduce the potential and consequences of accidents. In all cases, it is assumed that a major threat to one's national interest is at work.

The language of small wars is different. Here, we tend to start by talking about the reasons for wars, the **casus belli**. This is not to say that they do not involve the national interest but that, this phrase by itself, does not convey a sense of why the war began. They often appear to be wars of choice rather than wars of necessity implying the other means existed for solving the dispute which gave rise to the conflict. One major source of small wars involves access to energy supplies. Access to clean water and food supplies are also seen as potentially significant causes of small wars. Looking beyond natural resources, it is clear that ethnicity is a cause of small wars. In some cases, this takes the form of separatism, where one ethnic group seeks to leave a state and form a new state in order to better protect itself. In other cases, it takes the form of irredentism, where a state reaches out and tries to bring its kin group into the state by expanding its boundaries. In still other cases, it takes the form of genocide, as one group seeks to eliminate another ethnic group from its territory.

Deterrence and arms control become more complex in small wars. For example, it is argued by some that deterrence against terrorism can only be partially successful and that for deterrence to work terrorist networks must be broken down into their component parts with different deterrence strategies being employed against each.[2] Arms Control efforts can easily flounder when the target of concern is viewed by key states as a matter of domestic politics. This has been the case with conventional arms control efforts and concerns expressed in the United States that this would violate Second Amendment rights to bear arms.

Bridging the Conventional-Asymmetric Warfare Divide

Two forms of military action, often involving the use of conventional forces short of engaging in traditional wars, have had a recurring presence on the international scene. They are humanitarian/peacekeeping operations and stability forces. They serve as a bridge for our thinking about the use of military power as we move from big wars (discussed in the last chapter) to small wars even though they have the potential for involving large numbers of military forces.

Humanitarian/Peacekeeping Operations

Operation Restore Hope (Somalia), Operation Provide Comfort (Northern Iraq), Operation Restore Democracy (Haiti), and Operation Odyssey Dawn (Libya) are prominent examples of post–Cold War U.S. military interventions that at least in part can be classified as humanitarian in nature. The United States is the largest source of money for United Nations (UN) peacekeeping operations providing about one-quarter of its funds but among the least active in providing personnel, only eighty-two military personnel and police officers are assigned to them. In 2015 Obama promised to increase the U.S. participation in peacekeeping by providing logistical support, and building camps and airfields.

There is nothing easy about humanitarian operations. Among the most important lessons cited from past humanitarian interventions are the need to be timely and robust, U.S. forces should remain under U.S. or North Atlantic Treaty Organization (NATO) command, and regional organizations are not viable alternatives to the UN for carrying out such missions.[3]

Humanitarian military operations grew out of an earlier generation of efforts referred to as **peacekeeping** operations. Carried out by neutral UN forces, their original purpose was to provide a way to stabilize an international or domestic conflict without involving U.S. or Soviet forces or by creating a situation where either side had "lost" the conflict. They provided a second-best solution for each side. Peacekeeping forces did not arrive until all sides to the conflict were ready to end the fighting. Over time, the scope of these efforts was expanded to include interventions undertaken outside of the UN system and where fighting continues. In these situations, the word "peacemaking" is often used to describe the challenge facing the intervening military forces.

Opposition to humanitarian and peacekeeping undertakings has been expressed from across the political spectrum. Neoisolationist commentators have questioned whether humanitarian interventions are really in the American national interest. They compare it to bungee jumping: "A risky undertaking for which there is no compelling need."[4] Advocates of military humanitarian interventions reject this argument contending that definitions of American national interest that focus only on the physical security of the United States or the health of its economy are anachronistic.

Stability Forces

Peacekeeping and humanitarian interventions focus on developments in a state and generally occur after a crisis has already begun. **Stability operations** in contrast may focus on internal situations but may also have a broader focus seeking to prevent interstate violence from breaking out or trying to prevent an international conflict from spilling over into neighboring states.

One area in which stability operations are growing in importance to U.S. security interests is Africa. This recognition led, in 2007, to the creation of the U.S. Africa Command (AFRICOM). Its purpose is to work with other U.S. agencies and international organizations to strengthen regional stability and security and, if need be, to deter aggression and respond to crises. In the words of one commentator, AFRICOM's mission is conflict prevention not conflict reaction.[5] Already AFRICOM's goals are proving difficult to implement, as the marriage of political and military objectives has created concern in many quarters. American embassies in Africa are raising questions about who is in charge of U.S. policy. African governments are raising concerns about AFRICOM signaling a new wave of American imperialism on the continent, and many humanitarian and civic groups are reluctant to become identified with AFRICOM for fear of creating distrust among the people they rely upon to achieve their development and humanitarian objectives.

AFRICOM's five-year plan announced in 2016 shows in growing role of counter insurgency and counter terrorism in its operations. It contained five priority missions. The first was to neutralize the al-Shahab terrorist group in Somalia. The second was to contain instability in Libya. Containing Boko Haram in West Africa was the third mission. Fourth, AFRICOM would focus on disrupting illegal criminal activity in Central Africa. The fifth mission was to build the peacekeeping and disaster assistance capabilities of African partner states.

Asymmetric Warfare

Asymmetric warfare is military conflict between forces that have significantly different power resources and strategies. Where conventional warfare achieves victory by defeating enemy military forces and taking control of land leading to surrender, in asymmetric warfare the path to victory lies in inducing exhaustion that erodes the enemy's will to fight and leads to the collapse of its military and political base.[6]

The U.S. faces three major asymmetric conflict challenges today: **Hybrid warfare,** insurgencies, and terrorism. They are not three self-contained categories. The dividing line separating them is fluid and elements of each may be present to some degree in any given conflict situation of which there are many today. From January to March 2015 the CATO Institute think tank estimated that U.S. Special Forces were deployed in over eighty countries.

Hybrid Warfare

"Hybrid warfare" is a term with many different meanings. Perhaps the most frequently used definition is that by Frank Hoffman who defines a hybrid war as one which "incorporate(s) a range of different modes of warfare, including conventional capabilities, irregular tactics, and formations, terrorist acts including indiscriminate violence and coercion, and criminal disorder."[7] By 2010 the Army had already begun to alter its training programs to put greater emphasis on hybrid conflicts. Its Hybrid Threat Training Circular introduced soldiers to hybrid strategies and tactics and presented three hybrid conflict scenarios: offensive, defensive, and stability operations.[8]

Most observers agree that it is not a new form of warfare so much as one that combines different forms of warfare into a coordinated and controlled strategy of war that emphasizes avoiding predictability and engaging in combat in "contested zones" characterized as highly populated areas and ones of economic importance. In most accounts hybrid warfare also recognizes the importance of using information resources such as social media and the press to defeat the adversary.

Hybrid warfare may be carried out by both nonstate actors and states. Hezbollah's campaign against Israel is an example of the former and Russia's military operations in Crimea and the Ukraine are examples of the latter. By the end of the Ukrainian crisis Russia had sent in armed forces without uniforms, professional soldiers in uniforms without marking, and agents acting with indigenous separatist groups to seize public buildings. It also relied upon local agitators, a variety of militia groups. Sophisticated military technology such as antiaircraft weapons and surface-to-air missiles were provided to local fighters who also employed terrorist techniques and engaged in sabotage. Russia sought to control the information about the conflict and engage in deception through such means as Russia Today, a Russian controlled news network.

Lawrence Freedman urges caution in making overly positive evaluations of the success of Russia's Ukraine hybrid war strategy. He notes that while Russia achieved key objectives it had great difficulty controlling developments in the Ukraine. Differences in objectives with local forces created military and political coordination problems and its deception operations were largely unsuccessful.[9]

Counterinsurgency The *US Army/US Marine Counterinsurgency Field Manual* defines an "insurgency" as "an organized movement aimed at the overthrow of a constituted government through the use of subversion and armed conflict." **Counterinsurgency** (COIN) is the strategy the United States employs to defeat insurgencies. COIN is defined by the 2006 Field Manual (FM3-34) as a protracted conflict that involves a mix of offensive, defensive, and stability operations. It requires that soldiers be both "nation builders as well as warriors."[10] It is a strategy designed to get the support of the people that requires the coordinated use of military, paramilitary, political, economic, psychological, and civic actions.

Using a medical analogy, COIN operations are seen as moving through three stages. Stage 1 involves stopping the bleeding by providing the patient with emergency first aid. Here, the goal is to protect the population and break the insurgency's momentum. Stage 2 involves inpatient care. The goal is to restore the patient's health and move him on the way to a successful long-term recovery. Stage 3 is outpatient care. Here, the goal is to move the patient to self-sufficiency, with more and more of the governing functions being carried out by the patient. At each stage, attention needs to be given to a wide range of activities, including providing security, providing essential services, promoting good governance, and promoting economic development.

COIN is primarily associated with the U.S. military involvement in Iraq and Afghanistan following the removal of Saddam Hussein. In 2016 US Special Forces and advisors were dispatched to Yemen in what was termed a short-term military operation where they would support Arab forces fighting al-Qaeda in the Arabian Peninsula. The United States did have a military presence in Yemen until 2014 when they were removed after the pro-U.S. government collapsed. Two major critiques of COIN have emerged. The first has to do with the prerequisites for COIN success, most notably the character of the host government. COIN seeks to partner with the government-in-power to restore or enhance its legitimacy so that the insurgent's military capability will be severely diminished and it will become isolated from the public who will turn their loyalty to the government. As Iraq and Afghanistan demonstrated, not all local partners are in a position to capitalize on the successes of COIN. Rather than see their legitimacy grow the result is a growing political void that invites a renewed insurgency.

A second question focuses on COIN's internal logic. According to some analysts, COIN has three main strategic goals: force protection, distinguishing between combatants and noncombatants, and the physical destruction of insurgents. But, at any one time it is only capable of achieving two of them.[11] In the case of the U.S. surge in Iraq, COIN focused on protecting U.S. forces and civilians by distinguishing between them and enemy combatants but did so at the expense of destroying the insurgents. In Afghanistan COIN focused on discriminating between civilians and enemy combatants and physically destroying the insurgents at the cost of increasing the risks faced by U.S. troops.

Counterterrorism   Terrorism is violence employed for the purpose of political intimidation. Where counterinsurgency strategies focus on winning the collective "hearts and minds" of the public, military-oriented antiterrorism policies focus on taking out individual leaders and crippling terrorist organizations. The weapon of choice in combatting terrorism is air power. It is valued for its ability to strike deep behind enemy lines at significant targets with little warning and minimal loss of American lives. It has been criticized for being conducted with too little oversight from civilian leaders (including the president) and for resulting in the deaths of innocent civilians. Since mid-2015 air strikes against ISIS economic targets such as oil wells, tanker trucks, oil pipelines, and buildings within which cash is stored are major targets of U.S. air power. In 2016 it was estimated that production of oil had fallen by 30 percent, and revenues from oil sales were down some 50 percent. Moreover ISIS had lost 47 percent of its territory in Iraq and 20 percent in Syria. Its fighting force fell from thirty-three thousand in 2015 to eighteen thousand to twenty-two thousand in mid-2016.

In 2016 the Obama administration released its report on civilian casualties from drone strikes. It concluded that from 2009 to 2015, 473 drone strikes outside of war zones (Syria, Afghanistan, and Pakistan) had killed 2,372–2,581 combatants and around 64–116 civilians. These drone attacks took place in Pakistan, Libya, Somalia, and Yemen. The administration's figures were far lower than those calculated by human rights groups which placed them from as low as 207 to as high as 801.[12]

Prominent recent drone strikes include a November 2015 attack on ISIS targets in Libya. This marked the first time U.S. drones had struck at ISIS targets outside Iraq or Syria. Killed in this strike was Abu Nabil, an Iraqi and longtime member of al Qaeda operative and the ISIS leader in Libya. Also killed by a drone strike that month in Syria was "Jihadi John" who often appeared in ISIS videos dressed in black and wielding a knife at hostages. He was suspected in the beheadings of American journalists and the killing of an American aid worker. In May 2016 U.S. drones struck in Pakistan killing an important Taliban leader. It was the most aggressive military action undertaken by the United States in Pakistan since the raid that killed Osama bin Laden and was carried out without the knowledge of Pakistan. One of the most controversial drone strikes occurred in 2011 and involved the killing of an al Qaeda leader Anwar al-Aulaqi who was linked to the attempted 2009 Christmas Day bombing of a Detroit-bound airliner. He was the first American citizen added to the list of terrorist suspects the Central Intelligence Agency (CIA) was permitted to kill.

Small Wars by Other Means

We routinely think about wars as being fought by armies. There are, however, other instances—often referred to as grey zones—where adversaries engage in hostile actions that fall just below the level of overt military conflict. One example in which military power is used is the contest of wills being played out in the South China Sea between the U.S. and Chinese air forces and navies that we have already highlighted in the dateline section of chapter 2. Two types of grey zone conflicts not involving the use of military power are covert action and cyber warfare. As its name implies, **covert action** is conducted in secret. It seeks results by altering the internal balance of power in a foreign state. No instrument of foreign policy is more controversial or difficult to control. As the Tower Commission that investigated the Iran-Contra Affair during the Reagan administration stated in its report, "Covert action places a great strain on the process of decision making in a free society."[13] **Cyber warfare** refers to attacks on computers or information networks.

Cold War Covert Action

In popular usage, covert action is all but synonymous with secret paramilitary operations. This is not the case. A review of U.S. Cold War covert action shows that at least five different forms of covert action have been employed by the United States.[14] The most common form of covert action has been and remains providing clandestine support for individuals and organizations. This support takes many forms (financial, technical, or training) and can be directed at many targets (politicians, labor leaders, journalists, unions, political parties, church groups, or professional associations). Clandestine support was the major focus of CIA efforts in France, Italy, and West Germany in the immediate post–World War II era.[15] A widely publicized case of CIA clandestine support outside Europe involved efforts to block the election of Salvador Allende in Chile by training anticommunist organizers among Chilean peasants and slum dwellers.[16]

Another form of clandestine support is the provision of security assistance and intelligence training to foreign governments. A controversial example of such a training program was "Project X." This was a U.S. military training program that included instruction on clandestine activity against domestic political adversaries. In 1999 President Bill Clinton expressed regret for U.S. support of the Guatemalan military during that country's thirty-six-year civil war after an independent commission concluded that the U.S.-backed forces were responsible for the vast majority of the human rights abuses that occurred during that conflict.

A second category of covert action is propaganda. The CIA has used a number of techniques for dispensing its propaganda including radio broadcasts and placing stories in newspapers. One of the most primitive involved using loaded balloons with an assortment of leaflets, pamphlets, and newspapers in an effort to exploit dissatisfaction and increase internal unrest in China in the early Cold War era.[17]

A third category of covert action involves economic operations. According to one account, comparatively few economic operations have been undertaken by the CIA, and they have not been very successful.[18] Economic operations were an integral part of the CIA's efforts to stop Salvador Allende. The goal was "to make the economy scream." The most persistent target of CIA covert economic operations was Fidel Castro's Cuba. One of the most notorious programs is Operation Mongoose.[19] It succeeded in getting European shippers to turn down Cuban delivery orders and sabotaging British buses destined for Cuba. Other anti-Castro economic covert action programs included an effort at weather modification against Cuba's sugar crop and infecting Cuban pig herds with an African swine flu virus.

The fourth category of covert action involves **paramilitary** undertakings which are defined as furnishing covert military assistance and guidance to unconventional and conventional foreign forces and organizations. It is argued to be a highly valuable "third option" between sending in the marines and doing nothing.[20] Initially, paramilitary operations were targeted against the Soviet Union and its Eastern European satellite states.[21] Almost uniformly, they were failures. Numbered among them was an effort to establish an underground apparatus for espionage and revolution in Poland. Polish secret service co-opted the network and used it to acquire gold and capture anticommunist Poles.

More significant CIA paramilitary operations took place in the Third World. In 1953, the United States and Great Britain undertook a joint venture, Operation AJAX, to bring down the government of Iranian prime minister Mohammed Mossadeq and return the shah to power.[22] In 1954 the CIA helped bring down the government of Jacobo Arbenz in Guatemala.[23] As was the case with Iran, the paramilitary operation itself was relatively small in scale, and it was preceded by a propaganda campaign designed to frighten Arbenz into fleeing the country.

As the 1950s ended, so too did the string of CIA successes. In 1958, it supported an unsuccessful coup against President Sukarno of Indonesia. A still greater embarrassment came in 1961 with the Bay of Pigs invasion of Cuba. A brigade of some fifteen hundred Cuban exiles was put ashore in Cuba, where they were to link up with Cuban opposition forces and topple the Castro regime. Everything went wrong. On the first day of the invasion, two of the four supplies and ammunition ships were sunk, and the other two fled. On the second day, the brigade was surrounded by twenty thousand well-armed and loyal Cuban soldiers. On the third day, the twelve hundred surviving members of the invasion force surrendered. Almost two years later, most were released in exchange for $53 million in food and drugs.

The Bay of Pigs put a temporary dent in Washington's fascination with paramilitary covert action programs, but it did not put an end to it. By the mid-1970s, a controversial covert paramilitary operation was under way in Angola.[24] In January 1975 a transitional coalition government in Angola was formed uniting rival pro-independence groups that was to rule until October elections. After this agreement was reached the CIA secretly paid the pro-U.S. National Front for the Liberation of Angola (FNLA) to attack the Soviet supported Popular Movement for the Liberation of Angola (MPLA). Contrary to what was actually taking place in Angola, the CIA maintained that no U.S. personnel were directly involved in the fighting or that it was directly supplying the FNLA with funds. Congress reacted by passing the Tunney Amendment in 1975 and the Clark Amendment in 1976 that attempted to cut off all government spending in Angola.

The most controversial of the CIA's paramilitary programs in the 1980s was its Nicaraguan operation. The impetus for CIA involvement in Nicaragua lay with evidence collected in the late 1970s that the Nicaraguan Sandinista government was increasing its shipments of arms to El Salvadoran rebels, intensifying pressure on domestic opposition forces, and becoming the site of a substantial Cuban-backed military buildup. Both the Carter and Reagan administrations responded to these events with economic sanctions that had little impact. In 1981 the Reagan administration authorized a $19.5 million program of covert action to stop the flow of arms to El Salvador. By November 1981 the program's goals had expanded to include creating an anti-Sandinista force (the Contras) that might effectively challenge the "Cuban support structure in Nicaragua."[25]

The CIA's paramilitary program in Nicaragua is credited with having slowed down the shipment of arms to El Salvador and with hampering Sandinista offenses in 1983 and 1984. It was also the object of intense criticism. Congress became concerned that the scope of the CIA's program exceeded that which it had authorized. As a result, in 1982 and 1984, it passed Boland Amendments which forbade funding the Contras for the purpose of overthrowing the Nicaraguan government

The largest Third World paramilitary Cold War covert operation program run by the CIA was in Afghanistan. In FY 1985, the CIA spent about $250 million or more than 80 percent of its covert action budget, helping the Afghan guerrillas evict Soviet forces. An internal CIA study carried out in 2012–13 concluded that with the exception of Afghanistan covert CIA training and arms transfers insurgents only succeeded if Americans were on the ground working with foreign forces in combat zones. Even then the operation was not without its long-term costs. After defeating the Russian forces, U.S. weapons remained in Afghanistan and came under the control of the Taliban.

A final form of covert action involves the assassination of foreign leaders. The most thorough investigation into U.S. involvements in assassination plots was carried out by the Church Committee. It investigated five cases of alleged U.S. involvement: (1) Cuba: Fidel Castro, (2) Congo (Zaire): Patrice Lumumba, (3) Dominican Republic: Rafael Trujillo, (4) Chile: René Schneider, and (5) South Vietnam: Ngo Dinh Diem.

The committee concluded that only the Castro and Lumumba cases involved plots conceived by the United States to kill foreign leaders. It found concrete evidence of at least eight CIA plots to assassinate Fidel Castro between 1960 and 1965. One former CIA official characterized these efforts as ranging from "the vague to the weird."[26] Proposed assassination devices included arranging an "accident," poison cigars, poison pills, poison pens, placing deadly bacterial powder in Castro's scuba-diving suit, and rigging a seashell to explode while Castro was scuba diving.

In 1972, following the kidnapping and assassination of Chilean General René Schneider, Director of Central Intelligence Richard Helms issued a directive banning assassinations.[27] This ban has since been included in the presidential executive orders. Following the terrorist attacks on the World Trade Center and the Pentagon, President George W. Bush asserted that the ban on assassinations did not prohibit the United States from assassinating terrorists or acting in self-defense.

Post–Cold War Covert Action

Covert action programs did not disappear with the end of the Cold War. President-elect Barack Obama received a briefing on nine different types of on-going covert actions operations in over sixty countries including ones targeted on terrorism, proliferation, genocide, and drug trafficking. As president in 2013 he authorized a covert program to fund and assist Syrian rebels who sought to remove Bashar al-Assad from power. This program has not been without its problems. Training Syrian rebels has not gone well. Very few recruits joining the battle against Assad or ISIS distinguished themselves in combat. Evidence of blowback also emerged. It was discovered that some CIA weapons shipped into Jordan intended for the rebels were stolen by Jordanian intelligence officers and then sold on the black market for millions of dollars

The CIA ran a Cold War–style operation against Saddam Hussein between 1992 and 1996. The goal was to remove him from power by encouraging a military coup and reducing his control over Iraq's outlying regions, such as Iraqi Kurdistan. The cost of the program is estimated to have approached $100 million. Little was achieved. In June 1996 Saddam Hussein arrested and executed more than one hundred Iraqi dissidents and military officers associated with the CIA plan.

Historical Lesson

Into Afghanistan

The U.S. involvement in Afghanistan began following the 1979 Soviet invasion. Carried out by some 50,000 Soviet troops the Reagan administration saw the invasion as an attempt to increase Soviet influence in the region. Evidence suggests that the Soviet leadership was motivated more by fears of large-scale domestic unrest on its borders. The Soviets had planned on leaving the bulk of the fighting to the Afghan army but soon they were forced to increase their military presence to over 110,000 troops. Initially they used a conventional war strategy against the Mujahadin, a loose coalition of Islamic forces, but gradually embraced a search-and-destroy strategy in which they sought to establish control over strategic areas. The strategy failed and peace talks began in 1982 that led to the Soviet withdrawal in 1989 along with pledges by the United States and Soviet Union not to intervene into Afghanistan's internal affairs. One reason for the success of the Mujahadin was covert U.S. military support provided by the CIA that totaled $2.1 billion over the course of the fighting.

The Mujahadin refused to accept the peace agreement and continued fighting for control of the Afghan government. The communist Afghan government fell in 1992, but that did not bring peace. Fighting continued and in the midst of this fighting the Taliban, an Islamic fundamentalist movement, came into existence in 1994 with the support of neighboring Pakistan which saw the Taliban as an Afghan force that would protect its security interests in the ongoing civil war. By 1998 the Taliban had succeeded in taking control over most of Afghanistan. Initially the United States was not opposed to the Taliban because it saw them as capable of bringing order back to Afghanistan. This soon changed after the Taliban took control of the government and began trying to enforce a reform agenda designed to bring into existence an Islamic state and with al Qaeda's 1998 bombing of U.S. embassies in Kenya and Tanzania.

After the September 22, 2001, terrorist attacks President George W. Bush demanded that the Taliban expel Osama bin Laden and al Qaeda. The Taliban had given refuge to al Qaeda and bin Laden after it was expelled from Somalia in 1996. Founded in 1988, al Qaeda was no stranger to Afghanistan having fought against Soviet forces following its 1989 invasion of Afghanistan. The Taliban refused and on October 26 the

United States began air strikes against terrorist facilities and Afghan military targets.

Ground fighting was largely carried out by local forces known as the Northern Alliance whose efforts were guided and aided by CIA operatives. A small contingent of U.S. Special Operations forces entered Afghanistan shortly after fighting began and U.S. Marines arrived in November. At a December 10, 2011, news conference Deputy Secretary of Defense Wolfowitz stated, "We have accomplished one major objective, which is the defeat of the Taliban government." A few days earlier a Bonn Conference of Afghan opposition leaders selected Hamid Karzai to head the new Afghan Interim Authority. The UN announced the creation of an International Security Assistance Force that would be commanded by NATO to aid the new government in providing security.

From the outset the new Afghan government struggled to assert and build its legitimacy and expand its power. Taliban forces had fled to Pakistan and into rural areas of Afghanistan to evade capture. By the summer of 2003 they had begun to reassert their presence in Afghanistan. By July 2008 the situation in Afghanistan had deteriorated to the point that the chairman of the Joint Chiefs of Staff characterized it as "precarious and urgent"; 36,000 U.S. troops were present at the time. Three options were presented to Obama by the military: (1) 80,000 additional troops for a COIN operation to maximize success; (2) 40,000 with a medium likelihood of success; and (3) 20,000 to pursue a counterterrorism strategy. Taliban attacks continued as did the number of U.S. forces present. In February 2009 Obama announced that another 17,000

troops would be sent to Afghanistan. Some in the Obama administration saw the move as not likely to make an impact unless the Karzai government ended the widespread corruption and mismanagement of funds that had become so prevalent. A December 2009 briefing indicated that Taliban-sponsored incidents were now up 300 percent from 2007. That same month, President Barack Obama announced that an additional 30,000 U.S. troops would be sent to Afghanistan as part of a short-term surge operation.

Stating that "the tide of war is receding," in June 2011 Obama announced 10,000 U.S. troops would be withdrawn from Afghanistan by the end of the year and that another 23,000 would leave by summer 2012 leaving 65,000 troops there. A 2012 NATO Summit Conference decided to move forward with an exit strategy that would turn over command and control of combat mission to the Afghan army by mid-2013. On May 27, 2014, Obama announced that U.S. combat operations in Afghanistan would end in December. All but 9,800 troops would leave at this time. They would be tasked with training and counterinsurgency operations. All forces would be gone by the end of 2016, the end of his presidency.

Applying the Lesson

1. How similar were the U.S. and Soviet experiences in going into Afghanistan?

2. How much changed in U.S. military strategy between the initial entry into Afghanistan and the reentry?

3. What other options might the United States (and Soviets) have pursued to stabilize the situation in Afghanistan?

The most controversial post–Cold War covert action program became public on September 6, 2006, when George W. Bush acknowledged the existence of a renditions program in which suspected terrorists were kidnapped and taken to prisons located outside the United States, where they were subjected to what he referred to as "tough" but "safe and lawful and necessary" interrogation methods carried out by specially trained CIA officers. Others condemned them as torture. Interrogation techniques included feigned drowning ("waterboarding"), extreme isolation, slapping, sleep deprivation, semi-starvation, and light and sound bombardment.[28]

Public reports identified Thailand, Egypt, Indonesia, Poland, Romania, and Libya as among the countries to which suspects were taken. In August 2009 Obama announced that his administration would continue the renditions program but more closely monitor the interrogation methods used by assigning oversight responsibility to the National Security Council.

The Covert War against Osama bin Laden

Osama bin Laden was killed on May 2, 2011, in an attack carried out by U.S. Special Forces on his safe house in Abbottabad, Pakistan. Efforts to capture him predated the terrorist attacks of 9/11.[29] Perhaps the earliest involved the recruitment of a family-based team of Afghan tribal members who were given the task of trying to kidnap bin Laden so that he could be taken out of Afghanistan by U.S. Special Forces. The last effort before 9/11 involved the 1999 recruitment of a Northern Alliance guerrilla commander who had a long history of dealings with the CIA, many of which were not positive. In between these two operations, the CIA contacted and recruited at least three proxy forces in the region to try and capture or kill bin Laden. One plan involved using a Pakistani commando team that was trained, supported, and equipped by the CIA.

Formal authorization for the CIA to pursue bin Laden had been obtained in 1998, following the bombings of the American embassies in Kenya and Tanzania, when Bill Clinton signed the first of a series of findings consistent with the Hughes-Ryan Amendment. The original finding emphasized the goal of capturing bin Laden but permitted the use of lethal force. The first Memorandum of Notification expanded the covert operation to include using lethal force against bin Laden and his forces even when there was little chance of capturing him. The second expansion permitted the intelligence community to target his top aides. It is believed that fewer than ten individuals were identified and that they were to be captured or killed. The third expansion permitted the intelligence community to shoot down a private or civilian aircraft if bin Laden was a passenger.[30]

Cyber Warfare

The Defense Department now defines cyberspace as one of five distinct domains of warfare along with air, land, sea, and outer space. In its 2014 Worldwide Threat Assessment Report to Congress the intelligence community stated, "We assess that the likelihood of a destructive attack that deletes information or renders system inoperable will increase." It went on to note that "many countries are creating cyber defense institutions . . . we estimate that several of these will likely be responsible for offensive cyber operations as well." Among those singled out for special attention were Russia and China because of the scope of their cyber operations, Iran and North Korea because they were "unpredictable." The Defense Department's 2015 Cyber Strategy called for creating a 6,200-person Cyber Mission Force that will be divided into 133 teams by 2020.

Cyber threats are real. Since 2003 a series of coordinated attacks on U.S. computer systems have taken place. Referred to as "Titan Rain," these attacks are believed to be linked to China. Cyber-attacks have taken place against websites operated by the White House, Defense Department, Department of Homeland Security, and the Federal Aviation Administration. In spring 2007 Estonia was the target of a cyber-attack that effectively shut down its banking system. In 2008, prior to Russia's invasion of Georgia, Georgia government's websites were knocked offline. In both cases, the attacks were determined to have originated in Russia and were carried out by nationalistic hacker gangs. More recently, in 2016, the Obama administration accused Russia of stealing and publicizing emails from the Democratic National Committee and others in an attempt to influence the presidential election.

The United States has not just been the target of cyber-attacks it has also employed them. In late 2009 and early 2010 rather than engage in a military operation against Iran's Natanz nuclear facilities, cyber-attacks were launched against it. The Stuxnet computer virus that was central to the attack's success in 2010 caused 984 targeted centrifuges to spin wildly out of control while at the same time sending information back to those monitoring the system indicating that all was normal. While the United States and Israel were widely believed to be responsible for the attack neither country took official responsibility. Information made public as part of the 2013 NSA leaks revealed that in 2011 the United States carried out 231 offensive cyber operations, all of which were on a far smaller scale than the Stuxnet attack. In 2016 it was revealed that cyber-attacks were now being carried out against ISIS. Its goal is to disrupt communications and interrupt electronic transfers of money.

Three significant cases of nonuse of cyber-attack plans by the United States have also been revealed. First was the possibility of an offensive cyber warfare campaign against Libya in the early period of the uprising against Gaddafi. The plan was rejected for fear that it would set a precedent that might be used by Russia or China to justify a future offensive cyber-attack on their part. Second, the use of cyber weapons against the Syrian military and President Bashar-al Assad's communication networks was also raised. Obama rejected the option in part because Syria was not of sufficient strategic value to the United States to justify the risks such an attack could bring with it. Third, the Obama administration constructed a cyber-attack plan, Nitro-Zeus, whose mission it was to disable Iran's air defenses, communications systems, and crucial parts of its power grid if an arms control agreement with Iran was not reached.

Varying evaluations have been put forward of the 2010 cyber-attack on Natanz. Where once Israeli officials stated an Iranian nuclear capability was imminent after the cyber-attack they said it would not happen before 2015. Press accounts only two years later spoke of how quickly Iran was recovering from this attack even though the infected controllers were already on the economic embargo list put into place against Iran.

More generally, it has been argued that "the advantages of cyber war are swamped by the disadvantages if it cannot be kept under control."[31] The challenges of doing so are many ranging from the identifying the source of the attack, limiting the potential of vertical escalation from attacks on a specific target to attacks across a broad range of targets, and stopping horizontal escalation from military targets to civilian targets.

One line of thought that has emerged from studying offensive cyber war operations argues that it is imperative that laws-of-war standards govern military cyber operations in terms of the rationale for their use, the targets selected, and the principle of proportionality in conducting cyber operations. These principles lead them to argue against a first use of cyber weapons as well as avoiding using cyber weapons as an instrument of coercive diplomacy. They argue for limiting the use of cyber weapons against military targets during armed conflict or in retaliation for cyber-attacks as part of a strategy of deterrence.[32]

Conventional, Cyber, and WMD Arms Control

Nuclear weapons receive most of the attention when arms control is discussed, but they are not the only proliferation problem facing policy makers today. The proliferation of chemical and biological weapons (along with the missile delivery systems that they use) and conventional weapons has also been the subject of arms control efforts. Collectively, chemical, biological, and nuclear weapons are referred to as **weapons of mass destruction** (WMD).

Chemical and Biological Weapons

Chemical and biological weapons may be constructed around a number of different agents. Among the most significant chemical agents are mustard gas, which causes blistering over the entire body, blindness, and death by respiratory failure, and sarin, which interrupts the flow of oxygen to cells. Significant biological agents and toxins include anthrax, which causes pneumonia and organ failure; ricin, which attacks the circulatory system; and smallpox, which many consider the most deadly biological agent.

The modern historical record documenting the use of chemical and biological weapons dates to World War I when Germany used chemical weapons. Saddam Hussein employed chemical weapons, principally sarin and mustard gas, against Iran in the Iran-Iraq War as early as 1983. He then used poison gas and possibly anthrax against Kurds in northern Iraq to solidify his hold on power following that war. Evidence began to mount in late 2013 that Syria had used chemical weapons against rebel groups seeking to overthrow the government. At the time Syria had one of the world's largest stockpiles of chemical weapons. It began to acquire them in large numbers in the 1970s and 1980s to offset Israel's superior strength in conventional weapons. At the turn of the century,

Syria was one of an estimated about sixteen countries to have chemical weapons programs. Another twelve countries were believed to have offensive biological weapons programs.

Commonly discussed means for the delivery of WMD include dispersal from an aircraft or drone and from artillery shells, rockets, ballistic missiles, and cruise missiles. Of most concern are ballistic and cruise missiles. With few exceptions, countries in possession of, or seeking, such weapons all have ballistic missiles. Another fifteen countries have ballistic missiles but are not seeking WMD. The number of countries with cruise missiles is even greater. Some eighty countries have them, and eighteen countries make them.

The military value of chemical and biological weapons is disputed. For example, sarin is most effective against large concentrations of troops but is not very useful for fighting insurgent forces in close contact situations. A danger also exists that if winds change direction government forces and their supporters might be affected. At the same time it is recognized that the use of chemical weapons could have a devastating psychological impact on rebel forces and might succeed in denying opposition forces access to large areas due to the long-lasting effects of the poisons used. Biological weapons face similar problems. Microbes used for biological weapons often lose their effectiveness when exposed to sunlight, water, and other natural elements. They are also difficult to use militarily because of the challenges involved in spreading them out over large areas.

International treaties are in place for both chemical and biological weapons. The Chemical Weapons Convention outlaws the production, stockpiling, and use of chemical weapons. The United States signed and ratified the treaty which entered into force in 1997. With over thirty-five thousand tons of declared chemical weapons stockpiled, the United States had the second largest quantity of chemical weapons to destroy. April 2012 was set as the destruction target but this date was not met. As of January 2012 it had destroyed 90 percent of its chemical weapons. A Biological Weapons Convention also exists but the United States has not signed it. The Obama administration followed the path pursued by the Bush administration to support a more limited global biological weapons monitoring system.

Recovering Loose WMD Material

An additional serious arms control problem in the area of WMD involves preventing vulnerable WMD material from falling into the hands of terrorists, rogue governments, or criminals. The challenge is immense. In Iraq alone, from 2004 to early 2011, the United States recovered 4,996 discarded chemical weapons. Not all were lethal in their present condition. Some were found abandoned. Others were secretly purchased by the CIA in 2005–2006 as part of Operation Avarice. All were manufactured in the 1980s and early 1990s. They were destroyed by open air detonation.

At the global level following his 2009 address in Prague where he highlighted the dangers posed by unsecure nuclear material, President Obama organized a series of Nuclear Security Summits to address this problem. The first took place in

2010. The fourth, and probably last one, took place in 2016. The focus of these discussions was on increasing security around vulnerable military and civilian nuclear material, and how to better deal with the potential problem of nuclear terrorism. At that time it was estimated that twenty-four countries held nearly two thousand tons of nuclear weapons grade material. Twenty countries had atomic stockpile facilities or nuclear power plants judged to be vulnerable to cyber-attacks.[33] The largest amount of nuclear grade material is held in Russia which declined to attend the meeting due to worsening relations with the United States. In October, 2016, as U.S.-Russian relations worsened over Syria, Russia announced that it was suspending its participation in a 2000 agreement to dispose of surplus weapons-grade plutonium. Among the conditions Russia placed for resuming its participation were ending economic sanctions put in place after its annexation of Crimea , the deployment of NATO troops in the Baltics, and repeal of the Magnistsky Act which targeted Russian officials for their violation of human rights.

Cyberspace

While much of the discussion to date has been over questions of cyber warfare, the political contest to establish rules for the use of cyberspace is also under way.[34] For some, cyberspace is a region best seen as divided among states. It will be an area around which borders will be built and national legal and political rules will apply. For others cyberspace is and should remain a global commons to which all should have equal access and to which internationally agreed upon rules and norms should apply.

At present the policy debate between these two perspectives centers on calls for a cyber security treaty. In 2011 Russia and China jointly proposed a code of conduct among cyber-powers. The stated goal was to keep cyberspace from becoming a battleground and heading of a cyber-arms race. The United States objected citing a provision which asserted it was the right of states to protect their information space from attacks and sabotage on the grounds that this statement provided grounds for legitimizing censorship and curbing free speech. In 2014 the State Department's Office for Cyber Issues joined the discussion by calling for developing a set of confidence-building measures that would promote security in cyberspace and reduce the incentives for using it as a platform for attacks.[35]

The complexity and newness of cyberspace as an arms control issue have led many to call for changing the focus of negotiations away from cyberspace security issues to the problem of curbing cyber-crime. Others argue that the Chemical Weapons Convention might serve as a model for a cyber-security treaty.[36] According to its terms each country is responsible for enforcing the treaty's terms within its borders. The agreement also established an international office to provide help during crises.

Conventional Weapons

Several different types of conventional weapons exist. A commonly used classification distinguishes between heavy weapons system (such as missiles, tanks, attack helicopters, advanced artillery systems); small weapons (pistols and rifles that can be carried by one person); light weapons (heavy machine guns and anti-tank and antiaircraft munitions that are carried by two or more people or transported in light vehicles); cluster bombs (air or ground launched weapons that release smaller munitions); and land mines (an explosive device that his hidden underground and activated when stepped upon). Each of these has been subject to arms control efforts and has met with limited success.

Traditionally, efforts to curb conventional weapons proliferation have focused on restricting the sale or transfer of major weapons systems from one state to another. For a brief period of time, it appeared that conventional arms transfers were becoming less pronounced in world politics. Between 1989 and 1991, worldwide sales fell 53 percent and U.S. sales fell almost 34 percent. This downward trend has since been reversed. The volume of major weapons sold during 2011–15 was 14 percent higher than in the 2006–10 period. The United States was the largest exporter of weapons accounting for 33 percent of the total

The major international initiative in place to curb conventional proliferation is UN Arms Transfer Register.[37] It identifies seven different categories of heavy conventional weapons and countries are requested to submit an annual statement of the number of these items it exported or imported during the previous year. The goal is to bring a heightened degree of transparency to the arms transfer process and thereby reduce the military advantages that arms transfers bring to states. Some fear, however, that it may have the unintended effect of legitimizing those arms transfers that are registered.

In 2001 a voluntary international agreement was reached that was designed to stop the international trade in small arms. The United States blocked efforts to include regulations on civilian ownership of military weapons and to restrict small arms trade to rebel movements. It continued to oppose such an agreement even when after seven years of negotiation it finally produced a treaty in 2013 that covered trade in heavy, small, and light conventional weapons. Among its key features was a prohibition on selling weapons to countries that were engaged in genocide, war crimes, or crimes against humanity. While the United States voted for the treaty at the UN it raised objections that almost scuttled the talks insisting that any agreement "not impose any new requirements on the U.S. domestic trade in firearms or on U.S. exporters."

In 2008 ninety-four countries signed the Convention on Cluster Munitions that banned the production, stockpiling, transfer and use of cluster munitions. That agreement came into effect in 2010. The United States opposed the agreement maintaining that a separate treaty on cluster munitions was not needed; that it should be included in the broader conventional arms trade treaty then under discussion. Moreover, the United States argued that the development of "smart" munitions which contained automatic self-destruct capabilities had not only drastically reduced the scope of the problem but that a treaty banning their use was dangerous to civilians.

The Obama administration also continued the existing policy of not signing the 1997 Ottawa Treaty banning the use, prosecution, stockpiling, or transfer of antipersonnel landmines although it did send an observer to the 2009 Review Conference. The military has long opposed the ban arguing that landmines are necessary to ensure the protection of U.S. forces abroad. Some one million landmines remain in place along the North-South Korean border. Along with the United States, China, Russia, India, and Israel are the most prominent countries not to have signed the treaty.

Counterproliferation

One final arms control and disarmament strategy we will introduce is **counterproliferation**. Unlike the other approaches outlined here that rely heavily on diplomacy to achieve its ends counterproliferation historically had involved the use of military force to deter countries from acquiring and using WMD against the United States. Today one can extend the concept to include cyber-attacks such as the Stuxnet. Reports suggest that the Obama administration had developed a cyber-attack plan (Nitro Zeus) to be implemented against Iran should diplomacy fail to halt its nuclear program.[38]

Proponents of counterproliferation start from the premise that nonproliferation efforts have failed. It is not a new strategy but one that continues to evolve and is controversial.[39] Its principal targets are smaller states such as Iran and North Korea. Few historical examples of counterproliferation exist.[40] The most frequently cited are Israel's 1981 raid on Iraq's Osiraq nuclear reactor, the bombing of Iraq's unconventional weapons during the first phase of Operation Desert Storm in 1991, and U.S. cruise missile attacks on the al Shifa pharmaceutical plant in Sudan in 1998. Because the historical evidence is so limited strategists have turned to war games and simulations to help them judge the potential value of a specific counterproliferation strike. A 2012 Pentagon assessment based on a two-week war game that assumed Israel would attack four major Iranian nuclear sites concluded it would lead to a wide regional war.

Over the Horizon: The Future of COIN

For the better part of a decade COIN was the principal strategy embraced by the U.S. military. One of the most important decisions President Trump will make is whether to continue to give COIN this priority or to put U.S. military strategy and force composition back on a more traditional conventional war footing. As the Obama administration ended signs pointed to such a change taking place. The military's national security assessments budget requests for FY 2017 highlighted the dangers posed by "high end adversaries," namely, Russia and China. In 2016 General Mark Milley, the Army chief of staff, spoke to the need to move away from COIN saying that the emphasis on COIN had taken away from the Army's ability to fight a land war against more traditional military adversaries. "A major in the Army knows nothing but fighting terrorists and guerrilla . . . as we get to higher end threats, our skills have atrophied." There has been, he argued, "a loss of muscle memory."

Challenges to COIN come not only from those favoring a more conventional threat-oriented military establishment but also from those who question the ability of COIN to successfully address insurgent threats such as those faced in Iraq, Afghanistan, and more recently Syria. One line of criticism points to its lack of fit with the American national style of foreign policy that we discussed in chapter 2. Among the key characteristics of the American national style are a firm dividing line between war and peace, impatience, and an engineering approach to creating policy. COIN does not fit this profile. It is protracted warfare with no clear endpoint of victory or defeat. Critics also argue that COIN fashioned a strategy based on national solutions for local problems and that it is too expensive.

COIN is not without its defenders. They see many of the problems critics identify as not inherent in the concept of counterinsurgency warfare but as a product of a military culture that was slow to embrace the idea and then did so with little enthusiasm, and policy makers who made military decisions on going to war without plans that follow its conclusion. In the final analysis, some argue "counterinsurgency is sometime the least bad option available."[41]

Critical Thinking Questions

1. How can insurgents be best stopped from acquiring weapons?
2. What types of actions are best taken covertly and what actions should never be taken covertly?

3. What is the most likely cause of a U.S. small war in the next five years and in the next ten years?

Key Terms

casus belli, 324
counterinsurgency, 324
counterproliferation, 341
covert action, 324
cyber warfare, 324
hybrid warfare, 327

paramilitary, 328
peacekeeping, 325
stability operations, 326
weapons of mass destruction, 337
windows of fear, 324
windows of opportunity, 324

Further Reading

Thomas Barnet, *The Pentagon's New Map: War and Peace in the Twenty-First Century* (New York: Berkley Books, 2004).
The author argues that a new set of rules govern warfare today and examines the likely future locations of international conflicts, especially as they relate to the spread of globalization.
Richard Betts, *American Force* (New York: Columbia University Press, 2012).
Betts believes that policy makers have failed to recognize that with the end of the Cold War the strategic importance and military force in American foreign policy has been altered. He calls for greater caution and restraint in its use.

Lawrence Cavaiola, David Gompert, and Martin Libicki., "Cyber House Rules: On War, Retaliation, and Escalation," *Survival* 57 (March 2015), 81–104.

The authors argue that the advantages of cyber war are far outweighed by the disadvantages if it is not kept under control, something they assert is unclear. They identify and assess three basic offensive options: minimum deterrence, equivalence, and superiority.

Lawrence Freedman, "Ukraine and the Art of Limited War," *Survival* 25 (November 2014), 7–38.

In this work Freedman examines the intensification of the Ukraine crisis and the strategic lessons that can be drawn from it. It is one of a series he authored. Other focal points were crisis management and the strategy of exhaustion.

John Nagl, *Learning to Eat Soup with a Knife: Counterinsurgency Lessons from Malaya and Vietnam* (Chicago, IL: University of Chicago Press, 2005).

This book is frequently cited by proponents of counterinsurgency warfare. Its core argument is that to succeed the military must foster a spirit of innovation within its organizational culture.

Michael O'Hanlon, *The Future of Land Warfare* (Washington, DC: Brookings, 2015).

The author argues we should not be too confident that the era of land warfare is over. To this end he examines a series of possible scenarios in which land warfare might play a significant role ranging from deterring Russia and China to civil strife in Central American and Africa to humanitarian disaster relief.

Pavel Podvig, "Blurring the Line Between Nuclear and Nonnuclear Weapons," *Bulletin of the Atomic Scientists* 72 (2016), 145–49.

The decreased role of nuclear weapons in world politics has led to efforts to give strategic systems a useful role to play in conventional conflicts by allowing them to carry nonnuclear warheads. This article argues that this blurring of the line creates an increased risk of accidental nuclear war.

John Prados, *President's Secret Wars: CIA and Pentagon Covert Operations since World War II* (New York: William Morrow, 1986).

This book provides a thorough overview of covert operations through the Cold War and the politics surrounding them.

Notes

1 Azam Ahhmed and Joseph Goldstein, "Taliban Gains Pull U.S. Units Back Into Fight," *New York Times,* April 30, 2015, A1.

2 Matthew Kroenig and Barry Pavel, "How to Deter Terrorism," *Washington Quarterly* 35 (2012), 21–36.

3 Thomas G. Weiss, "Triage: Humanitarian Interventions in a New Era," *World Policy Journal* 11 (1994), 59–66.

4 Ted Galen Carpenter, "Foreign Policy Peril: Somalia Set a Dangerous Precedent," *USA Today,* May 1993, 13.

5 Sean McFate, "U.S. Africa Command: A New Strategic Paradigm?" *Military Review* 88 (2008), 10–21.

6 On the strategy of exhaustion, see Lawrence Freedman, "Ukraine and the Art of Exhaustion," *Survival* 57:5 (2015), 77–106.

7 Frank Hoffman, *Conflict in the 21st Century: The Rise of Hybrid Wars* (Arlington, VA: Potomac Institute, 2007), 14, http://www.potomacinstitute.org/images/stories/publications/potomac_hybridwar_0108.pdf.

8 *Hybrid Threats,* U.S. Army Training Circular, November 2010, http://www.benning.army.mil/mssp/security%20topics/Potential%20Adversaries/content/pdf/tc7_100.pdf.

9 Lawrence Freedman, "Ukraine and the Art of Limited War," *Survival* 56:6 (2015), 7–38.

10 *Counterinsurgency.* Field Manual 3–24, Department of the Army, December 2006.

[11] Lorenzo Zambernardi, "Counterinsurgency's Impossible Trilemma," *Washington Quarterly* 33 (2010), 21–34.

[12] Scott Shane, "Drone Strike Data Reveals Limits of Fighting Terrorists From Sky," *New York Times,* July 4, 2016, A1.

[13] The President's Special Review Board, *The Tower Commission Report* (New York: Bantam, 1987), 15.

[14] *Foreign Affairs* 93 (July 2014) presented a series of retrospective commentaries on Cold War covert actions in Bangladesh, Iran, Congo, and Chile.

[15] Jeffrey Richelson, *The U.S. Intelligence Community* (Cambridge, MA: Ballinger, 1985), 228–29.

[16] Morton Halperin, Jerry Berman, Robert Borosage, and Christine Mwarwick, *The Lawless State* (New York: Penguin, 1976), 15–29.

[17] Victor Marchetti and John Marks, *The CIA and the Cult of Intelligence,* (New York: Knopf, 1974), 167.

[18] Ibid., 72; Richelson, *The U.S. Intelligence Community*, 230–31. Steven Metz, "New Challenges and Old Concepts: Understanding 21st Century Insurgency," *Parameters* 37 (Winter 2007/2008), 20–32.

[19] Warren Hinckle and William Turner, *The Fish Is Red: The Story of the Secret War against Castro* (New York: Harper & Row, 1982).

[20] Theodore G. Shackley, *The Third Option: An American View of Counterinsurgency Operations* (New York: Reader's Digest Press, 1981).

[21] Trevor Barnes, "The Secret Cold War: The CIA and American Foreign Policy in Europe: 1946–1956," *Historical Journal* 24:25 (1981, 1982), 399–415, 649–70.

[22] Ray S. Cline, *Secrets, Spies and Scholars: The Essential CIA* (Washington, DC: Acropolis, 1970), 132–33; Barry Rubin, *Paved with Good Intentions: The American Experience and Iran* (New York: Penguin, 1981), chapter 3.

[23] Richard H. Immerman, *The CIA in Guatemala: The Foreign Policy of Intervention* (Austin: University of Texas Press, 1982).

[24] John Stockwell, *In Search of Enemies: A CIA Story* (New York: W. W. Norton, 1978).

[25] Christopher Dickey, "Central America: From Quagmire to Cauldron," *Foreign Affairs* 62 (1984), 669.

[26] Harry Rositzke, *The CIA's Secret Operations*, (New York: Readers Digest Press, 1977), 97.

[27] Bob Woodward, *Obama's War* (New York: Simon & Schuster, 2010), 50–55.

[28] Dan Eggen and Dafna Linzer, "Secret World of Detainees Grows More Public," *The Washington Post*, September 7, 2006, A18; Dana Priest, "Officials Relieved Secret Is Shared," *The Washington Post*, September 7, 2006, A17.

[29] Information in this section is drawn from various newspaper accounts. See Barton Gellman, "Broad Effort Launched After '98 Attacks," *The Washington Post*, December 19, 2001, A1; "Struggles Inside the Government Define Campaign," *The Washington Post*, December 20, 2001, A1; Bob Woodward and Thomas Ricks, "U.S. Was Foiled Multiple Times in Efforts to Capture bin Laden or Have Him Killed," *The Washington Post*, October 3, 2001, A1; Bob Woodward, "CIA Paid Afghans to Track bin Laden," *The Washington Post*, December 23, 2001, A1; Steve Coll, *Ghost Wars* (New York: Penguin, 2004).

[30] For critical accounts of the attempt to capture bin Laden, see Richard Clarke, *Against All Enemies* (New York: The Free Press, 2004); Anonymous, *Imperial Hubris* (Washington, DC: Brassey's, 2004).

[31] Lawrence Cavaiola, David Gompert, and Martin Libiki, "Cyber House Rules: On War, Escalation and Retaliation," *Survival* 57:1 (2015), 81–104.

[32] David C. Gompert and Martin Libicki, "Waging Cyber War the American Way," *Survival* 57:4 (2015), 7–28.

[33] See NTI Nuclear Security Index, http://ntiindex.org/data-results/country-profiles/?index=theft.

[34] Louise Arimatsu, A Treaty for Governing Cyber-Weapons, 2012, http://www.ccdcoe.org/publications/2012proceedings/2_3_Arimatsu_ATreatyForGoverningCyber-Weapons.pdf.

[35] For a discussion of cyber confidence control, see Paul Meyer, "Cyber-Security through Arms Control," *RUSI Journal* 156 (2011), 22–27.

[36] Kenneth Geers, "Cyber Weapons Convention," *Computer Law and Security Review* 26 (2010), 547–51.

[37] Edward J. Laurance, "Conventional Arms: Rationales and Prospects for Compliance and Effectiveness," *Washington Quarterly* 16 (1993), 163–72.

[38] David Sanger and Mark Mazzetti, "U.S. Drew Up Cyberattack Plan in Case Iran Nuclear Dispute Lead to Conflict," *New York Times*, February 17, 2016, A5.

[39] Henry Sokolski, "Mission Impossible," *Bulletin of the Atomic Scientists*, March/April 2001, 63–68.

[40] Robert Luttwak, "Nonproliferation and the Use of Force," in Jane Nolan, Bernard Finel, and Bryan Finlay (eds.), *Ultimate Security* (New York: The Century Foundation Press, 2003), 75–106.

[41] The quote is from John Nagl, "COIN Fights: A Response to Etzioni," *Small Wars and Insurgencies* 26 (2015), 379. For the debate over COIN, see Amatai Etzioni, "COIN: A Study of Strategic Illusion," *Small Wars & Insurgencies* 26:3 (2015), 345–76; Karl Eikenberry, "The Limits of Counterinsurgency Doctrine in Afghanistan," *Foreign Affairs,"* 92:5 (2013), 59–74; John Nagl, *Knife Fights* (New York: Penguin, 2014); and Gian Gentile, *Wrong Turn* (New York: Free Press, 2013).

14 Alternative Futures

Dateline: Obama Visits Cuba

On December 14, 2014, President Barack Obama announced that he was restoring full diplomatic relations with Cuba. Diplomatic relations were broken off by Dwight Eisenhower in January 1961—seven months before Obama was born. Obama would meet with Cuban president Raul Castro in March 2016. He was the first president to visit Cuba in eighty-eight years. Calvin Coolidge visited in 1928 arriving on a battleship to address a meeting of Western Hemisphere leaders. Coolidge sought to calm their anger with U.S. foreign policy. He spoke of "an attitude of peace and goodwill" in the hemisphere but did not address Cuba's unhappiness with the 1901 Platt Amendment which set the terms by which the United States would end its military presence in Cuba.

Obama's announcement came as a surprise. He was on record as favoring reestablishing diplomatic relations with Cuba but little had come of it. Now, with only two years left in his presidency and with Republicans having won control of Congress in the November 2014 election, it was not expected to happen. What was unknown at the time of the announcement was that for the past eighteen months secret negotiations had been taking place between the United

States and Cuba. Nine meetings, most of them in Canada, took place beginning in June 2013.

Numerous stumbling blocks stood in the way of reestablishing diplomatic relations. One was the release of USAID contractor Alan Gross who had been imprisoned in Cuba since 2009 and was serving a fifteen-year sentence for trying to covertly bring Internet and satellite communications connections into Cuba. Cuban officials claimed he was trying to incite a "Cuban Spring." Now in declining health many in Congress identified his release as being in the national interest. For its part Cuba sought the release of three Cubans held in the United States on espionage charges since 1998. In 2012 Cuba had offered to release Gross in return for the United States releasing the three Cubans. The United States rejected that deal.

This impasse was broken in October 2014 when Pope Francis wrote a letter to Obama and Raul Castro urging them to resolve their differences on the prisoner exchange. The Vatican then hosted a meeting between the U.S. and Cuban delegations. On the day Obama made his announcement Cuba released Gross as a "humanitarian" gesture of goodwill. There followed an exchange of spies. The United States released the three Cubans, and Cuba released a Cuban national to the United States whom it had held in prison for almost twenty years. Later Cuba released an additional fifty-three political prisoners from a list of names provided by the United States.

After the announcement that diplomatic relations would be resumed a series of official meetings were held between U.S. and Cuban officials. The first was held in January 2015 and focused on immigration issues with Cuba calling for an end to the policy which provided U.S. citizenship to any Cuban who reached U.S. soil. The United States stated that this policy would continue and called upon Cuba to provide greater freedom of speech and assembly to its citizens. Shortly after this meeting took place Raul Castro called for the United States to return the Guantanamo Naval Base to Cuba. The United States had obtained use of the naval base in 1903 when it signed an open-ended agreement with the Cuban government. Obama responded that this was out of the question.

A second meeting was held in February 2015 with the major issue of contention being Cuba's status as a sponsor of international terrorism. A third meeting was held in Havana in March 2015. It ended abruptly after one day and without any public statement being made by either side. The goal had been to have an agreement in place for officially reopening the embassies by the April 2015 Summit of the Americas conference where Obama and Castro planned to meet. This marked the first time a representative of Cuba participated in the meetings since its founding in 1994.

Momentum to normalizing relations continued in spite of this last meeting. In April 2015 Obama announced he planned to remove Cuba from the list of state sponsors of terrorism because it had provided support for international terrorism over the past nine months and pledged not to do so in the future. Congress could have stopped this decision by passing blocking legislation within forty-five days, but it did not do so and on May 29, 2015, Cuba was officially taken off the list.

Yet another complicating issue was the U.S. economic embargo. The full embargo cannot be removed without the consent of Congress since much of it is contained in legislation. Obama's strategy was to remove those portions that are in place because of past presidential executive orders. Numbered among them were easing restrictions on agricultural exports, establishing banking relations, and lifting the need for special permission for trips to Cuba. Secretary of State John Kerry made it clear in his August 2015 trip to Cuba to reopen the U.S. embassy that these steps could not occur without an improvement in Cuba's human rights record.

Obama's visit to Cuba did not signify that all these issues had been solved. One additional major remaining roadblock is the matter of compensation for properties seized in the 1960s by Cuba ($1.9 billion) and counterclaims of damages done by the United States ($1 trillion). Opponents to normalizing relations also remain. Fidel Castro wrote after Obama's visit, "We do not need the empire to give us anything." Senator Marco Rubio, a Cuban American, vowed to place a hold on the confirmation of any ambassador to Cuba. Still as one Cuban diplomat under Fidel Castro observed, "The genie is out of the bottle . . . you're not going to be able to put it back in."

Political controversy over normalizing relations with Cuba continued as the Obama administration came to an end. In September, Obama nominated a career diplomat to be the first ambassador to Cuba in over 50 years. In October the U.S. rather than vote no, abstained for the first time in 55 years on a United Nations vote condemning the U.S. embargo on Cuba. Meanwhile, Republicans in the Senate said they would block any effort to lift the economic embargo on Cuba.

Obama's trip to Cuba sensitizes us to the possibility of change, the unpredictability of actions, and the potential consequences of foreign policy choices. In this chapter, we introduce six competing visions of the future direction American foreign policy might take.

Foreign Policy Visions

Each of the six competing visions we are about to introduce provides a different starting point for making policy choices. We ask three questions of each alternative future: (1) What is the primary threat to U.S. national security? (2) What responsibility does the United States have to other states? (3) What responsibility does the United States have to the global community? The answers given reflect different views regarding the degree to which the United States should be involved in world politics, how much power it possesses, and the extent to which we think the future will differ from the past.

The United States as an Ordinary State

For some, the key to the future is realizing that foreign policy can no longer be conducted on the assumption of American uniqueness or that U.S. actions stand between anarchy and order. The American century is over, and the challenge facing policy makers is no longer that of managing alliances, deterring aggression, or ruling over the international system. It is now one of adjusting to a new role orientation, one in which the United States is an **Ordinary State**.[1] The change in outlook is necessary because international and domestic trends point to the declining utility of a formula-based response to foreign policy problems, be it rooted in ideology, concepts of power politics, or some vision of regional order. As a result, the United States is forced to pursue narrowly defined national interests at the expense of international collaborative and cooperative efforts. In this altered environment, flexibility, autonomy, and impartiality are to be valued over one-sided commitments, name calling, and efforts at the diplomatic, military, or economic isolation of states.

As an Ordinary State, the United States would not define its interests so rigidly that their defense would require unilateral American action. If the use of force is necessary, it should be a truly multilateral effort; if others are unwilling to act, there is no need for the United States to assume the full burden of the commitment. Stated as a rule: "The United States should not be prepared, on its own, and supported solely by its own means, to perform tasks that most other states would not undertake."[2] Ordinariness does not, however, mean passivity, withdrawal, or a purely defensive approach to foreign policy problems. The quality of U.S. participation in truly multilateral efforts to solve international problems will be vital, because the core ingredients of international influence in the future will be found in the fields in which the United States is a leader: economics, diplomacy, and technology. The goal of these collaborative efforts should be to "create and maintain a world in which adversaries will remain in contact with one another and where compromises are still possible."[3] To summarize, in the Ordinary State perspective:

1. The greatest threat to U.S. national security lies in trying to do too much and in having too expansive a definition of its national interest.
2. The United States' responsibility to other states must be proportionate and reciprocal to that which other states have to the United States.
3. The United States' responsibility to the global community is to be a good global citizen—nothing more and nothing less.

The imagery advanced by the Ordinary State perspective is one that most Americans find troubling.[4] Its denial of American uniqueness, its lack of optimism, its focus on restraints rather than opportunities, and its admonition not to try to do too much all run against the traditional American approach to world politics. For that reason, it is a perspective that is unlikely to be endorsed (at least by this name) by politicians. A variant of the Ordinary States perspective now voiced is that the United States must act like a normal state. It too taps into a feeling shared by many Americans that although the United States should not retreat into isolationism, it should not be the first to take risks that others are not willing to run.

Reformed America

According to proponents of the **Reformed America** perspective, U.S. foreign policy has traditionally been torn between pursuing democratic ideals and

empire.[5] The United States wants peace—but only on its own terms; the United States supports human rights—but only if its definitions are used; the United States wants to promote Third World economic growth—but only if it follows the U.S. model and does not undermine U.S. business interests abroad. Historically, the thrust toward empire (whether it is called containment or détente) has won out, and democratic ideals have been sacrificed or given only lip service. U.S. policy makers have given highest priority to maintaining the United States' position of dominance in the international system and promoting the economic well-being of U.S. corporations.[6]

The need now exists to reverse this pattern. Democratic ideals must be given primary consideration in the formulation and execution of U.S. foreign policy. Not doing so invites future Vietnams and runs the risk of undermining the very democratic principles for which the United States stands. Foreign policy and domestic policy are not seen as two separate categories. They are held to be inextricably linked, and actions taken in one sphere have effects on behavior and policies in the other. Bribery of foreign officials leads to bribery of U.S. officials; an unwillingness to challenge human rights violations abroad reinforces the acceptance of discrimination and violations of civil rights at home; and a lack of concern for the growing disparity in economic wealth on a global basis leads to an insensitivity to the problems of poverty in the United States.

The Reformed America perspective demands global activism from the United States. The much-heralded decline in American power is not seen as being so great as to prevent the United States from exercising a predominant global influence. Moreover, the United States is held to have a moral and political responsibility to lead by virtue of its comparative wealth and power. The danger to be avoided is inaction brought on by the fear of failure. The United States cannot be permitted to crawl into a shell of isolationism or to let itself be "Europeanized" into believing that there are limits to its power and accepting the world "as it is." The power needed for success in creating what amounts to a new world order that is faithful to traditional American democratic values is not the ability to dominate others but to renew the American commitment to justice, opportunity, and liberty. In sum, the Reformed America perspective holds that:

1. The primary threat to U.S. national security is a continued fixation on military problems and an attachment to power-politics thinking.
2. The United States' responsibility to other states is great, provided they are truly democratic, and the United States must seek to move those that are not in that direction.
3. The United States' responsibility to the global community is also great and centers on the creation of an international system conducive to the realization of traditional American values.

The values underlying this perspective were widely embraced in the early post–Cold War period, as many commentators urged presidents to move more aggressively toward a neo-Wilsonian foreign policy. After 9/11 a split occurred within the Reformed America movement with some, labeled liberal hawks, advancing a foreign policy that embraced the use of military power in places such as Iraq and Afghanistan to advance democracy and reconstruct societies.

Others continue to express concern over the extent to which the military has become the foreign policy instrument of choice to advance American foreign policy goals. Along these lines some commentators argue that the United States is far more secure today than is commonly believed, thus providing an opportunity for rejecting power-politics thinking.[7]

Pragmatic America

The **Pragmatic America** perspective holds that the United States can no longer afford foreign policies that are on the extreme ends of the political spectrum. Neither crusades nor isolationism serve America well. Some world problems require U.S. attention, but not all do. What is needed in U.S. foreign policy is "selectivity," a strong dose of moderation in means and ends.[8] To supporters of this view, the end of the Cold War vindicated a policy of moderation.[9]

The United States must recognize that the American national interest is not identical to the global interest, and that not all problems lend themselves to permanent resolution. The most pressing issue on the agenda is for the United States to develop a set of criteria for identifying these problems and then act in moderation to protect American interests.

Pragmatic America emphasizes a utilitarian outlook on world politics and recognizes the lessened ability of military force to solve many foreign policy problems; it also recognizes that the nature of the problems facing the United States has changed. The Cold War dragon represented by the Soviet Union has been slain. The world confronting the United States is now populated by large numbers of poisonous snakes.

One national security practitioner suggests that the ideal practical method for moving forward to deal with these poisonous snakes is through the creation of international posses.[10] Just as in the old American West, when security threats present themselves, the United States (the sheriff) should organize and deputize a posse of like-minded states that will end the threat. It will then disband. In sum, the Pragmatic America perspective holds that:

1. The primary threats to U.S. national security continue to be military in nature.
2. The United States has a responsibility to other states on a selective basis, and only to the extent that threats to the political order of those states would lessen American security.
3. The United States' responsibility to the global community is limited.

More pressing is a sense of responsibility to key partners whose cooperation is necessary to manage a threatening international environment.

President George H. W. Bush, in his farewell foreign policy address, argued for a position that is consistent with this view.[11] Warning against becoming isolationist, Bush asserted that the United States can influence the future, but that "it need not respond to every outrage of violence." Bush went on to note that no formula exists that tells with precision when and where to intervene. "Each and every case is unique . . . we cannot always decide in advance which interests will require our using military force." When force is used, Bush urged that the mission be clear and achievable, that a realistic plan exist, and that equally realistic criteria be established for withdrawing U.S. forces.

The Pragmatic America perspective is seen by some as well suited for an international system in a state of flux. Henry Kissinger argues that "conviction on what we are trying to achieve must be constant but their application has to be adjusted to specific conditions."[12] This measured approach to solving foreign policy problems is also a fundamental weakness. Because pragmatism can be interpreted differently by different people, the policy it produces tends to move forward in a series of disjointed steps. The result is that whereas defenders see it as producing flexibility and adaptability, detractors see in it a foreign policy by lottery, in which the past provides little guidance for friends or enemies as they seek to anticipate America's position.

American Crusader

The **American Crusader** sees the United States as having won the Cold War and being now intent on enjoying the fruits of its victory as the dominant global power. Victory brings with it an opportunity to act on America's historical sense of mission. It builds on an important strain in the American national style that defines security in absolute terms. The objective is "unconditional surrender." "For more than two centuries, the United States has aspired to a condition of perfect safety from foreign threats," both real and imagined.[13] Unlike the Reformed America perspective, the American Crusader perspective identifies military power as the instrument of choice. It is rooted firmly in that part of the American national style that rejects compromise and seeks engineering and permanent solutions to political problems.

Faint echoes of the American Crusader perspective can be found in post–World War II foreign policy. During the Eisenhower administration, some commentators called for rolling back the Iron Curtain, feeling that containment was too passive and accommodating a strategy. During the Persian Gulf War, there was a moment when defeating Saddam Hussein had the characteristics of a crusade, at least at a rhetorical level. The American Crusader perspective is most associated with neoconservative thinking on foreign policy and burst on the scene with full force following the terrorist attacks on the World Trade Center and the Pentagon. In sum, the American Crusader perspective holds that:

1. The international system holds real and immediate threats to American national security that must be unconditionally defeated.
2. The United States has a responsibility to help other states that are allies in its cause, because their security increases American security.
3. The United States' responsibility to the international community is great, but how that responsibility is defined is a matter for the United States to determine based on its historical traditions.

There are some who share the American Crusader view that the international system contains immediate and serious threats to American security but question its wisdom. One concern expressed is that it overlooks the fact that superpower status does not convey total power to the United States. The challenge of bringing means and ends into balance is an ongoing one, and "superpower fatigue" becomes a real danger.[14] A second concern is that by acting in this manner, the United States may hasten its own decline. Rather than staying on the American "bandwagon" as an ally, second-order states may decide that—because they too may become the object of an American crusade—it is necessary to build up their own power and balance that of the United States.

America the Balancer

Out of a conviction that unipolarity is bound to give way to a multipolar distribution of power in the international system, some commentators argue that the prudent course of action today is to adopt the role of balancer. The United States needs to stand apart from others, yet be prepared to act in concert with them. It cannot and should not become a rogue superpower, acting on its own impulses and imposing its vision on the world.[15]

The starting point of wisdom from this perspective is that not all problems are threatening to the United States or require its involvement. The United States has a considerable amount of freedom to define its interests. In addition, the United States must recognize that one consequence of having put a global security umbrella in place is that it has discouraged other states and regional organizations from taking responsibility for preserving international stability. This situation must be reversed. Others must be encouraged to act in defense of their own interests. Otherwise the United States runs the risk of becoming entrapped by commitments to unstable regimes.[16] Finally, the United States must learn to live with uncertainty. Absolute security is an unattainable objective and one that only produces imperial overstretch. In sum, the **America the Balancer** perspective holds the following:

1. The primary national security threats to the United States are self-inflicted. They take the form of a proliferation of security commitments designed to protect America's economic interests.
2. The United States has a limited responsibility to other states, because the burden for protecting a state's national interests falls on that state.
3. The United States' responsibility to the global community is limited. American national interests and the maintenance of global order are not identical.

Many advocates of balancing see a return to multipolarity as all but inevitable and believe that trying to reassert or preserve American preeminence and suppress the emergence of new powers is futile.[17] There is thus little reason for the United States to become deeply involved in the affairs of other states on a routine basis. What is needed is a **hedging strategy**, one that will allow the United States to realize its security goals without provoking others into uniting against it or accelerating their separate pursuits of power. Blessed by its geopolitical location, the answer for some lies in adopting the position of an offshore balancer.[18] The United States is positioned to allow global and regional power balances to ensure its strategic independence. Only when others prove incapable of acting to block the ascent of a challenging hegemony should the United States step in to affect the balance of power. Given its continued power resources, such an intervention is held likely to be decisive.

One issue that needs to be confronted by advocates of the America the Balancer perspective is how to exercise American military power most effectively. Traditionally, war was the mechanism by which a balance-of-power system preserved stability in the international system. Commentators positioned across the political spectrum have raised the question of whether wars can continue to play this role on a large scale. If they cannot, then how is the balancer to enforce its will? One possibility is that rather than using American power to deter or defeat an adversary, America the Balancer will play a central role in compelling adversaries to change their behavior. The distinction is potentially important. One commentator who has looked at compellence suggests that it is more of a police task than deterrence, which is a military task.

Disengaged America

The final alternative future put forward calls for the United States to selectively, yet thoroughly, withdraw from the world.[19] It is a perspective most often associated with the libertarian perspective on U.S. foreign policy.[20] The **Disengaged America** perspective sees retrenchment as necessary because the international system is becoming increasingly inhospitable to U.S. values and unresponsive to efforts at management or domination. Increasingly, the choices facing U.S. foreign policy will be ones of choosing what kinds of losses to avoid. Optimal solutions to foreign policy problems will no longer present themselves to policy makers, and if they do, domestic constraints will prevent policy makers from pursuing such a path. In the Disengaged America perspective, foreign policy must become less of a lance—a tool for spreading values—and more of a shield—a minimum set of conditions behind which the United States can protect its values and political processes.[21] In the words of one commentator writing after 9/11, the purpose of American foreign policy should be security first. Promoting democracy is fine so long as it is pursued by peaceful means and is seen as homegrown.[22]

Historical Lesson

Nixon's Trip to China

On July 15, 1971, President Richard Nixon announced to a stunned world that he had accepted Mao Zedong's invitation to visit the People's Republic of China (PRC), referred to in the U.S. media as Communist China. The visit, which occurred in February 1972, ended almost a quarter of a century of isolation, mutual suspicion, and occasional military crises.

Nixon's announcement resulted in strong public reactions for and against the president's planned trip. Reactions

were quick and varied. Senator Humbert Humphrey, whom Nixon defeated for the presidency in 1968, stated that if Nixon used the presidency to promote peace and security throughout the world, the price for his reelection would be small. Republican Senator John Tower asserted that Nixon owed the American people an explanation. United Nations secretary general U Thant said the trip would open a new chapter in international relations. Taiwanese officials asked Nixon to cancel the trip. North Vietnamese officials said the trip was to divert attention from Nixon's crimes. Pope Paul VI said it could change the face of the earth.

Nixon's diplomatic opening took observers by surprise because his entire political career had been based on demonstrating firm anticommunist credentials. He gained national notoriety as a member of the House Un-American Activities Committee that investigated allegations that State Department official Alger Hiss was a Soviet spy. Nixon used this visibility as a springboard to the Senate in a race in which he characterized his Democratic opponent as a left-wing communist sympathizer. Once in the Senate, he spoke out often against international communism and criticized Truman's handling of the Korean War.

Nonetheless, there were ample signs of Nixon's interest in dramatically changing the landscape of world politics. One year before becoming president, Nixon wrote on China that there was no reason for its people to live in "angry isolation." Early in his presidency, Nixon communicated to the Chinese his interest in ending this long period of isolation through the Romanian government, the U.S. ambassador to Poland, and Pakistan's president. He also began to refer to Communist China by its official name, the People's Republic of China. It was only in December 1970 that these initiatives produced a positive response from China. In late April 1971, China signaled its willingness to invite Nixon, and in July, National Security Advisor Henry Kissinger made a secret trip to China to finalize matters.

Nixon visited China from February 21 to February 28, 1972. The trip ended with the United States and China issuing the Shanghai Communiqué. In this document, the two countries agreed to work toward normalizing their relations, a statement that all understood to mean that the United States would drop its recognition of Taiwan as the government of China and recognize the PRC instead in spite of ambiguous language elsewhere in the document. The PRC and the United States also agreed that neither they nor any other power should seek "hegemony" over the Asia-Pacific region. The other unnamed power was the Soviet Union, and the Shanghai Communiqué thus served as an implicit alliance against Soviet infringement on Chinese territory or regional interests.

Nixon's diplomatic opening to China came against the backdrop of two significant developments for U.S. foreign policy. The first was growing conflict between the PRC and the Soviet Union. The United States had been slow to recognize the growing animosity in Sino-Soviet relations, but it was now clear that the United States was no longer opposed by a unified communist bloc. The second significant trend was the ongoing war in Vietnam. A widespread consensus existed inside and outside of the U.S. government that after Vietnam, the United States would have a difficult, if not impossible, time in opposing Soviet aggression. Its military was strained to the breaking point, and the American public would not support "another Vietnam."

The challenge, as Nixon and Kissinger saw it, was to position the United States in such a way that it would remain the dominant power in the international system but at a lesser cost. The answer they arrived at was a strategy designed to reduce Soviet hostility to U.S. leadership by recognizing the Soviet Union as a legitimate power in world politics, while at the same time finding allies to stand with the United States against the Soviet Union, should that be necessary. No country fitted that bill better than the

PRC. But being able to play the "China card" first required establishing working relations with it.

Applying the Lesson

1. What is the equivalent of the "China card" for U.S. foreign policy in today's international system?

2. Was Nixon's opening to China forward-looking or backward-looking in what it hoped to accomplish?

3. Is one peaceful foreign policy initiative really capable of changing the direction of world politics?

Becoming disengaged means that the United States will have to learn to live in a "second-best world," one that is not totally to its liking but one in which it can get by. Allies will be fewer in number, and those that remain will have to do more to protect their own security and economic well-being. Nonintervention will be the rule for the United States and self-reliance the watchword for others. The United States must be prepared to "let" some states be dominated and to direct its efforts at placing space between the **falling dominoes** rather than trying to define a line of containment. In the realm of economics, while free trade is supported, the objective should be to move toward autarchy and self-sufficiency so that other states cannot manipulate or threaten the United States. If the United States cannot dominate the sources of supply, it must be prepared to "substitute, tide over, [and] ride out" efforts at resource manipulation.[23] World order concerns must also take a backseat in U.S. foreign policy. As George Kennan has said about the food-population problem, "We did not create it and it is beyond our power to solve it."[24] Kennan argues that the United States needs to divest itself of its guilt complex and accept the fact that there is really very little that it can do for the Third World and very little that the Third World can do for the United States. In sum, the Disengaged America perspective holds the following:

1. The major threat to U.S. national security comes from an overactive foreign policy. Events beyond U.S. borders are not as crucial to U.S. security as is commonly perceived, and, moreover, the United States has little power to influence their outcome.
2. The United States' responsibility to other states is minimal. The primary responsibility of the United States is to its own economic and military security.
3. The United States' responsibility to the global community is also minimal. The issues on the global agenda, especially as they relate to the Third World, are not the fault of the United States, and the United States can do little to solve them.

From the Disengaged America perspective, traditional principles of defense planning are largely irrelevant.[25] Military power should no longer be employed to further human rights or economic principles beyond American borders. Rather than pursuing military goals, American foreign policy must concentrate on protecting American lives and property, the territorial integrity of the United

States, and the autonomy of its political system. Consistent with these priorities, American military power would be used for only three purposes: (1) to defend the approaches to U.S. territory, (2) to serve as second-chance forces to be used if deterrence fails or unexpected threats arise, and (3) to provide finite essential deterrence against attacks on the United States and its forces overseas.

The Disengaged America perspective has few qualms about the need to defend American interests or take action unilaterally and forcefully in doing so. Preemption as a means for dealing with terrorists is not a repugnant strategy to them. What concerns them is that the War on Terrorism has as its objective not simply the defeat of the enemy but its transformation. In the words of Pat Buchanan, the purpose of American foreign policy is "America First—and Second, and Third." Some twenty-five years later Buchanan reiterated this theme writing "This is not isolationism. It is putting our country first . . . It used to be called patriotism."[26]

Over the Horizon: Time for a Terrorism Long Telegram?

In the first chapter we presented the outlines of Obama's foreign policy doctrine. We found that it suffered from many of the same weaknesses as other presidential foreign policy doctrines. Not surprisingly these repeated shortcomings in U.S. grand strategies produce repeated calls for creating a new, more internally consistent, and effective grand strategy for promoting U.S. national interests. Added on to addressing these shortcomings are problems created by the changing nature of global politics. The extent to which the future will resemble the present or the past is unclear. Some go so far as to argue we are entering the **post-American world**.[27] This will not necessarily be an anti-American world, but one which would require adjustments in foreign policy strategies. In this chapter we have reviewed some of the major alternative visions to U.S. foreign policy now being debated.

One suggestion for moving forward is to reevaluate our thinking about the major challenges that the United States will face. To that end, Daniel Drezner has suggested it is time for a new long telegram.[28] The long telegram was a diplomatic cable sent to Washington by U.S. ambassador to the Soviet Union George Kennan on February 22, 1946. It came at a time when the United States was uncertain how to organize its relations with the Soviet Union. Some foreign policy specialists saw it as a possible partner just as it had been during World War II. Others saw it as an irreconcilable expansionist enemy. In his eight-thousand-word telegram Kennan argued the Soviet Union was neither. It was expansionist but lacked a blueprint for global domination. Its expansionist policies were driven by fear of foreign conquest and were defensive in nature. Kennan argued that a policy of steadfast counterpressure would cause the Soviet communist party Soviet Union to back away from its expansionist policy. His argument came to form the basis for a policy of containment. It did not end differences of opinion over the direction of U.S. foreign policy (Kennan would later criticize how this policy was implemented arguing that too much emphasis was being given by presidents to using military power) but it did raise important questions that needed to be addressed about the fundamental nature of Soviet and U.S. foreign policy.

Then as now world politics is in transition. When Kennan wrote his long telegram the United States had only recently entered the post–World War II era. A label such as this tells you where you have been but offers little guidance on where you are going or what comes next. Today the United States finds itself in a similarly ill-defined post–Cold War era. Then as now we find a great deal of disagreement about what motivates the foreign policies of other states. Where in the aftermath of World War II understanding Soviet foreign policy was the most pressing issue facing U.S. policy makers, today the most crucial issue may be not understanding the foreign policies of Russia or China so much as understanding ISIS and other terrorist groups. If, as President Obama asserted, ISIS represents a generational challenge the time might be right for a new long telegram to Washington to lay the groundwork for a new grand strategy against terrorism.

Critical Thinking Questions

1. In selecting a foreign policy for the future, which of the three questions we ask is most important?
2. Identify one foreign policy option that is missing and needs to be added to the list. Why is it needed?

3. What power resources are most needed by the United States in facing the future?

Key Terms

America the Balancer, 353
American Crusader, 252
Disengaged America, 354
empire, 348
falling dominoes, 356

hedging strategy, 353
Ordinary State, 349
post-American world, 357
Pragmatic America, 351
Reformed America, 349

Further Reading

Daniel Deudney and G. John Ikenberry, "Unraveling America the Great," *The American Interest* 11 (Summer 2016), 7–17.
The authors call for a renewal of the Rooseveltian (FDR) foundations of success and influence in the world. They express deep concern over the growing influence of radical conservative anti-internationalism.
Robert Kagan, "The Allure of Normalcy," *The New Republic*, June 9, 2014, 14–31.
The author calls for the United States to reject a return to normalcy that guided foreign policy in the post–World War I era. He argues that it must adopt a definition of the national interest that recognizes the need to defend the global liberal international order.

Anatol Lieven and John Hulsman, *Ethical Realism: A Vision for America's Role in the World* (New York: Pantheon, 2006).

The authors argue that what has failed recently in American foreign policy is not just the Bush administration's embrace of preemptive war but the whole way in which Americans look at the world.

Michael Lind, "The Case for American Nationalism," *The National Interest* 131 (May 2014), 9–20.

The author calls for a foreign policy of primacy rather than one of hegemony. To this end he favors an offshore balancing or concert balancing strategy and supports the call for the United States to become a normal country in world politics

Joseph Nye, *Is the American Century Over?* (Cambridge, MA: Harvard University Press, 2015).

This book argues that the American century is far from over because its military, economic, and soft power resources will continue to far exceed those possessed by its closest rivals for several decades.

David Shlapak, "Toward a More Modest American Strategy," *Survival* 57 (April 2015), 59–78.

The author argues that the United States needs to place limits on its global ambitions. He identifies five challenges that should drive force planning, and all focus on defeating an adversary's attempt to project power and not on internal Pentagon politics.

Fareed Zakaria, *The Post American World* (New York: Norton, 2009).

The author outlines the changing landscape of world politics and its implications for American foreign policy. He argues that the "rise of the rest" is not so much due to American failures but the very success of past U.S. policies.

Notes

[1] Richard Rosecrance, "New Directions?" in Richard Rosecrance (ed.), *America as an Ordinary Country: U.S. Foreign Policy and the Future* (Ithaca, NY: Cornell University Press, 1976). Reprinted in James O'Leary and Richard Shultz (eds.), *Power, Principles, and Interests* (Lexington, MA: Ginn, 1985), 433–44.

[2] O'Leary, and Shultz, *Power, Principles, and Interests*, 443.

[3] Ibid., 442.

[4] See, for example, the argument of Robert Kagan, "The Allure of Normalcy," *New Republic,* June 9, 2014, 14–31.

[5] On this theme, see Robert A. Isaak, *American Democracy and World Power* (New York: St. Martin's Press, 1977); Robert C. Johansen, *The National Interest and the Human Interest: An Analysis of U.S. Foreign Policy* (Princeton: Princeton University Press, 1980).

[6] Johansen, *The National Interest and the Human Interest.*

[7] Micah Zenko and Michael Cohen, "Clear and Present Safety," *Foreign Affairs* 91 (2012), 79–93.

[8] James Schlesinger, "Quest for a Post–Cold War Foreign Policy," *Foreign Affairs* 72 (1992/93), 17–28.

[9] Robert W. Tucker, "1989 and All That," in Nicholas X. Rizopoulos (ed.), *Sea-Changes: American Foreign Policy in a World Transformed* (New York: Council on Foreign Relations Press, 1990), 204–37.

[10] Richard Haass, "Military Force: A User's Guide," *Foreign Policy* 96 (1994), 21–38.

[11] George Bush, "Remarks at the United States Military Academy," *Public Papers of the President* (Washington, DC: U.S. Government Printing Office, 1993), 2230–31.

[12] Henry Kissinger, "Universal Values, Specific Policies," *National Interest* 84 (2006), 13.

[13] James Chace and Caleb Carr, *America Invulnerable* (New York: Summit, 1988), E318.

[14] Graham Fuller, "Strategic Fatigue," *National Interest* 84 (2006), 37–42.

[15] The merits of balancing are most often debated with reference to an offshore balancing strategy. For opposing views, see Hal Brands, "Fools Rush Out?" *Washington Quarterly* 38 (Summer

2015), 7–28; and John Mearsheimer and Stephen Walt, "The Case for Offshore Balancing," *Foreign Affairs* 95 (July 2016), 70–83.

16 Hilton Root, "Walking with the Devil," *National Interest* 88 (2007), 42–45.

17 Christopher Layne, "The Unipolar Illusion: Why Great Powers Will Rise," *International Security* 17 (1993), 5–51.

18 Christopher Layne is a major proponent of the end of unipolarity and the need for an offshore balancing strategy. See his "This Time It's Real," *International Studies Quarterly* 56 (2012), 203–13.

19 Earl C. Ravenal, *Never Again: Learning from America's Foreign Policy Failures* (Philadelphia, PA: Temple University Press, 1978). Also see Joseph Parent and Paul MacDonald, "The Wisdom of Retrenchment," *Foreign Affairs* 90 (2011), 32–47. For an opposing view, see Stephen Brooks, G. John Ikenberry, and William Wohlforth, "Don't Come Home, America," *International Security* 37 (2012/13), 7–51.

20 See "Toward a Libertarian Foreign Policy," CATO Policy Report, July/August 2015, for a discussion of what a more libertarian foreign policy would mean for the United States.

21 Ravenal, *Never Again*, 15.

22 Amitai Etzioni, "Security First," *National Interest* 88 (2007), 11–15.

23 Ravenal, *Never Again*, xv.

24 George Kennan, *Cloud of Danger: Current Realities of American Foreign Policy* (Boston, MA: Little, Brown, 1977), 32.

25 Earl Ravenal, "The Case for Adjustment," *Foreign Policy* 81 (1990/91), 3–19.

26 Patrick Buchanan, "America First, and Second, and Third," *National Interest* 19 (1990), 77–82; and "The U.S. Empire is Overextended," April 15, 2016.

27 Fareed Zakaria, *The Post-American World* (New York: W. W. Norton, 2009).

28 Drezner calls for a new long telegram focusing on Saudi Arabia. See "The United States Needs a New Long Telegram," https://www.washingtonpost.com/posteverything/wp/2016/02/22/the-united-states-needs-a-new-long-telegram-but-from-where.

Glossary

action channels Decision-making linkages between organizations and individuals that determine who participates in bureaucratic politics decision-making games. Important because not everyone "plays" in these games. Players and their power are determined by where they fit in the action channels.

action indispensability Decision-making situations in which action by policy makers is critical to success or failure. The identity of the actor is not essential because the response was standard and expected.

action policy U.S. foreign policy as it is actually carried out with respect to a problem. Refers to what is done rather than what is said. Often contrasts with declaratory policy. Originally used in the context of U.S. nuclear policy.

actor indispensability Decision-making situations in which not only is action by policy makers critical to success or failure but the identity of the actor is seen as being key to the outcome.

alliance A formal agreement among states to provide military assistance to each other. Alliances vary in the types of aid offered and the nature of the commitment.

America the Balancer A possible future foreign policy strategic orientation of U.S. foreign policy that is based on a limited and selective involvement in world affairs.

American Crusader A possible future foreign policy strategic orientation of U.S. foreign policy that is based on the idea that the United States faces real and immediate security threats and has the power and moral responsibility to lead.

"America first" perspective A perspective on foreign policy in which priority is given to the interests of American firms over those of other states. Identified with bureaucracies such as the Commerce and Agriculture Departments.

analogy Central to method of reasoning in which comparisons are made between events and objects as the basis for making judgments about similarities and differences. Foreign policy often involves comparison of present with past events.

arms control Policy designed to bring about restraint in the use of weapons. Generally involves reduction in numbers of weapons but does not have to do this. Often contrasted with disarmament.

arms sale Purchase of weapons by one state from another. The distinguishing feature of arms sales is the quality of the weapons obtained. Unlike in the case of arms transfers, these weapons tend to be among the most preferred in the seller's inventory.

arms transfer Process of providing weapons to another state for free or at greatly reduced prices. Typically, these weapons are characterized as being excess defense articles or emergency allocations.

assured destruction Nuclear strategy under Johnson predicated on U.S. ability to destroy a significant portion of Soviet population and economic capability in retaliation for a Soviet attack on the United States.

bargaining Process by which two or more states reach agreement on a policy through a process of give and take. It can take place in formal settings or informally. A subtype of negotiations.

barnacles Riders or amendments that are attached to foreign policy legislation. Often needed to secure its passage, they can result in features being added that complicate the conduct of U.S. diplomacy. Reporting requirements are an example.

bipartisanship Situation in domestic politics of American foreign policy, where a policy is supported by both political parties. Seen as a sign of national unity and communicates resolve to opponents. It came into use following World War II when foundations of containment policy were put into place.

bipolar Characterizes an international system that is conflict prone and divided into two competing and mutually exclusive blocs each led by a superpower. Often subdivided into loose and tight variants depending on the unity of the blocs and the distance separating them. The Cold War was a bipolar system.

black box Part of rational actor decision-making perspective. Assumes that foreign policy is a response to actions and events in the international system. Therefore, one does not need to examine domestic politics, and events inside the state can be ignored or black boxed.

blowback The negative consequences that result from foreign policy actions. Originally used with reference to CIA covert actions but now applied more generally to foreign policy initiatives.

boycott A refusal to buy or sell goods from a company or country. Alternatively, a refusal to attend a meeting or negotiations.

Bretton Woods system International economic order created after World War II consisting of the International Monetary Fund, the World Bank, and the General Agreement on Trade and Tariffs. Formally ended in 1974 when Nixon took the United States off the gold standard.

Bricker Amendment Failed attempt by Congress in the 1950s to limit the president's ability to use executive agreements in place of treaties as instrument of U.S. foreign policy. It would have required Senate advice and consent to executive agreements before they took effect.

bureaucratic politics Decision-making model that emphasizes the influence of bureaucratic factors, most notably,

self-interest. Policy is not decided upon so much as bargained into existence.

casus belli The factors or events used to justify going to war.

CEO system Presidential management system introduced by George W. Bush that emphasizes the importance of providing overall direction to policy and selecting qualified individuals and then removing oneself from the day-to-day affairs of governing.

civil-military relations The overarching relationship between professional military officers and civilian policy makers. Involves issues such as who has ultimate authority, the values to be pursued, and political neutrality.

closed belief system A belief system is a set of interrelated mental images about some aspect of reality. A closed belief system is one that does not change in spite of contradictory evidence. Contrasts with an open belief system.

CNN effect Phrase designed to convey increased importance of the media for determining the foreign policy agenda of the United States by its ability to arouse and shape public opinion and to force policy makers to respond quickly to unfolding events.

coalitions Informal alignment of states that come together out of self-interest to deal with a specific problem. Common forms include voting blocs at an international organization and combinations of military forces such as those in the Persian Gulf War and the Iraq War.

coercive diplomacy Use or threatened use of force against another state for political purposes. Typically refers to military force but can include economic force. Purposes can include deterrence and compellence.

cognitive consistency The tendency of individuals to seek out information and stimuli that are supportive of one's beliefs and attitudes.

collegial system Presidential management system that emphasizes cooperation, team work, and problem-solving as primary values for top presidential aides and department heads.

compellence Use or threat of using military force to prompt another state to undertake a desired action. Contrasts with deterrence in which force is used or threatened to prevent an action from taking place.

competitive system Presidential management system that emphasizes playing off aides against one another and assigning the same task to multiple units in order to maximize information flow and freedom of maneuver.

conference diplomacy Category of diplomacy that focuses on large international gatherings that are generally open to all states. Typically, they focus on a single problem or issue and attempt to lay down rules for addressing the problem. Differs from summit diplomacy where only a few states attend.

constructivism A theoretical perspective for studying international relations that emphasizes the subjectivity of actions. Emphasis is placed on understanding how the developments are viewed by the participants by examining ideas, culture, history, and the dynamics of interaction.

containment U.S. policy toward the Soviet Union for much of the Cold War. Predicated on the assumption that the potential for Soviet aggression was constant but could be checked by applying constant counterpressure to thwart it. Over time, this policy was expected to produce a mellowing of Soviet foreign policy.

counterinsurgency The military strategy for fighting an insurgency, which is defined as an armed rebellion against a recognized government. The military strategy counterinsurgency also contains political, economic, and psychological dimensions.

counterproliferation Military strategy designed to prevent the spread of weapons. Most frequently talked about in

context of weapons of mass destruction, it can be seen as a preemptive use of force.

country team Comprises the representatives from all U.S. agencies represented in an embassy. Headed by the ambassador. It is meant to signify that a united purpose exists to U.S. foreign policy in the country.

covert action Activities to influence military, economic, and political conditions abroad, where it is intended that the role of the U.S. government not be apparent.

cyber warfare A variety of attacks on computer and information systems for the purpose of causing damage or destruction through such means as computer viruses or denial of service attacks.

declaratory policy Public statements of U.S. foreign policy with regard to a problem. Refers to what is said rather than what is done. Often contrasted with action policy. Originally used in the context of U.S. nuclear policy.

denuclearizing Process by which a state that has acquired or is pursuing a nuclear weapon reverses course and agrees to forego it.

détente Foreign policy associated with Nixon. Rather than containing the Soviet Union, it sought to establish a working relationship by treating it as a legitimate power and engaging it in a series of mutually beneficial arms control and economic relationships that would reduce its threat to the United States, thus making global conflicts more manageable.

deterrence The use of power to prevent an unwanted action from taking place. Most frequently, it refers to the use of military power and in the context of the Cold War, the nuclear standoff between the United States and the Soviet Union.

digital diplomacy The use of the Internet and information and communication technologies such as social media and twitter to achieve diplomatic objectives.

disarmament Policy designed to reduce the number of weapons in existence. May be applied to specific weapons or inventories in general. Logical endpoint is zero weapons but need not necessarily reach this point. Often contrasted with arms control.

Disengaged America A possible future foreign policy strategic orientation of U.S. foreign policy that is based on minimal global engagement and learning to live in a second-best world.

economic statecraft The use of economic resources and tools to achieve foreign policy goals.

elite theory Decision-making model that stresses the overwhelming influence of economic class and ideology on policy. Contrasts with pluralism, arguing that there does not exist a system of checks and balances among competing interests.

embargo A prohibition of selling goods or services to another country.

empire A hierarchically structured grouping of states ruled from one power center. It is debated whether or not the U.S. position of dominance in the world qualifies it to be an empire. Similarly, it is debated how long the U.S. empire, if it exists, can survive.

executive agreement Arrangements entered into with other countries by the president that are not subject to a congressional vote. The Supreme Court has ruled executive agreements hold force of law as do treaties.

falling dominoes Term associated with the Cold War, it denotes the possibility that a U.S. foreign policy failure in a given country or military engagement may set off a chain reaction leading to the fall of many states, resulting in a major national security crisis.

fast track Today known as Trade Promotional Authority. Voted on by Congress for set periods of time, it gives the president the authority to enter into international trade negotiations, guarantees a prompt vote by Congress, and limits Congress's ability to modify treaties that come before it.

firewall A blockage or separation that is intended to stop the spread of a dangerous condition. In warfare, it is often used to signify attempts to create a dividing line between conventional and nuclear weapons.

flexible response Nuclear strategy under Kennedy that called for wide range of military responses, including a variety of nuclear options to deal with Soviet challenges.

foreign service officer Professional diplomatic corps of the United States. Has been controversial at times for its values and degree of separation from American society as a whole.

formalistic system Presidential management system that employs strict hierarchical decision-making structure on decision-making processes.

free trade International economic policy based on the principle of the open and nondiscriminatory flow of goods across borders. Achieved through the removal of government-imposed barriers to trade.

gadfly A congressional orientation to foreign policy in which an individual raises concerns about the direction of U.S. foreign policy not out of an interest in short-term electoral gains but with an eye toward affecting the long-term direction of policy.

gatekeeper An individual who determines the types of information and which individuals have access to a policy maker. Gatekeepers are crucial to establishing effective decision-making routines and yet also a liability because they can distort the information on which policy is made.

generational events Those highly visible and psychologically significant events that influence the worldview of a generation of individuals, whether they were experienced directly or not. The Great Depression, Pearl Harbor, and Vietnam are often given as examples.

globalization Refers to the process of the growing pace and density of economic, political, and cultural interactions in international affairs. Viewed by some in a positive light as a force that unites peoples; others see it as a threatening condition that fosters conflict among people and countries.

grand strategy Overarching conceptual framework for integrating and applying all elements of power. Establishes the general direction, purposes, and logic of U.S. foreign policy. Often associated with presidential doctrines.

groupthink Common consequence of small-group decision-making dynamics. Concurrence seeking behavior on the part of group members causes them to reach fundamentally flawed decisions.

guerrilla war Unconventional war strategy that emphasizes hit-and-run tactics and prolonged warfare rather than direct engagement of enemy forces in decisive battles. Ultimate objective is to get government to overreact and lose support of the people.

hard power The power to coerce. Generally associated with military power. It seeks to impose an outcome on an opponent.

hedging strategy A foreign policy strategy in which the United States acts cautiously to ensure that the failure of no single initiative can inflict great harm on U.S. national interests. It requires keeping open lines of communication with all states and not locking the United States into an all-or-nothing situation.

hegemony Domineering and uncontested leadership that is rooted in the political, economic, and military ability to impose one's will on others. Often used to characterize the position of the dominant state in a unipolar system and the U.S. position in the world after the end of the Cold War.

hybrid warfare A form of warfare that employs a combination of conventional and unconventional military strategies along with informational and other nonmilitary resources and societal resources to achieve victory.

imperialism A foreign policy of domination in which one state controls the people, resources, and political activity in other states generally by military force. Critics of U.S. foreign policy have often argued that it has been imperialist in dealings with developing countries.

intermestic Foreign policy problems that contain both domestic and foreign policy dimensions thus complicating efforts to solve them and defy the traditional dichotomy of foreign versus domestic policy.

internationalism An orientation to world affairs that stresses the importance of taking an active role in global decision-making in order to protect and promote national security and economic prosperity. Can be undertaken both in the pursuit of liberal or conservative goals.

Iraq syndrome Much speculated on possible negative public reaction to U.S. involvement in Iraq that will prevent policy makers from using force in the future, just as Vietnam syndrome did in the 1970s.

isolationism An orientation to world affairs that stresses the dangers of global involvement rather than its benefits. Strong defenses and unilateral action are seen as necessary to protect the national interest. A sharp distinction is drawn between the national interest and the global interest.

legalism Part of the American national style. The belief that foreign policy problems can be solved through the application of legal formulas and principles.

legislative veto A situation where Congress repeals presidential action or the decision of a Federal agency by writing legislation so that it can be overridden by a majority of one or both Houses. Contained in the War Powers Resolution.

Lippmann Gap The difference between a country's power resources and the goals it wishes to achieve. Named after political columnist Walter Lippmann, who argued that the larger this gap, the greater the likelihood that U.S. foreign policy would fail.

massive retaliation Nuclear strategy under Eisenhower that sought to deter the Soviet aggression throughout the world by threatening a large-scale retaliatory strike on the Soviet Union.

military after next Phrase used to describe need to think beyond immediate problems and focus on long-term bureaucratic requirements of U.S. foreign policy. Can also be "State Department after next" or "CIA after next."

military-industrial complex A phrase used in Eisenhower's farewell presidential address. Most narrowly used, it speaks to the unchecked influence of industry lobbyists and allies in the military to obtain funds for weapons systems and militarize American foreign policy.

models A simplified depictions of a complex process or structure used to generate insights into their nature. May be mathematical or descriptive.

moral pragmatism Part of the American national style. Brings together the belief that foreign policy ought to be driven by the pursuit of principles and that they can be solved by applying an engineering problem-solving logic.

multipolar Characterizes an international system in which there are at least five major powers. No permanent dividing line separates them into competing blocs; rather, the major states enter into a series of shifting alliances to preserve national interests. Nineteenth-century Europe is seen as a multipolar period.

national interest The fundamental goals and objectives of a state's foreign policy. Used as if it were self-explanatory, it is a contested concept that holds great emotional power in political debates.

national style Refers to deeply engrained patterns of thought and action on how to approach foreign policy problems and their solutions. More generally, it establishes the basis for how a country looks out at the international system and defines its role in world politics.

negotiation Broadly defined as a dialogue to resolve disputes. This result may be achieved through mediation, fact finding, or bargaining. On occasion, negotiations are entered into by states not to solve problems but to gain an advantage through obtaining information or the publicity it generates.

neoconservatism In foreign policy, it refers to an activist and unilateral orientation to involvement in world affairs for the purpose of promoting democracy and free trade that stresses the use of military power to defeat enemies. Seen by many as the dominant viewpoint of the George W. Bush administration following 9/11.

neoliberalism A theoretical perspective for studying international relations that stresses the ability of states to cooperate, solve problems, and defend their interests peacefully. Emphasis is placed on the importance of mutually beneficial economic interactions, the peaceful effects of democracy, and the importance of international laws and organizations.

noise Background clutter of irrelevant or misleading data that complicates the task of policy makers trying to identify important pieces of information or signals that will help them formulate policy.

nontariff barrier A nontax barrier to free trade. Generally takes the form of requirements to ship national vessels, purchase goods in a specific country of origin, or meet safety and health or environmental standards imposed on goods and their production.

opportunity costs In conducting foreign policy, states are faced with the reality of limited time and limited resources. The pursuit of any objective necessarily comes at the expense of pursuing other goals that now must be neglected.

Ordinary State A possible future foreign policy strategic orientation of U.S. foreign policy that is based on the presumption that the United States has no greater responsibility for maintaining global order than does any other state.

outsource To rely on nongovernmental or private sector agencies to carry out assigned tasks. Found throughout foreign policy area. Became controversial with large-scale use of private contractors during the Iraq War.

oversight Congressional regulatory supervision of the Federal bureaucracy. The stated objective is not day-to-day managerial control but ensuring accountability of decisions made and improving performance.

paramilitary Operations carried out by forces or groups distinct from the professional military for which no broad conventional military capability exists. They are often carried in hostile, politically sensitive, or denied areas.

peacekeeping Operations conducted in postconflict areas to observe the peace process and implement peace agreements. Although not exclusively military in nature, peacekeeping operations generally build upon a significant military presence in the country affected.

pledge system Form of international cooperation in which countries promise voluntarily to support an agreement. No enforcement mechanism is created.

pluralism Decision-making model that sees policy as the result of competing interest groups. The government is often pictured as a neutral umpire making policy to reflect position of strongest groups.

policy entrepreneur A congressional orientation to foreign policy, whereby the individual takes positions on foreign policy legislation, primarily with an eye toward the electoral advantage it might bestow rather than a long-range concern for the issue itself.

poliheuristic decision-making A model of decision-making that emphasizes the presence of a two-stage decision-making process only the second of which involves engaging in an analysis of options.

political creep The tendency for political criteria and considerations to replace professional ones in assignment of personnel to positions within foreign policy bureaucracy. Once identified with appointment of political fund-raisers to ambassadorships, it is now also an issue at lower levels of bureaucracies.

politicizing intelligence Situation where professional expertise and objectivity of intelligence reports is replaced by partisan political considerations. Associated with phrases such as intelligence-to-please and cherry-picking.

positional issues Refers to foreign policy issues in elections that find candidates taking opposite sides. The dominant logic of primary campaigns. A frequent result is to oversimplify issues.

post-American world An international system, some say, may come into existence in the near future. It is characterized by the rise in the power of competing states to create an international system in which the United States has reduced influence.

Pragmatic America A possible future foreign policy strategic orientation of U.S. foreign policy that is based on the view that the rapid changes in world politics make it inadvisable for U.S. foreign policy to be guided by a broad set of principles. Instead, it should focus on the particulars of each situation as they arise.

preemption Striking first in self-defense. In classical usage, a distinction is drawn between preemption, which occurs when the threat is immediate, and prevention, when it is more long term or generic.

presidential finding Mandated by the Hughes-Ryan Amendment, it requires that except under exceptional circumstances, presidents inform key members of Congress in advance of the scope of CIA operations.

presidential personality Refers to those traits of the president that are important for understanding how he defines problems and solutions as well as his outlook on the use of presidential power.

proliferation Spread of weapons. Two different versions exist. Horizontal, in which weapons spread to additional countries, and vertical, in which case, the inventories of states already possessing the weapon grow larger.

prospect theory Decision-making model that sees policy makers far more willing to take risks to defend what they have than to pursue new goals and objectives.

proxy war War fought on behalf of another state that does not actively participate in the war itself. Typically associated with a smaller or regional ally fighting on behalf of a major power.

public diplomacy Diplomatic activity that is directed at the public at large in a target state. Contrasts with classical diplomacy, which is conducted in secret and involves government-to-government relations. Based on the belief that the public can influence the foreign policy decisions of adversaries.

public goods Policy benefits that are not the object of competition among state and cannot be possessed by a state or group of states and denied to all others. Often characterized as goals that are in the global interest such as a clean environment, absence of disease, or an international stable economic order.

Quadrennial Defense Review Congressionally mandated four years of U.S. defense strategy. Used to identify scenarios that might confront the United States and forces that might be needed to meet that threat. In practice, has often been largely a symbolic exercise.

quota Quantitative restriction placed on the amount of goods allowed to enter a country from another country.

rally-around-the-flag effect Tendency for public opinion to coalesce and support the president's foreign policy position in times of crisis. Reflects both the power of the presidency and media to shape public opinion as well as the lack of in-depth knowledge that many Americans have on foreign policy matters.

ratify To give approval. Treaties in the United States are ratified by the president after the Senate has given its advice and consent by a two-thirds majority.

rational actor Decision-making model that stresses foreign policy; it should be viewed as a deliberate and calculated response to external events and actions. Values are identified, options are listed, and a choice is made that best ensures that the most important values will be realized.

realism A theoretical perspective for studying international relations that emphasizes the struggle for power carried out under conditions of anarchy. Conflict and competition are seen as permanent features of world politics. Security, not peace, is the central objective of foreign policy.

Reformed America A possible future foreign policy strategic orientation of U.S. foreign policy that is based on the belief that the time is appropriate to give preference to traditional American values over narrowly defined security interests in dealing with global problems.

reporting requirement A statement added on to legislation, requiring periodic reports by implementing agencies or the president on the status of a situation. They have been used by Congress as a means of keeping up the pressure on presidents to carry out foreign policy according to its wishes. Generally, escape hatches are included to give presidents freedom to act.

Revolution in Military Affairs Term used to capture the transformational power that modern information and communication technology were expected to have in conduct of military campaigns. Widely used in U.S. defense planning and weapons procurement decisions after Persian Gulf War. Now challenged by new emphasis on counterinsurgency warfare.

sanctions Penalties or other means of enforcement used to create incentives for countries to act in accordance with policy edicts of the sanctioning state. Typically involves the use of economic instruments of foreign policy.

shock and awe Massive bombing campaign used by United States in opening of

Iraq War. Designed as much to psychologically intimidate enemy as to defeat it on the battlefield. Associated with military logic of Revolution in Military Affairs.

shuttle diplomacy negotiations or talks mediated by a third party who travels frequently between the counties who are involved in the dispute.

signal Piece of information that will help policy makers formulate policy. Often difficult to identify because of the presence of noise that masks their presence and significance.

signing statement Comments made by the president when signing legislation into law and used to identify which parts of the legislation he objects to and will not enforce. Effectively allows the president to veto certain parts of a bill without having to veto the entire bill.

smart sanctions Penalties or other measures that are targeted on specific groups or individuals in a target state. Adopted out of a concern that sanctions, particularly economic sanctions, unfairly punish all individuals in a society rather than just those engaging in the disputed behaviors.

soft power The power to influence and persuade. It attracts others to one side rather than forcing them to support your cause as is the case with hard power. Often associated with diplomacy, positive economic incentives, and, more generally, the attraction of American culture, ideas, and values.

sovereignty The principle that no power exists above the state. The state alone decides what goals to pursue and how to pursue them. Its relevance as an absolute standard is questioned by many in today's world of globalization, terrorism, and large-scale power inequalities among states.

spiral of silence Tendency for those holding minority views to remain silent when they fail to see the media report stories that support their position. Results in an exaggerated sense of national unity.

stability operations Military operations undertaken to restore and maintain order and stability in regions or states where a competent civil authority no longer functions.

standard operating procedures Central part of bureaucratic politics model. States that policy is implemented not with an eye to the particulars of a situation or a problem but in a routine and predictable fashion, with the result that policies often fail to achieve their intended purpose.

sufficiency Nuclear strategy under Nixon that emphasized strategic equality with the Soviet Union and the possession of a minimum retaliatory threat.

summit conference Category of diplomacy that involves meetings of the heads of government of a small number of states. Popularized during World War II and the Cold War. They are now less negotiating sessions and more occasions to sign agreements reached in other settings.

tariff Tax on foreign products coming into a country. May be put in place to raise revenue, protect domestic industries from foreign competition, or punish another state.

terrorism Violence employed for purposes of political intimidation. It may be employed in the support of any set of goals and carried out by nonstate actors or state agencies. It may exist as a strategy in its own right or as the first stage in a larger guerrilla war conflict.

think tanks Generic phrase used to describe organizations that engage in policy analysis and advocacy. They may be nonprofits, represent corporate interests, or funded by governments.

tipping point Term used to describe foreign policy issues in which elite and public opinion are sufficiently divided that a shift in public opinion holds the potential for changing the direction of policy.

trade promotional authority Once known as fast-track authority. Voted on by Congress for set periods of time, it gives the president the authority to enter into international trade negotiations, guarantees a prompt vote by Congress, and limits Congress's ability to modify treaties that come before it.

unilateral president View of presidential power that emphasizes strength rather than weakness. By acting unilaterally to make policy statements, create organizations, appoint individuals to key positions, and take action, the president is seen as able to dominate the political agenda and outmaneuver Congress and the Courts, placing them in a reactive position.

unilateralism Part of the American national style. It is an orientation to action that emphasizes the value of going it alone. When cooperation with others is needed, it must be carried out on one's own terms and with a minimal level of commitment to joint action.

unipolar Characterizes an international system in which one power dominates over all others. No balancing or competing bloc exists. Rare at the international level, it has been more common at the regional level such as in Latin America and East Europe. Some see the contemporary international system as unipolar.

valence issues Refers to electoral foreign policy issues, which find all candidates taking the same side. Common in general elections. For voters, the choice becomes not what position to endorse but who they think is best capable of achieving the agreed-upon outcome.

Vietnam syndrome Refers to what many interpreted as the primary lesson of Vietnam. The perception that the American public will not again support long-term military engagements that result in the substantial loss of American lives.

Consequently, any military action must be quick and decisive.

War Powers Resolution The major Cold War attempt by Congress to limit a president's ability to use military force without its approval. Its constitutionality has never been tested. No president has officially recognized its binding nature on their decision-making power.

weapons of mass destruction Overarching term used to describe nuclear, biological, and chemical weapons. Radiological weapons and delivery systems are also often included in the definition. During the Cold War, the term related almost exclusively to nuclear weapons.

Wilsonianism A set of foreign policy ideas associated with Woodrow Wilson. The core essence of these ideas is contested. Generally seen as foundational is the notion that the United States has a moral and national security obligation to spread democracy and create a liberal international order.

window of fear The onset of a set of short-term conditions that lead policy makers rationally to conclude that military action needs to be taken, regardless of how small the prospects of victory are, because conditions will only get worse in the future.

window of opportunity The onset of short-term conditions that lead policy makers rationally to conclude that military actions needs to be undertaken because they possess a clear and distinct military advantage over the enemy.

yellow journalism Phrase used to characterize media coverage of foreign policy that stresses a provocative, overly dramatic, and sensationalistic treatment of events over measured reporting and a concern for factual accuracy.

Photo Credits

Index